Lecture Notes in Computer Science 2890

Edited by G. Goos, J. Hartmanis, and J. van Leeuwen

Springer

Berlin
Heidelberg
New York
Hong Kong
London
Milan
Paris
Tokyo

Manfred Broy   Alexandre V. Zamulin (Eds.)

Perspectives of System Informatics

5th International
Andrei Ershov Memorial Conference, PSI 2003
Akademgorodok, Novosibirsk, Russia, July 9-12, 2003
Revised Papers

Springer

Series Editors

Gerhard Goos, Karlsruhe University, Germany
Juris Hartmanis, Cornell University, NY, USA
Jan van Leeuwen, Utrecht University, The Netherlands

Volume Editors

Manfred Broy
Technische Universität München, Institut für Informatik
Boltzmannstr. 3, 85748 Garching, Germany
E-mail: broy@informatik.tu-muenchen.de

Alexandre V. Zamulin
Siberian Branch of the Russian Academy of Sciences
A.P. Ershov Institute of Informatics Systems
630090, Novosibirsk, Russia
E-mail: zam@iis.nsk.su

Cataloging-in-Publication Data applied for

A catalog record for this book is available from the Library of Congress.

Bibliographic information published by Die Deutsche Bibliothek
Die Deutsche Bibliothek lists this publication in the Deutsche Nationalbibliografie;
detailed bibliographic data is available in the Internet at <http://dnb.ddb.de>.

CR Subject Classification (1998): F.3, D.3, D.1, D.2, F.1

ISSN 0302-9743
ISBN 3-540-20813-5 Springer-Verlag Berlin Heidelberg New York

Springer-Verlag is a part of Springer Science+Business Media

springeronline.com

© Springer-Verlag Berlin Heidelberg 2003
Printed in Germany

Typesetting: Camera-ready by author, data conversion by PTP-Berlin, Protago-TeX-Production GmbH
Printed on acid-free paper   SPIN: 10976128   06/3142   5 4 3 2 1 0

Preface

The volume comprises final versions of the papers presented at the 5th International Andrei Ershov Memorial Conference "Perspectives of System Informatics," Akademgorodok (Novosibirsk, Russia), July 9–12, 2003. The main goal of the conference was to give an overview of research directions that are decisive for growth in the major areas of research activities in system informatics.

The conference was held to honor the 70th anniversary of Ershov's closest colleague, the late Prof. Igor Pottosin (1933–2001), and his outstanding contribution towards advancing informatics. The first four Andrei Ershov conferences were held in May 1991, June 1996, July 1999, and July 2001, and they proved to be significant international events.

Andrei Ershov was one of the early Russian pioneers in the field of theoretical and systems programming, a founder of the Siberian School of Computer Science. His closest colleague, Igor Pottosin, worked for the Siberian Branch of the Russian Academy of Sciences from 1958, step by step filling positions from junior researcher to director of the A. P. Ershov Institute of Informatics Systems. In later years he headed the Laboratory of Systems Programming in this institute and the Department of Programming at Novosibirsk State University.

I. V. Pottosin took a leading position among Russian specialists in computer science. It is hardly possible to overestimate his contribution to the formation and development of this research direction in the country. He obtained fundamental results in the theory of program optimization, formulated main principles and typical schemes of optimizing compilers, and suggested efficient algorithms for optimizing program transformations. One of the world's first optimizing compilers ALPHA, the ALPHA-6 programming system, and the multilanguage compiling system BETA were designed and developed on the basis of these results and with the direct participation of Igor Pottosin.

In later years he mainly concentrated on the problems of designing programming environments for efficient and reliable program construction, and headed the SOKRAT project aimed at producing software for embedded computers. Research in program analysis and programming methodology was essentially inspired and greatly influenced by his practical work. Prof. Pottosin was actively involved in the training of computer professionals, and there is a professor, 11 Ph.D. holders, and hundreds of graduates among his disciples.

The fifth conference followed the traditions of the previous ones and included many of their subjects, such as theoretical computer science, programming methodology, and new information technologies, which are the most important components of system informatics. The style of the previous conferences was preserved to a certain extent: a considerable number of invited papers in addition to contributed regular and short papers.

This time 110 papers (a record number!) were submitted to the conference by researchers from 28 countries. Each paper was reviewed by three experts, at least two of them from the same, or from a closely related one discipline as the authors. The reviewers generally provided high-quality assessments of the papers and often gave extensive comments to the authors for possible improvements of the presentations. The Programme Committee selected 25 high-quality papers as regular talks and 27 papers as short talks. A broad range of hot topics in system informatics was covered by five invited talks given by prominent computer scientists from different countries.

We are glad to express our gratitude to all the persons and organizations who contributed to the conference: to the sponsors for their moral, financial and organizational support, to the members of the Programme Committee who did their best to select the worthiest papers, and to the members of the Local Organizing Committee for their efforts towards the success of this event. We are especially grateful to N. Cheremnykh for her selfless labor when preparing the conference.

July, 2003   M. Broy,
                                                                                                  A. Zamulin

Organization

Conference Chair

Alexander Marchuk (Novosibirsk, Russia)

Programme Committee Co-chairs

Manfred Broy (Munich, Germany)
Alexandre Zamulin (Novosibirsk, Russia)

Conference Secretary

Natalia Cheremnykh (Novosibirsk, Russia)

Programme Committee

Egidio Astesiano (Italy)
Janis Barzdins (Latvia)
Frédéric Benhamou (France)
Nieves Brisaboa (Spain)
Mikhail Bulyonkov (Russia)
Albertas Čaplinskas (Lithuania)
Gabriel Ciobanu (Romania)
Alexander Dikovsky (France)
Alexander Gelbukh (Mexico)
Jan Friso Groote (The Netherlands)
Victor Ivannikov (Russia)
Victor Kasyanov (Russia)
Alexander Kleschev (Russia)
Gregory Kucherov (France)
Reino Kurki-Suonio (Finland)
Sergei Kuznetsov (Russia)
Giorgio Levi (Italy)
Dominique Méry (France)
Ruslan Mitkov (UK)
Bernhard Möller (Germany)
Hanspeter Mössenböck (Austria)
Peter Mosses (Denmark)
J. Strother Moore (USA)
Ron Morrison (UK)

Valery Nepomniaschy (Russia)
Peter Pepper (Germany)
Francesco Parisi-Presicce (Italy)
Jaan Penjam (Estonia)
Alexander Petrenko (Russia)
Jaroslav Pokorny (Czech Republic)
Wolfgang Reisig (Germany)
Fuji Ren (Japan)
Viktor Sabelfeld (Germany)
Don Sannella (UK)
Vladimir Sazonov (UK)
Timos Sellis (Greece)
Alexander Semenov (Russia)
Klaus-Dieter Schewe (New Zealand)
David Schmidt (USA)
Sibylle Schupp (USA)
Lothar Thiele (Switzerland)
Alexander Tomilin (Russia)
Enn Tyugu (Estonia)
Frits Vaandrager (The Netherlands)
Karin Verspoor (USA)
Andrei Voronkov (UK)
Tatyana Yakhno (Turkey)
Wang Yi (Sweden)

Additional Referees

H. Anderson	J. Iyoda	A. Sabelfeld
Th. Baar	Ch. Jermann	A. Sage
R. Bagnara	A. Kalnins	Th. Santen
V. Barichard	K. Kapp	B. Schätz
M. Bellia	R. Kaschek	K. Schneider
J. Bézivin	Yu. Khan	N. Shilov
L. Bordeaux	M. Kirchberg	D. Shkurko
M. Cebulla	L. Kof	A. Sinyakov
M.V. Cengarle	J. Küster Filipe	S. Skiadopoulos
A. Cisternino	J. Lawall	J. Souquieres
Th. Dalamagas	Le An Ha	K. Spies
O. Danvy	S. Link	A. Stasenko
M. Dekhtyar	R. Loukanova	A. Stefan
F. Dinenberg	P. Machado	Gh. Stefanescu
Th. Ehm	S. Merz	G. Struth
A. El-Sayed	A. Metzner	M. Südholt
P. Emelianov	B. Meyer	M. Sustik
J. Engblom	K. Michen	M. Syrjakow
J. Erickson	T. Mossakowski	P.S. Thiagarajan
R. Evans	S. Norcross	M. Tombak
M. Falaschi	M.E. Occhiuto	B. Trancón y Widemann
F.A. Ferrarotti	C. Orasan	A. Tretiakov
S. Frank	A. Pavlov	A. Tsois
P. Geibel	T. Pedersen	T. Uustalu
R. Glück	M. R. Penabad	M. K. Valiev
M. Glukhankov	P. Pettersson	S. Van Groningen
J. Golden	M. Pister	P. Vassiliadis
D. Gurov	M. Pizka	L. Vigneron
G. Hains	K. Podnieks	A. Vilbig
S. Hartmann	S. Ray	I. Virbitskaite
M. Henz	E. Reeber	M. Voorhoeve
D. Hofbauer	G. Reggio	W. Wesselink
P. Hofstedt	W.P. de Roever	J. Wieland
R.R. Hoogerwoord	J. Romberg	T. Willemse
F. Huber	A. Roychoudhury	

Sponsors

Support from the following institutions is gratefully acknowledged:

- Microsoft Research Ltd., UK
- US Air Force European Office of Aerospace Research and Development
- US Navy Office of Naval Research, International Field Office
- US Army Research Laboratory, European Research Office
- US Army Communications-Electronics Command (CECOM)

Table of Contents

Programming Issues

Software Engineering

Software Education

Program Synthesis, Transformation, and Semantics

Graphical Interfaces

Partial Evaluation and Supercompilation

Verification

Logic and Types

Concurrent and Distributed Systems

Concurrent and Reactive Systems

Program Specification

Verification and Model Checking

Constraint Programming

Documentation and Testing

Databases

Natural Language Processing

The Verifying Compiler:
A Grand Challenge for Computing Research

Tony Hoare

Microsoft Research Ltd., 7 JJ Thomson Ave, Cambridge CB3 0FB, UK
thoare@microsoft.com

Abstract. I propose a set of criteria which distinguish a grand challenge in science or engineering from the many other kinds of short-term or long-term research problems that engage the interest of scientists and engineers. As an example drawn from Computer Science, I revive an old challenge: the construction and application of a verifying compiler that guarantees correctness of a program before running it.

1 Introduction

The primary purpose of the formulation and promulgation of a grand challenge is to contribute to the advancement of some branch of science or engineering. A grand challenge represents a commitment by a significant section of the research community to work together towards a common goal, agreed to be valuable and achievable by a team effort within a predicted timescale. The challenge is formulated by the researchers themselves as a focus for the research that they wish to pursue in any case, and which they believe can be pursued more effectively by advance planning and co-ordination. Unlike other common kinds of research initiative, a grand challenge should not be triggered by hope of short-term economic, commercial, medical, military or social benefits; and its initiation should not wait for political promotion or for prior allocation of special funding. The goals of the challenge should be purely scientific goals of the advancement of skill and of knowledge. It should appeal not only to the curiosity of scientists and to the ambition of engineers; ideally it should appeal also to the imagination of the general public; thereby it may enlarge the general understanding and appreciation of science, and attract new entrants to a rewarding career in scientific research.

An opportunity for a grand challenge arises only rarely in the history of any particular branch of science. It occurs when that branch of study first reaches an adequate level of maturity to predict the long-term direction of its future progress, and to plan a project to pursue that direction on an international scale. Much of the work required to achieve the challenge may be of a routine nature. Many scientists will prefer not to be involved in the co-operation and co-ordination involved in a grand challenge. They realize that most scientific advances, and nearly all break-throughs, are accomplished by individuals or small teams, working competitively and in relative isolation. They value their privilege

M. Broy and A.V. Zamulin (Eds.): PSI 2003, LNCS 2890, pp. 1–12, 2003.

of pursuing bright ideas in new directions at short notice. It is for these reasons that a grand challenge should always be a minority interest among scientists; and the greater part of the research effort in any branch of science should remain free of involvement in grand challenges.

A grand challenge may involve as much as a thousand man-years of research effort, drawn from many countries and spread over ten years or more. The research skill, experience, motivation and originality that it will absorb are qualities even scarcer and more valuable than the funds that may be allocated to it. For this reason, a proposed grand challenge should be subjected to assessment by the most rigorous criteria before its general promotion and wide-spread adoption. These criteria include all those proposed by Jim Gray [1] as desirable attributes of a long-range research goal. The additional criteria that are proposed here relate to the maturity of the scientific discipline and the feasibility of the project. In the following list, the earlier criteria emphasize the significance of the goals, and the later criteria relate to the feasibility of the project, and the maturity of the state of the art.

- **Fundamental.** It arises from scientific curiosity about the foundation, the nature, and the limits of an entire scientific discipline, or a significant branch of it.
- **Astonishing.** It gives scope for engineering ambition to build something useful that was earlier thought impractical, thus turning science fiction to science fact.
- **Testable.** It has a clear measure of success or failure at the end of the project; ideally, there should be criteria to assess progress at intermediate stages too
- **Inspiring.** It has enthusiastic support from (almost) the entire research community, even those who do not participate in it, and do not benefit from it.
- **Understandable.** It is generally comprehensible, and captures the imagination of the general public, as well as the esteem of scientists in other disciplines.
- **Useful.** The understanding and knowledge gained in completion of the project bring scientific or other benefits; some of these should be attainable, even if the project as a whole fails in its primary goal.
- **Historical.** The prestigious challenges are those which were formulated long ago; without concerted effort, they would be likely to stand for many years to come.
- **International.** It has international scope, exploiting the skills and experience of the best research groups in the world. The cost and the prestige of the project is shared among many nations, and the benefits are shared among all.
- **Revolutionary.** Success of the project will lead to radical paradigm shift in scientific research or engineering practice. It offers a rare opportunity to break free from the dead hand of legacy.

- **Research-directed.** The project can be forwarded by the reasonably well understood methods of academic research. It tackles goals that will not be achieved solely by commercially motivated evolution of existing products.

- **Challenging.** It goes beyond what is known initially to be possible, and requires development of understanding, techniques and tools unknown at the start.

- **Feasible.** The reasons for previous failure to meet the challenge are well understood and there are good reasons to believe that they can now be overcome.

- **Incremental.** It decomposes into identified intermediate research goals, which can be shared among many separate teams over a long time-scale.

- **Co-operative.** It calls for planned co-operation among identified research teams and research communities with differing specialized skills.

- **Competitive.** It encourages and benefits from competition among individuals and teams pursuing alternative lines of enquiry; there should be clear criteria announced in advance to decide who is winning, or who has won.

- **Effective.** Its promulgation changes the attitudes and activities of research scientists and engineers.

- **Risk-managed**. The risks of failure are identified, symptoms of failure will be recognized early, and strategies for cancellation or recovery are in place.

The tradition of grand challenges is common in many branches of science. If you want to know whether a challenge qualifies for the title 'Grand', compare it with

- Prove Fermat's last theorem   (accomplished)
- Put a man on the moon within ten years   (accomplished)
- Cure cancer within ten years   (failed in 1970s)
- Map the Human Genome   (accomplished)
- Map the Human Proteome   (too difficult for now)
- Find the Higgs boson   (under investigation)
- Find Gravity waves   (under investigation)
- Unify the four forces of Physics   (under investigation)
- Hilbert's programme for mathematical foundations   (abandoned in 1930s)

All of these challenges satisfy many of the criteria listed above in varying degrees, though no individual challenge could be expected to satisfy all the criteria. The first in the list was the oldest and in some ways the grandest challenge; but being a mathematical challenge, my suggested criteria are considerably less relevant for it.

In Computer Science, the following examples may be familiar from the past. That is the reason why they are listed here, **not as recommendations,** but just as examples

- Prove that P is not equal to NP   (open)
- The Turing test   (outstanding)
- The verifying compiler   (abandoned in 1970s)
- A championship chess program   (completed)
- A GO program at professional standard   (too difficult)
- Automatic translation from Russian to English (failed in 1960s)

The first of these challenges is of the mathematical kind. It may seem to be quite easy to extend this list with new challenges. The difficult part is to find a challenge that passes the tests for maturity and feasibility. The remainder of this contribution picks just one of the challenges, and subjects it to detailed evaluation according to the seventeen criteria.

2   The Verifying Compiler: Implementation and Application

A verifying compiler [2] uses automated mathematical and logical reasoning methods to check the correctness of the programs that it compiles. The criterion of correctness is specified by types, assertions, and other redundant annotations that are associated with the code of the program, often inferred automatically, and increasingly often supplied by the original programmer. The compiler will work in combination with other program development and testing tools, to achieve any desired degree of confidence in the structural soundness of the system and the total correctness of its more critical components. The only limit to its use will be set by an evaluation of the cost and benefits of accurate and complete formalization of the criterion of correctness for the software.

An important and integral part of the project proposal is to evaluate the capabilities and performance of the verifying compiler by application to a representative selection of legacy code, chiefly from open sources. This will give confidence that the engineering compromises that are necessary in such an ambitious project have not damaged its ability to deal with real programs written by real programmers. It is only after this demonstration of capability that programmers working on new projects will gain the confidence to exploit verification technology in new projects.

Note that **the verifying compiler itself does not itself have to be verified.** It is adequate to rely on the normal engineering judgment that errors in a user program are unlikely to be compensated by errors in the compiler. Verification of a verifying compiler is a specialized task, forming a suitable topic for a separate grand challenge.

This proposed grand challenge is now evaluated under the seventeen headings listed in the introduction.

Fundamental. Correctness of computer programs is the fundamental concern of the theory of programming and of its application in large-scale software engineering. The limits of application of the theory need to be explored and extended. The project is self-contained within Computer Science, since it constructs a computer program to solve a problem that arises only from the very existence of computer programs.

Astonishing. Most of the general public, and even many programmers, are unaware of the possibility that computers might check the correctness of their own programs; and it does so by the same kind of logical methods that for thousands of years have conferred a high degree of credibility to mathematical theorems.

Testable. If the project is successful, a verifying compiler will be available as a standard tool in some widely used programming productivity toolset. It will have been tested in verification of structural integrity and security and other desirable properties of millions of lines of open source software, and in more substantial verification of critical parts of it. This will lead to removal of thousands of errors, risks, insecurities and anomalies in widely used code. Proofs will be subjected to check by rival proof tools. The major internal and external interfaces in the software will be documented by assertions, to make existing components safer to use and easier to reuse [3]. The benefits will extend also to the evolution and enhancement of legacy code, as well as the design and development of new code. Eventually programmers will prefer to confine their use of their programming language to those features and structured design patterns which facilitate automatic checks of correctness [4,5].

Inspiring. Program verification by proof is an absolute scientific ideal, like purity of materials in chemistry or accuracy of measurement in mechanics. These ideals are pursued for their own sake, in the controlled environment of the research laboratory. The practicing engineer in industry has to be content to work around the impurities and inaccuracies that are found in the real world, and often considers laboratory science as unhelpful in discharging this responsibility. The value of purity and accuracy (just like correctness) are often not appreciated until after the scientist has built the tools that make them achievable.

Understandable. All computer users have been annoyed by bugs in mass market software, and will welcome their reduction or elimination. Recent well-known viruses have been widely reported in the press, and have been estimated to cost billions of dollars. Fear of cyber-terrorism is quite widespread [6,7]. Viruses can often obtain entry into a computer system by exploiting errors like buffer overflow, which could be caught quite easily by a verifying compiler [8].

Trustworthy software is now recognised by major vendors as a primary long-term goal [9]. The interest of the press and the public in the project can be maintained, whenever dangerous anomalies are detected and removed from software that is in common use.

Useful. Unreliable software is currently estimated to cost the US some sixty billion dollars [10]. A verifying compiler would be a valued component of the proposed Infrastructure for Software Testing.

A verifying compiler may help accumulate evidence that will help to assess and reduce the risks of incorporation of commercial off-the-shelf software (COTS) into safety critical systems. The project may extend the capabilities of load-time checking of mobile proof-carrying code [11]. It will provide a secure foundation for the achievement of trustworthy software.

The main long-term benefits of the verifying compiler will be realised most strongly in the development and maintenance of new code, specified, designed and tested with its aid. Perhaps we can look forward to the day when normal commercial software will be delivered with an eighty percent chance that it never needs recall or correction by service packs, etc. within the first ten years after delivery. Then the suppliers of commercial and mass-market software will have the confidence to give the normal assurances of fitness for purpose that are now required by law for most other consumer products.

Historical. The idea of using assertions to check a large routine is due to Turing [12]. The idea of the computer checking the correctness of its own programs was put forward by McCarthy [13]. The two ideas were brought together in the verifying compiler by Floyd [14]. Early attempts to implement the idea [15] were severely inhibited by the difficulty of proof support with the machines of that day. At that time, the source code of widely used software was usually kept secret. It was generally written in assembler for a proprietary computer architecture, which was often withdrawn after a short interval on the market. The ephemeral nature and limited distribution for software written by hardware manufacturers reduced motivation for a major verification effort.

Since those days, further difficulties have arisen from the complexities of modern software practice and modern programming languages [16]. Features such as concurrent programming, object orientation and inheritance, have not been designed with the care needed to facilitate program verification. However, the relevant concepts of concurrency and objects have been explored by theoreticians in the 'clean room' conditions of new experimental programming languages [17,18]. In the implementation of a verifying compiler, the results of such pure research will have to be adapted, extended and combined; they must then be implemented and tested by application on a broad scale to legacy code expressed in legacy languages.

International. The project will require collaboration among leading researchers in America, China, India, Australasia, and many countries of Europe. Some of them are mentioned in the Acknowledgements and the References.

Revolutionary. At present, the most widely accepted means of raising trust levels of software is by massive and expensive testing. Assertions are used mainly as test oracles, to detect errors as close as possible to their place of occurrence [19]. Availability of a verifying compiler will encourage programmers to formulate assertions as specifications in advance of code, in the expectation that many of them will be verifiable by automated or semi-automated mathematical techniques. Existing experience of the verified development of safety-critical code [20,21] will be transferred to commercial software for the benefit of mass-market software products.

Research-Directed. The methods of research into program verification are well established in the academic research community, though they need to be scaled up to meet the needs of modern software construction. This is unlikely to be achieved solely in industry. Commercial programming tool-sets are driven necessarily by fashionable slogans and by the politics of standardisation. Their elegant pictorial representations can have multiple semantic interpretations, available for adaptation according to the needs and preferences of the customer. The designers of the tools are constrained by compatibility with legacy practices and code, and by lack of scientific education and understanding on the part of their customers.

Challenging. Many of the analysis and verification tools essential to this project are already available, and can be applied now to legacy code [22–27]. But their use is still too laborious, and their improvement over a lengthy period will be necessary to achieve the goals of the challenge. The purpose of this grand challenge is to encourage larger groups to co-operate on the evolution of a small number of tools.

Feasible. Most of the factors which have inhibited progress on practical program verification are no longer as severe as they were.

1. Experience has been gained in specification and verification of moderately scaled systems, chiefly in the area of safety-critical and mission-critical software; but so far the proofs have been mainly manual [20,21].
2. The corpus of Open Source Software [http://sourceforge.net] is now universally available and used by millions, so justifying almost any effort expended on improvement of its quality and robustness. Although it is subject to continuous improvement, the pace of change is reasonably predictable. It is an important part of this challenge to cater for software evolution.
3. Advances in unifying theories of programming [28] suggest that many aspects of correctness of concurrent and object-oriented programs can be expressed by assertions, supplemented by automatic or machine-assisted insertion of instrumentation in the form of ghost (model) variables and assignments to them.
4. Many of the global program analyses which are needed to underpin correctness proofs for systems involving concurrency and pointer manipulation have now been developed for use in optimising compilers [29].

5. Theorem proving technology has made great strides in many directions. Model checking [30–33] is widely understood and used, particularly in hardware design. Decision procedures [34] are beginning to be applied to software. Proof search engines [35] are now well populated with libraries of application-dependent theorems and tactics. Finally, SAT checking [36] promises a step-function increase in the power of proof tools. A major remaining challenge is to find effective ways of combining this wide range of component technologies into a small number of tools, to meet the needs of program verification.
6. Program analysis tools are now available which use a variety of techniques to discover relevant invariants and abstractions [37–39]. It is hoped that that these will formalize at least the program properties relevant to its structural integrity, with a minimum of human intervention.
7. Theories relevant for the correctness of concurrency are well established [40–42]; and theories for object orientation and pointer manipulation are under development [43,44].

Incremental. The progress of the project can be assessed by the number of lines of legacy code that have been verified, and the level of annotation and verification that has been achieved. The relevant levels of annotation are: structural integrity, partial functional specification, specification of total correctness. The relevant levels of verification are: by testing, by human proof, with machine assistance, and fully automatic. Most software is now at the lowest level – structural integrity verified by massive testing. It will be interesting to record the incremental achievement of higher levels by individual modules of code, and to find out how widely the higher levels are reasonably achievable; few modules are likely to reach the highest level of full verification.

Cooperative. The work can be delegated to teams working independently on the annotation of code, on verification condition generation, and on the proof tools.

1. The existing corpus of Open Source Software can easily be parcelled out to different teams for analysis and annotation; and the assertions can be checked by massive testing in advance of availability of adequate proof tools.
2. It is now standard for a compiler to produce an abstract syntax tree from the source code, together with a data base of program properties. A compiler that exposes the syntax tree would enable many researchers to collaborate on program analysis algorithms, test harnesses, test case generators, verification condition generators, and other verification and validation tools.
3. Modern proof tools permit extension by libraries of specialized theories [34]; these can be developed by many hands to meet the needs of each application. In particular, proof procedures can be developed that are specific to commonly used standard application programmer interfaces for legacy code [45].

Competitive. The main source of competition is likely to be between teams that work on different programming languages. Some laboratories may prefer to concentrate on older languages, starting with C and moving on to C++. Others may prefer to concentrate on newer languages like Java or C# .

But even teams working on the same language and on the same tool may compete in achieving higher levels of verification for larger and larger modules of code. There will be competition to find errors in legacy code, and to be the first to obtain mechanical proof of the correctness of all assertions in each module of software. The annotated libraries of open source code will be good competition material for the teams constructing and applying proof tools. The proofs themselves will be subject to confirmation or refutation by rival proof tools.

Effective. The promulgation of this challenge is intended to cause a shift in the motivations and activities of scientists and engineers in all the relevant research communities. They will be pioneers in the collaborative implementation and use of a single large experimental device, following a tradition that is well established in Astronomy and Physics but not yet in Computer science.

1. Researchers in programming theory will accept the challenge of extending proof technology for programs written in complex and uncongenial legacy languages. They will need to design program analysis algorithms to test whether actual legacy programs observe the constraints that make each theoretical proof technique valid.
2. Builders of programming tools will carry out experimental implementation of the hypotheses originated by theorists; following practice in experimental branches of science, their goal is to explore the range of application of the theory to real code.
3. Sympathetic software users will allow newly inserted assertions to be checked dynamically in production runs, even before the tools are available to verify them.
4. Empirical Computer Scientists will apply tools developed by others to the analysis and verification of representative large-scale examples of open code.
5. Compiler writers will support the proof goals by adapting and extending the program analyses currently used for optimisation of code; later they may even exploit for purposes of further optimization the additional redundant information provided with a verified program.
6. Providers of proof tools will regard the project as a fruitful source of low-level conjectures needing verification, and will evolve their algorithms and libraries of theories to meet the needs of actual legacy software and its users.
7. Teachers and students of the foundations of software engineering will be enthused to set student projects that annotate and verify a small part of a large code base, so contributing to the success of a world-wide project.

Risk-Managed. The main risks to the project arise from dissatisfaction of many academic scientists with existing legacy code and legacy languages. The low quality of existing software, and its low level of abstraction, may limit the benefit to be obtained from the annotations. Many failures of proof are not due to an error at all, but just to omission of a more or less obvious precondition. Many of the genuine errors detected may be so rare that they are not worth correcting. In other cases, preservation of an existing anomaly in legacy software may be essential to its continuing functionality. Often the details of functionality of interfaces, either with humans or with hardware devices, are not worth formalising in a total specification, because testing gives an easier but adequate assurance of serviceability.

Legacy languages add to the risks of the project. From a logical point of view, they are extremely complicated, and require sophisticated analyses to ensure that they observe the disciplines that make abstract program verification possible. Finally, one must recognize that many of the problems of present-day software use are associated with configuration and installation management, build files, etc, where techniques of program verification seem unable to contribute.

The idealistic solution to these problems is to discard legacy and start again from scratch. Ideals are (or should be) the prime motivating force for academic research, and their pursuit gives scope for many different grand challenges. One such challenge would involve design of a new programming language and compiler, especially designed to support verification; and another would involve a re-write of existing libraries and applications to the higher standards that are achievable by explicit consideration and simplification of abstract interfaces. Research on new languages and libraries is in itself desirable, and would assist and complement research based on legacy languages and software.

Finally, it must be recognized that a verifying compiler will be only part of a integrated and rational tool-set for reliable software construction and evolution, based on sound scientific principles. Much of its use may be confined to the relatively lower levels of verification. It is a common fate of grand challenges that achievement of their direct goal turns out to be less directly significant than the stimulus that its pursuit has given to the progress of science and engineering. But remember, that was the primary purpose of the whole exercise.

Acknowledgements. The content and presentation of this contribution has emerged from fruitful discussions with many colleagues. There is no implication that any member of this list actually supports the proposed challenge. Ralph Back, Andrew Black, Manfred Broy, Alan Bundy, Michael Ernst, David Evans, Chris George, Mike Gordon, Armando Haeberer, Joseph Halpern, He Jifeng, Jim Horning, Gilles Kahn, Dick Kieburtz, Butler Lampson, Rustan Leino, John McDermid, Bertrand Meyer, Jay Misra, J Moore, Oege de Moor, Greg Morrisett, Robin Milner, Peter O'Hearn, Larry Paulson, Jon Pincus, Amir Pnueli, John Reynolds, John Rushby, Natarajan Shankar, Martyn Thomas, Niklaus Wirth, Jim Woodcock, Zhou Chaochen, and many others.

This article is an extended version of a contribution [46] to the fiftieth anniversary issue of the *Journal of the ACM*, which was devoted to Grand Challenges in Computer Science. It is published here with the approval of the Editor and the kind permission of the ACM.

References

1. J. Gray, What Next? A Dozen Information-technology Research Goals, MS-TR-50, Microsoft Research, June 1999.
2. K.M. Leino and G. Nelson, An extended static checker for Modula-3. *Compiler Construction:, CC'98*, LNCS 1383, Springer, pp 302–305, April 1998.
3. B. Meyer, *Object-Oriented Software Construction*, 2nd edition, Prentice Hall, 1997.
4. A. Hall and R. Chapman: Correctness by Construction: Developing a Commercial Secure System, IEEE Software 19(1): 18–25 (2002)
5. T. Jim, G. Morrisett, D. Grossman, M. Hicks, J. Cheney, and Y. Wang, Cyclone: A safe dialect of C. In USENIX Annual Technical Conference, Monterey, CA, June 2002.
6. See http://www.fbi.gov/congress/congress02/nipc072402.htm, a congressional statement presented by the director of the National Infrastructure Protection Center.
7. F.B. Schneider (ed), *Trust in Cyberspace*, Committee on Information Systems Trustworthiness, National Research Council (1999).
8. D. Wagner, J. Foster, E. Brewer, and A. Aiken. A first step towards automated detection of buffer overrun vulnerabilities. In Network and Distributed System Security Symposium, San Diego, CA, February 2000
9. W.H. Gates, internal communication, Microsoft Corporation, 2002
10. Planning Report 02-3. The Economic Impacts of Inadequate Infrastructure for Software Testing, prepared by RTI for NIST, US Department of Commerce, May 2002
11. G. Necula. Proof-carrying code. In Proceedings of the 24th Annual ACM SIGPLAN-SIGACT Symposium on Principles of Programming Languages (POPL '97), January 1997
12. A.M. Turing, Checking a large routine,*Report on a Conference on High Speed Automatic Calculating machines,* Cambridge University Math. Lab. (1949) 67–69
13. J. McCarthy, Towards a mathematical theory of computation, Proc. IFIP Cong. 1962, North Holland, (1963)
14. R.W. Floyd, Assigning meanings to programs, *Proc. Amer. Soc. Symp. Appl. Math.*, **19,** (1967) pp 19–31
15. J.C. King, A Program Verifier, PhD thesis, Carnegie-Mellon University (1969)
16. B. Stroustrup, *The C++ Programming Language*, Adison-Wesley, 1985
17. A. Igarashi, B. Pierce, and P. Wadler. Featherweight Java: A Minimal Core Calculus for Java and GJ, OOPSLA'99, pp. 132–146, 1999.
18. Haskell 98 language and libraries: the Revised Report, Journal of Functional Programming 13(1) Jan 2003.
19. C.A.R. Hoare, Assertions, to appear, Marktoberdorf Summer School, 2002.
20. S. Stepney, D. Cooper and J.C.P.W. Woodcock, An Electronic Purse: Specification, Refinement, and Proof, PRG-126, Oxford University Computing Laboratory, July 2000.
21. A.J. Galloway, T.J. Cockram and J.A. McDermid, Experiences with the application of discrete formal methods to the development of engine control software, Hise York (1998)
22. W.R. Bush, J.D. Pincus, and D.J. Sielaff, A static analyzer for finding dynamic programming errors, Software – Practice and Experience 2000 (30): pp. 775–802.
23. D. Evans and D. Larochelle, *Improving Security Using Extensible Lightweight Static Analysis*, IEEE Software, Jan/Feb 2002.

24. S. Hallem, B. Chelf, Y. Xie, and D. Engler, A System and Language for Building System-Specific Static Analyses, PLDI 2002.
25. G.C. Necula, S. McPeak, and W. Weimer, CCured: Type-safe retrotting of legacy code. In 29th ACM Symposium on Principles of Programming Languages, Portland, OR, Jan 2002
26. U. Shankar, K. Talwar, J.S. Foster, and D. Wagner. Detecting format string vulnerabilities with type qualifiers, Proceedings of the 10th USENIX Security Symposium, 2001
27. D. Evans. Static detection of dynamic memory errors, SIGPLAN Conference on Programming Languages Design and Implementation, 1996
28. C.A.R. Hoare and H. Jifeng. *Unifying Theories of Programming*, Prentice Hall, 1998.
29. E. Ruf, Context-sensitive alias analysis reconsidered, Sigplan Notices, 30 (6), June 1995
30. G.J. Holzmann, *Design and Validation of Computer Protocols*, Prentice Hall, 1991
31. A.W. Roscoe, Model-Checking CSP, *A Classical Mind: Essays in Honour of C.A.R. Hoare*, Prentice-Hall International, pp 353–378, 1994
32. M. Musuvathi, D.Y.W. Park, A. Chou, D.R. Engler, D.L. Dill. CMC: A pragmatic approach to model checking real code, to appear in OSDI 2002.
33. N. Shankar, Machine-assisted verification using theorem-proving and model checking, *Mathematical Methods of Program Development*, NATO ASI Vol 138, Springer, pp 499–528 (1997)
34. M.J.C. Gordon, HOL: A proof generating system for Higher-Order Logic, *VLSI Specification, Verification and Synthesis*, Kluwer (1988) pp. 73–128
35. N. Shankar, PVS: Combining specification, proof checking, and model checking. FMCAD '96,LNCS 1166, Springer, pp 257–264, Nov 1996
36. M. Moskewicz, C. Madigan, Y. Zhao, L. Zhang, S. Malik, Chaff: Engineering an Efficient SAT Solver, 38th Design Automation Conference (DAC2001), Las Vegas, June 2001
37. T. Ball, S.K. Rajamani, Automatically Validating Temporal Safety Properties of Interfaces, *SPIN 2001*, LNCS 2057, May 2001, pp. 103–122.
38. J.W. Nimmer and M.D. Ernst, Automatic generation of program specifications, *Proceedings of the 2002 International Symposium on Software Testing and Analysis*, 2002, pp. 232–242.
39. C. Flanagan and K.R.M. Leino, Houdini, an annotation assistant for ESC/Java. *International Symposium of Formal Methods Europe 2001*, LNCS 2021, Springer pp 500–517, 2001
40. R. Milner, *Communicating and Mobile Systems: the pi Calculus*, CUP, 1999
41. A.W. Roscoe, *Theory and Practice of Concurrency*, Prentice Hall, 1998
42. KM Chandy and J Misra, *Parallel Program Design: a Foundation*, Adison-Wesley, 1988
43. P. O'Hearn, J. Reynolds and H. Yang, Local Reasoning about Programs that Alter Data Structures, Proceedings of CSL'01 Paris, LNCS 2142, Springer, pp 1–19, 2001.
44. C.A.R. Hoare and He Jifeng, A Trace Model for Pointers and Objects, ECOOP, LNCS 1628, Springer (1999), pp 1–17
45. A. Stepanov and Meng Lee, Standard Template Library, Hewlett Packard (1994)
46. C.A.R. Hoare, The Verifying Compiler: a Grand Challenge for Computer Research, JACM (50) 1, pp 63–69 (2003)

Linear Types for Cashflow Reengineering

Torben Æ. Mogensen

DIKU
University of Copenhagen
Universitetsparken 1
DK2100 Copenhagen O, Denmark
Phone: +45 35321404 Fax: +45 35321401
torbenm@diku.dk

Abstract. A while back a major Danish bank approached the programming language group at DIKU for help on designing a language for modelling cash flow reengineering: The process of issuing customised bonds based on income from existing bonds. The idea was to have a simple language that allows non-programmers to describe such reengineering and run statistical simulations of the structures.

We describe the problem and present the design of a cashflow-reengineering language based on the dataflow paradigm and linear types. This language has formed the basis of further development by the bank in question and a variant of it is now in use there.

1 Introduction

In the context of this paper, a *cashflow* is a bond or other financial obligation characterised by a sequence of payments of interest and principal on a sequence of specified dates. Both interest and principal payments may vary over time and can be influenced by outside forces such as interest rates, currency rates or stock market value. A cashflow may or may not have a *balance* that specifies the sum of the outstanding principal payments.

Banks often sell or buy cashflows tailor-made to specific customers. These are usually financed by buying and selling other cashflows and redirecting the payments between those that are bought and those that are sold. This is called *cashflow reengineering*[1]. Bank workers do this by combining and splitting cashflows in various ways such that the outcome is the desired cashflows and possibly some "residual" cashflows that the bank may keep for itself or try to sell. Typical operations on cashflows are:

Add: Two cashflows are combined into one, that gets the combined payments of the components.

Cleanup: When a certain condition occurs, all the remaining balance is paid as principal and no further payments are made.

---

[1] The term is in different contexts used for the process of restructuring the finances of a company.

M. Broy and A.V. Zamulin (Eds.): PSI 2003, LNCS 2890, pp. 13–21, 2003.

Divide: The cashflow is divided into two, each of which gets a specified fraction of the principal and/or interest payments.

Sequential: Until a certain condition occurs, all payments go to one cashflow, and subsequent payments go to another.

These operations are applied at every time step (i.e., at every payment date), but may have some degree of memory (e.g., of whether the specified condition has occurred in the past).

Since various parameters (such as future interest rates) can be unknown, it may not be possible to guarantee that the bank will get a profit from a deal. However, the bank can try to guess at these and try out various scenarios to get confidence that they are likely to make a profit. This can be done by *Monte Carlo simulation* [5]. To support this, the deal must be encoded in a program that does the simulation.

Some time ago, a Danish bank (which shall remain anonymous) used the practice of letting programmers code the deals in a standard programming language using some library functions for the simulation. The bank found this process tedious and prone to error, so they wanted to design a domain-specific language [12] that could be used directly by the bank workers without involving the programmers. The responsible people had no experience with language design, so after making a rough sketch of a possible language and finding the result unsatisfactory, they approached the programming language group at DIKU for help.

The sketch the bank provided was based on object-oriented notation, with variables having methods applied with dot-notation. There was no conscious consideration if this was suitable, it was just what the programmers in the bank were used to working with. A very simple example using this notation is

```
C = A + B;
D = C.divide(0.7);
```

In the first line, the cashflows A and B are added to form the cashflow C. In the second line, C is split such that 70% goes to the new cashflow D and the remaining 30% stays in C.

There were several problems with this design:

− The notation is not intuitive for nonprogrammers.
− It is difficult to check for *cashflow preservation.*

Cashflow preservation is the notion no cashflow is used twice or not at all, i.e., that you don't spend the same dollar more than once or forget you have it. To ensure this, the bank people suggested that side effects will empty cashflows as they are used, e.g., setting A and B to zero when they are added to form C in the example above. At the end, it is checked if all except the output cashflows are zero. While this strategy, indeed, ensures cashflow preservation, it doesn't catch all errors in a deal. For example, if a user had written a specification like this:

```
C = A + B;
 :
 :
E = D + A;
```

It just silently adds zero to D in the last line, where it would be appropriate to give a warning. Note that you can't just check for zero values when doing operations, as this will flag errors for sequential splits, where some payments are meant to be zero.

The rest of this paper will describe the design that was proposed by DIKU and briefly summarise the experiences of using the language.

2   Embedded vs. Stand-Alone Domain-Specific Languages

Domain-specific languages generally come in two flavours: They can be stand-alone languages with their own special syntax and compilers/interpreters, like the language described here, or they can be embedded languages. Embedded languages are, as the name indicates, implemented as a set of library functions, classes, macros or some other abstraction mechanism in an existing language.

An example of an embedded domain-specific language is the Lava hardware description language [4], while PostScript [1] is a stand-alone domain-specific language. It is possible to implement DSL's as both embedded and stand-alone languages. This is the case for, e.g., the query-language SQL [6], which is available both as a set of library functions and as a stand-alone notation used in interactive front ends to databases.

The two flavours of each have advantages and disadvantages:

Embedded languages: An embedded language inherits the full expressiveness of the host language, so constructs for conditionals, looping, recursion, etc. need not be explicitly added to the language. Furthermore, implementation and interoperability with other languages is more easily accomplished.
Stand-alone languages: The syntax can be chosen so it is natural for the problem domain without any limitations imposed by a host language. Furthermore, domain-specific consistency checks can be made at compile-time, and error-messages can be expressed in terms of the problem domain.

It is clear that the latter is most suitable for the problem presented here, both because cashflow preservation can be tested at compile time and because the language is intended for non-programmers.

The differences between embedded and stand-alone DSL's and their (dis)advantages is elaborated further in [12,11].

3   From Dataflow to Cashflow

The cashflow preservation property is similar to the property found in dataflow languages [9]: When a value is used, it is no longer available for further use (unless it is explicitly copied). In a dataflow language, a computation is represented as an acyclic directed graph, where the edges represent values and the nodes represent operations. Each operation has a fixed number of input and output edges, so you need an explicit copy node to use a value more than once. The same idea can be applied to cashflow reengineering: Each edge in the graph is a cashflow and the nodes are operations that combine or split cashflows. There are no copy nodes, as these would not preserve cashflow. Edges that aren't connected at both ends specify input or output cashflows.

Graphical notation is far from compact and it requires special tools for production and editing. So we define a textual notation similar to a traditional programming language for the graph: Edges are named and each name will be used exactly twice: Once for the place where the edge is given a value and once for the place where the value is used. Input and output edges are explicitly specified to preserve this definition/use property. The example from the introduction looks like this in the new notation:

```
declarations
  fraction = 0.7

input
  cashflow a, b

structure
  c = a + b
  (d,e) = Divide(c, fraction)

output
  cashflow d,e
```

The fraction 0.7 is now declared as a named constant. It could also have been specified as a numerical input parameter. Note that the Divide operation has two output values and that its parameter is completely consumed. Cashflow preservation is checked only for cashflow edges, so you can use numerical or boolean constants or parameters multiple times or not at all. Several operations can be combined on one line, so the structure part of the above example can be abbreviated to

```
(d,e) = Divide(a + b, fraction)
```

Names always refer to single edges/values, never to tuples. When expressions are nested, they may build tuples with tuples as elements. Such a nested tuple is flattened out to a single non-nested tuple. For example, the tuple $((2,3),4,(5,6,7))$ is flattened to the tuple $(2,3,4,5,6,7)$.

This is the basic core language, which is more or less what was implemented by the bank (see section 7 for more on this), but we can make various extensions that make the language more interesting and generally useful.

4   Function Definitions

These are trivial to add: A function declaration has exactly the same structure as a program: It consists of declarations, input, structure and output. A function is called exactly like a predefined operation, taking a tuple of parameters as input and returning a tuple as output.

Cashflow preservation for declared functions is checked in the same way as above: Each cashflow is defined and used exactly once in the function.

5   Conditionals

It is useful to construct cashflows depending on some condition. This condition can test current or past events. In the first case, the condition can change arbitrarily often over time, but since the latter tests if a certain event has happened at any point in the past, it can change status at most once (from false to true). We use two different conditionals for these two cases:

$$exp \to \textbf{if } cond \textbf{ then } exp_1 \textbf{ else } exp_2$$
$$exp \to \textbf{until } cond \textbf{ use } exp_1 \textbf{ thereafter } exp_2$$

Note that the conditionals are expressions, so they are used to the right of an assignment. It is a requirement that the two branches (exp_1 and exp_2) have identical cashflows, i.e., that they use the same cashflow variables and produce identical tuples. This isn't difficult to check, it gets more interesting when we consider the condition. A condition may want to check properties of cashflows, e.g., to see which has the highest interest payment. But this check doesn't actually use the money in the cashflows, so counting it as a use would go against cashflow preservation. Hence, we must distinguish between uses of a cashflow that build new cashflows and uses that inspect the cashflow without consuming it. We can do this by using *linear types* [7].

6   A Linear Type System

The basic idea is to use two different types for cashflows: *cashflow* for cashflows that are consumed when used and *cashflow0* for cashflows that aren't. Additionally, we have types for booleans and numbers and tuples of these atomic types. We denote an atomic type by σ (possibly subscripted) and atomic or tuple types by τ (also subscripted):

$$\sigma = bool \mid number \mid cashflow \mid cashflow0$$
$$\tau = \sigma \mid (\sigma_0, \dots, \sigma_n)$$

We will describe the type system by showing rules for type-correctness. For brevity, we show rules only for the subset of the language shown in Fig. 1. The rules for the rest of the language follow the same general structure. We have chosen $+$ as an example of a basic operation on cashflows and $<$ as an inspection operation. Note that $+$ can be used both on pairs of consumable cashflows, inspect-able cashflows and numbers. $<$ compares two numbers or the total payments (interest $+$ principal) of two cashflows. This is usually used in combination with an operator (not shown) that splits interest and principal payments into

$$Program \rightarrow \textbf{input } Decl \textbf{ structure } Stat \textbf{ output } Decl$$

$$
\begin{aligned}
Stat \quad &\rightarrow (x_1, \ldots, x_n) = Exp \\
&\mid Stat \; ; \; Stat
\end{aligned}
$$

$$
\begin{aligned}
Decl \quad &\rightarrow \tau \; x_1, \ldots, x_n \\
&\mid Decl \; ; \; Decl
\end{aligned}
$$

$$
\begin{aligned}
Exp \quad &\rightarrow x \\
&\mid Exp + Exp \\
&\mid Exp < Exp \\
&\mid \textbf{if } Exp \textbf{ then } Exp \textbf{ else } Exp
\end{aligned}
$$

Fig. 1. Syntax for a subset of the cashflow-reengineering language

$$\text{Weak} \quad \frac{\Gamma \vdash e : \tau}{\Gamma, x : \tau^{\blacksquare} \vdash e : \tau}, \quad \tau^{\blacksquare} \neq cashflow$$

$$\text{Exch} \quad \frac{\Gamma, x : \tau^{\blacksquare}, y : \tau^{\boxminus}, \Delta \vdash e : \tau}{\Gamma, y : \tau^{\boxminus}, x : \tau^{\blacksquare}, \Delta \vdash e : \tau}$$

$$\text{Copy} \quad \frac{\Gamma, x : \tau^{\blacksquare}, x : \tau^{\blacksquare} \vdash e : \tau}{\Gamma, x : \tau^{\blacksquare} \vdash e : \tau}, \quad \tau^{\blacksquare} \neq cashflow$$

$$\text{CopC} \quad \frac{\Gamma, x : cashflow0, x : cashflow \vdash e : \tau}{\Gamma, x : cashflow \vdash e : \tau}$$

Fig. 2. Structural rules

two different cashflows (so interest or principal can be compared separately). Note that the compared cashflows are not consumed, so the arguments can't be of type *cashflow*. We have omitted the constant declaration part of the program, so *Decl* refers to declarations of input and output variables.

We use a notation for linear types similar to [10]. Type environments (denoted by Δ, Γ and Θ) are lists of pairs of names and types (each written as $x : \tau$ and separated by commas). When typing expressions, we manipulate type environments with structural rules that can reorder, copy and delete pairs. We ensure that pairs where the type is *cashflow* can not be copied or deleted. The structural rules are shown in Fig. 2. Note that we (in rule CopC) can make an inspect-only copy of a cashflow variable.

We add rules for expressions, declarations and programs in Fig. 3.

Program:

$$\text{Prog}\ \dfrac{\vdash d_i : \Gamma \quad \Gamma \vdash s : \Delta \quad \vdash d_o : \Delta}{\vdash \textbf{input}\ d_i\ \textbf{structure}\ s\ \textbf{output}\ d_o}$$

Stat:

$$\text{Assg}\ \dfrac{\Gamma \vdash e : (\tau_1, \ldots, \tau_n)}{\Gamma, \Delta \vdash (x_1, \ldots, x_n) = e : (\Delta, x_1 : \tau_1, \ldots, x_n : \tau_n)},\ (\{x_1, \ldots, x_n\} \cap dom(\Delta)) = \emptyset$$

$$\text{Seq}\ \dfrac{\Gamma \vdash s_1 : \Delta \quad \Delta \vdash s_2 : \Theta}{\Gamma \vdash s_1\ s_2 : \Theta}$$

Decl:

$$\text{Decl}\ \dfrac{}{\vdash \tau\ x_1, \ldots, x_n : (x_1 : \tau, \ldots, x_n : \tau)}$$

$$\text{Dseq}\ \dfrac{\vdash d_1 : \Gamma \quad \vdash d_2 : \Delta}{\vdash d_1\ d_2 : \Gamma, \Delta},\ (dom(\Gamma) \cap dom(\Delta)) = \emptyset$$

Exp:

$$\text{Var}\ \dfrac{}{x : \tau \vdash x : \tau}$$

$$\text{AddC}\ \dfrac{\Gamma \vdash e_1 : cashflow \quad \Delta \vdash e_2 : cashflow}{\Gamma, \Delta \vdash e_1 + e_2 : cashflow}$$

$$\text{Add0}\ \dfrac{\Gamma \vdash e_1 : cashflow0 \quad \Delta \vdash e_2 : cashflow0}{\Gamma, \Delta \vdash e_1 + e_2 : cashflow0} \quad \text{AddN}\ \dfrac{\Gamma \vdash e_1 : number \quad \Delta \vdash e_2 : number}{\Gamma, \Delta \vdash e_1 + e_2 : number}$$

$$\text{LesC}\ \dfrac{\Gamma \vdash e_1 : cashflow0 \quad \Delta \vdash e_2 : cashflow0}{\Gamma, \Delta \vdash e_1 < e_2 : bool} \quad \text{LesN}\ \dfrac{\Gamma \vdash e_1 : number \quad \Delta \vdash e_2 : number}{\Gamma, \Delta \vdash e_1 < e_2 : bool}$$

$$\text{If}\ \dfrac{\Gamma \vdash c : bool \quad \Delta \vdash e_1 : \tau \quad \Delta \vdash e_2 : \tau}{\Gamma, \Delta \vdash \textbf{if}\ c\ \textbf{then}\ e_1\ \textbf{else}\ e_2\ :\ \tau}$$

Fig. 3. Typing rules

Most of the rules are straightforward. Note that the rule for assignment (Assg) splits the environment into the part that is consumed by the right-hand side and the part that is left alone. The latter is extended with the bindings made by the assignment, after checking that none of the defined names already occur in it. This actually allows reassignment of a name after it is consumed, but we don't find this a problem. In fact, the users of the language like it, as they don't have to invent new intermediate names all the time. Note how cashflow preservation is checked by verifying that the declaration of the output variables to a program correspond to the final environment. The rule is slightly simplified, as it doesn't allow non-cashflow variables to remain in the environment without being output, even though this is harmless. This weakness can be handled by applying variants of the structural rules to the final environment.

7   Conclusion

The bank has only implemented the core language as described in section 3, minus nested expressions. Their experiences are shown in the following fragment of a letter sent to DIKU a while after the language was put into use[2].

> After the initial pilot phase we can draw some conclusions about [the language]. The language works well in the intended context. We have achieved separation of the abstract description of structuring of bonds and the initial parameters, such as interest rates and principal balances, which later can be fine-adjusted to find optimal business opportunities. This has made the work considerably more efficient.
>
> We have not implemented the complicated structures, such as conditionals, but the basic dataflow model corresponds well to how people think about structuring of bonds. Using only the basic language primitives have lead to quite large and complex programs, but by making a library of the most used operations, we have simplified the use considerably.

The bank implemented the language entirely in-house from the design document. The choice to implement only the most basic subset of the language may be due to the bank first wanting to try out the basic design and finding that sufficient, perhaps combined not having people with background in type systems, which is required for the extensions.

The bank found it necessary to have a large set of primitive operations. It is my belief that the full version of the language would have allowed most of these operations to be defined in the language itself using only a few basic operations combined with conditionals and function declarations.

It is the opinion of the author that the financial world offers many opportunities for using small, well-defined domain-specific languages, as also evidenced in the section on related work below.

Related Work

The language Risal [11] is intended for the same purpose as our language: Describing and manipulating interest-rate products. As our language, it is actively in use in the bank world. The main new feature of our language is the linear type system for ensuring cashflow preservation.

Jones et al. [8] describe a language embedded in Haskell for describing financial and insurance contracts and estimating their worth through an evaluation semantics. The purpose is quite similar to what is done here, and one option for

---

[2] Translated from Danish and abbreviated slightly.

the evaluation semantics is, indeed, Monte Carlo simulation. The main differences, apart from the difference between the contracts modelled by the language in [8] and the cashflows modelled by our language is that Jones implements his language as a set of combinators in Haskell where we have chosen a stand-alone language. Furthermore, there is no notion of cashflow preservation or similar in [8]. According to the paper, the language may be implemented as a stand-alone language in the future.

[2] describes a domain-specific language for a quite different kind of financial application: Tracking and predicting stock-market values.

Linear types and related systems have been used for many purposes, for example converting call-by-need to call-by-name [10] and for ensuring single-threadedness for update-able structures in functional languages [3,13]. The first of these examples uses linear types *descriptively*, i.e., for identifying linear uses, while the latter uses the types *prescriptively* by disallowing non-linear uses of certain variables. As such, it is closest to our use of linear types, which also is intended to forbid nonlinear uses of cashflows.

References

1. Adobe postscript 3 home page.
   http://www.adobe.com/products/postscript/.
2. Saswat Anand, Wei-Ngan Chin, and Siau-Cheng Khoo. Charting patterns on price history. In *International Conference on Functional Programming*, pages 134–145, 2001.
3. Erik Barendsen and Sjaak Smetsers. Uniqueness typing for functional languages with graph rewriting semantics. In *Mathematical Structures in Computer Science 6*, pages 579 – 612, 1997.
4. Per Bjesse, Koen Claessen, Mary Sheeran, and Satnam Singh. Lava: Hardware design in Haskell. In *ICFP 1998*, 1998.
5. P. Boyle, M. Broadie, and P. Glasserman. Monte Carlo methods for security pricing. *Journal of Economic Dynamics and Control*, 21(1267), 1997.
6. C.J. Date and Hugh Darwen. *A Guide to The SQL Standard*. Addison-Wesley, third edition edition, 1993.
7. Jean-Yves Girard. Linear logic. *Theoretical Computer Science*, (50):1 – 102, 1987.
8. Simon Peyton Jones, Jean-Marc Eber, and Julian Seward. Composing contracts: an adventure in financial engineering. In *ICFP'00*. ACM Press, 2000.
9. P.C. Treleaven and R.P. Hopkins. Data-driven and demand-driven computer architecture. *ACM Computing Surveys*, 14(1), 1982.
10. David N. Turner, Philip Wadler, and Christian Mossin. Once upon a type. In *FPCA'95*, pages 1 – 11. ACM Press, 1995.
11. A. van Deursen. Domain-specific languages versus object-oriented frameworks: A financial engineering case study. In *Smalltalk and Java in Industry and Academia, STJA'97*, pages 35–39, 1997.
12. Arie van Deursen, Paul Klint, and Joost Visser. Domain-specific languages: An annotated bibliography. *SIGPLAN Notices*, 35(6):26–36, 2000.
13. Philip Wadler. Linear types can change the world! In *Programming concepts and methods*. North Holland, 1990.

Storing Properties in Grouped Tagged Tuples

Roland Weiss and Volker Simonis

Wilhelm-Schickard-Institut für Informatik, Universität Tübingen
Sand 13, 72076 Tübingen, Germany
{weissr,simonis}@informatik.uni-tuebingen.de

Abstract. A technique is presented that allows one to store groups of properties in C++, and single properties out of these groups can later be accessed by their name. Our approach refines previous work in this area and is an example for the application of template metaprogramming [1]. Typical usage examples of the introduced class templates are internal representations of serialized data, well suited for semi-automatic as well as manual generation of the corresponding class types.

1 Introduction

Cartesian product types are a fundamental building block for composite types in virtually all modern programming languages. For example, they are present as record types in Pascal, Ada, and Modula-3, in C/C++ [8] as structs, and functional languages often support tuple types, e.g. ML [10] and Haskell [9].

However, explicitly defining a new class in C++ in order to create a simple record type without advanced functionality was perceived as an unnecessary heavyweight process. Numerous approaches for integrating lightweight tuples were developed. Most notably, Jakko Järvi introduced a tuple library [7] that allows access to its elements by index or type, which finally resulted in the Boost Tuple Library [5]. He identified handling of multiple return values as one of the main applications of his tuple library [6].

Emily Winch proposed a tuple variant with access to its elements by name [16]. This comes closer to a typical record type. The advantage of the technique presented by Winch is that parts of a class can be generated with template metaprogramming. Therefore, tedious and error-prone class operations like constructors and the assignment operator can be generated from a formal description. Furthermore, she describes an iterator interface for manipulation of the tuple's elements with algorithms that execute at compile time.

We will identify a shortcoming in her implementation that may lead to inconsistencies and propose an adequate solution, which relies on template metaprogramming and is completely transparent to the user. We then show how this basic record type can be extended in order to group common properties in a composite data structure that still allows flat, direct access to single properties. Frequently, such a data structure is useful when creating an internal representation of serialized data.

M. Broy and A.V. Zamulin (Eds.): PSI 2003, LNCS 2890, pp. 22–29, 2003.

2 Named Objects Revisited

Winch shows in great detail how tuples of named objects can be created, manipulated and how they can help building complex classes on top of them. However, there is a fundamental problem in her approach for defining a tuple. This becomes apparent when looking at her introductory example:

⟨**Listing 1.** Code extracted from file src/named_objects.cpp, lines 9 to 12⟩ ≡
```
    struct myBigClass {}; struct age {}; struct myDatabase {};
    typedef makeVarlistType3<
      BigClass*, myBigClass, int, age, Database&, myDatabase
    >::list VarlistType;
```

First, one has to define empty structs in order to introduce their names for accessing tuple elements. Then, these names are used in the tuple's type definition. There, one has to pair them with what we call an *implementation type*. The tuple will actually hold elements of the implementation type, and these elements can be easily referenced by their *name type* later on. The problem arises when one creates other tuples using the same name type. Usually, the pair of implementation and name types is fixed, otherwise the resulting data structures would become very confusing for the user. So one has to remember this type pairing to keep the related data structures consistent. This represents a typical maintenance nightmare.

How can we deal with this problem? The desirable situation would be to permanently tie an implementation type to its corresponding name type. As structs can contain type definitions, this is achieved without problems. More challenging is the creation of a tuple type consisting of elements whose types are determined by associated implementation types. Our solution is sketched in the next paragraphs.

The definition of a tuple functionally equivalent to the one presented in listing 1 now looks like this:

⟨**Listing 2.** Code extracted from file src/named_objects.cpp, lines 20 to 24⟩ ≡
```
    struct myBigClass { typedef BigClass* type; };
    struct age { typedef int type; };
    struct myDatabase { typedef Database& type; };
    typedef Tagged_Tuple<
      TypeList<myBigClass, age, myDatabase>::type > PropType;
```

We see how a name type is permanently associated with its implementation type by nesting it directly inside the name type's struct. When defining a tagged tuple[1], one simply has to list the name types. Notice that the name types are passed inside a type list. This saves us from explicitly denoting the number of names as in the constructor function **makeVarlistType3**. The type list constructor used is an extension of the Loki library [1] which is based on an idea contributed to Thomas Becker [2].

Type lists are central to our approach for solving the problem of computing the type of the implementation tuple. Loki provides a tuple type that features a

---

[1] The term *tagged tuple* was coined by David Abrahams in this context.

constructor accepting a type list which contains its elements' types. Unfortunately, we cannot use the type list passed in the `Tagged_Tuple` constructor, because therein the implementation types are wrapped inside their name types. We employ a special template metaprogram `ExtractTypes` that creates a new type list from a type list consisting of name types with nested implementation types. It simply walks over all elements in the instantiation type list `TL` and extracts each nested implementation type, which is appended to the new list recursively. With this template metafunction at hand, the implementation tuple's type is computed like this:

⟨**Listing 3.** Code extracted from file `src/Named_Props.hpp`, line 104⟩ ≡
```
    typedef typename ExtractTypes<TL>::type types_tl;
```

This type list `types_tl` can now be used to instantiate the tuple `m_props` holding the actual elements. We face a final complication when implementing the tagged tuple's access methods. Access to an element is triggered by a name type given as instantiation parameter `PropT`, but the implementation tuple only knows its implementation types. We have to use the fact that an implementation type is located at the same position as its hosting name type in their corresponding type lists. Again, a template metaprogram computes the return type for us. The metafunction `return_t` expects three parameters: the name type for which the implementation should be located, and the type lists holding the implementation and name types, respectively. It returns the implementation type located at the same position as the name type. Now, we can define the mutating access function in terms of this helper function:

⟨**Listing 4.** Code extracted from file `src/Named_Props.hpp`, lines 137 to 141⟩ ≡
```
    template <class PropT>
    typename return_t<PropT, tuple_type, TL>::type at() {
      return Loki::Field<
        Loki::TL::IndexOf<props_tl, PropT>::value >(m_props);
    }
```

At this point, we supply the same functionality as Winch's heterogenous list, but with a more consistent definition for the name and implementation pair types. Type lists and template metaprogramming were instrumental in making the required computations transparent for the user.

3   Groups of Tagged Tuples

We now move on to a data structure that is tailored towards a special kind of problem. When internal data in serialized, these data often consists to a large degree of so called properties, e.g. the JavaBeans specifications [3] lists properties as one of its three main constituents. Properties describe the section of an object's internal state that is made visible to other entities, this means they usually can be read and set with simple access methods. Compared to other members, they have simple dependencies and can be changed in isolation.

The tagged tuple type described in the previous section is a good candidate for storing properties. In this section we present a convenient class template for combining groups of properties. This is especially useful if property groups are part of several components. Let us state the requirements we have on the class template `Named_Properties`.

1. Access to single properties is type safe, i.e. line numbers should be stored as integers, file names as strings, and so on.
2. Related properties can be grouped together, e.g. information relevant for debugging, or color information.
3. Groups of properties can themselves be combined to completely describe the visible part of a component's internal state exposed through properties.
4. Access to a single property should be possible simply by its name, i.e. the property group it belongs to should be deduced automatically.

The first two requirements are already fulfilled by `Tagged_Tuple`. Combining property groups is also achieved easily by putting tagged tuples into a tuple type themselves. The hardest part is providing *flat* access to single properties. This is not possible with standard record types, because one has to fully specify the target property, e.g. `Button.colors.foreground`, which selects a button's foreground color, which is part of the button's colors property group.

We will now develop the class template `Named_Properties`. It has one template parameter `TL`, which is a type list that should contain tagged tuple types. The named properties' single member is a tuple generated with this type list.

⟨**Listing 5.** Code extracted from file `src/Named_Props.hpp`, line 210⟩ ≡
```
template <class TL> class Named_Properties
```

In order to support the last requirement, we once again have to resort to extensive template metaprogramming. This is possible because we know at compile time which property groups make up the data structure, and we can look up the desired property inside these groups. The following listing shows how the element access method `at()` is realized.

⟨**Listing 6.** Code extracted from file `src/Named_Props.hpp`, lines 259 to 263⟩ ≡
```
template <class PropT>
typename return_t<PropT, tuple_type, TL>::type at() {
    return Loki::Field<IndexOfNP<TL, PropT>::value>(m_props).
        template at<PropT>();
}
```

The method's return type is computed with the local template metafunction `return_t`, which first determines the property group that contains the name type `PropT`, and then selects the implementation type at the name type's position. The same two-level process is applied in order to obtain the reference of the actual element. First, we select the property group containing the name type `PropT`, then retrieve the reference of the tuple element by this name. This can be seen directly in the body of method `at()` in listing 6. Fig. 1 depicts this two-level process of determining the property's reference. The reference of the shaded element belonging to `data` will be bound to `x`.

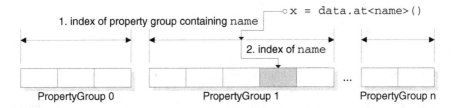

Fig. 1. The two-level selection process in method `at()`

At the moment, named properties support the presented two level access to elements. There is no conceptual obstacle to extending them to three or more levels, but it seems questionable if such class templates make sense. Name conflicts are more likely to arise, and tracing the property groups is a major challenge for the user.

Finally, we have to consider the requirements on the instantiation parameters of the class templates and their method templates. The grouping approach relies on the fact that a name type is only part of one property group. If this condition is not met, accessing such a property will only locate its first appearance in the property groups given in the instantiating type list. Furthermore, if method `at()` is instantiated with a name type that is not present in any property group this will result in a compile time error, a reasonable reaction. The only problem with this behavior are the confusing error messages generated by some compilers.

We also want to mention an alternative approach for fulfilling the stated requirements of class `Named_Properties`. Grouping properties can be achieved by appending type lists that constitute groups of properties. Then, this type list can be used to instantiate a tagged tuple. It will contain all properties and supports flat access to them for free. This approach has its merits in its simplicity, because it does not need class `Named_Properties` at all. However, we loose the ability to use different meta operations on isolated groups of properties, as describe in Winch's paper [16].

4   Example Applications and Performance Tests

Named properties are part of the support library in a compiler project [15]. The project's central intermediate representation consists of an abstract syntax tree. Nodes of this tree data structure contain named properties, which combine a node's general and specific property groups. General properties fall into categories like debugging information, type modifiers, or cross references. Local properties are put into one group and complement the global groups which are reused in several node types. For example, the properties of an algorithm node are defined like this:

⟨**Listing 7.** Code extracted from file `src/Algorithm.hpp`, lines 50 to 53⟩ ≡

```
    typedef Named_Properties< Loki::TypeList<
      id_property, idref_property, builtin_property,
      debug_property, access_mod_property>::type
    > algorithm_properties;
```

The named property is then aggregated by a generic syntax tree node, a technique similar to the one described in [14]. Named properties can be reused in several other application domains where the class types have a high percentage of property members. Examples are document management systems, or an internal representation of HTML nodes. In the HTML document type definition [11] *generic attributes* can be directly modeled with named properties. Of course, the same procedure can be applied to XML documents.

Finally, we want to compare the performance of our data structures generated with template metaprogramming to C++ classes written by hand. For this purpose, we use a little bench marking application. It first creates a huge vector, and then sets and reads all the properties of its element type, which is of course an instantiation of `Named_Properties`. Tables 1 and 2 summarize the results of the tests. The times in table 1 are given in microseconds and are computed by taking the arithmetic mean of five runs.

Table 1. Benchmark results for comparing named properties to handwritten classes with a vector of 2 million elements, performed on a Pentium 4 machine (2GHz, 512 MB) running Windows XP

compiler	handwritten classes				named properties				AP
	create	write	read	sum	create	write	read	sum	
g++ 3.2	739	2089	2155	*4983*	1104	2750	2952	*6806*	1.37
g++ 3.2 -O2	613	1614	1672	*3899*	661	1710	1767	*4138*	1.06
Metrowerks 8.3	431	4068	877	*5376*	495	4192	991	*5678*	1.06
Metrowerks 8.3 -O4	276	3801	495	*4572*	340	3908	583	*4831*	1.06
Visual Studio 7.1	470	4068	877	*5376*	495	4192	991	*5678*	1.51
Visual Studio 7.1 -O2	470	994	461	*1925*	481	1015	473	*1969*	1.02

Table 1 shows the results for three compilers, both with and without optimizations. We enumerate the results for initializing a vector, and subsequently writing to and reading from all its elements. Also, the sum of the runtimes is listed. In the last column the abstraction penalty (AP) is given, which is the ratio of dividing the runtime of the abstract version by the runtime of the one written at a lower level [12]. In our case, the code using handwritten classes represents the lower level version.

Table 2. Object size for data types used in benchmarks (see table 1)

compiler	object size	
	handwritten classes	named properties
g++ 3.2	32	32
Metrowerks 8.3	56	56
Visual Studio 7.1	104	112

Table 2 lists the sizes of the vector's element data types, both for handwritten classes and those using named properties. This is done for all tested compilers. The sizes for debug and release versions did not differ.

The abstraction penalty for using the class template `Named_Properties` is very low for optimized builds, between 1.02 and 1.06. And even for code produced without optimizations an AP ranging from 1.06 to 1.51 is quite moderate. This demonstrates that the tested compilers are effective at inlining the methods generated by the template mechanism.

The difference of the elements' object size is caused by the compilers' standard library implementation. The `std::string` class of the g++ compiler has size 4, Metrowerks' `string` class has size 12, and an object of class `string` in the Visual Studio amounts to 28 bytes. The named properties used in the benchmarks contain three strings, which accounts for the different object sizes. However, the object size of the handwritten classes and generated named properties are the same except for the Microsoft compiler[2], which is the primary observation to be made with respect to memory efficiency of named properties.

5   Conclusions

We have presented a technique that allows type-safe storage of groups of properties. Noteworthy for our implementation is the combination of class templates with metaprogramming on types. This integrated approach to code generation as provided by the C++ template mechanism has proven very successful for the development of efficient and type-safe components [4,13]. However, the actual incarnation of this metaprogramming environment leaves much to be desired, mainly motivated by the fact that it was a by-product not originally intended when designing C++'s template machinery. Further research should focus on identifying the typical needs for such a metaprogramming facility. The general technique could then be applied to languages other than C++.

---

[2] The C++ compiler packaged in Microsoft's Visual Studio 7.1 is their first C++ compiler that is able to handle advanced template metaprograms, therefore this peculiarity may disappear in subsequent releases.

References

1. Andrei Alexandrescu: *Modern C++ Design.* Addison-Wesley, 2001.
2. Thomas Becker: *STL & Generic Programming —- Typelists.* C/C++ Users Journal, December 2002.
3. Graham Hamilton (Editor): *JavaBeans^{TM}, V1.01.* Sun Microsystems, 1997.
4. Scott Haney, and James Crotinger: *How Templates Enable High-Performance Scientific Computing in C++.* Journal of Computing in Science and Engineering, Vol. 1, No. 4, IEEE, July/August 1999.
5. Jaakko Järvi: *Tuple types and multiple return values.* C/C++ Users Journal, August 2001.
6. Jaakko Järvi: *Tuples and multiple return values in C++.* Turku Centre for Computer Science, Technical Report 249, March 1999.
7. Jaakko Järvi: *ML-style Tuple Assignment in Standard C++ – Extending the Multiple Return Value Formalism.* Turku Centre for Computer Science, Technical Report 267, April 1999.
8. JTC1/SC22 – Programming languages, their environment and system software interfaces: *Programming Languages – C++.* International Organization for Standardization, ISO/IEC 14882, 1998.
9. Simon Peyton Jones, and John Hughes (eds.): *Haskell 98: A Non-strict, Purely Functional Language.* Language Report, 1998. Available at www.haskell.org.
10. Robin Milner, Mads Tofte, Robert Harper, and David MacQueen: *The Definition of Standard ML - Revised.* MIT Press, May 1997.
11. Dave Raggett, Arnaud Le Hors, and Ian Jacobs (editors): *HTML 4.01 Specification.* W3C Recommendation, December 1999. Available at www.w3.org/TR.
12. Arch D. Robertson: *The Abstraction Penalty for Small Objects in C++.* Workshop on Parallel Object-Oriented Methods and Applications (POOMA 96), Santa Fe, New Mexico, USA, February/March 1996.
13. Jeremy G. Siek, Lie-Quan Lee, and Andrew Lumsdaine: *The Boost Graph Library. User Guide and Reference Manual.* Addison-Wesley Publishing Company, 2001.
14. Volker Simonis, Roland Weiss: *Heterogeneous, Nested STL Containers in C++.* LNCS No. 1755 (PSI '99): p. 263–267, Springer, 1999.
15. Roland Weiss: *Compiling and Distributing Generic Libraries with Heterogeneous Data and Code Representation.* PhD thesis, University of Tübingen, 2003.
16. Emily Winch: *Heterogenous Lists of Named Objects,* Second Workshop on C++ Template Programming, Tampa Bay, Florida, USA, October 2001.

A Polymorphic Radix-n Framework for Fast Fourier Transforms

Marcin Zalewski and Sibylle Schupp

Dept. of Computer Science,
Rensselaer Polytechnic Institute (RPI), Troy, NY
{zalewm,schupp}@cs.rpi.edu

Abstract. We provide a polymorphic framework for radix-n Fast Fourier Transforms (FFTs) where all known kinds of monomoporhic radix-n algorithms can be obtained by specialization. The framework is mathematically based on the Cooley-Tukey mapping, and implemented as a C++ template meta-program. Avoiding run-time overhead, all specializations are performed statically.

1 Introduction

The Discrete Fourier Transform (DFT), one of the most fundamental operations in digital signal processing and many other application areas, is a complex matrix–vector–product. All algorithms that compute the DFT in $\mathcal{O}(N \log_2 N)$ time for an input vector of length N are collectively called Fast Fourier Transforms (FFTs). For composite N, $N = N_1 \cdot N_2$, Cooley and Tukey [1], introduced the family of *radix-n* FFTs ($n = \min\{N_1, N_2\}$), a divide-and-conquer strategy of 3 stages. First, N_1 DFTs of length N_2 are computed. Second, the results of these N_1 DFTs are multiplied by so-called *twiddle factors*. And third, N_2 DFTs of length N_1 are performed on the results of the second step. Eq. (1) lists the Cooley-Tukey mapping in closed form (W_N denotes an N-th root of unity, the respective stages 1 and 2 are indicated with an over- and underlining brace):

$$X_{k_1 N_2 + k_2} = \sum_{n_1=0}^{N_1-1} (\underbrace{ \sum_{n_2=0}^{N_2-1} x_{n_2 N_1 + n_1} W_{N_2}^{n_2 k} \overbrace{W_N^{n_1 k_2}}}) W_{N_1}^{n_1 k_1}. \tag{1}$$

Although the Cooley-Tukey mapping defines the entire family of radix-n FFTs, it usually is not implemented directly. Instead, current radix-FFTs are built from *butterfly* components, which greatly obscure their common core. In fact, the four major radix-2 algorithms — the most widely used FFTs at all — currently have little in common both with each other and with any other radix-n implementation.

In this paper, we provide a polymorphic framework for radix-n FFTs. Applying advanced techniques of generic programming, we are able to directly implement the Cooley-Tukey mapping so that the common radix-2, as well as all other radix-n algorithms can be obtained by specialization. Such a specialization

M. Broy and A.V. Zamulin (Eds.): PSI 2003, LNCS 2890, pp. 30–37, 2003.

need not incur any overhead in run time or space: in our C++ implementation, all relevant parameters are static parameters so that the dispatch to a particular, monomorphic radix-n algorithm happens at compile time.

The paper is organized in 3 sections: first we recapitulate the four kinds of monomorphic radix-2 algorithms. Next, we present our polymorphic radix-n framework. Lastly, we discuss related and future work.

2 Monomorphic Radix-2 FFT Implementations

One distinguishes two fundamental radix-2 decompositions: *decimation-in-time (DIT)* and *decimation-in-frequency (DIF)*. In DIT, subproblems are obtained by dividing the *input* series into an even-indexed set $\{x_{2k}\}_{k=0,\dots,N/2-1}$ and an odd-indexed set $\{x_{2k+1}\}_{k=0,\dots,N/2-1}$, whereas in DIF, the subproblems result from decimating the *output* series into an even-indexed set $\{X_{2k}\}_{k=0,\dots,N/2-1}$ and an odd-indexed set $\{X_{2k+1}\}_{k=0,\dots,N/2-1}$. The computations of DIT and DIF differ accordingly. In short, the DIT algorithm consists of three nested loops: the outermost loop, which controls the division into subsequences, the middle loop, which iterates over the resulting subsequences, and the innermost loop, which performs $N/2$ computations for subproblems of size 2. Each of these $N/2$ fundamental computations is called a *butterfly*, due to the shape of its flow graph. In contrast, the DIF algorithm, splitting the input sequence differently, has a different outermost and, as a consequence, different middle loop. Most importantly, the butterflies for DIFs and DITs differ, and the twiddle factors in the butterfly-loop are non-constant for DIFs, but constant for DITs.

Another characteristic feature of a radix-2 FFT is the order in which the output is computed. Since the algorithms are in-place, each butterfly overwrites two values of the input sequence. As a result, the output is permuted, albeit in a regular way: for radix 2 it is bit-reversed. If the output needs to be in natural order, it is easiest to bit-reverse the input.

Again, the different decomposition directions behave differently. In decimation-in-time with bit-reversed input, the twiddle factors in the butterfly-loop depend on the loop index, while in decimation-in-frequency with bit-reversal, the twiddle number in the innermost loop is constant. At the same time, both algorithms differ from their counterpart for natural input with respect to the iteration space that the butterfly-loop defines. In the radix-2 algorithms with natural order, the butterfly-loop initially has length $N/2$ and decreases by a factor of 2 in each iteration; in radix-2 algorithms with bit-reversed input, the inner loop has initial length 1 and increases by a factor of 2. No implementation we are aware of allows for any sharing between the implementation of any two of them: they constitute four entirely separate implementations.

3 A Polymorphic Radix-n Algorithm

The algorithm we present follows closely the Cooley-Tukey formula, i.e., it solves a given problem of length N recursively, by dividing it into N_1 subproblems of size N_2 and N_2 subproblems of size N_1, with $N = N_1 \cdot N_2$. The division stops at subproblems of size of the chosen radix and then applies a direct computation method. Now, how do we get from Eq. (1) to an effective procedure and how do we ensure that its specialization to a direct, monomorphic implementation happens entirely statically, without any overhead? In the following, we refer to the sizes of the subproblems by N_1 and N_2.

3.1   Design Issues

Obviously, the decomposition factors N_1 and N_2, since they control the specialization, can no longer be implicitly assumed in the algorithm. Instead, there has to be a way to bind them to different values. Moreover, their values need to be known statically since otherwise specializations cannot take place at compile time. Representing N_1 and N_2 as static parameters, however, raises the question how their decomposition is accomplished in the subsequent recursion stage and, more generally, how the divide-and-conquer scheme is defined both abstractly and statically. If users "select" the desired FFT via specialization at the top level of the polymorphic algorithm, its body needs to propagate their choice and to perform the appropriate recursion step then automatically. An abstract and static divide-and-conquer scheme provided, next, the twiddle factors and the input sequence need to be modeled so that they allow for the different access patterns that the different decimations require.

For efficiency reasons, twiddle factors usually are pre-computed rather than calculated on the fly, and stored in a container. Depending on the decimation chosen, the step-size varies with which this sequence is traversed. Again, the polymorphic algorithm can no longer implicitly operate with a particular step-size but has to refer to it abstractly. Similarly with the input sequence, which is given in natural order in some cases, in bit-reversed order in others. Looping over the input sequence has to be expressed abstractly, so that one instance of the loop steps through the sequence in the "random" fashion dictated by the bit-reversal, while another instance traverses it linearly. Finally, the view on the input and the twiddle sequence need to be coupled so that they always assume the same input order. How to properly identify the required parameters and how to design the parameterization to allow for compile-time specialization, is subject of the next section.

3.2   Data Abstraction

Essential for the intended code sharing is the ability to access data in a uniform and abstract manner, independently from the underlying container and the method of its traversal. The concept of an *iterator* proves to be the appropriate abstraction for this problem. An iterator adds a layer of abstraction between the data and its access by providing an interface between both. Different implementations of a particular iterator category, thus, can provide different traversal protocols while still complying to a common interface. Because of this indirection, iterators are widely used in generic programming and, through the Standard Template Library, standardized. In our algorithm, the iterator abstraction makes it in particular possible to abstract from the index-notation used in the mathematical representation of the Cooley-Tukey mapping. Abstracting from indices is necessary for a polymorphic algorithm, since the layout of the data may not correspond to the positions defined by an index.

Fig. 1 shows the structure of the body of the polymorphic radix-n algorithm, shared among its different specializations: in direct correspondence to the mathematical Cooley-Tukey mapping, it is a sequence of three loops. The first loop performs the DFTs of size N_2, the second loop defines the twiddle factor multiplication, and the last loop represents the DFTs of size N_1 computed in the outermost summation in Eq. (1). The two program variables *first_iterator* and *second_iterator*, in the first and the last loop, encapsulate the different advancement semantics of DIT or DIF, with natural or bit-reversed input. The multiplication by twiddle factors, in the middle loop, requires a traversal protocol other than sequential advancement, since the access to twiddle factors changes with the loop iteration. Besides, a twiddle factor with index $j * k$ is not necessarily located at the $(j * k)^{th}$ position of the twiddle container. We use a generic index operation, usually referred to as random access operation, to hide the location of the proper twiddle factor.

1.   **for** i **from** 1 **to** N_1
2.   perform DFT of size N_2 on data beginning at *first_iterator*
3.   advance *first_iterator* to the next position
4.   **for** j **from** 0 **to** $(N_1 - 1)$
5.   **for** k **from** 0 **to** $(N_2 - 1)$
6.   multiply k^{th} output from j^{th} DFT of size N_2 by $(j*k)^{th}$ *twiddle_iterator*
7.   **for** i **from** 1 **to** N_2
8.   perform DFT of size N_1 on data beginning at *second_iterator*
9.   advance *second_iterator* to next position

Fig. 1. Basic loop structure of polymorphic radix-n algorithm

Since N_1 and N_2 change in the course of the computation, the loops in Fig. 1 are not constant but change their iteration space from one recursion step to the next. Consequently, the behavior of the iterators has to be adjusted between the recursion steps, and this adjustment has to be done in a generic and statically decidable manner. In generic programming, *iterator adaptors* are used for that purpose, i.e., class templates that are parameterized by an iterator and modify or extend some of its functionality. Static adjustments of iterator properties, thus, can be achieved by type-based iterator adaptors, which modify the type of an iterator rather than a particular instance. The program variables *first_iterator*, *second_iterator*, and *twiddle factor*, therefore, may be iterator adaptors, and not necessarily iterators directly. In the actual implementation they adjust an iterator by modifying its stride, i.e., the step-size with which it traverses.

3.3 Implementation

The polymorphic radix-n algorithm is implemented as a C++ template meta-program. C++ is the most widely used language for generic programming since it supports parameterized types ("templates") as well as static meta-programming. In our particular application three additional properties of the template type system are worthwhile mentioning. First, template parameters include static expressions (*non-type template parameters*); constants such as the radix or the length of the input sequence thus map directly to them. Second, the instantiation, hence specialization, of parameterized types is done automatically rather than by hand. If the meta-program represents, for example, the factors N_1, N_2 of the input as static *expressions* in the template parameter list of a class, it forces the compiler to evaluate this expression at instantiation time; the (recursive) values of N_1, N_2 can thus be automatically computed. Third, C++ unifies templates in a best-fit manner, based on a partial order of templates. Thus, if the Cooley-Tukey recursion is represented by a pair of class templates, for the general and the base case, respectively, the compiler automatically detects and selects the base case when appropriate.

Designing the polymorphic radix-n framework as a meta-program, shifts much of the work to the C++ compiler; the remaining code becomes surprisingly slim. Its core is formed by two class templates, `radix_mapping`, which implement the Cooley-Tukey mapping: one class organizes the general case of the recursion (see appendix A), the other one the base case. In the latter case, the computation is forwarded to a direct computation of the FFT, encapsulated in the class template `small_dft`. There exists one `small_dft` per base case, e.g., `small_dft<2>` for radix-2 algorithms.

4   Related and Future Work

The work presented in this paper is rooted in the discipline of generic programming. Theoretically, the paper by Musser and Stepanov [5] was the first that postulated an "algorithm-oriented" approach and showed how to maximize the re-usability of an algorithm by reducing it to its minimal requirements. As we showed, crucial for the design and efficiency of our polymorphic radix-n FFT is the identification of the right abstractions and their representation as statically bound-able parameters. Methodologically speaking, our work is therefore closely related to the work by Lawall [4] and Glück et. al. [3], who both investigate binding-time analysis in the context of numerical algorithms. One of the first to see the connection between partial evaluation and the C++ template sub-language was Todd Veldhuizen [6], who demonstrated how compile-time recursion is possible if template parameters are appropriately chosen; today, it is known that the template sub-language is Turing-complete. Incidentally, Veld-huizen also used the FFT to illustrate meta-programming, but, in difference to our goal, has not attempted to build an entire FFT library.

In the immediate future, we want to further generalize the current algorithm from a polymorphic radix-n to a polymorphic *mixed-radix* and even polymorphic *split-radix* algorithm. The mixed-radix scheme allows users to choose different radices at different recursion steps, while the split-radix method, dividing an FFT computation in sub-computations of different sizes, changes the nature of the recursion and the declarative structure of the current radix-n algorithm. It furthermore requires a way to associate different recursion bases to the sub-computations of different sizes. Since the current program already uses meta-programming techniques, it should be possible to implement the necessary modifications as an extension. Our ultimate goal is to submit the FFT framework to Boost [2], the largest library initiative in C++.

References

1. J. W. Cooley and J. W. Tukey. An algorithm for the machine calculation of complex Fourier series. *Math. Comp.*, 19:297–301, April 1965.
2. B. Dawes and D. Abrahams. Boost. http://www.boost.org.
3. R. Glück, R. Nakashige, and R. Zöchling. Binding-time analysis applied to mathematical algorithms. In J. Dolezal and J. Fidler, editors, *System Modelling and Optimization*, pages 137–146. Chapman & Hall, 1995.
4. J. Lawall. Faster Fourier transforms via automatic program specialization. In J. Hatcliff, T. Mogensen, and P. Thiemann, editors, *Partial Evaluation: Practice and Theory. Proc. of the 1998 DIKU Internat. Summerschool*, volume 1706, pages 338–355. Springer-Verlag, 1999.
5. D. Musser and A. Stepanov. Algorithm-oriented generic libraries. *Software-practice and experience*, 27(7):623–642, Jul 1994.
6. T. L. Veldhuizen. C++ templates as partial evaluation. In *Partial Evaluation and Semantic-Based Program Manipulation*, pages 13–18, 1999.

A   C++-Interface of the Cooley-Tukey Mapping

```
// General radix_mapping stage
template<int length,      // length of the DFT
  int radix,              // desired radix, must have a small DFT
                          // implemented
  typename Decimation,    // DIT or DIF
  typename Order,         // input order: natural to bit-reversed
  typename Tag,           // reserved for future use
  bool verbose>           // debugging switch
class radix_mapping {
public:
  typedef radix_mapping<length,radix,Decimation,Order,Tag,verbose>self;

  // Factor 'length' into N1 and N2, based on 'Decimation'
```

```
typedef typename if_types<equal_types<Decimation,radix_dit>::equal,
    STATIC_INT<radix>, STATIC_INT<length / radix> >::if_t  N1_t;
typedef typename if_types<equal_types<Decimation,radix_dit>::equal,
    STATIC_INT<length / radix>,  STATIC_INT<radix> >::if_t  N2_t;
enum { N1 = N1_t::value};
enum { N2 = N2_t::value};
// Define the type for DFTs of length N1
typedef radix_mapping<N1,radix,Decimation,Order,Tag,verbose> stageN1;
// Define the type for DFTs of length N2
typedef radix_mapping<N2,radix,Decimation,Order,Tag,verbose> stageN2;

template<class RandomAccessIterator, class TwiddleIterator>
radix_mapping(const RandomAccessIterator& input_iterator,
              const TwiddleIterator&     twiddle_iterator)
{

    // Adjust access patterns of first_iterator by N2
    typedef typename adjusted_boost_iterator_trait<RandomAccessIterator,
        Order,STATIC_INT<N2> >::iterator               first_iterator;
    // Adjust access patterns of second_iterator by N1
    typedef typename adjusted_boost_iterator_trait<RandomAccessIterator,
        typename inverted_order_trait<Order>::order,STATIC_INT<N1> >
        ::iterator                              second_iterator;

    typedef typename adjusted_boost_iterator_trait<TwiddleIterator,
        radix_mapping_reversed,STATIC_INT<radix> >
        ::iterator                              twiddle_iterator_adj;

    // Copy the original iterator
    first_iterator in_it(input_iterator.base());
    stageN2 s(second_iterator(in_it.base()),
            twiddle_iterator_adj(twiddle_iterator.base()));
    in_it++;

    // Perform N1 stages of length N2
    for(int i = 1; i < N1; in_it++, i++) {
        stageN2 s(second_iterator(in_it.base()),
                twiddle_iterator_adj(twiddle_iterator.base()));
        second_iterator second(in_it.base());
        second++;
        for(int k2 = 1; k2 < N2; k2++, second++) {
            *second *= twiddle_iterator[i * k2];
        }
    }

    // Copy the original iterator; has to be a strided iterator
    // since stages in the second loop start at positions k2*N1
    // where k2 = 0, 1, ..., N2-1
    second_iterator in_it2(input_iterator.base());
```

```
// Perform N2 DFTs of length N1
for(int i = 0; i < N2; in_it2++, i++) {
    stageN1 s(first_iterator(in_it2.base()),
            twiddle_iterator_adj(twiddle_iterator.base()));}}};
```

Intersecting Classes and Prototypes

Wolfgang De Meuter, Theo D'Hondt, and Jessie Dedecker*

Programming Technology Lab
Vrije Universiteit Brussel
Pleinlaan 2
1050 Brussels, Belgium
{wdmeuter,tjdhondt,jededeck}@vub.ac.be

Abstract. The object-oriented programming language design space consists of class-based and prototype-based languages. Both families have
been shown to posses their advantages and disadvantages. Hybrid languages featuring both prototype-based and class-based mechanisms have
been proposed as a solution. Unfortunately these languages not only
unify the advantages but also the disadvantages of both families. We
propose a more intersectional point of view and propose a language that
inherits the advantages but shuns the disadvantages of both families.

1 Introduction

Object-oriented programming languages (OOPLs) can be divided into prototype-
based languages (PBLs) and class-based-languages (CBLs). In CBLs, objects are
created by *instantiating* a class. Classes can share behaviour by means of *inheritance*. In PBLs, objects are created *ex-nihilo* (e.g. by putting some fields and
methods between parenthesis), or by *cloning* other objects (called prototypes).
Sharing happens by an "inheritance relation" between objects, usually called
delegation. Examples of CBLs are Java, C++ and Smalltalk. Examples of PBLs
are Self [1], Agora [2], Kevo [3] and NewtonScript [4].

Some think that the controversy between CBLs and PBLs has become obsolete with the advent of Java as "the" standard OOPL. However, workshops such
as "Feyerabend" at OOPSLA'01, '02, ECOOP'02 and "Inheritance workshop"
at ECOOP'02 show that OOPL design is still alive and kicking. Moreover, recent
work also indicates that CBLs are gaining importance in agent technology where
objects can roam networks in unpredictable ways [5]. This was already predicted
by Cardelli in the mid nineties with Obliq [6].

Both CBLs and PBLs have advantages as well as drawbacks. A reaction
to avoid the shortcomings one gets by choosing a language from either family
is to design new languages that contain both CBL and PBL characteristics.
Unfortunately, such hybrid languages (like Hybrid [7] and JavaScript 2.0 [8])
are bold unions of the features of CBLs and PBLs. They unify the family's
advantages as well as their disadvantages and they tend to be large overfeatured
languages with non trivial combinations between PBL and CBL features.

---

* Research assistant of the Fund for Scientific Research - Flanders (Belgium) (F.W.O.)

M. Broy and A.V. Zamulin (Eds.): PSI 2003, LNCS 2890, pp. 37–45, 2003.

This paper presents a tiny language, called *Pic%* combining the CBL and PBL characteristics in an *intersection*, thereby combining their advantages but shunning their drawbacks.

2   PBLs vs. CBLs

Many PBLs exist. For a taxonomy, see [9]. In section 2.2 we list the CBL problems solved by PBLs. Section 2.3 lists the drawbacks of PBLs due to the absence of classes. First we review the most basic characteristics of PBLs.

2.1   Introducing Prototype-Based Languages

A PBL is often defined as "an OOPL without classes". In PBLs, objects are created *ex-nihilo* (by listing a number of fields and methods) and by *cloning* existing objects (called *prototype* of the clone). Whereas CBL allow classes to share attributes by inheritance, PBLs achieve the same effect by a (dynamic) mechanism called *delegation*: one object can dynamically decide another object to be its parent, and every message that is not handled by the object itself is (automatically) delegated to the parent. An important remark to make here is that this happens with *late binding of self* as illustrated in Fig. 1a. Messages send to the `self` (or `this`) variable in the parent will "come back" to the object that originally received the message. This is a crucial feature of delegation as originally defined by Lieberman [10]. The "delegation" described in "the" design patterns book is depicted in 1b. This might be called "message forwarding" but it does not meet the definition of delegation in PBLs.

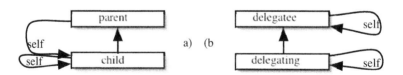

Fig. 1. Delegation vs. Messsage Forwarding

A problem with "naive prototype-based thinking" is that, when cloning objects, not only their state but also their behaviour gets copied. An object with 10 methods will give rise to 50 (pointers to the same) methods when cloned 5 times. A solution invented by the Self-group [11] is a programming technique called *traits objects*. The idea is to store the 10 methods in a special *traits* object and to let the 5 clones inherit them from that object. All 5 objects contain their specific state variables but share the behaviour of the traits parent.

Although traits objects are but a programming idiom, we have to face the fact that the technique *actually* boils down to writing class-based programs in a PBL: the traits objects play the role of a the classes. Therefore, Dony [9] argues in favour of object-centred programming, i.e. writing programs that do not use these "class-centered techniques" too much, but instead put the object as a "design entity" in a central position again.

2.2   Drawbacks of CBLs and Class-Centered Programming

The drawbacks of CBLs are divided into *language theoretical* and *philosophical* ones. From the philosophical side, modeling the world with static classifications is utopic. Furthermore, humans think in terms of concrete objects rather than abstractions. We refer to Taivalsaari's overview [3] for more information. The language theoretical drawbacks of CBLs are related to language design issues and interest us more. We merely summarize the analysis of [3]:

- In *uniform* CBLs, one ends up with **complex** concepts like meta classes and "the double hierarchy" in Smalltalk. In Java, classes are objects of the class `Class` and `Class` is an object that is its own class.
- Bugs in constructors can lead to **unmeaningfully initialized objects**. In PBLs, fields in clones always have a meaningful initial value, i.e. the value of the field of the object prototype.
- PBLs support **singleton objects** (such as True, False and singletons [12]) for which a class has to be constructed in CBLs. E.g. Smalltalk has the classes `True` and `False` with `True` and `False` as only instances.
- Classes play no less than 11 roles in CBLs [13].
- PBLs allow to re-introduce classes for **classification**: in StripeTalk [14] one can assign "stripes" to objects and classify objects based on the stripes.
- Most important, PBLs allow two 'views' or 'role objects' to delegate to the same parent object. Changes in the parent done by one child are also "felt" by the other child. This powerful mechanism, called *parent sharing*, allows for **views and roles on objects**. Simulating this in a CBL is very hard.

2.3   Drawbacks of PBLs and Object-Centred Programming

PBLs have been shown to be a solution to these problems. However, PBLs have their problems as well, most of them related to the absence of classes :

- The construction of certain objects requires a **construction plan** to be executed (e.g. building up a GUI). In CBLs, this is to formalized as a class constructor. In PBLs it requires a lot of discipline from programmers to make sure certain procedures are followed.
- The **prototype corruption problem** was put forward by Gunther Blashek [15]. Prototypes (e.g. the empty `String` prototype) can be inadvertently modified which might affect future clones. This can lead to subtle bugs.

– Without the traits technique, PBLs suffer from a **re-entrancy problem**: copying prototypes results in methods being copied. This is circumvented using a traits hierarchy for code reuse: objects inherit from their "real" parent *and* from their traits. In PBLs without multiple inheritance this is impossible and [16] shows that multiple inheritance in a PBL is problematic.
– Some concepts are **inherently abstract**. When writing a stack, the code for push and pop is written for *all* possible stacks (empty stacks, full stacks,...) and hence one is *by definition* working on the "class" level of abstraction. The problem is that "stack" is an inherently abstract concept.

Solving these problems by re-introducing classes implies re-introducing their problems as well. But they can also be solved without classes: Pic%[1] is an intersection of CBLs and PBLs, based on Pico, a tiny language sketched below. Sections 4 and 5 introduce Pic% and explain that it is indeed an intersection.

3   Pico: A Short Overview

A full explanation of Pico can be found on the internet [17]. The following implementation of the quicksort algorithm gives a general flavor of the language:

```
QuickSort(V, Low, High):
  { Left: Low;
    Right: High;
    Pivot: V[(Left + Right) // 2];
    until(Left > Right,  { while(V[Left] < Pivot, Left:= Left+1);
                           while(V[Right] > Pivot, Right:= Right-1);
                           if(not(Left > Right),
                             { Swap(V, Left, Right);
                               Left:= Left+1; Right:= Right-1 },
                           false) });
    if(Low < Right, QuickSort(V, Low, Right), false);
    if(High > Left, QuickSort(V, Left, High), false) }
```

Pico is an interpreted language that is based on Scheme [18]. All values are first class: basic values, functions and arrays can be passed around as arguments, returned from functions, used in assignments and so on. The major differences with Scheme are the surface syntax and the fact that Pico allows to define functions of which some parameters use lazy evaluation. This removed the need for special forms, while still allowing for a uniform extensible notation (see the usage of if, a function written in Pico). An expression is evaluated in an environment which is *a linked list of name-value associations*. Values no longer bound to a name in some environment get automatically garbage collected.

Table 1 shows the most frequently used syntactic constructions in Pico. New names are added to the 'current' environment using the colon notation. These names are bound to primitive values, arrays or functions. This is the second row of the table. Referring names, indexing arrays and calling functions make up the

---

[1] Read: Pic-oo

first row. The third row shows how variables are given a new value, how arrays our updated and how functions can get a new body. The curly braces as used in the quicksort teaser is mere syntactic sugar that is replaced - by the parser - to a call to the (lazily evaluated) **begin** function.

Table 1. Pico Basic Syntax

reference	nam	nam[exp]	nam(exp$_1$, ... ,exp$_n$)
definition	nam: exp	nam[exp1]: exp$_2$	nam(exp$_1$, ... ,exp$_n$): exp
assignment	nam:= exp	nam[exp$_1$]:= exp$_2$	nam(exp$_1$, ... ,exp$_n$):= exp

4   Pic%, an Intersection of PBLs and CBLs

Pic% is a PBL extension of Pico. The concepts of Pic% are based on previous research on Agora [2] of which we "proved" in [19] that it is an intersection of CBLs and PBLs in terms of denotational semantics. But Pic% is much simpler than Agora. The basic ideas we introduced to turn Pico into an OOPL are:

- The **capture()** primitive returns, at any point in the execution, a reference to the current environment. These captured environments are Pic%'s objects.
- The dot operator sends messages. If **e** is a captured environment, then **e.nam(e$_1$, ... ,e$_n$)** searches **nam** in that environment and invokes the associated function. The search starts, as in Pico, at the "bottom" and proceeds upward in the linked list of bindings. This corresponds to method lookup.

The following code shows how this enables OOP (more about :: later):

```
counter(n):
  { incr()::  n:= n+1;
    decr()::  n:=n-1;
    capture() }
```

The expression c:counter(10) creates an object c with methods incr and decr since the result of calling **counter** is a reference to the 'current' environment that was built up to the point where **capture** is called. **counter** is a *constructor function* because each call generates an object. Messages are sent to c with expressions like c.incr(). Inheritance comes for free in our model:

```
counter(n):
  { incr()::  n:= n+1;
    decr()::  n:=n-1;
    super: void;
    protect(limit)::
      { incr():: if(n=limit,error("overflow"),super.incr()) };
        decr():: if(n=-limit,error("underflow"),super.decr()) };
        capture() }
    super:= capture() }
```

Having constructed a counter c, the message c.protect(4) returns a *new* object whose parent is the receiver of the message, i.e. c. This is because objects are environments: upon entering protect, the 'current environment' is gradually extended with new incr and decr methods and the 'new current environment' is captured again. The resulting environment has the four methods and the super variable. Inheritance and overriding come for free as name lookup proceeds 'upward' in the environment. Methods like protect, that generate extensions of its receiver, are called a *mixin-method* (see [2] for more information).

This model misses 2 crucialities: super sends with late binding of self, and, cloning. Also, the biggest problem of PBLs (the re-entrancy problem) stays unsolved unless we use traits. The solution is to redesign our environments to consists of 2 parallel lists of bindings as shown in Fig. 2. One list is called the variable part (names defined with :) and the other is called the constant part (names defined with ::). The result is a very consistent object model:

- The constant part is the interface of objects: messages sent with the dot are looked for in the constant part. Methods are executed in the entire object. In a method, this() returns the current object. "Function calls" that are not qualified are implicit sends to this() such that calling a constructor function like counter(4) is actually a self-send to the "root environment".
- Every object understands clone, a method installed in the constant (i.e. public) part of the root environment. The entire point of objects being implemented as two lists of bindings and of the constant list to be the public part, is that clone will never copy the constant part of its receiver. Hence, by definition, the clone() method makes a new object consisting of the constant part of its receiver and a clone of the variable part of its receiver.
- Finally, a dot syntax *without receiver* is introduced. "Dotted messages" with no receiver are send to the parent object. Hence, .m() corresponds to super.m() in Java. The difference between this technique and the one with the super variable shown above is that the receiverless dot does not change the meaning of this() such that we have super sends with late binding.

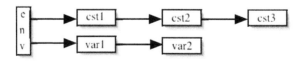

Fig. 2. Pic% Environment/Object Structure

Some Pic% Programming Patterns

- The following code exemplifies the programming style favored by Pic%.

```
Stack(n):
  { T[n]: void;  t: 0;
    empty()::  t=0;
    full()  :: t=n;
    push(x):: { T[t:=t+1]:=x; this() };
    pop()   :: { x: T[t]; t:=t-1; x };
    makeProtected()::
      { push(x):: if(full(),error("overflow"), .push(x) };
        pop()   :: if(empty(), error("underflow"), .pop()};
        capture() };
    capture() }
```

- The singleton in Pic% is a constructor that overrides clone() (to do nothing) and that replaces itself by its generated object:

```
constructor(args):{ ...<methods>...;
  clone():: this();
  constructor:=capture()}
```

- In [20] we explain that Pic% allows first class manipulation of methods. This is particularly useful in this model where all inheritance is accomplished by mixin-methods. Since the model requires the potential extensions to reside in mixin-methods *in* objects, extension "from the outside" would not be possible if it wasn't for the possibility to assign mixin-methods.
- The fact that the constants of an object are never cloned give us a powerful language feature called *cloning families* inside the implementation of Kevo [3]. We believe cloning families might be a good abstraction to think about the notion of replicas in a distributed system. we are currently investigating this in a version of Pic% that uses objects as mobile agents [5].

5   Evaluation and Epilog

We validate our claims. We omit the problems of CBLs: Pic% features only objects and constructor functions are methods in an object; 'calling' one is an implicit send to this(). Second, consider the drawbacks Of PBLs one by one:

- The **construction plan** problem was about the need for formalized construction plans. This need is clearly covered in Pic% by the constructor functions that generate objects using capture(). Constructor functions in Pic% are exactly the same as constructors in CBLs.
- The **prototype corruption** problem is solved by our proposal because constructor functions and overriding clone are two powerful techniques to *ensure* that fresh objects (constructed with a function or with clone) are always correctly initialized.

- Solving the **re-entrancy problem** is the most important technical contribution Pic% makes to the field. By structuring objects as 2 dictionaries of which only variables get copied by cloning, we ensure all clones of the prototype to share it constants. This "hidden traits" does *not* interfere with the inheritance hierarchy the way discussed before!
- The fact that some notions (like stacks) are **inherently abstract** is trivially covered because of the way constructor functions simulate classes.

Pic% has both PBL features (cloning) and CBL features (constructor functions). Nonetheless it does not inherit the problems from either language family. Furthermore we did not reintroduce classes as constructor functions are nothing but methods which in their turn reside in some environment (read: object). We therefore claim this tiny little language is a clean intersection of both families.

References

1. Ungar, D., Smith, R.: Self: The Power of Simplicity. In: Proceedings of OOPSLA. Volume 22., ACM Press (1987)
2. De Meuter, W.: Agora: The Scheme of Object-Orientation, or, the Simplest MOP in the World. In Noble, J., Taivalsaari, A., Moore, I., eds.: Prototype-based Programming: Concepts, Languages and Applications. (1998)
3. Taivalsaari, A.: Classes vs. Prototypes: Some Philosophical and Historical Observations. In Noble, J., Taivalsaari, A., Moore, I., eds.: Prototype-based Programming: Concepts, Languages and Applications. (1998)
4. Smith, W.: NewtonScript: Prototypes on the Palm. In Noble, J., Taivalsaari, A., Moore, I., eds.: Prototype-based Programming: Concepts, Languages and Applications. (1998)
5. Van Belle, W., D'Hondt, T.: Agent mobility and reification of computational state: An experiment in migration. Lecture Notes in Computer Science **1887** (2001)
6. Cardelli, L.: A language with distributed scope. Computing Systems **8** (1995)
7. Lieberman, H., Stein, L., Ungar, D.: Treaty of orlando. In: Addendum to OOPSLA. Volume 23., ACM Press (1988) 43–44
8. ECMAScript Edition 4: http://www.mozilla.org/js/language/es4/index.html.
9. Dony, C., Malenfant, J., Bardou, D.: Classifying Prototype-based Programming Languages. In Noble, J., Taivalsaari, A., Moore, I., eds.: Prototype-based Programming: Concepts, Languages and Applications. (1998)
10. Lieberman, H.: Using prototypical objects to implement shared behavior in object oriented systems. In Meyrowitz, N., ed.: Proceedings OOPSLA. Volume 22. (1987) 214–223
11. Ungar, D., Chambers, C., Chang, B., Hölzle, U.: Organizing programs without classes. Lisp and Symbolic Computation **4** (1991) 223–242
12. Gamma, E., Helm, R., Johnson, R., Vlissides, J.: Design Patterns. Addison-Wesley (1994)
13. Bracha, G., Lindstrom, G.: Modularity meets inheritance. In: Proceedings of IEEE Computer Society International Conference on Computer languages. (1992)
14. Green, T., Borning, A., O'Shea, T., Minoughan, M., Smith, R.: The Stripetalk Papers: Understandability as a Language Design Issue in Object-Oriented Programming Systems. In Noble, J., Taivalsaari, A., Moore, I., eds.: Prototype-based Programming: Concepts, Languages and Applications. (1998)

15. Blashek, G.: Object-Oriented Programming with Prototypes. Springer Verlag (1994)
16. Smith, R., Ungar, D.: Programming as an Experience: The inspiration for Self. In Noble, J., Taivalsaari, A., Moore, I., eds.: Prototype-based Programming: Concepts, Languages and Applications. (1998)
17. Pico Home Page: `http://pico.vub.ac.be/`.
18. Abelson, H., Sussman, G., J., S.: Structure and Interpretation of Computer Programs. 2nd edn. MIT Press (1996)
19. Steyaert, P., De Meuter, W.: A marriage of class-and object-based inheritance without unwanted children. Lecture Notes in Computer Science **952** (1995)
20. D'Hondt, T., De Meuter, W.: Of first-class methods and dynamic scope. In: Proceedings of LMO, France, to appear. (2003)

Bending without Breaking: Making Software More Flexible
Extended Abstract

Kim B. Bruce*

Department of Computer Science
Williams College
Williamstown, USA
`kim@cs.williams.edu`

Abstract. In this talk we discuss the problem of simultaneously refining mutually interdependent classes and object types. We discuss possible solutions using existing static type systems that include parametric polymorphism. A statically type-safe solution is presented that involves the introduction of type groups, a construct that can be understood as a generalization of the `MyType` construct introduced in a statically type-safe way in languages like PolyTOIL [3] and LOOM [2].

1 Introduction

One of the strong advantages of object-oriented programming languages is their support in making changes to programs and systems over time. For example, the use of inheritance to define subclasses makes it possible to create slight modifications of existing classes without actually changing the originals. Similarly, subtyping allows methods to be used with actual parameters whose types are subtypes of those for which the method parameters were originally specified. These features have been very helpful in allowing programmers to design reusable components as well as programs that are easier to modify over their lifetimes.

While early object-oriented languages had weak static type systems (e.g., Simula 67 [1]) or used dynamic rather than static typing (e.g., Smalltalk [9]), our understanding of static type systems for object-oriented languages has progressed significantly. While the static type systems for languages like C++, Java, and Object Pascal are more rigid than desired, and others like Beta [10] and Eiffel [12] require dynamic or link-time checks to guarantee type safety, research on the type systems of object-oriented languages (see [6] for a recent survey) has resulted in significant progress in designing static type systems for object-oriented languages that are both safe and expressive. However, there are areas in which static type systems are not sufficiently expressive.

Real systems are composed of collections of interacting objects from a variety of classes. Yet, object-oriented programming languages have provided few

---

* This research is partially supported by NSF grant CCR-9988210.

M. Broy and A.V. Zamulin (Eds.): PSI 2003, LNCS 2890, pp. 46–49, 2003.
© Springer-Verlag Berlin Heidelberg 2003

features to support working with these collections. Java's packages are a step in the right direction, but appear to be one of the least well thought-out features of the language.

In this talk we discuss an important way in which languages could provide better support for managing collections of interacting objects. The problem that we discuss is that of refining different classes simultaneously when their definitions are interdependent. We will see that popular static typing schemes fail either to be expressive enough or to preserve type-safety in supporting the kinds of changes that are desireable.

This particular issue is related to the general problem that the basic units for building programs in most object-oriented languages are classes or similarly fine-grained constructs. While there is not sufficient space here to present a detailed argument, we believe that language constructs, such as modules, that can be used to manage collections of classes used in building tightly intertwined systems are very useful in constructing and managing large systems.

In the rest of this talk we discuss why current languages fail to provide the support required for handling the refinement of interacting systems of objects and classes, and how the introduction of new language facilities can help.

2   Mutually Interdependent Object Types and Classes

Work on design patterns [8] in object-oriented programming languages has provided a rich source of examples of systems of interdependent classes. Examples include the Subject-Observer pattern, which models Java's event-driven programming style, the Interpreter pattern, and the Visitor pattern. In a previous paper [4], we used the Subject-Observer pattern as an example to show how currently popular static type systems failed to provide support when a programmer desires to simultaneously extend interdependent object types and classes.

In this talk we examine the "Expression problem" [13]. This is the problem of writing code to process in various ways the expressions of a simple programming language.

For example, suppose we wish to represent the expressions of a simple formal language that includes integer constants and negations of expressions in the language. We would also like to have an operation available that will return the value of an expression (*e.g.*, an expression interpreter). Once we have a design for such a system, we would like to examine how hard it is to add either a new kind of expression to the language or a new operation on expressions.

If we write the straightforward solution to this problem in a functional language like ML, we find that it is easy to add operations (such as an operation that takes an expression that returns a well-formatted string representation of the expression), but adding a new kind of expression (such as the sum of two expressions) would require extensive rewriting of already written code to accommodate the new case that existing operations must now handle.

On the other hand, a straightforward solution to this problem using the Interpreter pattern in an object-oriented language would result in code for which it is easy to add a new kind of expression (typically represented by a new class), but hard to add a new operation. In particular, to add the new operation, subclasses of all existing expression classes must be defined that add a new method supporting the operation. Moreover, though it has not been generally noted, typing problems sometimes result from adding new methods to subclasses representing the cases of a recursively defined type.

Thus programs written in functional languages are typically easily extended to add new operations, but are harder to extend (without modifying existing code) to support new kinds of expressions. Programs written in object-oriented languages are more easily extended to add new kinds of expressions, but adding new operations requires defining subclasses of all existing expression classes and may result in type problems. (See [14] for an early discussion of these differences in organization between programs written in functional and object-oriented languages.)

The Visitor pattern is often used in object-oriented languages in order to regain the advantages of functional languages in adding new operations, but at the cost of making it harder to add new kinds of expressions. However, we will see that extending programs that use the Visitor pattern gives rise to very difficult static typing problems that require rather sophisticated type systems.

After showing how attempted solutions relying on parametric polymorphism run into serious difficulties requiring casts or other dynamic checks, we introduce a construct called a "type group" that collects together related class and type definitions and allows simultaneous extensions of all. This approach provides a relatively straight-forward solution to these static typing problems.

3   Comparison with Other Work

Type groups are based on a generalization of the type rules associated with the "MyType" construct that is contained in our earlier languages PolyTOIL [3] and [2] (see [6] for a history of the use of MyType constructs in other languages). The construct MyType represents the type of self or this, and, like those terms, automatically changes its meaning in subclasses, providing a significant increase in the expressiveness of a static type system.

In type groups we generalize this by introducing a collection of mutually interdependent, but distinct "MyType"s. When a type group is extended, all of these MyTypes change simultaneously. Just as we have provided a set of provably safe static typing rules for languages that have a MyType construct, we can also provide a set of provably safe static typing rules for these collections of mutually interdependent MyTypes.

Type groups add additional expressiveness to the provision of parametric polymorphism (see also [5]). While they capture some of the expressiveness of the virtual classes [11] of Beta, they differ from Beta by providing static type safety, while virtual classes require dynamic checks to guarantee safety.

Type groups are most similar to Ernst's independently developed Family Polymorphism [7], but are based on a simpler and better understood type theory. In particular, the underlying theory of Family Polymorphism is based on dependent types, which is powerful enough to introduce difficulties with decidable type checking. By contrast, the underlying theory of type groups is based on the polymorphic lambda calculus with mutually recursive types, a much more tractable and well understood type system.

Type groups provide an expressive, yet statically type safe way of increasing the expressiveness of object-oriented programming languages, especially with regard to programs that involve the simultaneous refinement of collections of mutually interdependent classes and object types.

References

1. G.M. Birtwistle, O.-J. Dahl, B. Myhrhaug, and K. Nygaard. *SIMULA Begin.* Aurbach, 1973.
2. Kim B. Bruce, Adrian Fiech, and Leaf Petersen. Subtyping is not a good "match" for object-oriented languages. In *ECOOP '97*, pages 104–127. LNCS 1241, Springer-Verlag, 1997.
3. Kim B. Bruce, Angela Schuett, and Robert van Gent. PolyTOIL: A type-safe polymorphic object-oriented language. *TOPLAS*, 25(2):225–290, 2003.
4. Kim B. Bruce and Joseph C. Vanderwaart. Semantics-driven language design: Statically type-safe virtual types in object-oriented languages. In *Electronic notes in Theoretical Computer Science*, volume 20, 1999.
   URL: http://www.elsevier.nl/locate/entcs/volume20.html, 26 pages.
5. Kim Bruce, Marin Odersky, and Philip Wadler. A statically safe alternative to virtual types. In *ECOOP '98*, pages 523–549. LNCS 1445, Springer-Verlag, 1998.
6. Kim Bruce. *Foundations of Object-Oriented Languages: Types and Semantics.* MIT Press, 2002.
7. Erik Ernst. Family polymorphism. In Jørgen Lindskov Knudsen, editor, *ECOOP 2001 – Object-Oriented Programming*, LNCS 2072, pages 303–326, Heidelberg, Germany, 2001. Springer-Verlag.
8. E. Gamma, R. Helm, R. Johnson, and J. Vlissides. *Design Patterns: Abstraction and reuse of object-oriented designs.* Addison-Wesley, 1994.
9. A. Goldberg and D. Robson. *Smalltalk-80: The language and its implementation.* Addison Wesley, 1983.
10. Bent Bruun Kristensen, Ole Lehrmann Madsen, Birger Moller-Pedersen, and Kristen Nygaard. The beta programming language. In Bruce Shriver and Peter Wegner, editors, *Research Directions in Object-Oriented Programming*, pages 7–48. M.I.T. Press, Cambridge, MA.
11. Ole Lehrmann Madsen and Birger Moller-Pedersen. Virtual classes: A powerful mechanism in object-oriented programming. In *OOPSLA '89 Proceedings*, pages 397–406, 1989.
12. B. Meyer. *Eiffel: the language.* Prentice-Hall, 1992.
13. Philip Wadler. The expression problem. Message to Java-genericity electronic mail list, November 12, 1998.
14. W. Cook. Object-oriented programming versus abstract data types. In Proc. of the REX Workshop/School on the Foundations of Object-Oriented Languages (FOOL), pages 151–178. Springer-Verlag, LNCS 173, 1990.

Program Construction in the Context of Evolutionary Computation[*]

Jelena Sanko and Jaan Penjam

Institute of Cybernetics at TTU, Tallinn, Estonia
{jelena,jaan }@cs.ioc.ee

Abstract. Many optimization algorithms that imitate certain principles of nature have been proven useful in various application domains. The following paper shows how Evolutionary Algorithm (EA) can be applied to model (program) construction for solving the discrete time system identification problem. Non-linear system identification is used as an example problem domain for studying possibilities of EA to discover the relationship between parameters in response to a given set of inputs.

1 Introduction

Evolutionary computation is dealing with search and optimization algorithms. The evolutionary computation community uses Evolutionary Algorithms (EAs) as a general term for describing those paradigms that use computational models to simulate evolutionary process. These techniques of *Genetic Algorithms*, *Evolution Strategies* and *Evolutionary Programming* have one fundamental commonality: they all involve reproduction, random variation, competition, and selection of contending individuals in a population [1]. Though EAs belong to the class of probabilistic algorithms, they are very different from random algorithms as they combine elements of directed and stochastic search [2].

EAs applications appear as alternative to conventional approaches and in some cases are useful where other techniques have been completely unsuccessful. EAs are not fundamentally limited by restricted assumption about the search space, unimodality, existence of derivatives, and other matters [3]. Since EA simultaneously evaluates many points in the parameter space, it is more likely to converge towards the global solution. In each generation, it explores different areas of the parameter space, and then directs the search to regions where there is high probability of finding improved performance. By working with a population of solutions the algorithm can in effect search many local minima and thereby increase the likelihood of finding the global minima.

The paper is organized as follows. In Section 2, the motives of selection of EAs and the area of our research are explained. In Section 3, the essentials of system identification problems is outlined. The results of applying of EA for solving

---

[*] This work is partially supported by the Estonian Science Foundation under grant No 5567.

the system identification problem are described in Section 4. Finally, Section 5 summarizes the results and highlights further work. The basic principles of work of EAs can be found in many introductions (see e.g. [2,3]).

2 Motivation

One of the first descriptions of the evolutionary process use for computer problem solving appeared in the articles of Friedberg (1958) and Friedberg et al (1959). This represented some of the early work in machine learning and described the use of an evolutionary algorithm for *automated programming, program synthesis* or *program induction*, i.e. the task of finding a program that calculates a given input-output function.

During the past thirty years, a solid algorithmic and theoretical basis for understanding the power of EAs has been built. Koza (1992) developed a new methodology, named Genetic Programming (GP), which provides a way to run a search on the space of possible computer programs for the best one instead of solving a problem, and instead of building an evolution program to solve the problem [4]. GP can be defined as the direct evolution of programs or algorithms for inductive learning. The novelty of GP lies in its ability to abstract an underlying principle from a finite set of fitness cases and presenting them in the form of an algorithm or computer program to represent the simulation model [4,5].

In GP the individuals in the population are computer programs. Their fitness is usually calculated by running them one or more times with a variety of inputs (known as the training set) and seeing how close the program's output(s) are to some desired output(s) specified by the user.

GP is well suited for symbolic regression and many GP applications can be formulated as a variant of symbolic regression. Note that symbolic regression means finding both the coefficients and the form of the function itself. A GP system performing symbolic regression takes a number of input-output relations (i.e. fitness cases) and produces a function or program that is consistent with these fitness cases [5,6].

We would like to get a new method for automatic program construction that combines structural program synthesis (SSP) [7] with evolutionary learning via EAs. SSP method is a *deductive approach* for program synthesis that is carried out via special logical inference rules from general relational specification of the problem. This specification is often called as *computational model* of the problem (see Section 5). We design an *inductive approach* for automatic program construction based on the same specification language (computational model) that is augmented by experimental data that describe desirable input-output behaviour of the program to be composed. The commom specification would bridge deductive and inductive methods of program construction. As a case study for finding the relationship between parameters in response to a given set of inputs, a non-linear system identification problem was investigated. For solving system identification problem, a register based linear genetic programming technique was used.

3   System Identification

The subject of system identification is to build mathematical model of dynamical system based on experimental data [8]. Most of the identification methods, such as those based on least-squares or maximum likelihood estimates, are essentially techniques based on gradient following technique. It is well known that such approaches often fail to find the global optimum if the search space is multimodal, and also suffer from other drawbacks (e.g. unstable solution, *a priori* information on the system parameters is needed etc.) [9]. Several researches have applied evolutionary computation techniques to solve system identification problems [9, 10,11].

Dynamical systems are often characterized only in terms of the input-output behavior (i.e. black-box model), which illustrates the effects of the system inputs on the observed outputs. This problem is defined formally in the following way. Assume that the single-valued output y of an unknown system behaves as a function

$$y(t) = f(y(t-1), ..., y(t-n), u(t-1), ..., u(t-n)) \tag{1}$$

where n denotes the system order (i.e. the number of delayed inputs and outputs). Such kind of model establishes a non-libear relationship between the past inputs $(u(t-1), \ldots, u(t-n))$ and past outputs $(y(t-1), \ldots, y(t-n))$ and the predicted output $y(t)$.

Given N observations of these input-output data pairs the system identification problem consists in determining the input-output equation (i.e. function $\hat{f}$) that relates explicitly the sampled outputs of the system to the sampled inputs. So our task is to find such a function $\hat{f}$ that is approximate to the true function f according to some adequacy criterion. Normally, one would propose to solve the following minimization problem:

$$\sum_{i=1}^{N} (\hat{f}(y_{i1}, ..., y_{in}, u_{i1}, ..., u_{in}) - y_{io}) \rightarrow \min \tag{2}$$

where $y_{in} = y_i(t-n)$ and $u_{in} = u_i(t-n)$.

There is a clear difference between the parameter estimation with the fix model, and the system identification problem, in which the model is also searched for and optimized. Once the model to be identified is given, EAs are easily applicable to solving the system identification problem, in the form of certain parameter estimation. However, the identification problem is converted to a certain optimization when parameters to be estimated are defined.

4   An Experimental Test Problem

Within this paper we deal with identification of the non-linear third-order discrete-time single-input single-output model represented in the following form:

$$
\begin{aligned}
y(t+3) = {} & 0.43y(t+2) + 0.68y(t+1) - 0.149y(t) + 0.396u(t+2) + \\
& +0.014u(t+1) - 0.071u(t) - 0.351y(t+2)u(t+2) - \\
& -0.03y^2(t+1) - 0.135y(t+1)u(t+1) - 0.027y^3(t+1) - \\
& -0.108y^2(t+1)u(t+1) - 0.099u^3(t+1) + e(t)
\end{aligned}
\tag{3}
$$

where $e(t)$ is a sequence of normally distributed random variables with zero mean, which is similar to white noise. This equation represents a model of liquid level system of interconnected tanks [12].

To solve this problem at hand the Evolutionary Algorithm Program e was used. e was produced by the SDI (System Dynamics International) MEDIA GROUP in 1995. The EA has to "learn" how the output variables change if the input variables are changed.

To help teach or train EA to solve problem a training data set that contains numeric values is used. The training data were sampled using the equation (3) and the sinusoidal input $u(t) = \sin(0, 2t)$ and consisted of 300 pairs of data. A row of data across all used variables is an event the EA will use to learn the cause-effect dependence. Using observed values of training files, the EA tries to determine a solution that produces the actual value for each row of training data.

The EA evolve populations of entities (i.e. candidate models) that solve problems. These models are small programs or subroutines randomly generated from arithmetic operations, logical operations, and trigonometric functions. Randomly generated populations of computer code, which represent candidate solutions to problem, are evaluated for fitness. The *fitness* of an individual (solution) is a measure of how well it performs according to a particular problem specification. In our case the margin of square error between the actual solution (actual value) and the solution returned by the entity (predicted value) is the entity fitness score. Furthermore, no matter how well the entity does, no matter how good its fitness score, it also receives *penalty* points for being long in length.

$$
score = \frac{\sum\limits_{i=1}^{N} |predicted\ value - actual\ value|^2}{N-1} + Length\ Penalty
\tag{4}
$$

The fitness of an individual in the population determines the probability of its reproduction and to be selected for the next improved generations of programs. To implement selection *tournament* and *fitness proportionate* selection principles are used. The EA model then "trains" until the error between the predicted and actual value, across selected rows of data, is reduced to a satisfactory level.

To improve entity fitness, mutation and crossover/recombination operators are used to cause random changes in genetic material within the entities with highest fitness. To perform *mutation*, randomly selected part of instructions within entity is replaced by new, randomly selected genetic material. *Crossover (recombination)* starts with two parents and results in two offspring. The process begins by random selection of a point in each parent to be the crossover point. Genetic material from one side of the crossover point of one parent is recombined with genetic material from the other parent. Note that since each entity is of variable length, the two parents are usually unequal in size.

As the evolutionary process continues over a number of generations, the population at large adapts to the problem. Overall fitness and individual fitness will continue to increase until either a plateau is obtained (i.e. the problem is solved) or specific run limits (e.g. time limit, birth limit and/or error threshold) are reached. The purpose of evolution is to develop entities whose output values are as close as possible to their corresponding truth values for each row in the training data.

It took about 8-9 hours for e to generate the models like:

$$y(t+1) = -0.3807y(t)u^3(t) + 0.0943u^3(t) + 0.1488u(t) + 0.8486y(t) \qquad (5)$$

$$y(t+3) = -0.1126y(t+1) - 0.3627y(t+1)u(t) + 0.1771y(t+1)y(t+2) + \\ +0.1771u(t+1) + 1.2222y(t+2) - 0.5727 \qquad (6)$$

$$y(t+3) = 0.05514y^3(t+2)u(t+2) + 0.1119y^2(t+2)u(t+2) + \\ +2y(t+2) - y(t+1) - 0.01377 \qquad (7)$$

Note that the generated models differ sufficiently from the observed model (3) and much simpler. In addition, models (5) and (7) are presented by the ANARMA (Additive Non-linear AutoRegressive Moving Average) structure [12], i.e. is described in the following form:

$$y(t) = \sum_{i=1}^{n} \psi_i(y(t-i), u(t-i)) \qquad (8)$$

and thereby answer to the condition of system realization.

The notion of equivalence for non-linear input-output difference equation has been studied by Hammer (1984) [12]. In his approach, difference equations are called input-output equivalent, if, starting from zero initial conditions, they generate the same output sequence when excited by the same input sequence.

To the naked eye, the input-output performance of predicted and observed models appears to be similar (see Fig. 1). To measure the fitness of a predicted model structure the *coefficient of determination* was used, also called "R-squared" or "goodness of fit", which in general terms measures the percent of the variation of the observed variables that can be explained by the predicted variables. In our experiment R^2 for model (5) is 99.8138%, for model (6) is 99.9221%, for model (7) is 99.9057%.

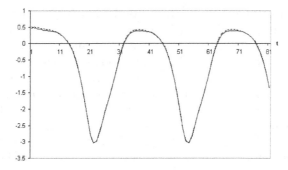

Fig. 1. Predicted (dashed) and true values (solid) for model (5)

5   Conclusions and Future Research Directions

In this paper it has been demonstrated how the EA can be used for solving the system identification problem. The method explored does not require prior information about the system (i.e. number and type of parameters, the system order etc.). Depending on the fitness function used, longer generated models were suppressed by the EA and, as the result, the generated models are shorter (i.e. lower order) than predicted by the system theory. These new models provide rather interesting preliminary data for the initial point of system analysis.

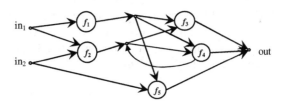

Fig. 2. Computational model

However, EA is not a panacea to every problem, because, as for other search and optimization methods, there are limitations to these methods. First of all, there are no known necessary and sufficient conditions for its convergence. Secondly, in systems like e it is usually difficult to get a model with an assumed structure because of a predefined set of instructions of the underlying abstract machine that is used as genetic material in the evolution process. So we cannot force the system to use a certain input variable (or a certain combination of input variables) and assure the realizability of generated models. To promote control over the evolution, we propose to use a configurable collection of instructions (i.e. computational models) instead (see Fig. 2). The computational model is a set of variables bound by partial relations. They initially were developed for specifications of engineering problems and were used in a problem solver Utopist (Tyugu 1970), which was a value propagation planner.

More precisely, we suggest using computational models as a source of genetic material. During the evolution process the individuals are generated from the programs $f_1, \ldots, f_5$ (see Fig.2) and the fitness function is built up in a way that suppresses individuals, which does not correspond to the data flow defined by the computational model. So the candidates for the best program could be e.g. $\langle f_1; f_3 \rangle$, $\langle f_1; f_5 \rangle$, $\langle f_1; f_2; f_4 \rangle$, $\langle f_1; f_2; f_4; f_4; f_4 \rangle$, etc. This allows usage of more powerful instructions as building bricks of programs and predefines structure of generated programs.

An important goal of research on evolutionary algorithms is to understand the class of problems for which EAs are more suited, and, in particular, the class of problems on which they outperform other search algorithms [2]. We should clearly define the domain of applicability of algorithms by presenting convergence proofs and efficiency results. Unfortunately, however, only by simplifying algorithms as well as the situations to which they are applied it is possible to prove abilities of them. The huge remainder of questions must be answered by means of (always limited) test series, and even that cannot tell much about an actual real-world problem-solving situation with yet unanalyzed features, that is, the normal case in applications [1].

Our goal is to get a new method for automatic program construction that combines SSP [7] (deductive method) with evolutionary learning via EAs (inductive method). On the basis of computational model EA can construct a program that is optimal, whereas SSP gives only "the first occasional solution" that fits the data flow and computes the output. In the framework of computational models and SSP, EAs could be effectively used for solving subproblems when training data that describes its input-output behavior is available.

So, much more work remains to be done but we strongly believe that further investigation of these evolutionary algorithm based methods will lead to success.

References

1. Bäck, T., Fogel, D.B., and Michalewicz, Z. (eds.): Handbook of Evolutionary Computation. IOP Publ. Co. & Oxford University Press (1997)
2. Michalewicz, Z. *Genetic Algorithms + Data Structures = Evolution Programs*, Springer-Verlag (1996)
3. Goldberg, D.E.: Genetic Algorithms in Search, Optimization, and Machine Learning. Addison-Wesley Reading Mass (1989)
4. Koza, J. *Genetic Programming: On the Programming of Computers by Means of Natural Selection.* MIT Press (1992)
5. Banzhaf, W., Nordin, P., Keller, R.E., Francone, F.D. *Genetic Programming , An Introduction On the Automatic Evolution of Computer Programs and Its Applications*, Morgan Kaufmann Publishers, Inc. (1998)
6. Langdon, W.B., Poli, R. *Foundations of Genetic Programming*, Springer-Verlag Publisher (2002)

7. Tyugu, E.: Knowledge-Based Programming. Addison-Wesley Publishing Company, Inc (1988)
8. Söderström, T, Stoica, P.: System Identification. Prentice Hall International, London (1989)
9. Tan, K.C., Li, Y., Murray-Smith, D.J., Sharman, K.: System identification and linearisation using genetic algorithms with simulated annealing. First Int. Conf. On CALESIA, University of Sheffield, UK (1995)
10. Kristinsson, K., Dumont, G. A.: Genetic Algorithms in system identification. Third IEEE Int. Symp. Intelligent Contr., Arlington, VA (1988) 597-602
11. Iba H.: System identification using structured genetic algorithms. In: Handbook of Evolutionary Computation. IOP Publ. Co. & Oxford University Press (1997), G1.4:1-11
12. Kotta, Ü., Nõmm, S., Chowdhury, F.N.: On a new type of neural-network-based input-output model: the ANARMA structure. IFAC (2001)

A Layered Architecture Sustaining Model-Driven and Event-Driven Software Development

Cindy Michiels, Monique Snoeck, Wilfried Lemahieu, Frank Goethals, and Guido Dedene

MIS Group, Dept. Applied Economic Sciences, K.U.Leuven,
Naamsestraat 69, 3000 Leuven, Belgium
{Cindy.Michiels, Monique.Snoeck, Wilfried.Lemahieu,
Frank.Goethals, Guido.Dedene}@econ.kuleuven.ac.be

Abstract. This paper presents a layered software architecture reconciling model-driven, event-driven, and object-oriented software development. In its simplest form, the architecture consists of two layers: an enterprise layer consisting of a relatively stable business model and an information system layer, containing the more volatile user functionality. The paper explains how the concept of events is used in the enterprise layer as a means to make business objects more independent of each other. This results in an event handling sublayer, allowing to define groups of events and handling consistency and transaction management aspects. This type of architecture results in information systems with a high-level modular structure, where changes are easier to perform as higher layers will not influence the inherently more stable lower layers.

1 Introduction

Separation of concerns can be pursued at different levels of abstraction in the software development process. In this paper we present a layered software architecture that represents a separation of concerns at a high level of abstraction: it classifies specifications in different layers according to a model-driven approach such that each layer only relies on concepts of the same layer or on concepts of the layers below. Such architecture results in information systems accounting for a high-level modular structure, where changes in higher layers will not influence the inherently more stable lower layers. At the same time, an event-driven approach is advocated as interaction paradigm for objects in the lowest layer: their interaction is modeled by identifying common involvement in business events. As such, these objects can be added and deleted from the bottom layer with no risk for severe maintenance problems, as is often the case in software development methodologies using method invocation as the main interaction method.

M. Broy and A.V. Zamulin (Eds.): PSI 2003, LNCS 2890, pp. 58–65, 2003.
© Springer-Verlag Berlin Heidelberg 2003

2   Model-Driven Development and Basic Layering

Model-driven development finds its origin in a reframed version of Zachman's Information Systems Architecture [1], which states that software requirements should be captured in different models according to their origin. As such, the Zachman framework recognizes four basic levels of abstraction in the software development process: the scope model, the business model, the information system model, and the technology model. Orthogonal to these basic abstraction layers, it identifies a number of aspects interacting with them, such as goals, data, process, and people. One of the main benefits of model-driven development is that it imposes a high-level modularity on the developed system: the inherently more stable business model can act as a foundation layer for the more volatile information system model. This facilitates maintenance dramatically.

The architecture presented in this paper builds upon model-driven development and as such retains two basic abstraction levels: the business model and the information system model. The scope model, defining the enterprise's direction and business purpose, is considered as a matter of ICT strategy development and is as a consequence left out of consideration [2]. The technology model, describing how technology may be used to address the information processing needs that were identified, is considered as an aspect orthogonal to the business model and the information system model, as different technology choices can be made for the realization of different layers [3]. One approach to deal with technology aspects will be the combination of code generation facilities with the reuse of patterns and frameworks [4].

The business model defines the fundamental business requirements using a set of business objects, business methods, and business rules to capture the entirety of the business. The Business Layer does not build upon an information system and is also valid if no information system is defined. The information system model is captured by an Information System Layer that actually builds upon an information system and covers all services related to the requested input and output functionality to the information system users. More precisely, the Information System layer is considered as a layer on top of the Business layer, because only the former is allowed to invoke services on the latter, and not the other way round (see Fig. 1). In adhering to this basic layering and to the principles of object-orientation, a flexible architecture is obtained, because input and output services can be plugged in and out of the Information System Layer with no side effects on the objects in the Business Layer.

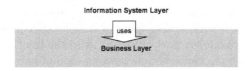

Fig. 1. Basic layers identified in architecture

3   Imposing an Event-Driven Approach

The introduction of a Business Layer, relating to the more stable business requirements, and an Information System Layer, capturing the more volatile input and output services of an information system, imposes a basic modularity upon the information system architecture. In this section it is argued that the modularity and, as a consequence, the flexibility of the architecture can be further enhanced by imposing an event-driven approach on the basic layering. This will result in a refinement of the Business Layer and the Information System Layer to account for business events and information system events respectively.

In most object-oriented approaches events are considered as subordinate to objects, because they only serve as a trigger for an object's method. The object interactions themselves are modeled by means of sequence and/or collaboration diagrams often involving long sequences of method invocations. As such, the specification of the dynamic behavior of a system can result in a complex network of method invocations between interacting objects. The main problem of this approach is that the addition or deletion of an object can involve severe maintenance problems, because all interaction sequences the object participates in are to be reconsidered.

In contrast, an event-driven approach raises events to the same level of importance as objects, and recognizes them as a fundamental part of the structure of experience [5]. A business event is now defined as an atomic unit of action that represents something that happens in the real world, such as the creation of a new customer, an order placement, etc. Without events nothing would happen: they reflect how information and objects come into existence (the creating events), how information and objects are modified (the modifying events), and how they disappear from our universe of discourse (the ending events). Object interaction can now be modeled by defining which objects are concurrently involved in which events. Object-event participations can be denoted by means of an Object-Event Table [6]. When an object participates in an event, it implements a method that defines the effect of the event on the object. On occurrence of the event all corresponding methods in the participating objects are executed in parallel. As such, the addition or deletion of an object will only involve the addition or deletion of all event participations of that object, without implications for other objects.

4   Implications on Basic Layering

The Business Layer can now be divided in two sublayers: the business objects, encapsulating data and behavior and defining business rules, constitute the lower sublayer. The business events, managing business object interaction, constitute the upper sublayer (see lower part of Fig. 2). Also the Information System Layer is split in two sublayers. The lower one is composed of information system transactions, managing a logical grouping of business events and of output services, implementing queries on business objects. The upper one consists of the user

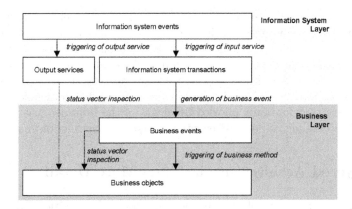

Fig. 2. Refinement of basic layers to sustain event-driven development

interface and its information system events triggering the input and output services (see upper part of Fig. 2).

Business events reflect those events that occur in the real world, even if there is no information system around. Examples of business events are the creation of a new course and the enrolment of a student. In contrast, information system events are inextricably linked with an information system and allow the external user to register the occurrence of a real world event in the information system by generating input for the information system, or to request data from the information system by generating output from the information system. An example of the former is a click on a Create button in a CreateNewCourse form. An example of the latter is a click on a ViewAllCourses button, resulting in the display of a list of courses. In fact, information system events do not relate only to user interface events but also to timer and sensor signals, etc.

The business objects of the Business Layer interact by means of common business events. For each business event a business object participates in, it implements a method. The triggering of this method will induce modifications in the attributes of the business object. On invocation of the business event, all related methods are executed in parallel. In addition to a method specification, a participating object can also specify a number of constraints that should be satisfied for the event to occur. For example, the class COURSE can specify that in order to accept an *enroll* event, the course should be in the state 'open_for_registration'. Such method preconditions and also class invariants can prevent the execution of the business event. Therefore, a business event will have to check the conditions imposed by all involved business objects before it is broadcast: all class invariants and sequence constraints should be met. This synchronization is performed by means of attribute inspections on all related business objects. If all constraints are met, the business methods can be triggered and as a consequence the modifications of the attributes will be made persistent. The invoking class is notified accordingly of the rejection, acceptance, and (un)successful execution of the event.

In the Information System Layer, information system events will trigger input and output services. Output services relate to information that is extracted from the business objects and are implemented by means of a set of corresponding attribute inspections (e.g. by means of a query). As attribute inspections do not involve changes in a business object, they are not the subjects of transaction management. In contrast, input services relate to modifications of business objects and are therefore only allowed by means of the intermediary of a business event. The handling of business events is subject to transaction management.

5   Layered Architecture in Some More Detail

To manage consistency of the Business Layer, business objects and business events are both modeled according to the principle of Design By Contract [7]. For each method they include a precondition clause, defining when method invocation is allowed, and a postcondition clause, defining what results are guaranteed after method invocation. As a result, a business event will first synchronize all involved business objects, i.e. check whether all method preconditions are fulfilled, and only if all agree trigger the corresponding business methods. In a similar way one layer up, an information system transaction will first check whether all involved business events agree before actually generating the business events.

However, the business events as considered so far actually all pertain to atomic business events, it is to say, they relate to atomic units of action. As atomic business events first synchronize all involved business objects, all class invariants and method sequence constraints are met before broadcasting the business event. If implemented well, the business objects are also in a consistent state after execution of the business event. Nevertheless, there remain some business rules that cannot be enforced at the level of atomic events but only by combining multiple atomic business events. As such, the layered architecture depicted in Fig. 2 can be refined somewhat further in distinguishing between two different kinds of business events, as explained in the example below.

Assume a course administration with a business rule stating that a student is mandatory enrolled for at least one course. In abstract terms, the atomic business event *create_student* is never allowed to happen alone, but should always be accompanied with at least one atomic business event *enroll*. This business rule can be formulated as a class invariant in the business class STUDENT, but cannot be dealt with by the atomic business event *create_student* or *enroll* alone. Actually, to enforce this mandatory relationship the atomic business events *create_student* and *enroll* are to be grouped in one consistent business event *C_create_student*. To ensure consistency, the consistent business event will be responsible for first checking whether its elementary atomic events agree and only in that case agree itself with a transaction.

Similar to the consistent event *C_create_student*, a consistent event *C_end_student* is defined, grouping the atomic business events *end_enrolment*, relating to the student's last enrolment, and *end_student*, relating to the student him/herself. Next to the consistent event *C_end_student*, a consistent event

C_end_enrolment has to be defined, imposing an extra constraint on atomic event *end_enrolment*, in stating that the event can only be invoked alone if STUDENT has more than one enrolment. Before and after the execution of consistent events *C_end_student*, and *C_end_enrolment*, all business objects are in a consistent state and thus all business rules are satisfied.

In this way, consistent events can be considered as a layer on top of part of the atomic events with a twofold responsibility: grouping of atomic events and/or imposing extra pre- and postconditions on atomic events. Now, information system transactions are considered as a layer invoking consistent events and those atomic events that are inherently consistent, for example *modify_student*. Transactions define a logical grouping of atomic and/or consistent events. For example, the transaction 'End Student' will involve the ending of the life cycle of a student together with all his/her enrolments because of referential integrity constraints. More precisely, the transaction will invoke a set of consistent events *C_end_enrolment* and one consistent event *C_end_student* the latter being composed of one atomic event *end_enrolment* and one atomic event *end_student* (see Fig. 3).

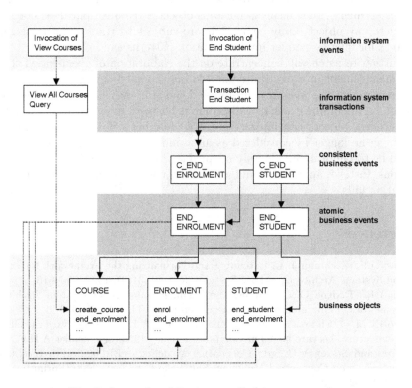

Fig. 3. Layered architecture applied to an example

6   Conclusions and Future Research

The architecture presented above adheres to the principles of model-driven and event-driven software development. The adoption of model-driven development resulted in the introduction of a Business Layer and an Information System Layer imposing a high-level modularity on the architecture. By adopting an event-driven approach the basic layers are further refined and deal respectively with business events and information system events. The modeling of business object interaction by means of business events allows for a loose coupling between the business objects. Atomic business events synchronize on business objects before they are triggered, i.e. all class invariants and method preconditions should be fulfilled. In order to guarantee full consistency of the Business Layer, business events are subdivided in atomic and consistent business events, because the former cannot deal with all kinds of business rules. Therefore, consistent events will be responsible for grouping and/or imposing extra business rules on part of the atomic events.

Another advantage of the event-driven approach is that it follows the Query-Command Separation Principle [7]: each service in the Information System layer is either a "command" which invokes business events but does not return values, or it is a "query" that inspects business object attributes, but does not modify or delete any object. Only commands are subject to transaction management whereas for queries simpler implementation patterns can be adopted.

Further research will concentrate on the elaboration of event-based transaction management in a distributed and loosely-coupled environment [8]. In such an environment the assumption of one global statically defined business model cannot be maintained: a set of distributed business models will exist of whom the business objects can interact in an ad hoc basis. Furthermore, a business event can no longer be considered as an atomic unit of action, as this approach would be too limiting in a loosely-coupled environment with long-standing transactions. Instead, an event should account for compensating actions if part of its execution fails.

References

1. Sowa J.F., Zachman J.A., Extending and Formalizing the Framework for Information Systems Architecture, IBM Systems Journal, 31(3), 1992, 590–616.
2. Maes R., Dedene G., Reframing the Zachman Information System Architecture Framework, Tinbergen Institute, discussion paper TI 9–32/2, 1996
3. Snoeck M., Poelmans S., and Dedene G., 2001, A Layered Software Specification Architecture, Lecture Notes in Computer Science 1920, in Laendler A.H.F., Liddle S.W., and Storey V.C., ed.: Conceptual Modeling – ER2000, 19th International Conference on Conceptual Modeling, Salt Lake City, Oct. 2000 (Springer Verlag), pp.454–469
4. Goebl W., Improving Productivity in Building Data-Oriented Information Systems — Why Object Frameworks are not Enough, Proc. of the 1998 Int. Conf. On Object-Oriented Information Systems, Paris, 9–11 September, Springer, 1998.

5. Cook S., Daniels J., Designing Object Systems: Object-Oriented Modeling with Syntropy, Prentice Hall, 1994.
6. Snoeck M., Dedene G., Existence Dependency: They Key to Semantic Integrity Between Structural and Behavioral Aspects of Object Types, IEEE Transactions on Software Engineering, Vol. 24, No. 24, April 1998, pp. 233–251.
7. Meyer B., Object-Oriented Software Construction, Prentice Hall, second edition, 1998
8. Lemahieu W., Snoeck M., Michiels C., and Goethals F., An Event Based Approach to Web Service Design and Interaction, Lecture Notes in Computer Science, accepted for APWeb2003.

The Outside-In Method of Teaching
Introductory Programming

Bertrand Meyer

ETH Zürich, Chair of Software Engineering
(Also Eiffel Software, Santa Barbara, and Monash University, Melbourne)
`se.inf.ethz.ch`

Abstract. The new design for the introductory programming course at
ETH relies on object technology, Eiffel, extensive reuse, a graphics-rich
library (TRAFFIC) built specifically for the course, a textbook (*"Touch
of Class"*) and an **Outside-In** approach based on "inverted curriculum"
ideas. This article presents the key aspects of the approach.
Note: readers interested in following the development of our course,
the "Touch of Class" textbook and the supporting TRAFFIC software
project may look up the page se.inf.ethz.ch/touch, where they can also
subscribe to mailing lists connected with the approach.

1   The Context

Many computer science departments around the world are wondering today how
best to teach introductory programming. This has always been a difficult task,
but new challenges have been added to the traditional ones:

- There is a strong pressure from many sources to emphasize directly operational skills over deeper, long-term concepts.
- Pressure also come from student families — more influential nowadays than
  in the past — who focus on the specific skills required in the job ads of
  the moment, and don't necessarily realize that four years later the acronyms
  listed in these ads might be different.
- Many academics who push fashionable technologies by invoking the demands
  of industry misunderstand industry's real needs: real industry recruiters —
  at least the good ones — know to look for problem-solving skills rather than
  narrow knowledge.
- Students come with a wide variety of backgrounds. Some have barely touched
  a computer; others may have programmed extensively before. It's tempting
  to assume programming experience, but this is unfair to students from the
  first category, who will then almost automatically fail, even though some
  may have developed other skills — such as mathematics — and have the
  potential to become good computer scientists.
- Of the students who have programming experience, some may actually possess skills (such as Web site programming) that the teacher doesn't.

M. Broy and A.V. Zamulin (Eds.): PSI 2003, LNCS 2890, pp. 66–78, 2003.
© Springer-Verlag Berlin Heidelberg 2003

- For exercises, if the programming language is C++ or Java, students increasingly resort to what may be called *Google-and-Paste* programming: find on the Web some existing program that — among other things — does the job, and turn off the irrelevant parts. It's a form of "reuse" not accounted for in the software engineering literature, and may yield solutions of 10,000 lines in which only a hundred are actually used. Unless we explicitly forbid this practice (should we?) it's not cheating, but it does raise interesting questions about our pedagogical techniques.
- Many courses use an object-oriented language, but not necessarily in an object-oriented way; few people have managed to blend genuine O-O thinking into the elementary part of the curriculum.
- In continental Europe a local phenomenon adds to the confusion: what we may call *Confetti Bolognese*, the tearing into pieces of national university systems — German, French, Italian..., each with its own logic and traditions — to make them all conform (as part of the "Bologna process") to a standard Bachelor's/Master's program, in principle devised from the US/UK model but in practice missing some of its ingredients. This is both an opportunity to take a fresh look at the curriculum and a source of instability.

The teaching of computer science at ETH, the Swiss Federal Institute of Technology in Zurich, is subjected to these contradictory pressures as in every other institution. What perhaps is most specific of ETH is its prestigious tradition of introducing new techniques both for programming and for teaching programming, epitomized in the line of languages designed by Niklaus Wirth: Pascal, Modula-2, Oberon. So it's not without trepidation that I accepted the invitation to take responsibility for "Introduction to Programming", formerly "Informatik I", starting in the Fall of 2004, and to teach it in Eiffel. Rather than using safe, time-honored approaches, I am taking the plunge and trying to apply ideas ("Progressive Opening of the Black Boxes", Inverted Curriculum, full use of object technology) which I previously described — from the comfort of a position in industry — in articles and books.

One of the remarkable traditions of computer science at ETH is the rule that introductory courses must be taught by senior professors. This contrasts with the practice of some institutions which view the teaching of introductory programming as a chore best handed over to part-timers or junior faculty. The ETH approach recognizes that those who have accumulated the most experience in their discipline are the ones who should teach it to newcomers at the most elementary level. Being asked to teach such a course is a great honor, and this article explains what I am trying to do, with my group, to fulfill that duty.

2   Components

The effort includes the following elements:

- The course itself: lecture schedule, overhead slides, exercises.

- A new textbook, "Touch of Class" [7], available to the students in electronic form for the first session, with the expectation of publishing it as an actual book in 2004. The developing manuscript is available to other interested parties from the URL listed at the beginning of this article.
- An extensive body of supporting software, called TRAFFIC, also under development.

3   Outside-In: The Inverted Curriculum

The order of topics in programming courses has traditionally been bottom-up: start with the building blocks of programs such as variables and assignment; continue with control and data structures; move on if time permits — which it often doesn't in an intro course — to principles of modular design and techniques for structuring large programs.

This approach gives the students a good practical understanding of the fabric of programs. But it may not always teach the system construction concepts that software engineers must master to be successful in professional development. Being able to produce programs is not sufficient any more today; many people who are not professional software developers can do this honorably. What distinguishes the genuine professional is a set of system skills for the development and maintenance of possibly large and complex programs, open for adaptation to new needs and for reuse of some of their components. Starting from the nuts and bolts, as in the traditional "CS1" curriculum, may not be the best way to teach these skills.

Rather than bottom-up — or top-down — the approach of the course is **Outside-In**. It relies on the assumption that the most effective way to learn software is to use good existing software, where "good" covers both the quality of the code — since so much learning happens through imitation of proven models — and, almost more importantly, the quality of its *interfaces*, in the sense of program interfaces (APIs).

From the outset we provide the student with powerful software: an entire set of sophisticated libraries — TRAFFIC — where the top layers have been produced specially for the course, and the basic layers on which they rely (data structures, graphics, GUI, time and date) are existing libraries that have stood the test of extensive commercial usage for many years.

All this library code is available in source form, providing a repository of high-quality models to imitate; but in practice the only way to use them for one's own programs, especially at the beginning, is through interfaces, also known as *contract views*, which provide the essential information abstracted from the actual code. By relying on contract views, students are able right from the start to produce interesting applications, even if the part they write originally consists of just a few calls to library routines. As they progress, they learn to build more elaborate programs, and to understand the libraries from the inside: to "open up the black boxes". The hope is that at the end of the course they would be able, if needed, to produce such libraries by themselves.

This Outside-In strategy results in an "Inverted Curriculum" where the student starts as a *consumer* of reusable components and learns to become a *producer*. It does not ignore the teaching of standard low-level concepts and skills, since at the end we want students who can take care of everything a program requires, from the big picture to the lowest details. What differs is the order of concepts and particularly the emphasis on architectural skills, often neglected in the bottom-up curriculum.

The approach is intended to educate students so that they will master the key concepts of software engineering, in particular *abstraction*. In my career in industry I have repeatedly observed that the main quality that distinguishes good software developers is their ability to abstract: to separate the essential from the accessory, the durable from the temporary, the specification from the implementation. All introductory textbooks indeed preach abstraction, but it's doubtful how effective such exhortations can be when all the student knows of programming is the usual collection of small algorithmic examples. I can pontificate about abstraction as much as the next person, but the only way I know to convey the concepts effectively is by example; in particular, by showing to the student how he or she can produce impressive applications through the reuse of existing software made of tens of thousands of lines, resulting from maybe a hundred person-years of work, so that trying to understand it from the inside, by reading the source code, would take months of study. Yet the student can, in the first week of the course, produce impressive results by reusing that software through its abstract interfaces — the contract views.

Here abstraction is not just a nice idea that we ask our students to heed, another parental incitation to be good and do things right. It's the only way to survive when faced with an ambitious goal that you can't fulfill except by standing on someone else's shoulders.

The student who has gone early and often through this experience of building a powerful application through interface-based reuse of libraries does not need to be harangued much more about the benefits of abstraction and reuse. These concepts become a second nature. Teaching is better than preaching, and if something is better than teaching it must be the demonstration, carried out by the students themselves, of the principles at work, producing "Wow!" results.

4   The Supporting Software

Central to the Outside-In approach of our course is the accompanying TRAFFIC software, available in source form on the book's CD and also on the Web. The choice of application area for the library required some care; the problem domain had to:

- Be immediately familiar to any student, so that we could spend our time studying software issues and solutions, not understanding the context.
- Provide a large stock of interesting algorithms and data structure examples, applications of fundamental computer science concepts, and new exercises that each instructor can devise beyond those in the *Touch of Class* textbook.

- Call for graphics and multimedia development as well as advanced Graphical User Interfaces — a requirement that is particularly important to capture the attention of a student generation which has grown up with video games and sophisticated GUIs.
- Unlike many video games, not involve violence and aggression, which would be inappropriate in a university setting (and also would not help correct the gender imbalance which plagues our field).

The application area that we retained meets these criteria. It's the general concept of *transportation in a city*: modeling, planning, simulation, display, statistics. The supporting TRAFFIC software is a library, providing reusable components from which students and instructors can build applications. Although still modest, the library has the basic elements of a Geographical Information System, and the supporting graphical display mechanisms.

Our example city is Paris, with its sights and transportation networks:

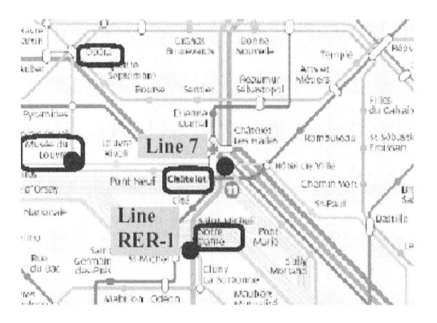

Since the city's description comes from XML files, it is possible to retarget the example to another city.

The very first application that the student produces displays a map, highlights the Paris Metro network on the map, retrieves a predefined route, and shows a visitor traveling that route through video-game-style graphical animation. The code is:

```
class PREVIEW inherit
       TOURISM
feature
       explore is
                       - - Show city info and route.
            do
                       Paris.display
                       Louvre.spotlight
                       Metro.highlight
                       Route1.animate
            end
end
```

The algorithm is four lines of code, and yet the effect is quite stunning, since these lines call powerful TRAFFIC mechanisms. In this example as in all subsequent ones, we remove any impression of "magic", since we can explain everything, at an appropriate level of abstraction. We avoid ever having to say "just code this the way you're told, it will work, you'll understand later". Such an approach is unsound pedagogically and does not create confidence in the subject. In this example, even the **inherit** clause can be explained in a simple fashion: we don't go into the theory of inheritance, of course, but simply tell the student that class *TOURISM* is a helper class introducing pre-defined objects such as *Paris*, *Louvre*, *Metro* and *Route1*, and that a new class can "inherit" from such an existing class to gain access to its features. They're also told that they don't need to look up the details of class *TOURISM*, but may do so if they feel the engineer's urge to know "how things work".

So the way we enable our students to approach the topics progressively is always to abstract and never to lie, even if it would be a pedagogical lie.

5   Object Technology and Model-Driven Architecture

Using an object-oriented language for introductory programming is not a new idea. But it's sometimes done halfheartedly, with the implicit view that students must be taken through the same set of steps that their teachers had to climb in their time. This approach continues the traditional bottom-up order of concept introduction, reaching classes and objects only as a reward to the students for having patiently climbed the *Gradus ad Parnassum* of classical programming constructs. There's no good reason for being so coy about O-O. After all, part of the pitch for the method is that it lets us build software systems as clear and natural *models* of the concepts and objects with which they deal. If it's so good, it should be good for everyone, beginners included. Or to borrow a slogan from the waiters' T-shirts at Anna's Bakery in Santa Barbara, whose coffee fueled some of the reflections behind this course: *Life is uncertain — Eat dessert first!*

Classes and objects appear indeed at the very outset, and serve as the basis for the entire course. I have found that beginners adopt object technology enthusiastically provided the concepts are introduced, without any reservations or excuses, as the normal, modern way to program.

One of the principal consequences of the central role of object technology is that the notion of *model* guides the student throughout. The emergence of "model-driven architecture" reflects the growing recognition of an idea central to object technology: that successful software development relies on the construction of models of physical and conceptual systems. Classes, objects, inheritance and the associated techniques provide an excellent basis to teach effective modeling techniques.

Object technology is not exclusive of the traditional approach. Rather, it subsumes it, much in the same way that relativity includes classical mechanics as a special case: an O-O program is made of classes, and its execution operates on objects, but the classes contain routines, and the objects contain fields on which programs may operate as they would do with traditional variables. So both the *static* architecture of programs and the *dynamic* structure of computations cover the traditional concepts. We definitely want the students to master the traditional techniques: algorithmic reasoning, variables and assignment, control structures, procedures, recursion...

6   Eiffel and Design by Contract

The approach relies on Eiffel and the EiffelStudio environment which students can download for free from www.eiffel.com. (Universities can also limit themselves to the free version, or they may get an academic license for extended functionality.) This choice directly supports the pedagogical concepts of the course:

- The Eiffel language is uncompromisingly object-oriented throughout.
- As many people have remarked, Eiffel provides an excellent basis to learn other programming languages, such as C#, Java, Smalltalk or C++. A software engineer must be multi-lingual, and in fact able to learn new languages regularly; but the first language you learn is critical since it can open or close your mind forever. Eiffel provides a general framework that is an excellent preparation for learning new paradigms later in the student's career.
- Eiffel is very easy to learn. In some other languages, before you can produce any result, you must include some magic formula which you don't understand, such as the famous *public static void main (string [] args)*. This is not the case in Eiffel. The concepts can be introduced progressively, without interference between basic constructs and those not yet studied.
- The EiffelStudio development environment uses a modern, intuitive GUI, with advanced facilities including sophisticated browsing, editing, debugging, automatic documentation (HTML or otherwise), even metrics. It produces architectural diagrams automatically from the code and, the other way around, lets a user draw diagrams from which the environment will produce the code, with round-trip capabilities.
- EiffelStudio is available on many platforms including Windows and Linux.

- The environment includes a set of carefully written libraries, which support the reuse concepts of our approach, and serve as the basis of the TRAFFIC library. The most directly relevant are *EiffelBase*, which by implementing the fundamental structures of computer science directly supports the study of algorithms and data structures in part III of the textbook, *EiffelTime* for date and time, and *EiffelVision*, an advanced portable graphical library serving as the basis for the graphical parts of TRAFFIC.
- Unlike tools designed for education only, Eiffel is used commercially for large mission-critical applications handling billions of dollars of investment, managing health care, performing large civil and military simulations, and others spanning a broad range of areas. This is in my opinion essential to effective teaching of programming; a tool that is really good should be good for the professionals as well as for the novices.
- Eiffel is not just a programming language but a method whose primary aim — beyond expressing algorithms for the computer — is to support thinking about problems and their solutions. It enables us to teach a **seamless approach** that extends across the software lifecycle, from analysis and design to implementation and maintenance. This concept of seamless development, supported by the two-way diagram tool of EiffelStudio, is in line with the key modeling benefits of object technology, and at the heart of the Eiffel approach.

To support these goals, Eiffel directly implements the concepts of **Design by Contract**^{TM}, which were developed in connection with Eiffel and are closely tied to both the method and the language. By equipping classes with preconditions, postconditions and class invariants, we let students use a much more systematic approach than is currently the norm, and prepare them to become successful professional developers able to deliver bug-free systems.

Along with these semantic concepts we shouldn't underestimate the role of *syntax*, both for experienced programmers and for beginners. Eiffel's syntax — illustrated by the above short example of the course's first program, to be compared to equivalents in other languages — seeks to facilitate learning, enhance program readability, and fight mistakes:

- The language avoids cryptic symbols.
- Every reserved word is a simple and unabbreviated English word (*INTEGER*, not *int*).
- The equal sign =, rather than doing violence to hundreds of years of mathematical tradition, means the same thing as in math. (How many students, starting with languages where = denotes assignment, have wondered what value a must have for $a = a + 1$ to make sense, and as noted by Wirth [9] why $a = b$ doesn't mean the same as $b = a$?)
- In many languages, program texts are littered with semicolons separating declarations and instructions. Most of the time there is no reason for these pockmarks; even when not consciously noticed, they affect readability. Being required in some places and illegal in others, for reasons not always clear

to beginners, they are also a source of small but annoying errors. Eiffel's syntax has been designed so that the semicolon, as instruction separator, is optional, regardless of program layout. With the standard layout style of writing separate instructions and declarations on separate lines, this leads to a neat program appearance.

Encouraging such cleanliness in program texts must be part of the teacher's pedagogical goals. Eiffel includes precise style rules, explained along the way in *Touch of Class* to show students that good programming requires attention to both the high-level concepts of architecture and the low-level details of syntax and style: quality in the large and quality in the small.

More generally, a good teaching language should be unobtrusive, enabling students to devote their efforts to learning the concepts (and professional programmers to applying the concepts). This is one of the goals of using Eiffel for teaching: that students, ideally, shouldn't even have to *know* what language they are using.

7   How Formal?

One of the benefits of the Design by Contract approach is to expose the students to a gentle dose of "formal" (mathematically-based) methods of software development.

The software world needs — among other advances — more use of formal methods. Any serious software curriculum should devote at least one course entirely to mathematics-based software development, for example in the second year, based on a mathematical specification language such as B, Z or HOL. In addition — although not as a substitute for such a course — the ideas should influence the entire software curriculum. This is particularly important at the introductory level. It is probably unrealistic, today at least, to subject beginners to a fully formal approach; this might turn off some of them who might otherwise become good computer scientists, and would miss the need to start mastering the concrete, practical skills of programming.

The challenge is not only to include an introduction to formal reasoning along with those practical skills, but to present the two aspects as complementary, closely related, and both indispensable. The techniques of Design by Contract, tightly woven into the fabric of object-oriented program structures, permit this.

Teaching Design by Contract awakens students to the idea of mathematics-based software development. Almost from the first examples of interface specifications, routines possess preconditions and postconditions, and classes possess invariants. These concepts are introduced in the proper context, treated — as they should, although many programmers still fear them, and most programming languages offer no support for contracts — as the normal, obvious way to reason about programs. Without intimidating students with a heavy-duty formal approach, we prepare the way for the introduction of formal methods, which they will fully appreciate when they have acquired more experience with programming.

Writing up the material has confirmed that reliance on mathematics actually helps following a practical, concrete, hands-on approach. For example we introduce loops as an *approximation* mechanism, to compute a solution on successively larger subsets of the data; then the notion of *loop invariant* comes naturally, as a key property of any kind of loop, expressing how big the approximation is at every stage. We hope that such techniques will help educate students for whom correctness concerns are a natural, ever-present component of the software construction process.

8   From Programming to Software Engineering

Programming is at the heart of software engineering, but is not all of it. Software engineering concerns itself with the production of systems that may be large, require long-running development, undergo many changes, meet strong constraints of quality, timeliness and cost. Although the corresponding techniques are usually not taught to beginners, it's important in our view to provide at least a first introduction. Topics include debugging and testing (even with the best of modern programming methodology, this will account for a good deal of the time spent on the job, so it would be paradoxical not to teach the corresponding skills), quality in general, lifecycle models, requirements analysis (the programmers we are educating shouldn't just be techies focused on the machinery but should also be able to talk to users and understand their needs), GUI design.

9   Topics Covered

The *Touch of Class* textbook, in its final form, is divided into five parts, which a course may not be able to cover entirely.

Part I introduces the basics. It defines the building blocks of programs, from objects and classes to interfaces, control structures and assignment. It puts a particular emphasis on the notion of contract, teaching students to rely on abstract yet precise descriptions of the modules they use and, as a consequence, to apply the same care to defining the interface of the modules they will produce. A chapter on "Just Enough Logic" introduces the key elements of propositional calculus and predicate calculus, both essential for the rest of the discussion. Back to programming, subsequent chapters deal with object creation and the object structure; they emphasize the modeling power of objects and the need for our object models to reflect the structure of the external systems being modeled. Assignment is introduced, together with references, only after program structuring concepts.

Part II, entitled "How things work", presents the internal perspective: basics of computer organization, programming languages, programming tools. It is an essential part of the abstraction-focused approach to make sure that students also master the concrete aspects of hardware and software, which define the context of system development. Programmers who focus on the low-level, machine-oriented, fine-control details are sometimes derided as "hackers" in the older sense (not the more recent one of computer vandal). There's nothing wrong with that form of hacking when it's the natural hands-on, details-oriented complement to the higher-level concepts of software architecture. Students must understand the constraints that computer technology puts on our imagination, especially orders of magnitude: how fast we can transmit data, how many objects we can store in primary and secondary memories, the ratio of access times for these two kinds.

Part III examines the fundamental "Algorithms and data structures" of computer science, from arrays and trees to sorting and some advanced examples. Here too the approach is object-oriented and library-based.

Part IV considers some more specialized object-oriented techniques such as inheritance, deferred features and constrained genericity, event-driven design, and a taste of concurrency.

Part V adds the final dimension, beyond mere programming, by introducing concepts of software engineering for large, long-term projects, with chapters on such topics as project management, requirements engineering and quality assurance.

Appendices provide an introduction to various programming languages of which the students should have a general understanding: C#, Java, C — described in some more detail since it's an important tool for accessing low-level details of the operating system and the hardware — and C++, a bridge between the C and O-O worlds.

10   Comparing with Other Approaches

Introductory programming education is a widely discussed issue and many techniques have been tried.

Today's commonly used textbooks tend to emphasize a particular programming language, often Java or C++. This has the advantage of practicality, and of easily produced exercises (sometimes subject to the Google-and-Paste attack cited above), but gives too much weight to the study of the chosen language, at the expense of fundamental conceptual skills. Eiffel as a language avoids making a fuss of itself; its aim, as noted, is to be unobtrusive, serving as a mere mode of expression for concepts of software architecture and implementation. That's what we teach, not the specifics of any language.

The justly famous MIT course based on Scheme [1] is strong on teaching the logical reasoning skills essential to a programmer. We definitely intend to retain this benefit, as well as the relationship to mathematics (especially in our case through Design by Contract), but feel that object technology provides students with a more concrete grasp of the issues of system construction. Not only is an O-O approach in line with the practices of the modern software industry, which has shown little interest in functional programming; more importantly for our pedagogical goals, it emphasizes **system building** skills and software architecture, which should be at the center of computer science education.

One may also argue that the operational, imperative aspects of software development, downplayed by functional programming, are not just an implementation nuisance but a fundamental component of the discipline of programming, without which many of its intellectual challenges disappear. If so, we are not particularly helping students by protecting them from this component at the beginning of their education, presumably leaving them to their own resources when they encounter it later.

At the other extreme, one finds suggestions by Guzdial and Soloway [3] to make full use of modern technologies, such as graphics and multimedia, to capture the attention of the *"Nintendo Generation"*. We retain this analysis, and include extensive graphics in the TRAFFIC software; but we strive to establish a proper balance, not letting technological dazzle push aside the teaching of timeless skills.

11   Outlook

The preparatory work described here is in a state of flux; the course has not yet been taught. In October of 2003 the first batch of ETH students will take it.

Only their reaction and, more significantly, their success in later parts of the computer science curriculum — if we can't wait for the ultimate test, their careers — will tell whether the Outside-In method can deliver on its promise of providing a modern computer science education based on reuse, object technology, Eiffel, Design by Contract and the principles of software engineering.

Acknowledgments. My understanding of how to teach programming has been shaped by discussions with numerous professional educators over the years, too numerous in fact to be listed here (see, however, the long list in chapter 29 of [5]). I should single out Bernard Cohen for his original work on the Inverted Curriculum [2], and Christine Mingins for implementing the ideas at Monash University, in a program [8] running continuously with Eiffel for almost ten years. Peter Henderson first pointed out to me the phenomenon called "Google-and-Paste programming" above. The work reported here is a collective effort of my group at ETH, involving in particular Susanne Cech, Karine Arnout, Bernd Schoeller and Michela Pedroni; the design and implementation of TRAFFIC is the work of Patrick Schoenbach and Till Bay with the support of the rest of the team and critical help from Julian Rogers and Ian King at Eiffel Software. I am grateful to other ETH professors, especially Jürg Gutknecht and Hans Hinterberger, for advice and numerous discussions, and to the FILEP project of ETH for financially supporting the development of the course and the software.

A preliminary version of this article appeared in the proceedings of the Japanese Symposium on Object Orientation (IPSJ-SIGSE), edited by Mikio Aoyama, Tokyo, August 2003.

References

1. Harold Abelson and Gerald Sussman, *Structure and Interpretation of Computer Programs*, 2nd edition, MIT Press, 1996.
2. Bernard Cohen: *The Inverted Curriculum*, Report, National Economic Development Council, London, 1991.
3. Mark Guzdial and Elliot Soloway: *Teaching the Nintendo Generation to Program*, in *Communications of the ACM*, vol. 45, no. 4, April 2002, pages 17–21.
4. Bertrand Meyer, *Towards an Object-Oriented Curriculum*, in *Journal of Object-Oriented Programming*, vol. 6, no. 2, May 1993, pages 76–81. Revised version in *TOOLS 11 (Technology of Object-Oriented Languages and Systems)*, eds. R. Ege, M. Singh and B. Meyer, Prentice Hall, Englewood Cliffs (N.J.), 1993, pages 585–594.
5. Bertrand Meyer, *Object-Oriented Software Construction*, *2nd edition*, Prentice Hall, 1997, especially chapter 29, *"Teaching the Method"*.
6. Bertrand Meyer, *Software Engineering in the Academy*, in Computer (IEEE), vol. 34, no. 5, May 2001, pages 28–35.
7. Bertrand Meyer, *Touch of Class: Learning to Program Well — With object technology, Design by Contract, and steps to software engineering*, to be published, draft versions currently available from se.inf.ethz.ch/touch
8. Christine Mingins, Jan Miller, Martin Dick, Margot Postema: *How We Teach Software Engineering*, in *Journal of Object-Oriented Programming* (JOOP), vol. 11, no. 9, 1999, pages 64–66, 74.
9. Niklaus Wirth: *Computer Science Education: The Road Not Taken*, opening address at ITiCSE conference, Aarhus, Denmark, June 2002, available (September 2003) at www.inr.ac.ru/ info21/greetings/wirth_doklad_eng.htm.

Design by Contract is a trademark of Eiffel Software.

Numeric Types in Formal Synthesis[*]

Viktor Sabelfeld and Kai Kapp

Institute for Computer Design and Fault Tolerance (Prof. Dr.-Ing. D. Schmid)
University of Karlsruhe, Germany
{Viktor.Sabelfeld,Kai.Kapp}@ira.uka.de
http://goethe.ira.uka.de/fsynth

Abstract. The Formal Synthesis methodology can be considered as the application of the transformational approach to circuit synthesis by logical transformations performed in a theorem prover. Additionally to the implementation of the circuit, the proof that the result is a correct implementation of a given specification is obtained automatically. In this paper, a higher-order formalisation for the arithmetic of bound numeric data types is given. We provide correct transformations implemented in the theorem prover HOL [4], to register-transfer level descriptions of arithmetic operations. For a restricted class of specifications, a correct transformation is described which eliminates the type num and replaces arithmetic operations by its bound variants.

Keywords: formal specification, correct hardware synthesis, higher-order logic, theorem prover, arithmetic operations.

1 Introduction

The correctness of the design is the most critical question in circuit synthesis. By correctness we mean that the synthesis result satisfies the specification, in a formal mathematical sense. Because of the size and complexity of today's synthesis tools they generally cannot be formally verified, but only be tested partially and bugs in the programs of these synthesis tools mostly lead to faulty implementations.

In formal synthesis, we derive the circuit implementation from a given specification by the application of elementary transformation rules which are formulated in higher-order logic and proved as theorems in a theorem prover. Since the composition of correct transformations is also correct, the resulting synthesised circuit is a correct implementation of the specification, and the proof of the correctness of this implementation ("correctness by construction") is obtained automatically.

In the formal synthesis, most approaches deal with the synthesis of digital systems at lower levels of abstraction [11], or with synthesis of pure data-flow descriptions at the algorithmic level [7].

---

[*] This work has been partly financed by the Deutsche Forschungsgemeinschaft, Project SCHM 623/6-3.

M. Broy and A.V. Zamulin (Eds.): PSI 2003, LNCS 2890, pp. 79–90, 2003.

The main related approach is known as "transformational design" and aims at "correctness by construction": The synthesis process is also based on correctness-preserving transformations[6]. However, the transformations are proved by paper & pencil and afterwards implemented in a complex software program. It is implicitly assumed that an automatic synthesis process is correct by definition. But there is no guarantee that the transformations have been implemented correctly and therefore, the correctness of the synthesis process cannot be regarded as proved.

In our approach to formal synthesis, we have developed the language *Gropius* [1] to describe the circuit specifications and implementations. The semantics of this language is mathematically exactly defined in the higher-order logic HOL [4].

In this paper, we give a higher-order formalisation for the arithmetic of the bound numeric data types, and provide correct transformations implemented in the theorem prover HOL to register-transfer level descriptions of the basic arithmetic operations.

1.1   Related Works

The last release *Kananaskis* of the theorem prover HOL contains a HOL-formalisation of the 32-bit machine arithmetic, due to Anthony Fox, but no optimisation theorems or circuit implementation theorems for the arithmetic operations.

The Intel Corporation has developed [8] a combination of model checking and theorem proving technique for the formal specification and verification of floating-point arithmetic hardware. Though this technique is not universally applicable to arbitrary bit width, it was successfully applied to formal specification and verification of the IEEE compliance of the gate-level descriptions of the Pentium Pro processor's floating-point arithmetic operations.

2   Gropius

The BNF rules below describes the simple syntactic structure of DFG-terms (acyclic **D**ata **F**low **G**raphs). They represent non-recursive programs that always terminate. Such descriptions are used in *Gropius1*, the register-transfer (RT) level of *Gropius*.

$$var\_struct \ ::= \ variable \ [\text{":"} type \ ] \ | \ \text{"("} \ var\_struct \ \text{","} \ var\_struct \ \text{")"}$$
$$expr \ ::= \ var\_struct \ | \ constant \ [\text{":"} type \ ]$$
$$| \ \text{"("} expr \ \text{","} expr \ \text{")"} \ | \ \text{"("} expr \ expr \ \text{")"}$$
$$DFG\text{-}term \ ::= \ expr$$
$$| \ \text{"λ"} \ var\_struct \ \text{"."} \{ \text{"let"} \ var\_struct = expr \ \text{"in"} \} \ expr$$

A *condition* is a DFG-term which produces a boolean output. At the algorithmic level, the *Gropius* circuits are described by P̲rogram terms. The following syntax definitions fix the core of this language. All other P-terms can be reduced to the semantically equivalent ones from the core.

$$P\text{-}term ::=$$
"DEF" *DFG-term* | "WHILE" *condition P-term*
| *P-term* "SER" *P-term* | *P-term* "PAR" *P-term*
| "IF" *condition P-term P-term*

To represent the data type of P-terms which may not terminate, the type α partial with constructor partial and type parameter α has been introduced. It extends an arbitrary type α by a new value $\bot$ which is interpreted as "undefined". That means that any value of the type α partial is either $\bot$ or Def x, where x is a value of type α. For example, the DEF-construct is defined by DEF $f\ x = $ Def$(f\ x)$ so that it delivers a "defined" value for all DFG-terms $f : \alpha \to \beta$ and $x : \alpha$, and never delivers the value $\bot$.

The P-terms have a type $\alpha \to \beta$ partial, where α and β are arbitrary type parameters.

The semantics of the P-term (WHILE *condition body*) is a higher-order function of type $\alpha \to \alpha$ partial such that there exists a function $(state : \text{num} \to \alpha)$ satisfying the condition $(state\ 0 = x)$, and

$$(\text{WHILE } condition\ body\ x = \text{Def } y) \Leftrightarrow$$
$$\exists t.\ \forall n.\ n < t \Rightarrow condition(state\ n) \wedge (state\ t = y) \wedge$$
$$(body(state\ n) = \text{Def}(state(\text{SUC } n))) \wedge \neg condition(state\ t)$$

In all other cases, i. e., when the sequence of states is infinite or it stops in a body computation delivering the value $\bot$, WHILE *condition body* $x = \bot$.

The SER and PAR constructs are the strict composition operators on P-terms. SER denotes the sequential composition: $(A$ SER $B)\ x = y$, iff

$$((x = \bot) \vee (A\ x = \bot)) \wedge (y = \bot), \text{ or } \exists u.\ (A\ x = \text{Def } u) \wedge (B\ u = y),$$

and PAR is the parallel composition operator:

$$(A \text{ PAR } B)\ x = \bot, \qquad \text{iff } (x = \bot) \vee (A\ x = \bot) \vee (B\ x = \bot),$$
$$(A \text{ PAR } B)\ x = \text{Def}(u, v), \text{iff } (A\ x = \text{Def } u) \wedge (B\ x = \text{Def } v). \qquad ^{\cdot}$$

At last, the semantics of the IF-construct with a condition $condition : \alpha \to \text{bool}$ and branches $(A : \alpha \to \beta$ partial) and $(B : \alpha \to \beta$ partial) is defined by

$$\text{IF } condition\ A\ B \overset{\text{def}}{=} \lambda x.\ \text{if } condition\ x \text{ then } A\ x \text{ else } B\ x.$$

More details about P-terms and the algorithmic level of *Gropius* can be found in [2].

At the system level of *Gropius*, the circuit description is represented as a system structure (*S-structure*) of communicating *processes* similar to Petri nets. The behavior of each process is specified by a P-term. We have studied the semantics of circuit descriptions at system level, and the problems of the correct transformation to lower levels of *Gropius*. Also we have described some optimisation transformations like partition and combination of processes, which are particularly important in software/hardware co-design [10].

3   Semantics for *Gropius* Bound Numeric Data Types

At the RT-level of *Gropius*, the natural numbers of the bit width W are represented by boolean functions which deliver the value F (false) for all arguments greater than W:

$$Bit\ W\ n\ i \stackrel{\text{def}}{=} i < W \wedge \mathsf{ODD}(n\ \mathsf{DIV}\ 2^i)$$

Now we want to introduce the natural and the integer numbers in *Gropius* in a more abstract way. The *Gropius* numbers ought to be independent from any concrete implementation by special generic circuits which model the execution of the basic arithmetic operations. This will decrease the number of the specification errors in arithmetic units caused by the circuit designer, and will give reason to develop some specific correct transformations intended for automatic optimisation of the arithmetic modules (e.g., the choice of the bit width, the selection of the types and of the number of adders, multipliers and so on).

In our first step, we have introduced the (width parametrised) arithmetic operations on W-bit natural numbers by the reduction to the arithmetic operations on the natural numbers in HOL, for example

$$\mathsf{plus}\ W\ m\ n \stackrel{\text{def}}{=} (m+n)\ \mathsf{MOD}\ 2^W$$
$$\mathsf{mult}\ W\ m\ n \stackrel{\text{def}}{=} (m*n)\ \mathsf{MOD}\ 2^W$$
$$\mathsf{less}\ W\ m\ n \stackrel{\text{def}}{=} m\ \mathsf{MOD}\ 2^W < n\ \mathsf{MOD}\ 2^W$$
$$\mathsf{lshift}\ W\ s\ n \stackrel{\text{def}}{=} (n*2^s)\ \mathsf{MOD}\ 2^W$$

The "bit by bit" operations on W-bit natural numbers can be defined by means of an auxiliary function $BinOp$ which models the bit by bit execution of a boolean operation $o : \mathsf{bool} \rightarrow \mathsf{bool} \rightarrow \mathsf{bool}$:

$$BinOp\ 0\ o\ m\ n \stackrel{\text{def}}{=} 0$$
$$BinOp\ (\mathsf{SUC}\ W)\ o\ m\ n \stackrel{\text{def}}{=}$$
$$(\text{if } o(\mathsf{ODD}\ m)(\mathsf{ODD}\ n)\text{ then }1\text{ else }0) + 2 * BinOp\ W\ o\ (m\ \mathsf{DIV}\ 2)(n\ \mathsf{DIV}\ 2)$$

So, the semantics of bit by bit AND operation is described by

$$BitAnd\ W \stackrel{\text{def}}{=} BinOp\ W\ \wedge$$

Some other arithmetic operations deliver an additional boolean value; for example, the operation plus_with_overflow_signal delivers additionally an overflow bit:

$$\mathsf{plus\_with\_overflow\_signal}\ W\ m\ n \stackrel{\text{def}}{=} ((m+n)\ \mathsf{MOD}\ 2^W, 2^W \leq m+n)$$

and the operation div_with_zero_division_signal delivers additionally a zero division bit.

Most arithmetic laws hold also for the basic arithmetic operations on W-bit natural numbers, for example operations plus and mult are commutative and associative, there exist the *zero* element for the addition and the *one* element for the multiplication. Of course, some usual arithmetic laws does not hold in the W-bit arithmetic, for example, all W-bit numbers are less than 2^W.

In the next step, we will introduce a new data type num32 for an abstraction of 32-bit natural numbers. To this end, we use the type definition package by Melham [9] and define a *representation function* _ :num32→num and its inverse *abstraction function* ¯ :num→num32, so that the following theorem holds:

$$\vdash (\forall x : \text{num32}. \overline{(\underline{x})} = x) \wedge \forall n : \text{num}. \, Is\_num\ 32\ n = (\,\underline{(\overline{n})} = n)$$

where $Is\_num \overset{\text{def}}{=} \lambda w\, n : \text{num}. \, n < 2^w$. Unfortunately, HOL has no dependent types, so we built a theory $num32Theory$ for the type num32 and can then automatically generate a new theory and transformation algorithms for W-bit natural numbers with any concrete width value W we need $(1 < W)$. The basic arithmetic operations of the type num32 are defined according to the above definitions of the parametrised W-bit operations. Using operation overloading allowed in HOL, we can reuse the inured names for the basic arithmetic operations and define its semantics for any arguments m, n of type num32 (here only for a few samples):

$$m + n \overset{\text{def}}{=} \overline{\text{plus } W\ \underline{m}\ \underline{n}} \qquad\qquad \text{addition}$$
$$m \uplus n \overset{\text{def}}{=} (m + n,\ 2^W \le \underline{m} + \underline{n}) \qquad \text{addition \& overflow}$$
$$m * n \overset{\text{def}}{=} \overline{\text{mult } W\ \underline{m}\ \underline{n}} \qquad\qquad \text{multiplication}$$
$$m/n \overset{\text{def}}{=} \overline{\underline{m}\ \text{DIV}\ \underline{n}} \qquad\qquad \text{division}$$
$$m\%n \overset{\text{def}}{=} \overline{\underline{m}\ \text{MOD}\ \underline{n}} \qquad\qquad \text{modulo operation}$$
$$m < n \overset{\text{def}}{=} \underline{m} < \underline{n} \qquad\qquad \text{less relation}$$
$$m \wedge n \overset{\text{def}}{=} \overline{\text{BitAnd } W\ \underline{m}\ \underline{n}} \qquad\qquad \text{bit by bit AND}$$
$$n << s \overset{\text{def}}{=} \overline{\text{lshift } W\ \underline{s}\ \underline{n}} \qquad\qquad \text{shift left}$$

The most of the well known arithmetic laws of the natural numbers hold also in our theory $numWTheory$, and we use them in our optimisation and synthesis algorithms:

$$\vdash \qquad \forall\ m\ n.\ m + n = n + m$$
$$\vdash \forall\ m\ n\ k.\ m + (n + k) = (m + n) + k$$
$$\vdash \qquad \forall\ m.\ m + 0 = m$$
$$\vdash \qquad \forall\ m.\ m << 1 = m * 2$$
$$\vdash \qquad \forall\ m.\ m \le m$$
$$\vdash \quad \forall\ m\ n.\ m \le n \wedge n \le m \Longrightarrow m = n$$
$$\vdash \forall\ m\ n\ k.\ m \le n \wedge n \le k \Longrightarrow m \le k$$

In a similar way, the theory $intWTheory$ for the W-bit bound integers has been constructed. Here is

$$Is\_int \overset{\text{def}}{=} \lambda\,(W : \text{num})(i : \text{integer}).(i < 2^{W-1}) \wedge (-2^{W-1} \le i)$$

the characteristic predicate for the type definition of the W-bit integers $(1 < W)$. Because of the asymmetry of the range, some arithmetic laws of the integer numbers do not hold in $intWTheory$, for example the addition and the multiplication operations are not associative.

4   Transformation to RT-Level

All levels of *Gropius* are embedded in the HOL language. Therefore, we can make use of the HOL theorem prover advantages. Such advantages are, for example, the strict mathematical semantics, the term polymorphism and the static type checking mechanism of HOL. For each construct we have introduced in *Gropius*, a correct transformation to register-transfer level was proposed [3]. So, we have described a set of regular structures as *generic extensions* of RT-level formulations. These extensions can contain additional parameters of the types num or α list which will be deleted by the subsequent HOL term rewriting. To guarantee that the reduction process always terminates we have to prove a theorem that states how to eliminate such extensions. Most important for the generic extensions are some specific regular structures which are intended to simplify the inductive proofs of the extension properties. Below we illustrate this procedure by an regular binary tree generic structure example. The simple generic tree structure is described in a recursive definition of the generic extension $BinTree$ where we use a parameter $op : \alpha \times \alpha \to \alpha$ for an arbitrary binary operation:

$$BinTree\ 0\ op\ (E : \mathsf{num} \to \alpha)\ i \overset{\text{def}}{=} E\ i$$
$$BinTree\ (\mathsf{SUC}\ n)\ op\ E\ i \overset{\text{def}}{=} op(BinTree\ n\ op\ E\ i, BinTree\ n\ op\ E\ (i + 2^n))$$

Suppose we have a circuit description $\otimes : \mathsf{matr} \times \mathsf{matr} \to \mathsf{matr}$ for the implementation of the matrix multiplication operation. The term $BinTree\ 2\ \otimes$ $(\lambda i : \mathsf{num}.\ M : \mathsf{matr})$, after instantiation of the constant 2 reduces to the term $M4 \overset{\text{def}}{=} (M \otimes M) \otimes (M \otimes M)$ which is a description of the full binary tree circuit for the parallel evaluation of the 4th power of the matrix M. Note that this description does not specify the order of the particular multiplication steps. By the means of simple equivalent transformations both circuits for the optimal parallel evaluation let $M2 = M \otimes M$ in $M2 \otimes M2$ and the full sequential (and slow) variant

$$\mathsf{let}\ M2 = M \otimes M\ \mathsf{in}\ \mathsf{let}\ M3 = M2 \otimes M\ \mathsf{in}\ M3 \otimes M$$

for the sequential evaluation can be deduced from $M4$. For the transformation to the last variant the associativity of the operation $\otimes$ was used.

A modification of the generic structure $BinTree$ is defined below for the implementation of the Carry-Lookahead adder.

As mentioned above, the integer and the natural numbers are represented in *Gropius1* by boolean functions of natural argument, which yield the value F (false) for all arguments greater than a parameter. We have proved theorems for the automatic correct transformation of arithmetic operations to several implementations as RT-level circuit descriptions. For example, we have provided several correct transformations of the addition operation to three different *Gropius* circuits *RC_adder*, *CLA_adder* and *OptCLA_adder*.

The ripple-carry adder *RC_adder* can be described in the following generic extensions

$$ripple\ W\ (a:\mathsf{num}\to\mathsf{bool})\ (b:\mathsf{num}\to\mathsf{bool})\ (c:\mathsf{bool})\ 0 \stackrel{\mathrm{def}}{=} (\mathsf{F},c)$$

$ripple\ W\ a\ b\ c\ (\mathsf{SUC}\ i) \stackrel{\mathrm{def}}{=}$
    if $i < W$
    then let $(sum, carry) = ripple\ W\ a\ b\ c\ i$ in $\mathsf{FADD}(carry, a\ i, b\ i)$
    else (F, F)

$RC\_adder\ W\ (a:\mathsf{num}\to\mathsf{bool})\ (b:\mathsf{num}\to\mathsf{bool}) \stackrel{\mathrm{def}}{=}$
    $(\lambda i:\mathsf{num}.\ \mathsf{FST}(ripple\ W\ a\ b\ \mathsf{F}\ i), \mathsf{SND}(ripple\ W\ a\ b\ \mathsf{F}\ W))$

where FADD denotes the full boolean adder

$$\mathsf{FADD}(c, x, y) \stackrel{\mathrm{def}}{=} \mathsf{let}\ (u, v) = (x\ \mathsf{XOR}\ y, x\ \mathsf{AND}\ y)$$
$$\mathsf{in\ let}\ z = c\ \mathsf{AND}\ u\ \mathsf{in}\ (c\ \mathsf{XOR}\ u, v\ \mathsf{OR}\ z)$$

For the correct transformation of P-terms containing arithmetic addition, to *Gropius1* circuit descriptions with ripple-carry adder implementation of addition, the following theorem has been proved for the bit width W:

$$\vdash \qquad \forall(m:\mathsf{num}W)(n:\mathsf{num}W).$$
$$\mathsf{let}\ (s, o) = m \uplus n\ \mathsf{in}\ (Bit\ W\ \underline{s}, o) = RC\_adder\ W\ (Bit\ W\ \underline{m})(Bit\ W\ \underline{n})$$

The structure of the ripple-carry adder of the bit width 8 is shown in the Fig. 1.

The description of the faster Carry-Lookahead adder [5] in *Gropius1* contains the definition of the generic circuit *PG* which implements the evaluation of the propagate-generate predicate pair for two given boolean functions a and b representing natural numbers:

$$PG\ 0\ i\ (a:\mathsf{num}\to\mathsf{bool})(b:\mathsf{num}\to\mathsf{bool}) \stackrel{\mathrm{def}}{=} ((a\ i)\mathsf{OR}(b\ i), (a\ i)\mathsf{AND}(b\ i))$$
$$PG(\mathsf{SUC}\ n)\ i\ a\ b \stackrel{\mathrm{def}}{=} \mathsf{let}\ (p_1, g_1) = PG\ n\ i\ a\ b\ \mathsf{and}\ (p_2, g_2) = PG\ n(i + 2^n)\ a\ b$$
$$\mathsf{in}\ (p_1\ \mathsf{AND}\ p_2, g_2\ \mathsf{OR}\ (g_1\ \mathsf{AND}\ p_2))$$

The characteristic property of this generic circuit can be proved as a theorem:

$$\vdash \forall\ n\ m\ (a:\mathsf{num}\to\mathsf{bool})(b:\mathsf{num}\to\mathsf{bool}).\ \mathsf{let}\ (p, g) = PG\ n\ m\ a\ b\ \mathsf{in}$$
$$(p = (\forall i.\ m \le i \wedge i < m + 2^n \Rightarrow a\ i \vee b\ i)) \wedge (g =$$
$$\exists k.\ (m \le k \wedge k < m + 2^n) \wedge a\ k \wedge b\ k \wedge (\forall i.\ k < i \wedge i < m + 2^n \Rightarrow a\ i \vee b\ i))$$

So, $PG\ n\ m\ a\ b$ delivers a pair (p, g), where p is true iff the positions $m \ldots m + 2^n$ propagate the carry and g is true iff the positions $m \ldots m + 2^n$ generate a carry during addition execution for vectors a and b.

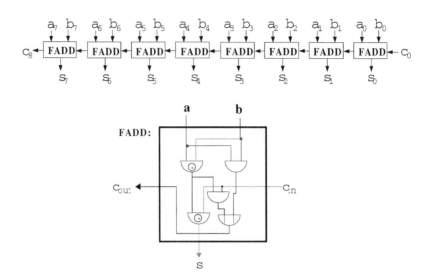

Fig. 1. Ripple-carry adder of the bit width 8

Another theorem very important for proving properties of the generic PG-circuits is the theorem

$$\vdash \qquad \forall\, n\, m\, x\, y. \text{ let } W = 2^n \text{ in}$$
$$\text{let } (p,g) = PG\ n\ m\ (Bit\ W\ x)\ (Bit\ W\ y)$$
$$\text{and } sum = (x\ \text{DIV}\ 2^m)\text{MOD}\ 2^W + (y\ \text{DIV}\ 2^m)\text{MOD}\ 2^W \text{ in}$$
$$(g = (2^W \le sum)) \wedge (\neg g \Rightarrow (p = (sum = 2^W - 1)))$$

which asserts a relation between the generate-propagate predicate pair and the inequality of the corresponding natural numbers.

The carry bits of the sum are defined in the second part of the Carry-Lookahead circuit description which we formulate below also as a generic extension:

$$Carry\ 0\ m\ (a : \text{num} \to \text{bool})(b : \text{num} \to \text{bool})(c : \text{bool})\ i \overset{\text{def}}{=} c$$
$$Carry\ (\text{SUC}\ n)\ m\ a\ b\ c\ i \overset{\text{def}}{=}$$
$$\quad \text{if } i < 2^n$$
$$\quad \text{then } Carry\ n\ m\ a\ b\ c\ i$$
$$\quad \text{else let } (p,g) = PG\ n\ m\ a\ b$$
$$\quad\quad \text{in } Carry\ n\ (m + 2^n)\ a\ b\ (g\ \text{OR}\ (c\ \text{AND}\ p))\ (i - 2^n)$$

In this recursive definition, $Carry\ n\ m\ a\ b\ c\ i$ denotes for $i = 0, \ldots, 2^n$ the carry bit at the position $m + i$ in the sum of vectors a and b supposed the incoming carry bit c stays in the position m.

In the third part of the generic Carry-Lookahead circuit, the carry bits are used for the parallel computation of the sum bits:

$$CLA\_adder\ h\ (a\!:\!\mathsf{num}\to\mathsf{bool})(b\!:\!\mathsf{num}\to\mathsf{bool}) \overset{\text{def}}{=} \text{let } W = 2^h \text{ in}$$
$$(\lambda i.\ (i < W) \wedge ((a\ i)\,\mathsf{XOR}\,(b\ i)\,\mathsf{XOR}\,(Carry\ h\ 0\ a\ b\ \mathsf{F}\ i)),$$
$$\mathsf{SND}(PG\ h\ 0\ a\ b))$$

Note we use here a bit width W which is equal to two to the power of some natural h, $W = 2^h$. We ensure the correctness of the transformation of the addition operation from the theory $numWTheory$ to the Carry-Lookahead adder by proving the theorem

$$\vdash \qquad\qquad \forall h\ (m\!:\!\mathsf{num}W)(n\!:\!\mathsf{num}W).$$
$$\text{let } (s,o) = m \uplus n \text{ in } (Bit\ W\ \underline{s},o) = CLA\_adder\ h\ (Bit\ W\ \underline{m})\,(Bit\ W\ \underline{n})$$

By subsequent applications of simple optimisation transformations, the definitions of functions PG, $Carry$, and CLA_adder are combined in a single circuit description $OptCarry$, and the repeated evaluation of PG-terms in $OptCarry$ is eliminated.

$$OptCarry\ 0\ m\ (a\!:\!\mathsf{num}\to\mathsf{bool})(b\!:\!\mathsf{num}\to\mathsf{bool})(c\!:\!\mathsf{bool})\ i \overset{\text{def}}{=}$$
$$(c, (a\ m)\mathsf{OR}(b\ m), (a\ m)\mathsf{AND}(b\ m))$$
$$OptCarry(\mathsf{SUC}\ n)\ m\ a\ b\ c\ i \overset{\text{def}}{=}$$
$$\text{let } (c1,p1,g1) = OptCarry\ n\ m\ a\ b\ c\ i$$
$$\text{in let } (c2,p2,g2) = OptCarry\ n\ (m+2^n)\ a\ b\ (g1\ \mathsf{OR}\ c\ \mathsf{AND}\ p1)(i-2^n)$$
$$\text{in let } (p,g) = (p1\ \mathsf{AND}\ p2, g2\ \mathsf{OR}\ g1\ \mathsf{AND}\ p2)$$
$$\text{in } (\text{if } i < 2^n \text{ then } c1 \text{ else } c2, p, g)$$

The basis for the correctness proof for the optimised version $OptCarry$ is the theorem

$$\vdash \qquad\qquad \forall\ n\ m\ x\ y\ (c\!:\!\mathsf{bool})\ i.$$
$$\text{let } (carry,pg) = OptCarry\ n\ m\ (Bit\ 2^n\ x)(Bit\ 2^n\ y)\ c\ i \text{ in}$$
$$(pg = PG\ n\ m\ (Bit\ 2^n\ x)(Bit\ 2^n\ y)) \wedge$$
$$(2^{n-1} \le m \wedge i < 2^n\ \Rightarrow (carry =$$
$$2^i \le (x\ \mathsf{DIV}\ 2^m)\mathsf{MOD}\ 2^i + (y\ \mathsf{DIV}\ 2^m)\mathsf{MOD}\ 2^i + (\text{if } c \text{ then } 1 \text{ else } 0)))$$

which says that the generic extension $OptCarry$ correctly computes the carry bits and the propagate-generate predicate pairs. As a result, the efficient Carry-Lookahead adder implementation

$$OptCLA\_adder\ h\ (a\!:\!\mathsf{num}\to\mathsf{bool})(b\!:\!\mathsf{num}\to\mathsf{bool}) \overset{\text{def}}{=}$$
$$(\lambda i\!:\!\mathsf{num}.\ (i < 2^h) \wedge ((a\ i)\ \mathsf{XOR}\ (b\ i)\,\mathsf{XOR}\ (OptCarry\ h\ 0\ a\ b\ \mathsf{F}\ i)),$$
$$\mathsf{SND}(PG\ h\ 0\ a\ b))$$

will be obtained together with its correctness proof:

$$\vdash \qquad\qquad \forall h\ (m\!:\!\mathsf{num}W)(n\!:\!\mathsf{num}W).$$
$$\text{let } (s,o) = m \uplus n \text{ in } (Bit\ W\ \underline{s},o) = OptCLA\_adder\ h\ (Bit\ W\ \underline{m})\,(Bit\ W\ \underline{n})$$

The structure of the optimised CLA-adder of the bit width 8 is shown in the Fig. 2.

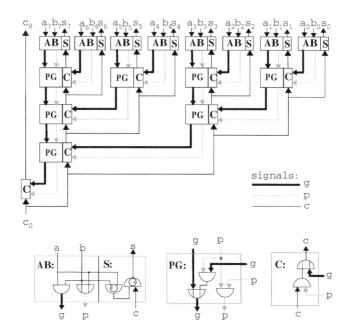

Fig. 2. Optimised CLA-adder of the bit width 8

5   Elimination of the Type num

We have introduced means for the W-bit arithmetic at the algorithmic level of *Gropius*. The theorems we have proved for several implementations of the arithmetic operations ensure the correctness of the automatic transformation to RT-level. But in some cases, it would be more convenient for the circuit designer to allow a restricted use of *manageable* natural numbers in specifications so that he needs not to care about the bit width. We have described a correct transformation eliminating such restricted use of the num type expressions from a *Gropius* term t satisfying following conditions

- The types of the input and of the output of t do not contain the type num.
- The operations + and * do not occur in WHILE loops.
- The DIV and MOD operations occur only with a constant second argument (the denominator) which is not zero.

This transformation is used also for the automatic correct elimination of the type num from our "state-representation" of P-terms

$$\text{Loop } (start : \text{num}) \ L \stackrel{\text{def}}{=} \text{DEF } (\lambda x : \alpha.(x, start))\text{SER}$$
$$\text{WHILE } (\lambda(x : \alpha, s).\text{StateExists } L \ s)(\text{StateFun } L)\text{SER DEF FST}$$

resulting from the single-loop transformation of the circuit description. In this state representation, a key list $L : (\text{num} \times (\alpha \rightarrow (\alpha \times \text{num})\text{partial}))\text{list}$ of alternatives and two derived constructs StateExists and StateFun are used. Each element of the list L is a pair $(state : \text{num}, f)$ consisting of a state $state$ and a function f that says how to evaluate the next state and a new value x of type α as the initial value for the next loop iteration. The predicate

$$\text{StateExists } L \; state \; \stackrel{\text{def}}{=} \; \exists \, x. \, MEM(state, x) \; L$$

checks the existence of a state $state$ in the list L and is used in the state representation for the loop exit test, and

$$\text{StateFun } L \; \stackrel{\text{def}}{=} \; (\lambda(x : \alpha, s : \beta). \; \text{StateCase } L \; s \; x)$$

is the "uncurried" version of the StateCase construct which means the choice of an element from the "selector list" L by the selector s:

$$\text{StateCase}((state, f) :: L) \; s \; \stackrel{\text{def}}{=} \; \text{if } s = state \text{ then } f \text{ else StateCase } L \; s$$

The elimination of the type num from the state representation of a Gropius specification has three essential elements:

- Determination of the maximal natural number which can ever arise in the program execution.
- Reduction of constant terms. We have implemented a conversion $reduceW$ which reduces constant terms of bit-width W, i.e. terms without variables, to constants. For example,

$$reduce32(1 << 4) = \vdash \; ((1 << 4) = 16)$$

  There are two exceptions in the reducing process: zero division and modulo zero terms are irreducible.
- Type change for the selector variable of the loop. First the range of the selector variable is restricted to the length of the selector list, afterwards the selector type is changed.

For example, to eliminate the type num from a loop with less than 2^{32} states, the following theorem is applied:

$\vdash \forall \; L \; (start : \text{num}). \; DisjointStates \; L \wedge (|L| < 2^{32}) \Rightarrow$
let $R = \iota(p : \text{num} \rightarrow \text{num32})$.
    $\forall i.(i < |L| \Rightarrow (p(\text{FST}(\text{EL } i \; L)) = \bar{i})) \wedge (\neg \, \text{StateExists } L \; i \Rightarrow (p \; i = \overline{|L|}))$
in Loop $start \; L \; =$
    Loop $(R \; start)(MAP(\lambda(s, f). \; (R \; s, f \; \text{SER DEF}(\lambda(x, s). \; (x, R \; s))))L)$

By an application of this theorem, the ith element $(state : \text{num}, f)$ of the list L will be replaced by a new element $(\bar{i} : \text{num32}, f \; \text{SER DEF}(\lambda(x, s).(x, R \; s)))$, for $i = 0, \ldots, |L| - 1$.

6   Conclusion

We have introduced W-bit natural and integer numbers in the hardware description language *Gropius* by reducing its semantics to the semantics of the HOL numbers. This makes our numbers independent from the circuit implementations and give rise to develop and to use correct transformations to implementations with automatic choice of the right bit width, with automatic selection of the type and of the number of arithmetic units with suitable speed and hardware costs. Another advantage of the abstract number types in *Gropius* is the static type checking mechanism inherited from HOL.

We succeed in simplifying our correctness proofs for transformations of arithmetic operations to RT-level circuit descriptions by dividing this proofs into two parts. In the first part, the quality of the circuit does not matter, only functional aspects are of importance. The resulting intermediate circuit description contains recursion equations which are close to the induction schemes used in the correctness proof. The second part contains the reduction to linear recursion, and some other optimisations, so that all terms are evaluated only once in the resulting circuit description.

References

1. Ch. Blumenræhr and D. Eisenbiegler. *Performing High-Level Synthesis via Program Transformations within a Theorem Prover*, In: Digital System Design Workshop at the 24th EUROMICRO 98 Conference, 1998.
2. Ch. Blumenræhr and V. Sabelfeld. *Formal Synthesis at the Algorithmic Level*, In: Correct Hardware Design and Verification Methods, Charme'99, 1999.
3. D. Eisenbiegler. *Ein Kalkül für die Formale Schaltungssynthese*, Karlsruhe University Dissertation (in German). Logos Verlag Berlin, 1999, 150 P.
4. M.J.C. Gordon and T.F. Melham. *Introduction to HOL: A Theorem Proving Environment for Higher Order Logic*, Cambridge University Press, 1993.
5. J.L. Hennessy, D.A. Patterson. *Computer Architecture — a Quantitative Approach*, 2nd Edition, 1996.
6. J. Iyoda, A. Sampaio, L. Silva. *ParTS: A Partitioning Transformation System*, In: FM'99 — Formal Methods, World Congress on Formal Methods in the Development of Computing Systems, LNCS 1709, pp. 1400–1419.
7. M. Larsson. *An engineering approach to formal digital system design.* The Computer Journal, 38(2):101–110, 1995.
8. J. O'Leary, X. Zhao, R. Gerth, C. H. Seger. *Formally Verifying IEEE Compliance of Floating-Point Hardware*, Intel Technology Journal, 1999, 14 p., http://www.intel.com/technology/itj/q11999/articles/art_5.htm
9. T.F. Melham. *Automating Recursive Type Definitions in Higher Order Logic*, In: G. Birtwistle and P. A. Subrahmanyam, eds., Current Trends in Hardware Verification and Automated Theorem Proving, pp. 341–386, Springer-Verlag, 1989.
10. V. Sabelfeld, Ch. Blumenræhr and K. Kapp. *Semantics and Transformations in Formal Synthesis at System Level*, In: Perspectives of System Informatics, PSI'2001, Novosibirsk, LNCS 2244, 2001, pp. 149–156.
11. R. Sharp, O. Rasmussen. *The T-Ruby design system.* In: IFIP Conference on Hardware Description Languages and their Applications, pp. 587–596, 1995.

On the Possibility of Provably Secure Obfuscating Programs*

Nikolay P. Varnovsky[1,3] and Vladimir A. Zakharov[2,3]

[1] Laboratory for Cryptography,
Lomonosov State University, Moscow, RU-119899, Russia
[2] Faculty of Computational Mathematics and Cybernetics,
Lomonosov State University, Moscow, RU-119899, Russia
zakh@cs.msu.su
[3] Institute for System Programming, Russian Academy of Sciences,
B. Kommunisticheskaya, 25, 109004 Moscow, Russia

Abstract. By obfuscation we mean any efficient semantic-preserving transformation of computer programs aimed at bringing a program into such a form, which impedes the understanding of its algorithm and data structures or prevents the extracting of some valuable information from the plaintext of a program. The main difficulty in designing an effective program obfuscator is to guarantee security, i.e. to prove that no algorithm can break software protection in reasonable time. All obfuscation techniques and tools developed so far rely on the informal concept of security and therefore can't be regarded as provably secure. In this paper we (1) introduce for the first time a formal information-theoretic definition of obfuscation security, (2) present a new obfuscation technique which takes advantage of cryptographic primitives (one-way functions, hard-core predicates), and (3) demonstrate, taking a conventional password identification scheme as a case study, how to prove security of the obfuscating transformations.

Keywords: program transformation, obfuscation, security, mutual information, one-way function, hard-core predicate.

1 Introduction

Protection of software against intelligent tampering and unauthorized purposeful modifications is one of the central issues in computer security. Almost every software-controlled system faces threats from potential adversaries, from Internet-aware client applications running on PCs, to complex telecommunications and power systems accessible over Internet, to commodity software with copy protection mechanisms. Various methods and tools are widely used for the purpose of software protection, including sophisticated security policies, network filters, cryptosystems, tamper-resistant hardware, etc. [1,8,10]. But no matter

---

* This work was supported by the Russian Foundation for Basic Research (grant 03-01-00880)

M. Broy and A.V. Zamulin (Eds.): PSI 2003, LNCS 2890, pp. 91–102, 2003.
© Springer-Verlag Berlin Heidelberg 2003

how powerful these techniques may be, they don't cover the case when an adversary, having in mind to make an illegal modification of a program or to gain some valuable knowledge about algorithms or data structures, gets an access to the plaintext of a program. The current trends in software engineering and communication technology make it common to distribute software in such a form that retains most of information presented in the program source code. This increases drastically the risk of reverse engineering attacks aimed at extracting secret information from a program.

An important example is Java bytecode. Java applications are distributed as Java class files, hardware-independent virtual machine codes that retains almost all information of the original Java source. The customary cryptographic tools can be very effective for protecting programs from illegal usage at the stage of their distribution. But when a program is decrypted, it becomes extremely vulnerable to software pirates seeking for private information (passwords, data-keys, etc.) or valuable pieces of code to incorporate them in their own applications.

In these cases the only way to prevent such malicious activity is to convert a program into some tamper-resistant form, which has the property that understanding and making purposeful modifications to it are rendered difficult while its original functionality and efficiency are preserved. Program transformations of this kind are called *obfuscating transformations*. The plaintext of an obfuscated program becomes itself the "ultimate defensive line" of the program.

Apart from software protection, program obfuscators could enjoy wide application in cryptography. When introducing the concept of public-key cryptosystem in the seminal paper [9], Diffie and Hellman noticed that, given any means for obscuring data structures in a symmetric-key encryption algorithm, one could convert this algorithm into a public-key cryptosystem. Obfuscators would also allow one to convert any public-key cryptosystem into a homomorphic one, i.e. a public-key cryptosystem which, given encryption of two bits, can securely compute an encryption of any Boolean operation of these bits. The existence of homomorphic encryption schemes is a long-standing open problem in cryptography.

The concept of obfuscating transformation was introduced in [4]. In this paper an obfuscator is defined informally as any efficient probabilistic compiler $\mathcal{O}$ which transforms any source program π into a new program $\mathcal{O}(\pi)$ satisfying the following requirements:

– $\mathcal{O}(\pi)$ has the same observable behavior, and
– $\mathcal{O}(\pi)$ is substantially less intelligible (readable) than π.

To get a formal definition of obfuscating transformation one has to clarify the terms "the same observable behavior" and "less intelligible". Now it is commonly accepted that when dealing with sequential deterministic programs the first term means that programs π and $\mathcal{O}(\pi)$ compute the same input-output relation and the complexity of $\mathcal{O}(\pi)$ (its size, time and space complexity, etc.) is at most polynomially larger than that of π.

The second term is still a topic for discussions. The authors of the most papers on program obfuscation restrict their consideration only to the expounding of the intuitive meaning of this term. Thus, Collberg and Thomborson [7] require an obfuscating transformation $\mathcal{O}$ to increase the *obscurity* of π so that the understanding and reverse engineering of $\mathcal{O}(\pi)$ will be strictly more time-consuming than the understanding and reverse engineering of π. Since static analysis of programs is in wide use for the purposes of program understanding and reverse engineering, this line of research on obfuscating transformations regards obfuscator as a tool for obstructing static analysis (see [18]). There have been many ad hoc obfuscating techniques proposed: a taxonomy of approaches is discussed in [4,5,18,19]. The most advanced of them are based on the following principle: find some NP-hard problem $\mathcal{P}$, define a class $\mathcal{F}$ of program fragments whose efficient analysis implies resolution of $\mathcal{P}$ in polynomial time, and develop a technique for inserting safely fragments from $\mathcal{F}$ into an arbitrary program. Collberg et al. [5,6] exploit NP-hardness of pointer alias analysis [13,14,17] for constructing opaque predicates, i.e. predicates whose behavior is difficult for understanding. The hard cases of points-to analysis problem is also used in [18] for increasing software tamper-resistance. In [3] a universal technique was proposed which makes it possible to "implant" uniformly and safely an arbitrary PSPACE-complete problem into any program.

The principal drawback of all these techniques is that none of them has a formal basis for making claims about the difficulty of understanding an obfuscated program. Therefore it is hardly possible to estimate to what extent such methods serve the purpose — only the reference to the intractability of some static analysis problems or to the hardness of combinatoric problem embedded into obfuscated programs is not sufficient. Meanwhile, the need for formalization of security requirements was realized in the earliest studies on foundation of cryptography, and a number of suitable security criteria were developed. M. Blum (see [15]) noticed that some ideas and techniques from cryptography are worthy of being adapted for program obfuscation. Unfortunately, the straightforward application of these techniques to the obfuscation problem is hardly possible, since obfuscating transformations ought to preserve functionality of source programs, whereas semantic-preserving encryptions are few and far between.

A formal investigation of the very concept of program obfuscation in the context of present-day cryptography was initiated in [2,12]. To formalize the "unreadability" requirement Barak, Goldreich, et al. introduced in [2] the concept of "perfect" obfuscation. Intuitively, a program obfuscator $\mathcal{O}$ is called *perfect* if it transforms any program π into a "virtual black box" $\mathcal{O}(\pi)$ in the sense that anything one can efficiently compute given $\mathcal{O}(\pi)$, one should be able to efficiently compute given just oracle access to π. The main result of [2] implies that perfect obfuscation is impossible. This is proved by constructing a family $\mathcal{F}$ of functions and a predicate $P : \mathcal{F} \to \{0,1\}$ such that, given any program that computes a function $f \in \mathcal{F}$, the value $P(f)$ can be efficiently computed, whereas no efficient algorithm, being given only oracle access to a randomly selected $f \in \mathcal{F}$, can compute $P(f)$ much better than by random guessing.

Our brief review shows that there is an amazing gap between the well-proved negative result of [2], which excludes the possibility of omnipotent obfuscators, and numerous heuristic algorithms [3,4,5,6,7,18,19] attempting some vague kind of obfuscation. The aim of our paper is to fill (at least partially) this gap. We put forward an alternative meaningful definition of obfuscation security which allows to estimate in information-theoretic terms the capability of a semantic-preserving program transformation $\mathcal{O}$ to obfuscate an individual property P for a given class of programs $\mathcal{H}$. Informally, $\mathcal{O}$ obfuscates securely a property P if any adversary A, being granted an access to programs from $\mathcal{O}(\mathcal{H})$, can extract in polynomial time only a "negligibly small" amount of information on P. To show that the new formalization of obfuscation security enables one to design provably secure program obfuscators we consider one meaningful example. We take for $\mathcal{H}$ a class of programs that implement a simple fixed password identification scheme, and for P the property of a program to execute actual password checking. Then, assuming that one-way permutations exist, we design a program compiler $\mathcal{O}$ and prove that $\mathcal{O}$ securely obfuscates P. Moreover, by demonstrating that a secure obfuscation of P implies the existence of one-way functions, we also reveal close relationships between obfuscation problem and basic cryptographic primitives.

The paper is organized as follows. In Section 2 we give some basic definitions along with some facts from complexity theory that are necessary for proving our main result. In Section 3 we introduce an information-theoretic definition of obfuscation security. Next (Section 4) we consider an obfuscation problem for a fixed password identification scheme, present an obfuscating transformation $\mathcal{O}$ and prove its security. Finally (Section 5) we show how to apply $\mathcal{O}$ in practice to strengthen the tamper resistance of an arbitrary program.

2   Preliminaries

We denote by B the set $\{0,1\}$, by B^n the set of all binary strings of length n, and by B^* the set of all finite binary strings. If x and y are binary strings of the same length, say n, then we write $\bigoplus(x,y)$ for $\bigoplus_{i=1}^{n} x_i y_i$. PPA is shorthand for probabilistic polynomial time algorithms. Each PPA A is associated with a pair of polynomials p_1, p_2. If A is a PPA then by $A(x,r)$ we refer to the result of running A within $p_1(|x|)$ steps on input x, $x \in B^*$, and a random string r choosing uniformly from $B^{p_2(|x|)}$. By $A(x)$ we refer to the distribution induced by choosing r uniformly and running $A(x,r)$. If D is a distribution then by $x \xleftarrow{R} D$ we mean that x is randomly distributed according to D. When writing $x \xleftarrow{R} B^n$ we mean that x is a random binary string distributed uniformly over the elements of B^n.

We denote by $\mathcal{U}$ some universe of computer programs. The nature of $\mathcal{U}$ is of minor importance; for definiteness sake we consider ALGOL-style programs. Each program π computes some recursive function $F_\pi : Dom_{In} \to Dom_{Out}$. Programs π_1 and π_2 are said to be equivalent ($\pi_1 \sim \pi_2$ in symbols) iff $F_{\pi_1} = F_{\pi_2}$. We denote by $comp_\pi$ some complexity measure of program π; for example, $comp_\pi(x)$ may be thought of as the number of basic actions (steps) to be executed by π for computing $F_\pi(x)$. When a program π is analyzed by an algorithm A, we assume that some suitable encoding is used to represent π as a binary string x, and by writing $A(\pi)$ we refer to the result of running A on such x. The length of such binary string x is denoted by $size(\pi)$.

A function $\mu : \mathbb{N} \to \mathbb{N}$ is called *negligible* if for any positive polynomial $p(\cdot)$ there exists $N \in \mathbb{N}$ such that $\mu(n) < 1/p(n)$ for any $n > N$. We will sometimes use $neg(\cdot)$ and $poly(\cdot)$ to denote unspecified negligible function and positive polynomial, respectively.

A sequence $\varphi = \{\varphi_n\}_{n \in \mathbb{N}}$ of functions $\varphi_n : B^n \to B^{m(n)}$ is called *one-way function* if the following conditions hold

1. $n < poly(m(n))$,
2. there is a deterministic polynomial time algorithm C such that $C(x) = \varphi_n(x)$ for every $x \in B^n$, $n \in \mathbb{N}$,
3. $\Pr_{x \xleftarrow{R} B^n}[\varphi_n(A(\varphi_n(x))) = \varphi_n(x)] = neg(n)$, for any PPA A.

This means that it is "easy" to compute φ for all binary strings x but for "essentially all" elements $y \in Im(\varphi)$ it is "computationally infeasible" to find any string x such that $\varphi(x) = y$. If every φ_n is a bijection then φ is called a *one-way permutation*. It is still unknown whether one-way functions exist since the existence of one-way functions implies P$\neq$NP. But nevertheless, some functions (discrete logarithm, RSA-function, etc., see [16]) are strongly believed to be one-way. One-way functions are used widely in cryptography for designing public-key cryptosystems, pseudorandom generators, hash-functions, etc. A cryptographic method is said to be *provably secure* if its defeating can be shown to be essentially as hard as solving a well-known and supposedly difficult problem (such as inverting one of the above functions).

A function $h : B^* \to B$ is said to be a *hard-core predicate* for a one-way function φ if the following conditions hold

1. there is a deterministic polynomial time algorithm C' which computes h,
2. if there is a PPA A_1 such that

$$\Pr_{x \xleftarrow{R} B^m}[A_1(\varphi_m(x)) = h(x)] > \frac{1}{2} + 1/poly(m)$$

holds for infinitely many $m \in \mathbb{N}$ then there exists a PPA A_2 such that

$$\Pr_{x \xleftarrow{R} B^n}[\varphi_n(A_2(\varphi_n(x))) = \varphi_n(x)] > 1/poly(n)$$

holds for infinitely many $n \in \mathbb{N}$.

In other words, an oracle which computes $h(x)$ with probability significantly greater than $1/2$, given only $\varphi(x)$, can be used to invert φ efficiently.

Goldreich and Levin [11] showed that any one-way function φ can be transformed into a one-way function ψ which has a hard-core predicate. Their construction is as follows. Define the function ψ by $\psi(u, x) = (u, \varphi(x))$, where u is a binary string of the same length as x. Then ψ is also a one-way function and $h(u, x) = \bigoplus(u, x)$ is a hard-core predicate for ψ.

3   Program Obfuscators

By program obfuscation we mean any semantic-preserving transformation aimed at bringing a program into such a form which impedes as much as possible the extracting of some valuable information from the plaintext of a program.

Definition 1. *A probabilistic algorithm $\mathcal{O}$ is a* program obfuscator *if for every program π, $\pi \in \mathcal{U}$, the following conditions hold:*

(1) $\pi \sim \mathcal{O}(\pi)$ *(functionality preserving);*
(2) $size(\mathcal{O}(\pi)) \leq poly(size(\pi))$ *(polynomial expansion);*
(3) $comp(\mathcal{O}(\pi)) \leq poly(comp(\pi))$ *(polynomial slowdown).*

But the most important issue which characterizes the capability of $\mathcal{O}$ to hide the specific properties of programs is security. Informally, an obfuscator $\mathcal{O}$ is called *secure* w.r.t. an ensemble of programs $\mathcal{H}$ and a secret property P if any (possible) adversary, when being granted a random access to obfuscated programs $\mathcal{O}(\pi)$, $\pi \in \mathcal{H}$, can extract in reasonable time only a negligibly small amount of information on P.

An *ensemble* of programs is a sequence $\mathcal{H} = \{(S_n, D_n)\}_{n \in \mathbb{N}}$, where S_n, $n \in \mathbb{N}$, is a sample set of programs from $\mathcal{U}$, and D_n is a probability distribution on S_n. Denote by $S_{\mathcal{H}}$ the set $\bigcup_{n \in \mathbb{N}} S_n$ of all programs that appear in $\mathcal{H}$.

Let $\mathcal{H}$ be an ensemble of programs. We call a *secret property* any predicate P defined on $S_{\mathcal{H}}$. For every $n \in \mathbb{N}$ such P can be considered as a random variable defined on S_n. We write $\Pr_{\pi \xleftarrow{R} D_n}[P(\pi) = \sigma]$, $\sigma \in B$, for the probability of a randomly chosen program π from S_n satisfying (case $\sigma = 1$) or not satisfying (case $\sigma = 0$) the secret property P. If for every pair of programs π_1, π_2, the equivalence $\pi_1 \sim \pi_2$ implies $P(\pi_1) = P(\pi_2)$ then P is called a *semantic property.*

By an *adversary* we mean any set $\mathcal{A}$ of PPAs; the elements from $\mathcal{A}$ will be called *attacks.* Each attack takes programs from $\mathcal{U}$ as inputs and outputs one bit. Thus, an attack A can be viewed as a randomized checker of a secret property of programs. To hamper the deducing of the secret property one could apply some obfuscator $\mathcal{O}$ to the source programs. When an ensemble $\mathcal{H}$ is fixed, this forces an adversary $\mathcal{A}$ to deal with the set of programs $\{\mathcal{O}(\pi) : \pi \in S_{\mathcal{H}}\}$. The result $A(\mathcal{O}(\pi))$ of an attack A on a randomly chosen obfuscated program $\mathcal{O}(\pi)$ can be considered as a random variable defined on the sample set of triples (π, x, y), where π is a program from $\mathcal{O}(S_n)$ and x, y are random bit strings used by the PPAs A and $\mathcal{O}$. We denote by $\Pr_{\pi \xleftarrow{R} D_n}[A(\mathcal{O}) = \delta]$, $\delta \in B$, the probability of the attack A completing with the result δ on obfuscated programs $\mathcal{O}(\pi)$, where π is distributed over S_n. In what follows we will write $\Pr_n$ instead of $\Pr_{\pi \xleftarrow{R} D_n}$ to simplify notation.

Definition 2. *Let $\mathcal{H}$ be an ensemble of programs, P be a secret property, $\mathcal{A}$ be an adversary, and $\mathcal{O}$ be an obfuscator. We say that $\mathcal{O}$ securely obfuscates P w.r.t. $\mathcal{H}$ and $\mathcal{A}$ if for every attack $A \in \mathcal{A}$ the following condition holds*

(4) $I_n(P, A(\mathcal{O})) = neg(n)$,   *(security)*

where $I_n(P, A(\mathcal{O}))$ is the mutual information of random variables P and $A(\mathcal{O})$,

$$I_n(P, A(\mathcal{O})) = \sum_{\alpha=0}^{1} \sum_{\beta=0}^{1} \Pr_n[P(\pi) = \alpha, A(\mathcal{O}(\pi)) = \beta] \times$$
$$\times \log \frac{\Pr_n[P(\pi)=\alpha, A(\mathcal{O}(\pi))=\beta]}{\Pr_n[P(\pi)=\alpha] \Pr_n[A(\mathcal{O}(\pi))=\beta]}.$$

Clearly, the possibility of designing secure obfuscators depends highly on the secret properties to be obfuscated and the capability of an adversary. For example, if $P(\pi)$ is specified by the assertion "the program π uses the variable PSI" then P can be readily and securely obfuscated w.r.t. any ensemble of programs and any set of attacks by renaming variables in π. Nontrivial cases are that of a secret property P being semantic, since such predicates are invariant with respect to any obfuscation $\mathcal{O}$. It is easy to see that some semantic properties P admit no obfuscation at all (e.g. when $P(\pi)$ is specified by $F_\pi(0) = 0$).

4   The Main Result

To demonstrate that the requirements (1)–(4) can be satisfied by some compiler we consider the obfuscation problem for the fixed password identification scheme as the case study.

Suppose that a software engineer Alice eventually decides to protect from unauthorized access certain of the programs she designed. When selecting a program to be protected she chooses randomly a binary string for a password and adds to the program a fixed password identification scheme. A tamper engineer Bob, given a program designed by Alice, attempts to compromise the software protection. To obstruct his activity Alice may apply some obfuscator to her programs so that Bob could not distinguish the programs that actually use password identification from those having free access.

To help Alice to attain these ends we consider an ensemble of programs $\mathcal{H}_0 = \{(S_n, D_n)\}_{n \in \mathbb{N}}$, where $S_n = \{\pi_0\} \cup \{\pi_1^w : w \in B^n\}$, and the probability distribution D_n is defined by $D_n(\pi_0) = 1/2$ and $D_n(\pi_1^w) = 1/2^{n+1}$. The programs π_0 and π_1^w are depicted in Fig. 1. The program π_0 simulates free access, whereas the programs π_1^w implement a simple identification scheme.

```
prog π₀;                          prog π₁ʷ;
var x: string, y: bit;            var x: string, y: bit;
input(x);                         input(x);
y:=0; output(y);                  if x=w then y := 1 else y:=0;
end of prog;                      output(y);
                                  end of prog;
```

Fig. 1.

Bob is aimed at checking whether a program contains some identification scheme. Therefore, the secret property $P_0(\pi)$ to be obfuscated is specified by the predicate $\exists x(F_\pi(x) = 1)$. Clearly, $P_0(\pi_0) = 0$ and $P_0(\pi_1^w) = 1$. Bob is allowed to apply any algorithm running in polynomial time to achieve his goal. Hence, by the adversary $\mathcal{A}_0$ we mean the set of all PPAs.

Theorem 1. *If one-way permutations exist then the secret property P_0 can be securely obfuscated w.r.t. $\mathcal{H}_0$ and $\mathcal{A}_0$.*

Proof. Suppose φ is a one-way permutation computed by some deterministic polynomial time algorithm ONE_WAY. We will assume that it is implemented as a built-in function. A compiler $\mathcal{O}$, given a program π from S_n, computes a quadruple (w, u, v, σ) and builds the program $\Pi^{w,u,v,\sigma}$ (see Fig. 2). This program uses values u, v and σ as constants. The quadruple (w, u, v, σ) is computed as follows. If $\pi = \pi_0$ then $\mathcal{O}$ chooses uniformly at random a pair of bit strings $w, u \in B^n$ and sets $v = \varphi(w)$, $\sigma = \bigoplus(w, u)$. If $\pi = \pi_1^w$ then $\mathcal{O}$ chooses uniformly at random a string $u \in B^n$ and sets $v = \varphi(w)$, $\sigma = 1 \oplus \bigoplus(w, u)$.

```
prog Π^{w,u,v,σ};                      function SUM (X,Y : string);
var x: string, y: bit;                 var Z: bit, i : integer;
const u, v : string, σ : bit;          Z:=0;
input(x);                              for i=0 to n do Z:=Z ⊕ X[i] * Y[i];
if ONE_WAY(x) = v then                 return Z;
      if SUM(x,u) = σ then y:=0        end of function;
      else y:=1
else y:=0
output(y);
end of prog;
```

Fig. 2.

It is easy to see that $\mathcal{O}$ is an obfuscator: for every program π from $S_{\mathcal{H}_0}$ a program $\mathcal{O}(\pi)$ is equivalent to π, the size of $\mathcal{O}(\pi)$ is almost the same as that of π, and the time complexity of an obfuscated program $\mathcal{O}(\pi)$ is at most polynomially larger than that of π.

To show that $\mathcal{O}$ securely obfuscates P_0 w.r.t. $\mathcal{H}_0$ and $\mathcal{A}_0$ one should notice that $\mathcal{O}(\pi) = \Pi^{w,u,v,\sigma}$ implies $P_0(\pi) = \sigma \oplus \bigoplus(w, u)$. Hence, if by applying some attack A to programs $\Pi^{w,u,v,\sigma}$ one could extract a "significant" amount of information on P_0 then A could be used for computing $h(u, w) = \bigoplus(w, u)$ efficiently on a "significant" amount of inputs $u, \varphi(w)$. But the latter is impossible, since $h(u, w)$ is a hard-core predicate for the one-way function ψ associated with the one-way function φ (see Sect. 2).

These intuitive considerations give rise to the formal proof as follows.

Suppose the obfuscator $\mathcal{O}$ doesn't satisfy security requirement (4) (see Definition 2), i.e. there exists a PPA A such that $I_n(P_0, A(\mathcal{O})) > 1/poly(n)$ holds for infinitely many $n \in \mathbb{N}$. In view of the definition of $I_n(P_0, A(\mathcal{O}))$ and the facts that

$$\Pr_n[P_0(\pi) = 0] = \Pr_n[P_0(\pi) = 1] = 1/2$$

and

$$\Pr_n[A(\mathcal{O}(\pi))=\delta] = \Pr_n[P_0(\pi)=0, A(\mathcal{O}(\pi))=\delta] + \Pr_n[P_0(\pi)=1, A(\mathcal{O}(\pi))=\delta]$$

this implies that for some pair $\alpha, \beta \in B$

$$\Pr_n[P_0(\pi) = \alpha, A(\mathcal{O}(\pi)) = \beta] > 1/poly(n),$$
$$\Pr_n[P_0(\pi) = \alpha, A(\mathcal{O}(\pi)) = \beta] - \Pr_n[P_0(\pi) = 1 - \alpha, A(\mathcal{O}(\pi)) = \beta] > 1/poly(n)$$

hold infinitely often. Consider an attack A' which operates as follows. Given a program $\pi' \in \mathcal{O}(S_{\mathcal{H}_0})$, it first applies A to π'. If $A(\pi', x) = 1 - \beta$ (recall that x is a random string used by A) then A' decides by tossing a coin. Otherwise, A' outputs α. It is easy to see that $\Pr_n[A'(\mathcal{O}(\pi)) = P_0(\pi)] > 1/2 + 1/poly(n)$. Thus, A' can be used for computing $\bigoplus(w, u)$ with a "significant" probability on infinitely many inputs $u, \varphi(w)$. Taking into account the result of [11] (see Section 2), we arrive at the contradiction with the assumption that φ is a one-way permutation.

Thus, $\mathcal{O}$ is a secure obfuscator of the secret property P_0 w.r.t. the ensemble $\mathcal{H}_0$ of the password identification programs and the set $\mathcal{A}_0$ of the probabilistic polynomial-time attacks.   □

Theorem 2. *If the secret property P_0 can be securely obfuscated in polynomial time w.r.t. $\mathcal{H}_0$ and $\mathcal{A}_0$ then one-way functions exist.*

Proof. Suppose that PPA $\mathcal{O}$ securely obfuscates P_0 w.r.t. $\mathcal{H}_0$ and $\mathcal{A}_0$. Consider a function φ_0 defined as follows:

$$\varphi_0(\sigma, w, z) = \begin{cases} \mathcal{O}(\pi_0, z), \text{ if } \sigma = 0, \\ \mathcal{O}(\pi_1^w, z), \text{ if } \sigma = 1, \end{cases}$$

where $\sigma \in B$ is a bit, and $w, z \in B^*$ are bit strings. Clearly, $Im(\varphi_0) = \mathcal{O}(S_{\mathcal{H}_0})$, and, moreover, for every pair w, z we have $\sigma = P_0(\varphi_0(\sigma, w, z))$. Suppose that some PPA A correctly inverts φ_0 for a "significant" amount of elements from $\mathcal{O}(S_{\mathcal{H}_0})$. In such an event, there exists a PPA A' which on inputs $\mathcal{O}(\pi)$ computes $\sigma = P_0(\pi)$ more accurately than by random guessing. This implies that the mutual information $I_n(P_0, A'(\mathcal{O}))$ is non-negligible in contrary to the assumption that $\mathcal{O}$ is a secure obfuscator.

More formally.

Suppose φ_0 is not a one-way function. Then there exists a PPA A such that

$$\Pr_{\sigma \overset{R}{\leftarrow} B, w \overset{R}{\leftarrow} B^n, z \overset{R}{\leftarrow} B^n} [\varphi_0(A(\varphi_0(\sigma, w, z))) = \varphi_0(\sigma, w, z)] > 1/poly(n)$$

holds for infinitely many $n \in \mathbb{N}$. This inequality can be also written as follows:

$$\Pr_n[\varphi_0(A(\mathcal{O}(\pi))) = \mathcal{O}(\pi)] > 1/poly(n). \qquad (*)$$

Now consider a PPA A' which operates as follows. Given a program $\pi' \in \mathcal{O}(S_{\mathcal{H}_0})$, it first applies A to π'. If A inverts φ_0 on input π' correctly (this can be checked effectively) then A' outputs the first bit of the string $A(\pi')$ which is $\sigma = P_0(\pi')$. Otherwise A' tosses a coin to output a random bit. It follows from $(*)$ that

$$\mathrm{Pr}_n[A'(\mathcal{O}(\pi)) = P(\pi)] > 1/2 + 1/poly(n)$$

holds for infinitely many n. Hence, at least for one value $\alpha \in B$ the attack A' guesses the secret property P_0 of obfuscated programs with a significant accuracy, i.e.

$$\mathrm{Pr}_n[P(\pi) = \alpha, A'(\mathcal{O}(\pi)) = \alpha] - \mathrm{Pr}_n[P(\pi) \neq \alpha, A'(\mathcal{O}(\pi)) = \alpha] > 1/poly(n)$$

holds for infinitely many $n \in \mathbb{N}$. In view of the facts that

$$\mathrm{Pr}_n[P_0(\pi) = \alpha] = 1/2$$

and

$$\mathrm{Pr}_n[A'(\mathcal{O}(\pi)) = \alpha] = \mathrm{Pr}_n[P_0(\pi) = \alpha, A'(\mathcal{O}(\pi)) = \alpha] + \mathrm{Pr}_n[P_0(\pi) \neq \alpha, A'(\mathcal{O}(\pi)) = \alpha]$$

holds, this implies

$$\mathrm{Pr}_n[P(\pi) = \alpha, A'(\mathcal{O}(\pi)) = \alpha] \times \log \frac{\mathrm{Pr}_n[P(\pi) = \alpha, A'(\mathcal{O}(\pi)) = \beta]}{\mathrm{Pr}_n[P(\pi) = \alpha]\mathrm{Pr}_n[A'(\mathcal{O}(\pi)) = \beta]} > 1/poly(n)$$

for infinitely many n. It immediately follows that $I_n(P, A'(\mathcal{O})) > 1/poly(n)$ in contrary to the assumption that $\mathcal{O}$ is a secure obfuscator.

Thus, φ_0 is a one-way function. □

5   Conclusions

We introduce a new formal definition of program obfuscation security which enables us to judge the capability of tools intended for obscuring individual semantic properties of programs. The essential feature required of a secure obfuscation is that there be only a negligible "leakage" of information on the secret property under the "pressure" of polynomial time algorithms. The new definition of obfuscation security agrees well with intuition, but at the same time it is much weaker than that from [2]. This opens up fresh opportunities for invoking complexity-theoretic and cryptographic techniques to software protection. To be certain that our approach has some success we consider a meaningful example of programs implementing a password identification scheme and demonstrate with the commonly accepted assumptions that some key property of such programs admits secure obfuscation. This simple case study results in the "perfect" obfuscator for the class of computer programs supplied with a password identification scheme.

The obfuscating transformation presented in the proof of Theorem 1 can be extended and adapted for strengthening tamper-resistance of an arbitrary computer program which uses fixed password identification scheme.

Consider some one-way function φ. The extended obfuscator $\mathcal{O}_{ext}$, given a program π protected by an identification scheme with a password w, operates as follows:

1. $\mathcal{O}_{ext}$ decomposes π into separate fragments $B_1, B_2, \ldots, B_n$ and forms a set of spurious fragments $S = \{B'_1, \ldots, B'_k\}$;
2. $\mathcal{O}_{ext}$ computes $v = \varphi(w)$ and adds to the program a new bit string variable x;
3. for every i, $1 \le i \le n$, the extended obfuscator $\mathcal{O}_{ext}$ chooses randomly a bit string u_i such that $|u_i| = |w|$, computes $\sigma_i = \bigoplus(u_i, w)$ and replaces the fragment B_i with a statement

   if $\bigoplus(u_i, x)$ then B^1 else B^0

   such that $B^{\sigma_i} = B_i$ and $B^{1-\sigma_i} \in S$;
4. protects the program through the use of the conventional identification scheme

   ```
   input(x);
   if  φ(x)              =              v then ACCESS_GRANTED else
   ACCESS_DENIED;
   ```

If we consider the limiting case, when each separate fragment B_i represents a single bit operation, then Theorem 1 guarantees that no adversary can extract any "significant" information on π from the plaintext of thus obfuscated program. This means that the "perfect" secure obfuscation of programs supplied with password identification scheme is possible. One could trace the parallels between the above obfuscating transformation and one-time pad symmetric-key cryptosystems [16].

References

1. Amoroso E.G. *Fundamentals of Computer Security Technology*. Englewood Cliffs, NJ: Prentice Hall PTR, 1994.
2. Barak B., Goldreich O., Impagliazzo R., Rudich S., Sahai A., Vedhan S., Yang K., On the (Im)possibility of obfuscating programs. *CRYPTO'01 — Advances in Cryptology*, Lecture Notes in Computer Science, **2139**, 2001, p. 1–18.
3. Chow S., Gu Y., Johnson H., Zakharov V., An approach to the obfuscation of control flow of sequential computer programs. *Information Security Conference*, Lecture Notes in Computer Science, **2200**, 2001, p. 144–156.
4. Collberg C., Thomborson C., Low D., A taxonomy of obfuscating transformations, Tech. Report, N 148, Dept. of Computer Science, Univ. of Auckland, 1997.
5. Collberg C., Thomborson C., Low D., Manufacturing cheap, resilient and stealthy opaque constructs. *Symposium on Principles of Programming Languages*, 1998, p.184–196.
6. Collberg C., Thomborson C., Low D. Breaking abstraction and unstructuring data structures. *IEEE International Conference on Computer Languages*, 1998, p.28–38.
7. Collberg C., Thomborson C., Watermarking, tamper-proofing and obfuscation — tools for software protection. *IEEE Transactions on Software Engineering*, **28**, N 2, 2002, p. 735–746.
8. Devanbu P.T., Stubblebine S. Software engineering for security: a roadmap. *Future of SE Track*, 2000, 227–239.
9. Diffie W., Hellman M.E., New directions in cryptography. *IEEE Transactions in Information Theory*, **22**, 1976, p. 644–654.

10. Gollmann D. *Computer Security*. New York: Willey, 1999.
11. Goldreich O., Levin L.A., A hard-core predicate for all one-way functions. *Proceedings of the 21st Annual ACM Symposium on Theory of Computing*, 1989, p. 25–32.
12. Hada S., Zero-knowledge and code obfuscation. *ASIACRYPT'2000 — Advances in Cryptology*, 2000.
13. Horwitz S., Precise flow-insensitive may-alias analysis is NP-hard. *ACM Transactions on Programming Languages and Systems*, **19**, N 1, 1997, p. 1–6.
14. Landi W. Undecidability of static analysis. *ACM Letters on Programming Languages and Systems*, **1**, N 4, 1992, p. 323–337.
15. MacDonald J. On program security and obfuscation. Technical Report, University of California, 1998.
16. Menezes A.J., Van Oorschot P.C., Vanstone S.A., *Handbook of Applied Cryptography*. CRC Press, 1997.
17. Ramalingam G., The undecidability of aliasing. *ACM Transactions on Programming Languages and Systems*, **16**, N 5, 1994, p. 1467–1471.
18. Wang C., Hill J., Knight J. Davidson J., Software tamper resistance: obstructing static analysis of programs, Tech. Report, N 12, Dep. of Comp. Sci., Univ. of Virginia, 2000.
19. Wroblewski G., General method of program code obfuscation, in *Proceedings of the International Conference on Software Engineering Research and Practice (SERP)*, 2002, p. 153–159.

Verification-Oriented Language C-Light and Its Structural Operational Semantics

Valery A. Nepomniaschy, Igor S. Anureev, and Alexey V. Promsky

A. P. Ershov Institute of Informatics Systems
Siberian Division of the Russian Academy of Sciences
6, Lavrentiev ave., Novosibirsk 630090, Russia
{vnep, anureev, promsky}@iis.nsk.su

Abstract. The paper presents the language C-light which is a representative verification-oriented subset of the standard C. This language allows deterministic expressions and a limited use of the statements switch and goto. C-light includes the C++ operators new and delete to manage the dynamic memory instead of standard C library functions. The structural operational semantics of C-light in the Plotkin style is outlined.

1 Introduction

Verification of programs presented in widely used programming languages, such as C and C++, is a subject of much current interest. An essential prerequisite for a programming language to be suitable for verification is its compact transparent formal semantics. The language C++ is not suitable for verification because there is no formal semantics for it. Therefore, a problem to find a representative subset of C++ which is suitable for verification is an actual problem. It is natural to investigate such a problem with respect to the language C. It should be noted that there is no formal semantics for the complete language C corresponding to the standard ISO/IEC 9899:1999 [4].

A rather representative subset of C with formal semantics has been proposed in [2,3]. Another representative subset of C with structural operational semantics has been proposed in [9,10]. This subset does not include library functions, the statements switch and goto, some types, such as unions, although it allows nondeterministic semantics of expressions. Operational semantics [10] is oriented to verification because of embedding it in the theorem prover HOL. However, the verification process in operational semantics is much more complicated as compared with axiomatic semantics based on Hoare logic [1].

The purpose of our paper is to present the verification-oriented language C-light and to outline its structural operational semantics. The language includes the statements switch and goto with some restrictions, as well as the operators new and delete of C++ for managing the dynamic memory.

A survey of the language C-light is given in Section 2. Section 3 presents such notions as a state language, abstract machine states and special functions on the

M. Broy and A.V. Zamulin (Eds.): PSI 2003, LNCS 2890, pp. 103–111, 2003.

states on which the semantics rules are based. The operational semantics of C-light is outlined in Section 4. Perspectives of the development of our approach are discussed in Section 5.

2   C-Light Programming Language

The C-light programming language covers a representative subset of ISO/IEC C [4]. Let us list the restrictions on C.

C-light includes the following base types of C [4]: integer types and enumerations, real floating types and the void type. The derived types of C-light are structures (struct(T_1, ..., T_n)), functions ($T_1 \times ... \times T_n \to T$), pointers ($T*$), and arrays ($T[n]$). Function pointers, incomplete types except for incomplete array types as function parameter types, and bit fields in structures are forbidden.

Restrictions on the C-light declarations are: 1) type qualifiers, variable argument lists, and tentative definitions are forbidden; 2) parameter lists do not contain abstract declarators; 3) the function main accepts an empty parameter list.

Restrictions on the C-light expressions are: 1) the expressions are evaluated from left to right; 2) the pointer arithmetics is only applied to array elements; 3) the C++ operators new and delete are used to manage memory.

There are two restrictions on the C-light statements: 1) case labels are on the top level of the switch statement; 2) the goto statement is enclosed by the block which contains a labeled statement with the same label.

A C-light program is a sequence of external declarations. Preprocessing directives and pragmas are forbidden.

3   C-Light Abstract Machine

State Language.   The state language (SL for short) is used for the description of the abstract machine states.

The base types of SL are: 1) the union *CTypes* of all types of the language C-light except functions; 2) the set *Names* of admissible names in C-light programs; 3) the set *Locations* of storage locations of objects of C-light programs; 4) the set *TypeSpecs* of abstract names of types [4]; 5) the set *Levels* whose elements (nonnegative integers) specify the nesting levels of program identifiers; 6) the set *FuncVal* of function definitions from which the function names are excluded.

The compound types of SL include: 1) functions ($T \to T'$); 2) Cartesian products ($T \times T'$); 3) references to storage locations ($\mathrm{lv}[T]$).

Variables and constants can be of any type except empty one. The set of all variables is denoted by *Var*. The variables of the base types, in addition to the values of these types, can take the undefined value ω.

The expressions of SL are defined by induction: 1) A variable or a constant of the base type T is an expression of the type T; 2) If $s_1, ..., s_n$ are expressions of the types $T_1, ..., T_n$ and s is a constant or a variable of the type $T_1 \times ... \times T_n \to T$, then $s(s_1, ..., s_n)$ is an expression of the type T.

The logical expressions are built from the expressions of the type _Bool with the help of the logic connectives and the quantifiers in a usual way.

Abstract Machine State. Let us introduce an auxiliary notation. Let ID be a set of all admissible identifiers of the C language. The fact that the element c does not belong to the domain of the map ϕ is written as $\phi(c) = \bot$, where $\bot$ is an undefined value for maps. Let $\sigma \models P$ denote that the property P is valid in the state σ.

A *state* of C-light's abstract machine is a map on the following variables:

1. MeM is a variable of the type ID $\times$ Levels $\rightarrow$ Locations. It associates identifiers (in accordance with its nesting levels) with storage locations;
2. MD is a variable of the type Locations $\rightarrow$ CTypes. It defines the values stored in the memory;
3. Γ is a variable of the type Locations $\rightarrow$ TypeSpecs. It defines the types of values;
4. STD is a variable of the type Names $\rightarrow$ TypeSpecs. It defines the information about tags and type synonyms (**typedef**-declarations);
5. Val is a variable of the type CTypes $\times$ TypeSpecs. It stores the value of the last calculated (sub)expression together with its type;
6. GLF is a variable of the type Levels. It determines the current nesting level.

For GLF two operators "$++$" and "$--$" are defined. They increment and decrement GLF, respectively. The latter one also removes the identifiers of the current nesting level from the domain of the map MeM.

Let *States* denote a set of all states. The Greek letters σ, τ,... with indices denote states. Let $upd(f, i, e)$ denote the function f' which coincides with the function f everywhere except for, possibly, the element i and $f'(i) = e$. For short, we write $\sigma(u \leftarrow e)$ instead of $\sigma \leftarrow upd(\sigma, u, e)$, and X_σ instead of $\sigma(X)$ for a variable X.

Special Functions and Values. The following functions are used to describe the action of the abstract machine:

1. Labels(S) defines the set of labels of the block S;
2. UnOpSem(op, v, τ) applies the unary operator op to the value v of the type τ;
3. BinOpSem($op, v_1, \tau_1, v_2, \tau_2$) applies the binary operator op to the values v_1 and v_2 of the types τ_1 and τ_2, respectively;
4. InstParms($argdecl\_list, val\_list$) substitutes the actual arguments val_list for the formal parameters $argdecl\_list$;
5. FindL(id) finds the nesting level of the identifier id.

We also list the exceptional values of the abstract machine which can be stored in the component Val in addition to the values of the program types. These values have no types. They signal about a change of the control flow. Let

OkVal denote that the statement has been terminated normally, GoVal(L) —
the statement `goto L` has been executed, BreakVal — the statement `break` has
been executed, ContVal — the statement `continue` has been executed, RetVal(e)
— the statement `return e` has been executed, CaseVal(e) — the statement
`switch(e){...}` is being executed, Fail — the statement has been terminated
in abnormal way.

An abstract machine *configuration* is a pair $\langle E, \sigma \rangle$, where σ is a state, P is
one of the following constructs: a program, a statement, a statement list, an
expression, or the intermediate forms loop and GotoTrap which are used in the
operational semantics rules.

4   C-Light Operational Semantics Outline

C-light semantics is defined by induction on the program structure in terms of
the transition relation $\rightarrow$.

An axiom and an inference rule conclusion look like $\langle A, \sigma \rangle \rightarrow \langle B, \tau \rangle$. It
means that one step of execution of the program fragment A starting in the
state σ results in the state τ, and B is the program fragment which remains for
execution. A premise of the rule consists of conditions $P_1,...,P_n$ which are to be
satisfied.

Let ϵ denote an empty fragment. It can be both an empty program and empty
expression. Further $\rightarrow^*$ stands for the reflexive transitive closure of $\rightarrow$.

Expression Semantics.   There are two groups of rules which define the expression semantics. The first group deals with normal expression evaluation. The
second one deals with errors of the expression evaluation. The final configuration
in every rule of the second group has the form $\langle \epsilon, \sigma(\mathrm{Val} \leftarrow \omega) \rangle$ and all subsequent
evaluations are ignored in accord with the rule

$$\frac{\mathrm{Val}_\sigma = \omega}{\langle e, \sigma \rangle \rightarrow \langle \epsilon, \sigma \rangle}.$$

Let us consider some rules of the first group.

The group of rules associated with values and lvalues includes the rules for
simple variables, arrays, the subscript operator, the comma operator, the address and indirection operators. As an example we give the rule for indirection
operator:

$$\frac{\sigma \models e : \mathrm{lv}[\tau*] \quad \langle e, \sigma \rangle \rightarrow^* \langle \epsilon, \sigma_1 \rangle \quad \mathrm{Val}_{\sigma_1} = (v, \tau*)}{\langle *e, \sigma \rangle \rightarrow \langle \epsilon, \sigma_1(\mathrm{Val} \leftarrow (\mathrm{MD}_{\sigma_1}(v), \tau))\rangle},$$

where τ is not an array or a functional type.

The rule for unary operators without side effects has the form:

$$\frac{\square \in \{+, -, !, \tilde{}\,, (.), \mathsf{sizeof}\} \quad \langle e, \sigma \rangle \rightarrow^* \langle \epsilon, \sigma' \rangle}{\langle \square e, \sigma \rangle \rightarrow \langle \epsilon, \sigma'(\mathrm{Val} \leftarrow \mathrm{UnOpSem}(\square, \mathrm{Val}_{\sigma'}))\rangle}.$$

The rule for binary operators without side effects is similar.

The logical operators and the conditional operator form a separate group because not all of their operands can be evaluated. As an example we give the rule for the && operator:

$$\frac{\langle e_1, \sigma \rangle \rightarrow^* \langle \epsilon, \sigma' \rangle \quad \mathrm{Val}_{\sigma'} = (0, \tau) \quad \tau \text{ is scalar type}}{\langle e_1 \text{\&\&} e_2, \sigma \rangle \rightarrow \langle \epsilon, \sigma'(\mathrm{Val} \leftarrow (\mathrm{FALSE}, \text{\_Bool})) \rangle}.$$

In our approach all side effects are evaluated immediately. This is one of the key distinctions from [10] where the bag of the pending side effects is used. The rule for the simple assignment has the form:

$$\frac{\begin{array}{ccc} \sigma_0 \models e_1 : \mathrm{lv}[\tau_1] & \tau_1 \text{ not an array type} & \langle e_2, \sigma_0 \rangle \rightarrow^* \langle \epsilon, \sigma_1 \rangle \\ \langle \text{\&} e_1, \sigma_1 \rangle \rightarrow^* \langle \epsilon, \sigma_2 \rangle & \mathrm{Val}_{\sigma_1} = (v, \tau_2) \quad \mathrm{Val}_{\sigma_2} = (c, \tau_1*) & IC(\tau_1, \tau_2) \end{array}}{\langle e_1 = e_2, \sigma_0 \rangle \rightarrow \langle \epsilon, \sigma_3 \rangle},$$

where $\sigma_3 = \sigma_2(\mathrm{MD} \leftarrow \mathrm{upd}(\mathrm{MD}, c, \gamma_{\tau_2, \tau_1}(v)))(\mathrm{Val} \leftarrow (\gamma_{\tau_2, \tau_1}(v), \tau_1))$ and IC stands for the relation of implicit coercibility on types. The abstract type-conversion function γ_{τ_2, τ_1} maps the values of type τ_2 into the values of type τ_1. For the set of basic C types the family of such functions is defined. The rule for the compound assignment is similar.

We use C++ operators new and delete for memory management. The rule for a simple new operator has the form:

$$\frac{\tau \text{ not a functional type} \quad \sigma' = \sigma(\mathrm{MD}(nc \leftarrow 0))(\mathrm{Val} \leftarrow (nc, \tau*)) \quad \mathrm{MD}_\sigma(nc) = \bot}{\langle \text{new } \tau, \sigma \rangle \rightarrow \langle \epsilon, \sigma' \rangle}.$$

Here and further nc stands for a new address, i.e. $(\sigma(\mathrm{MeM}))(nc) = \bot$. The rule for the array allocation (new $\tau[size]$) is similar. The argument $size$ is checked to be nonnegative and the set of new addresses is produced.

The rule for the delete operator has the form:

$$\frac{\sigma \models e : \mathrm{lv}[\tau*] \quad \tau \text{ not a functional type}}{\langle \text{delete } e, \sigma \rangle \rightarrow \langle \epsilon, \sigma' \rangle},$$

where $\sigma' = \sigma(\mathrm{MD} \leftarrow \mathrm{upd}(\mathrm{MD}, \mathrm{MD}(\mathrm{MeM}(e, \mathrm{GLF})), \omega))$. The rule for the array deallocation (delete[]) is the same because the first address is only removed.

The following rule describes the "pass-by-value" mechanism of function calls:

$$\frac{\begin{array}{c} \langle e_i, \sigma_{n-i} \rangle \rightarrow^* \langle \epsilon, \sigma_{n-i+1} \rangle \quad \mathrm{Val}_{\sigma_{i+1}} = (v_i, \tau_i') \quad IC(\tau_i, \tau_i') \quad \text{for each } i \in \{1..n\} \\ \sigma \models f : \tau_1 \times ... \times \tau_n \rightarrow \tau_r \quad \mathrm{MD}_{\sigma_0}(\mathrm{MeM}_{\sigma_0}(f, 0)) = [parms]\{S\} \\ \langle S, \mathrm{InstParms}(\sigma', parms, [v_1...v_n]) \rangle \rightarrow^* \langle \epsilon, \sigma'' \rangle \\ \mathrm{Val}_{\sigma''} = \mathrm{RetVal}(v, \tau') \vee \mathrm{Val}_{\sigma''} = \mathrm{OkVal} \quad IC(\tau_r, \tau') \end{array}}{\langle f(e_1, ..., e_n), \sigma_0 \rangle \rightarrow \langle \epsilon, \sigma''' \rangle},$$

where $\sigma' = \sigma_{n+1}(\text{MeM} \leftarrow \text{upd}(\text{MeM}, \{(\text{id}, k) \mid \text{id} \in Names, k > 0\}, \perp))$
$(\text{Val} \leftarrow \text{OkVal})(\text{GLF} \leftarrow 1),$
$\sigma''' = \sigma''(\text{MeM} \leftarrow \text{MeM}_\sigma)(\text{GLF} \leftarrow \text{GLF}_\sigma).$

If the return type τ_r is void, the return value is OkVal.

Declaration Semantics.   We consider here the rules for declarations with initialization. The rules for declarations without initialization are similar. The value of parameter i in the declaration rules is equal to 0, if *storage* is static and is equal to GLF_σ otherwise. We use the abstract initialization function $\mathcal{I}nit$. It has two fixed arguments: the object type and its storage class. The third argument denoting the initializer value is optional. If it is absent, the function implements the default initialization.

There are two axioms for typedef declarations. One of them is of the form:

$$\langle \texttt{typedef } t\_spec \texttt{ Id;}, \sigma \rangle \rightarrow \langle \epsilon, \sigma(\text{STD} \leftarrow \text{upd}(\text{STD}, \text{Id}, \text{STD}(t\_spec)))\rangle.$$

The group of rules for declaration of simple variables, arrays and pointers is presented by the rule for pointers:

$$\frac{\langle e, \sigma \rangle \rightarrow^* \langle \epsilon, \sigma' \rangle \quad \text{Val}_{\sigma'} = (v, \tau*)}{\langle storage \; \tau* \; \texttt{id} \; = \; e;, \sigma \rangle \rightarrow \langle \epsilon, \sigma'' \rangle},$$

where $\sigma'' = \sigma'(\text{MeM} \leftarrow \text{upd}(\text{MeM}, (\texttt{id}, i), nc))(\Gamma \leftarrow \text{upd}(\Gamma, nc, \tau*))$
$(\text{MD} \leftarrow \text{upd}(\text{MD}, nc, \mathcal{I}nit(\tau, storage, v)))(\text{Val} \leftarrow \text{OkVal}).$

The other rules are similar.

The rule for the function definition (and function prototype) has the form:

$$\frac{B \text{ is empty or compound statement}}{\langle \tau \; \texttt{id}(\tau_1 \; v_1, ..., \tau_n \; v_n) \, B, \sigma \rangle \rightarrow \langle \epsilon, \sigma' \rangle},$$

where $\sigma' = \sigma(\text{MeM} \leftarrow \text{upd}(\text{MeM}, (\texttt{id}, 0), nc))(\Gamma \leftarrow \text{upd}(\Gamma, nc, \tau_1 \times ... \times \tau_n \rightarrow \tau))$
$(\text{MD} \leftarrow \text{upd}(\text{MD}, nc, [v_1, ..., v_n]B))(\text{Val} \leftarrow \text{OkVal}).$

A C-light program is a sequence of external declarations. Its rule has the form:

$$\frac{\sigma \text{ is empty map} \quad \langle Program, \sigma' \rangle \rightarrow \langle \epsilon, \sigma'' \rangle \quad \text{MD}_{\sigma''}(\text{MeM}_{\sigma''}(\text{main})) = \{S\}}{\langle Program, \sigma \rangle \rightarrow \langle \{S\}, \sigma'' \rangle},$$

where $\sigma' = \sigma(\text{MeM}, \text{MD}, \Gamma, \text{STD} \leftarrow \emptyset)(\text{Val} \leftarrow \text{OkVal})(\text{GLF} \leftarrow 0)$. We form the initial state, analyze the external declarations and execute the main function body.

Statement Semantics.   Most of the following rules contain the implicit premise $\mathrm{Val}_\sigma = \mathrm{OkVal}$, where σ is a state of the initial configuration. If a rule requires another premise, it is given explicitly.

The base cases are the null statement rule $\langle\,;,\sigma\rangle \to \langle\epsilon,\sigma\rangle$ and the expression statement rules:

$$\frac{\langle e,\sigma_0\rangle \to^* \langle\epsilon,\sigma\rangle \qquad \mathrm{Val}_\sigma \neq \omega}{\langle e\,;,\sigma_0\rangle \to \langle\epsilon,\sigma(\mathrm{Val} \leftarrow \mathrm{OkVal})\rangle} \qquad \frac{\langle e,\sigma_0\rangle \to^* \langle\epsilon,\sigma\rangle \qquad \mathrm{Val}_\sigma = \omega}{\langle e\,;,\sigma_0\rangle \to \langle\epsilon,\sigma(\mathrm{Val} \leftarrow \mathrm{Fail})\rangle}\,.$$

The rules for the labeled statements are divided into groups depending on the label kind. As an example we give the rules for default labels.

$$\frac{\mathrm{Val}_\sigma = \mathrm{OkVal} \vee \mathrm{Val}_\sigma = \mathrm{CaseVal}(..)}{\langle \texttt{default}\colon\ S,\sigma\rangle \to \langle S,\sigma(\mathrm{Val}\leftarrow\mathrm{OkVal})\rangle} \qquad \frac{\mathrm{Val}_\sigma \neq \mathrm{OkVal} \wedge \mathrm{Val}_\sigma \neq \mathrm{CaseVal}(..)}{\langle \texttt{default}\colon\ S,\sigma\rangle \to \langle\epsilon,\sigma\rangle}\,.$$

The jump statement semantics is defined as follows. The jump statements generate the above-listed exceptional values. These values are trapped in the loops, blocks or labeled statements. One of the rules for the return-statement has the form:

$$\frac{\langle e,\sigma\rangle \to^* \langle\epsilon,\sigma'\rangle \qquad \mathrm{Val}_{\sigma'} = (v,\tau)}{\langle \texttt{return}\ e\,;,\sigma\rangle \to \langle\epsilon,\sigma(\mathrm{Val}\leftarrow\mathrm{RetVal}(v,\tau))\rangle}\,.$$

The other statements propagate exceptional values through the program according to the following rule:

$$\frac{\mathrm{P}_{exc}(S,\sigma(\mathrm{Val}))}{\langle S,\sigma\rangle \to \langle\epsilon,\sigma\rangle}\,,$$

where $\mathrm{P}_{exc}(S,\mathrm{V})$ means that the statement S does not trap the value V.

The rule for the statement sequence has the form:

$$\frac{S_1 \text{ is statement} \qquad \langle S_1,\sigma\rangle \to \langle S_2,\sigma'\rangle}{\langle S_1\,T,\sigma\rangle \to \langle S_2\,T,\sigma'\rangle}\,.$$

The block rule uses the intermediate form $\mathsf{GotoTrap}(S)$, where S is a statement sequence, to trap the exceptional value $\mathrm{GoVal}(..)$.

$$\frac{\langle \mathit{Stat\_list}\ \mathsf{GotoTrap}(\mathit{Stat\_list}),\sigma(\mathrm{GLF}\,{+}{+})\rangle \to^* \langle\epsilon,\sigma'\rangle}{\langle\{\mathit{Stat\_list}\},\sigma\rangle \to \langle\epsilon,\sigma'(\mathrm{GLF}\,{-}{-})\rangle}\,.$$

The semantics of $\mathsf{GotoTrap}(S)$ is given by the following rules:

$$\frac{\mathrm{Val}_\sigma = \mathrm{GoVal}(\mathrm{L}) \wedge \mathrm{L} \in \mathrm{Labels}(\mathit{Stat\_list})}{\langle\mathsf{GotoTrap}(\mathit{Stat\_list}),\sigma\rangle \to \langle\mathit{Stat\_list}\ \mathsf{GotoTrap}(\mathit{Stat\_list}),\sigma\rangle}\,,$$

$$\frac{\mathrm{Val}_\sigma \neq \mathrm{GoVal}(..) \vee (\mathrm{Val}_\sigma = \mathrm{GoVal}(\mathrm{L}) \wedge \mathrm{L} \notin \mathrm{Labels}(\mathit{Stat\_list}))}{\langle\mathsf{GotoTrap}(\mathit{Stat\_list}),\sigma\rangle \to \langle\epsilon,\sigma\rangle}\,.$$

There are four rules for the if statement. The first one adds the else branch if it has been omitted. The other rules deal with different (undefined, non-zero, or zero) values of the condition. For example:

$$\frac{\langle e, \sigma \rangle \to^* \langle \epsilon, \sigma' \rangle \qquad \mathrm{Val}_{\sigma'} = (0, \tau) \qquad IC(\tau, \mathsf{int})}{\langle \mathsf{if}\,(e)\ \ S_1\ \ \mathsf{else}\ \ S_2, \sigma \rangle \to \langle S_2, \sigma'(\mathrm{Val} \leftarrow \mathrm{OkVal}) \rangle}.$$

Using the value CaseVal(..) allows us to go to the body of the switch statement and not to look for the necessary branch. For example:

$$\frac{\langle e, \sigma \rangle \to^* \langle \epsilon, \sigma_1 \rangle \qquad \mathrm{Val}_{\sigma_1} = (v, \tau) \qquad IC(\tau, \mathsf{int})}{\langle B, \sigma_1(\mathrm{GLF} + +)(\mathrm{Val} \leftarrow \mathrm{CaseVal}(v)) \rangle \to^* \langle \epsilon, \sigma_2 \rangle \qquad \mathrm{Val}_{\sigma_2} \neq \mathrm{BreakVal}}{\langle \mathsf{switch}(e)\ \ \{B\}, \sigma \rangle \to \langle \epsilon, \sigma_2(\mathrm{GLF} - -) \rangle}.$$

We use the intermediate form $\mathsf{loop}(e, S)$ to handle the iteration statements. Intuitively it behaves like the while statement with the condition e and the body S, but in addition it can intercept the exceptional values raised by the jump statements. The semantics of $\mathsf{loop}(e, S)$ is given by six rules. As an example we consider the case when the statement break has been executed in the body S:

$$\frac{\mathrm{Val}_\sigma = \mathrm{BreakVal}}{\langle \mathsf{loop}(e, S), \sigma \rangle \to \langle \epsilon, \sigma(\mathrm{Val} \leftarrow \mathrm{OkVal}) \rangle}.$$

The iteration statements are defined via loop.

5   Conclusion

The language C-light forms the basis for the project aimed at the development of a method and tool for C-program verification. The advantages of C-light are the following: coverage of the representative verification-oriented subset of the language C, dynamic memory management, and compact transparent structural operational semantics.

The main distinction of the presented operational semantics of C-light from its description in earlier works [5,6] consists in more detailed specification of the abstract machine states and simplification of semantical rules.

To verify C-light programs, the two-level scheme is proposed. The translation of C-light into its subset C-light-kernel is fulfilled at the first stage [8]. The correctness conditions are generated with the help of axiomatic semantics of C-light-kernel at the second stage [7]. The translation allows the axiomatic semantics to be simplified. The formal proofs of correctness of the translation and soundness of axiomatic semantics of C-light-kernel w.r.t. its operational semantics play an important role in this project [7,8].

References

1. Apt K.R., Olderog E.R. Verification of sequential and concurrent programs. — Berlin a.o.: Springer Verlag, 1991.
2. Gurevich Y., Huggins J.K. The semantics of the C programming language. — Proc. of the Intern. Conf. on Computer Science Logic. — Berlin a.o.: Springer Verlag, 1993. — P. 274–309. — (Lect. Notes Comput. Sci.; Vol. 702).
3. Huggins J.K., Shen W. The static and dynamic semantics of C (extended abstract). — Local Proc. Int. Workshop on Abstract State Machines. — Zurich, 2000. — P. 272–284. — (ETH TIK-Rep.; N 87).
4. ISO/IEC 9899:1999, Programming languages — C, 1999.
5. Nepomniaschy V.A., Anureev I.S., Michailov I.N., Promsky A.V. Towards C program verificaton. The language C-light and its formal semantics. — Programmirovanie, 2002, N 6, p. 1–13 (in Russian).
6. Nepomniaschy V.A., Anureev I.S., Michailov I.N., Promsky A.V. Towards C program verificaton. Part 1. Language C-light. — A.P. Ershov Institute of Informatics Systems, Report N 84. — Novosibirsk, 2001 (in Russian).
7. Nepomniaschy V.A., Anureev I.S., Michailov I.N., Promsky A.V. Towards C program verificaton. Part 2. Language C-light-kernel and its axiomatic semantics. — A.P. Ershov Institute of Informatics Systems, Report N 87. — Novosibirsk, 2001 (in Russian).
8. Nepomniaschy V.A., Anureev I.S., Michailov I.N., Promsky A.V. Towards C program verificaton. Part 3. Translation from C-light into C-light-kernel and its formal justification. A.P. Ershov Institute of Informatics Systems, Report N 97. — Novosibirsk, 2002 (in Russian).
9. Norrish M. Deterministic expressions in C. — Proc. Europ. Symp. on Programming (ESOP99). — Berlin a.o.: Springer Verlag, 1999. — P. 147–161. — (Lect. Notes Comput. Sci.; Vol. 1576).
10. Norrish M. C formalised in HOL .— PhD thesis, Computer Lab., Univ of Cambridge, 1998.

Proofs-as-Imperative-Programs: Application to Synthesis of Contracts

Iman Poernomo

School of Computer Science and Software Engineering,
Monash University, Caulfield East, Victoria, Australia 3145.
ihp@csse.monash.edu.au

Abstract. Proofs-as-programs is an approach to program synthesis involving the transformation of intuitionistic proofs of specification requirements to functional programs (see, e.g., [1,2,12]). Various authors have adapted the proofs-as-programs to other logics and programming paradigms. This paper presents a novel approach to adapting proofs-as-programs for the synthesis of *imperative SML* programs with *side-effect-free return values*, from proofs in a constructive version of the Hoare logic. We will demonstrate the utility of this approach by sketching how our work can be used to synthesize assertion contracts, aiding software development according to the principles of design-by-contract [8].

1   Introduction

Proofs-as-programs is an approach to program synthesis based in intuitionistic logic. The idea is as follows. A description of the required program behaviour is given as a formula, P, for which an intuitionistic proof is given. The constructive nature of the proof allows us to transform this proof into a functional program whose behaviour meets the requirements of P.

This short paper describes an adaptation of intuitionistic proofs-as-programs to a constructive version of Hoare logic [4], with the purpose of synthesizing imperative, side-effect-producing *SML* programs together with side-effect-free return values. We base our work on the framework for proofs-as-programs given in [12], where a notion of *modified realizability* defines when side-effect-free functional programs satisfy intuitionistic formulae as specifications. The Hoare logic can already be used to synthesize programs — but not to synthesize return values. We use modified realizability to specify and prove properties about required return values within the logic, and an extraction map to synthesize required return values from proofs of specifications.

The advantage of our adaption is that the user need not think about the way the return value is to be coded, but can still reason about and later automatically generate required return values. Our methods are particularly effective when return values are complicated (involving, for instance, higher-order functionals), because we can then leverage the strengths of traditional proofs-as-programs.

We give an example of how our methods can be used to synthesize imperative programs with so-called *assertion contract* functions, used in design-by-contract

M. Broy and A.V. Zamulin (Eds.): PSI 2003, LNCS 2890, pp. 112–119, 2003.

[8]. An assertion contract is essentially a boolean function that evaluates at the beginning or end of a program for run-time testing. In certain cases, return values can be considered as end-of-program assertion contracts. This opens up a useful application of our methods — the synthesis of imperative programs with (potentially complex, higher-order) contracts to be used in run-time testing.

This paper proceeds as follows. Section 2 explains how the formulae of our calculus describe side-effect and return values of imperative programs. Section 3 outlines our treatment of the Hoare logic. We sketch the idea of proofs-as-imperative-programs in Section 4. Section 5 identifies how that result can be applied to the synthesis of of complex assertion contracts. We briefly review related work and provide concluding remarks in section 6.

Throughout this paper, we consider imperative *SML* programs whose side-effects only involve a presumed set of global state references. (See [10] for details on *SML*.)

2   Specification of Side-Effects and Return Values

We use Hoare logic to specify and reason about two aspects of imperative program behaviour: possible side-effects and possible return values. We use many-sorted formulae. Higher-order quantification is permitted, to represent and reason with pure, side-effect-free *SML* programs within formulae. We will only give informal definitions — see [11,13] for more detail.

Side-effects are specified as pre- and post-conditions, written as single formulae (as opposed to the semantically equivalent triples of [4]). Formulae involve special state reference variables, which denote initial and final state reference values, prior to and after execution of a required program. These are named by the state reference with a $()_i$ and $()_f$ subscript respectively. For instance, the formula $(r_f > r_i)$ describes every possible side-effect of the program $\mathbf{r} := !\mathbf{r} + 1$. It specifies side-effects whose final value of global state reference $\mathbf{r}$, denoted by r_f, is greater than the initial value, denoted by r_i.

We assume there is a canonical model of the data manipulated by our programs. We write $\Vdash F$ when a many-sorted formula F, not involving states, is true for of the model. Informally, a formula F is *true about the side-effects of a program* $\mathbf{p}$ when, for each possible execution, $\Vdash F'$ is true, where F' is F with initial and final values of global state references substituted for the corresponding state reference variables.

Possible *return values* are specified as the required constructive content of a formula. For instance, the formula $\exists y : int.Prime(y) \wedge y > r_i$ specifies a return value of a program as the witness for y, such that, for any side-effect, y is prime and greater than the final value of $\mathbf{r}$. In general, we extend the way that a formula of intuitionistic logic specifies a functional program according to proofs-as-programs, following [12].

To understand this form of return value specification, we first need to define Harrop formulae and the Skolem form.

F	$\mathsf{xsort}(F)$
$P(\bar{a})$	$\mathtt{Unit}$
$A \wedge B$	$\begin{cases} \mathsf{xsort}(A) & \text{if not } Harrop(B) \\ \mathsf{xsort}(B) & \text{if not } Harrop(A) \\ \mathsf{xsort}(A) * \mathsf{xsort}(B) & \text{otherwise} \end{cases}$
$A \vee B$	$\mathsf{xsort}(A)\|\mathsf{xsort}(B)$
$A \to B$	$\begin{cases} \mathsf{xsort}(B) & \text{if not } Harrop(B) \\ \mathsf{xsort}(A) \to \mathsf{xsort}(B) & \text{otherwise} \end{cases}$
$\forall x : S.A$	$s \to \mathsf{xsort}(A)$
$\exists x : S.A$	$\begin{cases} s & \text{if } Harrop(A) \\ s * \mathsf{xsort}(A) & \text{otherwise} \end{cases}$
$\perp$	$Unit$

Note: In this table, the disjoint union type $\mathtt{t}|\mathtt{u}$ *is shorthand for* $(\mathtt{t}, \mathtt{u})$ $\mathtt{disjointUnion}$ *an instantiation of the following parametrized SML data type*
$$\mathtt{datatype}\ (\mathtt{{}^{a}a, {}^{a}b})\ \mathtt{disjointUnion=Inl\ of\ {}^{a}a\ |\ Inr\ of\ {}^{a}b;;}$$

Fig. 1. The map $\mathsf{xsort}(F)$ from formulae to *SML* types

Definition 1 (Harrop formulae). *A formula F is a Harrop formula if it is 1) an atomic formula, 2) of the form $(A \wedge B)$ where A and B are Harrop formulae, 3) of the form $(A \to B)$ where B (but not necessarily A) is a Harrop formula, or 4) of the form $(\forall x : s.A)$ where A is a Harrop formula.*

We write $Harrop(F)$ if F is a Harrop formula, and $\neg Harrop(F)$ if F is not a Harrop formula.

We use the type extraction map of Fig. 1. This maps logical formulae to *SML* types.

Definition 2 (Skolem form and Skolem functions). *Given a closed formula A, we define the Skolemization of A to be the Harrop formula $Sk(A) = Sk'(A, \emptyset)$, where $Sk'(A, AV)$ is defined as follows. A unique function letter f_A (of sort corresponding to SML type $\mathsf{xsort}(A)$) called the Skolem function, is associated with each A. AV represents a list of variables which will be arguments of f_A. If A is Harrop, then $Sk'(A, AV) \equiv A$. If $A \equiv B \vee C$, then*
$$Sk'(A, AV) = (\forall x : \mathsf{xsort}(A).f_A(AV) = Inl(x) \to Sk'(B, AV)[x/f_B])$$
$$\wedge (\forall y : \mathsf{xsort}(B).f_F(AV) = Inr(y) \to Sk(C, AV)[y/f_C])$$
If $A \equiv B \wedge C$, then
$$Sk'(A, AV) = Sk'(B, AV)[fst(f_A)/f_B] \wedge Sk'(C, AV)[snd(f_A)/f_C]$$
If $A \equiv B \to C$, then
1) if B is Harrop, $Sk'(A, AV) = B \to Sk'(C, AV)[f_A/f_C]$.
    2) if B is not Harrop and C is not Harrop,
$$Sk'(A, AV) = \forall x : s.(Sk'(B, AV)[x/f_B] \to Sk'(C, AV)[(f_A x)/f_C])$$
If $A \equiv \exists y : s.P$, then
    1) when P is Harrop, $Sk'(A, AV) = Sk'(P, AV)[f_A(AV)/y]$
    2) when P is not Harrop, $Sk'(A, AV) =$

$$Sk'(P, AV)[fst(f_A(AV))/y][snd(f_A(AV))/f_P]$$

If $A \equiv \forall x : s.P$, then $Sk'(A, AV) = \forall x.Sk'(P, AV)[(f_A x)/f_P]$.

In typical proofs-as-programs approaches (such as those identified in [12]) a formula A specifies a functional program p if, and only if, the program can be represented as a Skolem function in the Skolem form of A, to form a true statement. In our approach, we extend realizability so that *a formula A specifies the return values of an imperative program* p if, and only if, for each evaluation of the program, $\Vdash Sk(A)'[a/f_A]$ is true, where a is a representation of the return value, and $Sk(A)'$ is $Sk(A)$ with initial and final state reference values substituted for the corresponding state reference variables. In this case, we write p retmr A.

3 The Calculus

Theorems of our calculus are pairs of the form p • A, consisting of a *SML* program p and a formula A. The formula is a statement about the side-effects of p, provided that p terminates. We use the usual rules of the Hoare logic, presented in natural deduction form, and using program/formula pairs instead of triples. These rules allow us to build new programs from old and to prove properties of these new descriptions For example, the conditional (if-then-else) rule allows us to build a conditional program from given programs and to derive a truth about the result:

$$\frac{\vdash l_1 \bullet \mathsf{tologic}_i(\mathsf{b}) = true \to C \quad \vdash l_2 \bullet \mathsf{tologic}_i(\mathsf{b}) = false \to C}{\vdash \mathtt{if\ b\ then\ l_1\ else\ l_2} \bullet C} \text{ (if-then-else)}$$

(The map $\mathsf{tologic}_i$ is used to represent a *SML* boolean function b as a corresponding boolean term for use in formulae — see [11,13].)

Hoare logic is defined with respect to a separate logical system. We use intuitionistic logic instead of the usual classical logic. The Hoare logic and the logical system interact via the consequence rule:

$$\frac{\vdash \mathtt{w} \bullet P \quad P \vdash_{\mathrm{Int}} A}{\vdash \mathtt{w} \bullet A} \text{ (cons)}$$

The meaning of this rule is that, if P implies A by intuitionistic deduction, and P is known to hold for the program w, then A must also hold for w. For the purposes of reasoning about a particular problem, black-box programs and domain knowledge, the calculus can be extended with axioms and schemata.

Our calculus forms a *logical type theory*, *LTT*, with proofs represented as terms (called proof-terms), program/formula pairs represented as types, and logical deduction given as type inference. (See [12] for a discussion of the general form of type theories for logics.) The proof-terms have a grammar similar to that of intuitionistic logic, but extended to incorporate rules of the Hoare logic. For example, the (if-then-else) rule corresponds to a type inference rule of the following form:

$$\frac{\vdash q_1^{l_1 \bullet \mathsf{tologic}_i(\mathsf{b}) = true \to C} \quad \vdash q_2^{l_2 \bullet \mathsf{tologic}_i(\mathsf{b}) = false \to C}}{\vdash \mathsf{ite}(q_1, q_2)^{\mathtt{if\ b\ then\ l_1\ else\ l_2} \bullet C}} \text{ (if-then-else)}$$

Proof-terms encode the derivation of the theorem. The full inference rules of the type theory are detailed in [11,13]. Because of the (*cons*) rule, proof-terms corresponding to Hoare logic rule application involve proof-terms corresponding to intuitionistic logic rule application.

As in the Curry-Howard isomorphism for intuitionistic logic, a proof normalization relation can be defined. It can be shown that our proofs are strongly normalizing.

4   Program Synthesis

We can extract an imperative program from a proof of a theorem, which satisfies the theorem as a specification. Here, a program p is said to satisfy a program/formula pair $(p \bullet A)$ when 1) the program's side-effects make the formula of true, and 2) the program's return value is a return-value modified realizer for the formula. In this case, we say that p is a *SML modified realizer* of $p \bullet A$, and write p mr $l \bullet A$.

We can define an extraction map extract : $LTT \to SML$, from the terms of the logical type theory, LTT, to imperative programs of SML. This map satisfies the following extraction theorem.

Theorem 1 (Extraction produces programs that satisfy proved formulae). *Given a proof* $\vdash_{LTT(\text{K})} p^{w \bullet P}$, *then* p mr $l \bullet A$.

Proof. The full proof and definition of extract are given in [11].

5   Synthesis of Contracts

Design-by-contract is a well established method of software development (see, e.g, [8]). Briefly, the idea is as follows. When a program is developed, it must be accompanied with two boolean-valued functions, called assertions. These form the so-called contract of the program. The boolean functions are called the pre- and post- condition assertions. Programs are tested at run-time by evaluating the values of the assertions in a dedicated test suite. If the pre-condition assertion evaluates to true before the program is executed, and the post-condition evaluates to false, then the program has an error and the designer is alerted by the test suite. The assertions are defined by the programmer to specify expectations as boolean functions. In this way, design-by-contract facilitates a logical, specification-oriented approach to run-time testing of programs.

However, as noted in [9], complex programs will often require correspondinly complex assertions. When this happens, there is a danger that an assertion can be incorrectly coded — in the sense that the boolean function does not correctly represent the expectation of the designer. It is therefore an interesting application of our methods to synthesize imperative programs with provably correct assertions.

For our purposes, we will consider only programs that use post-condition assertion contracts, without pre-conditions. We leave a full treatment of contracts for future research.

There is no native support for design-by-contract in *SML*. We will take a very simple approach. We can simulate post-condition assertions as *return values* of disjoint union type (defined in Fig. 1). That is, the post-condition assertion for a program is taken to be true if it is of the form Inl(a) and false if it is of the form Inr(b). For example, assume a program that s :=!s * 2; Even(!s) consists of some imperative code s :=!s * 2 with return values arising from Even(!s), of type (Unit|Unit). If the state value !s is even, then the return value of the program is Inl(()), and Inr(()) otherwise. We will assume that our programs with assertions are evaluated within a testing tool that will generate appropriate error reports whenever a post-condition is violated.

Because post-condition assertions are taken to be return values, we can employ our synthesis techniques to contracts. The specification of a required post-condition assertion is given by a disjunction of the form $(A \vee \neg A)$. The disjunction specifies the required post-condition as a return value realizer, of type $\mathsf{xsort}(A \vee \neg A) = (\mathsf{xsort}(A)|\mathsf{xsort}(\neg A))$. By Theorem 1, given a proof of the form

$$\vdash \mathbf{body} \bullet A \vee \neg A \qquad\qquad (*)$$

we can extract a program that has equivalent side-effect to body, but with an accompanying post-condition assertion that correctly expresses the expectations of the designer, as stated as the Skolem function for the disjunction specification.

By utilizing our synthesis methods, we can analyse programs that may be built from faulty sub-programs, complementing the ideas of design-by-contract. The designer uses the rules of our Hoare logic to make proofs of the form (*). As usual with the logic, only true, known properties about given programs are used. Faulty programs may, however, be used and reasoned about. Instead of using formulae that assert the correctness of programs, we use disjunctive statements stating that the program may or may not be faulty. Because disjunctive statements correspond to post-condition assertions, our synthesis enables the automatic construction of a program with accompanying assertion, through the reasoning about the potentential known faults of subprograms.

For example, consider a program designed to connect to a database, connectDB. The program is intended to always result in a successful connection, specified by formula $connected_f = true$. However, the program has a fault, and sometimes results in an unsuccessful connection. This situation is described truthfully by the disjunction

$$\vdash \mathbf{connectDB} \bullet connected_f = true \vee \neg connected_f = true$$

This property is true of the program, and so the program may be used within Hoare logic to develop a larger program/formula theorem, without jeapordizing the truth of the final result. But also, by our synthesis methods, proofs that involve this theorem can also be transformed into programs that use a version of `connectDB` with an accompanying assertion (the assertion is true when a connection has been made and false otherwise).

6   Related Work and Conclusions

Several authors have worked on imperative program synthesis using logical type theories. In [3], a Hoare-style logic was embedded within the Calculus of Constructions through a monad-based interpretation of predicate transformer semantics, with an implementation in the Coq theorem prover [2]. Various forms of deductive program synthesis, with its roots in constructive logic and the Curry-Howard isomorphism, have been used successfully by [6], [7] and [5] for the purposes of imperative synthesis. An important difference between our approach and these methods is that we do not use a meta-logical embedding of an imperative logic into a constructive type theory, but rather give a new logic that can be presented directly as a type theory. To the best of our knowledge, proofs-as-program style synthesis has never been adapted for synthesis of imperative programs with return values, nor to the case of assertion generation.

Our notion of proof-as-imperative-programs forms an example application of a general methodology for adapting proofs-as-programs to arbitrary logics and programming paradigms, called the Curry-Howard protocol, described in [12,11]. Our results show a successful and practical approach to merging constructive proofs-as-programs with Hoare logic. We retain the advantages of both methods, using them to target their concerns separately. Hoare logic is retained to reason about and develop a program in terms of side-effects. Constructive realizability is adapted to reason and develop functional return-values. Throughout the extraction process, programs with both aspects are synthesized from proofs.

In general, boolean assertions can contain complex functional aspects, such as higher-order abstractions. We have briefly shown by example how these assertions can be understood as functional return values of boolean range, and how they can be synthesized using our approach. It would be an interesting and potentially fruitful topic to develop these results further to an industrial strength approach to assertion synthesis, for a language such as Eiffel.

References

1. R. Constable, N. Mendler, and D. Howe. *Implementing Mathematics with the Nuprl Proof Development System.* Englewood Cliffs, NJ: Prentice-Hall, 1986.
2. Th. Coquand. Metamathematical Investigations of a Calculus of Constructions. In *Logic and Computer Science*, pages 91–122, 1990.
3. J.-C. Filliâtre. *Preuve de programmes impératifs en théorie des types.* Thése de doctorat, Université Paris-Sud, July 1999.
4. C. A. R. Hoare. An axiomatic basis for computer programming. *Communications of the Association for Computing Machinery*, 12:576–80, 1969.
5. A. Ireland and J. Stark. The automatic discovery of loop invariants, 1997.

6. Zohar Manna and Richard J. Waldinger. The deductive synthesis of imperative LISP programs. In *National Conference on Artificial Intelligence*, pages 155–160, 1987.
7. Mihhail Matskin and Enn Tyugu. Strategies of Structural Synthesis of Programs. In *Proceedings 12th IEEE International Conference Automated Software Engineering*, pages 305–306. IEEE Computer Society, 1998.
8. Bertrand Meyer. *Object-Oriented Software Construction*. Prentice-Hall, 1997.
9. Bertrand Meyer. Agents, iterators and introspection. Technology paper, ISE Corporation, available at
   `http://archive.eiffel.com/doc/manuals/language/agent/page.html`,
   May 2000.
10. Robin Milner, M. Tofte, and R. Harper. *The definition of Standard ML*. MIT Press, Cambridge, MA, 1990.
11. Iman Poernomo. *Variations on a theme of Curry and Howard: The Curry-Howard isomorphism and the proofs-as-programs paradigm adapted for imperative and structured program synthesis*. Phd thesis, Monash University, 2003. Available from the author on request.
12. Iman Poernomo and John N. Crossley. Protocols between programs and proofs. In Kung-Kiu Lau, editor, *Logic Based Program Synthesis and Transformation, 10th International Workshop, LOPSTR 2000 London, UK, July 24-28, 2000, Selected Papers*, volume 2042 of *Lecture Notes in Computer Science*. Springer-Verlag, 2001.
13. Iman Poernomo and John N. Crossley. The Curry-Howard isomorphism adapted for imperative program synthesis and reasoning. In Rod Downey, editor, *Proceedings of the 7th and 8th Asian Logic Conferences*. World Scientific, 2003, to appear.

On the Visualization and Aesthetics of Large Graphs
Short Abstract

David Harel

Faculty of Mathematics and Computer Science
The Weizmann Institute of Science
`dharel@weizmann.ac.il`

The talk will survey 14 years of our group's work on graph drawing. It will start with a simulated annealing algorithm we developed in 1989, that works well for graphs with 20–40 nodes, but has severe problems for larger graphs. It will culminate with extremely powerful multi-scale and algebraic approaches developed in the last few years that produce beautiful renditions of million-node graphs in very reasonable time. The work was done with Ron Davidson, Gregory Yashchin, Ronny Hadany, Liran Carmel and Yehuda Koren.

M. Broy and A.V. Zamulin (Eds.): PSI 2003, LNCS 2890, p. 120, 2003.

Data Mappings in the Model-View-Controller Pattern

Martin Rammerstorfer and Hanspeter Mössenböck

University of Linz, Institute of Practical Computer Science
{rammerstorfer,moessenboeck}@ssw.uni-linz.ac.at

Abstract. The model-view-controller pattern is used to keep a data model and its views consistent. Usually there is a one-to-one correspondence between the data in the model and its representation in the views, which is sometimes too inflexible. We propose to add so-called data mappings between the model and its views. Data mappings are components that can be plugged together hierarchically. They can perform any transformations on the data as well on notifications, thus allowing a more flexible collaboration between a model and its views. GUI builders can be extended so that a user can add data mappings to a graphical user interface interactively, i.e. without programming.

1 Motivation

Applications with graphical user interfaces (GUIs) usually rely on the *model-view-controller pattern* (MVC pattern) [1] that was first used in the Smalltalk system around 1980. The idea of this pattern is to decompose an application into three parts:

- The **model**, which stores the data of the application (e.g. a text, a drawing, or a table of numbers for a spreadsheet).
- One or several **views**, which show a representation of the model on the screen (e.g. a text window, a graphics window or a spreadsheet window). All views show the same model and are kept consistent whenever the model changes.
- One or several **controllers**, which handle user input and update the model accordingly. Every view has its own controller, which handle keyboard and mouse input in its own way.

Fig. 1 shows how these parts are connected and how they collaborate.

When the user presses a key the controller intercepts this event and updates the model (1), e.g. by inserting the typed character into a data structure. The model informs all its views about the modification by sending them notification messages (2). Each view in turn accesses the model to get the modification and updates its representation accordingly (3). The controller may also access the view directly, e.g. for scrolling or for setting a selection. All data modifications,

M. Broy and A.V. Zamulin (Eds.): PSI 2003, LNCS 2890, pp. 121–132, 2003.
© Springer-Verlag Berlin Heidelberg 2003

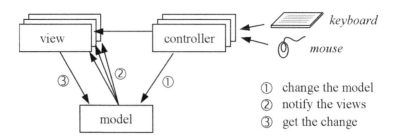

Fig. 1. Collaborations in the MVC pattern

however, are first done in the model and then propagated to the views. In this way, the MVC pattern guarantees that the views are consistent all the time.

Views and controllers always occur in pairs. Therefore they are sometimes merged into a single view/controller component that takes on the responsibilities of both the view and the controller.

If a user interface consists of multiple GUI elements such as text fields, checkboxes or radio buttons, the MVC pattern is applied for each of them. That means, for example, that every text field assumes the role of the view/controller component while the corresponding model is stored as a string in memory.

GUI Builders and Their Problems with MVC

Graphical user interfaces are often implemented with a GUI builder, which is a tool that allows the interactive composition of user interfaces by dragging and dropping GUI elements into a window, moving them to the desired position and specifying how they should react to input events.

One problem with current GUI builders is that they don't fully conform to the MVC pattern, i.e.:

– A GUI element (e.g. a text field) often already contains its model value (e.g. a string). There is no clear separation between the model and its view. The same object implements both concepts. Although some GUI builders (e.g. [8]) generate code such that the model value is kept as a separate variable outside the GUI element, it is usually not possible to connect the GUI element to an arbitrary variable in an already existing model.
– In most cases, GUI builders generate just one view for a given model. For example, a string usually cannot be shown and edited in multiple text fields.
– GUI builders require that the structure of a model exactly matches the structure of the view, therefore the design of the GUI often dominates the structure of the model. For example, if the GUI contains a color palette the corresponding model value is usually a RGB value and cannot easily be a string denoting the name of a color. Sometimes, an existing model also dominates the design of the GUI. For example, if a time value is stored in seconds the GUI cannot easily be made such that it shows the value in hours, minutes and seconds.

These problems arise because there is an unnecessarily close coupling between the model and the view, which does not allow multiple views or transformations between the values that are stored in the model and those that are shown in the view. Model-based user interface development environments (MB-UIDEs) [11,12] usually suffer from similar problems.

What we need is a more flexible framework that decouples a model from its views. It should not only allow a model to have several views but also to arbitrate between nonconforming models and views by using a sequence of data transformations. This led to the idea of so-called *data mappings* that can be inserted between a model and its views. Data mappings are described in the next section.

2   Data Mappings

A *data mapping* is a layer between the model and its views. It forwards the get and set requests from the view/controller component to the model as well as the change notifications from the model to the view/controller
(Fig. 2).

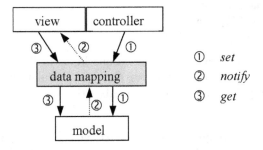

Fig. 2. A data mapping layer between model and view

Instead of just forwarding the requests, the mapping may also do some transformations between the data that is stored in the model and the data that is seen by the view. For example, an integer in the model may be transformed to a string in the view, or a string in the view may be transformed to a boolean in the model. By exchanging the data mapping one can adapt a given view to different models and a given model to different views. This includes the possibility to add multiple views to a model and to keep them consistent.

The data mapping layer may either consist of a single mapping or it may be composed from several mappings that together perform an arbitrarily complex transformation (similar to the way how Unix pipes work). The mapping layer may even be plugged together from prefabricated components using a tool that is similar to a GUI builder. This task can be done interactively, i.e. without programming, which saves considerable implementation time.

Data Mapping Elements

A data mapping layer consists of a number of *mapping elements* that can be plugged together to accomplish a certain transformation. All elements are derived from a common base class BaseMap, which has the following (simplified) interface:

```
public abstract class BaseMap implements ChangeListener {
    public BaseMap father;
    public abstract void set(Object model, Object data);
    public abstract Object get(Object model);
    public void notify(Object model) { father.notify(); }
}
```

The class BaseMap has three methods: set transfers data from the controller to the model, i.e. it changes the model; get reads data from the model and returns it to the view; notify finally forwards change notifications from the model to the view, i.e. it invalidates the view and causes a get operation.

BaseMap implements the ChangeListener interface, which allows descendants of this class to be registered as change listeners at variables in the model. If such a variable is changed, the notify method of the registered listener is invoked and the notification goes all the way up to the view.

```
public interface ChangeListener {
    public void notify(Object model);
}
```

Subclasses of BaseMap implement various kinds of data mappings such as conversions, access operations, notifications and calculations. We will look at some of these mappings in the following subsections.

Model References

The most basic data mapping is the *model reference*. It is used to connect a mapping to a variable of the model and to perform get and set operations on it. The reference is registered as a listener at the model variable and is notified whenever the underlying program changes this variable. Here is a simplified implementation:

```
public class RefMap extends BaseMap {
    private String name; // the referenced variable in the model

    public RefMap(String name, Object model) {
        this.name = name;
        use reflection to add this as a listener for name in model
    }

    public void set(Object model, Object data) {
        use reflection to set name in model to data
    }

    public Object get(Object model) {
```

```
      use reflection to get data from name in model
  }
}
```

If a data mapping consists just of a model reference it performs no transformation but only forwards get and set requests as well as notifications between the model and its view/controller.

Method Mappings

In addition to visualizing a model on the screen, a graphical user interface also has the task to respond to user input. For example, when a button is clicked a certain action should be performed. This behavior can be modeled by so-called *method mappings*, which encapsulate Java methods that are called during a set operation.

Method mappings and model references are those model-view connections that are usually also established by a traditional GUI builder. In contrast to the code generated by GUI builders, however, a data mapping layer consists only of data structures without generated code. It can be composed from prefabricated mapping elements without having to be coded and compiled. The layer can even be stored (e.g. in XML) and replaced at run time.

Decorator Mappings

Data mappings can be plugged together according to the *Decorator* design pattern [2]. This results in a chain of mapping elements, each doing a certain transformation on the data before forwarding them to the next mapping. We call this a *decorator mapping*.

A simple example of a decorator mapping is the *not mapping* (Fig. 3) that implements the boolean not operation. It inverts a boolean value during its get and set operations, i.e. a set(true) is forwarded as a false value and a set(false) is forwarded as a true value. If this mapping is applied the view shows the inverted value of the model.

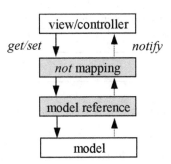

Fig. 3. A data mapping layer consisting of a *not*mapping and a model reference

Other examples of decorator mappings are:

- A mapping that inverts the sign of a number.
- A mapping that computes the absolute value of a number.
- A mapping that converts between numeric values in the model and string values in the view (e.g. "red", "blue" and "green")
- A mapping that implements a conditional set operation, i.e. it forwards a set(true) as a set(fixedValue) and ignores a set(false).

Note that some decorator mappings are symmetric (e.g. the *not* mapping or the sign inversion), while others are not symmetric (e.g. the conditional setting of a value) or not reversible (e.g. the computation of the absolute value).

Composite Mappings

Data mappings cannot only be plugged together sequentially (giving a chain of decorators) but also hierarchically (giving a tree of mappings). We call this a *composite mapping*. It is an application of the *Composite* design pattern [2] and allows a view value to be composed from several model values.

For example a date like "2/15/2003" can be composed from three numbers in the model representing the month, the day and the year, respectively. A composite mapping connects to multiple child mappings. It forwards a set(value) by splitting the value into parts and calling set(part) for each child. A get operation first gets the parts from the children and computes the combined value that it returns to its father. Notifications from the children are simply forwarded to the father (Fig. 4).

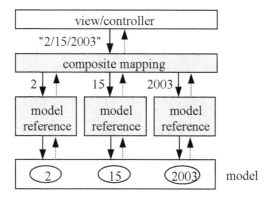

Fig. 4. A Composite mapping computing a date string from numeric values

All composite mappings are derived from a common base class CompositeMap with the following interface:

```
public abstract class CompositeMap extends BaseMap {
    public BaseMap[] components;
}
```

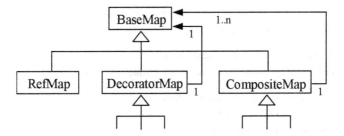

Fig. 5. Class diagram of mapping classes

Fig. 5 shows a class diagram combining the different kinds of mappings discussed so far.

Further examples of composite mappings include:

- A mapping that computes the sum of several model values.
- A mapping that copies a value from one mapping to another. This can be used to keep several model values synchronized. A **set** operation on the composite mapping **gets** a value from one of its components and **sets** it in the other components.
- A mapping that multiplexes its **set** and **get** operations to one of several other mappings depending on a special control value in the model.

3   An Example

We will now look at an example that shows how the date composition from Fig. 4 can be implemented in Java using the classes described in Section 2. We assume that we have a model that is stored in an object of the following class Date.

```
public class Date {
    private int year, month, day; // the variables of the model
    private ChangeListener[] yListeners, mListeners, dListeners;

    public Date(int month, int day, int year) {...}

    public void addChangeListener(String name, BaseMap map) {
        register map as a listener for the field name
    }

    public setYear(int y) {
        year = y;
        foreach (ChangeListener x in yListeners) x.notify(this);
    }
    ...
}
```

The model reference mappings are already available as RefMap objects so we don't have to implement them any more. The composite mapping, however, that combines the three parts of a date has to be implemented as a class DateMap, say, that is derived from CompositeMap and does the conversion.

```java
public class DateMap extends CompositeMap {
    public DateMap(BaseMap[] components) { super(components); }

    public void set(Object model, Object data) {
        split data into year, month and day;
        components[0].set(model, month);
        components[1].set(model, day);
        components[2].set(model, year);
    }

    public Object get(Object model) {
        return
            components[0].get(model).toString() + "/" +
            components[1].get(model).toString() + "/" +
            components[2].get(model).toString();
    }
}
```

Now we just have to instantiate and compose the mappings in the following way:

```java
Date date = new Date(2, 15, 2003); // the model
TextField f = new TextField(); // the view
f.setMapping(
    new DateMap( // the mapping
        new BaseMap[] {
            new RefMap("month", date),
            new RefMap("day", date),
            new RefMap("year", date)
        }
    )
);
```

In this example the composition is done in Java, but it is easy to imagine that a builder tool does it interactively once the mapping components are available. In fact, we are currently implementing such a builder tool that allows us to create and compose arbitrary data mappings from a growing catalog of available mappings.

The implementation of our data mapping framework heavily relies on *reflection*, i.e. on the use of metainformation to access and modify data at run time [3]. Reflection is used, for example, to connect model references to arbitrary variables in the model that can be specified by names or even by path expressions such as

```
x.y[3].z
```

We also use reflection in the implementation of the method mapping that identifies a method by its name. When a method mapping object is created, the method name is resolved using reflection and invoked whenever the set operation of this mapping is called.

4 Advanced Uses of Data Mappings

So far we have used data mappings only for simple transformations including the combination of several model values into a single view value. However, data mappings can also be used to accomplish more complex tasks, especially for optimizing the performance of the MVC pattern. Examples of such mappings include *caching*, *polling*, *lazy update*, *concurrency*, or *distribution*, which will be described in the following subsections.

Caching

A *cache mapping* is a decorator that remembers the result of the last get request. The next get is then answered from the cache. A change notification resets the cache and a set operation overwrites the cache contents.

The user may add a cache mapping to the mapping layer if the data retrieval from the model is too inefficient, e.g. if the calculation of the value is time consuming or if the data must be retrieved over a network first. With a builder tool, adding a cache mapping to an existing data mapping is as easy as adding scrollbars to a GUI element.

Polling

Polling allows one to retrieve data from models that do not offer change notifications. This may be useful for prototyped models where no notification mechanism is implemented yet or for debug views, which show internal data that is not intended to be displayed in the production view.

A *poll mapping* never forwards notifications from the model but uses a timer to generate notifications to the view in regular time intervals. The view in response to the notification issues a get operation on the mapping in order to retrieve the data.

Lazy Update

Some models change so rapidly that the high number of change notifications can become a burden to the system. This situation can be handled with a *lazy update mapping* that delays change notifications from the model until a certain time has elapsed and then forwards a single notification message to the view. This obviously reduces the total number of notification messages in the system. In contrast to the poll mapping, the lazy update mapping does not send notifications to the view if no notifications arrive from the model.

Concurrency

Modern GUI applications are event-driven, i.e. they wait for input events (keyboard input, mouse clicks, etc.) and then react to them. In order not to block the GUI for too long, every event usually causes a new thread to be started. The main thread just dispatches the events one after the other while the actual processing is done by separate threads in the background.

This behavior can be modeled with a so-called *concurrency mapping*. A concurrency mapping decorates some other mapping and starts a new thread whenever it performs its get or set operations. Change notifications, however, are immediately forwarded to the event-dispatching thread and are handled without delay, even if the last get or set operation is not yet finished (Fig. 6).

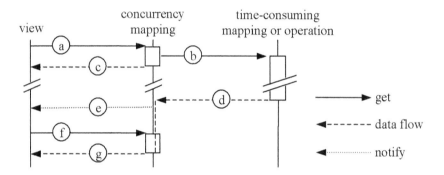

Fig. 6. Trace diagram of a concurrent get operation

While the set operation just starts a new thread to update the model and then returns, the get operation is a bit more complicated (see Fig.6), because the caller expects a result, but the event-dispatching thread cannot wait. After being invoked (a), the get operation starts a new working thread that performs the actual get on the model (b) and returns a default value immediately (c), so the calling thread will not be blocked. After the working thread has finished (d), the result remains in the concurrency mapping and a change notification (e) requests a get operation (f) to fetch the result (g).

Distribution

In some applications the model and its views reside on different computers. A *distribution mapping* can be used to hide the transfer of data and notifications over a network ([7]). Fig. 7 shows such a situation. The mapping has a server-side part and a client-side part both consisting of several decorator mappings that serialize, compress and encode the data.

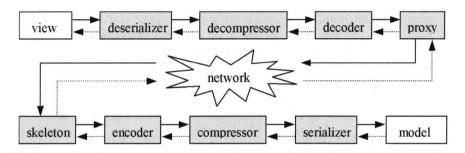

Fig. 7. A data mapping connecting a model on the server with a view on the client

5   Related Work

The MVC paradigm is also known as the *Observer* design pattern [2] where several observers can be attached to a model and are notified whenever the model is changed. The Observer pattern is more general than the MVC pattern because an observer can be any object, not just a graphical view. Similar to the MVC pattern, however, the Observer pattern does not define any mapping of the data or the notifications that flow between the model and its observers.

The same pattern also underlies the *Java event model* [4], where observers are called *listeners*. A listener is a class that implements a certain listener interface, which defines one or several call-back methods for notification. Listeners can be registered at other objects that assume the role of the model. When a certain event happens in the model the notification method of all registered listeners is called so that the listeners can react to the event. A special implementation of the Java event model can be found in the *JavaBeans* standard [6]. Again, however, the Java event model does not have the concept of mappings between an object and its listeners. Of course, a mapping transformation can be implemented by hand (e.g. by installing a special listener with glue code between the model and the actual listener) but this requires manual coding and cannot be automated easily.

GUI builders (e.g. Microsoft's Visual Studio [10], Sun ONE Studio [9] or IBM's Visual Age for Java [8]) allow a user to interactively compose a graphical user interface from prefabricated GUI elements by dragging and dropping them into a window and by modifying their properties. In most cases, however, the GUI elements do not implement the MVC pattern properly because the model data is stored directly in the GUI element, which plays also the role of the view. Thus, the model and the view are not separated and it is not possible to attach several views to a model.

Some GUI builders (e.g. [8]) allow a GUI element to be attached to a separate variable, which stores the model. However, this variable is generated by the builder and cannot be chosen to be a field of an already existing model, say. Other GUI builders allow glue code to be inserted at special places in the user interface, but this glue code has to be written by the user manually.

None of the GUI builders known to us has the concept of data mappings that can be plugged together from prefabricated mapping elements without coding. In this respect, our approach is novel and unique.

6   Summary

In this paper we have introduced the concept of a data mapping which is a layer between the model and its views in the MVC pattern. A data mapping is responsible for conciliating a model and its views if their structure is not identical. It can be hierarchically composed from simpler mappings using the Decorator and the Composite design patterns. We have shown how to use data mappings to accomplish data transformations as well as caching, polling, lazy update and concurrent model access.

Most current GUI builders do not allow transformations between a model and its views. Those, which allow such transformations, require the user to implement glue code by hand. We propose to extend GUI builders so that users can compose a data mapping from prefabricated mapping elements interactively, i.e. without coding. This is in accordance with component-based programming [5] and consistent with how a GUI is composed from GUI elements in a builder environment.

We are currently working on such an extended GUI builder, which separates a model from its views and allows the user to add a wide selection of data mappings between these two components in a plug and play manner.

References

1. Krasner G.E., Pope S.T.: A Cookbook for Using the Model-View-Controller User Interface Paradigm in Smalltalk-80. Journal of Object-Oriented Programming (JOOP), August/September (1988) 26–49
2. Gamma E., Helm R., Johnson R., Vlissides J.: Design Patterns—Elements of Reusable Object-Oriented Software, Addison-Wesley, 1995
3. Flanagan D.: Java in a Nutshell, 4th edition, O'Reilly, 2002
4. Campione M., Walrath K., Huml A.: The Java Tutorial—A Short Course on the Basics, 3rd edition, Addison-Wesley, 2000
5. Szyperski C.A., Gruntz D., Murer S.: Component Software, 2nd editions, Addison-Wesley, 2002
6. O'Neil J., Schildt H.: JavaBeans Programming from the Ground Up, McGraw-Hill, 1998
7. Hof M.: Composable Message Semantics in Object-oriented Programming Languages. Dissertation, University of Linz, 2000
8. Visual Age for Java: http://www-3.ibm.com/software/ad/vajava/
9. Sun ONE Studio 4 (formerly Forte): http://wwws.sun.com/software/sundev/jde/
10. Visual Studio .NET: http://msdn.microsoft.com/vstudio/
11. Griffiths T., et al.: Teallach: A Model-Based User Interface Development Environment for Object Databases. Proceedings of UIDIS'99. IEEE Press. 86–96.
12. Pinheiro da Silva P., Griffiths T., Paton N.W.: Generating User Interface Code in a Model Based User Interface Development Environment. Proceedings of AVI'00. ACM Press 155–160.

The Translation Power of the Futamura Projections

Robert Glück

PRESTO, JST & Institute for Software Production Technology
Waseda University, School of Science and Engineering
Tokyo 169-8555, Japan,
glueck@acm.org

Abstract. Despite practical successes with the Futamura projections, it has been an open question whether target programs produced by specializing interpreters can always be as efficient as those produced by a translator. We show that, given a Jones-optimal program specializer with static expression reduction, there exists for every translator an interpreter which, when specialized, can produce target programs that are at least as fast as those produced by the translator. This is not the case if the specializer is not Jones-optimal. We also examine Ershov's generating extensions, give a parameterized notion of Jones optimality, and show that there is a class of specializers that can always produce residual programs that match the size and time complexity of programs generated by an arbitrary generating extension. This is the class of generation universal specializers. We study these questions on an abstract level, independently of any particular specialization method.

1 Introduction

Program specialization, also known as partial evaluation, has shown its worth as a realistic program transformation paradigm. The *Futamura projections* [5] stand as the cornerstone of the development of program specialization. They capture a fundamental insight, namely that programs can be translated by specializing an interpreter. Several program specializers which perform these transformations automatically have been designed and implemented [14].

Despite these practical successes, it has been an open question (*e.g.*, [5,12, 16]) whether target programs produced by specializing interpreters can be as efficient as those produced by traditional translators, or whether there exist certain theoretical limitations to Futamura's method. We study these questions on an abstract level, independently of any particular specialization method or other algorithmic detail. We are interested in statements that are valid for all specializers and for all programming languages.

The results in this paper expand on previous work on Jones optimality [3, 8,13,17,23,24]. First, we show that, given a Jones-optimal program specializer with static expression reduction, there exists for every translator an interpreter which, when specialized, can produce target programs that are at least as fast

M. Broy and A.V. Zamulin (Eds.): PSI 2003, LNCS 2890, pp. 133–147, 2003.

as those produced by the translator. This is the class of *translation universal* specializers. We also show that a specializer that is not Jones-optimal is not translation universal. Finally, we introduce a parameterized notion of Jones optimality and show that there is a class of *generation universal* specializers that can always produce residual programs that match the size and time complexity of programs generated by an arbitrary generating extension. Previously, it was found intuitively [12,13] that Jones optimality would be a "good property". The results in this paper give formal status to the term "optimal" in the name of that criterion.

Our results do not imply that a specializer that is not Jones-optimal is not useful, but that there exists a *theoretical limit* to what can be achieved in general. They do not tell us when program generation by a specializer is preferable over program generation by a generating extension (parser generator, translator, *etc.*). This depends on pragmatic considerations and on the application at hand. We hope that the investigations in this paper will lead to a better understanding of some of the fundamental issues involved in automatic program specialization.

This paper is organized as follows. After reviewing standard definitions of several metaprograms (Sect. 2), we discuss translation by specialization (Sect. 3), Jones optimality (Sect. 4), and the degeneration of generating extensions (Sect. 5). Then, we present our main results on translation (Sect. 6) and program generation (Sect. 7). We discuss related work (Sect. 8) and finally conclude (Sect. 9). We assume that the reader is familiar with the ideas of partial evaluation, *e.g.*, as presented in [14, Part II].

2   Fundamental Concepts

What follows is a review of standard definitions of interpreters, translators, and specializers. We also formalize a notion of static expression reduction and define certain measures on programs. The notation is adapted from [14], except that we use divisions (SD) when classifying the parameters of a program as static or dynamic. We assume that we are dealing with universal programming languages.

We briefly review some basic notation. For any program text, p, written in language L, we let $[\![p]\!]_L\, d$ denote the application of L-program p to its input d. Multiple arguments are written as a list, such as $[\![p]\!]_L\,[\,d_1, ..., d_n\,]$. The notation is strict in its arguments. Programs and their input and output are drawn from the same data domain D. This is convenient when dealing with metaprograms which take programs and data as input. We define a program domain $P_L \subseteq D$, but leave the details of language L unspecified. Let P_L^p denote the set of all L-programs that are functionally equivalent to L-program p. Equality $(=)$ shall always mean strong (computational) equivalence: either both sides are defined and equal, or both sides are undefined. When we define a program using λ-notation, the text of the corresponding L-program is denoted by $\ulcorner \lambda ... \urcorner_L$. This mapping is fixed. The intended semantics of the λ-notation is call-by-value.

Definition 1 (interpreter). *An L-program int* $\in Int_{N/L}$ *is an N/L-inter-preter iff* $\forall p \in P_N, \forall d \in D$:

$$[\![int]\!]_L [p, d] = [\![p]\!]_N d .$$

Definition 2 (self-interpreter). *An L-program sint* $\in Sint_L$ *is a self-inter-preter for L iff sint is an L/L-interpreter.*

Definition 3 (translator). *An L-program trans* $\in Trans_{N \rightarrow L}$ *is an* $N \rightarrow L$-*translator iff* $\forall p \in P_N, \forall d \in D$:

$$[\![[\![trans]\!]_L p]\!]_L d = [\![p]\!]_N d .$$

Definition 4 (generating extension). *An L-program gen* $\in Gen_L^p$ *is an L-generating extension of a program* $p \in P_L$ *iff* $\forall x, y \in D$:

$$[\![[\![gen]\!]_L x]\!]_L y = [\![p]\!]_L [x, y] .$$

Definition 5 (specializer). *An L-program spec* $\in Spec_L$ *is an L-specializer iff* $\forall p \in P_L, \forall x, y \in D$:

$$[\![[\![spec]\!]_L [p, \mathrm{SD}, x]]\!]_L y = [\![p]\!]_L [x, y] .$$

For simplicity, we assume that the programs that we specialize have two arguments $[x, y]$, and that the first argument is static. Even though Def. 5 makes use of only one division 'SD', a constant, we keep the division argument. The program produced by specializing p is a *residual program*.

A specializer does not need to be total. Def. 5 allows *spec* to diverge on input $[p, \mathrm{SD}, x]$ iff p diverges on input $[x, y]$ for all y. Actual specializers often sacrifice the termination behavior implied by this definition and terminate less often. A specializer is *trivial* if the residual programs produced by the specializer are simple instantiations of the source programs. This trivial specializer never improves the efficiency because the source programs remain unchanged.

Definition 6 (trivial specializer).
An L-specializer $spec_{triv} \in Spec_L$ *is trivial iff* $\forall p \in P_L, \forall x \in D$:

$$[\![spec_{triv}]\!]_L [p, \mathrm{SD}, x] = \ulcorner \lambda y.[\![p]\!]_L [x, y] \urcorner_L .$$

More realistic specializers should evaluate as many static expressions as possible to improve the efficiency of the residual programs. However, an investigation [11] suggests that for universal languages, one cannot devise a specializer that makes '*maximal use*' of the static input in all programs. This makes it difficult to give a general definition of static expression reduction. Here, we define a special case that can be decided, namely static arguments that are always evaluated.

Definition 7 (static expression reduction). *An L-specializer spec $\in Spec_L$ has static expression reduction iff $\forall p, q, q' \in P_L, \forall x \in D$:*

$$p = \ulcorner \lambda(a, b).[\![q]\!]_L[[\![q']\!]_L a, b]\urcorner_L \implies$$
$$[\![spec]\!]_L[p, \mathrm{SD}, x] = [\![spec]\!]_L[q, \mathrm{SD}, [\![q']\!]_L x]$$

This definition tells us that there is no difference between specializing a program q with respect to a static value $[\![q']\!]x$ and specializing program p, the composition of programs q and q', with respect to a static value x. We expect that both residual programs are identical if *spec* fully evaluates the static expression $[\![q']\!]a$ in p.[1] Most specializers that have been implemented reduce more static expressions in p than what is required by Def. 7, for example, supported by a binding-time analysis as in offline partial evaluation [14].

A specializer with static expression reduction is not trivial; it can be viewed as a *universal program* (it is capable of simulating an arbitrary program q'). It cannot be total. A total specializer must be conservative enough to terminate on every static input. Finally, we introduce two measures on programs, namely *running time* and *program size*, and define two partial orders on programs, which we will use to discuss the transformation power of a specializer. The measure of the running time of a program can be based on a timed semantics (*e.g.*, counting the number of elementary steps a computation takes) [14]. The measure of program size can be the size of one of its representations (*e.g.*, the abstract syntax tree).

Definition 8 (time order). *For program $p \in P_L$ and data $d \in D$, let $Time(p, d)$ denote the* running time *to compute $[\![p]\!]_L d$. The partial order $\leq_{Time}$ on L-programs is defined by*

$$p \leq_{Time} q \stackrel{\mathrm{def}}{=} \forall d \in D: Time(p, d) \leq Time(q, d) .$$

Definition 9 (size order). *For program $p \in P_L$, let $Size(p)$ denote the size of p. The partial order $\leq_{Size}$ on L-programs is defined by*

$$p \leq_{Size} q \stackrel{\mathrm{def}}{=} Size(p) \leq Size(q) .$$

The corresponding equivalence relations, $=_{Time}$ and $=_{Size}$, are defined in the obvious way (by $=$ instead of $\leq$).

3   Translation by Specialization

The *Futamura projections* [5] stand as the cornerstone of the development of program specialization. They tell us how to translate programs by specializing

---

[1] Programs q and $q^\bullet$ can also be viewed as a decomposition of a program p into static and dynamic components. A method that transforms a program into a functionally equivalent program with strongly separated binding times can be found in [19].

interpreters, how to generate stand-alone translators and even a generator of translators. Here we discuss the 1st Futamura projection. A detailed account of all three projections can be found in [14]. Let p be an N-program, let $intN$ be an N/L-interpreter, and let $spec$ be an L-specializer. Then the *1st Futamura projection* is defined by

$$p' = [\![spec]\!]_L [\, intN, \mathrm{SD}, p\,] \ . \tag{1}$$

Here, the interpreter $intN$ is specialized with respect to program p. Using Defs. 1 and 5, we have the functional equivalence between p' and p:

$$[\![p']\!]_L\, d = [\![intN]\!]_L [\, p, d\,] = [\![p]\!]_N\, d \ . \tag{2}$$

We observe that p is written in language N, while p' is written in language L. This means that an N-to-L-translation was achieved by specializing $intN$ with respect to p. We say that p' is a *target program* of *source program* p. A trivial translation is always possible using a trivial specializer. The first argument of $intN$ is instantiated to p, and the result is a trivial target program:

$$[\![spec_{triv}]\!]_L [\, intN, \mathrm{SD}, p\,] = \ulcorner \lambda d.[\![intN]\!]_L [\, p, d\,] \urcorner_L \ . \tag{3}$$

The target program on the right hand side of (3) is inefficient: it contains an interpreter. Running this target program will be considerably slower than running the source program p, often by an order of magnitude. This is not the translation we expect.

Thus, a natural goal is to produce target programs that are at least as fast as their source programs. To achieve this goal, it is important that the specializer removes the *entire* interpretation overhead. Unfortunately, we cannot expect a specializer to achieve this optimization for *any* interpreter. As mentioned in Sect. 2, there exists no specializer that could make 'maximal use' of the static input in all programs, here, in all possible N/L-interpreters.

4   Jones Optimality

A specializer is said to be "strong enough" [13] if it can completely remove the interpretation overhead of a self-interpreter. The following definition is adapted from [14, Sect. 6.4]. It makes use of the 1st Futamura projection discussed in the previous section, but uses a self-interpreter instead of an N/L-interpreter.

Definition 10 (Jopt-$\leq_{Time}$). *Let $sint \in Sint_L$ be a self-interpreter, then a specializer $spec \in Spec_L$ is Jones-optimal for $sint$ with respect to $\leq_{Time}$ iff $Jopt_{\leq_{Time}}(spec, sint)$ where*

$$Jopt_{\leq_{Time}}(spec, sint) \stackrel{\mathrm{def}}{=} \forall p \in P_L : [\![spec]\!]_L [\, sint, \mathrm{SD}, p\,] \leq_{Time} p \ .$$

A specializer $spec$ is said to be *Jones-optimal* if there exists a self-interpreter $sint$ such that, for all source programs p, the target program produced by specializing the self-interpreter is at least as fast as p. This tells us that $spec$ can remove the interpretive overhead. The case of *self-interpreter specialization* is interesting because it is easy to judge to what extent the interpretive overhead has been removed by comparing the source and target programs, as they are written in the same language. In particular, when both programs are identical up to variable renaming, it is safe to conclude that this goal is achieved. When it is clear from the context, we will refer to the definition above simply as Jones optimality.

Remark. Jones optimality of a specializer is easier to state than to achieve. It was shown [20] that a specializer for a first-order functional language with algebraic data types requires a combination of several non-trivial transformation methods to become Jones-optimal (*e.g.*, partially static structures, type specialization). The first implementation of a Jones-optimal specializer was an offline partial evaluator for a Lisp-like language [21]. Jones optimality was first proven [23] for lambda-mix. Recent work [3,24] has focused on the problem of tag-elimination.

Existence of Jones-optimal Specializers. As discussed in [12], a Jones-optimal specializer can be built by a simple construction that just returns its third argument in case the first argument is textually identical to a particular self-interpreter (here, *mysint*); otherwise it performs a trivial specialization. Such a specializer can be defined by

$$spec_{jopt} \stackrel{\text{def}}{=} \ulcorner \lambda(p, \mathrm{SD}, x) \,.\, if \; equal(p, mysint) \; then \; x \\ else \; [\![spec_{triv}]\!]_L \, [\, p, \mathrm{SD}, x \,] \urcorner_L \tag{4}$$

This construction is not useful in practice, but it is sufficient to show that a Jones-optimal specializer can be built for every programming language. The specializer satisfies $Jopt_{\leq_{Time}}(spec_{jopt}, mysint)$.

Next, we show that there exists a Jones-optimal specializer with static expression reduction. This fact plays an important role later in this paper. Such a specializer can be defined by

$$spec_{jser} \stackrel{\text{def}}{=} \ulcorner \lambda(p, \mathrm{SD}, x) \,.\, case \; p \; of \\ \text{`}\lambda(a, b).[\![q]\!] \, [\![[\![q']\!] \, a, b \,]\text{'} \rightarrow [\![spec_{jser}]\!]_L \, [\, q, \mathrm{SD}, [\![sint]\!]_L \, [\, q', x \,] \,] \\ otherwise \qquad\qquad \rightarrow [\![spec_{jopt}]\!]_L \, [\, p, \mathrm{SD}, x \,] \urcorner_L \tag{5}$$

where *case* implements pattern matching: if program p consists of a composition[2] of two programs q and q', then q is specialized with respect to the result of evaluating $[\![sint]\!] \, [\, q', x \,]$ where *sint* is a self-interpreter; otherwise p is specialized with respect to x. Assume that program *mysint* does not suit the decomposition in *case*. Then we have $Jopt_{\leq_{Time}}(spec_{jser}, mysint)$ since for all L-programs p:

$$[\![spec_{jser}]\!]_L \, [\, mysint, \mathrm{SD}, p \,] \;=\; p \,. \tag{6}$$

The specializer has the static expression reduction property of Def. 7 since for all L-programs $p = \ulcorner \lambda(a, b).[\![q]\!]_L \, [\![[\![q']\!]_L \, a, b \,] \urcorner_L$ and for all data x:

$$[\![spec_{jser}]\!]_L \, [\, p, \mathrm{SD}, x \,] \;=\; [\![spec_{jser}]\!]_L \, [\, q, \mathrm{SD}, [\![q']\!]_L \, x \,] \,. \tag{7}$$

---

[2] We shall not be concerned with the technical details of parsing L-programs.

Remark. More realistic Jones-optimal specializers, for instance [18,20,21,23], do not rely on any of the constructions above. For several of these specializers, the target programs are *identical, up to variable renaming,* to the source programs. These specializers, as well as $spec_{jopt}$ and $spec_{jser}$ shown above, satisfy $Jopt_{=Time}$, which we obtain by replacing $\leq_{Time}$ by $=_{Time}$ in Def. 10. There exists no specializer that would satisfy $Jopt_{<Time}$. This would imply that we can improve the running time of a program infinitely often by repeated specialization, which is not possible – just consider an empty program that contains no operations.

5 Degeneration of Generating Extensions

The notion of a *generating extension* [4] describes uniformly the functioning of various program generators. This is a powerful concept because it captures the essence of different program generators, including diverse applications such as parsing, graphics, and pattern matching. Turning a general program into its generating extension has been intensively studied in the area of partial evaluation [14].

Consider the converse goal: turning a generating extension back into a general program. Given an L-generating extension *gen*, we can always construct a program p', a *degeneration of gen*, such that

$$\llbracket p' \rrbracket_L [x, y] = \llbracket \llbracket gen \rrbracket_L x \rrbracket_L y . \tag{8}$$

Let *sint* be a self-interpreter for L. Then we can immediately define a *trivial degeneration* of *gen* by

$$p' \stackrel{\text{def}}{=} \ulcorner \lambda(x, y).\llbracket sint \rrbracket_L [\llbracket gen \rrbracket_L x, y] \urcorner_L . \tag{9}$$

Program p' performs its computation in two stages: first, a specialized program is produced by *gen*, then the specialized program is evaluated by *sint*. For practical reasons, a trivial degeneration is not interesting, but it is sufficient to show that the computation of every generating extension can be unstaged by an interpreter.

The 2nd Futamura projection [5] asserts that for every interpreter there exists a translator ($\forall int \, \exists trans$). From the above construction we see that for every translator, there exists an interpreter ($\forall trans \, \exists int$). An $N \to L$-translator *trans* is an L-generating extension of an N/L-interpreter *int* since for all N-programs p and for all data d:

$$\llbracket int \rrbracket_L [p, d] = \llbracket \llbracket trans \rrbracket_L p \rrbracket_L d . $$

Remark. A more efficient degeneration may be obtained by applying a program composer to the composition of *sint* and *gen* in (9). An L-*composer* is an L-program such that, for all L-programs q, q' and for all data x, y:

$$\llbracket \llbracket komp \rrbracket_L [q, q'] \rrbracket_L [x, y] = \llbracket q \rrbracket_L [\llbracket q' \rrbracket_L x, y] . \tag{10}$$

Then the *1st degeneration projection* [10] is defined by

$$p'' = [\![komp]\!]_L [\, sint, gen\,] \; .$$

Programs p' and p'' are functionally equivalent. A non-trivial composer may generate a more efficient composition by eliminating intermediate code generation, parsing, and other redundant operations between the programs. A method for automatic program composition is deforestation, another is supercompilation. Different ways of degenerating generating extensions were studied in [10].

6   Translation Universality

The question has been raised, *e.g.*, [5,12,16], whether target programs produced by the Futamura projections can be as efficient as those produced by traditional, optimizing translators. We give a precise answer to this fundamental question.

We examine whether, for every translator *trans*, there exists an interpreter *int* such that the target programs produced by the 1st Futamura projection are at least as fast as the target programs produced by the translator. More formally, given a specializer *spec*, we examine the question whether $\forall trans, \exists int, \forall p$:

$$[\![spec]\!]_L [\, int, \mathrm{SD}, p\,] \leq_{Time} [\![trans]\!]_L \, p \; . \tag{11}$$

We call this property *translation universality* of a specializer. We will show that every Jones-optimal specializer with static expression reduction is translation universal. Thus, under these conditions, translation by the Futamura projections is as powerful as translation by any translator. We will also show that a specializer that is not Jones-optimal is not translation universal.

Theorem 1 (Jopt-$\leq_{Time}$ sufficient for Trans-univ-$\leq_{Time}$). *For all specializers* $spec \in Spec_L$ *with static expression reduction, the following holds:*

$$\exists sint \in Sint_L : \; Jopt_{\leq_{Time}}(spec, sint)$$
$$\Longrightarrow$$
$$\forall trans \in Trans_{N \to L}, \; \exists int \in Int_{N/L}, \; \forall p \in P_N :$$
$$[\![spec]\!]_L [\, int, \mathrm{SD}, p\,] \leq_{Time} [\![trans]\!]_L \, p \; .$$

Proof. We proceed in two steps. First, we show how to build for each translator *trans* an interpreter *int*; then we prove that the target programs produced by specializing *int* are at least as fast as those produced by *trans*.

1. For each $N \to L$-translator *trans*, define an N/L-interpreter *int* by

$$int \; \overset{\text{def}}{=} \; \underbrace{\ulcorner \lambda(p, d). [\![sint]\!]_L [\, [\![trans]\!]_L \, p, d\,] \urcorner_L}_{\text{trivial degeneration}} \; . \tag{12}$$

Given an N-program p and data d, the interpreter *int* performs p's computation in two stages: first, *trans* translates p into a target program written in

L; then the self-interpreter *sint* evaluates that program with input d. From Defs. 2 and 3 it follows that *int* is an N/L-interpreter since $\forall p \in P_N, \forall d \in D$:

$$[\![int]\!]_L [p, d] = [\![p]\!]_N d . \tag{13}$$

2. For each *trans*, let *int* be the interpreter defined in (12). Let p be an N-program. Then we obtain a target program p' by specializing *int* with respect to p (the 1st Futamura projection as discussed in Sect. 3):

$$p' = [\![spec]\!]_L [int, \mathrm{SD}, p] . \tag{14}$$

Since *spec* reduces static expressions and since *int* is of a form that suits Def. 7, we can rewrite (14) and obtain a program p''' as follows:

$$[\![spec]\!]_L [sint, \mathrm{SD}, [\![trans]\!]_L p] \tag{15}$$
$$= [\![spec]\!]_L [sint, \mathrm{SD}, p''] \tag{16}$$
$$= p''' . \tag{17}$$

When we evaluate the application of *trans* in (15), we obtain (16) where $p'' = [\![trans]\!] p$. Then p''' in (17) is the result of specializing *sint* with respect to p''. According to Def. 7, program p' in (14) is identical to program p''' in (17): $p' = p''$. We conclude from this identity, the specialization in (16) and property $Jopt_{\leq_{Time}}(spec, sint)$ that $p' \leq_{Time} p''$, and we have $[\![spec]\!]_L [int, \mathrm{SD}, p] \leq_{Time} [\![trans]\!]_L p$. This relation holds for any p.   □

The interpreter in (12) performs the computation in two stages: the first stage performs a transformation (translation) of the source program and the second stage evaluates the resulting program with a self-interpreter. Since the specializer performs static expression reduction, any computation can be performed on a program p. Jones optimality of the specializer then guarantees that the performance of the transformed program is not degraded by specialization through the self-interpreter *sint*. (A similar idea was used in [8] to show the power of binding-time improvements.)

We now prove that Jones optimality is a necessary condition for the specializer to be translation universal.

Theorem 2 (Jopt-$\leq_{Time}$ necessary for Trans-univ-$\leq_{Time}$). *For all specializers spec $\in Spec_L$, the following holds:*

$$\exists sint \in Sint_L : Jopt_{\leq_{Time}}(spec, sint)$$
$$\Longleftarrow$$
$$\forall trans \in Trans_{N \to L}, \exists int \in Int_{N/L}, \forall p \in P_N :$$
$$[\![spec]\!]_L [int, \mathrm{SD}, p] \leq_{Time} [\![trans]\!]_L p .$$

Proof. Assume that the *rhs* of the implication holds for all languages, in particular for languages $N = L$. Choose an $L \to L$-translator $trans_{id}$ such that $[\![trans_{id}]\!]_L p = p$ and let *sint* be the L/L-interpreter (= self-interpreter) that satisfies the *rhs* with respect to $trans_{id}$. Using the identity $[\![trans_{id}]\!]_L\, p = p$, the *rhs* of the implication can be simplified to

$$[\![spec]\!]_L\,[\,sint, \mathrm{SD}, p\,] \leq_{Time} p \; . \tag{18}$$

Since this relation holds for any p, we conclude from Def. 10 that *sint* is a self-interpreter for *spec* such that $Jopt_{\leq_{Time}}(spec, sint)$.   □

We conclude that, in terms of target-program efficiency, the translation power of a specializer that is not Jones-optimal is *strictly weaker* than a Jones-optimal specializer.

A specializer that is not Jones-optimal cannot always achieve the target-program efficiency a translator can, no matter how hard we try to find a suitable interpreter. The theorems hold for all specializers regardless of their source languages, their specialization methods, or any other operational details.

The proof of Thm. 1 is rendered by a trivial degeneration in (12). This construction is sufficient for theoretical purposes, but not very efficient: it incorporates an entire translator and uses trivial degeneration. In practice, there exist more customized interpreters that can induce the same target-program effect in connection with a particular specializer. For example, it is known how to build interpreters that are *not* based on trivial degeneration, while letting offline partial evaluators perform optimizing translations [15,22], deforestation or other supercompilation effects [9].

Given a particular specialization algorithm, only those fragments that are relevant for guiding that algorithm need to be considered in the design of a suitable interpreter. Fusing the self-interpreter with the translator in (12) by a program composer may eliminate redundant interface operations between the two programs. This may lead to a more 'natural' interpreter than the one used in our proof. There is room for more work on interpreter design for specialization.

The proof of Thm. 2 makes use of an identity translator $trans_{id}$. The theorem can also be proven using a *non-degrading self-translator*, that is, any $L \to L$-translator *trans* such that $\forall p \in P_L : [\![trans]\!]_L\, p \leq_{Time} p$. Conversely, if a specializer *spec* is not Jones-optimal, then it is not possible to self-translate programs without degrading the efficiency of some source programs: $sint \in Sint_L$, $\exists p \in P_L : [\![spec]\!]_L\,[\,sint, \mathrm{SD}, p\,] \nleq_{Time} p$.

Thus, a specializer that is not Jones-optimal, always degrades the performance of some target programs, and we have a good reason for not calling such a specializer translation universal.

The theorems do not imply that Jones optimality is necessary for every form of translation. A simple example is the class of *trivial translators*, that is, any $N \to L$-translator such that, for some N/L-interpreter *int*, we have $\forall p \in P_L : [\![trans_{triv}]\!]_L\, p = \ulcorner \lambda d.[\![int]\!]_L\,[\,p, d\,]\urcorner_L$. To match a trivial translator, all that is needed is a trivial specializer, but this translation is hardly interesting in practice. To summarize, there exist translators whose translation effect can be matched by a specializer without Jones optimality, but these translators *degrade the performance* of their source programs such that the specializer does not need to remove all of the interpretive overhead.

7 Generating Extensions and Jones Optimality

What we presented in the previous section can be generalized in two ways. First, instead of using a time order, we may want to use other orders on programs, such as a size order. Second, instead of using translators, we may want to consider generating extensions. A translator is just a special case of a generating extension. It is a generating extension of an interpreter.

First, the idea of Jones optimality can be applied to other partial orders or equivalence relations on programs. Let $\leq_R$ be such a binary relation on programs, then we define a parameterized form of Jones optimality and write $Jopt_{\leq_R}$. For instance, the relation could be $\leq_{Size}$ or $\leq_{Time}$. Since the relation is reflexive, we have $Jopt_{\leq_R}(spec_{jser}, mysint)$ for the specializer $spec_{jser}$ defined in Sect. 4.

Definition 11 (Jopt-$\leq_R$). *Let* $sint \in Sint_L$ *be a self-interpreter, then a specializer spec* $\in Spec_L$ *is Jones-optimal for* $sint$ *with respect to* $\leq_R$ *iff* $Jopt_{\leq_R}(spec, sint)$ *where*

$$Jopt_{\leq_R}(spec, sint) \stackrel{\text{def}}{=} \forall p \in P_L : [\![spec]\!]_L [\, sint, \text{SD}, p\,] \leq_R p .$$

Second, instead of translation universality, we now study the question whether, for every generating extension *gen* of a program p, there exists a program p' such that all programs produced by specializing p' are in relation $\leq_R$ with the programs produced by the generating extension. Given a specializer *spec*, we examine the question whether $\forall gen, \exists p', \forall x$:

$$[\![spec]\!]_L [\, p', \text{SD}, x\,] \leq_R [\![gen]\!]_L x . \tag{19}$$

In analogy to Sect. 6, we call this property *generation universality (with respect to* $\leq_R$). We generalize the two theorems by using $Jopt_{\leq_R}$ instead of $Jopt_{\leq_{Time}}$ and a generating extension *gen* instead of a translator *trans*.

Theorem 3 (Jopt-$\leq_R$ sufficient for Gen-univ-$\leq_R$). *For all specializers spec* $\in Spec_L$ *with static expression reduction, the following holds:*

$$\exists sint \in Sint_L : Jopt_{\leq_R}(spec, sint)$$
$$\Longrightarrow$$
$$\forall gen \in Gen_L^p, \exists p' \in P_L^p, \forall x \in D :$$
$$[\![spec]\!]_L [\, p', \text{SD}, x\,] \leq_R [\![gen]\!]_L x .$$

Theorem 4 (Jopt-$\leq_R$ necessary for Gen-univ-$\leq_R$). *For all specializers spec* $\in Spec_L$, *the following holds:*

$$\exists sint \in Sint_L : Jopt_{\leq_R}(spec, sint)$$
$$\Longleftarrow$$
$$\forall gen \in Gen_L^p, \exists p' \in P_L^p, \forall x \in D :$$
$$[\![spec]\!]_L [\, p', \text{SD}, x\,] \leq_R [\![gen]\!]_L x .$$

Proofs (outline). The proof of Thm. 3 follows the one of Thm. 1 except that it makes use of the trivial degeneration of *gen* in (9). The proof of Thm. 4 utilizes the fact that every translator is a generating extension ($Trans_{N \to L} = Gen_L^{int}$ where $int \in Int_{N/L}$) and then follows the argument for Thm. 2. $\qquad\square$

Example. Obtaining a linear string matcher out of a quadratic string matcher is a classic example in program specialization ([6]; see also [2]). This is a challenging problem because it is known that dedicated program generators exist that can produce efficient, specialized string matchers. For example, the Knuth-Morris-Pratt algorithm yields string matchers whose time complexity is linear in the length of the text and whose size is linear in the length of the pattern.

Let us look at the generation of specialized string matchers in an abstract way. A generator of specialized string matchers, such as the Knuth-Morris-Pratt algorithm, can be viewed as a generating extension *matchgen* of a general string matcher *match*. Let *pat* be a pattern and *txt* be a text, then *match* checks whether *pat* occurs in *txt*. The generator *matchgen*, and the specialized string matchers it produces, perform the same computation as the general string matcher, but in two stages. This is described by

$$[\![match]\!]_L [\, pat, txt \,] \;\; = \;\; [\![[\![matchgen]\!]_L \, pat]\!]_L \, txt \;.$$

As we recall from Sect. 4, specializers with static expression reduction exist that satisfy $Jopt_{=_{Text}}$ (where equivalence relation $=_{Text}$ relates programs that are textually identical up to variable renaming). Clearly, $p =_{Text} q \Rightarrow (p =_{Time} q \,\wedge\, p =_{Size} q)$. Let *spec* be such a specializer. This guarantees that for each generator *matchgen* a program *match* exists such that *spec* produces specialized string matchers that have the same time and size complexity as those produced by the generator *matchgen*. More precisely, given a specializer *spec* with static expression reduction and $Jopt_{=_{Text}}(spec, sint)$, we have $\forall matchgen, \exists match, \forall pat$:

$$[\![spec]\!]_L [\, match, \mathrm{SD}, pat \,] \;\; =_{Time} \;\; [\![matchgen]\!]_L \, pat \;,$$
$$[\![spec]\!]_L [\, match, \mathrm{SD}, pat \,] \;\; =_{Size} \;\; [\![matchgen]\!]_L \, pat \;.$$

This guarantees that for every specializer that satisfies the stated conditions, a string matcher *exists* such that the specialization of that matcher with respect to a pattern yields specialized string matchers of the desired time and size complexity. It does *not* tell us how 'naive' the string matcher *match* can be for a particular specialization method (*e.g.*, offline partial evaluation, supercompilation, partial deduction, generalized partial computation) or which binding-time improvements need to be applied to trigger the desired optimization. The degeneration construction used in the proof of Thm. 3 guarantees that for every *spec* a program *match* can be constructed that satisfies the stated conditions.

Also, the theorem does *not* tell us whether Jones optimality is needed for a particular specialization problem (*cf.* the discussion about simulating trivial translators at the end of Sect. 6). However, if a specializer is not Jones-optimal, then we know that the specializer is not generation universal and we cannot be sure to find the desired source program for every generating extension.

The practical challenge in making program specialization useful is to design specialization algorithms that are strong enough such that, *e.g.*, the string matcher *match* can be as simple as possible. This is the familiar tradeoff between improving the overall transformation by modifying the specializer, inserting an instrumented interpreter [7], or binding-time improving the source programs.

8 Related Work

The first version of optimality appeared in [12, Problem 3.8] where a specializer was called "strong enough" if program p and program $[\![spec]\!] [\, sint, SD, p\,]$ are "essentially the same". The definition of optimality used in Def. 10 appeared first in [13, p.650]; see also [14, Sect. 6.4]. These first studies were motivated by the problem of self-application. We applied the idea of self-interpreter specialization and obtained general statements about translation universality and generation universality of certain classes of specializers. In related work, the role of Jones optimality for universal binding-time improvements was investigated [8] and the idea of controlling the properties of residual programs by specializing suitable interpreters was studied [7,9,15,22].

It was also found [20] that a specializer is 'weak' in a more general sense if it cannot overcome inherited limits and that these limits are best observed by specializing a self-interpreter. Since the power of a specializer can be judged in different ways, it was suggested [17] to use the term "Jones optimality". Recent studies [3,24] focused on the problem of tag-elimination to achieve Jones optimality when specializing self-interpreters for strongly-typed languages.

9 Conclusion

We found that Jones optimality plays an important role in simulating translators and generating extensions by program specialization. We introduced a parameterized notion of Jones optimality and showed that, in principle, a Jones-optimal specializer with static expression reduction can always produce residual programs that match the size and time complexity of programs produced by an arbitrary generating extension. We say that such a specializer is generation universal. It is also reassuring to know that, in general, the method of translating programs by specializing interpreters is as powerful as translating programs by ordinary translators. In short, there is no theoretical limit that would make Futamura's method strictly weaker than ordinary translation.

We should reemphasize that our results imply neither that a specializer that is not Jones-optimal is useless nor that program generation by specialization is always a good idea. They show that there exists a theoretical limit to what can be achieved when a specializer is not generation universal. One of the main motivations for studying automatic program specialization is that a specializer has pragmatic success in producing efficient residual programs for a large class of source programs and, thus, a compromise between theory and practice needs to be found when designing a specializer.

We focused on the role of Jones optimality in specialization. We believe that the power to perform universal computations is another property necessary for generation universality. Thus, a total specializer can be said to be limited in its theoretical capability to simulate arbitrary translators and generating extensions. Whether the results in this paper can be adapted to other cases of non-standard interpreter hierarchies [1] is a topic for future work. We also did not explore the conditions for generating translators and generating extensions by specializing specializers (2nd Futamura projection). It is quite possible that the results in this paper can be carried to the next metasystem level.

Acknowledgments. We would like to thank Sergei Abramov, Mikhail Bulyonkov, Yoshihiko Futamura, Masahiko Kawabe, and the anonymous reviewers for valuable comments on an earlier version of this paper.

References

1. S. M. Abramov, R. Glück. Combining semantics with non-standard interpreter hierarchies. In S. Kapoor, S. Prasad (eds.), *Foundations of Software Technology and Theoretical Computer Science. Proceedings*, LNCS 1974, 201–213. Springer-Verlag, 2000.
2. M. S. Ager, O. Danvy, H. K. Rohde. On obtaining Knuth, Morris, and Pratt's string matcher by partial evaluation. In *Proceedings of the Asian Symposium on Partial Evaluation and Semantics-Based Program Manipulation*, 32–46. ACM Press, 2002.
3. O. Danvy, P. E. M. López. Tagging, encoding, and Jones optimality. In P. Degano (ed.), *Programming Languages and Systems. Proceedings*, LNCS 2618, 335–347. Springer-Verlag, 2003.
4. A. P. Ershov. On the partial computation principle. *Information Processing Letters*, 6(2):38–41, 1977.
5. Y. Futamura. Partial evaluation of computing process – an approach to a compiler-compiler. *Systems, Computers, Controls*, 2(5):45–50, 1971. Reprinted in Higher-Order and Symbolic Computation, 12(4): 381–391, 1999.
6. Y. Futamura, K. Nogi. Generalized partial computation. In D. Bjørner, A. P. Ershov, N. D. Jones (eds.), *Partial Evaluation and Mixed Computation*, 133–151. North-Holland, 1988.
7. R. Glück. On the generation of specializers. *Journal of Functional Programming*, 4(4):499–514, 1994.
8. R. Glück. Jones optimality, binding-time improvements, and the strength of program specializers. In *Proceedings of the Asian Symposium on Partial Evaluation and Semantics-Based Program Manipulation*, 9–19. ACM Press, 2002.
9. R. Glück, J. Jørgensen. Generating transformers for deforestation and supercompilation. In B. Le Charlier (ed.), *Static Analysis. Proceedings*, LNCS 864, 432–448. Springer-Verlag, 1994.
10. R. Glück, A. V. Klimov. A regeneration scheme for generating extensions. *Information Processing Letters*, 62(3):127–134, 1997.
11. J. Heering. Partial evaluation and ω-completeness of algebraic specifications. *Theoretical Computer Science*, 43(2–3):149–167, 1986.

12. N. D. Jones. Challenging problems in partial evaluation and mixed computation. In D. Bjørner, A. P. Ershov, N. D. Jones (eds.), *Partial Evaluation and Mixed Computation*, 1–14. North-Holland, 1988.

13. N. D. Jones. Partial evaluation, self-application and types. In M. S. Paterson (ed.), *Automata, Languages and Programming. Proceedings*, LNCS 443, 639–659. Springer-Verlag, 1990.

14. N. D. Jones, C. K. Gomard, P. Sestoft. *Partial Evaluation and Automatic Program Generation*. Prentice-Hall, 1993.

15. J. Jørgensen. Generating a compiler for a lazy language by partial evaluation. In *Conference Record of the Nighteenth Symposium on Principles of Programming Languages*, 258–268. ACM Press, 1992.

16. S. S. Lavrov. On the essence of mixed computation. In D. Bjørner, A. P. Ershov, N. D. Jones (eds.), *Partial Evaluation and Mixed Computation*, 317–324. North-Holland, 1988.

17. H. Makholm. On Jones-optimal specialization for strongly typed languages. In W. Taha (ed.), *Semantics, Applications, and Implementation of Program Generation. Proceedings*, LNCS 1924, 129–148. Springer-Verlag, 2000.

18. T. Æ. Mogensen. Partially static structures in a self-applicable partial evaluator. In D. Bjørner, A. P. Ershov, N. D. Jones (eds.), *Partial Evaluation and Mixed Computation*, 325–347. North-Holland, 1988.

19. T. Æ. Mogensen. Separating binding times in language specifications. In *Fourth International Conference on Functional Programming and Computer Architecture, London, UK*, 14–25. ACM Press and Addison-Wesley, Sept. 1989.

20. T. Æ. Mogensen. Evolution of partial evaluators: removing inherited limits. In O. Danvy, R. Glück, P. Thiemann (eds.), *Partial Evaluation. Proceedings*, LNCS 1110, 303–321. Springer-Verlag, 1996.

21. P. Sestoft. The structure of a self-applicable partial evaluator. In H. Ganzinger, N. D. Jones (eds.), *Programs as Data Objects*, LNCS 217, 236–256. Springer-Verlag, 1985.

22. P. Sestoft. ML pattern match compilation and partial evaluation. In O. Danvy, R. Glück, P. Thiemann (eds.), *Partial Evaluation. Proceedings*, LNCS 1110, 446–464. Springer-Verlag, 1996.

23. S. Skalberg. Mechanical proof of the optimality of a partial evaluator. Master's thesis, DIKU, Department of Computer Science, University of Copenhagen, 1999.

24. W. Taha, H. Makholm, J. Hughes. Tag elimination and Jones-optimality. In O. Danvy, A. Filinsky (eds.), *Programs as Data Objects. Proceedings*, LNCS 2053, 257–275. Springer-Verlag, 2001.

A Compiler Generator for Constraint Logic Programs

Stephen-John Craig and Michael Leuschel

Department of Electronics and Computer Science,
University of Southampton, Highfield SO17 1BJ
{sjc02r, mal}@ecs.soton.ac.uk

Abstract. The *cogen* approach to program specialisation, writing a compiler generator instead of a specialiser, has been used with considerable success. This paper demonstrates that the *cogen* approach is also applicable to the specialisation of constraint logic programs and leads to effective specialisers. We present the basic specialisation technique for CLP(Q) programs and show how we can handle non-declarative features as well. We present an implemented system along with experimental results.

1 Introduction

Program specialisation, also called partial evaluation (see, e.g., [9]), is an automatic technique for program optimization. Specialisation optimises programs by distinguishing between static and dynamic input data. Using the static data, parts of the original program can be evaluated at specialisation time, resulting in a hopefully more efficient residual program. The residual program is only dependent on the dynamic data (Fig. 1(a)) and can offer a substantial speed increase.

Despite some recent interest, there has been surprisingly little work on specialization of constraint logic programs. Indeed after some work in the early 90s [19,20] there has been a long period of relative inactivity, especially compared to the success that constraint logic programming has encountered for practical applications. Only very recently, new research is emerging [4,5,14,21] which is trying to tackle this difficult but practically relevant problem.

This paper presents an introduction to program specialisation of Constraint Logic Programs (CLP) and presents our newly developed technique and its implementation. We illustrate our technique and implementation on several examples and we also present experiments which evaluate the power and efficiency of our implementation. Our work presents the first offline specialiser for CLP, and it is also the first compiler generator for CLP. Our goal was to develop a system with fast and predictable specialisation times, and plan to integrate the tool into the Ciao Prolog system. To ensure wide applicability we also cater for non-declarative features.

M. Broy and A.V. Zamulin (Eds.): PSI 2003, LNCS 2890, pp. 148–161, 2003.
© Springer-Verlag Berlin Heidelberg 2003

Offline vs Online Specialisation. In an *offline* specialiser almost all the control decisions are taken before the actual specialisation phase in a preliminary analysis phase referred to as *binding-time analysis* (BTA). *Online* partial evaluators typically do not make use of such a preliminary phase phase but instead take their decisions on the fly, using the actual values of the static data. Note, however, that offline partial evaluators maintain — during specialisation — a list of calls that have been previously specialised or are pending [9]. This is called *memoisation*.

Online partial evaluators are in principle more powerful, as they base their control decisions on more precise information. However, one of the big advantages of the offline approach is the efficiency of the specialisation process itself: indeed, once the annotations have actually been derived, the specialiser is relatively simple, and can be made to be very efficient, since all decisions concerning local control are made before and not during specialisation. Other advantages of the offline approach is the better predictability of the output, i.e., it is easier to predict beforehand (based on the outcome of the BTA) what will happen during the specialisation phase. The simplicity of the specialiser also means that it is much easier to achieve *self-application*, i.e., specialise the specialiser itself using partial evaluation. Self-application enables a partial evaluator to generate so-called "compilers" from interpreters using the second Futamura projection and a compiler generator (*cogen*) using the third Futamura projection (see, e.g., [9]). However, the actual creation of the *cogen* according to the third Futamura projection is not of much interest to users since *cogen* can be generated once and for all when a specialiser is given. This is known as the *cogen-approach* and has been successfully applied in many programming paradigms [1,2,3,6,7,11,17].

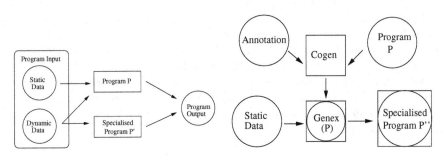

(a) The specialised program P' is only dependent on the dynamic input

(b) Overview of the Cogen approach.

Fig. 1. Overview of the Specialisation process

2   Logen

LOGEN [11] is an offline specialiser for logic programs which uses the *cogen* approach. Given an annotated version of program P, a(P), specifying for example which inputs will be static and dynamic, LOGEN produces a specialised specialiser, or Genex (generating extension) for the program P. Running the Genex with particular values for the static inputs produces the specialised program (Fig. 1(b)). As the Genex is not dependent on actual data values it can be reused to produce different specialised programs. Using this approach the efficiency of the specialisation process is greatly improved in situations where the same program is specialised multiple times. The annotated version a(P) employed by LOGEN contains:

1. for every predicate, a description of which arguments will be *static* or *dynamic*. It is also possible to only annotate certain parts of arguments as static.
2. for every predicate call in the program, whether this call should be *unfolded* or *memoised*, i.e., whether it should be performed within the specialiser or whether the call should be performed at runtime. In the former case, the Genex generated by LOGEN will replace (during specialisation) this predicate call in the body by its definition, performing all the needed substitutions. In the latter case, the predicate call will be *generalised* by replacing all parts which are marked as *dynamic* by a fresh variable. It will then be checked whether the generalised call has been encountered before. If it has not been encountered before, the original program will be specialised for this generalised call.

CLP(R) and CLP(Q). Constraint Logic Programming over the real domain, CLP(R) , and the rational domain, CLP(Q) , offer a powerful mathematical solver for the domains of real and rational numbers. The CLP(R) and CLP(Q) schemes used in this document and related tool are instances of the general Constraint Logic Programming Scheme introduced by Jaffar & Michaylov [8].

Constraint Logic Programming languages allow the programmer to express the probelm in a very high level language, specifying relationships or 'constraints' between objects, while the underlying engine uses powerful incremental constraint solvers.

Logen for CLP(R) and CLP(Q). Specialisation of CLP(R) or CLP(Q) programs using existing offline specialisation techniques causes problems as the program state is not limited to the goal stack but also populates a constraint store. This means that LOGEN cannot properly handle CLP programs. Indeed, LOGEN either performs *all* the constraint processing at specialisation time, or *all* the constraint processing at runtime — it is not possible to *partially evaluate* constraints. This is obviously a serious limitation and with the increasing adoption of CLP languages by industry it is important that tools allow for efficient specialisation of CLP programs.

Based upon the current LOGEN system we have thus developed a new version of LOGEN that can handle full CLP(R) or CLP(Q) programs. It supports constraint specialisation across predicates by memoising constraints and retains the full power of the original LOGEN to specialise ordinary logic programming constructs. In the next chapter we show how this is achieved.

3 Specialisation of Pure CLP(R) and CLP(Q) Programs

3.1 Unfolding and Simplification

The classical unfold transformation replaces a predicate call with the predicate body, performing all the needed substitutions. In CLP the state of uninstantiated variables is held in the constraint store, after unfolding the residual constraints have to be extracted from the constraint store, projected, simplified and then added back into the residual program.

Let us examine the trivial CLP(Q) program in Fig. 2, which multiplies X by an integer Y to give R. Fig. 3 demonstrates how to unfold this program for the call `multiply(X,2,R)`. After each recursive call to multiply, a new constraint is added to the constraint store ($C_{1..3}$). After the unfolding has completed the final constraints in C_3 and variable assignments can be extracted. These are then projected onto the variables X, R of the top-level query and simplified to produce the following residual program:

```
multiply(X,2.0,R) :-    {R = 2.0 * X}.
```

Careful attention must be paid to the simplification of the residual constraints. During unfolding an entailment check ensures that redundant clauses are removed from the specialised program. [12] demonstrates the optimizations available through constraint reordering and removal when the removal does not effect control flow. If a constraint is likely to fail and hence cause backtracking then it should be added to the constraint store as early as possible to ensure less time is wasted in unneeded calculations.

```
multiply(_,Y,R) :-  {Y = 0, R = 0}.
multiply(X,Y,R) :-  {Y > 0 ,Y1 = Y -1, R = X + R1},  multiply(X,Y1,R1).
```

Fig. 2. Trivial CLP(Q) Multiplication predicate

Definition 1 (Constraint Unfolding) *$CS' = unfold(Call, CS)$, where CS' is the simplified set of constraints obtained by calling Call with the initial constraints CS. For example, $unfold(multiply(X, 2, R), []) = \{R = 2 * X\}$ (using the definition of multiply/3 from Fig. 2)*

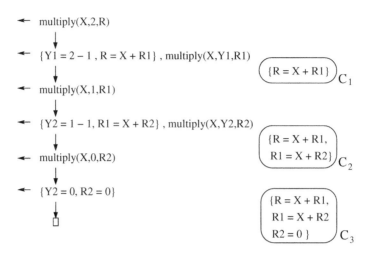

Fig. 3. The multiply predicate is unfolded, producing the residual constraints C_3

3.2   Memoisation

In the original LOGEN, when a call c is memoised it is first generalised, by re-placing any parts of the call that are marked as dynamic by a fresh variable. For example, if $c = p(2, 3)$ and if the second argument to p is marked dynamic, we obtain a generalised call $c' = p(2, V)$. LOGEN (or rather the generating extension generated by LOGEN) then searches its memo table for a variant of c'. If c' is a variant of any previously memoised call, c will be replaced with the residual call from the memo table (this might, e.g., be $p\_2(V)$). Otherwise c' has to be specialised on its own, and residual code has to be generated for it.

In the CLP setting the original LOGEN memoisation must be extended to take into account the constraint store. As a CLP variable may be uninstantiated but still bound to constraints it can not always be clearly marked as static or dynamic. A new variable type, *constraint*, was introduced so that the constraints can be propagated throughout the specialised program. A variable can still be marked as dynamic to limit constraint propagation.

When a call, c, is memoised for the first time the current constraints, pro-jected onto the arguments of c, must also be stored. During subsequent special-isation, constraints can be discarded if they are already entailed by the system. Therefore a memoised call can only be reused if the current constraints are at least as restrictive as the constraints stored for the memoised call.

Nonlinear Constraints. The $CLP(Q)$ system is restricted to solve only lin-ear constraints because the decision algorithms for general nonlinear constraints are prohibitively expensive to run [8]. However nonlinear constraints are col-lected by the $CLP(Q)$ engine in the hope that through the addition of further constraints they might become simple enough to solve. In Fig. 4 the constraint store has not failed but has become inconsistent, there are no values of X that will satisfy the set of equations. During memoisation a part of the constraint store is stored along with the residual call, subsequent calls are checked against the stored constraint set. Nonlinear constraints can not be tested for entailment and calculating a convex hull for nonlinear constraints is expensive. Therefor only linear constraints are stored inside the memoisation points, nonlinear constraints are simplified and added to the residual code. To do this we define the operation *removeNonLinear*.

```
| ?- {X * X = Y , X * X = Z, Z + 2 = Y }.
{Z= -2+Y},
clpq:{-(Z)+X^2=0},
clpq:{X^2-Y=0} ?
yes
```

Fig. 4. Nonlinear constraints can lead to an inconsistent constraint store

Definition 2 (Remove Nonlinear Constraints)

$$C' = removeNonLinear(C),$$

where C' is the set of linear arithmetic formulae occurring in C. For example,

$$removeNonLinear(\{X * X = Y \land Y + X = 6 \}) = \{Y + X = 6\}$$

Constraints Collection Points. During unfolding constraints are propagated through the program, in memoisation these constraints are collected in constraint collection points, simplified and added to the residual program. Fig. 5 is an extract from a CLP program, CS_{Label} represents a set of constraints. The call p in r has been annotated for memoisation, the calls to *foo* in both the p clauses have been annotated for unfolding. The clauses for *foo* are not shown in the example.

```
r[1] (X,Y,Z)  :- CS_r1 , memo(p(X,Y)), CS_r1.1.
p[1] (A,B)  :- CS_p1, unfold(foo(A)).
p[2] (A,B)  :- CS_p2, unfold(foo(B)).
```

Fig. 5. Extract from a CLP program

Definition 3 (Projection) $Project_V(C)$ is the projection of constraints C onto variables V. For example, $project_X(X = Y \land Y > 2) = \{X > 2\}$.

For simplicity it is assumed that the initial constraint store projected onto X, Y, Z is empty when the call to r is made. The memoisation table is used to keep track of previously memoised calls. Each entry consists of a call pattern, a set of assumed constraints and the residual call. In the example, Fig. 5, the current constraints are projected onto the variables X and Y and stored in CS_{mp} (Fig. 6). The residual call is a unique identifier for the new specialised call.

$$CS_{mp} = removeNonLinear(project_{vars(p(X,Y))}(CS_{r1}))$$
```
memo_table(p(X,Y) , CSmp, p_spec(X,Y))
```

Fig. 6. Memoisation table entry for p in Fig. 5

The two clauses for p are specialised using the initial constraints CS_{mp}, the calls to *foo* are unfolded and the become part of the residual code. As the constraint set CS_{mp} specifies a precondition for all calls to the residual code, $p\_spec(X,Y)$, all residual constraints entailed by CS_{mp} can be safely removed from the final code. If a subsequent call is made to $p(X,Y)$ it may reuse the specialised code $p\_spec(X,Y)$ iff the current linear constraints projected onto the variables X and Y are at least as restrictive as CS_{mp}.

Definition 4 (Remove Entailed Constraints)

$$removeEntailed(C', C) = \{c_i | c_i \in C \wedge C' \not\models c_i\}.$$

For example,

$$removeEntailed(\{X \geq 5 \wedge X \leq 12\}, \{ X > 2 \wedge X < 10 \}) = \{X < 10 \}.$$

$$CS_{pspec1} = removeEntailed(CS_{mp}, CS_{p1} \wedge unfold(foo(A), CS_{p1} \wedge CS_{mp}))$$
$$CS_{pspec2} = removeEntailed(CS_{mp}, CS_{p2} \wedge unfold(foo(B), CS_{p2} \wedge CS_{mp}))$$
```
r(X,Y,Z) :- CSr1 , p_spec(X,Y), CSr1.1
p_spec[1](A,B) :- CSpspec1.
p_spec[2](A,B) :- CSpspec2.
```

Fig. 7. Specialised fragment of Fig. 5

Convex Hull and Widening. If there is a subsequent call to a memoised predicate and it can not reuse the existing residual call then a new entry is added to the memoisation table and the call is respecialised for the new constraints. It may also be possible to widen the constraint to encompadd both the existing and the new call, reducing residual code size.

$CS_{mpq1} = \{X > 0, Y > 0, X + Y < 3\}$
`memo_table(q(X,Y)` , CS_{mpq1}, `q__1(X,Y))`

Fig. 8. Memoisation entry for q

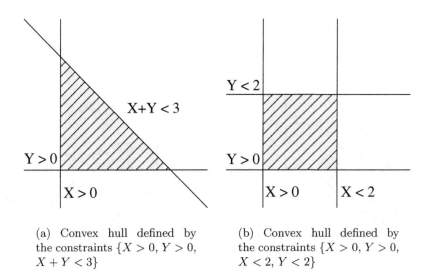

(a) Convex hull defined by the constraints $\{X > 0, Y > 0, X + Y < 3\}$

(b) Convex hull defined by the constraints $\{X > 0, Y > 0, X < 2, Y < 2\}$

Fig. 9. Constraint sets specify a convex hull in space

For example, consider the memoisation entry in Fig. 8, the constraints CS_{mpq} define the convex hull in Fig. 9(a). A subsequent call to $q(X, Y)$ can only reuse the entry if its constraints lie inside the defined hull.

A call to $q(X, Y)$ is made with constraints $\{X > 0, Y > 0, X < 2, Y < 2\}$ (Fig 9(b)), the existing memo entry can not be reused and the call to $q(X, Y)$ must be respecialised. Two strategies are available

1. Respecialise the predicate for the new constraints $\{X > 0, Y > 0, X < 2, Y < 2\}$ resulting in the memoisation table Fig 10. Two residual predicates for q are created, q_1 and q_2, possibly resulting in duplicated code in the specialised program.
2. Creating a new set of constraints to encompass both the existing and new constraints. The new constraint set is a convex hull encompassing the constraints Fig. 9(a) $\cup$ Fig 9(b) as shown in Fig. 11. Once the predicate has been specialised for these constraints the old residual call can be discarded and the new one used by both calls. It may also be necessary to widen the set by removing constraints to ensure termination.

Calculating the optimal convex hull (Fig. 11(b)) is computationally expensive but it can be approximated by shifting the existing constraints (possibly to infinity) until they enclose both of the original constraint spaces (Fig. 11(a)).

$CS_{mpq1} = \{X > 0, Y > 0, X + Y < 3\}$
$CS_{mpq2} = \{X > 0, Y > 0, X < 2, Y < 2\}$
```
memo_table(q(X,Y) , CS_mpq1, q__1(X,Y))
memo_table(q(X,Y) , CS_mpq2, q__2(X,Y))
```

Fig. 10. Memoisation table after respecialising for CS_{mpq2}

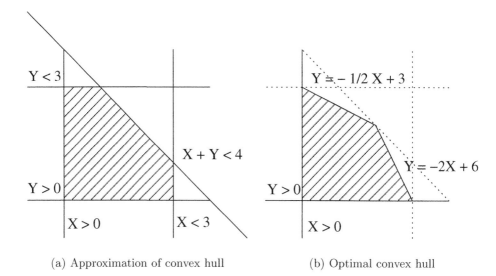

(a) Approximation of convex hull   (b) Optimal convex hull

Fig. 11. Convex hull for constraints Fig. 9(a) ∪ Fig. 9(b)

3.3   Rounding Errors with CLP(R)

Currently the specialisation phase uses the Rational domain, CLP(Q) , to generate specialised code for the CLP(R) engine. During the specialisation phase the residual constraint store becomes part of the specialised program. Fig. 12 demonstrates it is not always possible to retrieve exact numbers from the CLP(R) engine and therefore truncation errors can be introduced into the specialised program. A CLP(R) program can be specialised using the CLP(Q) engine however it may take quite big rationals to accommodate the required level of precision.

4   Examples and Experiments

In this section we illustrate our technique on a non-trivial example. Fig. 13 calculates the balance of a loan over N periods. *Balances* is a list of length N. The interest rate is controlled by the loan scheme and decided by the amount of the initial loan. The map predicate is used to apply the loan scheme over the list of balances.

```
| ?- {21/20 * Y > X},{21/20*X > Y}.
{Y-1.05*X<-0.0},
{Y-0.9523809523809523*X>0.0} ?
yes
```

Fig. 12. Demonstration of CLP(R) rounding problems. The output from the CLP engine is dependent on the ordering of the variables

```
%%% P = Principal, B = Balances, R = Repay, T = Term
loan(P, B, R) :- {P >= 7000}, T = [P|B], map(scheme1, T, R).
loan(P, B, R) :- {P>=4000,P<7000}, T = [P|B], map(scheme2, T, R).
loan(P, B, R) :- {P>=1000,P<4000}, T = [P|B], map(scheme3, T, R).
loan(P, B, R) :- {P>=0,P<1000}, T = [P|B], map(scheme4, T, R).

%%% A = Amount, NA = NewAmount, R = Repayment, I = Interest
scheme1(A, NA, R) :- {I = 0.005}, calcLoan(A, NA, I, R).
scheme2(A, NA, R) :- {I = 0.01 }, calcLoan(A, NA, I, R).
scheme3(A, NA, R) :- {I = 0.015}, calcLoan(A, NA, I, R).
scheme4(A, NA, R) :- {I = 0.02 }, calcLoan(A, NA, I, R).

map(_,[_],_).
map(SCHEME,[H1,H2|Tail], Repayment) :- Call =.. [SCHEME,H1,H2, Repayment],
          call(Call), map(SCHEME,[H2|Tail], Repayment).
calcLoan(Amount,NewTotal, Interest, Repayment) :-
          {NewTotal = Amount + (Amount * Interest) - Repayment}.
```

Fig. 13. Loan.pl calculates the balance of a loan over N periods for a given loan scheme and repayment

Unfolding Example. In Fig. 14 the loan predicate has been specialised to calculate the balances over two periods for a principal loan over 4000. As the length of the list is known all of the recursive calls can be executed at specialisation time. The map, scheme, and calcLoan calls have been unfolded and the resultant code has been inlined in the specialised code. The two redundant loan schemes have been removed from the final code. The specialised predicate (Fig. 14) runs 68% faster than the original predicate in Fig. 13.

Memoisation Example. In Fig. 15 the map predicate from the loan program has been specialised to use either scheme1 or scheme2. The length of the list has not been specified so the recursive call must be memoised. The calls in the body of map have been unfolded and the residual code inlined in the specialised code. The removal of the overhead from the univ (=..) and call operators combined with the simplification of the loan calculation to include the hard coded interest rate produces a 57% speed up over the original predicate.

```
loan__1(Principal,C,D,E) :-
  { Principal >= (7000), Principal = (((200/201)*C) + ((200/201)*E)),
    D = (((201/200) * C) - E) }.
loan__1(Principal,G,H,I) :-
 { Principal < (7000),
   Principal = (((100/101)*G) + ((100/101)*I)), H = (((11/10)*G) - I) }.
loan(Principal,[B,C],D) :- { Principal > (4000) }, loan__1(A,B,C,D).
```

Fig. 14. Specialised version of the loan predicate for $loan(X, [P1, P2], R)$ where $X > 4000$

```
map(scheme1,A,B) :- map__1(A,B).
map(scheme2,A,B) :- map__2(A,B).
map__1([B],C).
map__1([D,E|F],G) :- {E = ((201/200) * D ) - G }, map__1([E|F],G).
map__2([B],C).
map__2([D,E|F],G) :- { E = ((101/100) * D) - G }, map__2([E|F],G).
```

Fig. 15. Specialised version of the loan example for calls $map(scheme1, T, R)$ and $map(scheme2, T, R)$. In this example the recursive call to map_1 is memoed as the length of the list is not known at specialisation time

4.1 Summary of Experimental Results

Table 1 summarises our experimental results. The timings were obtained by using SICStus Prolog 3.10 on a 2.4 GHz Pentium 4. The second column contains the time spent by cogen to produce the generating extension. The third column contains the time that the generating extension needed to specialise the original program for a particular specialisation query. The fourth column contains the time the specialised program took for a series of runtime queries and the fifth column contains the results from the original programs. The final column contains the speedup of the specialised program as compared to the original. Full details of the experiments (source code, queries,...) can be found at [10].

Table 1. Experimental results

Program	Cogen Time	Genex Time	Runtime	Original	Speedup
multiply	0 ms	20 ms	10 ms	3780 ms	37800 %
loan_unfold	0 ms	0 ms	385 ms	647 ms	68 %
loan_map	0 ms	0 ms	411 ms	647 ms	57 %
ctl_clp	0 ms	100 ms	17946 ms	24245 ms	35 %

5 Non-declarative Programs

It is well known that to properly handle Prolog programs with non-declarative features one has to pay special attention to the left-propagation of bindings and of failure [18,16]. Indeed, for calls c to predicates with side-effects (such as nl/0) "$c, fail$" is not equivalent to "$fail, c$". Other predicates are called "propagation sensitive" [18]. For calls c to such predicates, even though $c, fail \equiv fail$ may hold, the equivalence $(c, X = t) \equiv (X = t, c)$ does not. One such predicate is var/1: we have, e.g., $(\texttt{var(X)},\texttt{X=a}) \not\equiv (\texttt{X=a},\texttt{var(X)})$. Predicates can both be propagation sensitive and have side-effects (such as print/1). The way this problem is overcome in the LOGEN system [11] is via special annotations which selectively prevent the left-propagation of bindings and failure. This allows the LOGEN system to handle almost full Prolog [1], while still being able to left-propagate bindings whenever this is guaranteed to be safe. In a CLP setting, the whole issue gets more complicated in that one also has to worry about the left-propagation of constraints. Take for instance the clause p(X) :- var(X),{X=<2} and suppose we transform it into p_1(X) :- {X=<2},var(X). The problem is now that the query {X>=2},p_1(X) to the specialised program fails while the original query {X>=2},p(X) succeeds with a computed answer X=2.0. To overcome this problem we have extended the scheme from [11] to enable us to selectively prevent the left-propagation of constraints. Using our new system we are now in a position to handle full CLP programs with non-declarative features. Take for example the following simple CLP(Q) program:

```
p(X,Y) :- {X>Y}, print(Y), {X=2}.
```

Using our system we can specialise this program for, e.g., the query p(3,Z) yielding the following, correct specialised program:

```
p__0(Y) :- {3>Y}, print(Y), fail.
```

6 Future, Related Work, and Conclusions

There has been some early work on specialization of CLP programs [20,19] and optimization [12]. There has been some recent interest in online specialisation techniques for constraint logic programs [4,5,14,21,15]. To the best of our knowledge there is no work on offline specialisation of CLP programs, and to our knowledge none of the above techniques can handle non-declarative programs.

The binding-time analysis of [11], based on a termination analysis for logic programs needs to be adapted to take constraints into account. At this stage it is not clear whether existing termination analysis techniques for constraint logic programs such as [13] can be used to that end.

There is still scope to improve the code generator of our system, e.g., by using more sophisticated reordering as advocated in [12]. Other possibilities might be to convert CLP operations into standard Prolog arithmetic (e.g., using is/2)

---

[1] Predicates which inspect and modify the clause database of the program being specialised, such as assert/1 and retract/1 are not supported; although it is possible to treat a limited form of them.

when this is safe. Extension to other domains, such as CLP(FD) are being investigated. Finally, we plan to integrate LOGEN into Ciao Prolog, making the use of our system more transparent.

The specialisation of CLP programs is an important research area for partial evaluation. We have implemented a working version of an offline CLP(R) specialiser and first results look promising.

References

1. Lars Ole Andersen. *Program Analysis and Specialization for the C Programming Language*. PhD thesis, DIKU, University of Copenhagen, May 1994. (DIKU report 94/19).
2. Lennart Beckman, Anders Haraldson, Östen Oskarsson, and Erik Sandewall. A partial evaluator and its use as a programming tool. *Artificial Intelligence*, 7:319–357, 1976.
3. Lars Birkedal and Morten Welinder. Hand-writing program generator generators. In M. Hermenegildo and J. Penjam, editors, *Programming Language Implementation and Logic Programming. Proceedings, Proceedings of PLILP'91*, LNCS 844, pages 198–214, Madrid, Spain, 1994. Springer-Verlag.
4. Fabio Fioravanti, Alberto Pettorossi, and Maurizio Proietti. Automated strategies for specializing constraint logic programs. In *Logic Based Program Synthesis and Transformation. Proceedings of Lopstr'2000*, LNCS 1207, pages 125–146, 2000.
5. Fabio Fioravanti, Alberto Pettorossi, and Maurizio Proietti. Verifying ctl properties of infinite-state systems by specializing constraint logic programs. In *Proceedings of VCL'2001*, Florence, Italy, September 2001.
6. C. K. Holst and J. Launchbury. Handwriting cogen to avoid problems with static typing. In *Draft Proceedings, Fourth Annual Glasgow Workshop on Functional Programming, Skye, Scotland*, pages 210–218. Glasgow University, 1991.
7. Carsten Kehler Holst. Syntactic currying: yet another approach to partial evaluation. Technical report, DIKU, Department of Computer Science, University of Copenhagen, 1989.
8. J. Jaffar, S. Michaylov, and R. H. C. Yap. A methodology for managing hard constraints in CLP systems. In *Proceedings of the ACM SIGPLAN '91 Conference on Programming Language Design and Implementation*, volume 26, pages 306–316, Toronto, Ontario, Canada, June 1991.
9. Neil D. Jones, Carsten K. Gomard, and Peter Sestoft. *Partial Evaluation and Automatic Program Generation*. Prentice Hall, 1993.
10. Michael Leuschel. The ECCE partial deduction system and the DPPD library of benchmarks. Obtainable via http://www.ecs.soton.ac.uk/~mal, 1996-2002.
11. Michael Leuschel, Jesper Jørgensen, Wim Vanhoof, and Maurice Bruynooghe. Offline specialisation in Prolog using a hand-written compiler generator. *Theory and Practice of Logic Programming*, page 52pp, 2003. To appear.
12. K. Marriott and P. Stuckey. The 3 r's of optimizing constraint logic programs: Refinement, removal, and reordering. In *Proceedings of POPL'93*, pages 334–344. ACM Press, 1993.
13. Fred Mesnard and Slavatore Ruggieri. On proving left termination of constraint logic programs. *ACM Transactions on Computational Logic*, 2003. to appear.

14. Julio C. Peralta and John P. Gallagher. Convex hull abstractions in specialization of clp programs. In Michael Leuschel, editor, *Proc. of 12th Int'l Workshop on Logic-based Program Synthesis and Transformation (LOPSTR'2002)*. Springer LNCS, 2002.

15. Julio C. Peralta. *Analysis and Specialisation of Imperative Programs: An approach using CLP*. PhD thesis, Department of Computer Science, University of Bristol, 2000.

16. Steven Prestwich. The PADDY partial deduction system. Technical Report ECRC-92-6, ECRC, Munich, Germany, 1992.

17. Sergei A. Romanenko. A compiler generator produced by a self-applicable specializer can have a surprisingly natural and understandable structure. In Dines Bjørner, Andrei P. Ershov, and Neil D. Jones, editors, *Partial Evaluation and Mixed Computation*, pages 445–463. North-Holland, 1988.

18. D. Sahlin. Mixtus: An automatic partial evaluator for full Prolog. *New Generation Computing*, 12(1):7–51, 1993.

19. Donald A. Smith. Partial evaluation of pattern matching in constraint logic programming languages. In N. D. Jones and P. Hudak, editors, *ACM Symposium on Partial Evaluation and Semantics-Based Program Manipulation*, pages 62–71. ACM Press Sigplan Notices 26(9), 1991.

20. Donald A. Smith and Timothy Hickey. Partial evaluation of a CLP language. In S.K. Debray and M. Hermenegildo, editors, *Proceedings of the North American Conference on Logic Programming*, pages 119–138. MIT Press, 1990.

21. Yi Tao, William Grosky, and Chunnian Liu. An automatic partial deduction system for constraint logic programs. In *9th International Conference on Tools with Artificial Intelligence (ICTAI '97)*, pages 149–157, Newport Beach, CA, USA, November 1997. IEEE Computer Society.

The Supercompiler SCP4: General Structure

Andrei P. Nemytykh[1,2]*

[1] Program Systems Institute RAS,
Pereslavl-Zalessky, Yaroslavl region, 152140 Russia
nemytykh@math.botik.ru
[2] State Key Lab of Software Engineering, Wuhan University,
Wuhan, 430072 Hubei, China
nemytykh@whu.edu.cn

Supercompilation is a program transformation technique introduced in the 1970s by V. Turchin [13,14,16]. His ideas were studied by a number of authors for a long time. We constructed an experimental supercompiler for a functional language Refal-5 [15]. The Scp4 project was discussed with V. Turchin. He initiated and supported our work. Scp4 has been implemented once again using Refal-5. Sources of Scp4 and the whole version of this paper are available for immediate download [8,9,17]. A user manual on Scp4 and reports on several interesting experiments can be found in [4,5,6]. Scp4 is a first experimental supercompiler for the real functional language Refal-5. The principal new tool in Scp4 is an online analysis of global properties of folded-components of the meta-tree MTr of all potential computations. Let a program P and a parameterized input of the P be given. Then such a pair defines a partial mapping. A supercompiler is a transformer of such pairs. The transformer must preserve the map values on the map domain. Scp4 unfolds a potentially infinite tree of all possible computations. It reduces in the process the redundancy that could be present in the original program. It folds the tree into a finite graph of states and transitions between possible configurations of the computing system. It analyses global properties of the graph and specializes this graph w.r.t. these properties. The resulting definition is constructed solely based on the meta-interpretation of the source program rather than by a step-by-step transformation of the program. The size of the Scp4 system is about 19500 lines of commented source code (800 KB).

The REFAL language: The following program written in Refal replaces every occurrence of the identifier Lisp with Refal in an arbitrary Refal datum:

```
$ENTRY Go { e.inp = <Repl (Lisp Refal) e.inp>; }
Repl {(s.x e.v) = ;
      (s.x e.v) s.x e.inp = e.v <Repl (s.x e.v) e.inp>;
      (s.x e.v) s.y e.inp = s.y <Repl (s.x e.v) e.inp>;
      (s.x e.v) (e.y) e.inp = (<Repl (s.x e.v) e.y>)<Repl (s.x e.v) e.inp>;}
```

On the right side of the first sentence of Repl we see the empty expression (we denote it with []). Additional information about Refal can be found in [8,15].

---

* The author's current address is the first one.

M. Broy and A.V. Zamulin (Eds.): PSI 2003, LNCS 2890, pp. 162–170, 2003.
© Springer-Verlag Berlin Heidelberg 2003

Layout of SCP4: Given a program P and a number of parameterized input entries `tasks` of P, Scp4 transforms the pair P and `tasks` to decrease their run-time on specific input values of the parameters preserving at the same time their run-time on all the other data. By the run-time we mean logical time rather than a precise value of any physical clock. The transformer is allowed to extend the domains of the defined maps. We refer to the entries as the tasks to be solved by Scp4. We start with an analogy between the interpreter and Scp4

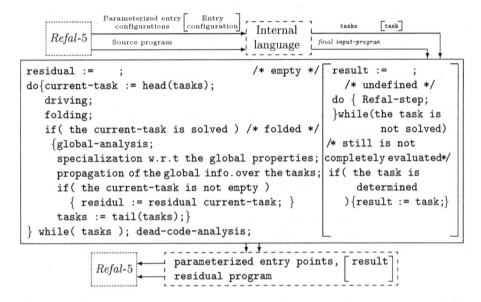

Fig. 1. General structure of Scp4 and [of the Refal interpreter]

(Fig. 1). Both the two systems work with an internal language, called Refal-graph language. Scp4 iterates an extension of the interpretation of Refal-graph steps, called *driving*, on parameterized sets of the input entries. Driving constructs a directed tree (cluster) of all possible computations for the given parameterized input entry and a given step. Edges of this tree are labeled with predicates over values of the parameters. The predicates specify concrete computation branches. Leaves contain parameterized entries to the next call of driving. The aim of driving is to perform as many actions uniformly on the parameterized input data as possible. The purpose of *folding* is to break up a task into subtasks, to transform the whole potential infinite tree derived by the driving iterations into a meta-structure – a graph of trees, and, finally, to fold infinite sub-branches of this graph of trees into some finite loops. The subtasks are the roots of the trees of possible computations. We say a task described in a node is solved if all branches starting in the node are folded. In this case some global properties of the sub-graph rooted in the node are analyzed and it is specialized w.r.t. the properties. If a current solved task is undefined on all values of the parameters then the branch incoming in the task node is pruned, otherwise the sub-graph outgoing from this node becomes a candidate for a residual function. Scp4 stops when the whole meta-graph has been folded, otherwise a strategy chooses a leaf for the following driving. The Scp4's output is defined in terms of the parameters.

1   Language of Parameters `ParL`

An input entry of a program, called a view field, determines the memory part to be evaluated by the abstract Refal-graph machine. One step of the machine is a logically closed transformation of the view field.

A language for describing some Refal datum sets.

```
pd  ::= [[ pos , neg ]]          neg ::= restriction, neg |[] | EMPTY-SET
pos ::= t pos₁ | empty           restriction ::= st₁ # st₂ | e.name # []
t   ::= p | DATA | (pos)         st ::= s.name | SYMBOL
p   ::= s.name | e.name | t.name empty ::= []              /* nihil */
```

A pair `[[pos,neg]]` is a positive and negative information. An `e.n` represents the set of all data, an `s.n` represents the set of the symbols and a `t.n` - the union of the symbol set and the set of all data enclosed in the parenthesis. `s.n1 # s.n2` means the parameters' ranges do not intersect. `[]` staying alone represents a tautology. "`,`" is a sign for intersection of the sets. *Parameterized sets of view fields and Refal-expressions:* There are no parameters, which domains contain function names or function application constructors. The encoded application constructor contains description of the domains of the function call arguments and the image of the call written in `pos`. The links between the elements of the stack are described by formal output variables `out.n`. E.g., `<F s.1>←out.1;` `<G <F e.2> out.1>←out.0;` The sign ← means an assignment of the left side to the right[1] one. We assume all trees are developed from the left to the right.

2   Internal Language

Input subset of the Refal-graph language is an applicative language based on pattern matching with syntactical means for describing the directed trees for analysis of all patterns (from a "function") at once. Nodes of the trees are functional, i.e. without backtracking. The patterns are explicitly decomposed using a finite set of patterns. Some negative information reflecting failure over the upper branches is written explicitly in `neg`. Every function is unary. The following two definitions specify a function `F` in Refal and in this input subset.

```
F { A   e.x = e.x;      │ F { +[1] e.inp→s.v e.u;
    s.y e.x = s.y e.x;  │     :{ +[1] s.v→A; {e.u←e.out;};};
          = ;           │        +[2] s.v # A; {s.v e.u←e.out;}; }
                        │    +[2] e.inp→[]; {[]←e.out;}; }
}
```

---

[1] We use the Turchin's arrow denotations [16] for describing the process of supercompiling. The meaning of the arrows is "the range of the part originating an arrow is narrowed to the range of the other part where the arrow incomes".

Where the arrow $\rightarrow$ is interpreted as matching of the variable's value from the left side with the pattern from the right side. The plus sign stands for an alternative.

Internal Language for Transformations. Programs in the input fragment are subjects only to be performed. Scp4 derives new programs in the whole transformation language. Colored graph nodes (see below) contain parameterized description of the stacks at the given points. The functionality of the nodes remains valid, they are named by their creation times. A function application may appear on an edge and its value may be tested along the edge. Functions may have nontrivial arities and co-arities. A fragment in the internal language:

```
F7 { +[1] e.1→[]; (I)←e.out;
     +[2] e.1→I e.11; {e.11←e.1;} <F7 e.1> {e.out←e.2;} e.2→(e.3);
         {e.11←e.1; e.3←e.4;} <F16 e.1, e.4> {e.out1←e.5;} {(e.5)←e.out;}
} /* Inductive Output Format: { (e.6)←e.out; } */
```

3 Driving

The driving is an extension of the interpretation of *one* graph (**gr**) **step** on the parameterized sets of the inputs. The aim is to perform as many actions of the machine uniformly on the parameter values as possible. A step of the machine consists of two stages. On the first stage the machine chooses a path from the root of a **gr** to a leaf, on the second the function stack is modified according to the environment **env** calculated on the first stage. The values of the variables from the current **env** match elementary patterns. Functionality of the nodes implies every node in the **gr**, for the sake of interpretation, is equal in its properties to the **gr** entry point: the pair (**gr**,**node**) can be considered as a function. The arity of the function is defined by the **env** of the node.Driving: $\mathbf{prog} \times \mathbf{name}_{node} \times \mathbf{PDenv} \mapsto \mathbf{Cluster}$, PDenv: vars $\mapsto$ pd   receives as an input a parameterized environment PDenv. When Driving reaches a branching-point (**bp**) it stores the current PDenv, takes the first edge outgoing from the node and tries consecutively to solve the equations with parameters p = pd, where the p-s are patterns labeling this edge and the pd-s are the parameterized values of the variables to be matched. Scp4 may extend the domain of the partial map defined by the parameterized entry and the program. That provides a possibility to use lazy evaluation in supercompile-time. I.e. the driving may be an extension of *one* step of a lazy graph machine. A *contraction* (contr) is var→pattern. Semantics: the value of the variable has to match the pattern. A contr is called elementary, iff contr $\in$ {e.n→(e.n$_1$) e.n$_2$, e.n→e.n$_1$ (e.n$_2$), e.n→S e .n$_1$, e.n→e.n$_1$ S, e.n→s.n$_1$ e.n$_2$, e.n→e.n$_1$ s.n$_2$, e.n→t.n$_1$ e.n$_2$, e.n→e.n$_1$ t.n$_2$, s.n→s .n$_1$, s.n→S, t.n→s.n$_1$, t.n→(e.n$_1$), t.n→S, e.n→[]}. S is a symbol. The patterns of the contr-s are called elementary.

Statement 1 *There is an algorithm [13] for solving any equation* $p = pexpr$ *(eq). p is an elementary pattern, pexpr is a parameterized expression. The result is: 1) the values of the p variables written in ParL; 2) or a directed finite tree* *splitting the eq parameters in the sub-cases, which predicates are written in the elementary contraction language and the leaves describe the pattern variables' values (from the right sides of these contr-s) written in ParL; 3) or information of eq has no roots; 4) or a call such that the eq solutions depend on its value.*

Reconstruction of the function stack: In the case of the lazy driving, a call <F_{nd} env> may be a hindrance for solving an equation. Then the call <F_{nd} env> is pushed out on the top of the stack in the closest bp. *The strategy for deriving of input formats:* The nodes of the driving cluster are painted in two colors distinguishing the *pivot* and the *secondary* points. If all leaves contain no function calls, then all bp-s are secondary, else 1) the left-most bp is pivot, all others are secondary; 2) if the root of the cluster is not a bp, then we paint it as secondary when there exist bp-s in the cluster. If there are no bp-s, then the step can be uniformly interpreted on the parameterized input data.

4   Folding

Folding folds the MTr of all possible computations in a finite graph. This tool takes into account only the pivot nodes. Those of them, which really fold the tree, are declared as basic. The tool tries to wrap the part of the path from the MTr root to a pivot node (CurNd) in the current driving cluster if such a node exists. The folding is divided in two tools: reducing and generalization.

Reducing: Let the call stack grow from the left to the right. Let it be split into a starting non-zero length segment (StSeg) and the tail part, then the computations on the stack are consequently performed by the StSeg and, afterwards, by the tail in the context of the env calculated during the first stage. Given a pivot CurNd, the reducing looks for another pivot node PrevNd on the above-mentioned path, such that there is a parameter substitution Subst that reduces the description of the previous set of stacks to the description of a StSeg of the CurNd. All computations defined by this StSeg, by means of the Subst, can be reduced to the computations defined by the PrevNd. The tail part of the current stack is declared as a separate task. If there is no suitable PrevNd, then the MTr remains unchanged, otherwise, the current stack is split into two; the first part of the task (defined in the current stack) for developing the MTr is reduced to the task considered before. An induction step on the structure describing the stack was exercised. Both the splitting of the stack and the reducing Subst define a set of sub-tasks: a decomposition of the tasks has occurred. The decomposition forms a sequence of the tasks for further developing. The subject to be folded is the path from the MTr root to the CurNd. The pivot nodes are run consequently along this path. Before every attempt to reduce the CurNd to the PrevNd, the reducing tries to reduce the CurNd to the basic nodes of the completely folded sub-trees. The parts of the MTr, which are under the basic nodes, are called the components of folding. They are the candidates for inclusion into the residual graph.

Generalization: From the point of view of generalization, the set of stacks in the pivot nodes from the partially folded `MTr` is a set of the induction hypotheses of every path in the tree will have a pivot node in a cluster of the driving such that the stack of the node will be completely reduced to the stacks of the other basic or pivot nodes existing in the `MTr` at the moment of the reducing attempt. The generalization is a tool for guaranteeing of finiteness of the number of these hypotheses. If the reducing did not find a pivot node to which the `CurNd` is reduced (maybe partially), then generalization looks for a pivot `PrevNd` (on the path from the root to the `CurNd`), which is "similar" to the pivot `CurNd`.

A Similarity relation links semantic loops in the `MTr` with syntactical structures in the `MTr`. The relation is the intersection of a relation of a pure function structure of the stacks (of a sequence of the call names syntactically being the uppermost calls (w.r.t. the composition) in each stack element) and similarity between the parameterized descriptions of the arguments of the different calls for the same functions. The following condition for approximation of loops in the `MTr` was suggested in Obninsk [14]. Let each function call for `F` be attributed by the time (F_t) the call was created during development of the `MTr`. Given two stacks labeled by the times - `Prev` and `Cur`, we say that this pair indicates a loop if the stacks can be represented in the form: `Prev = PrevTop; Context;` and `Cur = CurTop; Middle; Context; ,` where the bottom of the stacks is the length-most common part, i.e. this part nowise took part in the process developing of the stack along the path from the `PrevNd` to the `CurNd`, and their tops (`PrevTop =` $F1_{pt_1}, \dots,$ FN_{pt_n} and `CurTop =` $F1_{ct_1}, \dots,$ FN_{ct_n}) coincide modulo the times. `PrevTop` is called the entry point of the loop. The body of the loop is defined by the path from `PrevNd` to `CurNd`, that accumulates `Middle`. `Context` determines computations immediately after the loop. The definition reflects an assumed development of the stack as follows `PrevTop; Middle`^{n}`; Context` if `Middle` and `PrevTop` are considered modulo the times. In this case, if similarity of the considered nodes will be confirmed by other criteria, then the branches outgoing from the `PrevNd` are pruned and the task described in the node is split into the subtasks corresponding to the loop and the context. Consider a definition of the unary factorial.

```
$ENTRY IncFact { e.n = <Pl (I) (<Fact (e.n)>)>; }
Fact {     () = I;      (e.n) = <Times (e.n) (<Fact (<Min (e.n) (I)>)>)>;}
Times {(e.u) () = ;   (e.u) (I e.v) = <Pl (<Times (e.u) (e.v)>) (e.u)>;}
Pl { (e.u) () = e.u;          (e.u) (I e.v) = I <Pl (e.u) (e.v)>; }
Min { (I e.u) (I e.v) = <Min (e.u) (e.v)>;      (e.u) () = e.u; }
```

Lazy development of the stack along the main branch yields the sequence:
$\underline{1}$: $IncFact_1$;,$\underline{2}$: Pl_2;,$\underline{3}$: $Fact_4$; Pl_3;,$\underline{4}$: $Times_5$; Pl_3;,$\underline{5}$: $Fact_7$; $Times_6$; Pl_3;, ... The Obninsk condition indicates that the stack formed on the fifth step is similar to the stack created on the third step. A hypothesis is: the stack will further have the form `Fact`; `Times`^{n}; `Pl`$_3$;. Let a finite alphabet $A = \{a_i\}$, a $G: A \mapsto A^{\blacksquare}$ and an s $\in A^{\blacksquare}$ be given. Define a sequence st_n fixing the birth-times of the calls: (1) $st_0 =$ $(s,0)$; (2) defined $st_i = (a_i, t) \, u_i$, where $a_i \in A, t \in \mathbb{N}$ and u_i is the tail of st_i, then

st_{i+1} = Time(G(a_i),MaxTime) u_i, where MaxTime is the maximum on the second components of the pairs from st_i.Time(,t)=; Time(a w,t) = (a,t+1) Time(w,t+1); ,where a $\in A$, w $\in A^\square$. st_n is called the timed development of the stack (G,s).

Statement 1 *(V.F. Turchin [14]) Any development of a timed stack $stack_n$ is either finite or there exist natural numbers k , m such that $k > m$ and $stack_m$ = $(a_1, t_{m1})...(a_i, t_{mi})$* context*; $stack_k = (a_1, t_{k1})...(a_i, t_{ki})$* middle context*, where* middle *and* context *may have zero lengths. $(a_1, t_{m1})...(a_i, t_{mi})$ is called prefix.*

Every pivot node has a node - pro-image in the source graph. Every node in the input graph has a unique name. Scp4 considers the finite set of the names Fun_{nd} stored in the nodes by the driving and the stack reconstruction as an alphabet examined by Obninsk condition. Fun_{nd} completely specifies the structure of the env. A simplification ordering condition [11] specifies a similarity relation on the parts of the parameterized env-s $(a_j, t_{mj}),(a_j, t_{kj})$, which gives positive information of data. To fold the path in MTr, we have to reduce (by a Subst) the param. description of the env of the current prefix to the env of the previous prefix. If there are no such Subst-s, then the descriptions of these two env-s are subjects for generalization: a new parameterized env is constructed such the both prefix env-s can be reduced to the new env by some Subst-s of the parameters. The previous prefix is replaced with the generalized prefix. *Unfolding:* reconstructs the structures of the function stacks in the leaves of the driving cluster; chooses a leaf, which stack will be transformed by the next call for the driving.

5   Global Analysis

A pivot node was declared as basic and the sub-tree outgoing from the node is completely folded. An analysis of global properties of this component starts. The given component is the result of specialization of the program and simplification of its compositional structure. Any trivial transformations are very desirable at this moment of supercompilation, because further transformations of still unfolded parts of the MTr depend on their results. The principal point is to discover an output format of the component; breaking up a task into subtasks leads to the total loss of information about the images of the subtasks. An inductive output format is a common kind of the structure of the subtask image. The transformations on the basis of the global properties are able to decrease significantly time complexity of the programs [7,9]. *Derivation of the output formats* is critical when the length of the function stack of an input program is not uniformly bounded on the input data. Let us specialize the program: $ENTRY Go{e.n = <Pl (I I I) (e.n)>;}, where Pl (Sect.4) gives no information of the output structure of Pl. At the stage of constructing of its output format the folded component looks as: F7{+[1] e.1→[]; I I I←e.out;

+[2] e.1→I e.2; {e.2←e.1;} <F7 e.1> {e.out←e.3;};

I e.3←e.out;} (Output-Format e.out←e.out;)

Our algorithm constructs the inductive output format I e.4. *Analysis in terms of Refal* allows to transform simple recursive definitions to one-step programs. We give an example and refer the reader to [7]. `$ENTRY Go{e.str = <F e.str>;}` `F { s.1 = s.1; s.1 e.str = <F s.1> <F <F e.str>>; = ; }` The Scp4 output: `$ENTRY Go{e.inp = e.inp;}` The time complexity was decreased from $O(2^n)$ to $O(1)$. The domain of the partial map was extended. *Use of the global analysis results, repeated specialization:* An inductive output format of a recursive folded component P was constructed as a result of the analysis. We again are at the starting position to specialize P; because it may contain edge-references to itself and, hence, the information about the output structures was not used during the construction of P. Repeated specialization of P specializes P w.r.t. the structures of the output formats of the sub-graphs F_i, which P refers to. Let us change in Ex.1 Sect.4 only the entry point and the def. of Fact. `$ENTRY Go{e.n = <Fact (e.n)>;}`

`Fact{() = (I); (e.n) = (<Times (e.n) <Fact (<Min (e.n) (I)>)>>);}` The sub-graph corresponding to this task after the global analysis see in Sect.2,Ex.2.

Experiments:(P1,Min from Sect.4) (1) Specialization of P1 w.r.t. the 2nd arg. is not a surprise. Let us specialize it w.r.t. the 1st arg. The input entry: `$ENTRY Go{(e.n)(e.m)` `= <P1 (I e.n)(e.m)>;}`. The residual prog.: `$ENTRY Go{(e.n)(e.m) = I <F7 (e.n) e.m>;}` `F7{(e.1) = e.1; (e.1) I e.2 = I <F7 (e.1) e.2>;}` (2) Let the entry point for Min be `$ENTRY Go{(e.n) (e.m) = <Min (e.n) (I e.m)>;}`. The Scp4 output: `$ENTRY Go{(I e.n)(e.m) = <F6 (e.n) e.m>;}` `F6{ (I e.1) I e.2 = <F6 (e.1) e.2>;` `(e.1) = e.1;}` See the whole version of this paper [8] for examples of specialization of an interpreter w.r.t the examples given in this abstract and [4,5,6,9] for other examples.

References

1. A. P. Ershov. Mixed comp.: potential applications and problems for study. *Theoret. Comp. Science*, 18:41–67, 1982.
2. Y. Futamura and K. Nogi. Generalized partial computation. In *Proc. of the IFIP TC2 Workshop*, pp:133–151, 1988.
3. N. D. Jones, C. K. Gomard, P. Sestoft. *Partial Eval. and Automatic Program Generation*. Prentice Hall Intern., 1993.
4. A. V. Korlyukov. *User manual on the Supercompiler Scp4. (in Russian)*. http://www.refal.net/supercom.htm, 1999.
5. A. V. Korlyukov. *A number of examples of the program transformations with the supercompiler Scp4. (in Russian)*. http://www.refal.net/~korlukov/pearls/, 2001.
6. A. V. Korlyukov and A. P. Nemytykh. *Supercompilation of Double Interpretation*. http://www.refal.net/~korlukov/scp2int/Karliukou_Nemytykh.pdf , 2002.
7. A. P. Nemytykh. *A Note on Elimination of Simplest Recursions*. In *Proc. of ACM SIGPLAN Asia-PEPM'02*, 138–146, 2002.

8. A. P. Nemytykh. *The Supercomp. SCP4: Gen. Struct.* ftp://ftp.botik.ru/pub/local/scp/refal5/GenStruct.ps.gz, 2003.

9. A. P. Nemytykh and V. F. Turchin. *The Supercompiler Scp4: sources, on-line demonstration.* http://www.botik.ru/pub/local/scp/refal5/, 2000.

10. A. P. Nemytykh, V. A. Pinchuk, and V. F. Turchin. A Self-Applicable Supercompiler. *Proceeding of the PEPM'96, LNCS, Springer-Verlag*, 1110:322–337, 1996.

11. M. H. Sorensen, R. Glück. An algorithm of generalization in positive supercompilation. In *Logic Program.: Proc. of the 1995 Int. Symp.*, pp. 486–479. MIT, 1995.

12. V. F. Turchin, R. M. Nirenberg, D. V. Turchin. Experiments with a supercompiler. In *ACM Symposium on Lisp and Functional Programming*, ACM Press, 47–55, 1982.

13. V. F. Turchin. The concept of a supercompiler. *ACM TOPLAS*, 8:292–325, 1986.

14. V. F. Turchin. The algorithm of generalization in the supercompiler. In: *see reference to [2]*, pp. 531–549, 1988.

15. V. F. Turchin. *Refal-5, Programming Guide and Reference Manual.* New England Publishing Co.,1989.
(URL: http://www.botik.ru/pub/local/scp/refal5/ ,2000.).

16. V. F. Turchin. Supercompilation: Techniques and results. *Persp. of System Informatics, LNCS*, 1181:227–248, 1996.

17. V. F. Turchin, D. V. Turchin, A. P. Konyshev, and A. P. Nemytykh. *Refal-5: sources, executable modules.*
http://www.botik.ru/pub/local/scp/refal5/, 2000.

Partial Evaluation for Common Intermediate Language*

Andrei M. Chepovsky[1], Andrei V. Klimov[2], Arkady V. Klimov[2], Yuri A. Klimov[1], Andrei S. Mishchenko[1], Sergei A. Romanenko[2], and Sergei Yu. Skorobogatov[1]

[1] The CILPE Project, Department of Mechanics and Mathematics, Lomonosov Moscow State University, Vorobjovy Gory, Moscow, 119899, Russia
bfchep@mail.ru,
{yuri.klimov,andrei.mishchenko,sergei.skorobogatov}@cilpe.net
[2] Keldysh Institute for Applied Mathematics, Russian Academy of Sciences, 4 Miusskaya sq., Moscow, 125047, Russia
{klimov,arklimov,roman}@keldysh.ru

Abstract. Partial Evaluation is a well-established method for specialization of programs in functional languages. However, real-world applications demand specialization of object-oriented languages. With the advent of the Microsoft .NET platform with Common Intermediate Language (CIL), to which multiple languages are compiled, various program analysis and transformation techniques, including partial evaluation, can be developed once for a low-level language rather than over and over again to various high-level languages. The CILPE Project aims at developing a practical specializer for CIL programs based on Partial Evaluation with preliminary analysis referred to as Binding Time Analysis (BTA). The CILPE Specializer partially evaluates operations on values and objects determined by BTA as static. Static objects are created, processed and destroyed at specialization time; they may be mutable and can have some fields unknown (dynamic). Arbitrary verifiable CIL code is allowed as input.

Keywords: Program transformation, Partial Evaluation, polyvariant Binding-Time Analysis, mutable objects, object-oriented languages, Common Intermediate Language.

1 Introduction

Partial Evaluation is a well-established method for specialization of programs in functional languages with a track record of two decades of research [9]. However, neither it, nor its sister technology Supercompilation [15], is used in real-world applications yet. The most serious impediment was that only languages like C/C++ were considered industrial, while these were unsuitable for program analysis and transformation, because of the complexity of their semantics based

---

* Supported by Microsoft Research grant No. 2002-83.

M. Broy and A.V. Zamulin (Eds.): PSI 2003, LNCS 2890, pp. 171–177, 2003.

on explicit von Neumann memory model (unmanageable pointers). With the advent of such theoretically sound platforms as Java and Microsoft .NET, the way for Partial Evaluation and Supercompilation to industrial programming has got rid of the main obstacle.

The project codenamed CILPE (Partial Evaluation for Common Intermediate Language) aims at finding sufficient level of partial evaluation development to specialize real-world object-oriented programs. The CILPE specializer manipulates immutable data of value types like partial evaluators for first-order functional languages [9]. Additionally, the Binding Time Analysis (BTA) of the CILPE specializer separates out some possibly mutable objects as *static* as well. Static objects are created, processed and destroyed ("garbage-collected") at specialization time. Non-static objects are referred to as *dynamic*. No operations on dynamic objects are performed at specialization time; all of them are *residualized*, that is, put to a *residual* program. Static objects may have dynamic fields, which become local variables in the residual program. The main difference of static objects with (partially known) static values is the absence of "lifting" operation for objects: a static object exists only at specialization time and cannot remain for runtime, while a copy of a static data of value type can be reconstructed at a program point where it is needed at runtime.

The CILPE Binding Time Analysis is *polyvariant*, that is, it builds several separations of source program entities (classes, methods, statements, variables) into static and dynamic, if needed. The maximum number of variants is controlled by user-defined limits.

Terminological Note. The term "static" is used in this paper in the Partial Evaluation sense: it indicates program entities that deal with information known at specialization time. We avoid referring to the `static` modifier of class fields and methods, except example code in Fig.1.

2   Example

Fig. 1 shows the famous `ToPower` example (often used in papers on Partial Evaluation after the seminal paper [6]). It is rewritten in C# and augmented by an auxiliary object `a` to demonstrate a distinguishing feature of the CILPE specializer: the static object `a` disappears after specialization.

The `ToPower` method raises the first argument `float x` to power `n`, supplied by the second argument. The actual computation is done by the `Do_ToPower` method, which receives arguments `x` and `n` packed into the instance `a` of an auxiliary class `ArgsAndResult`, together with a field with initial value for `y`, which eventually contains the result of computation.

The `ToPower5` method is a use sample of method `ToPower`, where exponent `n` is set to known value 5. The residual code for the `ToPower5` method is shown in the right-hand side column. The invocations of methods `ToPower` and `Do_ToPower`, as well as the `while` and `if` statements are executed at specialization time, and only multiplications of dynamic values remain.

In this example, the result of BTA for the particular invocation of the ToPower is *monovariant*, than is, source code entities are annotated only once. Static variables, expressions and statements are underlined. Another usage of ToPower may give rise to another annotation; e.g., if one asks CILPE to optimize method ToPower, field n will be dynamic like x and y, while object a as a whole will remain static still.

After specialization, the dynamic fields a.x and a.y of static object a turn into local variables of the residual program, denoted as a_x and a_y in Fig.1.

To apply CILPE, one compiles the program from C# to CIL. Then the CIL code is submitted to the CILPE system along with a task to optimize method ToPower5. CILPE returns code in CIL; its equivalent in C# is shown in Fig.1.

```
class ArgsAndResult {
  public float x, y; public int n;
  public ArgsAndResult(float x, int n, float y) {
    this.x = x; this.n = n; this.y = y;
} }
static void Do_ToPower(ArgsAndResult a) {
  while (a.n != 0) {
    if (a.n % 2 == 1) {
      a.n--;
      a.y *= a.x;
    } else {
      a.n /= 2;
      a.x *= a.x;
} } }
static float ToPower(float x, int n) {
  ArgsAndResult a =
    new ArgsAndResult(x, n, 1);
  Do_ToPower(a);
  return a.y;
}
static float ToPower5(float x) {
  return ToPower(x, 5);
}
```

```
static float
  ToPower5(float x)
{
  float a_x;
  float a_y;
  a_x = x;
  a_y = 1;
  a_y *= a_x;
  a_x *= a_x;
  a_x *= a_x;
  a_y *= a_x;
  return a_y;
}
```

Fig. 1. An example of specialization: Static parts of source code in C# are underlined. See residual method ToPower5 on the right. CILPE returns an equivalent code in CIL

3 CILPE Architecture

A deployment program unit in the .NET framework is referred to as assembly. An assembly contains a collection of classes. The first version of the CILPE specializer takes one assembly as input along with information about specialization task given by a user, and returns an assembly, which looks like the original one from the outside, but part of its code has been replaced and some classes contain additional methods that are specialized versions of some of the original methods.

Information flows through CILPE subsystems in that order:

- *Assembly import:* An assembly is read, verified and converted to internal representation in form of Control Flow Graph (CFG).
- *Binding Time Analysis (BTA):* CIL instructions in CFG are annotated as static, dynamic or special. To represent polyvariant Binding Time annotation respective CFG parts are cloned.
- *Specializer proper:* The static part of the annotated code is interpreted with known data. Now CILPE specializes with respect to known information in source code only. In future, external sources like files will be used as well.
- *Post-processing:* Specialization clears the way for further optimizations. A variable use analysis along with some peephole optimizations are applied to find and delete extra local variables and operations.
- *Assembly export:* The residual CFG is converted to CIL and output to a file.

4   Basic Principles

The specializer performs computations on the values of local variables, parameters, evaluation stack slots, instances in heap and their fields, which are annotated by BTA as static. All operations on dynamic data are residualized, that is, put to the resulting program in the same order as they occur in the source program.

Data Representation. Static data can be either somehow encoded in the specializer, or represented "as is", in the same way as in ordinary computation. Starting from [11], all partial evaluators for untyped functional languages use the "as is" representation, which simplifies the system and speeds up specialization. However, specializers as well as interpreters of typed languages have to encode values, to wrap them in some universal data type.

Although CIL is a typed object-oriented language, it turned out that static objects can be represented "as is" by objects of respective classes, while the values of local variables, parameters and evaluation stack slots are wrapped in some universal class. The encoding is also required to manipulate boxed values and pointers.

Static objects exist only at specialization time. Unlike primitive values, static objects cannot be "lifted", i.e., get dynamic. Some fields of a static instance may be dynamic. Each dynamic field of a static instance is residualized as a new local variable. The specializer manipulates the values of static fields and does not look into dynamic fields, which carry zeros or nulls as fillers at specialization-time.

In contrast, all elements of a static array have the same binding time annotation. An array is static only if all accesses to its elements are performed by way of static indexes. In other respects, arrays are similar to objects. In future, we plan to evaluate constant subexpressions in BTA to distinguish array elements, where possible.

Dynamic objects are residualized, and no operations on them are partially evaluated. Hence, all fields of dynamic objects are dynamic. In future, we plan to elaborate a hybrid static-dynamic kind of objects, which are residualized but the information from part of their fields is known.

Aggregate data of value types pose no new problems as compared to objects. Values behave like immutable objects with equality by value rather than by reference. Locations where values are stored behave like mutable objects. Pointers can refer to locations or to the fields of stored values.

Graph Traversal. The specializer walks along the source program graph like an ordinary interpreter keeping the state of only static entities instead of the complete program state in the interpreter. But unlike the interpreter, after a branching the specializer has to walk though all branches in turn with the same initial state. In functional languages and in the limited case of immutable objects, it is sufficient to remember a reference to the representation of a state before branching and use it several times. However, mutable objects cannot be processed in this way. The CILPE specializer utilizes memoization to restore program states at branching points.

Memoization. To build loops and catch recursion, to generate several invocations to one residual method or several control transfers to one program point, the specializer memoizes certain residual program points, that is, stores the reference to a program point together with its static state. When a program point with an equal static state is met, a method invocation or a control transfer instruction is residualized.

Binding Time Analysis. BTA annotates source program instructions by information of the following kind:

- S (static): an instruction is to be executed by the specializer.
- D (dynamic): an instruction is to be residualized, that is, output to the residual program "as is".
- Static object creation instructions are supplied with the list of dynamic fields.
- Instructions to load/store a dynamic field (element) of a static object (array), including indirect ones, are annotated by a directive to turn it to an instruction to load/store a local variable.
- A method invocation instruction is annotated to be either inlined, or residualized. In the latter case, ether the original method is invoked, or a newly created specialized version of the original method. (There is no problem to invoke interface and virtual methods on static objects, since their types are known by the specializer proper, although BTA does not known them.)
- Special "lifting" instructions are inserted to turn a static value into instruction(s) to load an equal value onto the evaluation stack at runtime.

The details of the polyvariant BTA in CILPE will be described elsewhere.

5   Future Work

Future research into partial evaluation of CIL will include:

- Hybrid *static-dynamic* objects that remain in residual program, but some operations on them are executed (as in [1], but for objects)
- Evaluation of constant subexpressions in BTA to distinguish array elements
- Binding Time Analysis by a constraint solver to speed-up BTA
- Termination of the polyvariant BTA as well as that of the specializer
- A compiling version of the specializer, which produces a generating extension [6] of a source program with respect to an initial binding time annotation
- Self-application of the CILPE specializer
- Post-processing: better analysis to remove unneeded variables and computations; minimization of the number of local variables; arity raising [12] etc.
- Expansion of the methods to the next version of CIL with type polymorphism
- Last but not least: development of methods to successfully apply the specializer to real-world object-oriented programs

6   Related Work

A lot of research has been carried out in the field of Partial Evaluation and other program transformation for functional languages. The handbook [9] summed up the Partial Evaluation achievements obtained during 80s and early 90s. On the other hand, surprisingly little work has been done for object-oriented languages despite evident practical significance.

The first attempt to specialize object-oriented programs was made more than a decade ago [10]. Interestingly, the authors studied an online specializer, which does not contain BTA. They achieved some initial results for a toy language.

In [2] the problem of side-effect was studied in extended lambda-calculus. However, their single goal was to separate mutable and immutable data and to correctly residualize all accesses to mutable data. Only accesses to immutable data could be partially evaluated.

A similar goal to develop a partial evaluator for an object-oriented language (Java) is put forward in the COMPOSE Project [13]. However, the most recent publication [14] that we have found, deals only with immutable objects.

An interesting work was done by Peter Bertelsen [3] for a subset of Java byte code. The subset included primitive integer type and array type. No objects, no interfaces, all methods are static. Thus, it deals with only arrays of integers, arrays of arrays of integers etc. However, the main idea of partially static objects/arrays with dynamic fields/elements was demonstrated.

Partial evaluation of Evolving Algebras (a.k.a. Abstract State Machines) [8] resembles specialization of functional languages (even self-application has been achieved [4]). It is attractive to extend it to cover object-oriented notions.

A complementary approach to specialization is Supercompilation [15]. It would be interesting to compare the power of the CILPE specializer with that of the Java Supercompiler [7]. We expect CILPE will do its work much faster than the Supercompiler, but the later is capable of deeper specialization.

References

1. Kenichi Asai: Binding-Time Analysis for Both Static and Dynamic Expressions. In A. Cortesi, G. File (eds.): *Static Analysis, 6th International Symposium, SAS'99*, Venice, Italy, September 1999. LNCS 1694, Springer-Verlag 1999, pages 117–133.

2. Kenichi Asai, Hidehiko Masuhara, Akinori Yonezawa: Partial Evaluation of Call–by-value lambda-calculus with Side-effects. In *Proceedings of the 1997 ACM SIG-PLAN Symposium on Partial Evaluation and Semantics-based Program Manipulation*, ACM Press, New York, NY, USA, pages 12–21.

3. Peter Bertelsen: *Binding-time analysis for a JVM core language*, April 1999. ftp://ftp.dina.kvl.dk/pub/Staff/Peter.Bertelsen/bta-core-jvm.ps.gz

4. V. Di Iorio, R. Bigonha, and M. Maia: A Self-Applicable Partial Evaluator for ASM. In Y. Gurevich, P. Kutter, M. Odersky, and L. Thiele (eds.): *Abstract State Machines – ASM 2000, International Workshop on Abstract State Machines, Monte Verita, Switzerland, Local Proceedings*, number 87 in TIK-Report, pages 115–130. Swiss Federal Institute of Technology (ETH) Zurich, March 2000.

5. ECMA International: *Common Language Infrastructure (CLI), Standard ECMA-335*, 2nd edition (December 2002). http://www.ecma-international.org/publications/standards/ecma-335.htm

6. Andrei P. Ershov: On the essence of compilation. *Programmirovanie* (5):21–39, 1977 (in Russian). See translation in: E.J.Neuhold, ed., *Formal description of Programming Concepts*, North-Holland, 1978, pages 391–420.

7. Ben Goertzel, Andrei V. Klimov, Arkady V. Klimov: *Supercompiling Java Programs*, white paper, Supercompilers LLC, 2002. http://www.supercompilers.com

8. Y. Gurevich and J. Huggins: Evolving Algebras and Partial Evaluation. In B. Pehrson and I. Simon (eds.): *IFIP 13th World Computer Congress*, volume I: Technology/Foundations, pages 587–592, Elsevier, Amsterdam, 1994.

9. Neil D. Jones, Carsten K. Gomard, Peter Sestoft: *Partial evaluation and automatic program generation*. Prentice-Hall, Inc., Upper Saddle River, NJ, 1993.

10. Morten Marquard, Bjarne Steensgaard: *Partial Evaluation of an Object-Oriented Imperative Language*, Master's Thesis, Department of Computer Science, University of Copenhagen, Denmark, April 1992. ftp://ftp.research.microsoft.com/users/rusa/thesis.ps.Z

11. Sergei A. Romanenko: A Compiler Generator Produced by a Self-Applicable Specializer Can have a Surprisingly Natural and Understandable Structure. In D. Bjorner, A. P. Ershov, and N. D. Jones (eds.): *Workshop on Partial Evaluation and Mixed Computation*, GI. Avernaxs, Denmark, October 1987, North-Holland, 1988, pages 445–463.

12. Sergei A. Romanenko: Arity Raiser and Its Use in Program Specialization. In N.Jones (ed.): *ESOP'90, 3rd European Symposium on Programming*, Copenhagen, Denmark, May 15–18, 1990, LNCS 432, Springer-Verlag 1990, pages 341–360.

13. Ulrik P. Schultz, Julia L. Lawall, Charles Consel, Gilles Muller: Towards Automatic Specialization of Java Programs. *13th European Conference on Object-Oriented Programming (ECOOP'99)*, Lisbon, Portugal, June 1999. LNCS 1628, Springer-Verlag 1999, pages 367–390.

14. Ulrik P. Schultz: Partial Evaluation for Class-Based Object-Oriented Languages. In O. Danvy, A. Filinski (eds.): *Program as Data Objects, Second Symposium, PADO 2001*, Aarhus, Denmark, May 21-23, 2001. LNCS 2053, Springer-Verlag 2001, pages 173–197.

15. Valentin F. Turchin: The concept of a supercompiler. *ACM Transactions on Programming Languages and Systems*, 8, 1986, pages 292–325.

Timed Verification with μCRL

Stefan Blom[1], Natalia Ioustinova[1], and Natalia Sidorova[2]

[1] Department of Software Engineering, CWI
P.O. Box 94079, 1090 GB Amsterdam, The Netherlands
{Stefan.Blom, Natalia.Ioustinova}@cwi.nl
[2] Department of Mathematics and Computer Science
Eindhoven University of Technology
Den Dolech 2, P.O. Box 513, 5612 MB Eindhoven, The Netherlands
n.sidorova@tue.nl

Abstract. μCRL is a process algebraic language for specification and verification of distributed systems. μCRL allows to describe temporal properties of distributed systems but it has no explicit reference to time. In this work we propose a manner of introducing discrete time without extending the language. The semantics of discrete time we use makes it possible to reduce the time progress problem to the diagnostics of "no action is enabled" situations. The synchronous nature of the language facilitates the task. We show some experimental verification results obtained on a timed communication protocol.

Keywords: modelling, verification, discrete time, μCRL, model checking.

1 Introduction

The specification language μCRL [8] (micro Common Representation Language) is a process algebraic language that was especially developed to take account of data in the study of communicating processes. The μCRL toolset [5] provides support for enumerative model checking. One of the most important application areas for μCRL is specification and verification of communication protocols. Communication protocols are mostly *timed* systems. A common way to use time is the timeout. In some cases it is possible to abstract from duration and simulate timeouts with non deterministic choice. However, in other cases the lengths of the timeouts are essential to the correctness of the protocol. To deal with these cases one needs an explicit notion of time.

In [10], a timed version of the μCRL language is proposed where time is incorporated in μCRL as an abstract data type satisfying a few conditions plus a construct to make an action happen at a specific time. The timed version of the language turned out to be useful as a formalism for the specification and analysis of hybrid systems [9]. However, it is not clear yet whether timed μCRL can be used to analyse larger systems than the examples considered in the paper. Moreover, some of the existing tools cannot be used for timed μCRL without

M. Broy and A.V. Zamulin (Eds.): PSI 2003, LNCS 2890, pp. 178–192, 2003.
© Springer-Verlag Berlin Heidelberg 2003

modification. Most importantly, timed μCRL is incompatible with linearisation (translating a specification into the intermediate format) and with partial order reduction.

The goal of the work we present in this paper is to establish a framework in which timed verification may proceed using the existing untimed tools. The reason why we want to do this is that real life systems tend to consist of both timed and untimed components. Timed tools are very good at detailed analysis of the timed components of these systems, but cannot be used for analysing the whole system.

To achieve the goal of timed verification with untimed tools, we must restrict ourselves to discrete relative time: the state spaces of systems with dense or absolute time are almost always infinite. Techniques, such as regions and zones, which allow finite representations of such infinite state spaces, are not implemented in the untimed tools. Timestamping actions with "absolute" time, as is done in timed μCRL, leads to infinite state spaces in case of unbounded delays: Consider the process $X = \sum_{t=0}^{\infty} \mathsf{a}@t$ which uses time tags (the @ symbol must be read as "at time") and thus can do action a at any time. The transition system of X consists of 2 states and infinitely many transitions. For this reason, we have chosen a "relative" time solution. Namely, we introduce time through an action tick, which by convention expresses one unit of time elapsing. In this case we can specify the process that can do a at any time as $Y = \mathsf{tick}.Y + \mathsf{a}$. The transition system of process Y has two states and two transitions. The advantage of representing time progression as an action is that we stay within the syntax of μCRL. Moreover, the special use of tick is compatible with the semantics of μCRL and hence the existing toolset can be used for analysis and verification.

The proposed discrete time semantics is suitable to express time aspects and analyse time properties of a large class of systems. We argue the usefulness of our approach with the verification experiments on a μCRL specification of the positive acknowledgment retransmission protocol (PAR) [15], whose behaviour depends on the timers' settings.

To express *timed* properties of systems, we introduce an LTL-like timed temporal logic on actions and show how to encode its timed constraints with the use of tick, which results in *untimed* temporal formulas. These formulas can be then translated to μ-calculus and checked with the μCRL toolset.

The rest of the paper is organized as follows. In the following Section 2, we sketch the syntax and semantics of μCRL. In Section 3 we present the discrete time semantics that we work with and afterwards in Section 4 we explain how timed specifications can be developed within the untimed framework with following the proposed approach. In Section 5 we discuss some experimental results. In section 6 we introduce a timed temporal logic. We conclude in Section 7 with discussing the related works and the directions for the future work.

```
sort Bool
func T,F: ->Bool
map  eq,and:Bool#Bool->Bool
var  b:Bool
rew  eq(b,b)=T
     eq(T,F)=F
     eq(F,T)=F
     and(T,b)=b
     and(F,b)=F
```

Fig. 1. A μCRL specification of the sort Bool

```
act  a
     b,c:Bool
proc X=a.X
     Y=sum(b':Bool,b(b')).c(b').Y)
     Y'(b1:Bool,state:Bool)=
          sum(b':Bool,b(b')).Y'(b',F)<|eq(state,T)|>delta+
          c(b1).Y'(b',T)<|eq(state,F)|>delta
```

Fig. 2. Components in μCRL

2 μCRL: Basic Notions

The specification language μCRL (micro Common Representation Language) is essentially an extension of the process algebra ACP with abstract data types and recursive definitions. The μCRL toolset provides tool support for a subset of the μCRL language. In the remainder of this section, we will give an overview of both the language and its tool support. Details about the language can be found in [10]. Details about the tool support can be found in [5].

Data in μCRL is specified using equational abstract data types. Every μCRL specification must include a specification of the sort Bool, which represents the booleans. An example can be found in Fig. 1. Although the language specification does not require them, the tool support requires the function eq : D#D-> Bool for every sort D and the boolean function **and**. The equations following the keyword rew are oriented from left to right and used as rewrite rules by the tools, but may be used in both directions for reasoning.

The usual way of modeling a system in μCRL is to decompose the system into components and then specify the components and their interactions separately.

Components are usually recursively defined using atomic actions, alternative composition and conditionals. For example, in Fig. 2 we have specified processes X and Y. Process X simply repeats action a infinitely often. Process Y infinitely often chooses between T and F nondeterministically and performs b and c with the same choice as argument.

Component processes can be glued into a system using parallel composition, encapsulation, hiding and renaming operators. The parallel composition operator of μCRL combines two processes into a single process by allowing nondeterministic choice between interleaving the actions of the two processes and synchronous interaction (communication) of an action from each of the processes. Other types of parallel composition operators can be defined in terms of the basic operators. For example, the operator |{tick}| which lets the processes X and Y run interleaved except for the action tick, which must be performed synchronously by both X and Y may be encoded as follows:

```
act  tick tick'
comm tick|tick=tick'
     X |{tick}| Y = rename({tick'->tick},encap({tick},X||Y))
```

In this encoding we have a process X||Y where tick actions from X and Y may be performed interleaved or at the same time resulting in a tick'. In the process encap({tick},X||Y) the interleaved execution is disallowed by means of encapsulation. Finally the tick' is renamed to tick to get the desired result. Note that interaction is not limited to two parties. The result of an interaction may itself interact. For example, the interaction of actions a, b and c, resulting in action d can be expressed as

```
comm    a|b=ab b|c=bc a|c=ac    a|bc=d b|ac=d c|ab=d
```

Tool support for μCRL is centered around the linear process format. A linear specification consists of a single recursive process, which can choose between possibilities of the form action followed by a recursive call:

$$\text{proc } X(d_1 : D_1 \cdots, d_n : D_n) =$$
$$\sum_{e_{11}:E_{11}} \cdots \sum_{e_{1n_1}:E_{1n_1}} a_1(s_1).X(t_1) \lhd c_1 \rhd \delta+$$
$$\vdots$$
$$\sum_{e_{k1}:E_{k1}} \cdots \sum_{e_{kn_k}:E_{kn_k}} a_k(s_k).X(t_k) \lhd c_k \rhd \delta+$$
$$\text{init } X(t_0)$$

The toolset allows the transformation of specifications into linear form (on Fig. 2, process Y' is a linear equivalent of process Y), the optimisation of specification in linear form, the simulation of a linear specification, and the generation of a Labelled Transition System (LTS) from a linear specification. The toolset allows the user to apply a partial order method based on τ-confluence. Partial order reduction guarantees that the reduced state space is branching bisimilar to the original state space. Branching bisimulation preserves CTL*-X properties [13], so all CTL*-X properties are preserved by partial order reduction.

3   Semantics of Time

In this section we discuss what time semantics is appropriate for our purpose.

The first choice to be made is a choice between dense and discrete time. It is normally assumed that real-time systems operate in "real", continuous time (though some physicists contest against the statement that the changes of a system state may occur at any real-numbered time point). Due to the development of regions and zones techniques [1] the verification of real-time systems became possible. However, a less expensive, discrete time solution is for many systems as good as dense time in the modelling sense, and better than the dense one when the verification is concerned: [11] showed that discrete time suffices for a large and important class of systems and properties including all systems that can be modelled as timed transition systems and such properties as time-bounded invariance and time-bounded response. Another work that compares the use of dense and discrete time is [7]; the authors state that discrete time automata can be analysed using any representation scheme used for dense time, and *in addition* can benefit from enumerative and symbolic techniques (such as BDDs) which are not naturally applicable to dense time. Having in mind that we should not step out the current non-timed framework of μCRL the choice for discrete time is obvious.

The nature of systems under consideration suggests the choice for timers, not clocks: expiration of a timer is a natural way to model an interruption for hardware or a trigger for a software event. Both interrupt and software event must be handled, and they must be handled exactly once, i.e. with taking an event guarded by a timer condition, we assume that the timer which triggered this event became deactivated (otherwise, the system could handle one event several times). Time progresses by decreasing the values of all active timers by one time unit. We will refer to the time progress action as tick and to the period of time between two tick's as a time slice.

We consider a class of systems where delays are significantly larger than the duration of normal events within the system. Therefore, we assume system transitions to be instantaneous. This assumption leads us to the conclusion that time progress can never take place if there is still an untimed action enabled, or in other words, the time-progress transition has the least priority in the system and may take place only when the system is *blocked*: there is no any transition enabled except for time progress and communication with the environment.

4   Specifying Timed Systems in μCRL

In the μCRL framework, we can implement timers as data parameterising processes. Figure 3 shows the specification of the sort Timer. Terms on(n) stand for active timers (n is of sort natural numbers) while deactivated timers are represented by off terms. (Note that μCRL specifications containing sort Timer should also include sort Nat providing operation pred that decreases a non-zero natural number by one and operation eq checking for the equality of two numbers.) The operations we allow on timers are (1) setting a timer to a value given by a natural number that shows the time delay left until the timer expiration; (2) resetting a timer (setting it to off). Timer expiration condition given by

```
sort Timer                              var  t:Timer
func off:-> Timer                            n:Nat
     on:Nat->Timer                      rew  expired(off)=F
map  pred:Timer->Timer                       expired(on(n))=eq(0,n)
     expired:Timer->Bool                     pred(on(n))=on(pred(n))
     set: Timer # Nat -> Timer               pred(off)=off
     reset: Timer -> Timer                   set(t, n)=on(n)
                                             reset(t)=off
```

Fig. 3. A μCRL specification of the sort Timer

predicate `expired` is the check whether the delay until the timer expiration is zero. We assume that the action guarded by the timer expiration is normally resetting the timer or setting it to a positive value, though we leave the designer the freedom to continue considering the timer as set to `on(0)`.

Following the time semantics described in Section 3, we want to model the time progress by the `tick` action, which is a global action decreasing all active timers of the system by one and enabled only when the system is blocked. To achieve this, we enable the `tick` action in a component if that component is blocked and if every timer in that component is off or non-zero. By combining components with the `|{tick}|` operator as defined in Section 2 rather than the standard `||` operator we get precisely the desired behaviour.

A system is considered blocked if there are no *urgent* actions possible. As μCRL has no priority mechanism, there is a potential for technical problems, which we solve by following a specification discipline.

First, we classify a number of actions as *urgent*. Enabled *internal* operators are urgent — they take zero time and, hence, they may not be postponed until the next time slice, and `tick` may not be proposed as an alternative to an internal action. The situation with the *communication* is more complicated: When the two communicating parties are both ready to communicate, the communication should take place in the current time slice. Thus, no `tick` action can be given as an alternative to a communication action. However, when only one of the parties

$$\textbf{proc } A(t_1 : Timer \cdots, t_m : Timer, d_1 : D_1 \cdots, d_n : D_n) =$$
$$a_1.X_1(\boldsymbol{t}_1, \boldsymbol{y}_1) \triangleleft expired(t_1) \triangleright \delta+$$
$$\vdots$$
$$a_m.X_m(\boldsymbol{t}_m, \boldsymbol{y}_m) \triangleleft expired(t_m) \triangleright \delta+$$
$$tick.A(pred(\boldsymbol{t}), \boldsymbol{d}) \triangleleft not(\textstyle\bigvee_{j=1}^n expired(t_j)) \triangleright \delta+$$
$$\textstyle\sum_{d_{11}:D_{11}} \cdots \sum_{d_{1n_1}:d_{1n_1}} in_1(\boldsymbol{s}_1).X_1^{\blacksquare}(\boldsymbol{t}_1^{\blacksquare}, \boldsymbol{x}_1) \triangleleft c_1 \triangleright \delta+$$
$$\vdots$$
$$\textstyle\sum_{d_{k1}:D_{k1}} \cdots \sum_{d_{kn_k}:D_{kn_k}} in_k(\boldsymbol{s}_k).X_k^{\blacksquare}(\boldsymbol{t}_k^{\blacksquare}, \boldsymbol{x}_k) \triangleleft c_k \triangleright \delta$$

Fig. 4. Pattern of an input state

$$\text{proc } B(t_1 : Timer \cdots, t_m : Timer, d_1 : D_1 \cdots, d_n : D_n) =$$
$$\sum\nolimits_{d_{11}:D_{11}} \cdots \sum\nolimits_{d_{1n_1}:D_{1n_1}} a_1(s_1).X_1(t, x_1) \lhd c_1 \rhd \delta +$$
$$\vdots$$
$$\sum\nolimits_{d_{k1}:D_{k1}} \cdots \sum\nolimits_{d_{kn_k}:D_{kn_k}} a_k(s_k).X_n(t, x_n) \lhd c_k \rhd \delta$$

Fig. 5. Pattern of a non-input state

is willing to communicate, time progress should *not* be disabled, meaning that the process willing to communicate but not having this chance yet, should be able to take the `tick` action. We resolve the problem by introducing the asymmetry into communication: Though μCRL has no notions of "sender" and "receiver", it is rather usual for a large class of systems to distinguish between the sending and the receiving party in the communication action. Moreover, it is logical to expect for a correct specification that sendings take place in the time slice when they become enabled; otherwise the communication cannot be seen as synchronous and should go via a channel. Input, or reception, can be postponed until the next time slice. Consequently, we allow `tick` as an alternative to an input action and not to an output action.

The classification of actions results in the classification of process states: We require every state to be either an *input state*, i.e. a state where only input actions can be enabled, or a *non-input state*, i.e. a state where outputs and internal actions can be taken. The check that the specification meets this requirement can be easily automated by introducing conventional names for input and output actions. To simplify matters further, we have used patterns for specifying states of components as μCRL processes.

The patterns of input and non-input states are given in Fig. 4 and 5, respectively. In these patterns, all μCRL processes which correspond to states in a component have the same list of parameters. For a component with m timers and n other variables, the first m parameters are timers and the next n are the other variables. Input and non-input states have different transitions: In an input state, we have timer expiration events for expired timers, `tick` if no timer is expired and receive actions. In non-input states, we have send actions and internal actions. After a `tick` action, all active timers are decreased and everything else remains the same. After a read or send action, timers may be set or reset, data parameters can be modified and the state may change.

When we build a system from components, we must not only make sure that time progression is handled correctly but also that all messages sent on the set of internal channels I are kept within the system. The first means using $|\{tick\}|$, the latter means encapsulation of the send and receive actions for the channels in I. That is, a system with N components and internal channels I is described by the following μCRL init statement:

$$\text{init encap}(\{s_i, r_i\}_{i \in I}, C_1 \mid \{tick\} \mid \cdots \mid \{tick\} \mid C_N)$$

In Fig. 6 we give a pictorial representation and μCRL code of a simple watchdog. On channel 1, the watchdog receives a delay. While within that delay a new delay is sent the watchdog keeps waiting. If the watchdog times out then a message will be sent on channel 2.

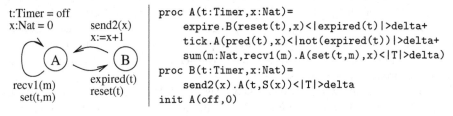

```
t:Timer = off                              proc A(t:Timer,x:Nat)=
x:Nat = 0           send2(x)                   expire.B(reset(t),x)<|expired(t)|>delta+
                    x:=x+1                      tick.A(pred(t),x)<|not(expired(t))|>delta+
    A         B                                 sum(m:Nat,recv1(m).A(set(t,m),x)<|T|>delta)
                                           proc B(t:Timer,x:Nat)=
recv1(m)            expired(t)                  send2(x).A(t,S(x))<|T|>delta
set(t,m)            reset(t)               init A(off,0)
```

Fig. 6. A simple component

5   Experiments

We have tested our approach on a number of examples one of which was a positive acknowledgment retransmission protocol (PAR) [15]. This is a classical example of a communication protocol in which time issues are essential for correct functionality. The usual scenario includes a sender, a receiver, a message channel and an acknowledgment channel. The sender receives a frame from the upper layer, sends it to the receiver via the message channel and waits for a positive acknowledgment from the receiver via acknowledgment channel. When the receiver delivered the message to the upper layer it sends the acknowledgement to the sender. After the positive acknowledgment is received, the sender becomes ready to send next message. The receiver needs some time to deliver the received frame to the upper layer. The channels delay the delivery of messages as well. Moreover, they can lose or corrupt messages. Therefore, the sender handles lost frames by timing out. If the sender times out, it re-sends the message.

The possible erroneous scenario is following. The sender times out while the acknowledgement is still on the way. The sender sends a duplicate, then receives the acknowledgment and believes that this is the acknowledgment for the duplicate. The sender sends the next frame, which gets lost. The sender receives however the acknowledgment for the duplicate, which it believes to be the acknowledgement for the last frame. Thus the sender does not retransmit the lost message and the protocol fails. To avoid the erroneous behaviour, the timeout interval must be long enough to prevent a premature timeout, which means that the timeout interval should be larger than the sum of delays on the message channel, acknowledgment channel and receiver.

We have specified PAR in μCRL using timers to represent delays on the channels and the receiver and timeout for the sender. Since the system is open, i.e. both the sender and the receiver communicate with upper layers, we have closed the system by the environment process that provides frames for the sender and receives frames delivered by the receiver. If the sender is ready to send next frame before the environment gets the previous frame delivered by the receiver, the environment process issues an error action `err`. The `err` action also occurs if the environment gets a wrong (not sent to the sender) frame from the receiver.

Using the μCRL toolset we have generated the state space for the μCRL specification of the protocol. With the CADP toolset, we have verified then a number of properties expressed by formulas of regular alternation-free μ-calculus [12]. One of the properties was absence of traces containing error action `err`: P1: `[T*."err"]F`, which held when the sender's timeout was large enough to avoid premature timeouts.

Another property, we have checked, was inevitable reachability of `__out` action after `__in` action meaning that the frame sent by the sender to receiver will always be delivered by the receiver to the environment:
P_2:`[T*."__in"] "mu" X.(<T>T and [not("__out")]X)`.
This property held neither for the system with correct timeout intervals nor for the system with premature timeouts. This can be explained by the fact that we do not use fairness, and hence the message channel may continue lose or corrupt frames forever, so the frame will never be delivered to the environment.

Using the notion of weak fairness, we have specified the property stating fair reachability of `__out` action after `__in`:
P_3:`[T*."__in".(not("__out"))*]<(not("__out"))*."__out">T`.
The property P_3 held for the system with correct timeout intervals and not for the system with wrong ones.

6   Timed Verification

In the previous sections we showed how to specify a timed system in μCRL and how to verify properties dependent on the settings of timers. In this section, we discuss how to verify *timed* properties. For this purpose, we introduce an LTL-like language that allows the direct use of timed constraints and then show how to encode those timed constraints with the use of `tick`.

6.1   Path Restricted LTL

First, we will give an untimed version. This untimed version is in fact a restriction of the μ-calculus, which is the input language used by the CADP toolset. Hence, the untimed formulas can be verified with the CADP toolset.

Let S be a set of states, and Act be a set of labels (actions). A path π of length N is a pair of functions

$$(s_\pi : \{0, \ldots, N\} \to S, \ a_\pi : \{1, \ldots, N\} \to Act)$$

Thus, $s_\pi(i)$ stands for the i-state of the path and $a_\pi(i)$ for the i-action of the path. Note that N may be infinite. We write $\pi(i, k)$ to denote a subpath of π starting at state $s_\pi(i)$ and ending at state $s_\pi(k)$ for $i = 0 \ldots N$.

Let Φ be a set of *state* formulas defined as $\Phi = \{true, false\}$, where *true* holds in all the states and *false* holds in none of them.

Let $\mathcal{R}$ be a set of *action* formulas, where an action formula r is defined as follows:

$$r ::= action \mid any \mid none \mid r_1 \ and \ r_2 \mid r_1 \ or \ r_2 \mid \neg r$$

Here $action \in Act$ is a formula satisfied by the corresponding label only. Any label from Act satisfies *any* and none of them satisfies *none*. A label satisfies $\neg r$ iff it does not satisfy r, a label satisfies r_1 *and* r_2 iff it satisfies both r_1 and r_2, and a label satisfies r_1 *or* r_2 iff it satisfies r_1 or r_2.

Using action formulas one can build *path* formula p as follows:

$$p ::= nil \mid r \mid p_1.p_2 \mid p_1 + p_2 \mid p^* \mid p^+$$

Here *nil* is an empty operator, $p_1.p_2$ is the concatenation, $p_1 + p_2$ is a choice operator, p^* is the transitive reflexive closure and p^+ is the transitive closure.

Let $\mathcal{P}$ be a set of all path formulas. We write $\pi(i,k) \models_{\mathcal{P}} p$ if $a_\pi(i+1) \ldots a_\pi(k)$ string matches path expression p.

Further we define a path-restricted LTL, where LTL modalities are parameterized by path formulas.

Definition 1 (Syntax of path restricted LTL).

$$\phi ::= \varphi \mid \langle p \rangle \phi \mid [p] \phi \mid \phi U(p) \phi \mid \phi \wedge \phi \mid \phi \vee \phi \mid \neg \phi$$

where p stands for a path formula and φ for a state formula.

First we give an intuition for formulas of the path-restricted LTL and then we provide more formal semantics.

$\langle p \rangle \phi$ holds on a path π if there exists a prefix $\pi(0,i)$ of π that matches p and ϕ holds on the suffix of π starting at $s_\pi(i)$.

$[p]\phi$ holds on a path π if for every its prefix $\pi(0,i)$ that matches p, ϕ holds on the suffix of π starting at $s_\pi(i)$.

$\psi U(p)\phi$ holds on a path π if there exists a state $s_\pi(i)$ on the path such that the path up to this state matches p, the path starting at $s_\pi(i)$ satisfies ϕ and the path starting at any state before this state satisfies ψ.

Definition 2 (Semantics of path restricted LTL). *Let π, i be the suffix of π starting at $s_\pi(i)$, then:*

- $\pi, i \models \varphi$ *where $\varphi \in \Phi$ if $s_\pi(i) \models \varphi$;*
- $\pi, i \models \langle p \rangle \phi$ *if there exists some $k \geq i$ such that $\pi(i,k) \models_{\mathcal{P}} p$ and $\pi, k \models \phi$;*
- $\pi, i \models [p]\phi$ *if for any $k \geq i$ such that $\pi(i,k) \models_{\mathcal{P}} p$ we have $\pi, k \models \phi$;*
- $\pi, i \models \psi U(p)\phi$ *if there exists some $k \geq i$ such that $\pi(i,k) \models_{\mathcal{P}} p$ and $\pi, k \models \phi$ and for any $j : i \leq j < k$ $\pi, j \models \psi$ holds.*

We say that π *satisfies* ϕ, denoted as $\pi \models \phi$, if $\pi, 0 \models \phi$. Formula ϕ is *satisfied* by an LTS T if all paths of T starting at the initial state satisfy the formula.

6.2   Path Restricted LTL with Time

Now we extend the path restricted LTL with time constraints of the form:

$$tc ::= \leq c \mid = c \mid \geq c$$

Let $d(\pi(i,k))$ denote the number of `tick` steps in $\pi(i,k)$. Then:

- $\pi(i,k) \models \leq c$ if $d(\pi(i,k)) \leq c$;
- $\pi(i,k) \models \geq c$ if $d(\pi(i,k)) \geq c$;
- $\pi(i,k) \models = c$ if $d(\pi(i,k)) = c$.

Then a path restricted LTL formula with time is defined as follows:

$$\phi ::= \varphi \mid \langle p \rangle_{tc}\phi \mid [p]_{tc}\phi \mid \phi U(p)_{tc}\phi \mid \phi \wedge \phi \mid \phi \vee \phi \mid \neg \phi \ ,$$

where none of the path formulas p refer to the action `tick`.

The intuitive semantics of the formulas is similar to those of path-restricted LTL. $\langle p \rangle_{tc}\phi$ holds on a path if there exists a state on that path such that the path up to that state satisfies both p and the time constraint and ϕ is satisfied by the path starting at that point.

$[p]_{tc}\phi$ holds on a path if for every prefix of the path that matches both p and the time constraint, ϕ holds the corresponding suffix of the path.

$\psi U(p)_{tc}\phi$ holds on a path if there exists a state on the path such that the path up to that state matches both p and tc, the path starting at that state satisfies ϕ and the path starting at any state before satisfies ψ.

The intuition about path formulas is that they hold on traces regardless of time progression. This means that a timed path satisfies a path formula if the path with the `tick` steps removed satisfies the path formula. Formally, we have

$$\pi(i,k) \models^{tick}_{\mathcal{P}} p \text{ if } a'_{\pi}(i+1)\ldots a'_{\pi}(k) \text{ matches } p, \text{ where } a' = \begin{cases} \epsilon \ , \text{ if } a = \texttt{tick} \\ a \ , \text{ otherwise} \end{cases}$$

Definition 3 (Semantics of path restricted LTL with time). *Let π, i is a suffix of π starting at $s_{\pi}(i)$, then:*

- *$\pi, i \models^{tick} \varphi$ where $\varphi \in \Phi$ if $s_{\pi}(i) \models \varphi$;*
- *$\pi, i \models^{tick} \langle p \rangle_{tc}\phi$ if there exists some $k \geq i$ such that $\pi(i,k) \models^{tick}_{\mathcal{P}} p$ and $\pi(i,k) \models tc$ and $\pi, k \models^{tick} \phi$;*
- *$\pi, i \models^{tick} [p]_{tc}\phi$ if for any $k \geq i$ such that $\pi(i,k) \models^{tick}_{\mathcal{P}} p$ and $\pi(i,k) \models tc$ we have $\pi, k \models^{tick} \phi$;*
- *$\pi, i \models^{tick} \psi U(p)_{tc}\phi$ if there exists some $k \geq i$ such that $\pi(i,k) \models^{tick}_{\mathcal{P}} p$ and $\pi(i,k) \models tc$ and $\pi, k \models^{tick} \phi$ and for any $j : i \leq j < k \quad \pi, j \models^{tick} \psi$ holds;*

We say that π *satisfies* ϕ denoted $\pi \models^{tick} \phi$ if $\pi, 0 \models^{tick} \phi$. Formula ϕ is *satisfied* by an LTS T if all paths of T starting at the initial state satisfy the formula.

Example 1: each *request* is followed by *answer* in at most 5 time units:

$$[any^*.request] < any^*.given >_{\leq 5} true$$

Example 2: "request" is never followed by "fail" within 2 time units.

$$[any^*.request][any^*.fail]_{\leq 2} false$$

6.3   tick-Encoding of Path Restricted LTL with Time

In this section we present a construction for translating a formula from path restricted LTL with time into path restricted LTL with tick. The key to this translation is the construction of a path formula over an action domain with tick from a path formula over a domain without tick but with a time constraint. This is done by translating both the path formula and the time constraint into a finite automaton, combining these automata into a single automaton and translating this automaton back into a path formula.

It is common knowledge that regular expression and finite automata have the same expressive power and can be translated into each other. Let $RE(\mathcal{A})$ be the translation from an automata $\mathcal{A}$ to an equivalent regular expression and let $\mathcal{A}(RE)$ be the transformation of a regular expression RE into a finite automaton.

Next, we will give the translation of time constraints into finite automata. But first, we give the formal definition of finite automata and languages recognized by finite automata.

Definition 4. *A finite automaton is a tuple $\mathcal{A} \equiv (S, \Sigma, T, I, F)$, where*

- S *is a set of states;*
- Σ *is a set of labels;*
- $T \subseteq S \times \Sigma \times S$ *is a set of transitions;*
- $I \subseteq S$ *is a set of initial states;*
- $F \subseteq S$ *is a set of final states.*

The set of strings recognized by $\mathcal{A}$ is given by

$$L(\mathcal{A}) = \{a_1 \ldots a_n \mid s_0 \in I, s_n \in F, \forall j = 1..n : (s_{j-1}, a_j, s_j) \in T\}$$

Definition 5. *The automata recognizing time constraints are:*

$\mathcal{A}(\leq c) =$
$(\{0, 1, \ldots, c+1\}, \{\text{tick}\}, \{(i, \text{tick}, i+1) \mid i = 0 \ldots c\}, \{0\}, \{0, 1, \ldots, c\})$
$\mathcal{A}(= c) =$
$(\{0, 1, \ldots, c+1\}, \{\text{tick}\}, \{(i, \text{tick}, i+1) \mid i = 0 \ldots c\}, \{0\}, \{c\})$
$\mathcal{A}(\geq c) =$
$(\{0, 1, \ldots, c\}, \{\text{tick}\}, \{(i, \text{tick}, i+1), (c, \text{tick}, c) \mid i = 0 \ldots c-1\}, \{0\}, \{c\})$

We now have a finite automaton corresponding to the path formula and a finite automaton corresponding to the time constraint. All we need to do is to build the product automata, which will recognize all interleavings of strings recognized by these two automata. The following definition gives such a construction:

Definition 6. *Given two finite automata* $\mathcal{A}_1 \equiv (S_1, \Sigma_1, T_1, I_1, F_1)$ *and* $\mathcal{A}_2 \equiv (S_2, \Sigma_2, T_2, I_2, F_2)$, *we define*

$$\mathcal{A}_1 \times \mathcal{A}_2 = (S_1 \times S_2, \Sigma_1 \cup \Sigma_2, T_1 \times S_2 \cup S_1 \times T_2, I_1 \times I_2, F_1 \times F_2), \; where$$

$$T_1 \times S_2 = \{((s_1, s_2), a, (t_1, s_2)) \mid (s_1, a, t_1) \in T_1 \wedge s_2 \in S_2\} \; ;$$

$$S_1 \times T_2 = \{((s_1, s_2), a, (s_1, t_2)) \mid s_1 \in S_1 \wedge (s_2, a, t_2) \in T_2\} \; .$$

We can now define the translation of path restricted LTL with time to path restricted LTL with `tick`.

Definition 7. *The function* $[\![\cdot]\!]$ *translating path restricted LTL with time to path restricted LTL with* `tick` *is given by:*

$$
\begin{aligned}
[\![\varphi]\!] &= \varphi \\
[\![\langle p \rangle_{tc} \psi]\!] &= \langle p \times tc \rangle [\![\psi]\!] \\
[\![[p]_{tc} \psi]\!] &= [p \times tc][\![\psi]\!] \\
[\![\psi_1 \, U (p)_{tc} \, \psi_2]\!] &= [\![\psi_1]\!] \, U (p \times tc) [\![\psi_2]\!] \\
[\![\psi_1 \wedge \psi_2]\!] &= [\![\psi_1]\!] \wedge [\![\psi_2]\!] \\
[\![\psi_1 \vee \psi_2]\!] &= [\![\psi_1]\!] \vee [\![\psi_2]\!] \\
[\![\neg \psi]\!] &= \neg [\![\psi]\!]
\end{aligned}
$$

where

$$p \times tc = RE(A(p) \times A(tc)) \; .$$

This translation preserves satisfaction:

Proposition 1. *For any LTS L and any path restricted LTL with time formula* ψ, *we have*

$$L \models^{tick} \psi \Longleftrightarrow L \models [\![\psi]\!] \; .$$

7   Conclusion

In this paper we proposed an approach to specification and verification of timed systems within the untimed μCRL framework. The experimental results confirmed the usefulness of the approach.

Related Works. Timed process algebras can be classified using three criteria. First, whether they use dense time or discrete time. Second, whether they use absolute or relative time. Third, whether they use time progression constructs or time stamping of actions. For example, timed μCRL [10] uses absolute time, time stamping of actions and leaves the choice between dense and discrete time open. Several versions of ACP with time have been studied. (E.g. [3,2].) These algebras use an operator σ to express time progression rather than an action. For example, the process $\sigma(P)$ in ACP with discrete relative time (ACP$_{drt}$ [2]) is intuitively the same as the process tick.P in μCRL with the tick-convention. For theoretical work the σ operator is more convenient. For tool support the tick action is easier. Hence in ACP one uses σ and in μCRL we use tick.

The use of the tick action results in a time semantics which is similar to the semantics used in others tools, such as DT Spin [6] and ObjectGeode [14]. However, the input languages of those tools restrict to one particular message passing model and in μCRL we are free to use whatever model we want. Moreover, Spin restricts to LTL model checking while in μCRL we can use regular alternation free μ-calculus.

Future Work. It will be interesting to find out if the framework presented in this paper can be extended to provide tool support for timed μCRL. Namely, we are going to investigate what class of specifications in timed μCRL can be adequately translated to the class of specifications described in the paper. Another research topic is the development of time-specific optimisation techniques, such as a tick-confluence based partial order method.

References

1. R. Alur. Timed Automata. In *Proceedings of CAV '99*, volume 1633 of *Lecture Notes in Computer Science*, pages 8–22. Springer-Verlag, 1999.
2. J. C. M. Baeten and J. A. Bergstra. Discrete time process algebra. *Formal Aspects of Computing*, 8(2):188–208, 1996.
3. J. C. M. Baeten and C. A. Middelburg. Process Algebra with Timing: Real Time and Discrete Time. In Bergstra et al. [4].
4. J. A. Bergstra, A. Ponse, and S. A. Smolka, editors. *Handbook of Process Algebra*. Elsevier, 2001.
5. S. C. C. Blom, W. J. Fokkink, J. F. Groote, I. A. van Langevelde, B. Lisser, and J. C. van de Pol. μCRL: a toolset for analysing algebraic specifications. In G. Berry, H. Comon, and A. Finkel, editors, *Proceedings 13th Conference on Computer Aided Verification (CAV'01), Paris, France*, volume 2102 of *Lecture Notes in Computer Science*, pages 250–254. Springer-Verlag, 2001.
6. D. Bošnački and D. Dams. Integrating real time into Spin: A prototype implementation. In S. Budkowski, A. Cavalli, and E. Najm, editors, *Proceedings of Formal Description Techniques and Protocol Specification, Testing, and Verification*. Kluwer Academic Publishers, 1998.
7. M. Bozga, O. Maler, and S. Tripakis. Efficient verification of timed automata using dense and disrete time semantics. In T. Kropf and L. Pierre, editors, *Proc.*

CHARME'99, volume 1703 of *Lecture Notes in Computer Science*, pages 125–141. Springer, September 1999.

8. J. F. Groote and M. Reniers. Algebraic process verification. In Bergstra et al. [4], pages 1151–1208.

9. J. F. Groote and J. J. van Wamel. Analysis of three hybrid systems in timed μCRL. *Science of Computer Programming*, 39:215–247, 2001.

10. J. F. Groote. The syntax and semantics of timed μCRL. SEN R9709, CWI, Amsterdam, 1997.

11. T. A. Henzinger, Z. Manna, and A. Pnueli. What good are digital clocks? In W. Kuich, editor, *ICALP*, volume 623 of *Lecture Notes in Computer Science*, pages 545–558. Springer, 1992.

12. R. Mateescu and M. Sighireanu. Efficient on-the-fly model-checking for regular alternation-free mu-calculus. In *Proceedings of the 5th International Workshop on Formal Methods for Industrial Critical Systems, FMICS'2000*, 2000.

13. R. D. Nicola and F. Vaandrager. Three logics for branching bisimulation. *Journal of the ACM(JACM)*, 42(2):458–487, 1996.

14. ObjectGeode 4. `http://www.csverilog.com/products/geode.htm`, 2000.

15. A. S. Tanenbaum. *Computer Networks*. Prentice Hall International, Inc., 1981.

Verification of Distributed Dataspace Architectures*

Simona Orzan[1,2] and Jaco van de Pol[1]

[1] Centrum voor Wiskunde en Informatica,
P.O.Box 94079, 1090 GB, Amsterdam, The Netherlands
[2] "A.I.Cuza" University, Iasi, Romania
{Simona.Orzan, Jaco.van.de.Pol}@cwi.nl

Abstract. The *space calculus* is introduced as a language to model distributed dataspace systems, i.e. distributed applications that use a shared (but possibly distributed) dataspace to coordinate. The publish-subscribe and the global dataspace are particular instances of our model. We give the syntax and operational semantics of this language and provide tool support for functional and performance analysis of its expressions. Functional behaviour can be checked by an automatic translation to μCRL and the use of a model checker. Performance analysis can be done using an automatically generated distributed C prototype.

1 Introduction

A distributed system is generally seen as a number of single-threaded applications together with a distributed communication layer that coordinates them. Various shared dataspace models have been proposed to solve the task of coordination for parallel computing applications (Linda [8], Gamma [1]), network applications (Bonita [23], WCL [24]), command and control systems (Splice [3]), management of federations of devices (JavaSpaces [15]).

A shared dataspace (or tuple space) architecture is a distributed storage of information and/or resources, viewed as an abstract global store, where applications read/write/ delete pieces of data. In this paper, we focus on the problem of designing, verifying and prototyping distributed shared dataspace systems. Building correct distributed systems is a difficult task. Typical required properties include transparent data distribution and fault-tolerance (by application replication and data replication), which are usually ensured at the price of giving up some performance. Many questions occur when deciding on the exact shape of the distributed dataspace. For instance: what data should be replicated (in order to prevent single points of failure or increase efficiency)? should the local storages be kept synchronized or should they be allowed to have different views on the global space? should the migration of data between local storages be on a subscription basis or rather "on demand"?

The space calculus, introduced in this paper, is an experimental framework in which verification and simulation techniques can be applied to the design of distributed systems that use a shared dataspace to coordinate their components.

---

* Partially supported by PROGRESS, the embedded systems research program of the Dutch organisation for Scientific Research NWO, the Dutch Ministry of Economic Affairs and the Technology Foundation STW, grant CES.5009.

M. Broy and A.V. Zamulin (Eds.): PSI 2003, LNCS 2890, pp. 192–206, 2003.

We provide a tool that translates a space calculus specification into a μCRL specification [16]. From this code a state space graph can be generated and analyzed by means of the model checker CADP [13]. A second tool generates distributed C code to simulate the system. System designers may use the automatic verification and simulation possibilities provided by the μCRL toolset [2] to verify properties of their architecture. Complementary, the distributed C prototype can be used for testing purposes, and to get an indication about the performance (e.g. number of messages, used bandwidth, bottlenecks). Several design choices can be rapidly investigated in this way. Ultimately, the prototype C implementation could even be used as a starting point for building a production version.

The operational semantics of our space calculus provides the formal ground for algebraic reasoning on architectures. Despite its apparent simplicity, our calculus is highly expressive, capable of modeling various destructive/non destructive, global/local primitives. By restricting the allowed space connectives and the allowed coordination primitives, we obtain well known instances, such as the kernels of Splice (a publish-subscribe architecture), and JavaSpaces (global space). Some specific features, like the transactions in JavaSpaces or dynamic publish/subscribe in Splice are out of our scope. Our goal is a uniform framework where core characteristics of various dataspace architectures should be present, in order to allow for studies and comparisons. The verification tool will help getting fast insights in the replication and distribution behaviour of certain architectures, for instance. The simulation tool can help identifying the classes of applications appropriate to each architecture.

Related Work. An overview of shared dataspace coordination models is given in [25]. Some work that studies different semantics has been done in [4,5,7,6], on which we based the style of our operational semantics. [18] proposes a compositional denotational semantics for Splice and proves it equivalent to an operational semantics. [7] compares the publish/subscribe with the shared dataspace architectural style by giving a formal operational semantics to each of them. We also aim at being able to compare the two paradigms, but we take a more unifying perspective: we consider both as being particular instances of the more general distributed dataspace model and express them in the same framework. [10] was the first attempt to use a Unity-like logic to reason on a shared dataspace coordination model (Swarm). [20] has goals similar to ours. It provides a framework for describing software architectures in the theorem prover PVS. However, it seems that the verification of functional behaviour is out of the scope of that paper. In [9], a language for specification and reasoning (with TLA) about software architectures based on hierarchical multiple spaces is presented. The focus there is on the design of the coordination infrastructure, rather than on the behaviour of systems using it. In [17], a translator from the design language VPL to distributed C++ code is presented. VPL specifications can be verified using the CWB-NC toolset. Compared to that approach, our work is more specific. We concentrate on shared dataspace architectures and define a "library" of carefully chosen set of primitives that are both handy and expressive. In [12], scenario-based verification is introduced as a useful technique in between verification and testing. Our language also supports that.

In section 2, we present the syntax and semantics of the space calculus and we comment its main characteristics. Then (section 3) we introduce the supporting tools. Section 4 contains two examples. We end with some concluding remarks (section 5).

2   The Space Calculus

2.1   Informal View

We model the shared space as a graph with atomic spaces as nodes (see Fig. 1). We consider two types of links between spaces: *eager* and *lazy*. When elements are written in a local space, they are asynchronously transferred over all eager links that start in this local space. Eager links can be used to model subscription and notification mechanisms. Lazy links, on the other hand, are demand driven. Only when a data item is requested in some atomic space, it is transferred via a lazy link from one of the neigbouring spaces. Besides modeling the shared space, the space calculus provides a set of coordination primitives for *applications*: write, blocking and non-blocking read, local and global delete operations. Applications are loosely coupled in the sense that they cannot directly address other applications.

With so many existing shared dataspace models, it is difficult to decide what features are the most representative. Some choices that we are faced to are: atomic spaces can be sets or multisets; when transferring data items between different spaces, they could be replicated or moved; the primitives can be location-aware or location-independent; the retrieve operation can be destructive or non-destructive, etc. The answers depend of course on the specific application or on the purpose of the architecture. In order to allow the modeling of as many situations as possible, we let the user make the distinction between data items that should be treated as *information* (e.g. data from a sensor), for which multiplicity is not relevant, and data items that should be treated as *resource* (e.g. numbers to be added, jobs to be executed), for which multiplicity is essential. When handling elements, the space takes into account their type. The transfer between spaces means "copy" for information items and "move" for resources. Similarly, the

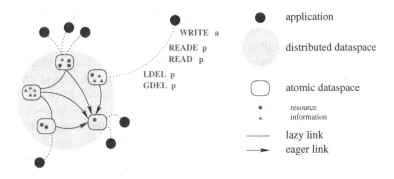

Fig. 1. A distributed dataspace architecture

lookups requested by applications are destructive for resources and non-destructive for information items.

The atomic spaces are multisets in which the elements tagged as information are allowed to randomly increase their multiplicity. As for the question whether to give to applications the possibility to directly address atomic spaces by using handles, like for instance in [23], we have chosen not to, in order to keep the application layer and the coordination layer as separated as possible. The advantage of a clear separation is that the exact distribution of the space is transparent to the applications.

2.2 Syntax and Semantics

As mentioned before, a system description consists in our view from a number of program applications and a number of connected atomic spaces. We refer to the topology of the distributed space by giving atomic spaces (abstract) locations, denoted by $i,j,\ldots$. The data items come from a set $\mathcal{D}$ of values, ranged over by $a,b,\ldots$. Furthermore, we assume a set of patterns $\mathcal{P}at(\mathcal{D})$, i.e. properties that describe subsets of $\mathcal{D}$. (in particular, $\mathcal{D} \subseteq \mathcal{P}at(\mathcal{D})$). $p,q,\ldots$ denote patterns. We also postulate two predicates on patterns: match : $\mathcal{P}at(\mathcal{D}) \times \mathcal{D} \rightarrow \{\top, \bot\}$ to test if a given pattern matches a given value, and inf : $\mathcal{P}at(\mathcal{D}) \rightarrow \{\top, \bot\}$ to specify whether a given pattern should be treated as information or as resource. The predicate res : $\mathcal{P}at(\mathcal{D})$ will be used as the complementary of inf.

A process ($[P]^i$) is a program expression P residing at a location i. A program expression is a sequence of coordination primitives: write, read, "read if exists", local delete, global delete. These primitives are explained later in this section. Formal parameters in programs are denoted by $x,y,\ldots$, the empty program is denoted by ε, and $\bot$ denotes a special error value.

The lazy and eager behaviours of the connections are specified as special marks: $\downarrow_p^i$ (meaning that atomic space i publishes data matching p), $\uparrow_p^i$ (i subscribes to data matching p), ι_i^j (i and j can reach each other's elements). If $\downarrow_p^i$ and $\uparrow_q^j$ are present, then all data matching $p \wedge q$ written in the space i by an application will be asynchronously forwarded to the space j. We say then that there is an eager link from i to j. The presence of ι_i^j indicates that there is a (symmetric) lazy link from space i to j. That is, all data items of i are visible for retrieve operations issued on to j by an application.

For administrative reasons, the set of data items (a) is extended with buffered items that have to be sent ($!a^j$), pending request patterns ($?p$) and subscription policies ($\bigcirc p, k$ and $\bigcirc p, k, t$). Subscription policies are inspired by Splice and their function is to filter the data coming into a space as consequence of a subscription. Based on *keys* and *timestamps*, some of the data in the space will be replaced (overwritten) by the newly arrived element. The parameters k, t are functions on data $k : \mathcal{D} \rightarrow \mathcal{K}eys, t : \mathcal{D} \rightarrow \mathsf{N}$ that dictate how the keys and the timestamps should be extracted from data items. If the newly arrived element a, matching p, meets the filter $\bigcirc p, k$, then a will overwrite all data with the key equal to that of a. If it meets the filter $\bigcirc p, k, t$, it will overwrite the data with the key equal to that of a and timestamp not fresher than that of a. With this second filter, it is also possible that a drops out and has no effect, if its timestamp is too old. A configuration ($\mathcal{C}$) then consists of a number of atomic dataspaces and applications, each bound to a location, and a number of links. The parallel composition operator $\parallel$ is associative and commutative.

$$\text{data} ::= a \mid !a^j \mid ?p \mid \bigcirc p, k \mid \bigcirc p, k, t$$
$$\text{Data} ::= \langle D \rangle^i, \text{ where } D \text{ is a finite set over data}$$
$$\text{Link} ::= \ ^j_i \mid \uparrow^i_p \mid \downarrow^i_p$$
$$\text{Conf} ::= \text{Data} \mid \text{Proc} \mid \text{Link} \mid \text{Conf} \parallel \text{Conf}$$

The operational semantics of the space calculus is defined as a labeled transition relation $\mathcal{C} \xrightarrow{a} \mathcal{C}'$, meaning that if the system is in configuration $\mathcal{C}$ then it can do an a-step to configuration $\mathcal{C}'$. The transition relation is defined inductively in Fig. 2. Note that the OS rules don't explicitly reflect the dual information/resource structure of the systems. This unitary appearance is possible due to a few operators on data, the definition of which (Fig. 3) encapsulates this distinction. D, B are multisets, $-$ and $+$ denote the usual difference and union of multisets and d is a *data* (a or $!a^j$ or $?p$ or $\bigcirc p, k$ or $\bigcirc p, k, t$). We will use the notation $\inf(d)$ to express the value of the predicate inf for the pattern occurring in d. That is, $\inf(!a^j) = \inf(a)$ and $\inf(?p) = \inf(\bigcirc p, k) = \inf(\bigcirc p, k, t) = \inf(p)$. The same holds for res.

$$\text{Prim} ::= write(a) \mid read(p, x) \mid read\exists(p, x) \mid ldel(p) \mid gdel(p)$$
$$P \quad ::= \varepsilon \mid \text{Prim}.P$$
$$\text{Proc} ::= [P]^i$$

We now explain the intuitive semantics of the coordination primitives.

$write(a)$: write data item a into the local dataspace, to be automatically forwarded to all subscribed spaces. a is added to the local dataspace (W1) and an auxiliary $w(i, a)$ step is introduced. When pushing $w(i, a)$ to the top level, if a matches a pattern published by i, then $!a^j$ items are introduced for all subscriptions $\uparrow^j_p$ matching a (rules W2, W3). At top level, the auxiliary $w(i, a)$ step gets promoted to a $write(a)$ step (W4). Finally, the a items are sent to the subscribed spaces asynchronously (W5). The operator $\uplus$ in the right hand side of rule (W5) states that the freshly received data item should be added to the local database taking into account the local subscription policies.

$read(p, x)$: blocking test for presence, in the local space and its lazy linked neigbouring spaces, of some item a matching p; x will be bound to a. This results in generating a $?p$ request, keeping the application blocked (Rτ). If a matching a has been found, it is returned and the application is unblocked (R). Meanwhile, the lazy linked neighbours of the local space asynchronously respond to the request $?p$, if they have an item matching p (TAU). $read\exists(p, x)$: non-blocking test for presence in the local space. If some item a matching p exists in the local space, it is bound to x; otherwise a special error value $\perp$ is returned. Delivers a matching a from the local space, if it exists (R$\exists$1). Otherwise an error value is returned (R$\exists$2). $ldel(p)$: atomically removes all elements matching p from the local space (LD). $gdel(p)$: this is the global remove primitive. It atomically deletes all items matching p, in all atomic spaces. Note that due to its global synchronous nature, $gdel$ can not be lifted over atomic spaces (GD2). Finally, the general parallel rule (act) defines parallelism by interleaving, except for $write$ and $gdel$ which have their own parallel rules to ensure synchronization.

$(\mathbf{W1})$ $\quad \langle D \rangle^i \ || \ [write(a).P]^i \ \overset{w(i,a,[a])}{\longrightarrow} \ \langle D \rangle^i \ || \ [P]^i$

$(\mathbf{W2})$ $\quad \dfrac{\mathcal{C} \ || \ \langle D \rangle^i \ \overset{w(i,a,B)}{\longrightarrow} \ \mathcal{C}^{\scriptscriptstyle\square} \ || \ \langle D \rangle^i}{\mathcal{C} \ || \ \langle D \rangle^i \ || \ \downarrow_p^i \ || \ \uparrow_q^j \ \overset{w(i,a,B \boxplus !a^j)}{\longrightarrow} \ \mathcal{C}^{\scriptscriptstyle\square} \ || \ \langle D \rangle^i \ || \ \downarrow_p^i \ || \ \uparrow_q^j}$

$$\mathsf{match}(p,a) \wedge \mathsf{match}(q,a)$$

$(\mathbf{W3})$ $\quad \dfrac{\mathcal{C} \ \overset{w(i,a,B)}{\longrightarrow} \ \mathcal{C}^{\scriptscriptstyle\square}}{\mathcal{C} \ || \ X \ \overset{w(i,a,B)}{\longrightarrow} \ \mathcal{C}^{\scriptscriptstyle\square} \ || \ X}$

$$X \in \{ \iota_j^k, [P]^j, \langle D \rangle^j, \downarrow_q^j, \uparrow_p^l \}, \quad p : \neg\mathsf{match}(p,a) \vee \downarrow_p^i \notin \mathcal{C}$$

$(\mathbf{W4})$ $\quad \dfrac{\mathcal{C} \ \overset{w(i,a,B)}{\longrightarrow} \ \mathcal{C}^{\scriptscriptstyle\square}}{\mathcal{C} \ \overset{w(i,a,B \boxplus a)}{\longrightarrow} \ \mathcal{C}^{\scriptscriptstyle\square}}$ $\qquad (\mathbf{W5})$ $\quad \dfrac{\langle D \rangle^i \ || \ \mathcal{C} \ \overset{w(i,a,B)}{\longrightarrow} \ \langle D \rangle^i \ || \ \mathcal{C}^{\scriptscriptstyle\square}}{\langle D \rangle^i \ || \ \mathcal{C} \ \overset{write(a)}{\longrightarrow} \ \langle D \oplus B \rangle^i \ || \ \mathcal{C}^{\scriptscriptstyle\square}}$

$(\mathbf{W6})$ $\quad \langle D + [!a^j] \rangle^i \ || \ \langle D^{\scriptscriptstyle\square} \rangle^j \ \overset{\tau}{\longrightarrow} \ \langle D \rangle^i \ || \ \langle D^{\scriptscriptstyle\square} \uplus a \rangle^j$

$(\mathbf{R}\tau)$ $\quad \langle D \rangle^i \ || \ [read(p,x).P]^i \ \overset{\tau}{\longrightarrow} \ \langle D + [?p] \rangle^i \ || \ [read(p,x).P]^i$ $\qquad ?p \notin D$

$(\mathbf{R})$ $\quad \langle D + [?p] \rangle^i \ || \ [read(p,x).P]^i \ \overset{read(p,a)}{\longrightarrow} \ \langle D - [?p] \ominus a \rangle^i \ || \ [P[x := a]]^i$

$$a \in D \wedge \mathsf{match}(p,a)$$

$(\mathbf{R\exists 1})$ $\quad \langle D \rangle^i \ || \ [read\exists(p,x).P]^i \ \overset{read\scriptscriptstyle\square(p,a)}{\longrightarrow} \ \langle D \ominus a \rangle^i \ || \ [P[x := a]]^i$

$$a \in D \wedge \mathsf{match}(p,a)$$

$(\mathbf{R\exists 2})$ $\quad \langle D \rangle^i \ || \ [read\exists(p,x).P]^i \ \overset{read\scriptscriptstyle\square(p,\scriptscriptstyle\square)}{\longrightarrow} \ \langle D \rangle^i \ || \ [P[x := \bot]]^i$

$$\nexists a \in D \ \mathsf{match}(p,a)$$

$(\mathbf{LD})$ $\quad \langle D \rangle^i \ || \ [ldel(p).P]^i \ \overset{ldel(p)}{\longrightarrow} \ \langle D - [a \in D \ | \ \mathsf{match}(p,a)] \rangle^i \ || \ [P]^i$

$(\mathbf{GD1})$ $\quad [gdel(p).P]^i \ || \ ||_j \ \langle D_j \rangle^j \ \overset{gdel(p)}{\longrightarrow} \ [P]^i \ || \ ||_j \ \langle D_j - [a \in D_j \ | \ \mathsf{match}(p,a)] \rangle^j$

$(\mathbf{GD2})$ $\quad \dfrac{\mathcal{C} \ \overset{gdel(p)}{\longrightarrow} \ \mathcal{C}^{\scriptscriptstyle\square}}{\mathcal{C} \ || \ X \ \overset{gdel(p)}{\longrightarrow} \ \mathcal{C}^{\scriptscriptstyle\square} \ || \ X}$ $\qquad\qquad X \neq \langle D \rangle^i$

$(\mathbf{TAU})$ $\langle D + [?p] \rangle^i \ ||\iota_i^j|| \ \langle D^{\scriptscriptstyle\square} \rangle^j \ \overset{\tau}{\longrightarrow} \ \langle D - [?p] \oplus a \rangle^i \ ||\iota_i^j|| \ \langle D^{\scriptscriptstyle\square} \ominus a \rangle^j$

$$a \in D^{\scriptscriptstyle\square} \wedge \mathsf{match}(p,a)$$

$(\mathbf{act})$ $\quad \dfrac{\mathcal{C} \ \overset{act}{\longrightarrow} \ \mathcal{C}^{\scriptscriptstyle\square}}{\mathcal{C} \ || \ \mathcal{C}^{\scriptscriptstyle\boxminus} \ \overset{act}{\longrightarrow} \ \mathcal{C}^{\scriptscriptstyle\square} \ || \ \mathcal{C}^{\scriptscriptstyle\boxminus}}$ $\qquad act \notin \{gdel(p), write(a), w(i,a)\}$

Fig. 2. Operational semantics of the space calculus

2.3 Modeling Some Dataspace Paradigms

The kernels of some well-known dataspace paradigms can be obtained by restricting the allowed configurations and primitives.

Splice [3] implements a publish-subscribe paradigm. It has a loose semantics, reflecting the unstable nature of a distributed network. Applications announce themselves

$$D \underset{p}{\uplus} a \quad = D + [\,a\,]$$

$$D \underset{p,k}{\uplus} a \quad = D - [\,b \in D \mid k(b) = k(a)\,] + [\,a\,]$$

$$D \underset{p,k,t}{\uplus} a \quad = D - [\,b \in D \mid k(b) = k(a)\,] + [\,a\,]$$

$$\text{if } \nexists b \in D \; k(b) = k(a) \wedge t(b) > t(a)$$
$$D \quad \text{otherwise}$$

$$D \underset{d}{\uplus} d \quad = D - [\,d \in D\,] + [\,d\,]$$

$$D \oplus d \quad = \begin{cases} D \underset{d}{\uplus} d & \text{if } \mathsf{inf}(d) \\ D + [d] & \text{if } \mathsf{res}(d) \end{cases} \qquad D \ominus a = \begin{cases} D & \text{if } \mathsf{inf}(a) \\ D - [a] & \text{if } \mathsf{res}(a) \end{cases}$$

$$D \oplus [\,d_1 \cdots d_n\,] = D \oplus d_1 \oplus \cdots \oplus d_n \qquad B \boxplus d = \begin{cases} B \underset{d}{\uplus} d & \text{if } \mathsf{inf}(d) \\ [\,d\,] & \text{if } \mathsf{res}(d) \end{cases}$$

$$D \uplus a \quad = \begin{cases} D \underset{p,k}{\uplus} a & \text{if } \bigcirc p, k \in D \wedge \mathsf{match}(p, a) \\ D \underset{p,k,t}{\uplus} a & \text{if } \bigcirc p, k, t \in D \wedge \mathsf{match}(p, a) \\ D \oplus a & \text{if } \nexists \bigcirc p, k, \bigcirc p, k, t \in D \text{ s.t. } \mathsf{match}(p, a) \end{cases}$$

Fig. 3. Auxiliary operators on multisets

as publishers or subscribers of data sorts. Publishers may write data items to their local agents, which are automatically forwarded to the interested subscribers. Typically, the Splice primitives are optimized for real-time performance, and don't guarantee global consistency. The space calculus fragment without lazy links and restricted to the coordination primitives *write*, *read*, *ldel* corresponds to the reliable kernel of Splice. Network searches (modeled by the lazy links) and global deletion (gdel) are typically absent. In Splice, data sorts have keys, and data elements with the same key may overwrite each other – namely at the subscriber's location, the "fresh" data overwrites the "old" one. The order is given by implicit timestamps that elements get in the moment when they are published. The overwriting is expressible in our calculus, by using the eager links with subscribe policies. The Splice's timestamps mechanism is not present, but some timestamping behaviour can be mimicked by explicitly writing and modifying an extra field in the tuples that models the data.

JavaSpaces [15] on the contrary can be viewed as a *global* dataspace. It typically has a centralized implementation, and provides a strongly consistent view to the applications, that can write, read, and take elements from the shared dataspace. The space calculus fragment restricted to a single atomic space to which all coordination primitives are attached, and with the primitives *write*, *read*, *read∃* forms a fragment of JavaSpaces. Transactions and leasing are not dealt with in our model. Note that with the mechanism of marking the data "information" or "resource", we get the behaviour of both destructive and non-destructive JavaSpaces lookup primitives: our *read*, *read∃* works, when used for information, like *read* and *readIfExists* from JavaSpaces, and like *take* and *takeIfExists* when called for resources.

So, interesting parts of different shared dataspace models are expressible in this framework.

3   The Verification and Prototyping Tools

We defined a mapping from every configuration in the operational semantics to a process in the μCRL specification language [16]. An incomplete description of this mapping is given later in this section. The generation of the μCRL specification following this mapping is automated. Therefore, the μCRL toolset [2] can be immediately used to simulate the behaviour of a configuration. This toolset is connected to the CADP [13] model checker, so that temporal properties on systems in the space calculus can be automatically verified by model checking. Typical verified properties are deadlock freeness, soundness, weak completeness, equivalence of different specifications.

The state of a μCRL system is the parallel composition of a number of processes. A process is built from atomic actions by sequential composition (.), choice (+,sum), conditionals ($\cdot \lhd \cdot \rhd \cdot$) and recursive definitions. For our purpose, we introduce processes for each atomic space and for each application. An additional process, called the TokenManager, has to ensure that operations requiring global synchronization ($gdel$) don't block each other, thus don't introduce deadlocks. Before initiating a global delete operation, a space has to first request and get the token from the manager. When it has finished, it has to return the token to the manager, therefore allowing other spaces to execute their $gdel$s. A second additional process, SubscriptionsManager, manages the list (multiset) of current subscriptions. When an item a is written to an atomic space, that space synchronizes with the SubscriptionsManager in order to get the list of the other atomic spaces where the new item should be replicated or moved.

For simplicity, we model the data items as tuples of natural numbers – fields are modeled by the μCRL datasort Nat, tuples by Tuple.

An atomic space has two interfaces: one to the application processes, and one to the other atomic spaces. In μCRL calls between processes are modeled as synchronization between atomic actions. The primitives of the space calculus correspond to the following atomic actions of Atomic: $\{W, R, RE, Ldel, Togdel, Gdel\}$. The interface to the other atomic processes is used to send/receive data items and patterns for read requests. In Fig. 4, the μCRL specification of a space's *write* behaviour is shown.

The application programs are also mapped to μCRL processes. Execution of coordination primitives is modeled as atomic actions, that synchronize with the corresponding local space's pair actions. This synchronization with the space is described by a communication function.

Another tool translates space calculus specifications to a distributed implementation in C that uses MPI (Message-Passing Interface) [14] for process communication. Different machines can be specified for different locations, thus getting a real distribution of spaces and applications. By instrumenting this code, relevant performance measures for a particular system under design can be computed. The result of the translation is

```
Atomic (id:Nat, D:TupleSet, Req: TupleSet,
        ToSend: NatTupleSet, todel:Tuple,
        LL: NatSet, PL: TupleSet, SL: SubscriptionList) =

%  W
  sum(v:Tuple,
      W(v). sum(NewToSend: NatTupleSet,
            sum(NewD: TupleSet,
                getToSend(v, ToSend, NewToSend, D, NewD).
                Atomic(id, NewD, Req, NewToSend,
                       todel, LL, PL, SL)))
      <| and(isData(v), match(v, PL)) |> delta)
+ sum(v:Tuple,
      W(v).
      Atomic(id, a(v,D), Req, ToSend, todel, LL, PL, SL)
      <| and(isData(v), not(match(v,PL)))|> delta )

% async send
+ sum(x:Nat, sum(y:Tuple,
      el_send(x,y).
      Atomic(id, D, Req, r(x,y,ToSend), todel, LL, PL, SL)
      <| in(x,y,ToSend) |> delta ))

% async receive
+ sum(x:Tuple,
      el_recv(id,x).
      Atomic(id, add(x,D,SL), Req, ToSend, todel, LL, PL, SL))
...
```

Fig. 4. Fragment from a μCRL specification of an atomic space

more than a software simulation. It is actually a prototype, that can be tested in real-time conditions, in a distributed environment.

3.1   The Space Calculus Tool Language

In order to make the space calculus usable as specification language, the tools supporting it work with a concrete syntax. The data universe considered is *tuples of naturals* and the patterns are incomplete tuples (e.g. <1,*,2>,<*>). Apart from the syntactical constructions already defined, we allow external actions (e.g. EXTping), *assignment* of data variables, assignment of tuple variables and *if* and *while* with standard semantics. We give now a brief description of this language, including a precise syntax written in a slightly simplified YACC format.

Since we allow exactly one space per location, it is nice to give *names* to spaces and to say, instead of saying that a program stays at location i, that the program runs at the space <name>. A specification of a configuration consists of:

EXTCOMMAND means $[E][X][T][a-zA-Z]+$
INTID means $[i][a-zA-Z0-9]^\star$
ID means $[a-zA-Z][a-zA-Z0-9]^\star$ (that is not INTID)
INT means $[0-9]^+$

configuration	: settings declarations
settings	:
	| setting settings
setting	: **nfields** = INT
	| **upbound** = INT
	| **res** pattern
declarations	: space declarations
	| link declarations
	| application declarations
space	: **space** ID (ID)
	| **space** ID
link	: **LL** (ID , ID)
	| ID $-$ > pattern
	| ID $<-$ pattern | ID $<-$ pattern intlist | ID $<-$ pattern intlist INT
pattern	: $<$ tuple $>$
tuple	: datum
	| tuple , datum
datum	: * | INT | INTID
intlist	: INT | intlist , INT
intexpression	: INT | INTID | projection | intexpression + intexpression
projection	: pattern / INTID | ID / INTID
application	: **app** ID @ ID { program }
program	:
	| command ; program
command	: **write** pattern
	| **write** ID
	| **read** pattern ID
	| **readE** pattern ID
	| ID := pattern
	| INTID := intexpression
	| **ldel** pattern
	| **gdel** pattern
	| **publish** pattern
	| **subscribe** pattern |**subscribe** pattern intlist |**subscribe** pattern intlist INT
	| **if** condition { program }
	| **while** condition { program }
	| EXTCOMMAND
condition	: ID | not(ID) | true | false

Fig. 5. The YACC style syntax definition

- (optional) fixing the tuple size (**nfields**) and the first natural value strictly greater than any field of any tuple (**upbound**). The default values are nfields=1, upbound=2.
- (optional) define the inf/res predicates, by mentioning the patterns for which res should be $\top$. Any pattern p not included by the **res** declaration has $\inf(p) = \top$.
- describing the spaces, by giving each space a name and, optionally, the machine where it's supposed to live. The default machine is "localhost".
- describing the applications, by specifing for each application its name, the name of the space with which it shares the location (the physical location as well) and its program.

Apart from the primitives **read, readE, write, ldel, gdel**, the actual language includes some extra constructions to provide easy data manipulation and control possibilities: natural variable names and expressions, projection of a tuple on a field, assignments, if, while, external actions that can be specified as strings.

The condition of *if* and *while* is very simple: a standard boolean value or a variable name that gets tested for correctness. Namely, "*if x*" means "if x is not *error*". Extending the conditions is further work.

The key and timestamp functions needed in the subscription policies are considered to be projections on the fields of the tuples – one field for the timestamp, possibly more for the key. Therefore, key functions are represented as lists of field indeces and timestamps functions as one field index.

4   Examples

We use the new language to specify two small existing applications, studied in [22] and [19], respectively. The goal of these examples is to show that our language is very simple to use and to illustrate the typical kind of problems that space calculus is meant for: transparent distribution of data and transparent replication of applications.

4.1   Towards Distributed JavaSpaces

One of the initial motivations of our work was to model a distributed implementation of JavaSpaces, still providing the same strongly consistent view to the applications. When restricting the primitives as discussed in section 2.3, the expression $\langle \emptyset \rangle^0$ represents the kernel of JavaSpaces and the expression $\langle \emptyset \rangle^0 \,||\, \langle \emptyset \rangle^1 \,||\, \downarrow_\star^0 \,||\, \uparrow_\star^0 \,||\, \downarrow_\star^1 \,||\, \uparrow_\star^1$ models a distributed implementation of it, consisting of two spaces eagerly linked by subscriptions matching any item.

Two rounds of the Ping-Pong game ([15], [22]) can be written in the space calculus as follows:

$$Ping = write(1).read(0, x).write(1).read(0, x)$$
$$Pong = read(1, x).write(0).read(1, x).write(0)$$

(with $\mathcal{D} = \{0, 1\}$ and $\inf(x) = \bot, \forall x$). We wish that the distribution of the space should be completely transparent to the applications, i.e. that they run on one space exactly the same that they run on two:

$$[Ping]^0 \,||\, [Pong]^0 \,||\, \langle \emptyset \rangle^0 = [Ping]^0 \,||\, [Pong]^1 \,||\, \langle \emptyset \rangle^0 \,||\, \langle \emptyset \rangle^1 \,||\, \downarrow_\star^0 \,||\, \uparrow_\star^0 \,||\, \downarrow_\star^1 \,||\, \uparrow_\star^1$$

```
nfields = 1                              nfields = 1
upbound = 2                              upbound = 2
res <*>                                  res <*>

space JS (mik.sen.cwi.nl)                space JS (mik.sen.cwi.nl)
                                         space JSbis (boeg.sen.cwi.nl)
app Ping@JS {                            JS -> <*>
  write <1>; EXTping; read <0> x;        JS <- <*>
  write <1>; EXTping; read <0> x;        JSbis -> <*>
}                                        JSbis <- <*>
app Pong@JS {
  read <1> x; write <0>; EXTpong;        app Ping@JS {
  read <1> x; write <0>; EXTpong;          write <1>; EXTping; read <0> x;
}                                          write <1>; EXTping; read <0> x;
                                         }
                                         app Pong@JSbis {
                                           read <1> x; write <0>; EXTpong;
                                           read <1> x; write <0>; EXTpong;
                                         }
```

(a) A Ping-Pong application on one JavaSpace (left) and on two (right)

```
nfields = 3                              nfields = 3
upbound = 3                              upbound = 3
space A1                                 space A1
space A2                                 space A2
space A3                                 space A3
A1 -> <1,*,*>                            space A4
A2 -> <2,*,*>                            A1 -> <1,*,*>
A2 <- <1,*,*> 1 3                        A2 -> <2,*,*>
A3 <- <2,*,*> 1 3                        A2 <- <1,*,*> 1 3
                                         A3 <- <2,*,*> 1 3
app Producer@A1 {                        A4 -> <2,*,*>
    itsp := 0; EXTin;                    A4 <- <1,*,*> 1 3
    write <1,0,itsp>;
    itsp := itsp + 1;                    app Producer@A1 {
    write <1,1,itsp>;                        itsp := 0; EXTin;
  }                                          write <1,0,itsp>;
app Transformer@A2 {                         itsp := itsp + 1;
    while (true) {                           write <1,1,itsp>;
      read <1,*,*> x;                     }
      ivx := x/2+1; itx := x/3;          app Transformer@A2 {
      write <2,ivx,itx>;                     while (true) {
    };                                         read <1,*,*> x;
  }                                            ivx := x/2+1; itx := x/3;
app Consumer@A3 {                              write <2,ivx,itx>;
    while (true) {                           };
      read <2,*,*> x;                      }
      EXTout;                            app Transformer@A4 {
    };                                       while (true) {
  }                                            read <1,*,*> x;
                                               ivx := x/2+1;
                                               itx := x/3;
                                               write <2,ivx,itx>;
                                             };
                                           }
                                         app Consumer@A3 {
                                             while (true) {
                                               read <2,*,*> x;
                                               EXTout;
                                             };
                                           }
```

(b) The Producer/Consumer/Transformer application with one (left) and two (right) transformers

Fig. 6. Space calculus program examples

We have checked this equivalence by writing the two specifications of the Ping-Pong game (with a single, respectively replicated space) in the "tool syntax" (Fig. 6(a)), generating the two statespaces and using the model checker to verify that they satisfy the *safety equivalence* relation.

4.2   Transparent Replication of Some Splice Applications

Some of the most interesting problems in a system with components are associated with *replication*: what components can be replicated, and at what costs? We claim that the space calculus is a good framework for studying this type of questions. In the sequel we give an example of how our space calculus can be used to rapidly check transparent replication of some applications on Splice.

Consider a simple Splice system, composed of three applications: a *Producer* that writes data to the Splice network, based on observations that it makes on the environment; a *Transformer* that reads the data, applies some transformations on it and writes it back; and a *Consumer* that reads the transformed data items and uses it further, for instance by displaying it on a screen. The producer and the consumer are the components that interact with the environment, while the transformer works "under water". Therefore it is reasonable to ask whether it is possible to replicate the transformer without affecting the (external) behaviour of the system.

This producer-transformer-consumer example illustrates a specific pattern in Splice systems. The transparent replication of the middle component was extensively studied in [19], using both μCRL and PVS. We show how to model the problem in space calculus (Fig. 6(b)), for the specific instance when two data items are produced, with values 0 and 1. The itsp variable models the local clock. The two specifications are proved safety equivalent by the model checker.

5   Conclusions

This paper presents our initial research in a unifying framework for the design and analysis of various distributed dataspace systems. We introduced the space calculus, in which basic concepts of some dataspace paradigms can be modeled. A formal syntax and operational semantics provides a rigorous basis to this calculus.

We aim at two goals: comparing the various paradigms with respect to their meta-properties and facilitating the analysis of individual systems based on heterogeneous shared dataspace architectures.

For the first goal, we view a particular dataspace paradigm as a fragment of the space calculus and we address questions like: does a fragment admit transparent replication of data/processes, what are the costs of a distributed implementation, what are the typical applications for a certain fragment. An answer to the last question would facilitate early architectural design decisions. Some of these questions have been answered for Splice already [11,19,21].

The second goal is supported by automatic translations to μCRL and to C. The μCRL specifications can be used as an input to a model checker, thus formally establishing the functional correctness of a system. The approach follows a previous successful attempt for JavaSpaces [22]. The distributed C simulator can be used to find performance bottlenecks in the high-level architecture. These could be solved by transforming the space calculus expression to a functionally equivalent one with a better performance.

As future work, we plan to investigate meta-properties for (fragments) of the space calculus and identify behaviour-preserving transformation rules. Also, we intend to study more examples, in order to establish the validity of our framework and to improve it where necessary. An interesting extension might be to allow dynamic creation of spaces and applications or the dynamic change of the link structure.

We like to acknowledge Michel Chaudron for initiating our quest for a unifying dataspace framework.

References

1. J.P. Banâtre and D. Le Métayer. The GAMMA model and its discipline of programming. *Science of Computer Programming*, 15:55–77, November 1990.
2. S.C.C. Blom, W.J. Fokkink, J.F. Groote, I.A. Langevelde, B. Lisser, and J.C. van de Pol. μCRL: a toolset for analysing algebraic specifications. In G. Berry, H. Comon, and A. Finkel, editors, *Proc. of 13th conference on Computer Aided Verification (CAV)*, pages 250–254, 2001. LNCS 2102.
3. M. Boasson. Control systems software. *IEEE Transactions on Automatic Control*, 38(7):1094–1106, July 1993.
4. M.M. Bonsangue, J.N. Kok, and G. Zavattaro. Comparing coordination models based on shared distributed replicated data. In J. Carroll, H. Haddad, D. Oppenheim, B. Bryant, and G.B. Lamont, editors, *Proceedings of the 1999 ACM Symposium on Applied Computing (SAC '99)*, pages 146 – 155, San Antonio, Texas, USA, February 1999. ACM press.
5. N. Busi, R. Gorrieri, and G. Zavattaro. Process calculi for coordination: From Linda to JavaSpaces. In T. Rus, editor, *8th International Conference on Algebraic Methodology and Software Technology*, number 1816 in LNCS, Iowa, USA, 2000. Springer-Verlag.
6. N. Busi, C. Manfredini, A. Montresor, and G. Zavattaro. Towards a data-driven coordination infrastructure for peer-to-peer systems. In *Proc. of Workshop on Peer-to-Peer Computing*, number 2376 in LNCS. Springer-Verlag, May 2002.
7. N. Busi and G. Zavattaro. Publish/subscribe vs. shared dataspace coordination infrastructures. In *Proc. of WETICE'01*. IEEE Press, 2001.
8. N. Carriero and D. Gelernter. *How to Write Parallel Programs: A First Course*. MIT Press, 1990.
9. P. Ciancarini, M. Mazza, and L. Pazzaglia. A logic for a coordination model with multiple spaces. *Science of Computer Programming*, 31(2–3):231–261, 1998.
10. H. Cunningham and G.-C. Roman. A Unity-style programming logic for shared dataspace programs. *IEEE Transactions on Parallel and Distributed Systems*, 1(3):365–376, July 1990.
11. P.F.G. Dechering and E. de Jong. Transparent object replication: A formal model. In *Fifth Workshop on Object-oriented Real-Time Dependable Systems (WORDS'99F)*, Monterey, California, USA, 2000. IEEE Computer Society.
12. P.F.G. Dechering and I.A. van Langevelde. The verification of coordination. In A. Porto and C. Roman, editors, *Proceedings of the Fourth International Conference on Coordination Models and Languages*, number 1906 in LNCS, Limassol, Cyprus, 2000. Springer-Verlag.
13. J.-C. Fernandez, H. Garavel, A. Kerbrat, L. Mounier, R. Mateescu, and M. Sighireanu. CADP – a protocol validation and verification toolbox. In *Proc. 8th Conference on Computer-Aided Verification*, number 1102 in LNCS, pages 437–440. Springer, 1996.

14. Message Passing Interface Forum. MPI: A Message-Passing Interface standard. Technical Report UT-CS-94-230, 1994.
15. E. Freeman, S. Hupfer, and K. Arnold. *JavaSpaces principles, patterns, and practice*. Addison-Wesley, Reading, MA, USA, 1999.
16. J.F. Groote and M.A. Reniers. Algebraic process verification. In J.A. Bergstra, A. Ponse, and S.A. Smolka, editors, *Handbook of Process Algebra*, chapter 17. Elsevier, 2001.
17. D. Hansel, R. Cleaveland, and S. Smolka. Distributed prototyping from validated specifications. In *12th IEEE International Workshop on Rapid System Prototyping*, pages 97–102. IEEE Computer Society Press, June 2001.
18. J.M.M. Hooman and J.C. van de Pol. Equivalent semantic models for a distributed dataspace architecture. In *Proceedings of the First International Symposium on Formal Methods for Components and Objects*, LNCS, 2002. To appear.
19. J.M.M. Hooman and J.C. van de Pol. Formal verification of replication on a distributed data space architecture. In *Proceedings of SAC 2002 (Madrid)*, pages 351–358. ACM, 2002.
20. K. Lichtner, P. Alencar, and D. Cowan. A framework for software architecture verification. In *Proc. of 12th Australian Software Engineering Conference*, pages 149–158. IEEE Computer Society, 2000.
21. Simona Orzan and Jaco van de Pol. Distribution of a simple shared dataspace architecture. In Antonio Brogi and Jean-Marie Jacquet, editors, *Electronic Notes in Theoretical Computer Science*, volume 68. Elsevier Science Publishers, 2002.
22. J.C. van de Pol and M. Valero Espada. Formal specification of JavaSpaces™ architecture using μCRL. In F. Arbab and C. Talcott, editors, *Proc. of COORDINATION*, number 2315 in LNCS, pages 274–290. Springer, 2002.
23. A.I.T. Rowstron and A.M. Wood. Bonita: a set of tuple space primitives for distributed coordination. In *Proceedings of the 30th Annual Hawaii International Conference on System Sciences*, pages 379–388. IEEE Computer Society Press, 1997.
24. Antony I. T. Rowstron. WCL: A co-ordination language for geographically distributed agents. *World Wide Web*, 1(3):167–179, 1998.
25. R. Tolksdorf and G. Rojec-Goldmann. The SPACETUB models and framework. In *Coordination Models and Languages*, pages 348–363, 2002.

Using SPIN and STeP to Verify Business Processes Specifications

Juan C. Augusto, Michael Butler, Carla Ferreira, and Stephen-John Craig

Declarative Systems and Software Engineering Research Group
Department of Electronics and Computer Science
University of Southampton, Southampton, UK
{jca, mjb, cf, sjc02r}@ecs.soton.ac.uk

Abstract. Business transactions are prone to failure and having to deal with unexpected situations. Some business process specification languages, e.g. StAC, introduce notions like *compensation* handling. Given the need of verification of correctness in business related software, it is important to fill in the gap between business process specification languages like StAC and the verification software already available.
We report on two of our previous attempts to develop a tool to allow verification of StAC specifications by using already existing systems, SPIN and STeP. We highlight some of the problems we faced during these attempts as they can prevent successful and widespread use of verification tools. Our experience can be used to make the available tools more versatile and hence, useful to a wider range of applications.

1 Introduction

Because of their complexity, business transactions are prone to failure in many ways. For example, a request that normally is satisfied under certain conditions can be unexpectedly rejected. That can be experienced in daily life when the book we requested is not anymore in stock, or when our trip is cancelled.

However systems are normally built considering the normal and expected pattern of behavior. A way to deal with this conflict is to supplement the usual pattern of behavior with mechanisms which allow the system to react more appropriately when an unexpected/undesired event occurs. One such mechanism proposed in the literature is to associate a *compensation* action to each action, which will repair or handle in an appropriate way abnormal situations. Offering alternatives and rescheduling can be ways to compensate previous actions. We focus on StAC (see [5] and [4]), a business process modelling language with a formal semantics which handles compensation.

We report here some of our attempts to provide a suitable verification framework for StAC specifications. We considered two systems with different characteristics, SPIN [7] and SteP [3]. The first option led us to consider a translation from the StAC specification language to Promela, the input language for SPIN. For the second option we considered instead a translation to SPL, the input language for STeP.

M. Broy and A.V. Zamulin (Eds.): PSI 2003, LNCS 2890, pp. 207–213, 2003.

This paper is an abstract of a larger article [1] which gives more details about the main contribution. After a brief introduction to StAC (section 2) we explain some of the main obstacles we found attempting to use SPIN (section 3) and STeP (section 4) to verify StAC specifications. We also provide a description on how we handled compensations (section 5) and samples of the verifications we were able to make (section 6). The conclusions (section 7) will summarize some of the features that need to be made available in the next generation of verification systems for business-related systems.

2 StAC

StAC (Structured Activity Compensation) is a language that, in addition to CSP-like operators [6], offers a set of operators to handle the notion of *compensation*. In StAC is possible to associate to an action a set of compensation actions providing a way to repair an undesired situation. Compensations are expressed as pairs with the form $P \div Q$, meaning that Q is the compensation planned in case that the effect of P needs to be compensated at a later stage. As the system evolves, compensations are remembered. Each compensation operator is bounded to a scope of application. If all the activities are successfully accomplished then the operator *accept*, ☑ , releases the compensations. If any activity fails then the operator *reverse*, ☒ , orders the system to apply all the recorded compensations for the current scope. The abortion of a process can be imposed by using the *early termination* operator, ⊙.

DEFINITION 1 Let A represent an activity, b a boolean condition, P and Q two generic processes, x a variable and X a set of values. Then, we can define as follows the set of well formed formulas in StAC:

$Process ::=$	A	(activity label)			
	0	(skip)		$b \rightarrow P$	(condition)
	$rec(P)$	(recursion)		$P; Q$	(sequence)
	$P \| Q$	(parallel)		$\| x \in X.P_x$	(generalised parallel)
	$P [] Q$	(choice)		$[] x \in X.P_x$	(generalised choice)
	⊙	(early termination)		$\{P\}$	(termination scoping)
	$P \div Q$	(compensation pair)		$[P]$	(compensation scoping)
	☒	(reverse)		☑	(accept)

In the examples below, processes written in boldface are intended to be basic activities. Each StAC specification is coupled with a B machine [2] describing the state of the system and its basic activities. We address the reader who want a more in-detail account of StAC to [5] and [4].

EXAMPLE 1 (*order fulfillment scenario* [5]) The whole process can be described throughout the following steps: a) an order is accepted from a customer; b) the warehouse prepares the order for shipment, including booking a courier for delivery; c) simultaneously with step (b) there is a credit check to verify if the customer can pay the order; d) if the check is successful the order completes, otherwise it is stopped and the compensation mechanism is started.

abc = (**acceptOrder** ÷ **restockOrder**);
    fulfillOrder;
    ((**okFulfillOrder** → ☑) ▯(**notokFulfillOrder** → ☒))
fulfillOrder = {**wareHousePackaging** ‖
                (**creditCheck** ;
                  ((**notokCreditCheck**→ ⊙)▯(**okCreditCheck** → 0)))}
wareHousePackaging = (**bookCourier** ÷ **cancelCourier**) ‖ packOrder
packOrder = ‖ i∈I .(**packItem**(i)÷ **unpackItem**(i))

△

3 Translating StAC to Promela

Model checking can be used to check whether a logical property is consistent with the specification of a system. A particularly successful implementation of this approach is SPIN, [7] that has been widely accepted as a tool for verification of software specifications. Promela is the specification language of SPIN. It is a C-like language enriched with a set of primitives allowing the creation and synchronization of processes, including the possibility to use both synchronous and asynchronous communication channels.

We refer the reader to the extensive literature about the subject as well as the documentation of the system at Bell Labs web site for more details: http://netlib.bell-labs.com/netlib/spin/whatispin.html We assume some degree of familiarity with this framework from now on.

Translating StAC specifications to Promela proved to be a non-trivial matter and, when possible, demanded more complex data and control structures to recreate StAC novel features.

Coordinating Nested Procedures. Calls to non-primitive processes in StAC behave as calls to procedures in programming languages. For example, a sequence of calls to non-primitive processes in the StAC specification must be executed without interleaving between them, while their proctype counterparts in Promela will allow interleaving. For example, "run P; run Q" will start P first and then will start Q without waiting for P to terminate. Q can be started at any time after P has been. The ; operator in this case does not have the usual semantics expected for procedures in high level programming languages as it is the case for StAC.

Synchronization can be achieved as expected in StAC through a fork & join mechanism forcing all subprocesses to be finished before the process that created them is considered finished. Broadly speaking, a way to introduce this mechanism in the translation, e.g. by using channels, is as follows: for every process P calling other subprocesses $p_1, \ldots, p_n$, i.e. implemented as **proctype** calls through the run sentence, we can a) add at the end of each p_i, with $i = 1, \ldots n$, a way to acknowledge that the process have finished, and b) after the call sentence in the caller process a way to recognize that the called processes finished before proceeding.

For parallel processes let us consider the general case: A(...) || B(...). We will call the parallel definition to be coordinated *a block*. A block A || B terminates when both A and B terminates. Differently from the sequential case we want to ensure that parallelism is restricted to those processes in the block. In this case the testing for acknowledgments is shifted immediately after the translation of the intervening processes inside the block.

If we use a parallel or a generalised parallel operator, we want to ensure that we consider the process finished if and only if all the processes being run concurrently are finished. Then again we need to address the coordination problem. Since Promela does not support generalised parallel we need to use a loop to create the appropriate number of parallel processes. Naturally the problem is far simpler when using *generalised choice* because when the choice involves a procedure call all we need to check is that one call was made.

StAC allows recursive definitions. In this particular case, we cannot adapt the idea of using channels as before. Messages to ensure termination will successfully ensure all the calls ended before proceeding to execute code after the recursive call but it could be the case that messages generated for an instance $i1$ of the recursive proctype will be allowing to finish an instance $i2, i1 \neq i2$. One option would be to generate "keys", which univocally tie each acknowledge with a call. Another simpler, but partial, solution to the problem is to translate tail-recursive specifications to an iterative one.

Enumerates. A problem that applies to both, *generalised parallel* and *generalised choice*, is that the above schema assumes the indexes of the generalised operators are numeric. But, the usual case is to provide different enumerates for each operator, representing names, brands, addresses and all sort of useful labels motivated by real life applications. So, if a more flexible set of values has to be used, the limitations imposed by Promela's restriction to define all enumerates by using just one `mtype` are obvious. Although it is possible, see [1], to overcome the restrictions imposed in Promela to the use of enumerates that makes the specification unnecessary complicated and inefficient.

Early Termination. The *early termination* operator, ⊙ (see example 1 for an illustration of its use), can be applied to force a process to terminate. Brackets can be used to delimitate the scope for the operator application. For example $\{P; \odot; Q\}; R$ specifies that after P is executed, Q will be forced to terminate. This will not affect R. If we apply ⊙ to a parallel process then all the parallel processes within the scope of the ⊙ are also terminated. For example, in $\{(P; \odot; Q)||R\}||S$ process R will also be terminated but S will not. We found that the implementation of this characteristic is particularly problematic in Promela.

The closest approach to a solution was the use of the label `provided` available in Promela which impose conditions to the executability of a proctype, provided some conditions are fulfilled. Unfortunately a note in Promela user's manual, `"provided clauses are incompatible with partial order reduction"`, deters us to do so.

4   Translating StAC to SPL

STeP ([3]) is a verification system for reactive systems based in a deductive approach. STeP provides a collection of tools allowing verification by deduction, sometimes with user interaction. Model checking is also available, and is a good complement to the deductive system providing counter examples to false properties. A system can be input to STeP as an SPL program or as a *Fair Transition System* [8].

The syntax of SPL programs follows that of traditional imperative languages such as Pascal. In addition to the basic constructs found in these languages, SPL supports nondeterminism by means of the selection statement 'or' and parallel composition by means of the cooperation statement ||. Parallel processes can interact through shared variables such as semaphores, as well as by synchronous and asynchronous channels. Execution of parallel processes is assumed to proceed by interleaving. The specification language for temporal properties to be checked is Linear-Time Temporal Logic [8]. More documentation about the system, including tutorials, demos for specific parts of the system and case studies can be found in the web page for STeP (http://www-step.stanford.edu/). Now we shortly describe some of the obstacles we faced translating StAC to SPL.

Recursive Specifications. Because "the parser just plugs in the bodies of procedures when it finds a procedure call" ([9], pp. 29), general recursion cannot be used as needed in StAC. To overcome that we have to resort to an equivalent translation, e.g. a While-like loop like we used for our translation to Promela. Naturally, with same limitations, i.e. it can be used just with tail-recursion cases.

Flexibility on Generalised Operators. An advantage of SPL in comparison with Promela is that provides generalised parallel and generalised choice sentences. The bad news being that SPL does not allow to use non-numeric enumerate values in generalised choice and parallel. For example, we cannot use: [or O[c:[java..xml]] :: . .... Again we have to resort to encodings, mapping strings into numbers and using numbers as a metaphor of the real information with the same negative consequences of the previous step.

Early Termination. SPL does not provide any constructor that can help to implement the *early termination* operator. There is nothing in SPL syntax similar to the label `provided` available in Promela to impose conditions on the executability of a process.

This forced us to implement that notion by using special structures and procedures. To detect when a concurrent process has finished we use a structure where to store inter-related processes and conditions of termination have to be inserted inside inter-related processes to make their executions threads dependent on each others computations.

Obtaining Counterexamples. Interpreting a counterexample given by the model checker is a very involved process as the steps that caused the unexpected situation are described in terms of internal variables acting as indirect references to the user's structures.

There seems to be no syntax description in any of the publicly available documentation for the system. This force users to have a deep knowledge of all the theoretical framework underlying the system in order to be able to understand a counterexample.

5   Handling of Compensations

A FIFO structure is used to record compensations, as a result, when the compensation mechanism is applied the compensation will be executed following that strategy. As the stack used to implement the notion of compensation is made up of global structures, access to these structures should be coordinated amongst the various concurrent processes.

Stored codes can be recovered later, if necessary, to know what compensations must be applied and in which order that must be done. Each possible compensation activity is identified with a code. To grant that each compensation has a different code we need to force each generalised parallel or generalised choice affecting a compensation pair to generate a disjoint set of codes from those used in other compensation pairs.

Both, the complexity of the structure dictated by the kind of compensations we need for some case studies, and the need of the generalised parallel to inspect the structure are serious drawbacks in terms of search complexity, an important issue for finite-state verification. Then, we found that implementing the very basic operations related to compensation handling was also a major issue in terms of the computational complexity required.

6   Verification

Because of all the problems mentioned before we were able to obtain fully automated verification just for a subset of StAC, e.g. excluding early termination, general recursion, and case studies demanding sophisticated use of enumerates in the case of the Promela specifications. The properties we verified by using SPIN and STeP were written in PLTL [8]. Some examples of properties we can verify by using SPIN in relation with the Fulfilment Order scenario follows. More case studies investigated can be found in [1].

No unmotivated courier cancellations: $\Box\neg$ (okCreditCheck $\wedge$ cancelCourier)

Each order will be packed: $\Box$ (acceptOrder $\rightarrow$ $\Diamond$ (packorder $\vee\neg$ okCreditCheck))

No unwanted unpacks: $\Box$ (acceptOrder $\rightarrow$ ($\neg$ unpackItem $W\neg$ okCreditCheck))

7   Conclusions

Business transactions can be very complex and ensuring correctness is a critical issue. We focused on the problem of providing automatic verification for a business-related specification language, StAC. We considered using two well-known tools in the literature of verification for hardware and software systems: SPIN and STeP. Although the goal of achieving full automatic support for StAC-based specifications was not completely achieved we have collected valuable experience from our research.

One of the results of our research is that we have have identified fragments of StAC that can be translated to Promela or SPL. Another very interesting outcome from our research was the detection of a list of features which are common to business-related specification languages and that are problematic to deal with, even for state of the art tools like SPIN and STeP. We provided in section 2 two case studies that are classic business-related specifications and cannot be satisfactorily mapped to either Promela or SPL.

Many, but not all, of the problems we faced are about mapping a high level language as StAC to the control and data structures provided in Promela and SPL. In some cases, the complexity of translation and space exploration of the resulting model check process increases up to an undesirable level. We think reporting this kind of experiences is very valuable in order to stimulate and guide improvement of state of the art tools towards their next stage. Overcoming this limitations should be part of the agenda to make model checking and other verification frameworks accessible to a broader class of problems.

References

1. J. Augusto and Michael Butler. Some Observations About Using SPIN and STeP to Verify StAC Specifications. Technical report, DSSE-TR-2002-9, 2002. Electronics and Computer Science Department, University of Southampton. 34 pages.
2. J. Abrial. *The B-Book: Assigning Programs to Meanings.* Cambridge University, 1996.
3. N. Bjorner, A. Browne, M. Colon, B. Finkbeiner, Z. Manna, B. Sipma, and T. Uribe. Verifying temporal properties of reactive systems: A step tutorial. *Formal Methods in System Design*, 16:227–270, 1999.
4. M. Butler and C. Ferreira. A process compensation language. In *IFM'2000 - Integrated Formal Methods*, LNCS 1945, pp. 61–76. Springer Verlag, 2000.
5. M. Chessell, C. Griffin, D. Vines, M. Butler, C. Ferreira, and P. Henderson. Extending the concept of transaction compensation. *IBM Journal of Systems and Development*, 41(4):743–758, 2002.
6. C. A. R. Hoare. *Communicating Sequential Processes.* Prentice-Hall, 1985.
7. Gerard Holzmann. The spin model checker. *IEEE Trans. on Software Engineering*, 23(5):279–295, 1997.
8. Z. Manna and A. Pnueli. *The Temporal Logic of Reactive and Concurrent Systems (Specification).* Springer Verlag, 1992.
9. Zohar Manna and the STeP group. STeP: The Stanford Temporal Prover (Educational Release), User's Manual. Technical report, 1995. STAN-CS-TR-95-1562, Computer Science Department, Stanford University. 138 pages.

Integrating Tools for Automatic Program Verification

Engelbert Hubbers

Nijmeegs Instituut voor Informatica en Informatiekunde,
University of Nijmegen, PO Box 9010, 6500 GL Nijmegen, The Netherlands
hubbers@cs.kun.nl

Abstract. In this paper we describe our findings after integrating several tools based upon the Java Modeling Language (JML) [1], a specification language used to annotate Java programs. The tools we consider are Daikon [2], ESC/Java [3], JML runtime assertion checker [1], and Loop/PVS tool [4]. The first one generates specifications; the others are used to verify them. We find that for the first three it is worthwhile to combine them because this is relatively easy and it improves the specifications. Combining Daikon and the Loop/PVS tool directly works in theory, but in practice it only works if the test suite is very good and hence it is not advisable.

1 Introduction

Specifying Java programs can be done by adding JML-assertions expressing preconditions, postconditions, invariants and lists of modified variables to the code. Verifying Java programs involves proving the source code correct with respect to the given specification. In this paper we present the results of an experiment where we have combined tools for both these tasks.

Note that this experiment describes some small steps toward the so-called *verifying compiler*, a compiler that guarantees program correctness before running the program, listed as one of the grand challenges of computer science [5].

1.1 Tools for Specification Generation

It is common knowledge that annotating programs with specifications or contracts increases their quality. It is also common knowledge that most programmers are not very fond of spending time on writing these specifications. Therefore some tools have been developed in order to assist programmers in writing these contracts. Houdini [6] and Daikon [7] are examples of such tools. In this paper we only use Daikon.

Daikon performs dynamic analysis. It starts with a large standard set of likely program invariants [2]. By executing test suites it deletes those invariants from the set that are falsified during the program run, leaving a set of possibly valid specifications. Some examples generated by Daikon:

M. Broy and A.V. Zamulin (Eds.): PSI 2003, LNCS 2890, pp. 214–221, 2003.
© Springer-Verlag Berlin Heidelberg 2003

```
/*@ invariant this.theArray != null; */
/*@ requires this.topOfStack < this.theArray.length-1; */
/*@ modifies this.theArray[*], this.topOfStack; */
/*@ ensures (\old(this.topOfStack) >= 0)   ==>
            (\old(this.topOfStack) == this.topOfStack + 1); */
```

Obviously this dependence on a specific test suite makes the tool unsound. Therefore we need a different tool in order to check the outcome generated by Daikon.

1.2   Tools for Proving Contracts

Several tools are available for checking Daikon's outcome when it is applied to Java programs: ESC/Java, JML , JACK [8], CHASE [9] and the Loop/PVS tool. Each of them has its special characteristics. In our experiment we use ESC/Java, JML and Loop/PVS. To avoid confusion between the language and the tool JML, we will use JMLRAC to refer to the tool.

1.3   The Specification Language JML

The binding factor between the tools we use is the specification language supported by all of them: JML, the Java Modeling Language. It can be used to specify the behavior of Java modules. It includes class invariants, constraints, method preconditions, and both normal and exceptional postconditions. The clauses are written between the code using special comment tags. Hence normal Java compilers do not notice these JML annotations. Goal of the JML project is to provide a language that resembles the Java programming language very closely, hereby making it easier to use for the actual Java programmers. Since JML is still under development it is almost impossible for the tools to keep up with full JML. Hence most tools use their own dialect of JML. The Java/JML combination has a great resemblance to the Eiffel 'design by contract language' [10]. However, because JML supports quantifiers such as \forall and \exists, and because JML allows so-called model fields, JML specifications can be more precise and complete than those typically given in Eiffel.

1.4   Related Work

This is not the first paper on integrating tools for specification generation and tools for specification verification. The papers [11,12] describe results of the integration of Daikon and ESC/Java. And the paper [13] describes an experiment of combining Daikon with the Larch Prover [14]. However, the combination of Daikon with the Loop/PVS tool and JMLRAC has not been described before.

In this paper we only look at Java and JML tools. However, tools for other languages also exist. See for instance Splint [15]. Using static analysis this tool checks whether a C program operates according to its user written annotations. And the SLAM/SLIC combination [16] resembles our experiment even better. It is a Microsoft tool that checks safety properties of C programs without the need for users to write annotations by hand because it generates them automatically.

In Sect. 2 we describe the tools used in more detail. In Sect. 3 we describe the experiment itself. In Sect. 4 we discuss the relevance of our findings.

2   Tools

2.1   Daikon

Daikon is developed at MIT. The tool dynamically generates specifications for input source code. We use Java source, but Daikon also supports C and Perl. Given this source file and a test suite it generates a file containing the original code annotated with JML assertions. These assertions are written in ESC-JML, the dialect of JML that is used by ESC/Java.

2.2   ESC/Java

ESC/Java stands for Extended Static Checker for Java. It is developed at Compaq Research. ESC/Java tries to prove complete programs correct with respect to their specification in ESC-JML using the theorem prover Simplify as engine. It is neither sound nor complete. However, this has been a design issue: one rather has a tool that is very easy to use and good at detecting certain type of errors than a sound and complete tool which is difficult to use. In particular ESC/Java is good in finding programming errors at compile time which are usually not detected before run time; for example null dereference errors, array bounds errors, type cast errors, and race conditions. Note that ESC/Java does not require any user interaction: once started it runs completely automatic.

2.3   JMLRAC

JMLRAC is being developed primarily at Iowa State University. It compiles JML assertions into an executable with runtime checks. If during execution these assertions do not hold, the program stops and reports a violation of the corresponding assertion. Like ESC/Java, JMLRAC doesn't require user interaction.

We have seen before that ESC/Java uses the so-called ESC-JML dialect of JML. JMLRAC uses the full JML syntax. Unfortunately there are some differences[1] between ESC-JML and JML as it is currently supported by the tools. However, JML is nearly a superset of ESC-JML, hence a program annotated in ESC-JML should almost always run without problems in JMLRAC.

It may seem strange to use a runtime assertion checker like JMLRAC to test whether specifications generated by Daikon are correct or not. If this checker is used on the same test suite as the specification generator Daikon, it is to be

---

[1] See [17, Ref. Manual, Sect. 16]. At the moment Kiniry and Cok have almost finished their project to adapt ESC/Java to full JML syntax. Their results will be made available on [4].

expected that no line generated by Daikon will lead to a violation of the runtime checks in JMLRAC. So if we do find these violations this might indicate that there is a problem with one of the two tools.

2.4 Loop/PVS

Loop stands for Logic of Object-Oriented Programming. It is the name of a research project carried out by our own Security of Systems group at the University of Nijmegen [4], and also the name of the tool that plays a central role in this project. The topic is formal methods for object-oriented languages. The aim is to specify and verify properties of classes in object-oriented languages, using proof tools like PVS [18].

The Loop project is centered around the Loop tool. Basically this is a compiler. The input for this compiler consists of Java source code annotated with JML specifications. The output are logical theories which can be loaded into the theorem prover PVS. If one succeeds in proving the corresponding theorems, one knows for sure that the JML specifications really match the code. Intrinsically, this process of proving requires a lot of user interaction and is very tedious work, which is a big contrast with ESC/Java and JMLRAC. Therefore an important part of our research involves writing sophisticated proof strategies that can automate the process as much as possible.

The Loop tool is not publicly available. Furthermore, it uses its own JML dialect. We will refer to it as Loop-JML. Although the Loop compiler and PVS are separate tools, we will use the term Loop/PVS as if it is one tool.

Note also that the goal of Loop/PVS is more ambitious than the goals of ESC/Java and JMLRAC. These two mainly serve the purpose to reduce the number of errors very easily, whereas Loop/PVS wants to show the absence of all errors at the cost of hard work.

3 Experiment

3.1 Test Suites

In order to stay close to the experiments already done by Nimmer and Ernst, we have used the same examples, originating from a textbook by Weiss [19]: DisjSets, QueueAr and StackAr. We have also added an example that comes from the tutorial for Loop/PVS [20]: Tutorial.

Weiss's examples come with minor test programs. The QueueAr and StackAr also come with the Daikon distribution where they have larger test suites. We used both of these suites. In the table of results we have made this distinction visible with a (W) for Weiss and (D) for Daikon. The Tutorial didn't have any test suite at all, so we made one ourselves.

3.2 Setup

The setup of this experiment is shown in Fig. 1. The dashed arrows indicate the desired situation where the code is proved correct with respect to the given specification. Both ESC/Java and JMLRAC report exactly which assertion is being

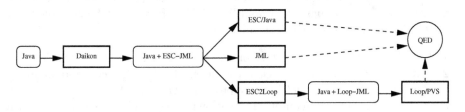

Fig. 1. From Java source file to a proof

violated. Loop/PVS combines all assertions and tries to prove them together. Hence it is more difficult to point out which annotation caused the problem if the whole set of assertions couldn't be proved in Loop/PVS. And therefore we split the experiment into two sub-experiments.

3.3 Daikon, ESC/Java, and JMLRAC Results

The results are related to the number of Daikon's annotations in Fig. 2. The figures in the Daikon columns reflect the number of `invariant`, `requires` and `ensures` annotations created by Daikon. The figures in the ESC/Java columns are the numbers of annotations that could not be verified by ESC/Java. And the figures in the JMLRAC columns are the numbers of annotations for which JMLRAC detected an assertion violation.

	Daikon (generated)			ESC/Java (rejected)			JMLRAC (rejected)		
	inv	req	ens	inv	req	ens	inv	req	ens
DisjSets	7	16	29	2*	1	0	0	0	0
QueueAr (W)	9	39	74	2*	6*	8*	0	1	2
QueueAr (D)	9	25	49	0	1	4	0	0	1
StackAr (W)	8	3	20	4*	0	4*	0	0	1
StackAr (D)	7	4	36	1	1	1	0	0	1
Tutorial	0	20	26	0	1	7	0	0	1

Fig. 2. Daikon, ESC/Java and JMLRAC results. Entries with a* include unverified clauses because of type check errors

Although in principle ESC/Java is able to read Daikon's output, we did encounter 'type check errors' running ESC/Java on all three examples with Weiss's test suites. By removing the corresponding assertions and counting them as un-verified and running ESC/Java again, we came up with the figures in Fig. 2.

A similar strategy is used for JMLRAC. The checker typically only mentions the first assertion violation. By removing this assertion and running JMLRAC again, we filled the whole table.

The problems we found here can be seen as interpretation differences be-tween the tools or as bugs. We would like to classify the first four problems as interpretation differences, the last one as a bug.

1. ESC/Java gives a type check error on Daikon's `this != null` invariant.
2. ESC/Java gives a type check error on Daikon's `requires` and `ensures` clauses with the construct `\elemtype(this.theArray)`.
3. JMLRAC detects postcondition violations on Daikon's postconditions with the construct `\typeof(\result) == \typeof(null)`. JML's `\typeof` refers to the dynamical type. But what is the dynamical type of `null`? And what is Daikon's interpretation of `\typeof`?
4. ESC/Java complains about the fact that Daikon uses `\old` on variables that are not mentioned in the `modifies` clause in its `ensures` clauses. In JML `\old(v)` refers to the value of v in the pre state. If v is not modified this implies that `\old(v)==v` in the post state and therefore it is usually written as v. However `\old(v)` is correct JML, so why is ESC/Java cautious about this? And what is Daikon's interpretation of `\old`?
5. JMLRAC reports a postcondition violation on `\result == this.i` execut-ing the `Tutorial` example. The code causing this problem is:

```
int tryfinally() {
    try { switch (i) { case 0:  throw (new Exception());
                       default: return i; }
        }
    catch(MyException e) { return --i; }
    catch(Exception e) { return ++i; }
    finally { i += 10;
              j += 100; }
}
```

Apparently Daikon gets confused because of the tricky `try-catch-finally` construction. It seems that Daikon only regards the `return` statements as exit points for the method and doesn't take into account that the finally part modifies some values afterwards.

3.4   Daikon and Loop Results

Because Loop-JML is not a superset of ESC-JML we use the script ESC2Loop to transform Daikon's output to a format that can be parsed by Loop/PVS. This transformation involves both pure syntax modifications as well as deletions of constructs that are not supported in Loop-JML.

The real work starts in PVS. Every method in the Loop-JML file has been translated to a lemma. If such a lemma is proved, one knows that the complete specification for this method is correct. If one doesn't succeed in proving this, it takes some experience to see which line of the specification is really causing the problem. Hence there is no easy reference back to the original line in the specification generated by Daikon.

We managed to prove the specifications for some of the methods. Unfortunately most method specifications lead to dead ends: situations where we don't know how to complete the proof. Sometimes this was because we could see that the specifications were incorrect. ESC/Java can help here: if it cannot establish the condition, it sometimes gives enough hints to construct a counterexample. However, more often this was because we got stuck in PVS technicalities and the complexity of the underlying formalism for the memory model as it is being used by Loop/PVS.

4   Conclusion

The original goal of this experiment was to test whether Daikon's results could be verified by other tools. We noticed that both ESC/Java and JMLRAC are well suited for this task. Mainly because they run without user interaction. The combination of Daikon and Loop/PVS is less suitable for this task. PVS is good at noticing that a proof has been completed. However, it is not good at detecting branches of proofs that will lead to contradictions. If one also takes into account that most proofs require a lot of work, it seems best not to feed Daikon's output directly to Loop/PVS. Note that this is in line with the earlier claim that Loop/PVS is more ambitious but requires more effort: if you decide to do the hard work with Loop/PVS then you should also invest more time in writing the specifications and not rely on a specification generation tool only. But if you do want to use a tool like Daikon, make sure that you also use a tool like ESC/Java to filter out the 'obvious' problems before feeding the specifications to Loop/PVS to formally prove their correctness.

During the experiment we found that combining tools also serves a second goal: to detect problems with the tools. As we have seen before, these problems can be real bugs or just differences of interpretation of the specification language JML. The fact that we got type check errors for Weiss's test suites is a good indication that there is a problem between Daikon's ESC-JML and ESC/Java's. And the fact that JMLRAC reports a postcondition violation although it is run on the same test suite as Daikon indicates that there must be something wrong with one of the programs. Furthermore, running Loop/PVS on Daikon's output revealed quite a few bugs in the parser of the Loop compiler. These bugs showed up because Daikon sometimes uses constructs that are valid JML, but would never have been written like this by a human. And hence Daikon's automatic output is interesting test input.

Finally, a tool for automatic derivation of test suites would be great. However, creating it might be an even greater challenge than Hoare's verifying compiler.

References

1. Leavens, G.T., Baker, A.L., Ruby, C.: Preliminary design of JML: A behavioral interface specification language for Java. Technical Report 98-06t, Iowa State University, Dep. of Computer Science (2002) See www.jmlspecs.org.
2. Ernst, M., Cockrell, J., Griswold, W., Notkin, D.: Dynamically Discovering Likely Program Invariants to Support Program Evolution. IEEE Trans. on Software Eng. **27** (2001) 99–123
3. Compaq Systems Research Center: Extended Static Checker for Java (2001) version 1.2.4, http://research.compaq.com/SRC/esc/.
4. Nijmeegs Instituut voor Informatica en Informatiekunde, University of Nijmegen, The Netherlands: Security of Systems group (2003) http://www.cs.kun.nl/ita/research/projects/loop/.
5. Hoare, T.: The verifying compiler: a grand challenge for computing research. Invited talk for PSI'03 conference (2003)
6. Flanagan, C., Leino, K.R.M.: Houdini, an annotation assistant for ESC/Java. In: Formal Methods Europe. Volume 2021 of LNCS., Berlin, Germany (2001) 500–517
7. Lab. for Computer Science, MIT: Daikon Invariant Detector (2003) version 2.4.2, http://pag.lcs.mit.edu/daikon/.
8. Lilian Burdy and Jean-Louis Lanet and Antoine Requet: JACK (Java Applet Correctness Kit) (2002) http://www.gemplus.com/smart/r_d/trends/jack.html.
9. Cataño, N., Huisman, M.: Chase: A Static checker for JML's Assignable Clause. In: Verification, Model Checking and Abstract Interpretation (VMCAI'03). Number 2575 in LNCS, Springer-Verlag (2003) 26–40
10. Meyer, B.: Eiffel: the language. Prentice Hall, New York, NY (1992)
11. Nimmer, J.W., Ernst, M.D.: Static verification of dynamically detected program invariants: Integrating Daikon and ESC/Java. In Havelund, K., Rosu, G., eds.: Electronic Notes in Theoretical Computer Science. Volume 55., Elsevier Science Publishers (2001)
12. Nimmer, J.W., Ernst, M.D.: Automatic generation of program specifications. In: ISSTA 2002, Proceedings of the 2002 International Symposium on Software Testing and Analysis, Rome, Italy (2002) 232–242
13. Win, T.N., Ernst, M.D.: Verifying distributed algorithms via dynamic analysis and theorem proving. Technical Report 841, MIT Lab. for Computer Science (2002)
14. Garland, S.J., Guttag, J.V.: A guide to LP, the Larch Prover. Technical Report 82, Digital Equipment Corporation, Systems Research Center (1991)
15. Evans, D., Larochelle, D.: Improving security using extensible lightweight static analysis. IEEE Software **19** (2002) 42–51
16. Ball, T., Rajamani, S.K.: Automatically validating temporal safety properties of interfaces. Lecture Notes in Computer Science **2057** (2001) 103–122
17. Gary Leavens et al.: Java Modeling Language (JML) (2003) http://www.jmlspecs.org/.
18. Computer Science Lab., SRI: The PVS Specification and Verification System (2002) version 2.4.1, http://pvs.csl.sri.com.
19. Weiss, M.A.: Data Structures and Algorithm Analysis in Java. Addison Wesley (1999) ISBN: 0-201-35754-2.
20. Jacobs, B.P.: A Tutorial for the Logic of JML in PVS. under development (2002)

A Logical Reconstruction of Reachability

Tatiana Rybina and Andrei Voronkov

University of Manchester
{rybina,voronkov}@cs.man.ac.uk

Abstract. In this paper we discuss reachability analysis for infinite-state systems. Infinite-state systems are formalized using transition systems over a first-order structure. We establish a common ground relating a large class of algorithms by analyzing the connections between the symbolic representation of transition systems and formulas used in various reachability algorithms. Our main results are related to the so-called *guarded assignment systems*.

Keywords: theoretical foundations, model theory, infinite-state systems, reachability analysis.

1 Introduction

Reachability properties arise is many applications of verification. In this paper we discuss reachability algorithms in infinite-state systems. Infinite-state systems are formalized using transition systems over a first-order structure. We analyze the connections between the symbolic representation of transition systems and formulas which are used in various reachability algorithms. Our main results are related to the so-called *guarded assignment systems*.

This paper serves two main purposes. First, it formalizes infinite-state systems using model-theoretic notions and discusses reachability algorithms based on this formalization. Though many results and observations of this paper form part of folklore circulating in the infinite-state model checking community, we believe that our formalization is useful since it gives a common model-theoretic approach to otherwise quite diverse formalizations. Second, we observe that for a large class of systems, called guarded assignment systems (GAS), the reachability analysis is simpler since only formulas of a special form are used for satisfiability- and entailment-checking. Many known formalizations of broadcast, cache coherence, and other protocols belong to the simplest kind of GAS, called simple GAS. It follows from our results that the so-called local backward reachability algorithms can be used for simple GAS over structures in which satisfiability-checking is decidable for conjunctions of atomic formulas. This, for example, allows one to extend the existing reachability algorithms to some theories of queues.

This paper is organized as follows. In Section 2 we briefly overview relevant parts of model theory and define several classes of first-order formulas. In Section 3 we give a model theory-based formalization of transition systems and

M. Broy and A.V. Zamulin (Eds.): PSI 2003, LNCS 2890, pp. 222–237, 2003.

their symbolic representations and introduce basic forward and backward reach-ability algorithms. We also discuss requirements on the underlying first-order structures. In Section 4 we define guarded assignment systems and reachability algorithms for them. In Section 5 we introduce local reachability algorithms for guarded assignment systems. Some other issues related to our formalization of infinite-state systems and reachability are discussed in a full version of this paper but not included here due to a lack of space.

2   Preliminaries

In this section we define notation and several classes of formulas which will be used in the rest of the paper. We assume knowledge of standard model-theoretic definitions, such as first-order formulas, structure and truth, which can be found in any standard textbook on logic or model theory.

Unless stated otherwise, we will deal with a fixed first-order structure $\mathbb{M}$ with a domain $\mathcal{D}$ and assume that all formulas are of the signature of this structure. A *valuation* for a set of variables V in $\mathbb{M}$ is any mapping $s : V \to \mathcal{D}$. We will use the standard model-theoretical notation $\mathbb{M}, s \models A$ to denote that the formula A is true in the structure $\mathbb{M}$ under a valuation s. When we use this notation, we assume that s is defined on all free variables of A.

A formula A with free variables V is said to be *satisfiable* (respectively, *valid*) in $\mathbb{M}$ if there exists a valuation s for V in $\mathbb{M}$ such that $\mathbb{M}, s \models A$ (respectively, for every valuation s we have $\mathbb{M}, s \models A$).

A formula A is called *quantifier-free* if A contains no quantifiers. A formula A is called *positive existential* if A can be built from atomic formulas using just $\exists, \wedge, \vee$. A is called a *conjunctive constraint* if it can be built from atomic formulas using just $\exists, \wedge$; and a *simple constraint* if it is a conjunction of atomic formulas.

3   Transition Systems and Reachability: A Formalization in Logic

Infinite-State Transition Systems and Their Symbolic Representation. Our formalization of transition systems is as follows. A transition system has a finite number of variables with values in a possibly infinite domain $\mathcal{D}$. A state is a mapping from variables to values. Transitions may change values of variables. A symbolic representation of such a system uses first-order formulas interpreted in a structure with the domain $\mathcal{D}$.

DEFINITION 1 (Transition System) A *transition system* is a tuple $\mathbb{S} = (\mathcal{V}, \mathcal{D}, \mathcal{T})$, where (i) $\mathcal{V}$ is a finite set of *state variables*; (ii) $\mathcal{D}$ is a non-empty set, called the *domain*. Elements of $\mathcal{D}$ are called *values*. A *state* of the transition system $\mathbb{S}$ is a function $s : \mathcal{V} \to \mathcal{D}$. (iii) $\mathcal{T}$ is a set of pairs of states, called the *transition relation* of $\mathbb{S}$.

A transition system $\mathbb{S}$ is *finite-state* if $\mathcal{D}$ is finite, and *infinite-state* otherwise. ❑

We call any set of pairs of states a *transition*. Transition systems arising in practical applications often have variables ranging over different domains. For example, some state variables may range over the natural numbers, while others over the boolean values or other finite domains. We introduce a single domain for simplicity. It is not hard to generalize our formalization to several domains using many-sorted first-order logic. In the sequel we assume a fixed transition system $\mathbb{S} = (\mathcal{V}, \mathcal{D}, \mathcal{T})$. Suppose that $\mathbb{M}$ is a first-order structure whose domain is $\mathcal{D}$. For example, if $\mathcal{D}$ is the set of natural numbers, then the structure $\mathbb{M}$ can be the set of natural numbers together with the order $<$, operation $+$ and constants $0, 1$. In addition to the set of state variables $\mathcal{V}$, we also introduce a set $\mathcal{V}'$ of *next state variables* of the same cardinality as $\mathcal{V}$. We fix a bijection $' : \mathcal{V} \to \mathcal{V}'$ so that for all $v \in \mathcal{V}$ we have $v' \in \mathcal{V}'$.

We can treat the variables in $\mathcal{V} \cup \mathcal{V}'$ also as logical variables. Then any mapping $s : \mathcal{V} \to \mathcal{D}$ can be considered as both a state of the transition system $\mathbb{S}$ and a valuation for $\mathcal{V}$ in the structure $\mathbb{M}$, and similarly for $s' : \mathcal{V}' \to \mathcal{D}$.

DEFINITION 2 (Symbolic Representation) Let S be a set of states and A be a formula with free variables in $\mathcal{V}$. We say that A *symbolically represents S in* $\mathbb{M}$, or simply *represents* S if for every valuation s for $\mathcal{V}$ in $\mathbb{M}$ we have $s \in S \Leftrightarrow \mathbb{M}, s \vDash A$. Likewise, we say that a formula B with free variables in $\mathcal{V} \cup \mathcal{V}'$ *(symbolically) represents a transition T in* $\mathbb{M}$ if for every pair of valuations s, s' in $\mathbb{M}$ for $\mathcal{V}$ and $\mathcal{V}'$ respectively we have $(s, s') \in T \Leftrightarrow \mathbb{M}, s, s' \vDash B$.   ❏

In the sequel we will follow the following convention. We will often identify a symbolic representation of a transition with the transition itself. For example, when T is a formula with free variables in $\mathcal{V} \cup \mathcal{V}'$ we can refer to T as a transition.

DEFINITION 3 We say that a state s_n is *forward reachable* from a state s_0 w.r.t. $\mathcal{T}$ if there exists a sequence of states $s_1, \ldots, s_{n-1}$ such that for all $i \in \{0, \ldots, n-1\}$ we have $(s_i, s_{i+1}) \in \mathcal{T}$. In this case we also say that s_n is reachable from s_0 *in n steps* and that s_0 is *backward reachable* from s_n in n steps.   ❏

Instead of "forward reachable" we will say "reachable". When we speak about reachability with respect to $\mathcal{T}$, and $\mathcal{T}$ is clear from the context, we will simply say "reachable". The reachability problem can now be defined as follows.

DEFINITION 4 (Reachability Problem) The *reachability problem for* $\mathbb{M}$ is the following decision problem. Given formulas *In*, *Fin*, and *Tr* such that
1. *In* represents a set of states I, called the set of *initial states*;
2. *Fin* represents a set of states F, called the set of *final states*;
3. *Tr* represents the transition relation of a transition system $\mathbb{S}$,
do there exist states $s_1 \in I$, $s_2 \in F$ such that s_2 is reachable from s_1 w.r.t. *Tr*?   ❏

In fact, reachability is a family of decision problems parametrized by the structure $\mathbb{M}$.

When we discuss instances of the reachability problem, we will call the formulas *In* and *Fin* the *initial* and *final conditions*, respectively, and *Tr* the *transition formula*.

The reachability problem for infinite-state systems is, in general, undecidable. Various results on reachability are discussed in many papers, including [9,1,13,2].

Algorithms for Checking Reachability. The algorithms for checking reachability are based on the idea of building a symbolic representation of the set of reachable states. There are two main kinds of reachability algorithms: *forward reachability* and *backward reachability*. Forward reachability algorithms try to build the set of states reachable from the initial states and check whether this set of states contains any final state. Backward reachability algorithms try to build the set of states backward reachable from the final states and check if this set of states contains any initial state.

Before defining these algorithms, let us discuss symbolic representations of forward and backward reachable states. We assume fixed initial and final conditions $In(\mathcal{V})$, $Fin(\mathcal{V})$ and the transition formula $Tr(\mathcal{V}, \mathcal{V}')$.

Let $A(\mathcal{V})$ be a formula which represents a set of states S. It is not hard to argue that the set of states reachable in one step from a state in S can be represented by the formula $\exists \mathcal{V}_1(A(\mathcal{V}_1) \wedge Tr(\mathcal{V}_1, \mathcal{V}))$. Likewise, the set of states backward reachable in one step from a state in S is represented by the formula $\exists \mathcal{V}_1(A(\mathcal{V}_1) \wedge Tr(\mathcal{V}, \mathcal{V}_1))$. This observation implies the following facts about forward and backward reachability.

LEMMA 5 (Forward Reachability) *Consider the sequence of formulas FR_i defined as follows: $FR_0(\mathcal{V}) = In(\mathcal{V})$; $FR_{i+1}(\mathcal{V}) = FR_i(\mathcal{V}) \vee \exists \mathcal{V}_1(FR_i(\mathcal{V}_1) \wedge Tr(\mathcal{V}_1, \mathcal{V}))$. Then each FR_i symbolically represents the set of states reachable from I in at most i steps.* ❏

LEMMA 6 (Backward Reachability) *Consider the sequence of formulas BR_i defined as follows: $BR_0(\mathcal{V}) = Fin(\mathcal{V})$; $BR_{i+1}(\mathcal{V}) = BR_i(\mathcal{V}) \vee \exists \mathcal{V}_1(BR_i(\mathcal{V}_1) \wedge Tr(\mathcal{V}, \mathcal{V}_1))$. Then each BR_i symbolically represents the set of states backward reachable from F in at most i steps.* ❏

Using these lemmas, one can prove two theorems which form the basis of reachability algorithms.

THEOREM 7 (Reachability) *(i) There exists a final state reachable from an initial state if and only if there exists a number $i \geq 0$ such that $\mathbb{M} \models \exists \mathcal{V}(FR_i(\mathcal{V}) \wedge Fin(\mathcal{V}))$. (ii) If there exists a number $i \geq 0$ such that $\mathbb{M} \not\models \exists \mathcal{V}(FR_i(\mathcal{V}) \wedge Fin(\mathcal{V}))$ and $\mathbb{M} \models \forall \mathcal{V}(FR_{i+1}(V) \rightarrow FR_i(\mathcal{V}))$, then there exists no final state reachable from an initial state. The same statements hold if one replaces FR by BR and Fin by In.*

This theorem reduces, in some sense, reachability-checking to checking whether formulas of a special form are true in the structure $\mathbb{M}$. The form of these formulas depends on the symbolic representations In, Fin, Tr of the sets of initial and finite states and the transition relation.

The basic reachability algorithms are based on explicit computation of the formulas FR_i and BR_i and the use of Theorem 7.

DEFINITION 8 The *forward reachability algorithm* Forward and the *backward reachability algorithm* Backward are shown in Figures 1 and 2. They are parameterized by a function simp, called a *simplification function*. ❏

procedure Forward
input: formulas In, Fin, Tr
output: "reachable" or "unreachable"
begin
  current($\mathcal{V}$) := $In(\mathcal{V})$
  while $\mathbb{M} \not\models \exists \mathcal{V}(\text{current}(\mathcal{V}) \wedge Fin(\mathcal{V}))$
    next($\mathcal{V}$) :=
      simp(current($\mathcal{V}$) $\vee$
            $\exists \mathcal{V}_1(\text{current}(\mathcal{V}_1) \wedge Tr(\mathcal{V}_1, \mathcal{V}))$)
    if $\mathbb{M} \models \forall \mathcal{V}(\text{next}(\mathcal{V}) \rightarrow \text{current}(\mathcal{V}))$
    then return "unreachable"
    current($\mathcal{V}$) := next($\mathcal{V}$)
  return "reachable"
end

procedure Backward
input: formulas In, Fin, Tr
output: "reachable" or "unreachable"
begin
  current($\mathcal{V}$) := $Fin(\mathcal{V})$
  while $\mathbb{M} \not\models \exists \mathcal{V}(\text{current}(\mathcal{V}) \wedge In(\mathcal{V}))$
    prev($\mathcal{V}$) :=
      simp(current($\mathcal{V}$) $\vee$
            $\exists \mathcal{V}_1(\text{current}(\mathcal{V}_1) \wedge Tr(\mathcal{V}, \mathcal{V}_1))$)
    if $\mathbb{M} \models \forall \mathcal{V}(\text{prev}(\mathcal{V}) \rightarrow \text{current}(\mathcal{V}))$
    then return "unreachable"
    current($\mathcal{V}$) := prev($\mathcal{V}$)
  return "reachable"
end

Fig. 1. Forward reachability algorithm   **Fig. 2.** Backward reachability algorithm

Usually, this formula transforms formulas into equivalent ones, i.e., $\mathbb{M} \models \forall \mathcal{V}(A \leftrightarrow \text{simp}(A))$ for all formulas A.

In different reachability algorithms, the simplification function simp may make a simple transformation, for example into a normal form, but may also perform more complex ones, such as quantifier elimination. We will sometimes need the simplification function simp to preserve some class of formulas. To this end, we introduce the following definition. We call a function simp on formulas *stable* w.r.t. a class of formulas $\mathcal{C}$, if for every formula $A \in \mathcal{C}$ we have $\text{simp}(A) \in \mathcal{C}$.

First-Order Theories of Infinite Structures. In this section we analyze first-order structures which are suitable for reachability algorithms. In both forward and backward reachability algorithms one has to solve repeatedly the following problems:

1. *Satisfiability:* whether the formula current($\mathcal{V}$) $\wedge Fin(\mathcal{V})$ or current($\mathcal{V}$) $\wedge In(\mathcal{V})$ is satisfiable in $\mathbb{M}$.
2. *Entailment:* whether the formula next($\mathcal{V}$) $\rightarrow$ current($\mathcal{V}$) or prev($\mathcal{V}$) $\rightarrow$ current($\mathcal{V}$) is valid in $\mathbb{M}$.

Of course the reachability algorithms of Figures 1 and 2 can only be considered as algorithms modulo the assumption that satisfiability- and entailment-checking are decidable.

It is not hard to argue that the formulas current($\mathcal{V}$) at the ith iteration of the while-loop are equivalent to the formulas FR_i for forward reachability and BR_i for backward reachability, provided that simp is equivalence-preserving. If $\text{simp}(A) = A$ for every formula A, then the formulas current($\mathcal{V}$) are exactly the formulas FR_i for the forward reachability algorithm and BR_i for the backward reachability algorithm. This implies that the reachability algorithms have the following properties.

THEOREM 9 (Soundness and Semi-Completeness) *The algorithms* Forward *and* Backward *have the following properties: (i) there is a final state reachable from an initial state if and only if the algorithm returns "reachable"; (ii) if the algorithm returns "unreachable", then there is no final state reachable from an initial state.* ❑

On some inputs the algorithms do not terminate. In this case we say that the reachability analysis *diverges*.

Complexity of the satisfiability and entailment problems depends on the structure $\mathbb{M}$ and the form of the formulas current used in the algorithm.

If the first-order theory of $\mathbb{M}$ is decidable, one can implement satisfiability- and entailment-checking using a decision procedure for the first-order theory of $\mathbb{M}$. In some cases, one can even use off-the-shelf decision procedures or libraries. For example, [5] use the Omega Library [16] for deciding Presburger arithmetic. The use of general-purpose algorithms to decide specific classes of formulas may be inefficient. Then specialized tools may be needed to decide these classes of formulas more efficiently.

It is not hard to see that in many important special cases the formulas FR_i and BR_i have a special form.

LEMMA 10 *Let In, Fin, and Tr be positive existential formulas and* simp *be stable w.r.t. positive existential formulas. Then the formulas* current *in the algorithms* Forward *and* Backward *are positive existential too.* ❑

It follows from this lemma that it is enough to solve satisfiability and entailment for positive existential formulas only, as soon as the initial and final conditions and the transition formula are positive existential formulas, which they often are. As we will see below, for some important special cases even quantifier-free formulas suffice.

If the first-order theory of $\mathbb{M}$ admits quantifier elimination, i.e., every formula is effectively equivalent to a quantifier-free formula, then it is enough to check satisfiability and entailment of quantifier-free formulas only. This can be achieved by applying quantifier elimination, i.e., replacing quantified formulas by equivalent quantifier-free formulas, whenever quantified formulas appear, for example, when transitions are applied. However, quantifier elimination may be expensive.

Integer Systems. Denote by I the set of integers. Consider the structure $\mathbb{I} = (I, >, <, \geq, \leq, +, -, 0, 1, 2, \ldots)$, where all the function and predicate symbols (for example, $>$) have their standard interpretation over integers. The first-order theory of $\mathbb{I}$ is decidable, which means that one can use the reachability algorithms Forward and Backward even when the initial and final conditions and the transition formula are arbitrary first-order formulas. In addition, infinite-state transition systems (of a very simple form) over the domain of integers can be used for specifying safety properties of large classes of protocols, for example, broadcast protocols [9]. The first-order theory of $\mathbb{I}$ (essentially, the Presburger arithmetic) admits quantifier elimination, if we extend the signature of $\mathbb{I}$ by the predicates expressing $m \mid (x - n)$ for concrete natural numbers m, n. We will call the transition systems over $\mathbb{I}$ the *integer transition systems* and the reachability problem over $\mathbb{I}$ the *integer reachability problem*. Off-the-shelf tools, such as Omega Library [16] or the Composite Library [20], are available to decide the Presburger arithmetic or its fragments.

The fact that satisfiability- and entailment-checking are decidable does not necessarily imply that the reachability problem is decidable. Neither does it imply that termination of the reachability algorithms is decidable. In this section we note the following undecidability result, which will carry over to all classes of transition systems and reachability algorithms studied in this paper.

THEOREM 11 *Consider the instances of the integer reachability problem with three state variables c_1, c_2, s whose transition relation is a disjunction of conjunctions of the following formulas: $c_i > 0$ or $s = n$, where n is a natural number, $c_i' = c_i + 1$, $c_i' = c_i - 1$, $c_i' = c_i$, or $s' = m$, where m is a natural number. There is exactly one initial and one final state. Then*

1. *the reachability problem for this class is undecidable;*
2. *termination of the algorithm* Forward *is undecidable;*
3. *termination of the algorithm* Backward *is undecidable.* ❏

One can easily prove this theorem by encoding two-counter machines by transition systems of this form. The systems used in the theorem are simple guarded assignment systems (the definition is given below).

Some decidability results for integer systems are given in e.g., [9,1]. For example, safety properties of broadcast protocols can be represented as instances of the integer reachability problem, and the backward reachability algorithm terminates on these instances [9].

4   Guarded Assignment Transition Systems

In this section we consider an important special case of transition systems in which quantifier-free formulas can be used for backward reachability, even without the use of expensive quantifier elimination algorithms. Guarded assignment systems lie in the heart of the model-checking system BRAIN [18].

Guarded Assignments. As usual, we assume that $\mathcal{V}$ is the set of state variables of the transition system.

DEFINITION 12 (Guarded Assignment) A *guarded assignment* is any formula (or transition) of the form $P \wedge v_1' = t_1 \wedge \ldots \wedge v_n' = t_n \wedge \bigwedge_{v \in \mathcal{V} - \{v_1, \ldots, v_n\}} v' = v$, where P is a formula with free variables $\mathcal{V}$, $\{v_1, \ldots, v_n\} \subseteq \mathcal{V}$, and $t_1, \ldots, t_n$ are terms with variables in $\mathcal{V}$. We will write guarded assignments as

$$P \quad \Rightarrow \quad v_1 := t_1, \ldots, v_n := t_n. \tag{1}$$

$$drinks > 0 \wedge customers > 0 \Rightarrow drinks \; := \; drinks - 1 \qquad \text{(* \texttt{dispense-drink} *)}$$
$$true \Rightarrow drinks \; := \; drinks + 64 \qquad \text{(* \texttt{recharge} *)}$$
$$true \Rightarrow customers \; := \; customers + 1 \; \text{(* \texttt{customer-coming} *)}$$
$$customers > 0 \Rightarrow customers \; := \; customers - 1 \; \text{(* \texttt{customer-going} *)}$$

Fig. 3. Guarded assignment system

The formula P is called the *guard* of this guarded assignment.

A guarded assignment is *quantifier-free* (respectively, *positive existential*), if so is its guard. A guarded assignment is called *simple existential* if its guard is a conjunctive constraint, and *simple* if its guard is a simple constraint.   ❏

Formula (1) represents a transition which applies to states satisfying P and changes the values of variables v_i to the values of the terms t_i. Note that a guarded assignment T is a deterministic transition: for every state s there exists at most one state s' such that $(s, s') \in T$. Moreover, such a state s' exists if and only if the guard of this guarded assignment is true in s, i.e., $\mathbb{M}, s \vDash P$.

DEFINITION 13 (Guarded Assignment System) A transition system is called a *guarded assignment system*, or simply *GAS*, if its transition relation is a union of a finite number of guarded assignments. A GAS is called *quantifier-free* (respectively, *positive existential*, *simple existential*, or *simple*) if every guarded assignment in it is also quantifier-free (respectively positive existential, simple existential, or simple).   ❏

An example integer guarded assignment system for representing a drink dispenser is given in Fig. 3. This system is a union of transitions shown in this figure. Since all guards are simple constraints, the system is simple.

Note that every guarded assignment represents a deterministic transition, but a guarded assignment system may represent a non-deterministic transition system because several guards may be true in the same state. Not every transition system is a guarded assignment system. Indeed, in every guarded assignment system with a transition relation $\mathcal{T}$ for every state s there exists a finite number of states s' such that $(s, s') \in \mathcal{T}$. The greatest transition *true* over any infinite structure $\mathbb{M}$ does not have this property.

THEOREM 14 *Every integer quantifier-free GAS is also a simple GAS.*   ❏

One can generalize this theorem to structures different from $\mathbb{I}$. Indeed, the only property of $\mathbb{I}$ used in this proof is that the negation of an atomic formula is equivalent to a positive quantifier-free formula.

The notion of a guarded assignment system is not very restrictive. Indeed, broadcast protocols and Petri nets can be represented as integer simple guarded assignment systems. All transition systems for cache coherence protocols described in [6] are integer simple GAS.

Let us note one interesting property of GAS related to properties other than reachability. Let us call a state s a *deadlock state* if there is no state s' such that $(s, s') \in \mathcal{T}$, where $\mathcal{T}$ is the transition relation.

THEOREM 15 *Let the transition relation $\mathcal{T}$ be a union of guarded assignments $(P_1 \Rightarrow A_1), \ldots, (P_n \Rightarrow A_n)$. Then the set of all deadlock states is represented by the formula $\neg(P_1 \vee \ldots \vee P_n)$.* ❏

This theorem shows that checking *deadlock-freedom* (i.e., non-reachability of a deadlock state) of GAS may be as easy as checking reachability properties, for example, if the GAS is quantifier-free, then the set of deadlock states can also be represented by a quantifier-free formula. Theorem 15 is also used in the system BRAIN to generate the deadlock-freedom conditions automatically.

Reachability Algorithms for Guarded Assignment Systems. We introduced simple guarded assignment systems because they have a convenient property related to backward reachability algorithms. Essentially, one can use backward reachability algorithms for these systems when the underlying structure has a much weaker property than the decidability of the first-order theory.

Let us see how the formulas FR_i and BR_i look like in the case of simple guarded assignment systems. Let u be a guarded assignment of the form $P(v_1, \ldots, v_n) \Rightarrow v_1 := t_1, \ldots, v_n := t_n$. For simplicity we assume that $\mathcal{V} = \{v_1, \ldots, v_n\}$. This can be achieved by adding "dummy" assignments $v := v$ for every variable $v \in \mathcal{V} - \{v_1, \ldots, v_n\}$. Let also $A(v_1, \ldots, v_n)$ be a formula whose free variables are in $\mathcal{V}$. For every term t denote by t' the term obtained from t by replacing every occurrence of every state variable v_i by v_i'.

Define the following formulas: $A^{\square u}(v_1, \ldots, v_n) \overset{\text{def}}{=} P(v_1, \ldots, v_n) \wedge A(t_1, \ldots, t_n)$; $A^u(v_1, \ldots, v_n) \overset{\text{def}}{=} \exists \mathcal{V}^{\square}(A(v_1^{\square}, \ldots, v_n^{\square}) \wedge P(v_1^{\square}, \ldots, v_n^{\square}) \wedge v_1 = t_1^{\square} \wedge \ldots \wedge v_n = t_n^{\square})$.

LEMMA 16 *Let a formula $A(v_1, \ldots, v_n)$ represent a set of states S. Then (i) the formula $A^u(v_1, \ldots, v_n)$ represents the set of states reachable in one step from S using u; (ii) the formula $A^{-u}(v_1, \ldots, v_n)$ represents the set of states backward reachable in one step from S using u.* ❏

One can deduce from this lemma that the formulas A^u and A^{-u} have a special form, as expressed by the following lemma.

LEMMA 17 *Let u be a guarded assignment. Then the function $A \mapsto A^u$ is stable w.r.t. positive existential formulas and conjunctive constraints. The function $A \mapsto A^{-u}$ is stable w.r.t. positive existential formulas, conjunctive constraints, quantifier-free formulas, and simple constraints.* ❏

Before this lemma, forward and backward reachability were treated symmetrically. This lemma shows an asymmetry between forward and backward reachability for simple GAS: the predicate transformer corresponding to backward reachability yields simpler formulas. Using Lemma 16, one can modify forward and backward reachability algorithms of Figures 1 and 2 for guarded assignment transition systems.

DEFINITION 18 *The forward reachability algorithm* GASForward *and the backward reachability algorithm* GASBackward *for GAS are shown in Figures 4 and 5.* When we check reachability for a GAS whose transition relation is a union of guarded assignments $u_1, \ldots, u_n$, we let $U = \{u_1, \ldots, u_n\}$ in the input of the algorithm. ❏

procedure GASForward
input: formulas $In, Fin,$
        finite set of guarded assignments U
output: "reachable" or "unreachable"
begin
  current := In
  while $\mathbb{M} \not\models \exists \mathcal{V}(\text{current} \wedge Fin)$
    next := current $\vee \bigvee_{u \boxdot U}$ current^u
    if $\mathbb{M} \models \forall \mathcal{V}(\text{next} \rightarrow \text{current})$
      then return "unreachable"
    current := next
  return "reachable"
end

procedure GASBackward
input: formulas $In, Fin,$
        finite set of guarded assignments U
output: "reachable" or "unreachable"
begin
  current := In
  while $\mathbb{M} \not\models \exists \mathcal{V}(\text{current} \wedge In)$
    prev := current $\vee \bigvee_{u \boxdot U}$ current$^{\boxdot\,u}$
    if $\mathbb{M} \models \forall \mathcal{V}(\text{prev} \rightarrow \text{current})$
      then return "unreachable"
    current := prev
  return "reachable"
end

Fig. 4. Forward reachability algorithm for GAS

Fig. 5. Backward reachability algorithm for GAS

THEOREM 19 *If the input GAS and the formulas In, Fin are quantifier-free, then all of the formulas* current *in the algorithm* GASBackward *are quantifier-free too. If, in addition, the input GAS and In, Fin are negation-free, then* current *is also negation-free.* ❑

This theorem shows that for quantifier-free GAS satisfiability and entailment in the algorithm GASBackward should only be checked for quantifier-free formulas. It does not hold for the forward reachability algorithm GASForward. Checking satisfiability and validity of quantifier-free formulas is possible if the existential theory (i.e., the set of all sentences of the form $\exists X A$, where A is quantifier-free) of the structure $\mathbb{M}$ is decidable. There exist theories whose full first-order theory is undecidable but existential theory is decidable. A simple example is Presburger arithmetic extended by the divisibility predicate though it is not clear how useful is this theory for applications. A more practical example are some theories of queues considered in [4,3]. This shows that there are infinite domains for which backward reachability may be easier to organize than forward reachability. Of course one can omit the entailment checks from the algorithms, but then they will only be applicable for checking reachability, but not for checking non-reachability.

5   Local Algorithms

In this section we study so-called *local* algorithms, which are different from the algorithms discussed above. They are simpler since checking for satisfiability and entailment for simple GAS is only performed for conjunctive constraints, but not so powerful since they may diverge for instances of reachability for which the previously described algorithms terminate. The idea of these algorithms is to

procedure LocalForward
input: sets of formulas IS, FS,
        finite set of guarded assignments U
output: "reachable" or "unreachable"
begin
  if there exist $I \in IS, F \in FS$ such that
        $M \vDash \exists \mathcal{V}(I \wedge F)$ **then**
    return "reachable"
  $unused := IS$
  $used := \emptyset$
  while $unused \neq \emptyset$
    $S := select(unused)$
    $used := used \cup \{S\}$
    $unused := unused - \{S\}$
    forall $u \in U$
      $N := S^u$
    if there exists $F \in FS$ such that
        $M \vDash \exists \mathcal{V}(N \wedge F)$ **then**
      return "reachable"
    if for all $C \in used \cup unused$
        $M \nvDash \forall \mathcal{V}(N \rightarrow C)$ **then**
      $unused = unused \cup \{N\}$
      forall $C' \in used \cup unused$
        if $M \vDash \forall \mathcal{V}(C' \rightarrow N)$ **then**
          remove C' from $used$ or $unused$
  return "unreachable"
end

Fig. 6. Local forward reachability algorithm

procedure LocalBackward
input: sets of formulas IS, FS,
        finite set of guarded assignments U
output: "reachable" or "unreachable"
begin
  if there exist $I \in IS, F \in FS$ such that
        $M \vDash \exists \mathcal{V}(I \wedge F)$ **then**
    return "reachable"
  $unused := FS$
  $used := \emptyset$
  while $unused \neq \emptyset$
    $S := select(unused)$
    $used := used \cup \{S\}$
    $unused := unused - \{S\}$
    forall $u \in U$
      $N := S^{-u}$
    if there exists $I \in IS$ such that
        $M \vDash \exists \mathcal{V}(N \wedge I)$ **then**
      return "reachable"
    if for all $C \in used \cup unused$
        $M \nvDash \forall \mathcal{V}(N \rightarrow C)$ **then**
      $unused = unused \cup \{N\}$
      forall $C' \in used \cup unused$
        if $M \vDash \forall \mathcal{V}(C' \rightarrow N)$ **then**
          remove C' from $used$ or $unused$
  return "unreachable"
end

Fig. 7. Local backward reachability algorithm

get rid of disjunctions which appear in the formulas current even when the input contains no disjunctions at all. Instead of a disjunction $C_1 \vee \ldots \vee C_n$, one deals with the set of formulas $\{C_1, \ldots, C_n\}$. The entailment check is not performed on the disjunction, but separately on each member C_i of the disjunction, and is therefore called a *local entailment check*.

DEFINITION 20 (Local Reachability Algorithms) The *local forward reachability algorithm* LocalForward and *local backward reachability algorithm* LocalBackward are given in Figures 6 and 7. They are parametrized by a function *select* which selects a formula in a set of formulas. The input set of guarded assignments U is defined as in the algorithms GASForward and GASBackward. The input sets of formulas IS and FS are any sets of formulas such that $In = \bigvee_{A \in IS} A$ and $Fin = \bigvee_{A \in FS} A$. ❑

Local algorithms can be used not only for guarded assignment systems, but for every system in which the transition relation is represented by a finite union of transitions. One can prove soundness and semi-completeness of the algorithms LocalForward and LocalBackward similar to that of Theorem 9. However, we cannot guarantee that the algorithms terminate if and only if their non-local counterparts terminate.

As an example, consider an integer GAS with one variable v whose transition relation is represented by a single guarded assignment $true \Rightarrow v := v - 1$. Take $0 > 0$ as the initial condition and $v \neq 0$ as the final condition. The non-local backward reachability algorithm for GAS at the second iteration will generate the formula $v \neq 0 \lor v \neq 1$, and at the third iteration $v \neq 0 \lor v \neq 1 \lor v \neq 2$. Since these formulas entail each other, the algorithm terminates. However, the local backward reachability algorithm for GAS generates formulas $v \neq 0$, $v \neq 1$, $v \neq 2, \ldots$ which do not entail one another, and hence diverges. One can give a similar example for forward reachability.

THEOREM 21 *If* LocalForward *(respectively,* LocalBackward*) terminates, then so does* GASForward *(respectively,* GASBackward*).*   ❏

Note that termination of the local algorithms may depend on the selection function *select*. Let us call the selection function *fair* if no formula remains in *unused* forever.

THEOREM 22 *If the local forward (respectively backward) algorithm terminates for some selection function, then it terminates for every fair selection function.*❏

It is difficult to say whether there are problems coming from real applications for which a non-local algorithm terminates but its local counterpart does not. One can prove, for example, that for broadcast protocols LocalBackward always terminates. The main property of the local algorithms is that subsumption and entailment-checking is only performed on simpler classes of formulas.

THEOREM 23 *If the input GAS is conjunctive and the sets IS, FS are sets of conjunctive constraints, then all of the formulas* current *in the algorithms* LocalForward *and* LocalBackward *are conjunctive constraints. If the input GAS is simple and the sets IS, FS are simple constraints then all of the formulas* current *in* LocalBackward *are simple constraints too.*   ❏

The last property of local reachability algorithms is heavily used in the system BRAIN. For some structures (for example the reals or the integers) the algorithms for satisfiability-checking of simple constraints are a heavily investigated subject. If the structure is $\mathbb{I}$, then a simple constraint is essentially a system of linear equations and inequations. Checking satisfiability of simple constraints means solving such a system. For solving systems of linear equations and inequations over integers or reals several off-the-shelf tools are available. For example, [7] implement satisfiability- and entailment-checking for conjunctive constraints over real numbers using the corresponding built-in functions of the SICStus Prolog constraint library.

When a backward reachability algorithm is performed on GAS, we get a quantifier elimination effect due to the special form of formulas A^{-u}. Theorems 19 and 23 show that in many cases entailment can be checked only between quantifier-free formulas or even simple constraints. Let us show that in some cases entailment-checking can be performed using satisfiability-checking. It is easy to see that a formula $\forall \mathcal{V}(A \to B)$ is valid if and only if the formula $\exists \mathcal{V}(A \land \neg B)$ is unsatisfiable. Therefore, for quantifier-free GAS and backward reachability algorithms one can use satisfiability-checking for quantifier-free formulas also for entailment-checking.

In the case of simple GAS the situation is not much more complicated. Suppose that we would like to check an entailment problem of the form $\forall \mathcal{V}(A_1 \wedge \ldots \wedge A_n \rightarrow B_1 \wedge \ldots \wedge B_m)$. This problem is equivalent to unsatisfiability of the formula $\exists \mathcal{V}(A_1 \wedge \ldots \wedge A_n \wedge (\neg B_1 \vee \ldots \vee \neg B_m))$. This formula is equivalent to $\exists \mathcal{V}(A_1 \wedge \ldots \wedge A_n \wedge \neg B_1) \vee \cdots \vee \exists \mathcal{V}(A_1 \wedge \ldots \wedge A_n \wedge \neg B_m)$. Therefore, to check the original entailment problem, one has to check m satisfiability problems for the formulas $A_1 \wedge \ldots \wedge A_n \wedge \neg B_i$. These formulas are not simple constraints any more, but can be made into simple constraints or disjunctions of simple constraints if the first-order theory of the structure $\mathbb{M}$ has the following property: the negation of any atomic formula is effectively equivalent to a disjunction of atomic formulas. The first-order theory of $\mathbb{I}$ has this property, for example the formula $\neg x = y$ is equivalent to $x > y \vee y > x$.

This observation shows that in many situations it is enough to implement satisfiability-checking for simple constraints in order to implement backward reachability. For example, for $\mathbb{I}$ it is enough to implement algorithms for solving systems of linear equations and inequations.

One general obstacle for efficiency of reachability algorithms is the problem of *accumulated variables*, i.e., existentially quantified variables introduced by applications of the corresponding predicate transformers. We have shown that for quantifier-free GAS and backward reachability algorithms no new variables are accumulated. For forward reachability algorithms, GAS still have an advantage of (normally) accumulating only a small number of extra variables. Indeed, consider a guarded assignment u of the form $P(v_1, \ldots, v_k) \Rightarrow v_1 := t_1, \ldots, v_n := t_n$ and assume that $\mathcal{V} = \{v_1, \ldots, v_n, v_{n+1}, \ldots, v_k\}$. Denote by $t'_1, \ldots, t'_n$ the terms obtained from $t_1, \ldots, t_n$ by replacing each variable v_i for $i \in \{1, \ldots, n\}$ by v'_i (note that the variables $v_{n+1}, \ldots, v_k$ are not replaced). It is not hard to argue that $A^u(v_1, \ldots, v_k)$ is equivalent to

$$\exists v'_1 \ldots \exists v'_n (A(v'_1, \ldots, v'_n, v_{n+1}, \ldots, v_k) \wedge P(v'_1, \ldots, v'_n, v_{n+1}, \ldots, v_k) \wedge \\ v_1 = t'_1 \wedge \ldots \wedge v_n = t'_n).$$

In this formula the new quantifiers bind the variables $v'_1, \ldots, v'_n$, i.e., only those variables whose values are changed by the transition. In transition systems formalizing protocols (e.g., from [6]) the number of variables whose values are changed by the transition is usually small compared to the overall number of state variables.

In some cases accumulated existentially quantified variables are not the only source of complexity. For example, for finite domains the number of variables is usually large, and repeated substitutions of terms t_i for v_i make the formula current grow exponentially. One way to make current shorter is to introduce extra existentially quantified variables to name common subexpressions, in which case the formulas current will not be quantifier-free even for simple GAS.

6   Related Work

Podelski [15] and Delzanno and Podelski [7] formalize model checking procedures as constraint solving using a rather general framework. In fact, what they call constraints are first-order formulas over structures. They treat a class of properties more general than reachability and use GAS and local algorithms. Our formalization has much in common with their formalization but our results are, in a way, orthogonal, because they do not study special classes of formulas. Among all results proved in this paper, only soundness and semi-completeness are similar to those studied by Delzanno and Podelski. All other results of this paper are new. In addition, Delzanno and Podelski do not discuss selection functions, so their algorithms are less general than ours. The class of systems for which Delzanno and Podelski's algorithms can be applied is also less general than the one studied here. Indeed, they require a constraint solver also to implement variable elimination. If a theory has such a solver, then this theory also has quantifier-elimination (every formula is equivalent to a boolean combination of constraints). The solver is also able to decide satisfiability of constraints, so in fact they deal with theories which are both decidable and have quantifier elimination. They do not notice that in many special cases (as studied in this paper) quantifier elimination is not required. Thus, our results encompass some important theories (such as those of queues in Bjørner [3]) not covered by the results of Delzanno and Podelski.

An approach to formalizing reachability for hybrid systems using first-order logic is presented by Lafferriere, Pappas, and Yovine [14]. They also note that one can use arbitrary first-order formulas (over reals) due to quantifier elimination. Henzinger and Majumdar [10] present a classification of state transition systems, but over the reals.

Lemma 16 which observes that for GAS backward reachability algorithms do not introduce extra variables is similar to the axiom of assignment for the weakest preconditions. This property is heavily used in BRAIN [18]. It is possible that it has been exploited in other backward reachability symbolic search tools but we could not find papers which observe this property.

Non-local reachability procedures for model checking were already formulated in Emerson and Clarke [8], Queille and Sifakis [17]. Delzanno and Podelski [7] studied algorithms based on local entailment in the framework of symbolic model checking. They do not consider the behaviour of local algorithms for different selection functions. Local algorithms could be traced to early works in automated reasoning and later works on logic programming with tabulation (e.g., Warren [19]), constraint logic programming, and constraint databases (e.g., Kanellakis, Kuper, and Revesz [11]).

Kesten, Maler, Marcus, Pnueli, and Shahar [12] present a general approach to symbolic model checking of infinite-state systems, but based on a single language rather than different languages for different structures.

Guarded assignment systems (under various names) are studied in many other papers, too numerous to be mentioned here. There are also many papers on (un)decidability results for infinite-state systems, both over integers and other structures, not mentioned here.

Our paper, as well as Delzanno and Podelski's [7], was inspired by works of Bultan, Gerber and Pugh (e.g., [5]) on symbolic model checking for systems with unbounded integer variables using decision procedures for Presburger arithmetic. Delzanno and Podelski observe that the implementation of constraint-based model checking in their system DMC is by an order of magnitude faster than that of [5]. We implemented GAS and backward reachability algorithms based on the results of our paper in the integer symbolic model checker BRAIN [18]. The experimental results reported in [18] show that on difficult problems BRAIN is several orders of magnitude faster than DMC. In particular, there are several protocols which are currently only solved by BRAIN.

Acknowledgments. We thank Howard Barringer, Giorgio Delzanno, and Andreas Podelski for their comments on earlier versions of this paper.

References

1. P.A. Abdulla, K. Cerans, B. Jonsson, and Y.-K. Tsay. Algorithmic analysis of programs with well quasi-ordered domains. *Information and Computation*, 160(1-2):109–127, 2000.
2. P.A. Abdulla and B. Jonsson. Ensuring completeness of symbolic verification methods for infinite-state systems. *Theoretical Computer Science*, 256:145–167, 2001.
3. N.S. Bjørner. *Integrating Decision Procedures for Temporal Verification*. PhD thesis, Computer Science Department, Stanford University, 1998.
4. N.S. Bjørner. Reactive verification with queues. In *ARO/ONR/NSF/DARPA Workshop on Engineering Automation for Computer-Based Systems*, pages 1–8, Carmel, CA, 1998.
5. T. Bultan, R. Gerber, and W. Pugh. Model-checking concurrent systems with unbounded integer variables: symbolic representations, approximations, and experimental results. *ACM Transactions on Programming Languages and Systems*, 21(4):747–789, 1999.
6. G. Delzanno. Automatic verification of parametrized cache coherence protocols. In A.E. Emerson and A.P. Sistla, editors, *Computer Aided Verification, 12th International Conference, CAV 2000*, volume 1855 of *Lecture Notes in Computer Science*, pages 53–68. Springer Verlag, 2000.
7. G. Delzanno and A. Podelski. Constraint-based deductive model checking. *International Journal on Software Tools for Technology Transfer*, 3(3):250–270, 2001.
8. E.A. Emerson and E.M. Clarke. Using branching time temporal logic to synthesize synchronization skeletons. *Science of Computer Programming*, 2(3):241–266, 1982.
9. J. Esparza, A. Finkel, and R. Mayr. On the verification of broadcast protocols. In *14th Annual IEEE Symposium on Logic in Computer Science (LICS'99)*, pages 352–359, Trento, Italy, 1999. IEEE Computer Society.
10. T.A. Henzinger and R. Majumdar. A classification of symbolic state transition systems. In H. Reichel and S. Tison, editors, *STACS 2000*, volume 1770 of *Lecture Notes in Computer Science*, pages 13–34. Springer Verlag, 2000.
11. P. Kanellakis, G.M. Kuper, and P.Z. Revesz. Constraint query languages. *Journal of Computer and System Sciences*, 51:26–52, 1995.
12. Y. Kesten, O. Maler, M. Marcus, A. Pnueli, and E. Shahar. Symbolic model checking with rich assertional languages. *Theoretical Computer Science*, 256(1-2):93–112, 2001.

13. O. Kupferman and M. Vardi. Model checking of safety properties. *Formal Methods in System Design*, 19(3):291–314, 2001.
14. G. Lafferriere, G.J. Pappas, and S. Yovine. Symbolic reachability computation for families of linear vector fields. *Journal of Symbolic Computations*, 32(3):231–253, 2001.
15. A. Podelski. Model checking as constraint solving. In J. Palsberg, editor, *Static Analysis, 7th International Symposium, SAS 2000*, volume 1924 of *Lecture Notes in Computer Science*, pages 22–37. Springer Verlag, 2000.
16. W. Pugh. Counting solutions to Presburger formulas: how and why. *ACM SIG-PLAN Notices*, 29(6):121–134, June 1994. Proceedings of the ACM SIGPLAN'94 Conference on Programming Languages Design and Implementation (PLDI).
17. J.P Queille and J. Sifakis. Specification and verification of concurrent systems in Cesar. In M. Dezani-Ciancaglini and M. Montanari, editors, *International Symposium on Programming*, volume 137 of *Lecture Notes in Computer Science*, pages 337–351. Springer Verlag, 1982.
18. T. Rybina and A. Voronkov. Using canonical representations of solutions to speed up infinite-state model checking. In E. Brinksma and K.G. Larsen, editors, *Computer Aided Verification, 14th International Conference, CAV 2002*, pages 386–400, 2002.
19. D.S. Warren. Memoing for logic programs. *Communications of the ACM*, 35(3):93–111, 1992.
20. T. Yavuz-Kahveci, M. Tuncer, and T. Bultan. A library for composite symbolic representations. In T. Margaria, editor, *Tools and Algorithms for Construction and Analysis of Systems, 7th International Conference, TACAS 2001*, volume 1384 of *Lecture Notes in Computer Science*, pages 52–66, Genova, Italy, 2001. Springer Verlag.

Recent Advances in Σ-Definability over Continuous Data Types*

Margarita Korovina

BRICS **, Department of Computer Science, University of Aarhus,
Ny Munkegade, DK-8000 Aarhus C, Denmark,
on leave from A. P. Ershov Institute of Informatics Systems,
Lavrent'ev ave., 6, 630090, Novosibirsk, Russia
korovina@brics.dk
http://www.brics.dk/~korovina

Abstract. The purpose of this paper is to survey our recent research in computability and definability over continuous data types such as the real numbers, real-valued functions and functionals. We investigate the expressive power and algorithmic properties of the language of Σ-formulas intended to represent computability on continuous data types. In the case of the real numbers we illustrate how computability can be expressed in the language of Σ-formulas.

1 Introduction

In order to motivate the reader, we start with an informal introduction to problems and solutions considered in this paper. It is well-known that the classical theory of computation, which works with discrete structures, is not suitable for formalisation of computations that operate on real-valued data. Most computational problems in physics and engineering are of this type, e.g. problems related to the complexity of dynamical and hybrid systems. As a consequence, computability on continuous data types has become a subject of great interest and study in Computer Science [4,6,11,10,14,17,21,27,26,32,37]. Since computational processes are discrete in their nature and objects we consider are continuous, formalisation of computability of such objects is already a challenging research problem. This has resulted in various concepts of computability over continuous data types. If we consider the case of the real numbers there are at least two main nonequivalent models of computability. The first one is related to abstract finite machines and schemes of computations (e.g. [4,15,31,29,35]) where real numbers are considered as basic entities which can be added, multiplied, divided or compared in a single step, and computations are finite processes. In this approach equality is usually used as a basic relation, consequently a computable function can be discontinuous. It differs from the situation in concrete

---

* This research was partially supported by the Danish Natural Science Research Council, Grant no. 21-02-0474, RFFI-DFG Grant no. 01-01-04003 and Grant Scientific School-2112.2003.1

** funded by the Danish National Research Foundation.

M. Broy and A.V. Zamulin (Eds.): PSI 2003, LNCS 2890, pp. 238–247, 2003.

computability over the reals, particularly, in computable analysis. The second model (e.g. [6,11,10,14,17,21,32,37]) is closely related to computable analysis. In this approach real numbers are given by appropriate representations and computations are infinite processes which produce approximations to the results. This model is more satisfying conceptually, conforming to our intuition of reals, but depends on representations of the reals. In some cases it is not clear which representations are preferable. In this paper we survey the logical approach to computability on continuous structures, which have been first proposed in [27, 26]. On the one hand, the logical approach agrees with the second model mentioned above (i.e. mathematical intuition), on the other hand it does not depend on representations of reals.

In order to introduce the logical approach to computability over continuous data types we consider the following problems.

1. *Which data structures are suitable for representing continuous objects?*
2. *Which logical language is appropriate to express computability on continuous data types?*
3. *Can we treat inductive definitions using this language?*
4. *What is the expressive power of this language?*

In this paper we represent continuous data types by suitable structures without the equality test. This is motivated by the following natural reason. In all effective approaches to exact real number computation via concrete representations [14,17,32], the equality test is undecidable. This is not surprising, because an infinite amount of information must be checked in order to decide that two given real numbers are equal. In order to do any kind of computation or to develop a computability theory, one has to work within a structure rich enough for information to be coded and stored. For this purpose we extend a structure A by the set of hereditarily finite sets $HF(A)$. The idea that the hereditarily finite sets over A form a natural domain for computation is discussed in [1,13,33]. Note that such or very similar extensions of structures are used in the theory of abstract state machines [3,2], in query languages for hierarchic databases [7], and in Web-like databases [33].

In order to express computability on continuous data types we use the language of Σ-formulas. This approach is based on definability and has the following beneficial features.

- *Notions of Σ-definable sets or relations generalise those of computable enumerable sets of natural numbers.*
- *It does not depend on representations of elements of structures.*
- *It is flexible: sometimes we can change the language of the structure to obtain appropriate computability properties.*
- *We can employ model theory to study computability.*
- *One can treat inductive definitions using Σ-formulas.*
- *Formulas can be seen as a suitable finite representation of the relations they define.*

Now we address problems 3-4, listed above, regarding the language of Σ-formulas. These problems are closely related to the well-known Gandy Theorem which states that the least fixed point of any positive Σ-operator is Σ-definable. Gandy Theorem was first proven for abstract structures with the equality test (see [1,13,16]). In our setting it is important to consider structures without the equality test. Let us note that in all known proofs of Gandy Theorem so far, it is the case that even when the definition of a Σ-operator does not involve equality, the resulting Σ-formula usually does. Only recently we have shown in [25,24] that it is possible to overcome this problem. In particular we have proved that Gandy Theorem holds for abstract structures without the equality test. The following several applications of Gandy Theorem demonstrate its significance. One of them is that we can treat inductive definitions using Σ-formulas. The role of inductive definability as a basic principle of general computability is discussed in [19,30]. It is worth noting that for finite structures the least fixed points of definable operators give an important and well studied logical characterisation of complexity classes [9,20,36]. For infinite structures fixed point logics are also studied e.g. [8]. In the case of the real numbers, as in the case of discrete structures, inductive definitions allow us to define universal Σ-predicates. Another application is that Gandy Theorem can be used to reveal algorithmic aspects of Σ-definability.

In order to investigate algorithmic aspects of Σ-definability over the reals without the equality test we use a suitable fragment of the constructive infinite language $L_{\omega_1 \omega}$ [1,34]. Certain fragments of constructive $L_{\omega_1 \omega}$ have been used to study the expressive power of formal approaches to computability such as search computability [30], 'While'-computability [35], $\forall$-recursiveness [28], dynamic logics [18] and fixed-point logics [9]. We show that a relation over the real numbers is Σ-definable if and only if it is definable by a disjunction of a recursively enumerable set of quantifier free formulas. Let us note that the proof of the 'if' direction follows from Engeler's Lemma for Σ-definability, which have been recently proved for the reals without equality in [23], and the proof of the 'only if' direction uses methods based on Gandy Theorem. It is worth noting that both of the directions of this characterisation are important. Engeler's Lemma gives us an effective procedure which generates quantifier free formulas approximating Σ-relations. The converse direction provides tools for descriptions of the results of effective infinite approximating processes by finite formulas.

For an illustration of the concepts of the logical approach, we consider computability on the real numbers. We show that computability of continuous objects, i.e. real numbers, real-valued functions, can be characterised by finite Σ-formulas. For complete proofs we refer to the paper [22].

The structure of this paper is as follows. In Section 2 we recall the notion of Σ-definability. In Section 3 we show that we can treat inductive definitions using Σ-formulas. Section 4 introduces a certain fragment of the constructive infinite logic. In Section 5 we present a characterisation of the expressive power of Σ-definability on the reals without the equality test. Section 6 illustrates how computability on the real numbers can be expressed in the language of Σ-formulas. We conclude with a discussion of future work.

2 Σ-Definability on Continuous Data Types

We start by recalling the notion of Σ-definability. The concept of Σ-definability is closely related to the generalised computability on abstract structures [1,13, 31,35], in particular on the real numbers [27,26,35]. Notions of Σ-definable sets or relations generalise those of computable enumerable sets of natural numbers, and play a leading role in the specification theory that is used in the higher order computation theory on abstract structures. In the case of the continuous data types it is natural to consider Σ-definability in a language without equality.

Let us consider an abstract structure A in a finite language σ_0 without the equality test. In order to do any kind of computation or to develop a computability theory one has to work within a structure rich enough for information to be coded and stored. For this purpose we extend the structure A by the set of hereditarily finite sets $\mathrm{HF}(A)$. We will construct the set of hereditarily finite sets over the model without equality. This structure permits us to define the natural numbers, and to code and store information via formulas. We construct the set of hereditarily finite sets, $\mathrm{HF}(A)$, as follows:

1. $\mathrm{HF}_0(A) \rightleftharpoons A$,
2. $\mathrm{HF}_{n+1}(A) \rightleftharpoons \mathcal{P}_\omega(\mathrm{HF}_n(A)) \cup \mathrm{HF}_n(A)$, where $n \in \omega$ and for every set B, $\mathcal{P}_\omega(B)$ is the set of all finite subsets of B.
3. $\mathrm{HF}(A) \rightleftharpoons \bigcup_{n \in \omega} \mathrm{HF}_n(A)$.

We define $\mathbf{HF}(A)$ as the following model:

$$\mathbf{HF}(A) \rightleftharpoons \langle \mathrm{HF}(A), U, S, \sigma_0, \emptyset, \in \rangle \rightleftharpoons \langle \mathrm{HF}(A), \sigma \rangle ,$$

where the constant $\emptyset$ stands for the empty set, the binary predicate symbol $\in$ has the set-theoretic interpretation. Also we add predicate symbols U for urelements (elements from A) and S for sets.

The notions of a term and an atomic formula are given in the standard manner. We use a standard shorthand notation $(\exists x \in y)$ and $(\forall x \in y)$ for $\exists x(x \in y \wedge \Psi)$ and $\forall x(x \in y \rightarrow \Psi)$ respectively.

The set of Δ_0-*formulas* is the closure of the set of atomic formulas under $\wedge, \vee, \neg$, and bounded quantifiers $(\exists x \in y)$ and $(\forall x \in y)$ such that in all formulas predicates from the language σ_0 can occur only positively.

The set of Σ-*formulas* is the closure of the set of Δ_0 formulas under $\wedge, \vee$, $(\exists x \in y)$, $(\forall x \in y)$, and $\exists$.

We are interested in Σ-definability of subsets on A^n which can be considered as a generalisation of recursive enumerability. The analogy of Σ-definable and recursive enumerable sets is based on the following fact. Consider the structure $\mathbf{HF} = \langle \mathrm{HF}(\emptyset), \in \rangle$ with the hereditarily finite sets over $\emptyset$ as its universe and membership as its only relation. In $\mathbf{HF}$ the Σ-definable sets are exactly the recursively enumerable sets. The notion of Σ-definability has a natural meaning also in the structure $\mathbf{HF}(A)$.

Definition 1. *1. A relation $B \subseteq \mathrm{HF}^n(A)$ is Δ_0 (Σ)-definable, if there exists a Δ_0 (Σ)-formula Φ such that*

$$\bar{b} \in B \leftrightarrow \mathbf{HF}(A) \models \Phi(\bar{b}).$$

2. A function is Δ_0 (Σ)-definable if its graph is Δ_0 (Σ)-definable.

Note that the sets A and ω are Δ_0-definable. This fact makes $\mathbf{HF}(A)$ a suitable domain for studying subsets of A^n.

3   Gandy Theorem and Σ-Inductive Definitions

Let $\Phi(a_1, \ldots, a_n, P)$ be a Σ-formula where P occurs positively in Φ and the arity of Φ is equal to n. We think of Φ as defining an *effective operator*

$$\Gamma : \mathcal{P}(\mathrm{HF}(A)^n) \to \mathcal{P}(\mathrm{HF}(A)^n)$$

given by

$$\Gamma(Q) = \{\bar{a} | \, (\mathbf{HF}(A), Q) \models \Phi(\bar{a}, P)\}.$$

Since the predicate symbol P occurs only positively we have that the corresponding operator Γ is monotone i.e. for any sets B and C, from $B \subseteq C$ follows $\Gamma(B) \subseteq \Gamma(C)$. By monotonicity, the operator Γ has the least (w.r.t. inclusion) fixed point which can be described as follows. We start from the empty set and apply operator Γ until we reach the fixed point:

$$\Gamma^0 = \emptyset, \quad \Gamma^{n+1} = \Gamma(\Gamma^n), \quad \Gamma^\gamma = \cup_{n < \gamma} \Gamma^n,$$

where γ is a limit ordinal.

One can easily check that the sets Γ^n form an increasing chain of sets: $\Gamma^0 \subseteq \Gamma^1 \subseteq \ldots$. By set-theoretical reasons, there exists the least ordinal γ such that $\Gamma(\Gamma^\gamma) = \Gamma^\gamma$. This Γ^γ is the least fixed point of the given operator Γ.

Theorem 1 (Gandy Theorem). *Let $\Gamma : \mathcal{P}(\mathrm{HF}(A)^n) \to \mathcal{P}(\mathrm{HF}(A)^n)$ be an effective operator. Then the least fixed-point LFP_Γ of Γ is Σ-definable, and the least ordinal γ such that $LFP_\Gamma = \Gamma^\gamma$ is less or equal to ω.*

Proof. For the complete proof we refer to [24].

Definition 2. *A relation $B \subset A^n$ is called Σ-inductive if it is the least-fixed point of an effective operator.*

Corollary 1. *Every relation on A is Σ-inductive if and only if it is Σ-definable.*

4   Constructive Infinitary Logic $L_{\omega_1\omega}$

We consider a fragment of the constructive infinite language $L_{\omega_1\omega}$ described below. Constructive $L_{\omega_1\omega}$ (cf. [34]) allows finitary quantification and infinitary disjunctions of recursively enumerable sets of formulas. We will use a certain fragment of constructive $L_{\omega_1\omega}$ which can be introduced in the following way.

The set of *basic formulas* is the smallest set of formulas containing all atomic formulas in the language σ_0 and closed under finite conjunctions. An $\bigvee$-formula is the formula of the form $\bigvee_{i \in E} \Phi_i$ where $\{\Phi_i | i \in E\}$ is an indexed family of basic formulas all of the variables of which belong to a finite set and E is recursively enumerable.

An computational counterpart of infinitary $\bigvee$-formulas is described in [18]. For example, a suitable encoding might represent the formula $\bigvee_{i \in E} \Phi_i$ as a code of a Turing machine which enumerates the codes of the formulas in the computably enumerable set E.

5   The Expressive Power of Σ-Definability over the Reals without the Equality Test

Now we consider the standard model of the real numbers

$$\langle \mathbb{R}, 0, 1, +, \cdot, < \rangle = \langle \mathbb{R}, \sigma_0 \rangle ,$$

denoted also by $\mathbb{R}$, where $+$ and $\cdot$ are regarded as the usual arithmetic operations on the reals. We use the language of strictly ordered rings, so we assume that the predicate $<$ occurs positively in all formulas. In order to investigate algorithmic aspects of Σ-definability over the reals without the equality test we use the fragment of the constructive infinite language introduced in Section 4. Various fragments of constructive $L_{\omega_1\omega}$, as we mentioned in the introduction, have been used to study the expressive power of formal approaches to computability. One of the most interesting and important results in the area is Engeler's Lemma (c.f. [12,35]) which states that any semi-computable relation is definable by a disjunction of a recursively enumerable set of quantifier free formulas. Engeler's Lemma was first proven for formal computability on abstract structures with the equality test (see [12,13,30,35]). We consider Σ-definability as a basic notion for computability on the reals [27,26]. The natural question to ask is does Engeler's Lemma hold for Σ-definability over the reals without the equality test. We answer this question positively, moreover we show that the converse statement of Engeler's Lemma over the reals holds too i.e. if a relation over the reals is definable by a disjunction of a recursively enumerable set of quantifier free formula then it is Σ-definable.

Theorem 2. *A relation $B \subset \mathbb{R}^n$ is Σ-definable if and only if it is definable by an $\bigvee$-formula, moreover $\bigvee$-formula (Σ-formula) can be constructed effectively from the corresponding Σ-formula ($\bigvee$-formula).*

Proof. The compete proof can be found in [23].

This theorem, as we mentioned in the introduction, reveals algorithmic aspects of Σ-definability. Indeed, suppose $\Phi(\bar{x})$ is a Σ-formula which defines a relation over the reals and we have $\mathbf{HF}(A) \models \Phi(\bar{x}) \leftrightarrow \bigvee_{i \in A} \Psi_i(\bar{x})$. Then each basic formula $\Psi_i(\bar{x})$, such that $i \in A$, represents a simple approximation of the relation definable by $\Phi(\bar{x})$ and there exists a Turing machine that computes these approximations (i.e., enumerates $\Psi_i(\bar{x})$). A universal Turing machine and a universal Σ-predicate for algebraic formulas can then be used to enumerate and check validity of each approximation Ψ.

As straightforward corollaries we obtain the following results. For the definition of semi-algebraic sets we refer to [5].

Proposition 1. *1. A relation $B \subset \mathbb{R}^n$ is Σ-definable if and only if it is an effective union of open semi-algebraic sets.*
2. A relation $B \subset \mathbb{R}^n$ is Σ-definable if and only if there exists an effective sequence $\{A_i\}_{i \in \omega}$ of open semi-algebraic sets such that
a) It monotonically increases: $A_i \subseteq A_{i+1}$, for $i \in \omega$;
b) $B = \bigcup_{i \in \omega} A_i$.

Corollary 2. *Every Σ-definable subset of $\mathbb{R}^n$ is open.*

Let $\Sigma_{\mathbb{R}}$ denote the set of all Σ-definable subsets of $\mathbb{R}^n$, where $n \in \omega$.

Corollary 3. *1. The set $\Sigma_{\mathbb{R}}$ is closed under finite intersections and effective infinite unions.*
2. The set $\Sigma_{\mathbb{R}}$ is closed under Σ-inductive definitions.
3. The set $\Sigma_{\mathbb{R}}$ is closed under projections.

6   Computability and Definability on the Reals

In this section we illustrate how computability can be expressed in the language of Σ-formulas. As a simple example, we first consider computability of real numbers.

Definition 3. *A real number x is called computable (c.f. [17,32]) if there exists an effective sequence of rational numbers $\{q_i\}_{i \in \omega}$ such that*

$$|x - q_i| < \frac{1}{2^i}.$$

Proposition 2. *A real number is computable if and only if the left Dedekind cut and the right Dedekind cut are Σ-definable.*

Proof. See [22].

Now we consider computability of real-valued functions. For this purpose we adopt the notion of majorant-computability [27,26] to the case of the reals without equality test. A real-valued function is said to be *majorant-computable* if we can construct a special kind of nonterminating process, which is expressed in the language of Σ-formulas, computing approximations to the result.

Definition 4. *A function $f : \mathbb{R}^n \to \mathbb{R}$ is called majorant-computable if there exist effective sequences of Σ-formulas $\{\Phi_s(\mathbf{x}, y)\}_{s \in \omega}$ and $\{\Psi_s(\mathbf{x}, y)\}_{s \in \omega}$ such that the following conditions hold.*

1. *For all $s \in \omega$, $\mathbf{x} \in \mathbb{R}^n$, the formula Φ_s defines an interval $< \alpha_s, \beta_s >$, and the formula Ψ_s defines the complement of a nonempty interval $[\delta_s, \gamma_s]$.*
2. *For all $\mathbf{x} \in \mathbb{R}^n$, the sequences $\{< \alpha_s, \beta_s >\}_{s \in \omega}$ and $\{[\delta_s, \gamma_s]\}_{s \in \omega}$ decrease monotonically and $< \alpha_s, \beta_s > \subseteq [\delta_s, \gamma_s]$ for all $s \in \omega$.*
3. *For all $\mathbf{x} \in \mathrm{dom}(f)$, $f(\mathbf{x}) = y \leftrightarrow \bigcap_{s \in \omega} < \alpha_s, \beta_s > = \{y\} \leftrightarrow \bigcap_{s \in \omega}[\delta_s, \gamma_s] = \{y\}$; for all $\mathbf{x} \notin \mathrm{dom}(f)$, $\| \bigcap_{s \in \omega} [\delta_s, \gamma_s] \| > 1$.*

As we can see, the process which carries out the computation is represented by two effective procedures. The first procedure produces Σ-formulas Φ_i which define real numbers that are close to the result, the second one produces Σ-formulas which define real numbers that are away from the result.

Theorem 3. *A total real-valued function is majorant-computable if and only if its epigraph and hypergraph are Σ-definable.*

Proof. See [22].

An important corollary is that every majorant-computable function is continuous. Now we compare majorant-computability and definability in the sense of computable analysis [17,32].

Definition 5. *A function $f : \mathbb{R} \to \mathbb{R}$ is called computable if*

1. *it maps computable sequences to computable sequences;*
2. *it is effectively uniformly continuous on intervals $[-n, n]$ for all n.*

In other words, a function $f : \mathbb{R} \to \mathbb{R}$ is *computable* if there exists a Turing machine which transforms Cauchy sequences of rationals, rapidly converging to an input x, into Cauchy sequences of rationals, rapidly converging to the output $f(x)$.

Theorem 4. *The class of computable real-valued functions coincides with the class of majorant-computable real-valued functions.*

Proof. See [22].

Using the language of Σ-formulas it is easy to prove well-known facts about total computable functions, i.e. computability of the maximal value, computability of the unique root, etc. Thus, we can see that the logical approach provides a convenient framework to investigate computability. For the case of the reals this yields a new characterisation of the classical notion of computable real function: a real-valued function is computable if and only if its epigraph and hypergraph are Σ-definable.

7   Future Work

In this paper we have shown that the logical approach provides a convenient framework to investigate computability on continuous data types. In this respect the following direction of research is of special interest: to propose and study descriptive complexity of computational processes over continuous data types.

References

1. J. Barwise. *Admissible sets and structure*. Springer Verlag, Berlin, 1975.
2. A. Blass and Y. Gurevich. Background, reserve and gandy machines. In *Proc. CSL'2000*, volume 1862 of *Lecture Notes in Computer Science*, pages 1–17, 2000.
3. A. Blass, Y. Gurevich, and S. Shelah. Choiceless polynomial time. *APAL*, pages 141–187, 1999.
4. L. Blum, F. Cucker, M. Shub, and S. Smale. *Complexity and Real Computation*. Springer Verlag, Berlin, 1996.
5. J. Bochnak, M. Coste, and M.-F. Roy. *Real Algebraic Geometry*. Springer Verlag, Berlin, 1999.
6. V. Brattka and P. Hertling. Topological properties of real number representations. *TCS*, 284(2):1–17, 2002.
7. E. Dahlhaus and J. A. Makowsky. Query languages for hierarchic databases. *Information and Computation*, pages 1–32, 1992.
8. A. Davar and Y. Gurevich. Fixed-point logics. *BSL*, pages 65–88, 2002.
9. H. Ebbinghaus and J. Flum. *Finite Model Theory*. Springer Verlag, Berlin, 1999.
10. A. Edalat and M. Escardo. Integration in real pcf. In *Proc. IEEE Conference on Logic in Computer Science (LICS)*, pages 382–393, 1996.
11. A. Edalat and A. Lieutie. Domain theory and differential calculus (function of one variable. In *Proc. IEEE Conference on Logic in Computer Science (LICS)*, pages 277–298, 2002.
12. E. Engeler. *Formal Languages: Automata and Structures*. Markham Publishing Co, 1968.
13. Yu. L. Ershov. *Definability and computability*. Plenum, New-York, 1996.
14. H. Freedman and K. Ko. Computational complexity of real functions. *TCS*, pages 323–352, 1992.
15. H. Friedman. Algorithmic procedures, generalized Turing algorithms, and elementary recursion theory. In C. M. E. Yates R. O. Gandy, editor, *Logic colloquium 1969*, pages 361–390. C.M.E, Hollang, Amsterdam, 1971.
16. R. Gandy. Inductive definitions. In J. E. Fenstad and P. D. Hinman, editors, *Generalized Recursion Theory*, pages 265–300. North-Holland, Amsterdam, 1974.
17. A. Grzegorczyk. On the definitions of computable real continuous function. *Fundamenta Mathematik*, pages 61–71, 1957.
18. D. Harel, D. Kozen, and J. Tiuryn. *Dynamic Logic*. The MIT press, Cambridge, MA, 2002.
19. P. G. Hinman. Recursion on abstract structure. In E. R. Griffor, editor, *Handbook of Computability Theory*, pages 317–359. Elsevie, Amsterdam-Tokyo, 1999.
20. N. Immerman. *Descriptive Complexity*. Springer Verlag, New-York, 1999.
21. Ulrich Kohlenbach. Proof theory and computational analysis. *Electronic Notes in Theoretical Computer Science*, 1998.

22. M. Korovina. Computability and Σ-definability over the reals. Technical report, BRICS, 2003. www.brics.dk/~korovina/compreals.ps.
23. M. Korovina. Computational aspects of Σ-definability over the real numbers without the equality test. To appear. www.brics.dk/~korovina/definability.ps.
24. M. Korovina. Fixed points on the abstract structures without the equality test. Technical report, BRICS, 2002. http://www.brics.dk/RS/02/26/index.html.
25. M. Korovina. Fixed points on the reals numbers without the equality test. *Electronic Notes in TCS*, 66(1), 2002.
26. M. Korovina and O. Kudinov. Characteristic properties of majorant-computability over the reals. In *roc. of CSL'98*, volume 1584 of *Lecture Notes in Computer Science*, pages 188–204, 1999.
27. M. Korovina and O. Kudinov. Some properties of majorant-computability. In M. Arslanov and S.Lempp, editors, *Recursion Theory and Complexity", Proceedings of the Kazan-97 Workshop, July 14-19*, pages 97–115. de Gruyter Series in Logic and its Applications, Berlin - New York, 1999.
28. D. Locombe. Recursion theoretical structure for relational systems. In R. O. Gandy and C. M. E. Yates, editors, *Proc. of Logic Colloquium'69*, pages 3–17. "North-Holland", Amsterdam-London, 1971.
29. K. Meer. Counting problems over the reals. *TCS*, 242(1-2):41–58, 2000.
30. Y. N. Moschovakis. Abstract first order computability. i, ii. *Transactions of the American Mathematical Society*, pages 427–46, 1969.
31. Y. N. Moschovakis. *Elementary Induction on Abstract Structur*, volume 77 of *Studies in Logic and the Foundations of Mathematics*. North-Holland Publishing Co., Amsterdam-London; American Elsevier Publishing Co, 1974.
32. M. B. Pour-El and J. I. Richards. *Computability in Analysis and Physics*. Springer Verlag, Berlin, 1988.
33. V. Sazonov. Using agents for concurrent querying of web-like databases via hyper-set-theoretic approach. In *Proc. of PSI'01*, volume 2244 of *Lecture Notes in Computer Science*, pages 378–394, 2001.
34. G. Takeuti and A. Kino. On predicates with constructive infinitary long expressions. *J. Math. Soc. Japan*, pages 176–190, 1963.
35. J. V. Tucker and J. I. Zucker. Computable functions and semicomputable sets on many-sorted algebras. In T. S. E. Maibaum S. Abramsky, D. M. Gabbay, editor, *Handbook of Logic in Computer Science*, pages 397–525. Oxford University Press, Oxford, 2000.
36. M. Vardi. The complexity of relational query languages. In *In Proc. of the 14th ACM Symposium on the Theory of Computing*, pages 37–146, 1982.
37. Klaus Weihrauch. *Computable analysis*. Springer Verlag, Berlin, 2000.

Open Maps and Trace Semantics for Timed Partial Order Models*

Irina B. Virbitskaite and Nataly S. Gribovskaja

A.P. Ershov Institute of Informatics Systems
Siberian Division of the Russian Academy of Sciences
6, Acad. Lavrentiev avenue, 630090, Novosibirsk, Russia
virb@iis.nsk.su

Abstract. The intention of the paper is to show the applicability of the general categorical framework of open maps to the setting of partial order models with a dense time domain. In particular, we define a category of timed event structures, where the morphisms are to be thought of as simulations, and an accompanying (sub)category of timed pomsets which provides us with a notion of open maps. Then, we show that the abstract equivalence obtained from the framework of open maps coincides with a timed extension of the well-known trace equivalence based on Pratt's partial orders.

Keywords: Category theory, timed event structures, partial order semantics, trace equivalence

1 Introduction

Category theory has proven itself very useful in many fields of theoretical computer science. We mention just one example which is directly related to concurrency theory. Over the past several years, various equivalence notions have been defined in concurrency theory. In an attempt to explain and unify apparent differences between the extensive amount of research within the field of behavioral equivalences, several category theoretic approaches to the matter have appeared (see [12,13] among others). One of them was initiated by Joyal, Nielsen, and Winskel in [13] where they proposed an abstract way of capturing the notion of bisimulation through the so-called spans of open maps: first, a category of models of computations is chosen, then a subcategory of observation is chosen relative to which open maps are defined; two models are bisimilar if there exists a span of open maps between the models. The abstract definition of bisimilarity makes possible a uniform definition of bisimulation over different models ranging from interleaving models like transition systems to 'true concurrency' models like event structures. On transition systems, abstract bisimilarity readily corresponds to Milner's strong bisimulation. On event structures, it leads to a strengthening

---

* This work is partially supported by the Russian Ministry of Education (grant No A03-2.8-353).

M. Broy and A.V. Zamulin (Eds.): PSI 2003, LNCS 2890, pp. 248–259, 2003.
© Springer-Verlag Berlin Heidelberg 2003

of history preserving bisimulation. Furthermore, this setting turned out appropriate for defining, among others, trace and testing equivalences, barbed and probabilistic bisimulations, following the line of [18].

In more recent years, great efforts have been made to develop formal methods for real time and other timing-based systems, i.e. systems whose correctness depends crucially upon real time considerations. As a result, timed extensions of interleaving models have been investigated thoroughly. Various recipes on how to incorporate time in transition systems — the most prominent interleaving model — are, for example, described in [2,10]. On the other hand, the situation is less settled in the case of noninterleaving models — few timed extensions of the models are known (see, for example, [5,7,16,17]).

The contribution of the paper is first to show the applicability of the general categorical framework of open maps to the setting of noninterleaving models with dense time. Here, we define a category of timed event structures, where the morphisms are to be thought of as simulations, and an accompanying (sub)category of timed pomsets, which, following [13], provides us with a notion of open maps. Then we use the framework of open maps to obtain the abstract equivalence that is established to coincide with a timed generalization of the well-known trace equivalence based on Pratt's partial orders [19]. Using the fact, we finally show decidability of the timed trace equivalence in the setting of a special class of timed event structures.

There have been several motivations for this work. One has been given by the papers [22,23] which have proposed and investigated categorical characterizations of event structure models. A next origin of this study has been a number of papers which have extensively studied time-sensitive equivalence notions for timed interleaving models. For instance, timed interleaving bisimulation was shown decidable for finite timed transition systems by Čerāns in [8], and since then more efficient algorithms have been discovered in [15,21]. However, to our best knowledge, the literature on timed partial order models has hitherto lacked such equivalences. In this regard, the papers [3,17] are a welcome exception, where the decidability question of timed interleaving testing in the framework of event structures with time notions has been treated. Furthermore, in the paper [20], timed variants of partial order based equivalences have been provided for timed event structures. Finally, another motivation has been given by the paper [11] that illustrates the use of open maps for providing an alternative proof of decidability of interleaving bisimulation for finite timed transition systems.

The rest of the paper is organized as follows. The basic notions concerning timed event structures and a timed trace equivalence based on Pratt's partial orders are introduced in the next section. A category of timed event structures is defined and studied in Section 3. A notion of open maps and its alternative characterization in the setting of timed event structures are provided in Section 4. Also, based on spans of open maps, the resulting abstract equivalence is studied, and shown to coincide with the timed trace equivalence. Section 5 is devoted to decidability of the equivalences in the framework of a special class of timed event structures. Section 6 contains conclusion and future work. Some of the proofs are relegated to an Appendix when they disturb the exposition.

2 Timed Event Structures

In this section, we introduce some basic notions and notations concerning timed event structures and a partial order based trace equivalence between them.

We first recall a notion of event structures [22] which constitute a major branch of partial order models. The main idea behind event structures is to view distributed computations as action occurrences, called events, together with a notion of causality dependency between events (which is reasonably characterized via a partial order). Moreover, in order to model nondeterminism, there is a notion of conflicting (mutually incompatible) events. A labelling function records which action an event corresponds to.

Let L be a finite set of actions. A *(labelled) event structure* over L is a tuple $S = (E, \leq, \#, l)$, where E is a countable set of events; $\leq \subseteq E \times E$ is a partial order (the *causality relation*), satisfying the *principle of finite causes*: $\forall e \in E \circ \{e' \in E \mid e' \leq e\}$ is finite; $\# \subseteq E \times E$ is a symmetric and irreflexive relation (the *conflict relation*), satisfying the *principle of conflict heredity*: $\forall e, e', e'' \in E \circ e \# e' \leq e'' \Rightarrow e \# e''$; $l : E \longrightarrow L$ is a labelling function.

For an event structure $S = (E, \leq, \#, l)$, we define $\smile = (E \times E) \setminus (\leq \cup \leq^{-1} \cup \#)$ (the *concurrency relation*). Let $C \subseteq E$. Then C is *left-closed* iff $\forall e, e' \in E \circ e \in C \wedge e' \leq e \Rightarrow e' \in C$; C is *conflict-free* iff $\forall e, e' \in C \circ \neg(e \# e')$; C is a *configuration of S* iff C is left-closed and conflict-free. Let $\mathcal{C}(S)$ denote the set of all finite configurations of S. For $C \subseteq E$, the *restriction* of S to C, denoted $S{\restriction}C$, is defined as $(C, \leq \cap(C \times C), \# \cap (C \times C), l \mid_C)$. We shall use $\mathcal{O}$ to denote the empty event structure $(\emptyset, \emptyset, \emptyset, \emptyset)$.

We next present a dense time variant of event structures, called *timed event structures*, because it is well recognized that the dense time approach looks more suitable to model realistic systems (see [1] for more explanation). In our model, we add time constraints to event structures by associating their events with earliest and latest times (w.r.t. a global clock) at which the events can occur. Following [14,16], the occurrence of an enabled event itself takes no time but it can be suspended for a certain time (between its earliest and latest times) from the start of the system. The reason for not using what is often referred to as local clocks (i.e., each event has its delay timer attached and the timer is set when the event becomes enabled and reset when the event is disabled or started to be executed) is that the operational semantics to timed models is more simple by avoiding local clocks (see [14] among others).

Before introducing the concept of a timed event structure, we need to define some auxiliary notations. Let $\mathbf{N}$ be the set of natural numbers, and $\mathbf{R}$ the set of nonnegative real numbers.

Definition 1. *A (labelled) timed event structure over L is a triple $TS = (S, Eot, Lot)$, where $S = (E, \leq, \#, l)$ is a (labelled) event structure over L; Eot,*

$Lot : E \to \mathbf{R}$ *are functions of the* earliest *and* latest occurrence times *of events,* satisfying $Eot(e) \leq Lot(e)$ *for all* $e \in E$.

A timed event structure is said to *have a correct timing*, if $e' \leq_S e \Rightarrow Eot(e') \leq Eot(e)$, and $Lot(e') \leq Lot(e)$, for all $e, e' \in E$. In the following, we will consider only timed event structures having a correct timing and call them simply timed event structures.

For depicting timed event structures, we use the following conventions. The action labels and timing constraints associated with events are drawn near the events. If no confusion arises, we will often use action labels rather event identities to denote events. The $<$-relation is depicted by arcs (omitting those derivable by transitivity), and conflicts are also drawn (omitting those derivable by conflict heredity). Following these conventions, a trivial example of a labelled timed event structure is shown in Fig. 1.

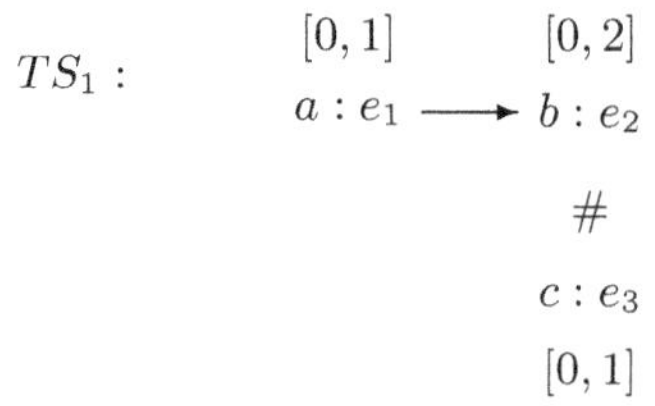

$$TS_1 : \quad \begin{array}{cc} [0,1] & [0,2] \\ a : e_1 \longrightarrow b : e_2 \end{array}$$

$$\#$$

$$c : e_3$$

$$[0,1]$$

Fig. 1.

Timed event structures TS and TS' are *isomorphic* (denoted $TS \simeq TS'$), if there exists a bijection $\varphi : E_{TS} \longrightarrow E_{TS'}$ such that $e \leq_{TS} e'$ iff $\varphi(e) \leq_{TS'} \varphi(e')$, $e \mathbin{\#_{TS}} e'$ iff $\varphi(e) \mathbin{\#_{TS'}} \varphi(e')$, $l_{TS}(e) = l_{TS'}(\varphi(e))$, and $Eot_{TS}(e) = Eot_{TS'}(\varphi(e))$, $Lot_{TS}(e) = Lot_{TS'}(\varphi(e))$, for all $e, e' \in E_{TS}$.

An execution of a timed event structure is a *timed configuration* which consists of a configuration and a timing function recording global time moments at which events occur, and satisfies some additional requirements. Let $TS = (S, Eot, Lot)$ be a timed event structure, $C \in \mathcal{C}(S)$, and $T : C \longrightarrow \mathbf{R}$. Then $TC = (C, T)$ is a *timed configuration* of TS iff the following conditions hold: (i) $\forall e \in C \circ Eot(e) \leq T(e) \leq Lot(e)$; (ii) $\forall e, e' \in C \circ e \leq_{TS} e' \Rightarrow T(e) \leq T(e')$. Informally speaking, the condition (i) expresses that an event can occur at a time when its timing constraints are met; the condition (ii) says that for all two events e and e' occurred if e causally precedes e' then e should temporally precede e'. Thus, we explicitly avoid the ill-timedness phenomena [4,14], because it seems more realistic to assume that the causal precedence of events does reflect their order in time. Moreover, unlike [4,16]), we do not force events to occur once they are ready, i.e. their causal predecessors have occurred and their timing constraints are respected, since the concept of urgent events is sometimes quite constraining in the timing actions (see [5,14] for more explanation). In our model, all events are non-urgent, allowing idling to be modelled. The *initial timed configuration* of TS is $TC_{TS} = (\emptyset, \emptyset)$. We use $\mathcal{TC}(TS)$ to denote the set of timed configurations of TS. To illustrate the concept, consider the set of possible timed configurations of the timed event structure TS_1 shown in Fig. 1: $\{(\emptyset,\emptyset),$ $(\{e_1\},T_1), (\{e_3\},T_2), (\{e_1,e_3\},T_3), (\{e_1,e_2\},T_4) \mid T_1(e_1) \in [0,1]; T_2(e_3) \in [0,1];$ $T_3(e_1),T_3(e_3) \in [0,1]; T_4(e_1) \in [0,1], T_4(e_2) \in [0,2], T_4(e_1) \leq T_4(e_2)\}.$

The semantics of timed event structures is defined by means of timed pomsets. First, define a *timed partial order set* as a timed event structure $TP = (S_{TP} = (E_{TP}, \leq_{TP}, \#_{TP}, l_{TP}), Eot_{TP}, Lot_{TP})$ with $\#_{TP} = \emptyset$ and $Eot_{TP}(e) = Lot_{TP}(e)$, for all $e \in E_{TP}$. Isomorphism classes of timed partial order sets are called *timed pomsets*. The *empty timed pomset* is $(\emptyset,\emptyset,\emptyset,\emptyset)$. We use $\mathcal{TPom}_L$ to indicate the set of finite timed pomsets labelled over L.

For a timed event structure TS and a timed configuration $TC = (C,T) \in \mathcal{TC}(TS)$, the *restriction* of TS to TC, denoted $TS\lceil TC$, is defined as an isomorphism class of $(S\lceil C, T)$. For $TC_1 = (C_1,T_1), TC_2 = (C_2,T_2) \in \mathcal{TC}(TS)$, from now on, we shall write $TC_1 \longrightarrow TC_2$ iff $C_1 \subseteq C_2$, $T_2|_{C_1} = T_1$, and $\forall e \in C_1 \ \forall e' \in (C_2 \setminus C_1) \circ T_1(e) \leq T_2(e'); TC_1 \xrightarrow{TP} TC_2$ iff $TC_1 \longrightarrow TC_2$ and TP is an isomorphism class of $(S_{TS}\lceil(C_2 \setminus C_1), T_2|_{(C_2\setminus C_1)}).$

We need to introduce some auxiliary notions and notations. Let TP and TP' be timed pomsets (isomorphism classes of $(E, \leq, l, Eot)$ and $(E', \leq', l, Eot')$, respectively). Then TP' is a *prefix* of TP, if E' is a left-closed subset of E, $\leq' = \leq \cap (E' \times E')$, $l' = l \mid_{E'}$, and $Eot' = Eot \mid_{E'}; TP'$ is an *augment* of TP, if there exists a bijection $\phi : E' \longrightarrow E$ such that $e \leq' e'$ if $\phi(e) \leq \phi(e'), l'(e) = l(\phi(e)),$ $Eot(e) = Eot'(\phi(e))$, for all $e, e' \in E'$. The set $L_{tp}(TS) = \{TP' \mid TP'$ is an augment of TP, and $TC_{TS} \xrightarrow{TP} TC$ for some $TC \in \mathcal{TC}(TS)\}$ is the *timed pomset language (tp-language)* of TS.

We are now ready to introduce a notion of trace equivalence based on timed pomsets (TP-equivalence), in the setting of timed event structures.

Definition 2. *Timed event structures TS and TS' are TP-equivalent (denoted by $TS \equiv_{TP} TS'$) iff $L_{tp}(TS) = L_{tp}(TS')$.*

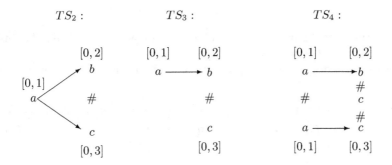

Fig. 2.

Considering the timed event structures shown in Fig. 2, we have $TS_3 \equiv_{TP}$ TS_4 but $TS_2 \not\equiv_{TP} TS_3$ because a timed pomset $\overset{[t_1,t_1]}{a} \ \overset{[t_2,t_2]}{c}$ ($t_1 \in [0,1]$, $t_2 \in [0,3]$) belongs to $L_{tp}(TS_3)$ but does not to $L_{tp}(TS_2)$.

3 A Category of Timed Event Structures

In this section, we define a category of timed event structures. The morphisms of our model category will be simulation morphisms following the approach of [13]. This leads to the following definition of a morphism that is a function, mapping events of the simulated system to simulating events of the other, satisfying some requirements.

Definition 3. *A morphism between timed event structures* $TS = (E, \leq, \#, l,$ $Eot, Lot)$ *and* $TS' = (E', \leq', \#', l', Eot', Lot')$, $\mu : TS \to TS'$, *is a function* $\mu : E \to E'$ *such that:*

- $l' \circ \mu = l$;
- $TC = (C,T) \in \mathcal{TC}(TS) \ \Rightarrow \ (\mu\, C, T') \in \mathcal{TC}(TS')$ *with* $T' \circ \mu = T$, *and*
  $\forall e, e' \in C \circ \mu(e) = \mu(e') \Rightarrow e = e'$.

As an illustration, consider a morphism from the timed event structure TS_5 in Fig. 3 to the timed event structure TS_1 in Fig. 1 mapping events e'_i to e_i ($1 \leq i \leq 3$). It is easy to check that the constraints in Definition 3 are satisfied.

TS_5 :

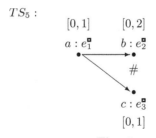

Fig. 3.

For a timed configuration $TC = (C,T)$, from now on, we write $\mu\, TC$ instead of $(\mu\, C, T')$ with $T' \circ \mu = T$.

Let us consider a simulation property of the morphisms defined prior to that.

Theorem 1. *Given a morphism* $\mu : TS \to TS'$ *and a timed pomset* TP. *If* $TC_{TS} \xrightarrow{TP} TC$ *in* TS, *then* $TC_{TS'} \xrightarrow{TP'} TC'$ *in* TS' *and* $\mu\, TC = TC'$, *where* TP *is an augment of* TP'.

Proof. It is straightforward, using the definitions of a timed configuration, morphism and augment. □

Thus, in the formal sense of Theorem 1, we have shown that the morphisms from Definition 3 represent a notion of simulation. Notice, on timed pomsets TP and TP', a morphism from TP to TP' amounts to 'TP being an augment of a prefix of TP''. So, define a category of timed event structures as follows.

Definition 4. *Timed event structures (labelled over L) with morphisms between them form a category of timed event structures $\mathcal{TS}_L$, in which the composition of two morphisms $\mu_1 : TS_0 \longrightarrow TS_1$ and $\mu_2 : TS_1 \longrightarrow TS_2$ is $(\mu_2 \circ \mu_1) : TS_0 \longrightarrow TS_2$, and the identity morphism is the identity function.*

Proposition 1. *$\mathcal{TS}_L$ is a category.*

4   Characterizations

Following the standards of timed event structures and the paper [13], we would like to choose timed pomsets with special morphisms between them so as to form a full subcategory of the category of timed event structures. With respect to a set of actions L, let $\mathcal{TP}_L^0$ denote the subcategory of the category $\mathcal{TS}_L$ whose objects are from $\mathcal{TPom}_L$, and whose morphisms are the identities and morphisms with the empty timed pomsets as domain. Given our categories of timed event structures and timed pomsets, we first apply the general framework from [13], defining the concept of $\mathcal{TP}_L^0$-open morphisms.

Definition 5. *A morphism $\mu : TS \to TS'$ in $\mathcal{TS}_L$ is called $\mathcal{TP}_L^0$-open iff whenever there exists $\mu' : TP \to TP'$ in $\mathcal{TP}_L^0$, $\mu'' : TP \to TS$ and $\mu''' : TP' \to TS'$ in $\mathcal{TS}_L$ such that $\mu \circ \mu'' = \mu''' \circ \mu'$, there exists a morphism $\widetilde{\mu} : TP' \to TS$ in $\mathcal{TS}_L$ such that $\mu'' = \widetilde{\mu} \circ \mu'$ and $\mu''' = \mu \circ \widetilde{\mu}$.*

Our next aim is to characterize $\mathcal{TP}_L^0$-openness of morphisms.

Theorem 2. *A morphism $\mu : TS \to TS'$ is $\mathcal{TP}_L^0$-open iff whenever $TC_{TS'} \xrightarrow{TP} TC'$ in TS', $TC_{TS} \xrightarrow{TP} TC$ in TS and $\mu\, TC = TC'$.*

Proof. It follows similar lines as other standard proofs of the characterization of openness of maps (see e.g., [11]).   □

As was reported in [13], the open map approach provides the general concept of bisimilarity for any categorical model of computation. We next introduce abstract bisimilarity, given in terms of a span of $\mathcal{TP}_L^0$-open morphisms.

Definition 6. *Timed event structures TS_1 and TS_2 are called $\mathcal{TP}_L^0$-bisimilar iff there exists a span $TS_1 \xleftarrow{\mu} TS \xrightarrow{\mu'} TS_2$ with vertex TS of $\mathcal{TP}_L^0$-open morphism.*

Notice that it follows from [13] and Theorem 3 (see below) that $\mathcal{TP}_L^0$-bisimulation is exactly the equivalence generated by $\mathcal{TP}_L^0$-open morphisms.

Theorem 3. *Let $\mu_1 : TS_1 \to TS$ and $\mu_2 : TS_2 \to TS$ be $\mathcal{TP}_L^0$-open morphisms. There exists a timed event structure TS_x and $\mathcal{TP}_L^0$-open morphisms $\mu_1' : TS_x \to TS_1$, $\mu_2' : TS_x \to TS_2$ such that $\mu_1 \circ \mu_1' = \mu_2 \circ \mu_2'$.*

Proof. See Appendix.   □

Finally, the coincidence of abstract bisimilarity and TP-equivalence is established.

Theorem 4. *Let TS_1 and TS_2 be timed event structures. Then TS_1 and TS_2 are $\mathcal{TP}_L^0$-bisimilar iff they are TP-equivalent.*

Proof. See Appendix.   □

5 Decidability

In this section, we first consider the decidability question for $\mathcal{TP}_L^0$-openness of morphisms in the setting of a special subclass of timed event structures, i.e. structures with finite sets of events and for which all constants referred to in the earliest and latest occurrence times of events are natural valued. The subclass of timed event structures is denoted by $\mathcal{TS_N}$.

As for many existing results for timed models, including results concerning verification of real-time systems, our decision procedure relies heavily on the idea behind regions (equivalence classes of states) [2], which essentially provides a finite description of the state-space of timed event structures.

Given a timed event structure $TS = (S = (E, \leq, \#, l), Eot, Lot)$, $E' \subseteq E$ and $T, T' \in [E' \longrightarrow \mathbf{R}]$, we let $T \simeq T'$ iff (i) for each $e \in E'$ it holds: $\lfloor T(e) \rfloor = \lfloor T'(e) \rfloor$, and (ii) for each $e, e' \in E'$ it holds: $\wr T(e) \wr \leq \wr T(e') \wr \Leftrightarrow \wr T'(e) \wr \leq \wr T'(e') \wr$, and $\wr T(e) \wr = 0 \Leftrightarrow \wr T'(e) \wr = 0$. Here, for $d \in \mathbf{R}$, $\wr d \wr$ and $\lfloor d \rfloor$ denote its fractional and smallest integer parts, respectively. For $(C, T) \in \mathcal{TC}(TS)$, $[T]$ denotes the *region* to which T belongs. An *extended timed configuration* of TS is defined as $[TC] = (C, [T])$ with $TC = (C, T) \in \mathcal{TC}(TS)$. We consider $[TC_{TS}] = (\emptyset, [\emptyset])$ as the *initial extended timed configuration* of TS. For an extended timed configuration $[TC] = (C, [T])$, we shall use $\mu\,[TC]$ instead of $(\mu\,C, [T'])$ with $T' \circ \mu = T$. For extended timed configurations $[TC] = (C, [T])$, $[TC'] = (C', [T'])$, we shall write $[TC] \xrightarrow{TP} [TC']$, if $(C, T) \xrightarrow{TP} (C', T')$.

We now give a characterization of $\mathcal{TP}_L^0$-openness of morphisms in terms of extended timed configurations.

Theorem 5. *Let $TS_1, TS_2 \in \mathcal{TS_N}$. A morphism $\mu : TS \to TS'$ is $\mathcal{TP}_L^0$-open iff whenever $[TC_{TS'}] \xrightarrow{TP} [TC']$ in TS', $[TC_{TS}] \xrightarrow{TP} [TC]$ in TS and $\mu\,[TC] = [TC']$.*

Proof. Follows from the definition of a region and Theorem 2.   □

Notice that the theorem above implies decidability of $\mathcal{TP}_L^0$-openness of morphisms between TS and TS' from $\mathcal{TS_N}$.

Theorem 6. *Let $TS_1, TS_2 \in \mathcal{TS_N}$. If there exists a span of $\mathcal{TP}_L^0$-open morphisms $TS_1 \xleftarrow{\mu_1} TS \xrightarrow{\mu_2} TS_2$, then there exists $TS' \in \mathcal{TS_N}$ of size bounded by the size of TS_1 and TS_2 and with $\mathcal{TP}_L^0$-open morphisms $TS_1 \xleftarrow{\mu_1'} TS' \xrightarrow{\mu_2'} TS_2$.*

Proof. See Appendix.   □

Corollary 1. *For $TS_1, TS_2 \in \mathcal{TS_N}$, $TS_1 \equiv_{TP} TS_2$ is decidable.*

6 Conclusion

In this paper, we have tried in practice to investigate the applicability of Joyal, Nielsen, and Winskel's theory of open maps [13], to providing a meaningful trace equivalence in a category of a dense time variant of a partial order model — timed event structures. This allows us to take into account the processes' timing behaviour in addition to their degrees of relative concurrency and nondeterminism, and to apply the categorical framework to characterize and, also, to decide the time-sensitive trace equivalence based on Pratt's partial orders, when restricted to a special class of finite timed event structures.

A natural continuation of this work is to check whether the result can be directly applied to timed extensions of partial order bisimulations [6]. Also, in the category of timed event structures, we expect to be able to capture timed variants of partial order testing [9] by defining a new morphism which intuitively corresponds to the testing semantics. Some categorical investigation on weak behavioural equivalences are now under way, and we plan to report on this work elsewhere.

References

1. R. ALUR, C. COURCOUBETIS, D. DILL. Model checking in dense real time. *Information and Computation* **104** (1993) 2–34.

2. R. ALUR, D. DILL. The theory of timed automata. *Theoretical Computer Science* **126** (1994) 183–235.

3. M.V. ANDREEVA, E.N. BOZHENKOVA, I.B. VIRBITSKAITE Analysis of timed concurrent models based on testing equivalence. *Fundamenta Informaticae* **43**(1-4)(2000) 1–20.

4. L. ACETO, D. MURPHI. Timing and causality in process algebra. *Acta Informatica* **33**(4) (1996) 317–350.

5. C. BAIER, J.-P. KATOEN, D. LATELLA. Metric semantics for true concurrent real time. Proc. *25th Int. Colloquium, ICALP'98*, Aalborg, Denmark (1998) 568–579.

6. M.A. BEDNARCZYK. Hereditory history preserving bisimulation or what is the power of the future perfect in program logics. Technical Report, Polish Academy of Science, Gdansk, 1991.

7. J. BENGTSSON, B. JONSSON, J. LILIUS, W. YI. Partial order reductions for timed systems. *Lecture Notes in Computer Science* **1466** (1998) 485–496.

8. K. ČERĀNS. Decidability of bisimulation equivalences for parallel timer processes. *Lecture Notes in Computer Science* **663** (1993) 302–315.

9. U. GOLTZ, H. WEHRHEIM. Causal testing. *Lecture Notes in Computer Science* **1113** (1996) 394–406.

10. T.A. HENZINGER, Z. MANNA, A. PNUELI. Timed transition systems. *Lecture Notes in Computer Science* **600**(1991) 226 – 251.

11. T. HUNE, M. NIELSEN. Timed bisimulation and open maps. *Lecture Notes in Computer Science* **1450** (1998) 378–387.

12. B. JACOBS, J. RUTTEN. A tutorial on (Co)algebras and (Co)induction. *EATCS Bulletin* **62** (1997) 222–259.

13. A. JOYAL, M. NIELSEN, G. WINSKEL. Bisimulation from open maps. *Information and Computation* **127(2)** (1996) 164–185.

14. J.-P. KATOEN, R. LANGERAK, D. LATELLA, E. BRINKSMA. On specifying real-time systems in a causality-based setting. *Lecture Notes in Computer Science* **1135** (1996) 385–404.

15. F. LAROUSSINIE, K.G. LARSEN, C. WEISE. From timed automata to logic and back. *Lecture Notes in Computer Science* **969** (1995) 529–539.

16. A. MAGGIOLO-SCHETTINI, J. WINKOWSKI. Towards an algebra for timed behaviours. *Theoretical Computer Science* **103** (1992) 335–363.

17. D. MURPHY. Time and duration in noninterleaving concurrency. *Fundamenta Informaticae* **19** (1993) 403–416.

18. M. NIELSEN, A. CHENG. Observing behaviour categorically. *Lecture Notes in Computer Science* **1026** (1996) 263–278.

19. V.R. PRATT. Modeling concurrency with partial orders. *Int. Journal of Parallel Programming* **15(1)** (1986) 33–71.

20. I.B. VIRBITSKAITE. An observation semantics for timed event structures. *Lecture Notes in Computer Science* **2244** (2001) 215–225.

21. C. WEISE, D. LENZKES. Efficient scaling-invariant checking of timed bisimulation. *Lecture Notes in Computer Science* **1200** (1997) 176–188.

22. G. WINSKEL. An introduction to event structures. *Lecture Notes in Computer Science* **354** (1988) 364–397.

23. G. WINSKEL, M. NIELSEN. Models for concurrency. In *Handbook of Logic in Computer Science* **4** (1995).

Appendix

Proof Sketch of Theorem 3. W.l.o.g. assume $TS_i = (E_i, \leq_i, \#_i, l_i, Eot_i, Lot_i)$ for $i \in \{1, 2\}$. As a first step, we construct a structure $TS_x = (E_x, \leq_x, \#_x, l_x, Eot_x, Lot_x) = +(TS_{TC_1 \times TC_2} \mid TC_i = (C_i, T_i) \in \mathcal{TC}(TS_i)$ for all $i \in \{1, 2\}$, $\mu_1\, TC_1 = \mu_2\, TC_2$, and $TS\lceil \mu_j\, TC_j \simeq TS_j \lceil TC_j$ for some $j \in \{1, 2\})$ with $TS_{TC_1 \times TC_2} = (E_{TC_1 \times TC_2}, \leq_{TC_1 \times TC_2}, \#_{TC_1 \times TC_2}, l_{TC_1 \times TC_2}, Eot_{TC_1 \times TC_2}, Lot_{TC_1 \times TC_2})$ defined as follows:

- $E_{TC_1 \times TC_2} = \{(e_1, e_2)_{TC_1 \times TC_2} \in C_1 \times C_2 \mid \mu_1(e_1) = \mu_2(e_2)\}$;
- $(e_1, e_2)_{TC_1 \times TC_2} \leq_{TC_1 \times TC_2} (e_1', e_2')_{TC_1 \times TC_2} \iff e_i \leq_i e_i'$, for some $i \in \{1, 2\}$;
- $\#_{TC_1 \times TC_2} = \emptyset$;
- $l_{TC_1 \times TC_2}((e_1, e_2)_{TC_1 \times TC_2}) = l_i(e_i)$, for all $(e_1, e_2)_{TC_1 \times TC_2} \in E_{TC_1 \times TC_2}$ and some $i \in \{1, 2\}$;
- $Eot_{TC_1 \times TC_2}((e_1, e_2)_{TC_1 \times TC_2}) = T_i(e_i)$, for all $(e_1, e_2)_{TC_1 \times TC_2} \in E_{TC_1 \times TC_2}$ and some $i \in \{1, 2\}$;
- $Lot_{TC_1 \times TC_2}((e_1, e_2)_{TC_1 \times TC_2}) = T_i(e_i)$, for all $(e_1, e_2)_{TC_1 \times TC_2} \in E_{TC_1 \times TC_2}$ and some $i \in \{1, 2\}$.

Here, '+' denotes an algebraic operation that can be 'interpreted' by indicating that all events in one component are in the #-relation with all events in the other. It is a routine to show that TS_x is a timed event structure.

Next, define maps $\mu_i' : TS_x \longrightarrow TS_i$ as follows: $\mu_i'((e_1, e_2)_{TC_1 \times TC_2}) = e_i$, for all $(e_1, e_2)_{TC_1 \times TC_2} \in E_x$ $(i = 1, 2)$. It is straightforward to check that μ_1' and μ_2'

are indeed morphisms. The fact that $\mu_1 \circ \mu_1' = \mu_2 \circ \mu_2'$ immediately follows from the construction of TS_x and the definition of μ_1' and μ_2'.

Finally, we have to show that μ_i' is a $\mathcal{TP}_L^0$-open morphism $(i \in \{1,2\})$. W.l.o.g. assume that $TC_{TS_i} \overset{TP}{\to} TC_i$ in TS_i. We then have that $TC_{TS} \overset{TP'}{\to} \mu_i \ TC_i$ in TS, and TP is an augment of TP', by Theorem 1. This implies that $TC_{TS_{3-i}} \overset{TP'}{\to} TC_{3-i}$ in TS_{3-i}, and $\mu_i \ TC_i = \mu_{3-i} \ TC_{3-i}$, according to Theorem 2. This means that $TS\lceil\mu_{3-i} \ TC_{3-i} \simeq TS_{3-i}\lceil TC_{3-i}$. Then we can construct $TS_{TC_1 \times TC_2}$ as a part of TS_x. It is now easy to show that $TC_x = (E_{TC_1 \times TC_2}, Eot_{TC_1 \times TC_2}) \in \mathcal{TC}(TS_x)$, and $TS_x\lceil TC_x \simeq TS_i\lceil TC_i$, using the construction of TS_x. This implies that $TC_{TS_x} \overset{TP}{\to} TC_x$ in TS_x. Moreover, we have that $\mu_i' \ TC_x = TC_i$, due to the definition of μ_i'. Thus, μ_i' is a $\mathcal{TP}_L^0$-open morphism $(i \in \{1,2\})$, by Theorem 2. $\square$

Proof Sketch of Theorem 4. $(\Rightarrow)$ Suppose $TS_1 \overset{\mu_1}{\leftarrow} TS \overset{\mu_2}{\to} TS_2$ to be a span of $\mathcal{TP}_L^0$-open morphisms. Let us prove that $L_{tp}(TS_1) \subseteq L_{tp}(TS_2)$ (the proof of $L_{tp}(TS_2) \subseteq L_{tp}(TS_1)$ is symmetric). Take an arbitrary $TP \in L_{tp}(TS_1)$. This implies that $TC_{TS_1} \overset{TP'}{\to} TC_1$ in TS_1, and TP is an augment of TP'. By Theorem 2, we have that $TC_{TS} \overset{TP'}{\to} TC$ in TS, and $\mu_1 \ TC = TC_1$. From Theorem 1, it follows that $TC_{TS_2} \overset{TP''}{\to} \mu_2 \ TC$ in TS_2, and TP' is an augment of TP''. Hence, TP is an augment of TP'', i.e. $TP \in L_{tp}(TS_2)$. Thus, we get that $L_{tp}(TS_1) = L_{tp}(TS_2)$.

$(\Leftarrow)$ Suppose that $L_{tp}(TS_1) = L_{tp}(TS_2)$. W.l.o.g. assume $TS_i = (E_i, \leq_i, \#_i, l_i, Eot_i, Lot_i)$ for $i \in \{1,2\}$. As a first step, we construct a structure $TS = (E, \leq, \#, l, Eot, Lot) = +(TS_{TC_1 \times TC_2} \mid TC_i = (C_i, T_i) \in \mathcal{TC}(TS_i)$ for all $i \in \{1,2\}$, and $TS_j\lceil TC_j$ is an augment of $TS_{3-j}\lceil TC_{3-j}$ for some $j \in \{1,2\})$ with the augment function $\phi : E_{TS_j\lceil TC_j} \longrightarrow E_{TS_{3-j}\lceil TC_{3-j}}$, and $TS_{TC_1 \times TC_2} = (E_{TC_1 \times TC_2}, \leq_{TC_1 \times TC_2}, \#_{TC_1 \times TC_2}, l_{TC_1 \times TC_2}, Eot_{TC_1 \times TC_2}, Lot_{TC_1 \times TC_2})$ defined as follows:

- $E_{TC_1 \times TC_2} = \{(e_1, e_2)_{TC_1 \times TC_2} \in C_1 \times C_2 \mid \phi(e_j) = e_{3-j}\}$;
- $(e_1, e_2)_{TC_1 \times TC_2} \leq_{TC_1 \times TC_2} (e_1', e_2')_{TC_1 \times TC_2} \iff e_i \leq_i e_i'$, for some $i \in \{1,2\}$;
- $\#_{TC_1 \times TC_2} = \emptyset$;
- $l_{TC_1 \times TC_2}((e_1, e_2)_{TC_1 \times TC_2}) = l_i(e_i)$, for all $(e_1, e_2)_{TC_1 \times TC_2} \in E_{TC_1 \times TC_2}$ and some $i \in \{1,2\}$;
- $Eot_{TC_1 \times TC_2}((e_1, e_2)_{TC_1 \times TC_2}) = T_i(e_i)$, for all $(e_1, e_2)_{TC_1 \times TC_2} \in E_{TC_1 \times TC_2}$ and some $i \in \{1,2\}$;
- $Lot_{TC_1 \times TC_2}((e_1, e_2)_{TC_1 \times TC_2}) = T_i(e_i)$, for all $(e_1, e_2)_{TC_1 \times TC_2} \in E_{TC_1 \times TC_2}$ and some $i \in \{1,2\}$.

Here, '+' denotes an algebraic operation that can be 'interpreted' by indicating that all events in one component are in the #-relation with all events in the other. It is a routine to show that TS is a timed event structure.

Next, define maps $\mu_i : TS \longrightarrow TS_i$ as follows: $\mu_i((e_1, e_2)_{TC_1 \times TC_2}) = e_i$, for all $(e_1, e_2)_{TC_1 \times TC_2} \in E$ $(i = 1, 2)$. It is straightforward to check that μ_1 and μ_2 are indeed morphisms.

Finally, we have to show that μ_i is a $\mathcal{TP}_L^0$-open morphism ($i \in \{1,2\}$). W.l.o.g. assume that $TC_{TS_i} \overset{TP}{\to} TC_i$ in TS_i. We then have that $TP \in L_{tp}(TS_i)$. Since $L_{tp}(TS_1) = L_{tp}(TS_2)$, it implies that $TC_{TS_{3-i}} \overset{TP'}{\to} TC_{3-i}$ in TS_{3-i}, and TP is an augment of TP'. This means that $TS_i \lceil TC_i$ is an augment of $TS_{3-i} \lceil TC_{3-i}$. Then we can construct $TS_{TC_1 \times TC_2}$ as a part of TS. It is now easy to show that $TC = (E_{TC_1 \times TC_2}, Eot_{TC_1 \times TC_2}) \in \mathcal{TC}(TS)$, and $TS \lceil TC \simeq TS_i \lceil TC_i$, using the construction of TS. This means that $TC_{TS} \overset{TP}{\to} TC$ in TS. Moreover, we have that $\mu_i\, TC = TC_i$, due to the definition of μ_i. Thus, μ_i is a $\mathcal{TP}_L^0$-open morphism ($i \in \{1,2\}$), by Theorem 2. $\qquad\square$

Proof Sketch of Theorem 6. Suppose $TS_1 \overset{\mu_1}{\longleftarrow} TS \overset{\mu_2}{\longrightarrow} TS_2$ to be a span of $\mathcal{TP}_L^0$-open morphisms. W.l.o.g. assume $TS_i = (E_i, \leq_i, \#_i, l_i, Eot_i, Lot_i)$ for $i \in \{1,2\}$. First, we construct a structure $TS' = (E', \leq', \#', l', Eot', Lot') = +(TS_{C_1 \times C_2} \mid \exists TC = (C,T) \in \mathcal{TC}(TS),\ \exists TC_i = (C_i, T_i) \in \mathcal{TC}(TS_i) \diamond \mu_i\, TC = TC_i$ for all $i \in \{1,2\}$, and $TS \lceil TC \simeq TS_j \lceil \mu_j\, TC$ for some $j \in \{1,2\}$) with $TS_{C_1 \times C_2} = (E_{C_1 \times C_2}, \leq_{C_1 \times C_2}, \#_{C_1 \times C_2}, l_{C_1 \times C_2}, Eot_{C_1 \times C_2}, Lot_{C_1 \times C_2})$ defined as follows:

- $E_{C_1 \times C_2} = \{(e_1, e_2)_{C_1 \times C_2} \in C_1 \times C_2 \mid \exists e \in C \diamond \mu_i(e) = e_i$ for all $(i = 1, 2)\}$;
- $(e_1, e_2)_{C_1 \times C_2} \leq_{C_1 \times C_2} (e_1', e_2')_{C_1 \times C_2} \Leftrightarrow e_i \leq_i e_i'$, for some $i \in \{1,2\}$;
- $\#_{C_1 \times C_2} = \emptyset$;
- $l_{C_1 \times C_2}((e_1, e_2)_{C_1 \times C_2}) = l_i(e_i)$, for all $(e_1, e_2)_{C_1 \times C_2} \in E_{C_1 \times C_2}$ and some $i \in \{1,2\}$;
- $Eot_{C_1 \times C_2}((e_1, e_2)_{C_1 \times C_2}) = \max\{Eot_1(e_1'),\ Eot_2(e_2') \mid (e_1', e_2')_{C_1 \times C_2} \leq_{C_1 \times C_2} (e_1, e_2)_{C_1 \times C_2}\}$, for all $(e_1, e_2)_{C_1 \times C_2} \in E_{C_1 \times C_2}$;
- $Lot_{C_1 \times C_2}((e_1, e_2)_{C_1 \times C_2}) = \min\{Lot_1(e_1'),\ Lot_2(e_2') \mid (e_1, e_2)_{C_1 \times C_2} \leq_{C_1 \times C_2} (e_1', e_2')_{C_1 \times C_2}\}$, for all $(e_1, e_2)_{C_1 \times C_2} \in E_{C_1 \times C_2}$.

Here, '$+$' denotes an algebraic operation that can be 'interpreted' by indicating that all events in one component are in the $\#$-relation with all events in the other. Using the construction of TS', it is a routine to show that $TS' \in \mathcal{TS}_\mathbf{N}$, and the size of TS' is bounded by the size of TS_1 and TS_2.

Next, define maps $\mu_i' : TS' \to TS_i$ as follows: $\mu_i'((e_1, e_2)_{C_1 \times C_2}) = e_i$, for all $(e_1, e_2)_{C_1 \times C_2} \in E'$ ($i = 1, 2$). It is straightforward to check that μ_1' and μ_2' are indeed morphisms.

Finally, we have to show that μ_i' is a $\mathcal{TP}_L^0$-open morphism ($i \in \{1,2\}$). W.l.o.g. assume that $TC_{TS_i} \overset{TP}{\to} TC_i$ in TS_i. By Theorem 2, we have that $TC_{TS} \overset{TP}{\to} TC$, and $\mu_i\, TC = TC_i$. This means $TS \lceil TC \simeq TS_i \lceil TC_i$. From Theorem 1, it follows that $TC_{TS_{3-i}} \overset{TP'}{\to} TC_{3-i} = \mu_{3-i}\, TC$, and TP is an augment of TP'. Then we can construct $TS_{C_1 \times C_2}$ as a part of TS'. Define $TC' = (C', T')$ as follows: $C' = E_{C_1 \times C_2}$, and $T'((e_1, e_2)_{C_1 \times C_2}) = T_i(e_i)$ for all $(e_1, e_2)_{C_1 \times C_2} \in E_{C_1 \times C_2}$. It is now easy to show that $TC' \in \mathcal{TC}(TS')$, and $TS' \lceil TC' \simeq TS_i \lceil TC_i$, using the construction of TS'. This implies that $TC_{TS'} \overset{TP}{\to} TC'$ in TS'. Moreover, we have that $\mu_i'\, TC' = TC_i$, due to the definition of μ_i'. Thus, μ_i' is a $\mathcal{TP}_L^0$-open morphism ($i \in \{1,2\}$), by Theorem 2. $\qquad\square$

Confidentiality for Multithreaded Programs via Bisimulation[*]

Andrei Sabelfeld

Department of Computer Science, Cornell University, Ithaca, NY 14853, USA
Fax: +1 607 255 4428
andrei@cs.cornell.edu

Abstract. Bisimulation has been a popular foundation for characterizing the confidentiality properties of concurrent programs. However, because a variety of bisimulation definitions are available in the literature, it is often difficult to pin down the "right" definition for modeling a particular attacker. Focusing on timing- and probability-sensitive confidentiality for shared-memory multithreaded programs, we clarify the relation between different kinds of bisimulation by proving inclusion results. As a consequence, we derive the relationship between *scheduler-specific*, *scheduler-independent*, and *strong* confidentiality definitions. A key result justifying strong confidentiality is that it is the most accurate (largest) compositional indistinguishability-based confidentiality property that implies scheduler-independent confidentiality.

1 Introduction

Modern computing systems are increasingly vulnerable to application-level attacks. These attacks are particularly dangerous because they circumvent the standard low-level protection mechanisms (such as OS-based monitors and access control). Furthermore, application-level attacks are easier to create (or simply download and launch) exactly because of their high-level nature. Because standard security low-level enforcement mechanisms offer only limited protection against application-level attacks, there is high demand for models of *language-based security* [17,31,28] aimed at defending against threats at the programming-language and, hence, application level.

In this paper, we concentrate on *confidentiality* for multithreaded computation (we assume that security is synonymous with confidentiality in the rest of the paper). The objective is to prevent shared-memory multithreaded applications (programs) from leaking confidential information to the attacker. Such an information leak (or *information flow*) may take place when executing a (potentially untrusted) program on a trusted machine with legitimate access

---

[*] This research was supported by the Department of the Navy, Office of Naval Research, ONR Grant N00014-01-1-0968. Any opinions, findings, conclusions, or recommendations contained in this material are those of the author and do not necessarily reflect the views of the Office of Naval Research.

M. Broy and A.V. Zamulin (Eds.): PSI 2003, LNCS 2890, pp. 260–274, 2003.

to confidential data. Because modern computing systems incorporate much untrusted code (and/or unintended bugs), undesired leaks pose a serious threat to security-critical applications. This threat is of major concern for business, medical, and military computing systems that access and manipulate highly sensitive information.

Noninterference [12] is widely used to ensure that programs do not introduce undesired information flow. Noninterference requires that the publicly-observable behavior of a program does not depend on the program's secret inputs. The absence of dependency means that the publicly-observable behavior of the program does not vary (or is indistinguishable) as secret inputs are varied. Hence, central to the noninterference approach is the notion of *indistinguishability* of program behaviors by the attacker. *Bisimulation* has been a popular foundation for process indistinguishability and, thus, for characterizing the confidentiality properties of concurrent programs (e.g., [8,9,29,34,33,4,2,27,11]). Different kinds of bisimulation allow for modeling different kinds of the attacker's observational power. For example, the attacker's power in *timing attacks* [16,7] includes the ability to observe the timing behavior of the system. This can be captured by timing-sensitive attacker models. The attacker's power in *probabilistic attacks* [13,22] includes the ability to iteratively run computation and collect the stochastic properties of public data. This can be captured by probability-sensitive attacker models.

Timing- and probability-sensitive bisimulation [36,5,18] provides a suitable abstraction to characterize these attackers. However, because a variety of bisimulation definitions are available in the literature, it is often difficult to pin down the "right" definition for modeling a particular attacker. In this paper, building on earlier work on timing- and probability-sensitive confidentiality [29], we clarify the relation between different kinds of bisimulation by proving inclusion results. As a consequence, we derive the relationship between *scheduler-specific*, *scheduler-independent*, and *strong* security definitions. A key result justifying strong security is that it is the most accurate (largest) compositional indistinguishability-based security property that implies scheduler-independent security.

In the rest of the paper, we present a simple multithreaded language with dynamic thread creation (Section 2); give the definitions of scheduler-specific, scheduler-independent, and strong security (Section 3); argue that strong security is the largest compositional indistinguishability-based security property that implies scheduler-independent security, illustrate the security hierarchy by examples (Section 4); and, finally, conclude by a discussion on related and future work (Section 5).

2   A Language with Dynamic Thread Creation

In this section, we sketch a simple multithreaded language with dynamic thread creation. Our confidentiality conditions will be defined in terms of the semantics of this language. For brevity, we only give an informal description of the syntax and semantics.[1]

We consider an imperative language with skip, assignment, sequential composition, conditional, while, and fork operators. The semantics of the language are defined by two kinds of transitions: deterministic ($\rightarrow$) and probabilistic ($\rightarrow_p$ for some p where $0 < p \leq 1$ or simply $\rightarrow$ when the exact value of p is unimportant). Semantic rules are defined as transitions between configurations. A configuration $\langle C, s \rangle$ consists of a command (or a command thread pool represented by a vector of commands) C and a state s (memory). For example, the transition defining the semantics for the fork operator

$$\langle \mathsf{fork}(C, \vec{D}), s \rangle \rightarrow \langle C\vec{D}, s \rangle$$

states that $\mathsf{fork}(C, \vec{D})$ spawns a collection (vector) of threads $\vec{D}$ in parallel to the main thread C without changing the program state s.

Probabilistic transitions are defined through deterministic transitions (where $\{\!|\acute{u}|\!\}$ denotes a multiset):

$$(\text{Pick}) \frac{\langle C_i, s \rangle \rightarrow \langle \vec{C}, s' \rangle}{\{\!|\langle C_0 \ldots C_{n-1}\rangle, s \rangle \rightarrow^i_{\sigma(i,n)} \{\!|\langle C_0 \ldots C_{i-1}\vec{C}C_{i+1} \ldots C_{n-1}\rangle, s' \rangle}$$

$$(\text{Sum}) \frac{p = \sum \{\!|q | \langle \vec{C}, s \rangle \rightarrow^i_q \langle \vec{D}, s' \rangle |\!\} \quad p \neq 0}{\langle \vec{C}, s \rangle \rightarrow_p \langle \vec{D}, s' \rangle}$$

A probabilistic transition originates from a configuration if a thread from the configuration's thread pool can make a deterministic step under the configuration's memory. The probability $\sigma(i,n)$ of the transition may depend on both the number i of the picked thread and the size n of the thread pool. Because no information about previous thread choices is used for determining the probability of the transition, this corresponds to a *history-independent* scheduler.[2] We assume that $\forall n(n > 0), i(i \in \{0, \ldots, n-1\}).\sigma(i,n) > 0$ and $\forall n(n > 0). \sum_{i \in \{0,\ldots,n-1\}} \sigma(i,n) = 1$. The labeling in the rule Pick together with the rule Sum ensure that $\forall \vec{C}, s. \sum_{D,s'} \{\!|p \mid \langle \vec{C}, s \rangle \rightarrow_p \langle \vec{D}, s' \rangle |\!\} = 1$. For example, instantiating σ as $uni(i,n) = \frac{1}{n}$ corresponds to the *uniform* scheduler that picks threads with uniform probability.

For simplicity, we assume that variables are partitioned into two classes — of *high* and *low* confidentiality (with typical variables h and l of respective confidentiality levels). We define *low equality* $=_L$ on memories by $s_1 =_L s_2$ if and only if s_1 and s_2 agree on the low variables.

---

[1] The complete syntax as well as deterministic and probabilistic semantics are given in Figures 2, 3, and 4, respectively, in Appendix A.

[2] This simple scheduler model is sufficient for our purposes. It is an instance of a general model of history-dependent schedulers [29].

3   Bisimulation-Based Confidentiality

As foreshadowed in Section 1, we can conveniently apply the machinery of bisimulation to characterizing security. The intuition is that a program is secure when a variation of the values of the high variables does not influence the low-observable behavior of the program. We have already defined the low equality of memories to represent the variation of the values of the high variables. What helps us model whether the low-observable behavior of the program is unchanged is *low-bisimulation*. This security-sensitive bisimulation captures whether two program behaviors are different through the view of an attacker. In the rest of this section, we present (with some simplifications) the bisimulation-based definitions of scheduler-specific, scheduler-independent, and strong security [29].

3.1   Scheduler-Specific Security

The worst-case-scenario attacker is capable of observing the timing and probabilistic properties of program execution. Hence, our goal is to capture probabilistic- and timing-sensitive security properties. Therefore, a suitable low-bisimulation definition is a timing-sensitive *probabilistic low-bisimulation*. Suppose we have a fixed scheduler σ for our semantics. Under this scheduler, let us state the definition of σ-*probabilistic low-bisimulation*.

Definition 1 *A partial equivalence relation R is a σ-probabilistic low-bisimulation on programs if whenever $\vec{C}\ R\ \vec{D}$ then*

$$\forall s_1 =_L s_2. \langle \vec{C}, s_1 \rangle \to \langle \vec{C'}, s'_1 \rangle \implies \exists \vec{D'}, s'_2. \langle \vec{D}, s_2 \rangle \to \langle \vec{D'}, s'_2 \rangle \ \textit{such that}$$

$$(i) \sum \{p | \langle \vec{C}, s_1 \rangle \to_p \langle \vec{S}, s \rangle, \vec{S} \in [\vec{C'}]_R, s =_L s'_1 \} =$$
$$\sum \{p | \langle \vec{D}, s_2 \rangle \to_p \langle \vec{S}, s \rangle, \vec{S} \in [\vec{D'}]_R, s =_L s'_2 \}$$

$$(ii) \ \vec{C'}\ R\ \vec{D'}, s'_1 =_L s'_2$$

where $[\vec{E}]_R$ stands for the R-equivalence class which contains $\vec{E}$.

(Observe that the probabilities p are determined by the scheduler σ according to the semantic rules Pick and Sum.) The intuition is that under arbitrary variations of the high-confidentiality data of a state two related commands must execute in lock-step, affect the low memory in the same way, and the summed probability of stepping to the configurations of commands and memories from the same equivalence class must be the same. Note that low-bisimulation is defined directly on programs (with the variation of high data built in). Hence, the low-bisimulation relation is not necessarily reflexive (the intention is that reflexivity breaks on insecure programs), and, thus, is a partial equivalence relation. Two commands C and D are *low-bisimilar* $(C \sim^\sigma_L D)$ *under σ-probabilistic low-bisimulation* if there exists a σ-probabilistic low-bisimulation that relates the commands. One can show that $\sim^\sigma_L$ itself is a σ-probabilistic low-bisimulation. The definition of σ-security is now straightforward:

$$\vec{C} \text{ is } \sigma\text{-secure} \iff \vec{C} \sim_L^\sigma \vec{C}$$

Examples of *uni*-secure programs are $h := l + 3; l := l + 1$ (h is not accessed), if $l > 0$ then $h := h + 1$ else $h := 0$ (l is not assigned), $\mathsf{fork}(l := l + 1, h := h - 1)$ (independent threads), and if $h > 0$ then $\mathsf{fork}(l := 0, l := 1)$ else $\mathsf{fork}(l := 1, l := 0)$ (secure because $\mathsf{fork}(l := 0, l := 1) \sim_L^{uni} \mathsf{fork}(l := 1, l := 0)$). These programs are secure because for each of them we can construct a partial equivalence relation that relates the program to itself and satisfies Definition 1.

Examples of *uni*-insecure programs are $l := h$ (explicit leak), if $h > 0$ then $l := 1$ else $l := 0$ (implicit leak [6]), while $h > 0$ do $h := h - 1$ (timing leak), if $h > 0$ then $\mathsf{fork}(l := 0, l := 1)$ else (skip; $l := 0; l := 1$) (which fails because $\mathsf{fork}(l := 0, l := 1) \not\sim_L^{uni}$ (skip; $l := 0; l := 1$)). We will return to some of these examples later in this section and in Section 4.

3.2 Scheduler-Independent Security

Scheduler algorithms are typically not specified by implementations. Thus, a higher security assurance than scheduler-specific security is needed — a security specification that is robust with respect to all schedulers. A stronger *scheduler-independent* security gives such assurance by quantifying over all schedulers. We now define both scheduler-independent low-bisimulation $\approx_L$ and scheduler-independent security (SI-bisimulation and SI-security for short):

$$\vec{C} \approx_L \vec{D} \iff \forall \sigma. \vec{C} \sim_L^\sigma \vec{D} \qquad\qquad \vec{C} \text{ is } SI\text{-secure} \iff \vec{C} \approx_L \vec{C}$$

Clearly, $\approx_L \subseteq \sim_L^\sigma$ for all σ. An example from the previous section shows that the converse inclusion does not hold. More precisely, the example illustrates that the uniform scheduler assumption does not imply security for other schedulers. Recall the program:

$$\text{if } h > 0 \text{ then } \mathsf{fork}(l := 0, l := 1) \text{ else } \mathsf{fork}(l := 1, l := 0)$$

While this is a secure program for the uniform scheduler, it is insecure for any other scheduler. Although the attacker may not know the scheduling algorithm in advance, he or she may infer it with sufficient certainty (using a program which does not touch high data) and apply the knowledge to deduce the value of h.

3.3 Strong Security

SI-security guarantees robustness with respect to all schedulers. However, the universal quantification used in its definition complicates direct proofs for SI-security. A compositional property that implies SI-security is an attractive alternative to verifying SI-security directly. Such a compositional property is of particular benefit if it is the *largest* compositional indistinguishability-based property that implies SI-security. We will prove that *strong security* (defined below) is indeed such a property.

Definition 2 *Define the* strong *low-bisimulation* $\approxeq_L$ *to be the union of all symmetric relations* R *on thread pools of equal size, so that whenever* $\langle C_0 \ldots C_{n-1} \rangle$ R $\langle D_0 \ldots D_{n-1} \rangle$ *then*

$$\forall s_1 =_L s_2 \forall i.\langle C_i, s_1 \rangle \twoheadrightarrow \langle \vec{C'}, s_1' \rangle \implies$$
$$\exists \vec{D'}, s_2'.\langle D_i, s_2 \rangle \twoheadrightarrow \langle \vec{D'}, s_2' \rangle, \vec{C'} R \vec{D'}, s_1' =_L s_2'$$

Two strongly low-bisimilar thread pools must have the same number of threads, and each thread must execute in lock-step and affect the low memory in the same way as the respective thread in the related thread pool. The strong security specification is given by the following definition:

$$\vec{C} \text{ is } strongly \text{ secure} \iff \vec{C} \approxeq_L \vec{C}$$

Recalling *uni*-secure examples, programs $h := l + 3; l := l + 1$, if $l > 0$ then $h := h + 1$ else $h := 0$, and fork($l := l + 1, h := h - 1$) are still secure under strong security. However, the *uni*-secure program if $h > 0$ then fork($l := 0, l := 1$) else fork($l := 1, l := 0$) is not strongly secure because the component-wise low-bisimilarity for the commands under the fork is broken: $l := 0 \not\approxeq_L l := 1$.

In general, strong low-bisimulation is indeed stronger than the scheduler-independent one: as desired, strong security implies SI-security (and, thus, all scheduler-specific security properties).

Proposition 1 ([29]) $\approxeq_L \subseteq \approx_L$.

Corollary 1 $\vec{C}$ *is strongly secure* $\implies \vec{C}$ *is SI-secure.*

Clearly, the converse does not hold. For example, the program

$$\text{if } h > 0 \text{ then fork(skip, skip) else skip; skip; skip}$$

is SI-secure (because fork(skip, skip) $\approx_L$ skip; skip; skip) but not strongly secure because the number of threads depends on high data (we have fork(skip, skip) $\not\approxeq_L$ skip; skip; skip).

Strong security features a number of compositionality properties. In particular, if a collection of commands are strongly secure then both the sequential (via ";") and parallel (via thread juxtaposition or fork) compositions of the commands are also strongly secure [29]. These are essential properties for modular security program analysis.

4 The Accuracy of Compositional Security

Let us show that strong security relation is the largest compositional relation contained in the SI-security relation. Observe that the combination of scheduler-independence and compositionality results in the condition that two low-bisimilar programs must have the same number of threads. The following example clarifies why this is the case. Consider these programs: the double-threaded $\langle l := 1, l := 1 \rangle$ and the single-threaded $l := 1; l := 1$. These programs are SI-bisimilar, i.e., $\langle l := 1, l := 1 \rangle \approx_L (l := 1; l := 1)$. Under any scheduler, no attacker is able to distinguish between the executions of the programs. However, the parallel composition of these programs with the thread $l := 2$ breaks low-bisimilarity: $\langle l := 1, l := 1, l := 2 \rangle \napprox_L \langle (l := 1; l := 1), l := 2 \rangle$. To see this, it is sufficient to observe that for the uniform scheduler, $\langle l := 1, l := 1, l := 2 \rangle \napprox_L^{uni} \langle (l := 1; l := 1), l := 2 \rangle$ as the probability of the value of l being 1 after the first step is $\frac{2}{3}$ for the first program and $\frac{1}{2}$ for the second. (The probabilities of the terminal values of l also differ for the two programs.) In order to prove a result formalizing the observation that compositionality requires the same number of threads, let us first rigorously define what a compositional indistinguishability relation on thread pools is. For our purposes, it is sufficient to consider a weak definition of compositionality: the compositionality of the parallel composition, requiring $l := 0$ and $l := 1$ to be secure ground contexts (for stronger notions of compositionality our results hold as well).

Definition 3 *An indistinguishability relation R on programs is* compositional *whenever $(l := 0)\ R\ (l := 0), (l := 1)\ R\ (l := 1)$ for some low variable l and if $\vec{C}\ R\ \vec{D}, \vec{C}'\ R\ \vec{D}'$ then $\langle \vec{C}\vec{C}' \rangle\ R\ \langle \vec{D}\vec{D}' \rangle$.*

Clearly, programs $l := 0$ and $l := 1$ are strongly secure. Because strong low-bisimulation is preserved under parallel composition, the strong low-bisimulation security definition is an example of a compositional indistinguishability relation.

4.1   The Accuracy Result via a Special-Purpose Scheduler

A *superincreasing* sequence of integers is a sequence where each element is greater than the sum of all previous elements. Let us define a scheduler *sup* (based on superincreasing sequences). This scheduler will be used for proving the main result of this section. The key property we desire for *sup* is the following. Suppose $X \subseteq \{0 \ldots n\}$, $X \neq \{0 \ldots n\}$, and $Y \subseteq \{0 \ldots m\}$ for some natural n and m. Then

$$\sum_{i \in X} sup(i, n) = \sum_{i \in Y} sup(i, m) \Longleftrightarrow X = Y \ \& \ n = m \qquad (*)$$

For the scheduler to distinguish between n and m we will use different prime numbers in the denominators of the fractions of the probability values, so that the sum of the probability values for X never equals the sum of the scheduler values for Y (because X is a proper subset of $\{0 \ldots n\}$ the values never sum up to 1). If $n = m$ then we use the numerators in the fractions as decimal encodings of X and Y based on a superincreasing sequence $1, 2, 4, 8, \ldots$. These encodings are equal if and only if the subsets are equal (no number in a superincreasing sequence can be written as the sum of other elements). Formally, the sequence $d_1, d_2, \ldots$ of denominators is formed by the rules:

$$d_1 = 1 \qquad d_n = \min\{p \mid p \text{ is prime} \ \& \ p > d_{n-1} \ \& \ p \geq 2^n - 1\}$$

Note that $\forall n, m(n \neq m). \gcd(d_n, d_m) = 1$. The scheduler sup is defined by:

$$sup(i, n) = \begin{cases} \frac{2^i}{d_n}, & \text{if } i \neq n-1 \\ \frac{d_n - (2^{n-1} - 1)}{d_n}, & \text{if } i = n-1 \end{cases}$$

Clearly, sup is a valid scheduler that satisfies the property $(*)$.

Proposition 2 $\langle \vec{C}, l := 0, l := 1 \rangle \sim_L^{sup} \langle \vec{D}, l := 0, l := 1 \rangle \Longrightarrow |\vec{C}| = |\vec{D}|$.

Proof. Consider states s_1 and s_2 such that $\forall Id.\, s_1.Id = s_2.Id = 0$. We have $\langle\langle \vec{C}, l := 0, l := 1 \rangle, s_1 \rangle \to \langle\langle \vec{C}, l := 1 \rangle, s_1 \rangle$. By the definition of sup-probabilistic low-bisimulation $\exists \vec{D}', s_2'.\, \langle\langle \vec{D}, l := 0, l := 1 \rangle, s_2 \rangle \to \langle \vec{D}', s_2' \rangle$ so that $s_1 =_L s_2'$ and

$$\sum \{p \mid \langle\langle \vec{C}, l := 0, l := 1 \rangle, s_1 \rangle \to_p \langle \vec{S}, s \rangle, \vec{S} \in [\langle \vec{C}, l := 1 \rangle]_{\sim_L^{sup}}, s =_L s_1 \} =$$
$$\sum \{p \mid \langle\langle \vec{D}, l := 0, l := 1 \rangle, s_2 \rangle \to_p \langle \vec{S}, s \rangle, \vec{S} \in [\vec{D}']_{\sim_L^{sup}}, s =_L s_2' \}$$

Under the scheduler sup, the probability of getting from a configuration with the program $\langle \vec{C}, l := 0, l := 1 \rangle$ to a configuration a state s such that $s.l = 0$ is less than 1 (because the last thread is possible to execute). Hence, we can rewrite the above sum equality as

$$\sum_{i \in X} sup(i, n) = \sum_{i \in Y} sup(i, m)$$

for some $X \subseteq \{0 \ldots (n+2)\}$, $X \neq \{0 \ldots (n+2)\}$, and $Y \subseteq \{0 \ldots (m+2)\}$ where $n = |\vec{C}|$ and $m = |\vec{D}|$. We conclude that $n = m$ by the property $(*)$. $\square$

Proposition 3 *Strong security is the largest compositional indistinguishability relation contained in the SI-security relation. I.e., if R is a compositional indistinguishability relation and $R \subseteq \approx_L$ then $R \subseteq \cong_L$.*

Proof. Define the projection $\vec{C} \!\downarrow_X$ for a thread pool $\vec{C}$ and $X \subseteq \{0, \ldots, |\vec{C}| - 1\}$ to be the thread pool formed only by those threads from $\vec{C}$ that are indexed in X. Given a relation R satisfying the premises of the proposition, we construct a relation Q such that $R \subseteq Q$ and $Q \subseteq \cong_L$. Define Q by

$$\{(\vec{C} \!\downarrow_X, \vec{D} \!\downarrow_X) \mid X \subseteq \{0, \ldots, |\vec{C}| - 1\}, \langle \vec{C}, l := 0, l := 1 \rangle \sim_L^{sup} \langle \vec{D}, l := 0, l := 1 \rangle\}$$

The projection $\vec{D} \!\downarrow_X$ is well-defined in this definition because the size of $\vec{C}$ and $\vec{D}$ must be the same by Proposition 2. To see that $R \subseteq Q$, suppose $\vec{C}\, R\, \vec{D}$ for some programs $\vec{C}, \vec{D}$. By the compositionality of R, we have $\langle \vec{C}, l := 0, l := 1 \rangle\, R$ $\langle \vec{D}, l := 0, l := 1 \rangle$. Because $R \subseteq \approx_L$ and $\approx_L \subseteq \sim_L^{sup}$, we receive $\langle \vec{C}, l := 0, l := 1 \rangle \sim_L^{sup} \langle \vec{D}, l := 0, l := 1 \rangle$. Hence, $\vec{C}\, Q\, \vec{D}$ (setting $X = \{0, \ldots, |\vec{C}| - 1\}$).

It remains to show that $Q \subseteq \cong_L$. In order to prove this inclusion, we argue that the relation Q is one of the relations from the union that defines strong low-bisimulation (cf. Definition 2). In other words, we need to show that Q is a symmetric relation on thread pools of equal size such that whenever $\langle C_0 \ldots C_{n-1} \rangle \, Q \, \langle D_0 \ldots D_{n-1} \rangle$ then

$$\forall s_1 =_L s_2 \forall i. \langle C_i, s_1 \rangle \rightarrow \langle \vec{C'}, s_1' \rangle \implies$$
$$\exists \vec{D'}, s_2'. \langle D_i, s_2 \rangle \rightarrow \langle \vec{D'}, s_2' \rangle, \vec{C'} \, Q \, \vec{D'}, s_1' =_L s_2'$$

The symmetry of the relation Q follows from that of $\sim_L^{sup}$. Recall that only thread pools of equal size may be related by Q by Proposition 2. Suppose $\vec{C} \restriction_X Q \, \vec{D} \restriction_X$ for some $\vec{C} = \langle C_0 \ldots C_{n-1} \rangle, \vec{D} = \langle D_0 \ldots D_{n-1} \rangle$ where $X \subseteq \{0, \ldots, n-1\}$ and $\langle \vec{C}, l := 0, l := 1 \rangle \sim_L^{sup} \langle \vec{D}, l := 0, l := 1 \rangle$. Assume $\langle C_i, s_1 \rangle \rightarrow \langle \vec{C'}, s_1' \rangle$ for some $i(i \in X)$ and s_1. Hence, we have $\langle \langle \vec{C}, l := 0, l := 1 \rangle, s_1 \rangle \rightarrow \langle \langle C_0 \ldots C_{i-1} \vec{C'} C_{i+1} \ldots C_{n-1}, l := 0, l := 1 \rangle, s_1' \rangle$. Because $\langle \vec{C}, l := 0, l := 1 \rangle \sim_L^{sup} \langle \vec{D}, l := 0, l := 1 \rangle$ for all s_2 such that $s_1 =_L s_2$ we have

$$\exists \vec{E}, s_3. \langle \langle \vec{D}, l := 0, l := 1 \rangle, s_2 \rangle \rightarrow \langle \vec{E}, s_3 \rangle \text{ such that}$$

$(i) \sum \{p | \langle \langle \vec{C}, l := 0, l := 1 \rangle, s_1 \rangle \rightarrow_p \langle \vec{S}, s \rangle,$
$$\vec{S} \in [\langle C_0 \ldots \vec{C'} \ldots C_{n-1}, l := 0, l := 1 \rangle]_{\sim_L^{sup}}, s =_L s_1' \} =$$
$$\sum \{p | \langle \langle \vec{D}, l := 0, l := 1 \rangle, s_2 \rangle \rightarrow_p \langle \vec{S}, s \rangle, \vec{S} \in [\vec{E}]_{\sim_L^{sup}}, s =_L s_3 \}$$

$(ii) \langle C_0 \ldots \vec{C'} \ldots C_{n-1}, l := 0, l := 1 \rangle \sim_L^{sup} \vec{E}, s_1' =_L s_3$

The probability equality (i) has the form $\sum_{k \in Y} sup(k, n) = \sum_{k \in Z} sup(k, n)$ for some $Y, Z \subsetneq \{0, \ldots, n-1\}$. The sets Y and Z correspond to different choices of the scheduler that takes the two configurations to the same equivalence classes. As we have observed earlier, the probability equality holds if and only if $Y = Z$. Thus, $\exists \vec{D'}. \langle D_i, s_2 \rangle \rightarrow \langle \vec{D'}, s_2' \rangle$ so that $\vec{E} \sim_L^{sup} \langle D_0 \ldots D_{i-1} \vec{D'} D_{i+1} \ldots D_{n-1}, l := 0, l := 1 \rangle$ and $s_3 =_L s_2'$. Therefore, due to $\langle C_0 \ldots \vec{C'} \ldots C_{n-1}, l := 0, l := 1 \rangle \sim_L^{sup} \langle D_0 \ldots \vec{D'} \ldots D_{n-1}, l := 0, l := 1 \rangle$, we have $\vec{C'} \, Q \, \vec{D'}$ which can be seen as $\langle C_0 \ldots \vec{C'} \ldots C_{n-1}, l := 0, l := 1 \rangle \restriction_{\{i, \ldots, (i+m)\}} Q \, \langle D_0 \ldots \vec{D'} \ldots D_{n-1}, l := 0, l := 1 \rangle \restriction_{\{i, \ldots, (i+m)\}}$ where $m = |\vec{C'}| = |\vec{D'}|$. $\qquad \square$

4.2   Security Hierarchy

The formal hierarchy of low-bisimulation allows us to derive the relationship between the corresponding security properties. The diagram in Fig. 1 illustrates the inclusion relation between security properties. On the right side of the figure we present examples that demonstrate the depicted inclusions. The smallest set on the diagram is the set of *typable* programs. A program is typable if it can be given a type. In the context of security-type systems, programs are given types in order to enforce security. Considering type systems enforcing strong security (e.g., [29]), Program 1 is an example of a typable and, thus, strongly secure program. Because type systems are (necessarily) conservative, there are

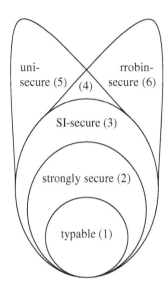

1. $h := l$
2. $l := h - h$
3. if $h > 0$ then fork(skip, skip)

   else skip; skip; skip
4. if $h > 0$ then fork$((l := 0; l := 1), l := 0)$

   else fork$(l := 0, (l := 0; l := 1))$
5. if $h > 0$ then fork$(l := 0, l := 1)$

   else fork$(l := 1, l := 0)$
6. if $h > 0$ then fork$(l := 0, l := 1)$

   else skip; $l := 0; l := 1$

Fig. 1. Security hierarchy

programs (such as Program 2) that are strongly secure but rejected by most type systems (e.g., [35,1,29]).

By Corollary 1, strong security implies scheduler-independent security. However, this inclusion is not strict. Recall that while Program 3 is secure under an arbitrary scheduler (because fork(skip, skip) $\approx_L$ skip; skip; skip), it is not strongly secure because the number of threads depends on high data. Program 4 is secure under both the uniform and round-robin[3] schedulers. However, there are schedulers that can be used by the attacker to leak high data through this program. One such scheduler is sup. Under this scheduler, the first and second threads are executed with the probabilities $\frac{1}{3}$ and $\frac{2}{3}$. If $h > 0$ then the probability that the final value of l is 1 is $\frac{8}{9}$ whereas if $h \leq 0$ then this probability is only $\frac{5}{9}$. Because of this undesired flow, Program 4 is not SI-secure.

As we pointed out in Section 3, Program 5 is secure under the uniform scheduler, but insecure under any other scheduler (including round-robin). Conversely, program 6 is secure under the round-robin scheduler but not under

---

[3] A round-robin scheduler is a deterministic scheduler that executes a thread for one step before switching to the next thread in the configuration (returning to the first thread after executing the last thread). Note that this is a history-dependent scheduler, and, thus, cannot be directly expressed as σ in the semantics. However, we use this scheduler as an example because our results apply to the more general history-dependent scheduler model of [29].

the uniform scheduler. The security under the uniform scheduler fails because $\mathsf{fork}(l := 0, l := 1) \not\approx_L^{uni} (\mathsf{skip}; l := 0; l := 1)$.

5   Conclusion

We have investigated the relation between different kinds of timing- and probability-sensitive bisimulation for multithreaded programs. Due to the direct connection between bisimulation (as indistinguishability) and confidentiality, our results have been insightful for relating different confidentiality definitions. In particular, we have proved that strong security is the largest compositional security relation contained in the scheduler-independent security relation. This provides a forceful argument in favor of the strong security definition. The main benefit of the strong security definition is compositionality, which is critical for modular security analysis. Clearly, compositionality comes at a price of losing accuracy with respect to scheduler-independent security. However, our results show that we pay the least possible price — there exists no other compositional security relation that subsumes strong security and implies scheduler-independent security.

Related Work. There is a large body of work on language-based information security (see [28] for a recent survey). Because compositionality is absolutely crucial for scalable security analysis, it has been an important topic in the context of programming languages [23,29,30,26,27,20] as well as process algebra [8,24,25, 32,9,10], and other frameworks [21,15,19].

Focardi et al. [9,10] and Aldini et al. [2,3] investigate timing- and probability-sensitive informaion-flow security as independent extensions of Focardi and Gorrieri's security process algebra (SPA) [8]. Both studies explore the relation between different bisimulation-based definition establishing similar inclusion results as in the original security hierarchy.

Focardi et al. [9,10] follow a similar methodology to ours. Their bisimulation-based timed nondeducability on compositions (*tBNDC*) characterizes a noninterference-like property. It is difficult to verify *tBNDC* directly because it involves a quantification over all contexts. They identify a compositional (in the parallel composition) security property *tSBSNNI* that is amenable to modular analysis and contained in *tBNDC*. However, there are no compositionality results for the probability-sensitive definitions by Aldini et al. [2,3]. Furthermore, because of an intricate interplay between timing and probabilistic attacks, it appears essential to us to be able to model combined attacks (which is left for future work in [10]). Because our bisimulation-based characterizations are sensitive to both timing and probabilities, combined attacks are a natural part of the attacker model in this paper.

Future Work. An important problem for further explorations is whether the argument in favor of strong security can be extended to a multithreaded language with synchronization [26]. As a prerequisite, scheduler-specific and scheduler-independent security properties have to be defined for the extended language.

In a more general perspective, an intriguing direction for future work is integrating bisimulation-based security for programming languages into general bisimulation-based security frameworks (see, e.g., [14] for a step in this direction). A rigorous connection could illuminate the relation between security properties and aid in designing hybrid mechanisms for their validation. This is a noteworthy goal for future work.

Acknowledgments. Thanks are due to Roberto Gorrieri, David Sands, and Björn Victor for stimulating discussions that have motivated this paper, and to Stephen Chong for valuable comments.

References

1. J. Agat. Transforming out timing leaks. In *Proc. ACM Symp. on Principles of Programming Languages*, pages 40–53, January 2000.
2. A. Aldini. Probabilistic information flow in a process algebra. In *Proc. CONCUR'01*, volume 2154 of *LNCS*, pages 152–168. Springer-Verlag, August 2001.
3. A. Aldini, M. Bravetti, and R. Gorrieri. A process algebraic approach for the analysis of probabilistic non-interference. Technical Report UBLCS-2002-02, University of Bologna, Bologna, Italy, 2002.
4. G. Boudol and I. Castellani. Noninterference for concurrent programs. In *Proc. ICALP*, volume 2076 of *LNCS*, pages 382–395. Springer-Verlag, July 2001.
5. K. Cerans. Decidability of bisimulation equivalences for parallel timer processes. In *Proc. CAV 1992*, volume 663 of *LNCS*, pages 302–315. Springer-Verlag, June 1992.
6. D. E. Denning and P. J. Denning. Certification of programs for secure information flow. *Comm. of the ACM*, 20(7):504–513, July 1977.
7. E. W. Felten and M. A. Schneider. Timing attacks on web privacy. In *ACM Conference on Computer and Communications Security*, pages 25–32, 2000.
8. R. Focardi and R. Gorrieri. A classification of security properties for process algebras. *J. Computer Security*, 3(1):5–33, 1995.
9. R. Focardi, R. Gorrieri, and F. Martinelli. Information flow analysis in a discrete-time process algebra. In *Proc. IEEE Computer Security Foundations Workshop*, pages 170–184, July 2000.
10. R. Focardi, R. Gorrieri, and F. Martinelli. Real-time information flow analysis. *IEEE J. Selected Areas in Communications*, 21(1):20–35, January 2003.
11. P. Giambiagi and M.Dam. On the secure implementation of security protocols. In *Proc. European Symposium on Programming*, volume 2618 of *LNCS*, pages 144–158. Springer-Verlag, April 2003.
12. J. A. Goguen and J. Meseguer. Security policies and security models. In *Proc. IEEE Symp. on Security and Privacy*, pages 11–20, April 1982.
13. J.W. Gray III. Probabilistic interference. In *Proc. IEEE Symp. on Security and Privacy*, pages 170–179, May 1990.
14. K. Honda and N. Yoshida. A uniform type structure for secure information flow. In *Proc. ACM Symp. on Principles of Programming Languages*, pages 81–92, January 2002.

15. J. Jürjens. Secure information flow for concurrent processes. In *Proc. CONCUR 2000*, volume 1877 of *LNCS*, pages 395–409. Springer-Verlag, August 2000.
16. P. C. Kocher. Timing attacks on implementations of Diffie-Hellman, RSA, DSS, and other systems. In *Proc. CRYPTO'96*, volume 1109 of *LNCS*, pages 104–113. Springer-Verlag, 1996.
17. D. Kozen. Language-based security. In *Proc. Mathematical Foundations of Computer Science*, volume 1672 of *LNCS*, pages 284–298. Springer-Verlag, September 1999.
18. K. G. Larsen and A. Skou. Bisimulation through probabilistic testing. *Information and Computation*, 94(1):1–28, September 1991.
19. H. Mantel. On the composition of secure systems. In *Proc. IEEE Symp. on Security and Privacy*, pages 81–94, May 2002.
20. H. Mantel and A. Sabelfeld. A unifying approach to the security of distributed and multi-threaded programs. *J. Computer Security*, 2003. To appear.
21. D. McCullough. Specifications for multi-level security and hook-up property. In *Proc. IEEE Symp. on Security and Privacy*, pages 161–166, April 1987.
22. J. McLean. Security models and information flow. In *Proc. IEEE Symp. on Security and Privacy*, pages 180–187, May 1990.
23. J. McLean. A general theory of composition for trace sets closed under selective interleaving functions. In *Proc. IEEE Symp. on Security and Privacy*, pages 79–93, May 1994.
24. P. Ryan and S. Schneider. Composing and decomposing systems under security properties. In *Proc. IEEE Computer Security Foundations Workshop*, pages 9–15, March 1995.
25. P. Ryan and S. Schneider. Process algebra and non-interference. In *Proc. IEEE Computer Security Foundations Workshop*, pages 214–227, June 1999.
26. A. Sabelfeld. The impact of synchronisation on secure information flow in concurrent programs. In *Proc. Andrei Ershov International Conference on Perspectives of System Informatics*, volume 2244 of *LNCS*, pages 227–241. Springer-Verlag, July 2001.
27. A. Sabelfeld and H. Mantel. Static confidentiality enforcement for distributed programs. In *Proc. Symposium on Static Analysis*, volume 2477 of *LNCS*, pages 376–394. Springer-Verlag, September 2002.
28. A. Sabelfeld and A. C. Myers. Language-based information-flow security. *IEEE J. Selected Areas in Communications*, 21(1):5–19, January 2003.
29. A. Sabelfeld and D. Sands. Probabilistic noninterference for multi-threaded programs. In *Proc. IEEE Computer Security Foundations Workshop*, pages 200–214, July 2000.
30. A. Sabelfeld and D. Sands. A per model of secure information flow in sequential programs. *Higher Order and Symbolic Computation*, 14(1):59–91, March 2001.
31. F. B. Schneider, G. Morrisett, and R. Harper. A language-based approach to security. In *Informatics—10 Years Back, 10 Years Ahead*, volume 2000 of *LNCS*, pages 86–101. Springer-Verlag, 2000.
32. S. Schneider. May testing, non-interference, and compositionality. Technical Report CSD-TR-00-02, Royal Holloway, University of London, January 2001.
33. G. Smith. A new type system for secure information flow. In *Proc. IEEE Computer Security Foundations Workshop*, pages 115–125, June 2001.
34. D. Volpano and G. Smith. Verifying secrets and relative secrecy. In *Proc. ACM Symp. on Principles of Programming Languages*, pages 268–276, January 2000.
35. D. Volpano, G. Smith, and C. Irvine. A sound type system for secure flow analysis. *J. Computer Security*, 4(3):167–187, 1996.

36. Y. Wang. Real-time behaviour of asynchronous agents. In *Proc. CONCUR 1990*, volume 458 of *LNCS*, pages 502–520. Springer-Verlag, August 1990.

Appendix A

$$C ::= \text{ skip} \mid Id := Exp \mid C_1; C_2$$
$$\mid \text{ if } B \text{ then } C_1 \text{ else } C_2 \mid \text{ while } B \text{ do } C \mid \text{fork}(C, \vec{D})$$

Fig. 2. Command syntax

$$\langle \text{skip}, s \rangle \twoheadrightarrow \langle \langle \rangle, s \rangle$$

$$\frac{\langle Exp, s \rangle \downarrow n}{\langle Id := Exp, s \rangle \twoheadrightarrow \langle \langle \rangle, [Id = n]s \rangle}$$

$$\frac{\langle C_1, s \rangle \twoheadrightarrow \langle \langle \rangle, s' \rangle}{\langle C_1; C_2, s \rangle \twoheadrightarrow \langle C_2, s' \rangle} \qquad \frac{\langle C_1, s \rangle \twoheadrightarrow \langle C_1' \vec{D}, s' \rangle}{\langle C_1; C_2, s \rangle \twoheadrightarrow \langle (C_1'; C_2)\vec{D}, s' \rangle}$$

$$\frac{\langle B, s \rangle \downarrow \text{True}}{\langle \text{if } B \text{ then } C_1 \text{ else } C_2, s \rangle \twoheadrightarrow \langle C_1, s \rangle}$$

$$\frac{\langle B, s \rangle \downarrow \text{False}}{\langle \text{if } B \text{ then } C_1 \text{ else } C_2, s \rangle \twoheadrightarrow \langle C_2, s \rangle}$$

$$\frac{\langle B, s \rangle \downarrow \text{True}}{\langle \text{while } B \text{ do } C, s \rangle \twoheadrightarrow \langle C; \text{while } B \text{ do } C, s \rangle}$$

$$\frac{\langle B, s \rangle \downarrow \text{False}}{\langle \text{while } B \text{ do } C, s \rangle \twoheadrightarrow \langle \langle \rangle, s \rangle}$$

$$\langle \text{fork}(C, \vec{D}), s \rangle \twoheadrightarrow \langle C\vec{D}, s \rangle$$

Fig. 3. Small-step deterministic semantics of commands

$$\text{(Pick)} \frac{\langle C_i, s \rangle \twoheadrightarrow \langle \vec{C}, s' \rangle}{\langle \langle C_0 \ldots C_{n-1} \rangle, s \rangle \rightarrow^i_{\sigma(i,n)} \langle \langle C_0 \ldots C_{i-1} \vec{C} C_{i+1} \ldots C_{n-1} \rangle, s' \rangle}$$

$$\text{(Sum)} \frac{p = \sum \{q | \langle \vec{C}, s \rangle \rightarrow^i_q \langle \vec{D}, s' \rangle \} \quad p \neq 0}{\langle \vec{C}, s \rangle \rightarrow_p \langle \vec{D}, s' \rangle}$$

Fig. 4. Probabilistic semantics of thread pools

Dynamic Modification of System Structures Using LLPNs

Berndt Farwer[1] and Kundan Misra[2]

[1] University of Hamburg, Department of Computer Science,
farwer@informatik.uni-hamburg.de
[2] Department of Computer Science, University of Warwick,
kundan@dcs.warwick.ac.uk

Abstract. In this paper we aim to set up a framework for object Petri net semantics, allowing the modification of object net structures at runtime. The approach uses linear logic Petri nets (LLPNs) and performs the structure modification on a linear logic encoding of the object net. In addition, Valk's self-modifying Petri nets are shown to be subsumed by LLPNs.

We expand on the existing theory of Farwer's LLPNs, which are Petri nets with linear logic formulae as tokens. This work in progress uses intuitionistic linear logic as the basis of a method for ensuring desirable properties — such as termination or non-termination — of P/T nets, coloured Petri nets and LLPNs.

1 Background and Motivation

Petri nets are well-known models for concurrent and reactive systems. A place-transition net (P/T net) is a type of Petri net with places which can contain tokens and transitions that are connected by directed, weighted arcs. Diagramatically, places are represented by circles and transitions by rectangles. The *precondition* of a transition is the number of tokens needed in each place for the transition to be enabled, and is indicated by the weights of the incoming arcs. The *postcondition* of a transition is the number of tokens generated in each place by the firing of the transition, and is indicated by the weights of the outgoing arcs. A transition fires when its precondition is satisfied, after which its postcondition is generated. This is shown in Fig. 1.

P/T nets have been extended in several ways. Coloured Petri nets (CPNs) were introduced under the name of "high-level Petri nets" by Jensen [16]. CPNs

Fig. 1. Transition firing in a P/T net

M. Broy and A.V. Zamulin (Eds.): PSI 2003, LNCS 2890, pp. 274–293, 2003.

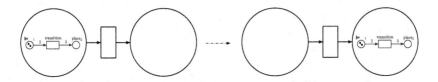

(a) Transition firing in an object Petri net

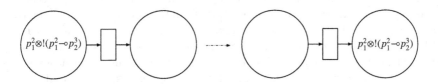

(b) Corresponding transition firing in an LLPN

Fig. 2. Object Petri net vs. linear logic Petri net

allow tokens to have different values. Each place is associated with a set of allowable values ("colours") and that set corresponds to a data type ("colour set"). The tokens inside a place must be taken from the colour set associated with the place. Any transition in a CPN may have a "guard function", which allows the designer to specify complex criteria on the incoming arcs. An equivalent CPN without a guard can always be constructed by unfolding the CPN. Some work has been done to express CPNs using linear logic [8]. Also, Lilius explains how CPNs can be described using linear logic by first converting a CPN to a corresponding P/T net [18] by creating a place for each value/colour. This quickly becomes unworkable for any practical use, because the colour set (i.e. data type) of any place is often infinite (e.g., $\mathbb{N}$).

Object Petri nets allow various structured objects as tokens, including P/T nets themselves. When P/T nets are used as tokens of a CPN, the token P/T nets are called *object nets* and the CPN whose places contain token nets is called the *system net*. A simple example of an autonomous system net transition firing is shown in Fig. 2. Here the object net is simply moved to a different place of the system net. Other more complex moves involving synchronisation of system and object net transitions are possible, but cannot be discussed here.

Farwer devised a type of CPN in which the tokens are formulae from linear logic formulae called linear logic Petri nets (LLPNs) [9]. LLPNs are distinct from CPNs because they allow tokens (linear logic formulae) to *interact* in the places under the proof rules of linear logic. Suppose the linear logic formulae $J \multimap K$ and J enter a place b. Then J and $J \multimap K$ are consumed to produce K. Now K alone is available to the output transitions of b. The *firing rule* of LLPNs is that a transition will fire if for each input place of the transition, the proof tree of the formulae in the place has a step with the transition's precondition [8]. LLPNs are convenient for modelling real-world systems and make the large body of linear logic theory available for modelling and analysing complex systems.

Linear logic has been used as a medium through which to talk about sequential and concurrent programming-language semantics [1], and has been facilitated for giving semantics for P/T nets [3,7,9,23]. Usually, these treatments are restricted to intuitionistic linear logic (**ILL**). Thus, we restrict the formulae tokens of LLPNs to **ILL** formulae.

Brown, Gurr and de Paiva developed an **ILL** proof theory for P/T nets [4]. They also gave a category theoretic proof that linear logic is a specification language for P/T nets. These last two results have been extended to LLPNs [21]. Meseguer and others used functorial embeddings of the category of P/T nets into categories related to linear logic to explain the connection between P/T nets and linear logic [19,20]. A categorical semantics of the simulation (i.e. refinement and abstraction) of P/T nets has also been developed [4] and this has been extended to LLPNs [21]. Treatments by Engberg, Winskel and Farwer do not rely so much on category theory [7,8,9].

As put by Sangiorgi and Walker [22], "Mobile systems, whose components communicate and change their structure, now pervade the informational world and the wider world of which it is a part." Heeding this observation requires that dynamic modification of Petri net structures be included in any serious object Petri net formalism. In this paper we give some ideas of how this can be achieved and study a possible application.

It is often necessary to ensure that a system has some desirable property, such as that it must or must not terminate. We will show how the use of linear logic, first order linear logic and second order linear logic can greatly simplify the augmenting of P/T nets, CPNs and LLPNs to ensure desirable properties. This is a seminal stage in developing a framework for systems that are modelled by Petri nets to ensure their own desirable behaviour without external intervention. This might lead towards a standard environment into which we can "plug" a Petri net to ensure that it has desirable properties.

2   Translation between LLPNs and Object Petri Nets

A revision of the rules of intuitionistic linear logic and the definition of object Petri nets are given in the appendices. Note, that the definition of a linear logic Petri net in the following section differs slightly from the definition given in [11], in that it generalises the arc inscriptions to multisets of linear logic formulae, rather than multisets of variables only. Also, a capacity is introduced for the places of an LLPN. Finally, the firing rule is generalised to incorporate autonomous derivation of the token formulae.

A variety of different high-level Petri nets are actively used for systems engineering (cf. [30]), all of which extend the basic formalism of place/transition nets or P/T nets. The definition of P/T nets is now recalled for reference.

Definition 1 (P/T net). *A P/T net is a tuple* (P, T, F, W) *with disjoint sets of places* P *and transitions* T; *the function* $F \subseteq (P \times T) \cup (T \times P)$ *defines the flow relation; and the function* $W : (P \times T) \cup (T \times P) \to \mathbb{N}$ *with* $W(x, y) = 0$ *if and only if* $(x, y) \notin F$ *defines the arc weights.*

A marked P/T net *or* P/T net system *is a tuple* $(P, T, F, W, \mathbf{m_0})$ *where* (P, T, F, W) *is a P/T net and* $\mathbf{m_0} : P \to \mathbb{N}$ *is the initial marking.*

An arc with weight zero has the same practical effect as an arc that does not exist, and so we regard these notions as equivalent. In the following, a P/T net is called an *ordinary Petri net* if $\forall (x, y) \in F.W(x, y) = 1$ is true for that P/T net.

2.1   Linear Logic Petri Nets

We denote by L_A the set of all **ILL** formulae over the alphabet A and by S_{L_A} the set of sequents over L_A. The shorthand B^A, where A and B are sets, denotes the set of all functions $A \to B$. We take $0 \in \mathbb{N}$.

Definition 2 (Linear Logic Petri net, LLPN). *A* linear logic Petri net *is a 6-tuple* $(P, T, F, \Lambda, G, \mathfrak{v}, \mathbf{m_0})$, *where:*

- P *is the set of places*
- T *is the set of transitions, such that* $P \cap T = \emptyset$
- $F \subseteq (P \times T) \cup (T \times P)$ *is the flow relation*
- Λ *maps each element of* $P \cup T$ *to a fragment of (propositional) linear logic*
- $\mathfrak{v}$ *is a function defined on* $(P \times T) \cup (T \times P)$ *which maps pairs* (x, y) *to multisets of variables drawn from the set of variables* $\mathfrak{V}$ *in* $L_{\Lambda(p)}$ *where* $p \in \{x, y\}$. *Denote by* $\mathfrak{V}_t$ *the set of variables on arcs adjacent to* t, *i.e.* $\mathfrak{V}_t = \{v \in \mathfrak{V} \mid \exists p \in {}^\bullet t \cup t^\bullet . v \in \mathfrak{v}(p, t) \cup \mathfrak{v}(t, p)\}$
- *the guard function* $G : T \to 2^{L_{\Lambda(t)}}$ *maps each transition to a set of sequents over* $L_{\Lambda(t)}$
- *the initial marking is some function* $\mathbf{m_0}$ *with* $p \mapsto n_p$ *for every* $p \in P$ *where* $n_p \in \mathbb{N}^{L_{\Lambda(p)}}$.

For a formula $l \in L_A$ we denote by $m_l(p)$ the number of occurrences of the formula l in the place p for the marking m. The marking of a place is extended to a set of places $M \subseteq P$ by the multiset union, i.e. $\mathbf{m}(M) := \sum_{p \in M} \mathbf{m}(p)$. The weight function $\mathfrak{v}$ assigns to each arc a multiset of variables. If there is no arc between nodes x and y the weight function denotes the empty multiset. In symbols, if $(x, y) \notin F$ then $w(x, y)$ is the empty multiset.

We denote the precondition of a transition t by ${}^\bullet t := \{p \in P \mid (p, t) \in F\}$ and the postcondition of t by $t^\bullet := \{p \in P \mid (t, p) \in F\}$.

Definition 3 (marking's proof trees). *Given a marking* m *and place* p, *the proof trees of* $\mathbf{m}(p)$ *are all possible proof trees that can be formed with at most the formulae from the multiset* $\mathbf{m}(p)$ *together with some axioms and tautologies of the calculus as their premises, i.e. leaves of the proof trees. We denote this set of proof trees by* $\Phi(\mathbf{m}(p))$. *The set of proof trees of a marking* m *is denoted* $\Phi(m)$ *and is given by* $\Phi(m) := \bigcup_{p \in P} \Phi(\mathbf{m}(p))$.

Definition 4 (independent formulae). *The set of multisets of formulae that can hold independently in a proof tree Φ is denoted $I(\Phi)$.*

This means that for every multiset of formulae $\Phi_F \in I(\Phi)$, all formulae in Φ_F can hold independently in the proof tree Φ. For example, suppose Φ is the proof tree [24]:

$$\frac{\dfrac{C, \Gamma, A \quad\quad C, \Gamma, B}{C, \Gamma, A\&B} \quad\quad D, \Gamma'}{C \otimes D, \Gamma, \Gamma', A\&B}$$

For $\Phi_{F_1} = \{\{C, \Gamma, A\}, \{C, \Gamma, B\}, \{D, \Gamma'\}\}$, $\Phi_{F_2} = \{\{C, \Gamma, A\&B\}, \{D, \Gamma'\}\}$ and $\Phi_{F_3} = \{\{C \otimes D, \Gamma, \Gamma', A\&B\}\}$, we get $I(\Phi) = \Phi_{F_1} \cup \Phi_{F_2} \cup \Phi_{F_3}$.

Definition 5 (binding). *A binding for a Linear Logic Petri net transition t is a mapping $\beta : \mathfrak{v}_t \to L_\Lambda$, such that*

$$\beta(x) \in \bigcap_{p \in \,^\bullet t \cup t^\bullet} \bigcap_{x \in \mathfrak{V}_t} L_{\Lambda(p)}$$

and all sequents $\sigma \in G(t)(\beta)$ are derivable in $\Lambda(t)$.

As we are only discussing propositional calculi there is no need for unification at this point.

Definition 6 (enablement). *A transition $t \in T$ is enabled with binding β if and only if there exists a t-binding satisfying $G(t)$, such that there is one occurrence of $\beta(X)$ in the place $p \in \,^\bullet t$ for each occurrence of X in $W(p,t)$, i.e.*

$$\forall p \in \,^\bullet t. \forall X \in W(p,t).\mathbf{m}(p)(\beta(X)) \geq W(p,t)(X)$$

The satisfaction of a guard formula is defined as its derivability in the Linear Logic sequent calculus.

Definition 7 (successor marking). *Transition t may occur taking the marking m to reach the successor marking m' according to the following rule for every place p in P and every variable X that appears in the arc inscription of any arc connected to t:*

$$\mathbf{m}'(p)(\beta(X)) = \mathbf{m}(p)(\beta(X)) - W(p,t)(\beta(X)) + W(t,p)(\beta(X))$$

Autonomous derivations among formulae residing in the same place are possible iff there exists a proof tree with the derived formula as consequence. Since the firing rule depends also on proof trees, a large number of markings are equivalent. For example, the marking $\mathbf{m}(p) = \{A\}$ will enable a transition t if and only if the marking $\mathbf{m}'(p) = \{B \multimap A, B\}$ enables the transition t, as does the markings $\{(B \multimap A) \otimes B\}$ This means that it is often convenient to think in terms of sets of equivalent markings with respect to the enablement of transitions.

We can express the equivalence between $\mathbf{m}(p)$ and $\mathbf{m}'(p)$ by $I\Big(\Phi\big(\mathbf{m}(s)\big)\Big) = I\Big(\Phi\big(\mathbf{m}'(s)\big)\Big)$. Since equality is an equivalence relation, we immediately obtain equivalence classes of markings.

2.2 Interpreting Object Petri Nets as LLPNs

There is a strong correspondence between intuitionistic linear logic (**ILL**) formulae and P/T nets [6,3,7,11,12]. This means that the object nets of an object Petri net can be regarded as **ILL** formulae. In this way, we can regard an object Petri net as an LLPN. Conversely, an LLPN can be regarded as an object Petri net. We recall Farwer's canonical **ILL** formula for a P/T net.

Definition 8 (canonical formula for a P/T net). *Let $N = (P, T, F, W, \mathbf{m_0})$ be a P/T net system. Then the canonical formula $\Psi_{\mathbf{ILL}_{PN}}(N)$ for N is the tensor product of the following formulae:*

- *For each transition $t \in T$ with non-empty preconditions $^\bullet t$ and non-empty postconditions $t^\bullet$,*

$$! \left(\bigotimes_{p \in {}^\bullet t} p^{W(p,t)} \multimap \bigotimes_{q \in t^\bullet} q^{W(t,q)} \right).$$

- *For the current marking m and each place $p \in P$ with $\mathbf{m}(p) = n \geq 1$, we include p^n.*

The special cases of where the precondition or postcondition of transition t is empty are accounted for in Definition 8. Explicitly, for each transition t where $^\bullet t = \emptyset$, we include the formula

$$! \left(1 \multimap \bigotimes_{q \in t^\bullet} q^{W(t,q)} \right) \text{ or equivalently } ! \left(\bigotimes_{q \in t^\bullet} q^{W(t,q)} \right),$$

and for each transition t where $t^\bullet = \emptyset$, we include the formula

$$! \left(\bigotimes_{p \in {}^\bullet t} p^{W(p,t)} \multimap \perp \right) \text{ or equivalently } ! \left(\left(\bigotimes_{p \in {}^\bullet t} p^{W(p,t)} \right)^{\perp} \right).$$

It is now clear that, given an object Petri net, we can regard the object nets as **ILL** formulae using Definition 8. Thus, we can regard any object Petri net, as defined in Appendix A as an LLPN.

The above suggests a reverse translation, from **ILL** to P/T nets. In order to interpret **ILL** formulae without the modality ! as P/T nets, we require *extended* P/T nets which include the concept of *disposable transitions* [10]. However, we will not require the reverse translation in this work. Aside from the reverse of the translation suggested by Definition 8, works by other authors provide a P/T net interpretation of full **ILL** [6,7].

3   Why Study Dynamic Structures?

At first glance the notion of "dynamic structure" may seem to be an oxymoron. Taking a closer look at the direction of information technology and its applications, it is clear that the connectedness of remote systems has become the major factor in many areas of computation and communication. The main example is of course the Internet. The Internet and even metropolitan and wide area networks (MANs and WANs) are reconfigured frequently, and so there is dynamism in the overall structure of these networks. This is accommodated, for instance, by the development of dynamic databases, where the topology is subject to permanent changes which must be taken into account by each new request.

There are different kinds of dynamism, two of which will be discussed in this paper:

(i) dynamic reconfiguration of resource-related quantitative aspects of systems, and

(ii) dynamic change of data flow, i.e. modification of the physical layout of a system.

The former is a kind of modification tackled by the self-modifying nets defined by Valk [25]. The latter has not yet been convincingly integrated into a Petri net-based modelling formalism. We show that both modification approaches are subsumed by LLPNs in Section 4 and in Section 5.

4   Self-Modification and LLPNs

In this section some aspects of self-modification for Petri nets are discussed. In particular, it is shown that the self-modifying nets of Valk [25] can be simulated by LLPNs.

A self-modifying Petri net is essentially a P/T net that can have linear expressions, with variables drawn from the place names of the net, as arc weights. That is, the weight of an arc from place p to transition t is given by an expression

$$\sum_{q \in P} a_q q \text{ where } a_q \in \mathbb{N} \text{ for all } q \in P, \text{ with the meaning } W(p,t) = \sum_{q \in P} a_q \mathbf{m}(q).$$

If the arc expression for an arc $(p,t) \in F$ of a self-modifying net includes a coefficient for p greater than one, then the net is not well-formed since transition t cannot be enabled. The self-modifying nets discussed below will be assumed to be well-formed.

An example of a self-modifying net transition is given in Fig. 3(a). This transition can be simulated by the LLPN transition shown in Fig. 3(b). Construction 9 gives a general transformation of self-modifying nets into LLPNs.

Construction 9. *Let N be a well-formed self-modifying Petri net with set of places P, set of transitions T, flow relation F, and initial marking $\mathbf{m_0}$. Construct an LLPN $N' := (P, T, F', \Lambda, G, \mathfrak{v}, \mathbf{m_0}')$ such that*

$$F' := F \cup F^{-1}$$
$$\cup \{(p,t) \in P \times T \mid \exists p' \in P.p \text{ has non-zero coefficient in } W(p',t)\}$$
$$\cup \{(t,p) \in T \times P \mid \exists p' \in P.p \text{ has non-zero coefficient in } W(t,p')\}$$

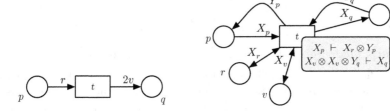

(a) Transition of a self-modifying net referring to places r and v

(b) LLPN transition simulation t from subfigure (a)

Fig. 3. A transition of a self-modifying net with arc weights referring to the markings of places r and v simulated by an LLPN transition

Λ is the set of all finite tensor products built with the single propositional variable $\mathfrak{a}$. The initial marking is given as follows:

$$\forall p \in P.\mathbf{m_0}'(p) := \mathfrak{a}^{\mathbf{m_0}(p)}$$

The arc inscriptions and guards of N' are defined according to the following rules: [1]

1. If $(p,t) \in F$ has an arc expression $\alpha_{(p,t)}$ that does not contain p, then the LLPN will have an arc from each place $q \in P$ occurring in α to t with inscription X_q. A reversed arc (t,p) with inscription Y_p is introduced. The guard for transition t then includes the sequent

$$X_p \vdash Y_p \otimes \bigotimes_{q \in \alpha_{(p,t)}} X_q.$$

   This tensor product depends on the multiset $\alpha_{(p,t)}$ and so it takes into account the coefficients in the arc inscription of N.
2. If the arc expression of $(p,t) \in F$ contains p (with coefficient one) then the arc acts as a reset arc and is represented by $(p,t) \in F'$ with inscription X_p and with guard $G(t) = \{X_p \vdash X_p\}$. The reverse arc (t,p) has no inscription and so can be omitted. If other place names appear in the arc expression of $(p,t) \in F$, then they are treated as in case 1.
3. If $(t,p) \in F$ has an arc expression $\alpha_{(p,t)}$, then the LLPN will have an arc from each place $q \in P$ occurring in α to t with inscription X_q. A reversed arc (t,p) with inscription Y_p is newly introduced.

---

[1] Arc inscriptions of self-modifying nets can be viewed as multisets of place names. In the sequel, multisets are sometimes written as formal sums for convenience.

In addition to the sequents introduced to the guard in 1 and 2, the guard for transition t contains the sequent

$$Y_p \otimes \bigotimes_{q \in \alpha_{(t,p)}} X_q \vdash X_p$$

where the tensor product depends on the multiset $\alpha_{(t,p)}$.

The flow relation F' in Construction 9 unfolds the arcs of the self-modifying net so that each arc depends on the marking of only one place. Note also that in any reachable marking of the LLPN from Construction 9, the entire marking of each place is treated as (at most) one formula.

Theorem 1. *The LLPN labelled N' in Construction 9 simulates the self-modifying net N with respect to the following simulation relation on markings, mapping multiplicities of tokens to tensor products:*

$$\sim \subseteq \mathbb{N}^{|P|} \times \left(\bigcup_{n \in \mathbb{N}} \mathfrak{a}^n \right)^{|P|} \quad where \quad (n_1, \ldots, n_{|P|}) \sim (\mathfrak{a}^{n_1}, \ldots, \mathfrak{a}^{n_{|P|}}).$$

In Theorem 1, N and N' have the same set of possible firing sequences and the same reachability set with respect to the $\sim$ relation.

Proof. Immediate from the construction, since no autonomous derivations are possible for the restricted class of formulae allowed as tokens.

Intuitively, the marking of each $p \in P$ given by $\mathbf{m}(p) = n$ in N is simulated by $\mathbf{m}(p) = \underbrace{\mathfrak{a} \otimes \ldots \otimes \mathfrak{a}}_{n} = \mathfrak{a}^n$ in N'.

Using ideas from Farwer and Lomazova [13], a self-modifying net transition can be encoded by a first-order intuitionistic linear logic formula containing a binary locality predicate P to specify that some formula ϕ resides in place p by $P(p, \phi)$. For example, the transition from Fig. 3(a) would be represented as the universally quantified formula

$$!(p(X_r \otimes Y_p) \otimes q(Y_q) \otimes r(X_r) \otimes v(X_v) \multimap p(Y_p) \otimes q(X_v \otimes X_v \otimes Y_q) \otimes r(X_r) \otimes v(X_v))$$

where $p(X)$ is short for $P(p, X)$. A similar encoding is possible, when enriching **ILL** with a modality for locality, such as the modal linear logic for distribution and mobility (DMLL) [2].

The simulation in Theorem 1 does not faithfully retain concurrency. To remedy this, we would have to equip LLPNs with the concept of test arcs, which are used in other areas of Petri net theory. Nevertheless, our result shows that in interleaving semantics, self-modifying nets can concisely be simulated by LLPNs.

Self-modifying nets have already been generalized to G-nets [5]. G-nets are a type of self-modifying net which allow polynomials of degree greater than one, where the variables of the polynomials are the place names of the net. There is no obvious way of extending Construction 9 to G-nets. Indeed, it is not possible to express polynomials of degree greater than one in propositional **ILL** if we use the **ILL**-representation of linear polynomials given in Construction 9. Further discussion of G-nets is beyond the scope of this paper due to space limitations.

5   Structural Modification

5.1   Motivating Object Net Modification

Many common P/T net properties have an evident extension to LLPNs. Some examples follow.

Definition 10 (termination). *An LLPN is* terminating *if there is no infinite firing sequence.*

Definition 11 (deadlock-freedom). *An LLPN is* deadlock-free *if each reachable marking enables a transition.*

Definition 12 (liveness). *An LLPN is* live *if each reachable marking enables a firing sequence containing all transitions.*

These properties point the way to a large class of situations in which it is necessary to be able to represent modification of object nets by the system net. For example, it is often necessary to ensure that some software process terminates. On the other hand, it might be necessary to ensure that a communication or control process never terminates.

There are standard ways of detecting termination without using LLPN features which addresses the first of these. Below, the possibility of unwanted non-termination in the form of infinite loops will be addressed.

Our approach will involve the modification of a transition in the object net (or, to be more precise, the linear logic encoding of the transition). In order to be able to ensure that exactly and only the desired modification is carried out, we first introduce the *s-canonical formula* of a P/T net. This modification of the standard canonical formula defined by Farwer [10] adds a fresh propositional symbol to the premise of each linear implication representing a transition. The reason for introducing this additional premise is to force the transition to synchronise with a system net transition, whereby we will be able to take some action after any object net transition fires.[2]

Definition 13 (s-canonical formula). *Let* $N = (P, T, F, W, \mathbf{m_0})$ *be a P/T net. Then the* **s-canonical formula** *for N is the tensor product of:*

- *For each transition $t \in T$ with non-empty preconditions $^\bullet t$ and non-empty postconditions $t^\bullet$*

$$! \left(\bigotimes_{p \in {}^\bullet t} p^{W(p,t)} \otimes \delta \multimap \bigotimes_{q \in t^\bullet} q^{W(t,q)} \otimes \overline{\delta} \right),$$

where δ and $\overline{\delta}$ are fresh propositional variables, and
- $p^{\mathbf{m}(p)}$ *for the current marking $\mathbf{m}$ and each place $p \in P$ with $\mathbf{m}(p) \geq 1$.*

---

[2] This restricts concurrency in the object net, which can granularly be regained by introducing additional modes for the respective system net transition(s). This is not discussed further here, in order not to distract the reader from the main idea and to keep the examples simple.

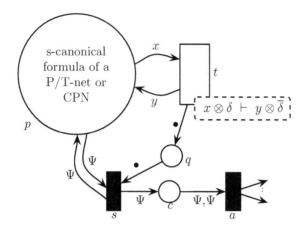

Fig. 4. Petri net augmentation to detect a repeated net marking

5.2 Detecting and Addressing Infinite Loops

A net with initial marking $\mathbf{m_0}$ is potentially non-terminating if (but not only if) the same marking appears twice in the firing sequence starting at initial marking $\mathbf{m_0}$. That is, we have:

$$\mathbf{m_0} \rightarrow m_1 \rightarrow \cdots \rightarrow m_k \rightarrow m_{k+1} \rightarrow \cdots \rightarrow m_n \rightarrow m_k \rightarrow \ldots.$$

for some $0 \leq k \leq n$. A method follows for augmenting a net to detect and address non-termination in this class of cases.

Non-termination in a CPN $\mathcal{N}$ can be detected by a concise LLPN construction. A "camera" place connects to all other places via "snapshot" transitions. Every transition of $\mathcal{N}$ is augmented so that each occurrence of the net adds an "unsnapped marker" token to all places. The presence of unsnapped marker tokens causes a snapshot to be taken of the entire net. That is, a token that is an **ILL** formula representation of the current marking of $\mathcal{N}$ is stored in a camera place with LLPN functionality. An evident **ILL** formula denoted Ψ can be added to the camera place as a token which responds to the presence of two identical snapshots. The formula Ψ quantifies over values drawn from all colour sets of the CPN. When there are two identical snapshots in the camera place, a token is sent to a place to indicate non-termination. Fig. 4 illustrates this.

The token formula in place p represents the original net $\mathcal{N}$ under consideration, encoded here in s-canonical form. Transition t allows any derivation that corresponds to the firing of an enabled transition in the object net. Each occurrence of t places a black token in the place triggering transition s that places a snapshot of the encoded object net in the camera place c.

By requiring the presence of two identical object net snapshots in c, transition a is only enabled if a marking in the object net has recurred. Transition a can then trigger an action not shown in this figure. For practical use, the two solid

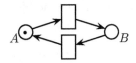

Fig. 5. Object net corresponding to $A\otimes!(B\!-\!\circ A)\otimes!(A\!-\!\circ B)$

transitions have to be "immediate transitions", meaning that they have to fire immediately when they are enabled.

Thus, the type of potential non-termination described above can be detected in an LLPN. But how is a loop to be addressed when it arises? We consider a specific case.

Consider a formula of the form $A\otimes!(B\!-\!\circ A)\otimes!(A\!-\!\circ B)$ where A and B are atomic, appearing in $m_k m_{k+1}\ldots m_n$ the part of the firing sequence that repeats. Note that this linear logic formula corresponds to the object net in Fig. 5. Suppose that many transitions require something representing an energy token denoted E. An obvious way of checking the progress of the repeating firing sequence is to substitute for any token of the form $!(A\!-\!\circ B)$ the token $!(A\otimes E\!-\!\circ B)$ using:

$$\left[!(B\!-\!\circ A)\otimes!(A\!-\!\circ B)\right] \;-\!\circ\; \left[!(B\!-\!\circ A)\otimes !(A\otimes E\!-\!\circ B)\right]. \tag{1}$$

A net to which the above can be applied might typically have a place containing some finite supply of energy, represented by a finite number of E tokens.

In order that a token of the form $!(A\!-\!\circ B)$ be recognizable and the formula (1) sent to the appropriate places, variables are needed for atomic symbols. In particular, the following formula could be used in the guard of the transition t of the LLPN:

$$!(x\!-\!\circ y) \;-\!\circ\; !(x\otimes E\!-\!\circ y),$$

which allows the derivation of:

$$\left[[!(x\!-\!\circ y) \;-\!\circ\; !(x\otimes E\!-\!\circ y)] \otimes !(y\!-\!\circ x)\otimes!(x\!-\!\circ y)\right] \;\vdash\; \left[!(y\!-\!\circ x) \otimes !(x\otimes E\!-\!\circ y)\right].$$

The energy requirement represented by E must be made specific to the applicable formula $!(x\!-\!\circ y)$ to ensure that these behaviour-modification linear logic formulae do not interfere with such formulae in other places. Therefore, the symbol E_{xy} is used to index the E.

Another possible way of dealing with this kind of modification is to provide additional formulae within the places that contain token formulae that are to be modified and rely on the autonomous derivations possible in LLPNs. This approach, while possible, would offer little control over the time at which modification occurs. This approach would also require quantification over atomic symbols for detecting the *need* for a modification and subsequent deployment of appropriate subformulae to carry out the modification:

$$\forall x, y \in \mathcal{A}.$$
$$\left[!(y{\multimap}x) \otimes !(x{\multimap}y)\right] \multimap \left[\left[!(x{\multimap}y) \multimap !(x \otimes E_{xy}{\multimap}y)\right] \otimes !(y{\multimap}x) \otimes !(x{\multimap}y)\right] \quad (2)$$

Using the formula (2) will cause the infinitely cycling process to cease when the energy is exhausted *or* the energy requirement will be stepped up if the process repeats again.

A problem remains in $!(A{\multimap}B)$ producing an indeterminate number of duplicates of $A{\multimap}B$. At present, the only known way of addressing this problem is by partitioning the reduction (according to the rules of linear logic) of linear logic formulae using a method by Farwer which develops Girard's multi-region logical calculus [14,15,12]. This method was originally motivated by the need to deal with *disposable transitions*, i.e. transitions that are allowed to occur only a finite number of times and which no longer exist as soon as this "capacity" is exceeded.

It is possible to progress even further, beyond (2) to second-order **ILL** , by quantifying in the following way: $\forall x, y \in L_{\mathcal{A}}$ and this would prevent non-termination in a much larger class of situations.

5.3   Alternative Approach Using Transition Guard

We now outline a different approach for the modification of the object net encoding. In this approach, the net modification is carried out by the guard of a single transition. The steps follow:

- Define a partial order $\prec$ on the set of canonical formulae for a Petri net.
  The partial order can be defined on the length of a formula and is introduced to deal with the non-uniqueness of Petri net encodings due to the possible replication of the exponential subformulae representing the transitions.
- A formula for a net is in **reduced canonical form** (RCF) if it is a lower bound of the canonical net representations with respect to $\prec$.
  In general, there is not a unique representation in RCF, since the tensor is commutative. Thus, there exist equivalent formulae of the same length.
- Apply the modification on an s-canonical net representation in RCF utilising a guard of the LLPN.
  For example, let x and y be in RCF and let x_1 and x_2 comprise tensor products of atoms, representing markings of the object net. Then the following guard of a system net transition can be used to modify the object net encoding according to the ideas in Section 5.2:

$$\{x \;\vdash\; \Gamma \otimes !(x_1 \otimes A{\multimap}x_2),$$
$$\Gamma \otimes !(x_1 \otimes A{\multimap}x_2) \otimes (!(x_1 \otimes A{\multimap}x_2) \multimap !(x_1 \otimes A \otimes E{\multimap}x_2))$$
$$\vdash\; \Gamma \otimes !(x_1 \otimes A \otimes E{\multimap}x_2),$$
$$\Gamma \otimes !(x_1 \otimes A \otimes E{\multimap}x_2) \;\vdash\; y\} \;.$$

By restricting the formulae to the reduced canonical formulae of nets, we avoid the replication anomalies discussed in previous papers.

6 Conclusions and Future Work

We have shown a straightforward way to simulate self-modifying Petri nets by linear logic Petri nets. Furthermore, we have given a framework for using LLPNs to modify at run-time a token formula representing an object net. This continues our investigation into appropriate semantics for object Petri net formalisms by giving, for the first time, the possibility of dynamic structural modifications. This extends the benefits of object-based modelling with the flexibility needed for modelling highly dynamic distributed systems that have gained an immense importance in recent years.

From a practical point of view, we are seeking to leverage the theory of **ILL** to do essentially what a compiler does with a computer program. That is, a software program is made to sit in a certain infrastructure which ensures that the program executes in a way that has certain desirable properties. However, the tokens that are used to produce a desired, or more desirable, behaviour may not be so obvious as in the case given in this paper. A general framework is required to systematically determine by using first or second-order **ILL** the most appropriate **ILL** formula tokens to use.

Linear logic allows far reaching modifications to be modelled. It is an open problem, how these possibilities should be restricted in order to retain desirable properties and preserve traditional results on Petri nets.

References

1. S. Abramsky. Computational interpretations of linear logic. *Theoretical Computer Science*, 111:3–57, 1993.
2. N. Biri and D. Galmiche. A modal linear logic for distribution and mobility. Talk given at LL'02 of FLoC'02, 2002.
3. C. Brown. *Linear Logic and Petri Nets: Categories, Algebra and Proof*. PhD thesis, AI Laboratory, Department of Computer Science, University of Edinburgh, 1991.
4. C. Brown, D. Gurr, and V. de Paiva. A linear specification language for Petri nets. Technical Report 363, Computer Science Department, Aarhus University, 1991.
5. C. Dufourd, A. Finkel, and Ph. Schnoebelen. Reset nets between decidability and undecidability. In *Proceedings of the 25th International Colloquium on Automata, Languages, and Programming (ICALP'98)*, volume 1443 of *LNCS*. Springer-Verlag, 1998.
6. U. Engberg and G. Winskel. Petri nets as Models of Linear Logic. In A. Arnold, editor, *Proceedings of Colloquium on Trees in Algebra and Programming*, volume 389 of *Lecture Notes in Computer Science*, pages 147–161, Copenhagen, Denmark, 1990. Springer-Verlag.
7. U. H. Engberg and G. Winskel. Linear logic on Petri nets. Technical Report ISSN 0909-0878, BRICS, Department of Computer Science, University of Aarhus, DK-8000 Aarhus C Denmark, February 1994.

8. B. Farwer. Towards linear logic Petri nets. Technical report, Faculty of Informatics, University of Hamburg, 1996.

9. B. Farwer. A Linear Logic View of Object Systems. In H.-D. Burkhard, L. Czaja, and P. Starke, editors, *Informatik-Berichte, No. 110: Workshop Concurrency, Specification and Programming*, pages 76–87, Berlin, September 1998. Humboldt-Universität.

10. B. Farwer. *Linear Logic Based Calculi for Object Petri Nets*. PhD thesis, Fachbereich Informatik, Universität Hamburg, 1999. Published by Logos Verlag, 2000.

11. B. Farwer. A Linear Logic View of Object Petri nets. *Fundamenta Informaticae*, 37:225–246, 1999.

12. B. Farwer. A multi-region linear logic based calculus for dynamic petri net structures. *Fundamenta Informaticae*, 43(1–4):61–79, 2000.

13. B. Farwer and I. Lomazova. A systematic approach towards object-based petri net formalisms. In D. Bjørner and A. Zamulin, editors, *Perspectives of System Informatics, Proceedings of the 4th International Andrei Ershov Memorial Conference, PSI 2001, Akademgorodok, Novosibirsk*, pages 255–267. LNCS 2244. Springer-Verlag, 2001.

14. J.-Y. Girard. Linear logic: its syntax and semantics. In Girard et al. [15], pages 1–42.

15. J.-Y. Girard, Y. Lafont, and L. Regnier, editors. *Advances in Linear Logic*. Number 222 in Lecture notes series of the London Mathematical Society. Cambridge University Press, 1995.

16. K. Jensen. An Introduction to High-Level Petri nets. Technical Report ISSN 0105-8517, Department of Computer Science, University of Aarhus, October 1985.

17. T. Kis, K.-P. Neuendorf, and P. Xirouchakis. Scheduling with Chameleon Nets. In B. Farwer, D. Moldt, and M.-O. Stehr, editors, *Proceedings of the Workshop on Petri Nets in System Engineering (PNSE'97)*, pages 67–77. Universität Hamburg, 1997.

18. J. Lilius. High-level nets and Linear logic. In Kurt Jensen, editor, *Application and Theory of Petri nets*, volume 616 of *Lecture Notes in Computer Science*, pages 310–327. Springer, 1992.

19. N. Marti-Oliet and J. Meseguer. From Petri nets to linear logic. *Mathematical Structures in Computer Science*, 1:69–101, 1991.

20. J. Meseguer, U. Montanari, and V. Sassone. Representation Theorems for Petri nets. In *Foundations of Computer Science: Potential - Theory - Cognition*, pages 239–249, 1997.

21. K. Misra. On LPetri nets. In K. Streignitz, editor, *Proceedings of 13th European Summer School on Logic, Language and Information*. European Association for Logic, Language and Information — FoLLI, European Association for Logic, Language and Information — FoLLI, May 2001.

22. D. Sangiorgi and D. Walker. *The Pi-Calculus: A Theory of Mobile Processes*. Cambridge University Press, 2001.

23. V. Sassone. On the Algebraic Structure of Petri nets. *Bulletin of the EATCS*, 72:133–148, 2000.

24. A. Troelstra. *Substructural Logics*, chapter Tutorial on linear logic. Clarendon Press, 1993.

25. R. Valk. Self-modifying nets, a natural extension of petri nets. In Ausiello, G. and Böhm, C., editors, *Automata, Languages and Programming (ICALP'93)*, volume 62 of *Lecture Notes in Computer Science*, pages 464–476, Berlin, 1978. Springer-Verlag.

26. R. Valk. Petri nets as token objects. an introduction to elementary object nets. In J. Desel and M. Silva, editors, *Applications and Theory of Petri Nets 1998. Proceedings*, volume 1420, pages 1–25. Springer-Verlag, 1998.
27. R. Valk. Reference and value semantics for object petri nets. In H. Weber, H. Ehrig, and W. Reisig, editors, *Colloquium on Petri Net Technologies for Modelling Communication Based Systems*, pages 169–188. Fraunhofer Institute for Software and Systems Engineering ISST, Berlin, 1999.
28. R. Valk. Relating Different Semantics for Object Petri nets. Technical Report B-226-00, TGI - Theoretical Foundations of Computer Science Group, Computer Science, University of Hamburg, June 2000.
29. R. Valk. Concurrency in Communicating Object Petri nets. In G. Agha, F. de Cindio, and G. Rozenberg, editors, *Concurrent Object-Oriented Programming and Petri Nets*, Lecture Notes in Computer Science, pages 164–195. Springer-Verlag, 2001.
30. R. Valk and C. Girault, editors. *Petri Nets for Systems Engineering – A Guide to Modeling, Verification, and Applications*. Springer-Verlag, 2003.

Appendix

A   Object Petri Nets

Informally, an object Petri net is a CPN with tokens which are P/T nets. The definitions given in this section are partly based on those of chameleon nets [17] and object systems [26,29]. The following definition of an object Petri net refers to a synchronisation relation, which is given in Definition 22. The other components of an object Petri net are a system net (Definition 15) and a set of object nets (Definition 16).

Definition 14 (object Petri net, OPN). *An object Petri net is a triple* $OPN = (SN, \{ON_i\}_{i \in I}, S)$ *where SN is a system net, the ON_i are object nets, I is a finite indexing set and S is a synchronisation relation.*

An OPN is essentially a system net with an associated set of object net tokens and a synchronisation relation between transitions of the system net and object nets. Throughout this paper, we only allow 2-level nesting of nets. Fig. 6 portrays a simple example of an object Petri net.

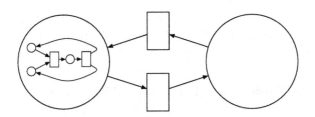

Fig. 6. An object Petri net with a system net and an object (token) net

Definition 15 (system net). *A system net is a tuple* $SN = (\Sigma, P, T, F, C, V, E)$ *where the following hold:*

(i) *Σ is the set of types or colours with a subtype relation $\sqsubseteq$ that is reflexive and transitive*

(ii) *P is the set of system net places and T is the set of system net transitions such that $P \cap T = \emptyset$*

(iii) *$F \subseteq (P \times T) \cup (T \times P)$ is the flow relation, also called the set of arcs*

(iv) *$C : P \to \Sigma$ is a total function, called the typing function or colouring function of the system places*

(v) *V is the set of variable symbols and to every $v \in V$ there is associated a type $type(v) \in \Sigma$*

(vi) *$E : F \to Bags(V)$ is the arc labelling function*

(vii) *The set of variables on the incoming arcs of transition t is denoted V_t and, for every variable v on an outgoing arc, $v \in V_t$ is true. of t. The set $V = \bigcup_{t \in T} V_t$ is the set of variables of SN.*

In Definition 16 an object net is defined to be a P/T net. As with the system net from Definition 15 we have omitted the marking, which is introduced in the respective net systems.

Definition 16 (object net). *An object net $ON = (P, T, F, W)$ is a P/T net.*

Remark 1. It will be assumed that different object nets have pairwise disjoint sets of places and transitions. Similarly, it will be assumed that the names of system net places and transitions are pairwise disjoint with the transitions and places of all object nets.

A basic object Petri net is essentially an ordinary Petri net regarded as the system net with P/T nets as tokens. For this purpose we define a basic system net as a special case of the system net from Definition 15.

Definition 17 (basic system net). *A basic system net is a system net $SN = (\Sigma, P, T, F, C, V, E)$, such that the following conditions hold:*

1. *$|\Sigma| = 1$, i.e. there is a unique type σ with $\Sigma = \{\sigma\}$*
2. *$\forall p \in P.C(p) = \sigma$*
3. *$\forall (x, y) \in F.|E(x, y)| = 1$, i.e. the arc labelling is a single variable*
4. *$\forall (x, y), (x', y) \in P \times T.(x, y), (x', y) \in F \Rightarrow x = x' \vee E(x, y) \neq E(x', y)$, i.e. all incoming arcs of a transition carry disjoint labels.*

With Definition 17 in hand, basic object Petri nets (BOPNs) can be defined. A BOPN can be seen as an OPN with only one type and one variable on each arc. For BOPNs we assume pairwise disjoint variables for any incoming arcs adjacent to the same transition.

Definition 18 (basic object Petri net, BOPN). *A basic object Petri net is a triple $BOPN = (SN, \{ON_i\}_{i \in I}, \mathcal{S})$ where $SN = (P, T, F)$ is an basic system net, the $ON_i = (P_i, T_i, F_i)$ are object nets, and $\mathcal{S}$ is a synchronisation relation for BOPN.*

In the sequel, by the term "object Petri net" we mean a basic object Petri net.

To study the dynamics of OPNs we must introduce the notion of a marking for OPNs, i.e. a token distribution adhering to the typing constraints of the system net. The definition uses the notation from Definitions 14, 15, and 16.

Definition 19 (OPN marking). *A marking* $\mathfrak{m}$ *of an OPN* $(SN, \{ON_i\}_{i \in I}, \mathcal{S})$ *is a function*

$$\mathfrak{m} : P \to Bags(\{(ON_i, m) \mid m : P_i \to \mathbb{N}\}_{i \in I}),$$

such that $\forall p \in P. \forall (x, m) \in \mathfrak{m}(p).type(x) \sqsubseteq C(p).$

Recall that an object Petri net does not include reference to a marking. When an OPN marking is associated with an OPN, then something new is derived: an object Petri net *system*.

Definition 20 (object Petri net system, OPNS). *An* object Petri net system *is a pair* $(OPN, \mathfrak{m})$, *where OPN is an object Petri net and* $\mathfrak{m}$ *is a suitable marking of OPN.*

We generalise the synchronisation relation from earlier work on object Petri nets by introducing *synchronisation expressions* for each transition of the system net. This reflects the view that the system net may invoke a synchronisation in several different ways. That is, the synchronisation may require a finite set of object net transitions to occur simultaneously with its own firing. This more general approach to synchronisation admits the standard *binary* synchronisation as a special case.

Synchronisation expressions from Definition 21 are used as a rule for synchronisation of a transition u of a given net with other transitions of a (not necessarily distinct) net or nets. Definition 21:

(a) assumes that the sets of transition labels for all nets in the object Petri net are pairwise disjoint, and
(b) defines synchronisation expressions in disjunctive normal form (DNF).

These requirements are for convenience and are not onerous: (a) is a matter of relabelling and, for (b), it is clear that every formula containing only conjunctions and disjunctions can be transformed into DNF.

Definition 21 (synchronisation expression and evaluation). *Let* $OS = (SN, \{ON_i\}_{i \in I}, \mathcal{S})$ *be an object Petri net with system net* $SN = (P, T, F)$ *and object nets* $ON_i = (P_i, T_i, F_i)$.

Denote the set of object net transitions by $\hat{T} := \biguplus_{i \in I} T_i$ *and define a context-free grammar* $G = (V_N, V_T, R, D)$ *where* $V_N = \{A, C, D\}$, $V_T = \hat{T} \uplus \{(,), \wedge, \vee\}$, *D is the initial symbol, and R comprises the following rules:*

$$D \to D \vee (C) \mid C$$
$$C \to C \wedge A \mid A$$
$$A \to u \ \text{for all } u \in \hat{T}.$$

We denote by $L(G)$ the language generated by the grammar G. The synchronisation expression of system net transition t is a pair (t, E_G) where $E_G \in L(G)$.

We say that $E_G \in L(G)$ is true if it is mapped to $\top$ under the evaluation function and is otherwise false. The evaluation function is given by:

$$L(G) \to \mathbb{B}$$
$$u \mapsto \top \quad \text{if and only if } u \text{ can fire in its net}^3$$
$$E_{G1} \wedge E_{G2} \mapsto \top \quad \text{if and only if } E_{G1} \text{ and } E_{G2} \text{ are simultaneously true}$$
$$E_{G1} \vee E_{G2} \mapsto \top \quad \text{if and only if } E_{G1} \text{ or } E_{G2} \text{ (or both) are true.}$$

The semantics of synchronisation expressions is given by the synchronisation evaluation function:

$$T \times L(G) \to \mathbb{B}$$
$$(t, E_G) \mapsto \top \quad \text{if and only if } t \text{ is enabled in the system net}^4 \text{ and } E_G \text{ is true.}$$

A transition appearing in an interaction expression can fire if and only if the interaction expression evaluates to true. Only transitions of the system net or the object nets that do not appear in any synchronisation expression of $\mathcal{S}$ may fire autonomously.

In Definition 21 the first component of a synchronisation expression is a transition in T, i.e. from the system net. This portrays the view of the system net controlling the object Petri net and reflects locality conditions that should also be taken into account for the generalised case of multi-level object Petri nets. In restricting synchronisations to take place only between adjacent levels we impose a locality condition. Object-object synchronisation is prohibited in the present model. Object nets can synchronise among each other only indirectly by synchronising with a net that takes the rôle of the system net.

If $u \in \hat{T}$ is not synchronised with a particular transition t, then this could be seen in the fact that u does not appear in the expression $E_G(t)$.

The following definition of synchronisation relation uses the notation of Definition 21.

Definition 22 (synchronisation relation). *A **synchronisation relation** for a system net with set of transitions T is given by:*

$$\{(t, E_G(t)) \mid t \in T, E_G(t) \in L(G)\}$$

where $E_G(t)$ is the synchronisation expression of transition t as defined in Definition 21.

---

[3] For this definition the object net is viewed as an isolated ordinary net system.

[4] Enablement and transition firing in the system net is discussed below.

To give an intuitive feel for synchronisation expressions, if the synchronisation expression for t were $(t, u_1 \wedge u_2)$ then both transitions u_1 and u_2 of the object net must simultaneously be able to fire in order that transition t of the system net be enabled. Thus enabled, transition t can fire forcing the object net to pass while changing the marking of the object net according to the firing of u_1 and u_2. If $(t, u_1 \vee u_2)$ were the element of the synchronisation relation involving t, then it would be sufficient for either transition u_1 or u_2 of the object net to be enabled in order that transition t be enabled in the system net.

While a variety of different firing rules have been discussed in earlier literature, the main differences are characterised by the proposed semantics of the respective approaches. Two main directions are noteworthy: reference semantics and value semantics (cf. [11,27,28]). While the former views an object net as an integral item that cannot be locally modified without the knowledge of this being transferred to all referring instances, the latter takes the viewpoint of local copies that can act as individuals.

Principles for Entity Authentication[*]

Michele Bugliesi, Riccardo Focardi, and Matteo Maffei

Dipartimento di Informatica, Università Ca' Foscari di Venezia,
{michele,focardi,maffei}@dsi.unive.it

Abstract. We study the roles of message components in authentication protocols. In particular, we investigate how a certain component contributes to the task of achieving entity authentication. To this aim, we isolate a core set of roles that enables us to extract general principles that should be followed to avoid attacks. We then formalize these principles in terms of rules for protocol parties and we prove that protocols designed according to these rules will achieve entity authentication.

1 Introduction

Security protocols, also known as cryptographic protocols, are designed to reach specific security goals in (possibly) hostile environments, like, e.g., Internet. Typical goals include the communication of a secret between two trusted entities, an authenticated message exchange, the generation and the sharing of a session key, the authentication of an entity with respect to another entity (e.g., to a server), and more. The design of security protocols is complex and often error prone, as witnessed by the many attacks to long standing protocols reported in the recent literature on the subject (see, e.g., [6,8,13, 16,19,20]). Most of these attacks do not need to break cryptography to be performed. Indeed, even when cryptography is assumed as a fully reliable building-block, an intruder can engage a number of potentially dangerous actions: it can intercept messages before they reach their destination, insert new messages, read those that travel along the communication links and forge new ones using the knowledge it has previously gained. All these actions are available to an intruder willing to try and break a protocol by exploiting a flaw in the underlying protocol logic.

In this paper, we focus on (shared-key based) cryptographic protocols for *entity authentication*, i.e. on protocols that enable one entity to prove its claimed identity to another entity [14,18,9], and discuss a novel method to protect such protocols from attacks to their logic.

A typical source of flaws in security protocols, and specifically in authentication protocols, is a poor interpretation of messages, whereby certain messages are believed to convey more guarantees than they really do. As observed in [2] "every message should say what it means, i.e., its interpretation should depend only on its content". As a trivial example of a message exchange that fails to comply with this principle consider the protocol:

$$A \rightarrow B : \{\text{"Here I am!"}\}_{K_{AB}}$$

[*] Work partially supported by MIUR project "Modelli formali per la sicurezza" and EU Contract IST-2001-32617 "Models and Types for Security in Mobile Distributed Systems" (MyThS).

in which *Alice* is sending to *Bob* the message "Here I am!" encrypted with a long-term key shared between them. When Bob receives the message, he could erroneously deduce that it has been generated by Alice since it is encrypted with a key that only Alice (besides Bob himself) knows. However, this is not true if Bob previously ran the same protocol with Alice (with exchanged roles). In that case, the following, well-known, *reflection attack* could be exploited by an intruder E:

$$a) \quad B \rightarrow E(A) : \{\text{"Here I am!"}\}_{K_{AB}}$$
$$b) \quad E(A) \rightarrow B : \{\text{"Here I am!"}\}_{K_{AB}}$$

In the first run a, E pretends to be A (denoted with $E(A)$) and intercepts the message sent by Bob; in the second run b, $E(A)$ replays the same message back to Bob. As a consequence, B erroneously interprets his own message as sent by Alice. The problem is that Bob is assuming that the message has been generated by Alice without this being explicitly indicated in the message. A simple solution is to provide this additional information within the message, as in $A \rightarrow B : \{A, \text{"Here I am!"}\}_{K_{AB}}$, where the first component now signals that A is the 'claimant' of the protocol.

Motivated by this need to make the interpretation of messages unambiguous, we investigate the roles of message components in authentication protocols. In particular, we study how entity identifiers, associated with the entity roles in the protocols, contribute to the task of achieving entity authentication. We identify three fundamental roles: (i) *Claimant*, the role of a principal willing to authenticate itself to some other principal; (ii) *Intended verifier*: the role of a principal that a claimant wants to act as a verifier for its response; (iii) *Key owner*: the role of a principal that owns a session key. These roles apply well, and uniformly, for a wide class of entity authentication protocols.

We propose a number of principles to be followed by the trusted parties of a protocol. These principles formalize provably safe ways for generating new encrypted blocks containing roles – called *authentication blocks* – from existing ones, and provide a formal basis for reasoning on authentication in terms of the authentication guarantees that are provided by decrypting such special blocks. For example, a trusted server S can assign to an entity A the claimant role in a message directed to another entity B, provided it has enough information to guarantee to B that A is indeed the claimant, i.e., provided that S has decrypted an authentication block stating that A is willing to authenticate with B. Dually, if an entity B decrypts a block where A is playing the claimant role, then he is guaranteed that A is indeed the identity of the claimant and that A was recently running the authentication protocol with him, i.e., A is authenticated to B.

We formalize these principles in terms of rules for protocol parties and we prove that protocols designed according to these rules will achieve entity authentication.

The rest of the presentation is organized as follows. § 2 describes the general assumptions of the model we work with, and introduces the notion of authentication block. § 3 defines the design principles, formalized as inference rules, and illustrates them with several examples. § 4 concludes with final remarks and a discussion on related work.

2   Protocol Roles and Authentication Blocks

As we stated in the introduction, our focus is on protecting protocols from attacks that are based on flaws in the protocols' logic and do that not exploit any weakness of the underlying cryptographic primitives. We thus make the so called *perfect cryptography* assumption, i.e. we abstract away from security issues regarding cryptographic primitives and specific cryptographic algorithms, and we assume every cryptographic operation to be a secure building-block. Moreover we assume that keys are carefully managed, i.e., long-term keys are safely distributed to participants and can never be learned by any intruder and, similarly, session keys are never circulated within messages once they have been first distributed.

Authentication protocols can be partitioned into two classes depending on whether or not they are based on a *Trusted Third Party* (TTP), i.e., a trusted entity that acts as intermediate party for the authentication task. As we shall see, our principles allow us to deal with both kinds of authentication in a uniform way.

The following conventions are assumed throughout. The capital letters A and B denote protocol *principals*, which are distinguished from TTPs denoted by S. Instead, we use I and J to refer to generic participants in the protocol, either principals or TTP's. We use K and N to denote keys and nonces, respectively. The notation K_{IJ} indicates a long-term key shared between I and J. We assume that $K_{IJ} = K_{JI}$. Finally, V is used to denote either a key or a nonce and R ranges over the roles Claim, Verif and Owner.

As discussed earlier, we consider three possible roles that entities can play during the authentication task: *Claimant*, *Intended verifier*, and *Key owner*. There are other message components that are necessary to make these roles useful for the purpose of authentication. In particular, each role needs a time-dependent element, like e.g., nonces, timestamps, sequence numbers, that provides *freshness*. Here we only consider *nonces*, i.e., numbers that are used only once: they are typically generated as challenges, and sent back inside encrypted messages, to be *checked* and thus prove that a certain message is not a replay of an old one. Together with nonces, we associate entities with the session key they possess (this is always true of entities playing the *Key owner* role). This is useful for distribution of session keys, where a trusted server wants to communicate that a certain entity owns a certain session key.

Authentication blocks are abstractions of encrypted messages which only contain the message components that are directly relevant to authentication, plus the role of such components in the authentication task. Formally,

Definition 1. *An authentication block is a tuple of the form* $\langle R, I, N, K \rangle_{K_{I_1 I_2}}$. *The session key K is mandatory only for the role* Owner: *when it is missing the block is denoted by* $\langle R, I, N \rangle_{K_{I_1 I_2}}$.

The use of roles and nonces within authentication blocks conveys useful information and guarantees to any entity which successfully decrypts them. Specifically, assume that entity I_1 decrypts the authentication block $\langle R, I, N, K \rangle_{K_{I_1 I_2}}$ and checks the nonce N (it had previously generated), and let $I_1 \neq I_2$. Then the following can be inferred: "Entity I is the owner of the fresh key K (if K is present), and is recently playing the role R with respect to I_1 and I_2", that is:

– if R = Claim, I_1 is not a TTP and $I_1 \neq I$ then I_1 is guaranteed that I has recently initiated an authentication session with I_1;
– if R = Verif, I_1 is a TTP and $I_1, I_2 \neq I$ then I_1 is guaranteed that I_2 has recently initiated an authentication session with I;
– if R = Owner then I_1 is guaranteed that I knows the fresh session key K;

In all the remaining cases, no guarantee can be made based on the decryption of the block.

As we mentioned earlier, "checking the nonce" provides the freshness guarantees on authentication blocks that are needed to counter replay attacks. Also note that guarantees are provided by decrypting authentication blocks only in some specific situations. In particular, since the Claim role is used to authenticate I to I_1 (possibly through a TTP), we require I_1 to be a party other than a TTP and that $I_1 \neq I$, i.e., that I_1 does not accept authentication requests from itself (which is a typical source of "reflection attacks"). Since the Verif role is used by I_2 to communicate to a TTP I_1 that I_2 itself intends to authenticate with I, we ask that I_1 be a TTP and that I be different from the other two identities. Finally, the assumption that $I_1 \neq I_2$ implies that we disregard all issues related to self-authentication.

Example 1. We illustrate the use of authentication blocks in reasoning on the interpretation of messages and in making their interpretation unambiguous. Consider a message $\{M, A, N\}_{K_{BS}}$ encrypted with a long-term key shared between principal B and TTP S, and containing a message M, the entity identifier A and a nonce N. One can deduce that this message is probably used to authenticate something, as a nonce is present, but nothing more can be said from the message itself. If instead, we represent it as an authentication block, we recover a precise, and unambiguous semantics. For example we can represent $\{M, A, N\}_{K_{BS}}$ as the block $\langle \text{Claim}, A, N \rangle_{K_{BS}}$, meaning that this message can be used to authenticate entity A to B, once nonce N has been checked by B. Alternatively, $\{M, A, N\}_{K_{BS}}$ could be mapped to $\langle \text{Verif}, A, N \rangle_{K_{BS}}$ to represents a request from B to authenticate with A through the TTP S. Note that we cannot map the message to a block of the form $\langle \text{Owner}, A, N, K \rangle_{K_{BS}}$ as no session key K is present in the message and K is mandatory for role Owner. In other words, to see a message as an authentication block, we need that every element required by the block is present in the original message. Note also that M is "discarded" in authentication blocks. This reflects the fact that it is irrelevant for entity authentication.

3   Principles for Entity Authentication

The formalization of our principles draws on a trace-based model that we adopt for describing protocol executions. The principles are stated as inference rules that specify (i) the format of the ciphertexts that a trusted party should generate to complete an authentication session, and (ii) the conditions under which such ciphertexts should be generated to provide the intended authentication guarantees.

The ciphertexts can be in two forms: either authentication blocks encrypted with long-term keys (which we assume to be robust) or any other message encrypted with session keys which are possessed by the trusted parties, and are only circulated among them within authentication blocks.

The inference rules predicate the generation of new messages or actions by each trusted principal on (i) previous actions by the same principal and (ii) on the structure of the ciphertexts that principal received at earlier stages of the protocol. Hence, the rules effectively assume that all the ciphertexts reach *all* parties, included their intended recipients. This may at first be understood as a limitation on the power of the intruder, because it prevents attacks to be mounted based on the interception (i.e., subtraction from the net) of ciphertexts. This is not the case, however, as intercepting a message may only break liveness properties, such as *fairness* in contract-signing, where two parties seek guarantees that none of them will get the contract signed before the other one (see, e.g., [21,25]). Authentication, instead, is (formalized as) a *safety* property, which is immune to attacks based on message interception. We start by formalizing the notion of safety.

3.1   Traces, Markers and Events

We represent (possibly concurrent) protocol runs in terms of traces that collect the sequence of encrypted messages generated during the runs as well as additional *marker* actions that we use to state our safety result. The structure of traces is defined as follows:

$$
\begin{array}{lll}
Markers & \mu ::= run_{\mathsf{R}}(I_1, I_2) \mid commit(I_1, I_2) \mid check(I, N) \\
Actions & \alpha ::= \mu \mid I \triangleright \{M\}_K \mid I \triangleright \langle \mathsf{R}, J, N, K \rangle_{K_{I_1 I_2}} \\
Traces & \sigma ::= \varepsilon \mid \alpha :: \sigma
\end{array}
$$

The two actions $I \triangleright \{M\}_K$ and $I \triangleright \langle \mathsf{R}, J, N, K \rangle_{K_{I_1 I_2}}$ represent the generation by entity I of $\{M\}_K$ and $\langle \mathsf{R}, J, N, K \rangle_{K_{I_1 I_2}}$, respectively. As for the markers, they are not part of the protocol runs: we include them in the traces to help define the desired safety property. Specifically, $check(I, N)$ indicates the checking of the nonce N by the entity I. Marker $run_{\mathsf{R}}(I_1, I_2)$ indicates the intention of (equivalently, the start of a protocol run by) I_1 to authenticate itself with I_2, by exploiting the role R. Note that there might be many $run_{\mathsf{R}}(I_1, I_2)$ markers corresponding to many (either parallel or sequential) protocol sessions (but we will require that all have the same role R). We write $run(B, A)$ instead of $run_{\mathsf{R}}(B, A)$ when the role R is immaterial. Finally, $commit(I_1, I_2)$ marks the completion of the authentication session.

We can now define the desired property of entity authentication in terms of a *correspondence* between actions of the participants [23,17], checked on the protocol traces.

Definition 2 (Safety). *A trace σ is safe if and only if whenever $\sigma = \sigma_1 :: commit(B, A) :: \sigma_2$, one has $\sigma_1 = \sigma_1' :: run(A, B) :: \sigma_1''$, and $\sigma_1' :: \sigma_1'' :: \sigma_2$ is safe.*

Intuitively, a trace is safe if every $commit(A, B)$ in the trace is preceded by a corresponding $run(B, A)$ action. Next, we discuss the rules for forming safe traces.

Table 1. Inference Rules

Environments

EMPTY

$$\dfrac{}{\emptyset \vdash \diamond}$$

NEW

$$\dfrac{\Gamma \vdash \diamond \quad V \textit{ fresh in } \Gamma \quad V \textit{ key or nonce}}{\Gamma, new(I, V) \vdash \diamond}$$

Principles

ENV

$$\dfrac{\Gamma \vdash \diamond}{\Gamma \vdash \varepsilon}$$

PRINCIPLE 1

$$\dfrac{\Gamma \vdash \sigma \quad run_R(A, B) \in \sigma \Rightarrow R = \mathsf{Claim}}{\Gamma \vdash \sigma :: run_{\mathsf{Claim}}(A, B) :: A \triangleright \langle \mathsf{Claim}, A, N \rangle_{K_{AB}}}$$

PRINCIPLE 2

$$\dfrac{\Gamma \vdash \sigma \quad run_R(A, B) \in \sigma \Rightarrow R = \mathsf{Verif}}{\Gamma \vdash \sigma :: run_{\mathsf{Verif}}(A, B) :: A \triangleright \langle \mathsf{Verif}, B, N \rangle_{K_{AS}}}$$

PRINCIPLE 3

$$\dfrac{\Gamma, new(S, N) \vdash \diamond \quad \Gamma \vdash \sigma \quad I \triangleright \langle \mathsf{Verif}, B, N \rangle_{K_{AS}} \in \sigma}{\Gamma, new(S, N) \vdash \sigma :: check(S, N) :: S \triangleright \langle \mathsf{Claim}, A, N \rangle_{K_{BS}}}$$

PRINCIPLE 4

$$\dfrac{\Gamma \vdash \sigma \quad I \triangleright \langle \mathsf{Verif}, B, N \rangle_{K_{AS}} \in \sigma}{\Gamma \vdash \sigma :: S \triangleright \langle \mathsf{Claim}, A, N \rangle_{K_{BS}}}$$

PRINCIPLE 5

$$\dfrac{\Gamma, new(S, K) \vdash \diamond \quad \Gamma \vdash \sigma}{\Gamma, new(S, K) \vdash \sigma :: S \triangleright \langle \mathsf{Owner}, A, N_A, K \rangle_{K_{BS}} :: S \triangleright \langle \mathsf{Owner}, B, N_B, K \rangle_{K_{AS}}}$$

PRINCIPLE 6

$$\dfrac{\Gamma \vdash \sigma \quad I \triangleright \langle \mathsf{Owner}, B, N, K \rangle_{K_{AS}} \in \sigma \quad run_R(A, B) \in \sigma \Rightarrow R = \mathsf{Owner}}{\Gamma \vdash \sigma :: run_{\mathsf{Owner}}(A, B) :: A \triangleright \{M\}_K}$$

Authentication Guarantees

AUTHENTICATION 1

$$\dfrac{\Gamma, new(B, N) \vdash \diamond \quad \Gamma \vdash \sigma \quad J \triangleright \langle \mathsf{Claim}, A, N \rangle_{K_{IB}} \in \sigma \quad I \in \{S, A\}}{\Gamma, new(B, N) \vdash \sigma :: check(B, N) :: commit(B, A)}$$

AUTHENTICATION 2

$$\dfrac{\Gamma, new(B, N) \vdash \diamond}{\Gamma \vdash \sigma \quad I \triangleright \langle \mathsf{Owner}, A, N, K \rangle_{K_{SB}} \in \sigma \quad J \triangleright \{M\}_K \in \sigma \quad J \neq B}{\Gamma, new(B, N) \vdash \sigma :: check(B, N) :: commit(B, A)}$$

3.2   Principles as Inference Rules

The inference rules, reported in Table 1, derive judgments of the form $\Gamma \vdash \sigma$, where σ is a trace, and Γ is an environment. Environments collect the *events* of the protocols, i.e. the creation of session keys and nonces:

$$\textit{Environments} \quad \Gamma ::= \emptyset \mid \Gamma, new(I, V)$$

where $new(I, V)$ traces the generation of the nonce or key V by the entity I. Environments are used in the inference system to ensure the freshness of nonces and session keys. The intuition is as follows: when a new nonce is generated, or a session key created, it is included in the environment. A nonce (key) can only be generated if it does not occur in the current environment. Nonces can be checked, (keys used) only if they are available in the environment, and once a nonce is checked (a key used) the corresponding event is discarded from the environment, and hence it is never available again for checking (usage).

The purpose of the inference rules is to generate *safe* traces, that is traces that provide the intended authentication guarantees for a protocol session. Indeed, we can prove the following result, stating that protocols designed according to our principles do achieve the desired authentication guarantees.

Theorem 1 (Safety). *If $\Gamma \vdash \sigma$ then σ is safe.*

We now proceed with the description of the deduction rules. The first block of rules derive auxiliary judgments $\Gamma \vdash \diamond$, that decree environments "well-formed": these rules should be self-explanatory: an environment is well-formed just in case it does not contain duplicate nonces and/or keys. The remaining rules, which formalize our principles, have the following uniform structure:

$$\frac{\Gamma \vdash \sigma \quad (\text{side conditions})}{\Gamma' \vdash \sigma'}$$

where σ' extends σ, and define the conditions under which the judgment in the conclusion may be derived from the judgment in the premise by including further actions in the trace. The side conditions only test the presence of certain ciphertexts, and marker actions, in the current trace σ.

Protocols without TTP (Direct Authentication). Principal A may authenticate with B by using a long-term key she shares with B.

PRINCIPLE 1 *Principal A may start authenticating with principal B by generating an authentication block of the form $\langle \text{Claim}, A, N \rangle_{K_{AB}}$.*

Since this is the start of an authentication session, it is marked by including $run_{\text{Claim}}(A, B)$ in the current trace. Other concurrent runs $run_R(A, B)$ are possible, given that $R = \text{Claim}$. Note that this principle is consistent with the intended guarantees provided by decrypting a block with Claim role. When B decrypts the block $\langle \text{Claim}, A, N \rangle_{K_{AB}}$, and verifies the nonce N, he is guaranteed that A has initiated an authentication session with him; moreover, if A receives such a message, she will discard it as the block is declaring herself as claimant.

Example 2. To motivate, consider the following protocol inspired to the ISO symmetric-key, two-pass unilateral authentication protocol [18,15]:

$$1) \; B \rightarrow A : N_B \qquad\qquad 2) \; A \rightarrow B : \{M, A, N_B\}_{K_{AB}}$$

B, the verifier, sends a freshly generated nonce to A as a challenge. A, the claimant, completes the authentication session by sending a message M, A and N_B encrypted using K_{AB}. This proves to B the identity of the claimant A, as only A and B know K_{AB}. Since identifier A represents the *claimant* of the protocol run, we make this information explicit by mapping message 2 into the authentication block $\langle \mathsf{Claim}, A, N_B \rangle_{K_{AB}}$ (note that M is not in the block as it is unessential for authentication). The protocol is a "good one" as it follows principle 1.

Interestingly, we can show that failing to comply with the previous principle may lead to protocol flaws. In particular, we consider the cases in which either A or N_B are missing in Message 2. In both cases there is no way to represent the message as a valid authentication block as one of the fundamental components is missing. And in both cases the protocol is insecure. Suppose first that A is missing: Message 2 becomes $\{M, N_B\}_{K_{AB}}$. Observing message $\{M, N\}_{K_{AB}}$, there is no way to tell who between A and B is the claimant, so it is impossible to distinguish between messages that belong to a protocol run and messages that belong to another concurrent protocol run with reversed roles. This fact can be used effectively by an adversary as follows:

$$1.a)\ B \rightarrow E(A) : N_B$$
$$1.b)\ E(A) \rightarrow B : N_B$$
$$2.b)\ B \rightarrow E(A) : \{M, N_B\}_{K_{AB}}$$
$$2.a)\ E(A) \rightarrow B : \{M, N_B\}_{K_{AB}}$$

With such a "reflection attack" an enemy can trick B into believing that A has been actively involved in the protocol run "a", while in fact it has not. As a further example, consider a version of the protocol that disregards the nonce, i.e., one in which message 2) is replaced by the message $\{A, M\}_{K_{AB}}$. Here the problem is that there is no way for B to tell if the message belongs to the current run or to a previous one, so an adversary can convince B that it is talking to A without A actively participating:

$$\text{old)}\ A \rightarrow B : \{A, M\}_{K_{AB}} \quad \ldots\ldots \quad \text{new)}\ E(A) \rightarrow B : \{A, M\}_{K_{AB}}$$

Protocols with TTP (Indirect Authentication). When a TTP is present, Alice may authenticate to Bob using the TTP as a mediator. In this setting, we assume that the only way for Alice and Bob to communicate is via the TTP, with which they share a long-term key. The role Verif aims at dealing with this kind of indirect authentication.

The second principle is similar to the previous one, only, it marks the start of the authentication session with $run_{\mathsf{Verif}}(A, B)$ and represents the start of an authentication session through a TTP.

PRINCIPLE 2 (Authentication through TTP) *Principal A may start authenticating herself with principal B by generating an authentication block* $\langle \mathsf{Verif}, B, N \rangle_{K_{AS}}$.

Note that this principle is consistent with the intended semantics of Verif role: it allows A to communicate to a TTP her intention of authenticating with B. This principle is useful when combined with other principles that allow the TTP to forward authentication to the intended verifier B. Notice that, as in the previous principle, A may be running other concurrent authentication sessions, provided that they are all marked with run_{Verif}.

PRINCIPLE 3 (Verified authentication forwarding) *TTP S may declare to a principal B that a principal A has recently started an authentication session with B, if S has decrypted a block $\langle \text{Verif}, B, N \rangle_{K_{AS}}$ and checked the validity of N. To do so, S generates an authentication block $\langle \text{Claim}, A, N' \rangle_{K_{BS}}$.*

The principle above states that a TTP can forward authentication from A to B if the TTP is guaranteed that A has recently initiated an authentication session with B. This guarantee is provided by the decryption (and the nonce checking) of the authentication block $\langle \text{Verif}, B, N \rangle_{K_{AS}}$, and this principle is thus consistent with the intended semantics of Claim and Verif roles.

Notice that to guarantee that N is never used again in the execution, PRINCIPLE 3 discards the event $new(S, N)$ from Γ.

Example 3 (nonce-based Wide Mouth Frog Protocol [1]). The Wide Mouth Frog Protocol [5] achieves unilateral authentication using a TTP. The original version is based on timestamps, here we consider the nonce-based version presented in [12].

1) $A \rightarrow S : A$ 4) $S \rightarrow B : *$
2) $S \rightarrow A : N_S$ 5) $B \rightarrow S : N_B$
3) $A \rightarrow S : A, \{B, K_{AB}, N_S\}_{K_{AS}}$ 6) $S \rightarrow B : \{A, K_{AB}, N_B\}_{K_{BS}}$

This protocol can be seen as a direct application of principles 2 and 3. As a matter of fact, the two encrypted messages 3 and 6, can be abstracted as the two authentication blocks $\langle \text{Verif}, B, N_S \rangle_{K_{AS}}$ and $\langle \text{Claim}, A, N_B \rangle_{K_{BS}}$, respectively. The latter block provides an authentication guarantee to B. Note that the two encrypted messages have the same form. Assigning them to two different authentication blocks make their interpretation very different and allows us to easily reason about which guarantees the two messages provide.

The next principle captures a variant of authentication forwarding that allows the TTP to forward authentication even if it has not verified the claimant's nonce. The idea is that the nonce sent by the claimant is forwarded to the verifier who is in charge of checking its validity.

PRINCIPLE 4 (Non-verified authentication forwarding) *TTP S may declare to a principal B that a principal A has started an authentication session with B, if S has decrypted a block $\langle \text{Verif}, B, N \rangle_{K_{AS}}$. To do so, S generates an authentication block of the form $\langle \text{Claim}, A, N \rangle_{K_{BS}}$.*

The difference with respect to principle 3 is that N is not checked by the TTP but is forwarded to B, in order to let him check its validity. This principle is again consistent with the intended semantics of authentication blocks: the TTP is assured that A has started authenticating with B even though it does not know anything about the freshness of this intention; for this reason, the TTP forwards the nonce N to B so that B may check it and verify that the authentication session started by A is also recent.

---

[1] This protocol has a *type-flaw* attack (cf. [12,2,3]) which we disregard, because of the perfect cryptography assumption.

A possible scenario is the following: the nonce is originated by the verifier, sent to the claimant who inserts it into the authentication request to the TTP; finally the nonce is forwarded back to the verifier for the final check. This is what the "Woo and Lam Shared-Key Protocol" does [24].

Example 4 (Flaws in the original Woo and Lam Protocol). Here we report the original (flawed) version of the protocol [24].

$$1)\ A \to B : A \qquad\qquad 4)\ B \to S : \{A, \{N_B\}_{K_{AS}}\}_{K_{BS}}$$
$$2)\ B \to A : N_B \qquad\qquad 5)\ S \to B : \{N_B\}_{K_{BS}}$$
$$3)\ A \to B : \{N_B\}_{K_{AS}}$$

Message 3 is encrypted with the key shared with S and is thus directed to S (even if it is sent to B who is in charge of forwarding it to S inside message 4). It represents the declaration of the intention of A to authenticate with B. However, note that A does not include in the ciphertext of message 3 the label of B. Thus, it is not possible to apply principle 2. The same happens in the last message, where S does not include any identity label. This makes Principle 4 inapplicable. It is interesting to remark that the corrected version of this protocol [12] uses the identifiers exactly as required by our principles.

Protocols with TTP Based on Session Keys. Another way for Alice to authenticate with Bob through a TTP is to establish a fresh session key with Bob and then use it to authenticate her. PRINCIPLE 5 states how key distribution should happen:

PRINCIPLE 5 (Session key distribution) *TTP S may distribute to principals A and B a freshly generated key K by generating two authentication blocks* $\langle \text{Owner}, B, N, K \rangle_{K_{AS}}$ *and* $\langle \text{Owner}, A, N', K \rangle_{K_{BS}}$.

The principle above shows how the Owner role is used: the TTP communicates to A (B) that B (A) owns the key K. Note that, in order to guarantee the secrecy of the session key, we are assuming that the TTP will never send other messages containing K. As in Table 1, the event $new(S, K)$ is discarded from Γ to ensure that K is never used again.

The next principle allows A to send to B a message encrypted with a session key K.

PRINCIPLE 6 (Authentication through session-keys) *Principal A may start an authentication session with B, by generating a ciphertext $\{M\}_{K_s}$, provided that A has decrypted a block* $\langle \text{Owner}, B, N, K \rangle_{K_{AS}}$ *and checked the validity of N.*

The condition $I \triangleright \langle \text{Owner}, B, N, K \rangle_{K_{AS}} \in \sigma$, binds K to the principal which shares K. Applying this principle, B may conclude that A has initiated an authentication session with him, if he receives a message $\{M\}_{K_s}$ and knows that (i) K is a fresh key owned by A and (ii) he did not generate $\{M\}_{K_s}$. An example of a protocol based on this kind of authentication is the Amended Needham Schroeder Shared-Key Protocol [19].

Authentication Guarantees. In view of the principles we have outlined, there are two situations that can drive an entity to accept an authentication request. An entity B accepts the authentication request of A whenever one of the following two conditions holds:

AUTHENTICATION 1   either B receives and checks (the nonce of) an authentication block
$\langle \mathsf{Claim}, A, N \rangle_{K_{IB}}$, or $\langle \mathsf{Claim}, A, N, K \rangle_{K_{IB}}$, where I is either A or a TTP identifier;
AUTHENTICATION 2   or, B has received and checked (the nonce of) an authentication
block in the form $\langle \mathsf{Owner}, A, N, K_s \rangle_{K_{SB}}$, with S a TTP, and receives a message
$\{M\}_K$ that he did not generate.

In condition AUTHENTICATION 1, if I is A, then the authentication request is *directly* made by A. Otherwise, I must be a TTP, say S, and the request is indirectly made S on behalf of A. A further remark is in order for the side-condition $J \neq B$ in AUTHENTICATION 2 . Here we are assuming that B, which is *committing* (hence completing the authentication session) has the ability to tell that he is not the originator of the ciphertext $\{M\}_K$ (see, e.g., the Amended Needham Schroeder Shared-Key Protocol [19]).

4   Conclusion and Related Work

We have given an in-depth analysis of the roles that message components play in authentication protocols, and we have investigated how a certain component contributes to the task of achieving entity authentication. We identified three simple roles, namely *Claimant*, *Intended verifier* and *Key owner*, that allow us to extract general principles to be followed to protect protocols against attacks. These principles are formalized in terms of rules for protocol parties and lead us to prove that any protocol following these rules (i.e., designed according to the principles) achieves entity authentication. Our approach should be understood as a first step of the development a new analysis technique for authentication protocols. Our goal is to develop (possibly automated) static analysis of authentication protocols based on the principles explained in this paper. At the present stage, we are able to judge if a certain trace is obtained according to the principles: if this is the case, we are guaranteed that such a trace is safe with respect to a specific notion of entity authentication. The next step is to have a language for specifying cryptographic protocols and a technique for proving that a certain protocol specification is designed according to the principles. This would imply that all the execution traces of the protocol are safe and, consequently, that the protocol guarantees entity authentication. We are presently studying how to obtain this on a language similar to spi calculus [1].

The formal model we have developed appears to be fairly general, but a number of extensions would be desirable to capture a wider class of protocols. We are currently studying how to extend the model in order to manage asymmetric and nested encryption, and in order to capture other important security properties such as message authentication and key distribution.

The idea of associating to principals the roles played in a cryptographic protocol is not completely new. Drawing on earlier work by Bieber in [4], in [22] Snekkenes develops a logic for the analysis of cryptographic protocols, to detect multi-role flaws, i.e., flaws that may result from a principal taking on multiple roles during different sessions of a protocol (an instance of this situation is the reflection attack of Example 3, where A plays both the initiator and responder roles). Our idea of role is however appreciably different. In particular, we focus on the role that principals play in an authentication task (e.g. claimant or verifier) instead of considering usual protocol roles like initiator and responder. Notice that reasoning on usual protocol roles does not always give information about "who is willing to authenticate with who". For example in mutual authentication protocols both initiator and responder act as claimant and verifier simultaneously, since in such protocols there are two authentication tasks (the authentication of A to B and vice versa).

In [12,11] Gordon and Jeffrey provide the spi calculus with a type system for analyzing authentication protocols based on symmetric and asymmetric encryption, respectively. These papers are very related to our work. First, their definition of safety exploits, as we do, the Woo and Lam idea of correspondence assertions [23]. Moreover, as stated above, our final aim is to obtain a static analysis of cryptographic protocols as they already do. There are however several important differences. The underlying idea of using roles and principles for generating authentication blocks is new and seems to be promising for obtaining simpler static analyses. Indeed, type definitions are the only human task required in [12,11], but types are quite complex, as the type of nonces keeps all the information regarding authentication tasks between principals. This implies dependent types and forces the use of casting inside processes. Our approach is completely different. We focus on the guarantees that the reception of a given ciphertext, as a whole, gives to a principal and we do not reason about single components. For instance, in our model a nonce does not, by itself, convey any information regarding principals. It is just used for ensuring freshness to the enclosing authentication block. We expect that a static analysis based on these ideas will be simpler as the only human effort required is the binding of every identity label present in a ciphertext to one of the three roles.

Further related work, which aims at reasoning about authentication guarantees provided by messages, is the one based on belief logics, like, e.g., BAN [5], GNY [10]. The main difference with such an approach is that we do not have any kind of protocol idealization. Indeed, we reason about "concrete" execution traces, directly connected to the structure of ciphertexts. An interesting paper that goes in the direction of eliminating the idealization step of the approaches above is [7] by Durgin, Mitchell and Pavlovic. They propose a logic for proving security properties, which is designed around a process calculus derived from Strand Spaces. The calculus has a semantics based on sets of traces and deals with asymmetric encryption. Our model is not directly comparable with the one proposed in the above mentioned paper, since we consider symmetric encryption and rely on a different formalization of authentication properties. Further work needs to be put in place to gain a deeper understanding of the relationships between the two approaches.

References

1. M. Abadi and A. D. Gordon. "A Calculus for Cryptographic Protocols: The Spi Calculus". *Information and Computation*, 148(1):1–70, 1999.
2. M. Abadi and R. Needham. Prudent engineering practice for cryptographic protocols. *IEEE Transactions on Software Engineering*, 22(1):6–15, 1996.
3. R. Anderson and R. Needham. Programming satan's computer. In Jan van Leeuwen, editor, *Computer Science Today — Recent Trends and Developments*, volume 1000 of *ln-cs*, pages 426–440. 1995.

4. P. Bibier. A logic of communication in a hostile environment, 1990. Proceedings the Computer Security Foundations Workshop III. IEEE Computer Society Press, 1422.

5. M. Burrows, M. Abadi, and R. Needham. "A Logic of Authentication". *Proceedings of the Royal Society of London*, 426(1871):233–271, 1989.

6. J. Clark and J. Jacob. "A Survey of Authentication Protocol Literature: Version 1.0". http://www.cs.york.ac.uk/~jac/papers/drareview.ps.gz, November 1997.

7. N. Durgin, J. Mitchell, and D. Pavlovic. A compositional logic for proving security properties of protocols, 2001. 14-th IEEE Computer Security Foundations Workshop, Cape Breton, Nova Scotia, June 11–13.

8. R. Focardi, R. Gorrieri, and F. Martinelli. Non interference for the analysis of cryptographic protocols. In *Proceedings of ICALP'00*, pages 354–372. Springer LNCS 1853, July 2000.

9. D. Gollmann. "What do we mean by Entity Authentication". In *Proceedings of the 1996 Symposium on Security and Privacy*, pages 46–54. IEEE Computer Society Press, 1996.

10. L. Gong, R. Needham, and R. Yahalom. Reasoning About Belief in Cryptographic Protocols. In Deborah Cooper and Teresa Lunt, editors, *Proceedings 1990 IEEE Symposium on Research in Security and Privacy*, pages 234–248. IEEE Computer Society, 1990.

11. A. D. Gordon and A. Jeffrey. Types and effects for asymmetric cryptographic protocols. In *15th IEEE Computer Security Foundations Workshop — CSFW'01*, pages 77–91, Cape Breton, Canada, 24–26 June 2002. IEEE Computer Society Press.

12. A. Gordon and A. Jeffrey. Authenticity by typing for security protocols. In 14th IEEE Computer Security Foundations Workshop (CSFW-14),pages 145–159, June 2001.

13. J. Heather, G. Lowe, and S. Schneider. How to prevent type flaw attacks on security protocols. In *13th IEEE Computer Security Foundations Workshop — CSFW'00*, pages 255–268, Cambridge, UK, 3–5 July 2000. IEEE Computer Society Press.

14. ISO/IEC. *Information Technology-Security Tecniques-Entity Authentication Mechanisms, Part 1:General Model.* 1991.

15. ISO/IEC. *Information Technology-Security Tecniques-Entity Authentication Mechanisms, Part 2:Entity Authentication using Simmetric Tecniques.* 1993.

16. G. Lowe. Breaking and fixing the Needham-Schroeder public-key protocol using FDR. In *Tools and Algorithms for the Construction and Analysis of Systems (TACAS)*, volume 1055, pages 147–166. Springer-Verlag, Berlin Germany, 1996.

17. G. Lowe. "A Hierarchy of Authentication Specification". In *Proceedings of the 10th Computer Security Foundation Workshop*. IEEE press, 1997.

18. A.J. Menezes, P.C. van Oorschot, and S.A. Vanstone. *Handbook of Applied Cryptography*. CRC Press, 1996.

19. R. M. Needham and M. D. Schroeder. Authentication revisited. *ACM SIGOPS Operating Systems Review*, 21(1):7–7, 1987.

20. Lawrence C. Paulson. Relations between secrets: Two formal analyses of the yahalom protocol. *Journal of Computer Security*, 9(3):197–216, 2001.

21. S. Schneider. Formal analysis of a non-repudiation protocol. In *Proceedings of CSFW'98*, pages 54–65. IEEE Press, 1998.

22. E. Snekkenes. Roles in cryptographic protocols, 1992. In Proceedings of the 1992 IEEE Symposium on Security and Privacy, pages 105-119. IEEE Computer Society Press.

23. T.Y.C. Woo and S.S. Lam. "A Semantic Model for Authentication Protocols". In *Proceedings of 1993 IEEE Symposium on Security and Privacy*, pages 178–194, 1993.

24. T. Y. C. Woo and S. S. Lam. Authentication for distributed systems, from computer, january, 1992. In *William Stallings, Practical Cryptography for Data Internetworks, IEEE Computer Society Press, 1992.* 1992.

25. J. Zhou and D. Gollman. A fair non-repudiation protocol. In *Proc. of Symposium in Research in Security and Privacy*, pages 55–61. IEEE Press, 1996.

Causality and Replication
in Concurrent Processes[*]

Pierpaolo Degano[1], Fabio Gadducci[1], and Corrado Priami[2]

[1] Dipartimento di Informatica, Università di Pisa
via F. Buonarroti 2, 56127 Pisa, Italia
{degano, gadducci}@di.unipi.it
[2] Dipartimento di Informatica e Telecomunicazioni, Università di Trento
via Sommarive 14, 38050 Povo, Italia
priami@science.unitn.it

Abstract. The replication operator was introduced by Milner for obtaining a simplified description of recursive processes. The standard interleaving semantics denotes the replication of a process P, written $!P$, a shorthand for its unbound parallel composition, operationally equivalent to the process $P \mid P \mid \ldots$, with P repeated as many times as needed.
Albeit the replication mechanism has become increasingly popular, investigations on its causal semantics has been scarce. In our work we consider the interleaving semantics for the operator proposed by Sangiorgi and Walker, and we show how to refine it in order to capture causality. Furthermore, we prove that a basic property usually associated to these semantics, the so-called *concurrency diamond*, does hold in our framework, and we sketch a correspondence between our proposal and the standard causal semantics for recursive process studied in the literature, for processes defined through constant invocations.

Keywords: Causal semantics, process calculi, replication operator.

1 Introduction

The replication operator offers a suitable tool for the description of distributed systems with resources that can serve iterated requests. For instance, the handler of a printer can be seen as a process which replicates itself any time a request arrives. Even if there is a single printer, a copy of it handles the current request, while another is willing to accept new requests. The syntax is $!P$ (*bang P*), intuitively meaning $P \mid P \mid \ldots$ as many times as needed.

According to its operational semantics, the execution of an action from a process $!P$ results in $!P \mid Q$, where Q is the residual of a finite process $P \mid \ldots \mid P$ after the action, and the new $!P$ is willing to generate other copies of P if needed. For this reason, quite often $!P$ is postulated equivalent to $!P \mid P$.

---

[*] This work has been partially supported by the Italian MIUR project COMETA (*Computational Metamodels*); and by EU within the FET – Global Computing initiative, project DEGAS IST-2001-32072 (*Design Environments for Global Applications*).

M. Broy and A.V. Zamulin (Eds.): PSI 2003, LNCS 2890, pp. 307–318, 2003.

The replication mechanism was not the original proposal for the handling of potentially infinite behaviour in process calculi. Standard specifications are based either on recursion operators or on constant definitions, on the form $A = P$, with A possibly occurring in P. In [13], Milner showed how to translate a process built up with constant definitions into a process containing only occurrences of the replication operator, at the price of an extra synchronisation that has to be ignored to preserve the semantics of processes.

The late introduction of the replication operator may explain why, to the best of our knowledge, investigations on its causal semantics are scarce in the literature. We are only aware of the work by Engelfriet (see e.g. [10]), where a Petri nets semantics for the π-calculus with replication is proposed, using possibly infinite markings. Such a state of affairs is unfortunate, since causality is often advocated to sharpen the description of distributed systems, because it may lead to more accurate guidelines to implementors and it offers a more precise analysis. In fact, causal semantics for concurrent systems in the setting of process calculi has been largely presented in the literature, see e.g. [1,2,4,5,7, 8,11,15]. It is remarkable that for CCS, maybe the best known calculus [12], all of them do agree, so either description is *the* causal semantics of the calculus.

Our goal here is to define a causal semantics for CCS extended with replication that agrees with the standard causal semantics of the calculus, in which constant definition is adopted for the specification of recursive processes. In order to accomplish that, we find it difficult to stick to the usual operational presentation of the operator, resorting instead to a proposal in [16]. Then, we exploit the technique used in [8] to define non interleaving semantics for the π-calculus [14], and we extend it to include the case of the replication operator, considering, for the sake of presentation, only pure CCS [12]. The essence of the enhanced SOS semantics proposed in [8,9] consists in encoding (portions of) the proof of a transition in its label. The resulting labelled transition system is thus called *proved*. Enhanced labels are sufficient to derive a causal semantics of the calculus.

In the next section we briefly define the proved operational semantics of CCS with replication. In Section 3 we adapt the definition of dependency between transitions given in [9] to cope with !, proving in Section 4 that two transitions are concurrent if and only if they form a so-called *concurrency diamond* in the proved transition system, i.e., roughly, if they can execute in any order. Instead, in Section 5 we sketch a correspondence between the new notion of causality and the one defined in the literature for processes built up using constant definitions.

2   Proved Transition Systems

We start introducing the syntax of CCS. As usual, we assume a countable set of *atomic actions*, denoted by $\mathcal{A}$ and ranged over by a; a bijective function $: \mathcal{A} \to \mathcal{A}$, assuming that $a = \overline{\overline{a}}$; and an *invisible action* $\tau \notin \mathcal{A}$, so that $\mathcal{A} \cup \{\tau\}$ is ranged over by μ. Processes (denoted by $P, Q, R, \ldots \in \mathcal{P}$) are built from actions and agents according to the following syntax

$$P ::= \mathbf{0} \mid \mu.P \mid P + P \mid P|P \mid (\nu a)P \mid !P$$

We assume that the operators have decreasing binding power, in the following order: $(\nu a), \mu., !, |, +$. Hereafter, both the parallel composition and the nondeterministic choice are left associative. Also, we usually omit the trailing **0**, whenever clear from the context. We slightly modified the original syntax in [12]: the replication operator ! replaces the recursion operators, and relabelling is omitted because irrelevant for the present study.

We assume the reader to be familiar with the interleaving operational semantics of CCS [12], and we concentrate on its proved semantics. We start enriching the labels of the standard transition system of CCS, in the style of [2,5]. This additional structure encodes some information on the *derivation* of the transitions, that is, on the inference rules actually used to obtain that derivation.

We jointly define the notion of *enhanced labels* and two functions on them. So, ℓ takes an enhanced label to the corresponding action. Instead, ∂ takes a label to its "static" component: thus, it basically discards all the information on nondeterministic choices from the labels, whilst replacing the ! operator with the occurrence of a $||_1$ operator (see also Theorem 1).

Definition 1. *Let ϑ range over the strings in $\{||_0, ||_1, +_0, +_1, !\}^*$. Then, the enhanced labels (denoted by metavariable θ) are defined by the following syntax*

$$\theta ::= \vartheta\mu \mid \vartheta\langle||_0\vartheta_0 a, ||_1\vartheta_1\overline{a}\rangle$$

The function ℓ is defined as

$$\ell(\vartheta\mu) = \mu \qquad \ell(\vartheta\langle||_0\vartheta_0 a, ||_1\vartheta_1\overline{a}\rangle) = \tau$$

The function ∂ is defined as (for $i = 0, 1$)

$$\partial(\mu) = \mu \qquad\qquad \partial(+_i\theta) = \partial(\theta) \qquad \partial(!\theta) = ||_1\partial(\theta)$$

$$\partial(||_i\theta) = ||_i\partial(\theta) \qquad \partial(\langle||_0\vartheta_0 a, ||_1\vartheta_1\overline{a}\rangle) = \langle\partial(||_0\vartheta_0 a), \partial(||_1\vartheta_1\overline{a})\rangle$$

By abuse of notation we will sometimes write $\partial(\vartheta)$ for $\partial(\vartheta\mu)$.

The rules of the proved transition system for CCS are in Table 1, where we omitted the symmetric Par_1 and Sum_1. As it will be made precise later on by Definition 2, the leftmost tag of a transition is in correspondence with the top-level operator of its source process (except for (νa)). Accordingly, rule Par_0 (Par_1) adds to the label a tag $||_0$ ($||_1$) to record that the left (right) component is moving. Similarly for the rules Sum_i.[1] The rule Com has in its conclusion a pair instead of a τ to record the components which interact. The rule $Bang$ for replication has in its premise a transition, tagged by θ, from its "body" P to a target P'. This rule adds in its conclusion the tag ! to the label of the transition, that now exits from $!P$ and reaches a state where $!P$ itself is put in parallel with P'; similarly for $Bang_C$, where two copies of P communicate with each other.

The interleaving transition system is derived from the proved one by relabelling each proved transition through function ℓ in Definition 1.

---

[1] This tag was not considered in [8], and it is really needed only in Definition 6 below.

Table 1. The proved transition system for CCS

$$Act : \frac{-}{\mu.P \xrightarrow{\mu} P} \qquad Sum_0 : \frac{P \xrightarrow{\theta} P^\square}{P + Q \xrightarrow{+_0\theta} P^\square} \qquad Par_0 : \frac{P \xrightarrow{\theta} P^\square}{P|Q \xrightarrow{\|_0\theta} P^\square|Q}$$

$$Bang : \frac{P \xrightarrow{\theta} P^\square}{!P \xrightarrow{!\theta} !P|P^\square} \qquad Bang_C : \frac{P \xrightarrow{\vartheta_0 a} P^\square, P \xrightarrow{\vartheta_1 \bar{a}} P^{\blacksquare}}{!P \xrightarrow{!\blacksquare\|_0\vartheta_0 a, \|_1\vartheta_1\bar{a}\blacksquare} !P|(P^\square|P^{\blacksquare})}$$

$$Com : \frac{P \xrightarrow{\vartheta_0 a} P^\square, Q \xrightarrow{\vartheta_1 \bar{a}} Q^\square}{P|Q \xrightarrow{\blacksquare\|_0\vartheta_0 a, \|_1\vartheta_1\bar{a}\blacksquare} P^\square|Q^\square} \qquad Res : \frac{P \xrightarrow{\theta} P^\square}{(\nu a)P \xrightarrow{\theta} (\nu a)P^\square} \quad \ell(\theta) \notin \{a, \bar{a}\}$$

Let us provide now a simple example of a proved computation. Consider the process $P = !(a|!b)$. The first four steps of a computation originating from P are indicated by the sequence of transitions below

$$P \xrightarrow{!\|_0 a} P|(0|!b) \xrightarrow{\|_1\|_1 !b} P|(0|(!b|0)) \xrightarrow{\|_0!\|_1 !b} \qquad (1)$$
$$(P|(a|(!b|0))) \mid (0|(!b|0)) \xrightarrow{\|_1\|_1\|_0 !b} \dots$$

A few comments are in order now, to vindicate our choice of inference rules for the replication operator. Our proposal follows [16], and its rational is that making a copy of a process is an activity in itself, even if hidden, that models the invocation of a run-time support routine. The actions performed by subsequent copies will then be caused by the first activation. (Of course, according to our semantics, the process $!(a|b)$ can perform two causally independent actions; each of them, in turn, causes any further subsequent action.) The standard rule

$$\frac{!P|P \xrightarrow{\mu} P'}{!P \xrightarrow{\mu} P'}$$

would allow for a recursive activation of a copy of P at any depth. This solution would make it difficult to obtain any result concerning causality in our approach, which is based on enhanced labels, hence it relies on proofs by structural induction over the entailment of the possible derivations of a transition.

In the next sections, our informal argument in favour of the chosen semantics for the replication operator will also be supported by a correspondence with the causal semantics of recursive processes (Section 5) and by mimicking the standard results on concurrent processes, as typically exemplified by the occurrence of concurrency diamonds (Section 4).

3   Causality

We introduce now the notion of causal dependency. Following [8], an auxiliary relation of dependency is introduced on the transitions that may occur along a computation, making explicit the causality between their actions. From this relation, it is straightforward to recover the more standard representation of causality as a partial ordering of events, and that of concurrency (see [9]). Both notions do coincide with those defined in the literature (see, e.g., [2,4]).

Definition 2 (dependency relation). *The* dependency *relation on enhanced labels is the relation induced by the axioms below (for $i \in \{0,1\}$)*

1. $\mu \lessdot \theta$
2. $+_i\theta \lessdot \theta'$ *if* $\theta \lessdot \theta'$
3. $\|_i\theta \lessdot \|_i\theta'$ *if* $\theta \lessdot \theta'$
4. $\langle\theta_0, \theta_1\rangle \lessdot \langle\theta_0', \theta_1'\rangle$ *if* $\exists i . \theta_i \lessdot \theta_i'$
5. $\langle\theta_0, \theta_1\rangle \lessdot \theta'$ *if* $\exists i . \theta_i \lessdot \theta'$
6. $\theta \lessdot \langle\theta_0', \theta_1'\rangle$ *if* $\exists i . \theta \lessdot \theta_i'$
7. $!\theta \lessdot \|_0\theta'$
8. $!\theta \lessdot \|_1\theta'$ *if* $\theta \lessdot \theta'$

Intuitively, each rule indicates that a dependency between the labels may occur. More precisely, $\theta_0 \lessdot \theta_1$ implies that if there exists a computation in which an occurrence of label θ_0 takes place before an occurrence of label θ_1, then the two associated transitions are causally related. For example, consider the computation $a.b.a.\mathbf{0} \xrightarrow{a} b.a.\mathbf{0} \xrightarrow{b} a.\mathbf{0} \xrightarrow{a} \mathbf{0}$. Now, the occurrence of the first a causes the transition labelled b, which in turns causes the second instance of a.[2]

So, the relation has to be specialised for each computation. From now onward, unless otherwise specified, ξ denotes a generic proved computation of the form $P_0 \xrightarrow{\theta_0} P_1 \xrightarrow{\theta_1} \ldots \xrightarrow{\theta_n} P_{n+1}$, whose *length* is n; furthermore, each label θ_i actually stands for the pair $\langle\theta_i, i\rangle$, thus uniquely identifying a single position of the label in the computation, hence the associated transition.

Definition 3 (causality partial order). *Let ξ be a computation, and let $i, j \in \{1, \ldots, n\}$ with $i < j$. Then, we say that θ_i causes θ_j in ξ (in symbols $\theta_i \lessdot_\xi \theta_j$) iff $\theta_i \lessdot \theta_j$.*

The relation $\preceq_\xi$ (or simply $\preceq$ when unambiguous) of causal dependency is the reflexive and transitive closure of $\lessdot_\xi$, further restricted over the transitions θ with $\ell(\theta) \neq \tau$.

The causality dependency is obtained for a computation ξ by first restricting $\lessdot$ to the transitions of ξ according to their occurrence in the computation, thus obtaining $\lessdot_\xi$; and then freely closing $\lessdot_\xi$ by reflexivity and transitivity. The resulting relation is a partial order, since antisymmetry is immediate by the condition $i < j$. Finally, the partial order is restricted to those transitions with visible actions, getting $\preceq_\xi$.

---

[2] In fact, the relation ensures that such a causal dependency holds for at least a computation, but it is neither reflexive, nor transitive. For instance, label $+_0\|_0a$ never occurs twice in a computation; and $\|_0b$ and $\|_1c$ are not dependent, even if $\|_0b \lessdot \langle\|_0a, \|_1\overline{a}\rangle$ and $\langle\|_0a, \|_1\overline{a}\rangle \lessdot \|_1c$, and the three labels occur exactly in that order in the unique computation starting from $(\nu a)(b.a|\overline{a}.c)$.

The intuitive idea behind $\theta_i \preceq_\xi \theta_j$ is that θ_i is a *necessary condition* in ξ for θ_j to occur. Such a condition is discovered on the enhanced labels by exploiting a prefix relation between them. Indeed, consider two transitions which are labelled ϑa and $\vartheta \vartheta' b$. Then, the action prefixes a and $\vartheta' b$ which originate the given transitions are within the same context. The dependency relation implies that two transitions have been derived by using the same initial set of inference rules, and this is verified when a and b are nested in the *same* prefix chain. Thus, b occurs in the process prefixed by a, and the occurrence of a is a necessary condition for b to occur.

More precisely, our definition of dependency relation inductively scans the common prefix of two labels. Item (1) of Definition 2 is one base case. It says that the action at the left-hand side was prefixed to the action at the right-hand side; so we postulate a causal dependency between the two labels, in the style of [8]. The other base case is in item (7). Any transition with a label starting with ! causes those with labels starting with a $||_0$. Indeed, the transition corresponding to the label on the right-hand side is fired by a replica of the !-process that fired the left-hand transition. The intuition is that a bang application generates a copy of itself and thus causes any subsequent action of that copy. Technically, subsequent applications of the same bang introduce on the labels of the corresponding transitions tags $||_0!, .., ||_0^k!$, where $||_0^k$ is a string of k tags $||_0$. Indeed, the second application of a bang is in the left component of a parallel composition (see the conclusion of the rules for bang in Table 1). Instead, if the right-hand label starts with a $||_1$, we continue scanning labels, as item (8) says. This case corresponds to having the transition with the label on the right being originated by an action of the residual process after the original ! activation. Item (2) reflects the fact that a choice has been resolved in the transition occurring first, and therefore the "+" will no longer appear in its derivatives. In item (3), labels are scanned as long as they have the same initial tag ($||_i$). As far as synchronisations are concerned, item (4) applies the definition component-wise, while items (5) and (6) compare visible actions with the components of the synchronisation.

Consider again the computation (1) in Section 2. It turns out that $!||_0 a$ and $||_1||_1!b$ are not related, whilst $!||_0 a \preceq ||_0!||_1!b$ by item (4) in Definition 2. It holds also $||_1||_1!b \preceq ||_1||_1||_0!b$ by two applications of item (2) and one application of item (4) in Definition 2.

4   Concurrency

We now introduce the notion of *concurrency* between the transitions of a computation. It is simply the complement of causality as in [8].

Definition 4 (concurrency relation). *Let ξ be a computation, and let $i, j \in \{1, \ldots, n\}$ with $\tau \notin \{\ell(\theta_i), \ell(\theta_j)\}$. Then, we say that θ_i is* concurrent *with θ_j (in symbols $\theta_i \smile_\xi \theta_j$, or simply $\theta_i \smile \theta_j$ when unambiguous) iff neither $\theta_i \npreceq_\xi \theta_j$ nor $\theta_j \npreceq_\xi \theta_i$.*

The definition of concurrency says that no necessary condition exists between two transitions such that $\theta_i \smile \theta_j$. This leads to the more usual statement that the execution ordering of concurrent transitions is irrelevant.

The theorem below extends a classical property of concurrency to CCS processes including replication. It states that two concurrent transitions, originated by the same process P, can be fired one before the other *and* vice versa, thus forming a so-called concurrency diamond in the transition system.

Theorem 1. *Let* $R \xrightarrow{\theta} U \xrightarrow{\theta'} S$ *be a computation such that* $\theta \smile \theta'$. *Then, in the proved transition system there exists the concurrency diamond below, where* $\partial(\theta) = \partial(\hat{\theta})$ *and* $\partial(\theta') = \partial(\hat{\theta}')$.

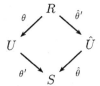

Consider again the process $P = !(a|!b)$. Its computation

$$P \xrightarrow{!||_1!b} P|(a|(!b|0)) \xrightarrow{||_1||\circ a} P|(0|(!b|0))$$

originates a diamond with the first two transitions in (1), our example in Section 2. Note that the leftmost ! in the first transition above becomes a $||_1$ in the second transition of (1), and the ! in the first transition of (1) becomes $||_1$ in the second transition above. Our function ∂ handles the situation.

Indeed, the main problem in defining a causal semantics for the replication operator was linked to obtaining a concurrency diamond property like the above. Our solution, based on the dependency relation in Definition 2, clearly states the dual nature of the bang: it behaves as a prefix $||_1$ when observed, even if it imposes a dependency on subsequent activations of its copies.

Given two concurrent transitions along a computation, it would be possible to prove, by repeated applications of the theorem above, the existence of another computation with the same source and the same target, in which those two transitions occur one after the other and in reverse order. This result establishes a classical property of causal semantics, often expressed by saying that "concurrent transitions may fire in any temporal order". Indeed, a *concurrent computation* could then be defined as the equivalence class of those computations that only differ in the order in which concurrent transitions occur, disregarding the actual identity of the processes involved.[3]

We close the section by providing a sketch of the proof for Theorem 1.

Proof. The proof proceeds by induction on the length of the deduction for derivation $\xi_1 = R \xrightarrow{\theta} U$, i.e., on the number of rules from Table 1 that are applied.

---

[3] The relation of "reachability by application of permutations" is clearly reflexive and transitive. In order to prove symmetry, a stronger version of Theorem 1 is needed, stating that a permutation gives back the initial computation when applied twice.

So, assume that the length is 1, hence, that ξ_1 has been obtained by a single application of rule Act. We can conclude that $R = \mu.U$ for a label μ and, more important, that $\theta = \mu \lessdot \theta'$, according to the definition of dependency relation in Definition 2. Then $\theta \not\smile \theta'$, and the proposition vacuously holds.

Consider now the inductive case, and assume that the last rule has been Sum_0 (the symmetric case is analogous). Then we may infer that $R = R_1 + R_2$ and $\theta = +_0\theta_1$ for suitable processes R_1 and R_2 and label θ_1. That is, ξ_1 has a deduction tree of the following shape

$$\mu.P \xrightarrow{\mu} P$$
$$\vdots$$
$$\frac{R_1 \xrightarrow{\theta_1} U}{R_1 + R_2 \xrightarrow{+_0\theta_1} U}$$

Consider the computation $R_1 \xrightarrow{\theta_1} U \xrightarrow{\theta'} S$. Since $\theta = +_0\theta_1 \smile \theta'$, by the definition of the dependency relation we infer that $\theta_1 \smile \theta'$. By induction hypothesis, there is a computation $R_1 \xrightarrow{\hat{\theta}'} \hat{U} \xrightarrow{\hat{\theta}_1} S$ such that $\partial(\theta_1) = \partial(\hat{\theta}_1)$ and $\partial(\theta') = \partial(\hat{\theta}')$. We then obtain the computation $R_1 + R_2 \xrightarrow{+_0\hat{\theta}'} \hat{U} \xrightarrow{\hat{\theta}_1} S$, and the proposition holds.

The application of Res as last rule is entirely analogous.

If $Bang$ was the last rule applied, then we may infer that $R = !R_1$, $\theta = !\theta_1$, and $U = !R_1 \mid U_1$ for suitable processes R_1 and U_1 and label θ_1. This amounts to say that ξ_1 has a deduction tree of the following shape

$$\mu.P \xrightarrow{\mu} P$$
$$\vdots$$
$$\frac{R_1 \xrightarrow{\theta_1} U_1}{!R_1 \xrightarrow{!\theta_1} !R_1 \mid U_1}$$

Thus, θ' must be a synchronization, or it must be either $\|_0 \theta_1'$ or $\|_1 \theta_1'$ for a suitable label θ_1'. The first two choices are not viable because $\theta \smile \theta'$, and this would not fit the definition of the dependency relation; the third choice implies $R_1 \xrightarrow{\theta_1} U_1 \xrightarrow{\theta_1'} U_2$, such that $\theta_1 \smile \theta_1'$. By induction hypothesis there exists a computation $R_1 \xrightarrow{\hat{\theta}_1'} \hat{U}_1 \xrightarrow{\hat{\theta}_1} U_2$, which implies the existence of computation $!R_1 \xrightarrow{!\hat{\theta}_1'} !R_1 \mid \hat{U}_1 \xrightarrow{\|_1\hat{\theta}_1} !R_1 \mid U_2$, and the latter satisfies the proposition.

The proofs for the remaining cases (namely $Bang_C$, Par_0 and its symmetric, and Com) follow the same pattern. $\qquad\square$

5 Causality for Replication and Recursion

We now compare our notion of causality with the others presented in the literature. More precisely, we show that the relation $\preceq$ coincides with the one in [7,8], that has been proved to coincide with the causal relation defined in [4], hence accounting for *the* causal semantics of the calculus, as argued in the Introduction.

First, some definitions from [12]. Given a set of *process constants*, ranged over by $A, B, \ldots$, an environment $\mathcal{E}$ is a set of equations $A_i = P_i$, for disjoint constants A_i's and *guarded* CCS processes P_i's. Those processes may then possibly contain occurrences of the constants, always inside the scope of a prefix operator μ, but no occurrence of the ! operator. The rule for constants is given by

$$\frac{P \xrightarrow{\theta}_{\mathcal{E}} P'}{A \xrightarrow{\theta}_{\mathcal{E}} P'} \quad A = P \in \mathcal{E}$$

and it is dependent from the chosen environment.

We let $\sqsubseteq^{\mathcal{E}}$ denote the causal dependency that is obtained (according to Definition 2 and Definition 3) on computations originating from processes with respect to a given environment $\mathcal{E}$, and with the inference rule presented above: it corresponds to the causality partial order given in [8], Definition 4.1.

It is folklore that the replication operator is less expressive than constant definitions in calculi without name mobility [3]. We can however sketch a simple correspondence between these two alternative presentations for recursive processes by restricting our attention to environments containing only one equation, and exploiting a translation proposed by Milner in [13].

Definition 5 (from constants to replication). *Let $\mathcal{E}$ be the environment defined by the equation $A = P$, and let a be an action not occurring in P. Then, the function $\phi_{\mathcal{E}}$, that translates processes possibly containing occurrences of the constant A into processes without them, is defined as*

$$\phi_{\mathcal{E}}(R) = R\{(\nu\, a)(\overline{a} \,|\, !a.P\{\overline{a}/A\})/A\}.$$

The process $(\nu\, a)(\overline{a} \,|\, !a.P\{\overline{a}/A\})$ replaces every occurrence of the constant A, insisting that a is a fresh action not occurring in P. The substitution of $\overline{a}$ for A in its body P is needed to activate other copies of P, possibly available later on. Indeed, the implementation performs a τ-transition (called below !-synchronisation) involving the $!a.P$ component of the translation, that enables a new instance of P. On the other hand, no τ occurs in the constant activation, so that the discrepancy has to be taken into account.

In the following, we will just fix an environment $\mathcal{E}$, composed by a single equation on the constant A, dropping all the subscripts referring to it.

Before comparing our causal relation $\preceq$ on the computations of R with the relation $\sqsubseteq$ on the computations of $\phi(R)$, we shall have a closer look at the labels of the transitions in corresponding computations. We start by defining the selector operator, $@\vartheta$, that applied to a process R singles out its sub-process P reachable at position ϑ in the abstract syntax tree (with nodes $||_i$, $+_i$ or ! and leaves $\mu.Q$ or $\mathbf{0}$) of R, and it is not defined otherwise.

Definition 6 (selectors). *Let P be a process and $\vartheta \in \{||_0, ||_1, +_0, +_1, !\}^*$. Then $P@\vartheta$ is defined by (for $i = 0, 1$)*

$$P@\epsilon = P \qquad (\nu\, a)P@\vartheta = P@\vartheta \qquad !P@!\vartheta = P@\vartheta$$
$$(P_0 \mid P_1)@||_i\vartheta = P_i@\vartheta \qquad (P_0 + P_1)@ +_i \vartheta = P_i@\vartheta$$

The newly defined operator will be later used to select within a process R its sub-process responsible for a transition $R \xrightarrow{\vartheta\mu} R'$.

We now compare a computation of the process R with the corresponding computation of $\phi(R)$. Intuitively, the transitions not originated by a constant invocation have the same labels in both. So, R and its translation $\phi(R)$ pass through the same states, up to the substitution of the occurrences of a constant with its translation, until the first invocation of a constant is fired. At that point, $\phi(R)$ performs a !-synchronisation that enables the first action of (the body of) the activated constant. The !-synchronisation introduces a tag $||_1$ followed by a ! in its label: the tag ! is added by the application of rule *Bang* that creates a new copy of $!a.P\{\overline{a}/A\}$. This copy is responsible for a $||_1$ tag in the labels of the transitions fired from the right component in the conclusion of that rule. The other transitions fired by (the body of) the constant have an additional tag $||_1$, due to the context $\overline{a}|-$ responsible for the !-synchronisation in $\phi(R)$. In the proposition below we shall point out this additional !-synchronisation and its target state, S_i, that has no corresponding state in the selected computation of R. Afterward, the two processes R and $\phi(R)$ evolve similarly until the next constant invocation, and if their transitions have different enhanced labels, this is only because of the additional tags $||_1||_1$ mentioned above.

Consider the process $c.A \mid R$, where $A = b.A \mid d$, which can evolve as

$$c.A \mid R \xrightarrow{||_0 c} A \mid R \xrightarrow{||_0||_0 b} (A|d) \mid R$$

Its translation is the process $c.(\nu\, a)(\overline{a}|!a.(b.\overline{a}|d)) \mid R$, and the computation corresponding to the one we have just seen is

$$c.(\nu\, a)(\overline{a}|!a.(b.\overline{a}|d)) \mid R \xrightarrow{||_0 c} (\nu\, a)(\overline{a}|!a.(b.\overline{a}|d)) \mid R \xrightarrow{||_0 \langle ||_0\overline{a}, ||_1 !a\rangle}$$
$$(\nu\, a)(\mathbf{0}|(!a.(b.\overline{a}|d))|(b.\overline{a}|d)) \mid R \xrightarrow{||_0||_1||_1||_0 b} (\nu\, a)(\mathbf{0}|(!a.(b.\overline{a}|d))|(\overline{a}|d)) \mid R$$

In the last transition of the translation we can see where the additional tags $||_1||_1$ are needed. Note also that in the last transition of both computations, the leftmost $||_0$ corresponds to the context of A and of its translation, while the rightmost $||_0$ encodes the context of b within the body of A.

The next proposition formalises the considerations above. For the sake of simplicity, we restrict our attention to computations with a single constant activation, and with a visible action. Our argument could be easily repeated for subsequent activations, possibly occurring inside a communication.

Proposition 1. *Let $\mathcal{E}$ be the environment defined by the equation $A = P$, and let ξ be the computation*

$$R_0 \xrightarrow{\theta_0} R_1 \xrightarrow{\theta_1} \ldots R_i \xrightarrow{\vartheta\theta_i} R_{i+1} \ldots \xrightarrow{\theta_n} R_{n+1}$$

such that $R_i \xrightarrow{\vartheta\theta_i} R_{i+1}$ is the only transition using a constant invocation, and moreover $R_i@\vartheta = A$. Then, $\phi(R_0)$ may perform the computation $\phi(\xi)$ below

$$\phi(R_0) \xrightarrow{\theta_0} \phi(R_1) \xrightarrow{\theta_1} \ldots \phi(R_i) \xrightarrow{\vartheta\langle\|_0\overline{a},\|_1!a\rangle} S_i \xrightarrow{\phi(\theta_i)} S_{i+1} \ldots \xrightarrow{\phi(\theta_n)} S_{n+1}$$

where

$$\begin{aligned}
S_i &= \phi(R_{i+1})[\partial(\vartheta) \mapsto Q] \\
S_j &= \phi(R_j)[\partial(\vartheta) \mapsto Q_j] \quad \text{for } j = i+1 \ldots n+1 \\
\phi(\theta_i) &= \partial(\vartheta)\|_1\|_1\theta_i \\
\phi(\theta_j) &= \begin{cases} \partial(\vartheta)\|_1\|_1\theta & \text{if } \theta_j = \partial(\vartheta)\theta \\ \theta_j & \text{otherwise} \end{cases} \quad \text{for } j = i+1 \ldots n
\end{aligned}$$

(for $R[\vartheta_R \mapsto S]$ denoting the process obtained from R when the process S substitutes the sub-process $R@\vartheta_R$), and

$$\begin{aligned}
Q &= (\nu\, a)(\mathbf{0} \mid (!a.P\{\overline{a}/A\} \mid P\{\overline{a}/A\})) \\
Q_j &= Q[\|_1\|_1 \mapsto R_j\{\overline{a}/A\}@\partial(\vartheta)] \quad \text{for } j = i+1 \ldots n+1
\end{aligned}$$

Hence, we end up with a function ϕ between computations with a different presentation for recursive processes (the source may contain constants, the target the replication operator), which relates in a precise way the single transitions. This allows for showing that the causal relation $\preceq$ coincides with the relation $\sqsubseteq$ described in the literature (e.g. in [2,4]), over computations related via ϕ.

Theorem 2. *Let $\mathcal{E}$ be the environment defined by the equation $A = P$, and let ξ be a computation originated by a finite CCS term, possibly involving some constant invocation. Then, $\sqsubseteq_\xi$ coincides with $\preceq_{\phi(\xi)}$, in that, for any two transitions θ_i, θ_j in ξ, $\theta_i \sqsubseteq_\xi \theta_j$ if and only if $\phi(\theta_i) \preceq_{\phi(\xi)} \phi(\theta_j)$.*

Thus, $\sqsubseteq_\xi$ and $\preceq_{\phi(\xi)}$ represent the same partial order of transitions, up to relabeling. The two partial orders are actually isomorphic, since the transitions in $\phi(\xi)$ which are not in the image of a transition in ξ are communications.

6   Conclusions

We extended the results in [8] showing how proved transition systems may help in defining non interleaving semantics of calculi including the replication operator. Our causal semantics for CCS with replication enjoys the classical "concurrency diamond" property, concerning the execution order of independent transitions; also, it coincides with the usual semantics for CCS with constant definition.

Our result extends a previous attempt concerning the causal semantics of processes with an operator for *replicated input*, denoted $!_a$, such that the process $!_a P$ may perform a move labelled a, becoming $!_a P \mid P$ [6]. In fact, our proved semantics for the replication operator is based on the intuition that making a copy of a process requires to invoke a run-time support routine, and thus subsequent copies will be causally linked.

Our proposal seems robust: no problem arises when dealing with name passing, because the replication operator only induces structural dependencies on transitions. Hence, a causal semantics for the π-calculus with ! can be defined, carrying over the present definitions the relevant ones of [8].

References

1. M. Boreale and D. Sangiorgi. A fully abstract semantics for causality in the π-calculus. *Acta Informatica*, 35:353–400, 1998.
2. G. Boudol and I. Castellani. A non-interleaving semantics for CCS based on proved transitions. *Fundamenta Informaticae*, 11:433–452, 1988.
3. N. Busi, M. Gabbrielli, and G. Zavattaro. Replication vs. recursive definitions in channel based calculi. In J.C.M. Baeten, J.K. Lenstra, J. Parrow, and G.J. Woeginger, editors, *Automata, Languages and Programming*, volume 2719 of *Lect. Notes in Comp. Science*, pages 133–144. Springer, 2003.
4. Ph. Darondeau and P. Degano. Causal trees. In G. Ausiello, M. Dezani-Ciancaglini, and S. Ronchi Della Rocca, editors, *Automata, Languages and Programming*, volume 372 of *Lect. Notes in Comp. Science*, pages 234–248. Springer, 1989.
5. P. Degano, R. De Nicola, and U. Montanari. Partial ordering derivations for CCS. In L. Budach, editor, *Fundamentals of Computation Theory*, volume 199 of *Lect. Notes in Comp. Science*, pages 520–533. Springer, 1985.
6. P. Degano, F. Gadducci, and C. Priami. A concurrent semantics for CCS via rewriting logic. *Theoret. Comput. Sci.*, 275:259–282, 2002.
7. P. Degano and C. Priami. Proved trees. In W. Kuich, editor, *Automata, Languages and Programming*, volume 623 of *Lect. Notes in Comp. Science*, pages 629–640. Springer, 1992.
8. P. Degano and C. Priami. Non interleaving semantics for mobile processes. *Theoret. Comput. Sci.*, 216:237–270, 1999.
9. P. Degano and C. Priami. Enhanced operational semantics: A tool for describing and analysing concurrent systems. *ACM Computing Surveys*, 33:135–176, 2001.
10. J. Engelfriet. A multiset semantics for the pi-calculus with replication. *Theoret. Comput. Sci.*, 153:65–94, 1996.
11. A. Kiehn. Comparing causality and locality based equivalences. *Acta Informatica*, 31:697–718, 1994.
12. R. Milner. *Communication and Concurrency*. Prentice Hall, 1989.
13. R. Milner. The polyadic π-calculus: A tutorial. In F.L. Bauer, W. Brauer, and H. Schwichtenberg, editors, *Logic and Algebra of Specification*, volume 94 of *Nato ASI Series F*, pages 203–246. Springer, 1993.
14. R. Milner, J. Parrow, and D. Walker. A calculus of mobile processes. Part I and II. *Information and Computation*, 100:1–77, 1992.
15. D. Sangiorgi. Locality and interleaving semantics in calculi for mobile processes. *Theoret. Comput. Sci.*, 155:39–83, 1996.
16. D. Sangiorgi and D. Walker. *The π-calculus: A Theory of Mobile Processes*. Cambridge University Press, 2001.

Event-Driven Traversal of Logic Circuits for Re-evaluation of Boolean Functions in Reactive Systems

Valeriy Vyatkin

Martin Luther University of Halle-Wittenberg,
Dept. of Engineering Science,
D-06099 Halle, Germany
phone: +49-(345)-552-5972; fax:+49-(345)-552-7304
Valeriy.Vyatkin@iw.uni-halle.de

Abstract. This paper presents an efficient algorithm for re-evaluation of a Boolean function represented as a logic circuit. The algorithm consists of pre-computation and re-evaluation parts. For a given logic circuit and initial input bits, the pre-computation constructs the data structure for the re-computation. The re-evaluation accepts a list of changed input bits and updates the output of the circuit. The pre-computation runs in time linear to size of the circuit and the re-computation performs in time linear to the number of triggered input bits.

Keywords: Boolean computation, Logic circuits, Incremental computation.

1 Motivation

In this paper we continue discussion of discrete computation methods for real-time reactive systems started in [6]. A typical example of such systems are real-time control systems as exemplified in Figure 1. A controller communicates with the controlled system (called *plant*) by means of signals, which relay values of sensors to inputs of the controller and values of the outputs to the actuators of the plant. The controller is a computing device, implementing a control algorithm, which can be for simplicity considered as a set of Boolean functions.

The usual way of the computation is cyclic. First, the current status of the plant, which is indicated by sensors, is stored in an input buffer, then the whole control program (Boolean functions) is executed, while the values of inputs in the buffer remain unchanged, and in the last step the calculated outputs are transmitted to the actuators of the plant. Such a procedure, called *scan* repeats itself over and over again. The duration of the scan determines the response characteristic of controller. The shorter response is, the better the quality and reliability of the control are expected.

As the measurement and control systems become distributed, agent-based, etc., it requires to substitute the traditional computation framework by an event-driven

M. Broy and A.V. Zamulin (Eds.): PSI 2003, LNCS 2890, pp. 319–328, 2003.

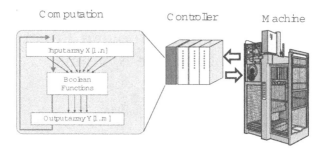

Fig. 1. A schematic picture of the computation process in discrete control systems

one. In our previous work [6] a method of re-computation was suggested that, in short, is as follows:

The change Δ to the input array is induced by an event and it initiates reevaluation of the function. *Precomputation*, placed between events prepares some auxiliary data which is used upon events to accelerate the *on-line reevaluation*.

We have found that:

Theorem 1. *On-line reevaluation of a Boolean function $f : \{0,1\}^n \to \{0,1\}$ after a change Δ to the input X can be done in time $O(|\Delta|)$ at the precomputation of $O(|V|\,n)$ time, where $|V|$ is the size of Binary Decision Diagram (BDD) of the given function.*

This result, while it shows optimal on-line performance, requires precomputations linear in time to the size of BDD representing the computed function. For those functions, which cannot be represented by a BDD of feasible size the application of that result becomes questionable. In this paper we attempt to suggest a certain trade-off between the on-line re-evaluation and pre-computation, applying logic circuit as an underlying graph structure instead of the BDD.

2   Introduction

Evaluation of a Boolean function $f : \{0,1\}^n \to \{0,1\}$ denoted by the analytic expression in terms of variables, brackets and Boolean operations is performed given an instance of input argument $X \in \{0,1\}^n$. First, values of X substitute the variable entries of the formula, and then the Boolean operations are performed over the constant terms, computing $f(X)$ in time linear to the length of the expression. This way of computation is called *start-over* or full evaluation.

As opposed to the evaluation, reevaluation finds $f(X_{new})$ given the change $\Delta \in \{0,1\}^n$ to the input X_{old} such that $X_{new} = X_{old} \oplus \Delta$. The change usually occurs just in a few bits of the input array X, so the reevaluation is expected to take much less time than the full evaluation. In terms of Boolean expressions the reevaluation can be formulated as follows: Given the expression where variables are replaced by constants from X_{old} and positions of changed terms, determined by Δ, find whether the expression changes its value, as compared with $f(X_{old})$.

The previous study of Boolean reevaluation includes the work [5] by Welch, where the principle of event (i.e. a change) propagation was used. The problem of function's reevaluation is related to the *incremental* methods of computations. More specifically, it is a particular case of the incremental circuit annotation problem, which in [1,4] was proved to have the complexity exponential to the size of the change.

The algorithm, presented in this paper, reevaluates the expression in terms of the change propagation in the corresponding circuit. The reevaluation time is linear in the number of changed formula's entries at cost of precomputation, linear to the size of the circuit.

3   Logic Expressions and Logic Circuits

3.1   Notation

According to [3] a Boolean (or logic) circuit is a directed acyclic graph (dag) $C = (V, E, root \in V)$, where the nodes $V = V_l \cup V_g$ can be either input nodes (V_l) with indegree equal to 0, or gates V_g. Conversely, the set of nodes of the circuit C will be denoted as $V(C)$.

Even though each gate can be an arbitrary Boolean function, for simplicity we assume that sort of gate is limited to binary operations $\{and, or, nand, nor\}$. Predecessors of a gate v are termed $left(v)$ and $right(v)$ respectively. Each input is associated with a variable and possibly with a negation attribute which is depicted as a mark on the outgoing edge.

A specific case of the circuits is those straightforwardly composed for Boolean expressions and represent their structure as it is illustrated in Figure 2. In this case the circuit is a tree, each input corresponds to the variable entry, and each gate - to the Boolean operation in the expression.

Each vertex $v \in V$ roots a *subcircuit* denoted as C_v. A circuit rooted in node v denotes a Boolean function f_v. If each vertex v in C has an attribute assigned with value of f_v, it is said that the circuit is correctly annotated with the function value.

For the sake of simplicity in the further explanations, we replace the original circuit with arbitrary types of gates by circuits with only $\{or, nor\}$ gates, which preserves the topological structure of the circuit. In the figures we depict the NOR-gate with a mark on its outgoing edge, similarly to the inputs which have the negation attribute.

For any two $a, b \in V$, there exist at least one common ancestor c, i.e. the node such that $a \in C_c$ and $b \in C_c$. The farthest among such nodes from the root is

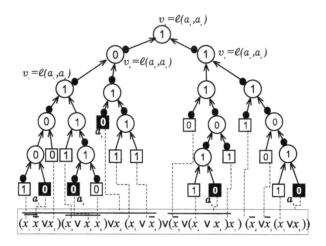

Fig. 2. An annotated logic circuit with switched inputs

called the *least common ancestor* (LCA) of the two nodes, which is denoted by $\ell(a, b)$.

A vertex w dominates on v and v, correspondingly, is subordinate to vertex w, if v belongs to the subtree rooted in $w : v \in C_w$. This fact will be denoted as $v<w$. Comparison of two nodes on domination/subordination can be made in a constant time. Two vertices $v_1, v_2 \in V$ are *independent* $v_1 \sim v_2$ if none of them belongs to the subtree rooted in the other: $(v_1 \notin C_{v_2})\&(v_2 \notin C_{v_1})$. For two independent vertices $v \sim w$ it is said that v precedes w, and denoted $v{\prec}w$ iff $v \in C_{left(\ell(v,w))}$ and $w \in C_{right(\ell(v,w))}$.

Thus, we defined two types of orders for vertices in logic circuit: the domination between successor/predecessor vertices and the precedence for independent vertices. Both these order relations are transitive: $(a{\prec}b)\&(b{\prec}c) \Rightarrow (a{\prec}c)$ and $(a<b)\&(b<c) \Rightarrow (a<c)$. The computational complexity of checking a pair of nodes on domination and precedence can be expressed also in terms of LCA computation. Really, if $\ell(a, b)$ does not coincide neither with a nor with b, that means that a and b are independent. Iff $\ell(a, b) = a$ then $a{\geq}b$. According to [2], the LCA for a pair of nodes in a binary tree can be found in a constant time provided the precomputation of time linear to the size of the tree is applied to the tree to assign some attribute to each node.

3.2   Re-evaluation in Terms of Circuits

A change of the variables' value leads to the change of the expression entries. Correspondingly, it causes the change in the function value attributes of some inputs of the circuit. We call the set of such inputs as the *initial switched set* V_l^δ, whose size is denoted by $m = |V_l^\delta|$. Furthermore, a change in V_l^δ may cause the *change propagation* to some other nodes of the circuit. We present the algorithm which finds $f(X_{new})$ as a propagation of changes from nodes of V_l^δ through the circuit.

Suppose there is one more, the difference annotation of nodes $\delta(v)$, which is equal to 1 if the function value $f_v(X_{new}) \neq f_v(X_{old})$. Let us term the set of all nodes where $\delta(v) = 1$ as V^δ and assume that initially the difference values are set to the value "Unknown" in all the nodes except for $V_l^\delta \subseteq V^\delta$, where it is 1. Re-evaluation in terms of logic circuit has to set the difference in the root, that automatically gives the new function value: $f_v(X_{new}) = f_v(X_{old}) \oplus \delta(v)$.

According to the re-evaluation/precomputation pattern, our algorithm first attempts to find the difference in the root of the circuit, and after that, during the precomputation, updates the functional annotation in all the other nodes of V^δ.

The algorithm rests on the following principle of the middle point: once the difference is established in an intermediate vertex w, the problem of re-evaluation of the circuit C rooted in v with set of switched inputs V_l^δ, is replaced by the re-evaluation of the circuit C' whose set of nodes is formed as:

$$V(C') = V(C) - V(C_w) + \{w\} ;$$

with set of switched inputs $V_l^{\delta'} = V_l^\delta - (V_l^\delta \cap V(C_w)) + [\delta(w) = 1]\{w\}$. This operation is called the reduction of re-evaluated sub-circuit.

4   Algorithm of Re-evaluation

4.1   Single switching case

Let us use the inductive approach to develop the re-evaluation algorithm. First, consider the case $m = 1$, i.e. when it is guaranteed that only one input of the circuit has changed and its location is given. The question is, how fast it is possible to compute the difference in the root.

Evident and correct answer is that this can be done in time linear to the distance between the switched input and the root. In the singular switch case, the change propagates only along this path. Assume that $V_l^\delta = \{v\}$, i.e. v is the only input in the circuit such that initially $\delta(v) = 1$. Denote the *singular propagation mapping* $p : V \to V$ as follows: $p(v)$ is the nearest node to the root among the nodes of V^δ, i.e. the node where the change propagation stops, assuming $|V_l^\delta| = 1$. In the root of the circuit $p(root) = 1$.

Precomputation of $p(v)$ for all the nodes in the circuit can be done in time linear to the circuit's size by a straightforward recursive algorithm. The check for OR,NOR gates is performed as follows: the change propagates from $left(v)$ to v if $f_{right(v)} = 0$ and from $right(v)$ to v if $f_{left(v)} = 0$; So, the algorithm sets the $p(v)$ in every node of the circuit in $O(|V|)$ time because every node from V is visited only once. Obviously, the difference in v can be found as $\delta(v) = 1$ iff $p(a) \geq v$.

Once the switched input w is given, it is enough to check, whether $p(w)$ is the root of the circuit. If not, that means that the function remains unchanged, otherwise the function switches its value to the opposite.

Lemma 1. *Re-evaluation of the singular switch circuit is done in a constant time provided the correct value of the singular propagation mapping is pre-assigned to every vertex of the circuit.*

The algorithm of singular switch circuit re-evaluation will be further referred to as the function *Single Switch Re-evaluation*(v: root of the circuit):Boolean which returns $\delta(v)$.

4.2   Double Switching Case

In the case the circuit has exactly two switched inputs a and b, consider its least common ancestor $v = \ell(a,b)$. Its predecessors $left(v)$ and $right(v)$ root the singular switching sub-circuits, so the difference in those can be assigned in a constant time according to Lemma 1. Once the differences are set in both $left(v)$ and $right(v)$, the difference in v is computable in a constant time as follows:

$$\delta(v) = \delta(left(v)) \wedge \delta(right(v)) \wedge [f_{left(v)} = f_{right(v)}] \vee$$
$$\delta(left(v)) \wedge \overline{\delta(right(v))} \wedge [f_{right(v)} = 0] \vee$$
$$\overline{\delta(left(v))} \wedge \delta(right(v)) \wedge [f_{left(v)} = 0]$$

So, we conclude with the following lemma:

Lemma 2. *Re-evaluation of the dual switch circuit is done in a constant time provided the correct value of the singular propagation mapping is pre-assigned to every vertex of the circuit.*

Similar to the singular case, the algorithm reevaluating the dual switching circuits will be referred to as the function *Double Switch Reevaluation*(v:root of the circuit), returning a Boolean value.

4.3   General case

In the general case the set V_l^δ contains an arbitrary number of switched inputs. It can be easily proved that among the nodes of V_l^δ there exist a pair, to say a, b, of nodes, LCA of which doesn't contain any other node from V_l^δ. We will call such a pair as *a pair with minimal LCA*. The subcircuit rooted in $\ell(a,b)$ is a dual switching subcircuit with the set of switched nodes $\{a, b\}$. It can be re-evaluated in a constant time according to Lemma 2. The general algorithm of the circuit re-evaluation looks like as follows:

algorithm Circuit Re-evaluation (V_l^δ: set of switched inputs);
[1] **while** $V_l^\delta \neq \varnothing$ **do**
[2]   **if** $|V_l^\delta| = 1$ **then** *Single Switch Re-evaluation*(a_1);
[3]   **elseif** $|V_l^\delta| = 2$ **then** *Double Switch Re-evaluation*(a_1, a_2);
[4]   **elseif** Select out of V_l^δ a pair (a, b) with minimal LCA
[5] Δ:=Double Switch Re-evaluation($\ell(a, b)$)
[6]   Apply Reduction of Re-evaluated subcircuit to $C_{\ell(a,b)}$
[7] **end**
end

The running time of the algorithm is $O(T_s \times m)$, where T_s is the time required to select a pair with minimal LCA out of V_l^δ. The only remained problem with the algorithm of circuit evaluation is how to choose a pair $a, b \in V_l^\delta$ with a minimal LCA. A naive approach could be to try every of $\frac{m(m-1)}{2}$ pairs of the vertices in V_l^δ and check whether the tree rooted in its LCA contains any of the remained $m - 2$ vertices, that totals in $\frac{m(m-1)(m-2)}{2}$ checks. Then for the total algorithm the complexity would be: $O(m^4)$. In fact, we will show that there is a way to select a minimal LCA pair which makes the *Circuit Re-evaluation* algorithm running in $O(m)$ time. The algorithm exploits some properties of adjacent switched vertices which are formulated below.

In V_l all the vertices are mutually independent, so that a set $V_l^\delta \in V_l$ of switched vertices, also holds this property. From now on assume the set of event nodes be sorted in ascending order as follows: $V_l^\delta = \{a_1, a_2, \ldots, a_m\}$. The following properties hold for an arbitrary triple of independent nodes, so they are valid for a sequence of three nodes in V_l^δ:

Lemma 3. *For an arbitrary triple of independent nodes $a, b, c \in V$ such that $a \prec b \prec c$, the following holds: 1)$\ell(a, b) \leq \ell(a, c)$;2) Either $\ell(a, b) < \ell(b, c)$, or $\ell(b, c) < \ell(a, b)$;*

Consider three consequent nodes a_1, a_2, a_3 from V_l^δ. According to Lemma 3, there are two possible cases of their pair-wise LCAs' mutual relationship: either $\ell(a_1, a_2) < \ell(a_2, a_3)$ (a), or $\ell(a_2, a_3) < \ell(a_1, a_2)$ (b).

If $\ell(a_1, a_2) < \ell(a_2, a_3)$ then $C_{\ell(a_1, a_2)}$ is a double switching subtree, since no other nodes from V_l^δ can be in it. The difference in $\ell(a_1, a_2)$ can be found in a constant time and the subtree can be exposed to the reduction.

Otherwise, if $\ell(a_2, a_3) < \ell(a_1, a_2)$, we add to the consideration the next node a_4. If $\ell(a_2, a_3) < \ell(a_3, a_4)$ then $C_{\ell(a_2, a_3)}$ is a minimal LCA, which roots a double switching subtree and can be reduced. This explains the basic idea of the algorithm: scan the sequence from left to right until such a pair a_j, a_{j+1} is found that

$$\ell(a_{j-1}, a_j) > \ell(a_j, a_{j+1}) < \ell(a_{j+1}, a_{j+2}).$$

This pair has to be reduced and the process continues. Finally we get the sequence, in which all pair-wise LCAs are ordered in the descending order, so the reduction is applicable from right to left until the sequence V_l^δ is empty.

The explained above rule of finding the pair with minimal LCA among the pairs of adjacent vertices in the sequence V_l^δ is formulated as the following criterion:

Lemma 4 (Criterion of minimality). *In the ordered sequence of switched nodes $V_l^\delta = \{a_1 \prec a_2 \ldots \prec a_m\}$*

1. The LCA $\ell(a_1, a_2)$ is minimal iff
   $\ell(a_1, a_2) < \ell(a_2, a_3)$;
2. $\forall 1 < j < m - 2$ LCA $\ell(a_j, a_{j+1})$ is minimal iff $\ell(a_{j-1}, a_j) > \ell(a_j, a_{j+1})$
   $< \ell(a_{j+1}, a_{j+2})$;
3. The LCA $\ell(a_{m-1}, a_m)$ is minimal iff $\ell(a_{m-1}, a_m) < \ell(a_{m-2}, a_{m-1})$;

Thus selection of the pair with minimal LCA for the reduction can be done by the linear lookup in the sequence of pairs (a_i, a_{i+1}) for $i(1 \le i < m)$. As a result of the reduction, nodes a_j, a_{j+1} are deleted from V_l^δ and the node $w = \ell(a_j, a_{j+1})$ adds to V_l^δ if $\delta(w) = 1$.

The following properties provide consistency of the set V_l^δ after the reduction is done.

Lemma 5. *For* $w = \ell(a_j, a_{j+1})$ *such that* $\ell(a_{j-1}, a_j) > w < \ell(a_{j+1}, a_{j+2})$ *it holds that:*

1. *Either* $\ell(a_{j-1}, a_j) < \ell(a_{j+1}, a_{j+2})$ *or* $\ell(a_{j-1}, a_j) > \ell(a_{j+1}, a_{j+2})$;
2. $\ell(a_{j-1}, v) = \ell(a_{j-1}, a_j)$ *and* $\ell(v, a_{j+2}) = \ell(a_{j+1}, a_{j+2})$;
3. $(w \sim a_{j-1}), (w \sim a_{j+2})$ *and* $(a_{j-1} \prec v \prec a_{j+2})$;
4. $\ell(a_{j-1}, a_{j+2}) = \max(\ell(a_{j-1}, a_j), \ell(a_{j+1}, a_{j+2}))$;

From the latter lemma it directly follows, that if the node $w = \ell(a_j, a_{j+1})$ is added to V_l^δ as a result of the reduction, then it is mutually independent with all the remaining vertices in V_l^δ and takes the place between a_{j-1}, a_{j+2} in the sequence. Its LCAs with adjacent vertices a_{j-1} and a_{j+2} are nothing but already computed LCAs $\ell(a_{j-1}, a_j)$ and $\ell(a_{j+1}, a_{j+2})$ respectively. If the reduction only removes the two vertices a_j, a_{j+1} from V_l^δ, then a new pair of adjacent vertices emerges in the sequence. This is the pair a_{j-1}, a_{j+2} with LCA equal to maximum among the LCA's $\ell(a_{j-1}, a_j), \ell(a_{j+1}, a_{j+2})$. As a result of the reduction the set V_l^δ remains to be an ordered set of independent nodes.

The first step of the algorithm processes the sequence V_l^δ from left to the right. The left part $a_1, a_2, \ldots a_i$ of the sequence is said to be *processed*. In the processed part the LCAs of the sequent pairs must follow to the descending order:

$$Processed = \{\ell(a_1, a_2) > \ell(a_1, a_2) \ldots > \ell(a_{i-1}, a_i)\}. \tag{1}$$

If $\ell(a_i, a_{i+1}) < \ell(a_{i-1}, a_i)$ then a_{i+1} is just added to the processed pair. Otherwise, i.e. if $\ell(a_i, a_{i+1}) > \ell(a_{i-1}, a_i)$, the pair (a_{i-1}, a_i) satisfies to the criterion of minimality and has to be exposed to the *Double Switching Re-evaluation* and, further, to the reduction. The processed part shrinks to $a_1, \ldots, a_{i-1}$ and the routine repeats. As a result of the first step the remained nodes of V_l^δ satisfy to (1).

The second step, thus, is given the sequence where the last pair has a minimal LCA. After its reduction this property holds, so the algorithm subsequently reduces all the pairs in the sequence from the last to the first, until the sequence either contains the only entry, or is empty. In the former case the circuit is reevaluated by the *Single Switch*, while in the latter the reevaluation has already established that the function does not switch.

To store the nodes during the processing we will use two stacks: one for the processed part, called *Proc* and the other for remaining part, called *Remain*. All the switched inputs are placed initially to the *Remain* stack. The overall algorithm computes Δf - the difference in the root of the circuit, which says whether the function switches or not.

The running time of the algorithm exploiting the above property is $O(m)$, provided the following auxiliary data are precomputed in all $v \in V$:

1. The value of *singular propagation mapping* $p(v)$;
2. The index for finding LCA in constant time;
3. Value of f_v.

Consider the example of re-evaluation of the logic circuit from Figure 2. The current values of argument are $X = \{1,0,0,1,0,0,1\}$. A change of two variables x_2, x_5 causes the switching of 5 circuit inputs, termed in the figure as a_1, a_2, a_3, a_4, a_5.

First, the nodes a_1, a_2 are placed into the stack *Proc*, and the nodes a_2, a_3, a_4 remain to be in the *Remain* stack. Since $\ell(a_1, a_2) < \ell(a_2, a_3)$, the subtree, rooted in $\ell(a_1, a_2)$ is exposed to the *Double Switch Re-evaluation*. As a result $\delta(\ell(a_1, a_2)) = 0$ and a_1, a_2 are removed from the *Proc* stack. Next, pair a_3, a_4 is placed to *Proc* and since $\ell(a_3, a_4) > \ell(a_4, a_5)$, then a_5 is also added to *Proc*. The *Remain* stack becomes empty and the first part of the algorithm halts.

In course of the second part, first the subcircuit $\ell(a_4, a_5)$ is exposed to the *Double Switch Re-evaluation* and a_4, a_5 are removed. The only node a_3 remains in the *Proc*. The *singular propagation mapping* of a_3 equals to the root of the circuit, so the function changes.

5   Conclusion

An algorithm of Boolean expression re-evaluation is suggested, which finds the new value of the expression in the on-line time linear to the number of changed formula's entries. The algorithm requires the precomputation linear to the size of the circuit.

Application of the algorithm is beneficial as compared to the full evaluation, which takes time linear to size of the circuit. It can be applied, for example, in the computer control of discrete event systems, which requires a huge number of Boolean functions to be computed in the real time mode.

As compared to the other methods of Boolean function re-evaluation, the logic circuits boast the compact size as compared with Binary Decision Diagrams (BDD). Therefore, they require much shorter precomputation and less space for storage than BDDs. But the on-line time of re-evaluation of the circuits (the number of changed formula's entries) is worse than that of the BDDs (the number of changed variables). We think that this a reasonable compromise of memory/speed for many applications.

Acknowledgement. Author is very grateful to Prof. Koji Nakano for discussions and critics. This work was partially supported by the DFG grant VY 5/3-1.

References

1. B. Alpern, R. Hoover, B.K. Rosen, P.F Sweeney, and K. Zadeck. *Incremental evaluation of computational circuits*, pages 32–42. Proceedings of First Annual ACM-SIAM symposium on Discrete Algorithms, 1990.

2. Sheiber B. and Vishkin U. On finding lowest common ancestors: Simplification and parallelization. *SIAM J.Comput.*, 17(6):1253–1262, 1988.
3. C.H.Papadimitriou. *Computational Complexity*. Addison-Wesley, 1994.
4. Ramalingam G. *Bounded Incremental Computation*, volume 1089 of *Lecture Notes in Computer Science*. Springer-Verlag, New York, 1996.
5. John T.Welch. The clause counter map: An event chaining algorithm for online programmable logic. *IEEE Trans. on Robotics and Automation*, 2, 1995.
6. Vyatkin V. *Optimal Algorithms of Event-driven Re-evaluation of Boolean Functions*, volume 2244 of *Lecture Notes in Computer Science*, pages 55–63. Springer-Verlag, Berlin, 2001.

Teams of Pushdown Automata[*]

Maurice H. ter Beek[1], Erzsébet Csuhaj-Varjú[2], and Victor Mitrana[3]

[1] Istituto di Scienza e Tecnologie dell'Informazione, CNR, Via G. Moruzzi 1,
56124 Pisa, Italy
mtbeek@iei.pi.cnr.it
[2] Computer and Automation Research Institute, Hungarian Academy of Sciences,
Kende utca 13–17, 1111 Budapest, Hungary
csuhaj@sztaki.hu
[3] University of Bucharest, Faculty of Mathematics, Str. Academiei 14,
70109 Bucharest, Romania,
mitrana@funinf.cs.unibuc.ro

Abstract. We introduce team pushdown automata as a theoretical framework capable of modelling various communication and cooperation strategies in complex, distributed systems. Team pushdown automata are obtained by augmenting distributed pushdown automata with the notion of team cooperation or — alternatively — by augmenting team automata with pushdown memory. Here we study their accepting capacity.

1 Introduction

During the last decade communication and cooperation strategies in complex, distributed systems have received considerable attention in many research areas. Examples include problem solving, multi-agent systems, groupware systems, and computer supported cooperative work (CSCW). Along this line of development, many attempts were made to provide theoretical models for such systems. These models often abstract from concrete data, configurations, and actions, but describe the system solely in terms of *(pushdown) automata*. The *team pushdown automata (team pda's)* we introduce here are in many ways a continuation of two such attempts, viz. the *distributed pushdown automaton* model [13,14,18] and the *team automaton* model [7,15]. However, team pda's also borrow ideas from other models, in particular from the theory of *grammar systems* [10,23].

Grammar systems consist of a set of grammars that, by interacting according to a protocol of communication and cooperation, generate one language. Best known are the sequential *cooperating distributed (CD) grammar systems* and the *parallel communicating (PC) grammar systems*. The grammars in CD grammar systems work together, in turn, by rewriting a common string [8]. When to

[*] ter Beek was supported by an ERCIM postdoctoral fellowship and his research was fully carried out during his stay at the Computer and Automation Research Institute of the Hungarian Academy of Sciences. Mitrana was supported by the Centre of Excellence in Information Technology, Computer Science and Control, ICA1-CT-2000-70025, HUN-TING project, WP5.

transfer control from one grammar to another is determined by the CD grammar system's cooperation strategy. The classic cooperation strategies are $*$, t, $\leq k$, $=k$, and $\geq k$, for some $k \geq 1$, by which a grammar rewrites the string any number of times, as long as it can, less than k times, exactly k times, and at least k times, resp. We call these *CD strategies*. In [11] CD grammar systems were recognized as the formal language-theoretic counterpart of blackboard systems [21], multi-agent systems used in the blackboard model of problem solving [20]. The common string models the blackboard containing the current state of the problem solving, the grammars represent knowledge sources contributing to the problem solving by changing the contents of the blackboard based on their competence, and the CD strategies regulate the control mechanism directing the problem solving by allowing the knowledge sources to access the blackboard.

The concept of *teams* was introduced in CD grammar systems by grouping grammars that, in turn, rewrite a common string in parallel [17,22]. Teams are prescribed or formed automatically, and the CD strategies determine when to transfer control from one team to another. Since well-structured groups outperform individuals in a variety of tasks, the concept of teams has a clear practical motivation [24]. The concept of *competence* was introduced in CD grammar systems by defining the "cleverness" of a grammar w.r.t. a certain string as the number of nonterminals of this string it is able to rewrite [2,3,9]. This recognizes the practical reality of members of a group possessing different skills.

Replacing the grammars in CD grammar systems by (pushdown) automata leads to *distributed (pushdown) automata* [13,18]. Their pushdown memories (a.k.a. stacks) model the memory, or a notebook, of the knowledge sources of blackboard systems. A similar operation was carried out for PC grammar systems [12]. Independently, *multistack pushdown automata* with CD strategies controlling the use of the stacks were introduced [14]. These two models thus differ conceptually: in the latter case there is one pushdown automaton (pda) with n stacks, while in the former case the n stacks are distributed over n pda's. The distributed pda's of [18] moreover communicate by allowing transitions from states of one pda to states of another pda. We refer to both models as a *CD pda*.

CD pda's accept languages similar to the way ordinary pda's do. Given a number of stacks and a tape with an input word on it, some central unit has a state and two reading heads. A fixed head scans the tape from left to right, one symbol at a time, while a mobile head inspects the topmost symbol of each stack. Based on some predefined transitions, the central unit reads the current symbol on the tape, replaces the topmost symbol of one of the stacks by a string, and changes state. This procedure is repeated until in accordance with the CD strategy used, the mobile head is moved to another stack. This other stack is chosen among those for which there exists a predefined transition allowing the central unit to read the current symbol on the tape, replace the topmost symbol of this stack, and change state. The word on the tape is part of the language accepted by a CD pda accepting by final state if it can be completely read in this way and the central unit has reached a final state. If, on the other hand, the word on the tape can be completely read in this way and all stacks are empty, then it is part of the language accepted by a CD pda accepting by empty stack.

Team automata form a formal framework capable of modelling groupware systems [15], multi-user software systems used in CSCW [1,16]. Inspiration came from a call for models capturing concepts of group behaviour [24]. Technically, team automata are an extension of I/O automata [19]. Team automata consist of a set of component automata interacting in a coordinated way by synchronizations of common actions. Component automata differ from ordinary automata by their lack of final states and the partition of their sets of actions into input, output, and internal actions. Internal actions have strictly local visibility and thus cannot be observed by other components, while external actions are observable by other components. The latter are used for communication between components and comprise both input and output actions. Through the partition of their sets of actions and the synchronizations of shared actions, a range of intriguing coordination protocols can be modelled by team automata, thus showing their usefulness within CSCW [5,6,7]. Research on team automata focuses on their modelling capacity rather than on their accepting capacity.

Like CD pda's and team automata, team pda's are comprised of a specific type of automata — pda's in this case — that by means of a certain strategy accept one language. Abstracting from the alphabet partition, we thus augment team automata with stacks. Seen as memories, or as notebooks in which the components can make sketches, these stacks thus enhance the modelling capacity of team automata. A team pda accepts languages similar to the way CD pda's do. However, whereas a CD pda reads the current symbol on the tape, replaces the topmost symbol of *one* stack, and changes state, a team pda replaces the topmost symbol of a *team* of stacks. We thus augment CD pda's with team behaviour. The size of a team is based on the so-called *mode of competence* a team pda is working in. These modes of competence are inspired by the CD strategies and result in the topmost symbol of an arbitrary one, less than k, exactly k, or at least k, for some $k \geq 1$, stacks to be replaced. By requiring the topmost symbol of each stack of a team to be equal, we model that the components forming a team are equally competent, i.e. have the same skills.

In this paper we focus on team pda's with non-deterministic pda's and acceptance by empty stack. We show that team pda's consisting of two pda's can generate non-context-free languages, while team pda's consisting of three pda's can accept all recursively enumerable languages. All proofs can be found in [4].

2   Preliminaries

We assume the reader to be familiar with the basic notions from formal language theory and automata theory, in particular concerning pushdown automata [23].

Set inclusion is denoted by $\subseteq$, while $\subset$ denotes strict inclusion. Set difference of sets V and W is denoted by $V \setminus W$. We denote the cardinality of a finite set V by $\#V$. The powerset of a set V, formed by finite parts of V only, is denoted by $\mathcal{P}_f(V)$. We denote the set $\{1, \ldots, n\}$ by $[n]$. Then $[0] = \varnothing$. The empty word is denoted by λ and the empty word vector $(\lambda, \ldots, \lambda)$, its dimension being clear from the context, is denoted by Λ. We consider languages L_1 and L_2 to be equal, denoted by $L_1 = L_2$, iff $L_1 \setminus \{\lambda\} = L_2 \setminus \{\lambda\}$. The classes of context-free and recursively enumerable languages are denoted by $\mathcal{L}(\mathrm{CF})$ and $\mathcal{L}(\mathrm{RE})$, resp. The family of context-free languages that do not contain λ is denoted by $\mathcal{L}(\mathrm{CF}-\lambda)$.

A *pushdown automaton* (pda) is a sixtuple $\mathcal{A} = (Q, \Sigma, \Gamma, \delta, q^0, Z^0)$, with set Q of states, input alphabet Σ, pushdown alphabet Γ, transition mapping $\delta : Q \times (\Sigma \cup \{\lambda\}) \times \Gamma \to \mathcal{P}_f(Q \times \Gamma^*)$, initial state $q^0 \in Q$, and initial stack content $Z^0 \in \Gamma$. The family of languages recognized by [λ-free] pda's is denoted by $\mathcal{L}(\mathrm{PDA}[-\lambda])$ and it is known that $\mathcal{L}(\mathrm{PDA}[-\lambda]) = \mathcal{L}(\mathrm{CF}[-\lambda])$.

The *shuffle* of $u, v \in \Sigma^*$, denoted by $u \,\|\, v$, is defined as $u \,\|\, v = \{u_1 v_1 \cdots u_n v_n \mid u_i, v_i \in \Sigma^*, i \in [n], u_1 \cdots u_n = u, v_1 \cdots v_n = v\}$. The shuffle of $L_1, L_2 \subseteq \Sigma^*$, denoted by $L_1 \,\|\, L_2$, is defined as $L_1 \,\|\, L_2 = \{w \in u \,\|\, v \mid u \in L_1, v \in L_2\} = \bigcup_{u \in L_1, v \in L_2} u \,\|\, v$. The shuffle operation is commutative and associative. The family of shuffles of n languages from language family $\mathcal{L}(F)$, denoted by n-$Shuf(F)$, is defined as n-$Shuf(F) = \{L_1 \,\|\, \cdots \,\|\, L_n \mid L_i \in \mathcal{L}(F), i \in [n]\}$. It is known that the shuffle of n context-free languages need not be context-free, for any $n \geq 2$.

3   Teams of Pushdown Automata

In the sequel we assume that $n \geq 2$ unless otherwise stated.

Given a set $\mathcal{S} = \{\mathcal{A}_i \mid i \in [n]\}$ of pda's $\mathcal{A}_i = (Q_i, \Sigma_i, \Gamma_i, \delta_i, q_i^0, Z_i^0)$, the *team pushdown automaton* of degree n (n-team pda) composed over $\mathcal{S}$ is the quintuple

$$\mathcal{T} = (Q, \Sigma, \Gamma, q^0, Z^0),$$

where $Q = Q_1 \times \cdots \times Q_n$ is its set of *states*, $\Sigma = \bigcup_{i \in [n]} \Sigma_i$ is its *input alphabet*, $\Gamma = \Gamma_1^* \times \cdots \times \Gamma_n^*$ is its *pushdown alphabet*, $q^0 = (q_1^0, \ldots, q_n^0)$ is its *initial state*, and $Z^0 = (Z_1^0, \ldots, Z_n^0)$ is *initial stack contents*. The pda's in $\mathcal{S}$ are called the *component pda's* of $\mathcal{T}$. We assumed $n \geq 2$ since a 1-team pda would be a pda.

Configuration of $\mathcal{T}$ contain its current — global — state defined by the — local — states its component pda's reside in, the part of the input word still to be read, and the current contents of its n stacks, i.e. they are triples

$$((p_1, \ldots, p_n), aw, (Z_1 \beta_1, \ldots, Z_n \beta_n)),$$

with $(p_1, \ldots, p_n) \in Q$, $a \in \Sigma \cup \{\lambda\}$, $w \in \Sigma^*$, and $(Z_1 \beta_1, \ldots, Z_n \beta_n) \in \Gamma$. Component pda $\mathcal{A}_j$, $j \in [n]$, is *competent* in such a configuration if $\delta_j(p_j, a, Z_j)$ is defined.

$\mathcal{T}$ can *move* from a configuration τ to a configuration τ', denoted by $\tau \vdash \tau'$, if one of its component pda's is competent in τ. Assuming that $\mathcal{A}_j$, with $j \in [n]$, is competent, then $\mathcal{A}_j$ can cause $\mathcal{T}$ to change state by changing state locally, reading the first letter of the remaining part of the input word to be read, and replacing the topmost symbol of the j-th stack. Formally,

$$((p_1, \ldots, p_n), aw, (Z_1 \beta_1, \ldots, Z_n \beta_n)) \vdash ((q_1, \ldots, q_n), w, (\alpha_1 \beta_1, \ldots, \alpha_n \beta_n))$$

if there exists a $j \in [n]$ for which $(q_j, \alpha_j) \in \delta_j(p_j, a, Z_j)$ and for all $i \in [n] \setminus \{j\}$, $q_i = p_i$ and $\alpha_i = Z_i$. If $a = \lambda$, then such a move is called a λ-*move*, and an n-team pda without λ-moves is called λ-*free*.

From an *initial configuration* (q^0, w, Z^0), consisting of its initial state q^0, a word w to be read, and its initial stack content Z^0, $\mathcal{T}$ *accepts* w if its stack content is the empty word vector when w has been completely read. All words that can be accepted in this way together form the language of $\mathcal{T}$. Consequently, the language accepted by $\mathcal{T}$, denoted by $L_*(\mathcal{T})$, is thus defined as

$$L_*(\mathcal{T}) = \{ w \in \Sigma^* \mid (q^0, w, Z^0) \overset{*}{\vdash} (q, \lambda, \Lambda) \text{ for some } q \in Q \},$$

with $\overset{*}{\vdash}$ as reflexive transitive closure of $\vdash$. The family of languages recognized by [λ-free] n-team pda's is denoted by $\mathcal{L}(n\text{-PDA}[-\lambda], *\text{-comp})$.

Example 1. Consider the pda's $\mathcal{A}_1 = (Q_1, \{a, b, c\}, \{A\}, \delta_1, p^0, A)$ and $\mathcal{A}_2 = (Q_2, \{a, b, c\}, \{A\}, \delta_2, q^0, A)$, where $Q_1 = \{p^0\} \cup \{p_i \mid i \in [3]\}$ and $Q_2 = \{q^0\} \cup \{q_i \mid i \in [3]\}$, and whose transition mappings δ_1 and δ_2 are defined by

$$
\begin{aligned}
\delta_1(p^0, a, A) &= \{(p_1, AA)\}, & \delta_2(q^0, a, A) &= \{(q_1, AA)\}, \\
\delta_1(p_1, a, A) &= \{(p_1, AA)\}, & \delta_2(q_1, a, A) &= \{(q_1, AA)\}, \\
\delta_1(p_1, b, A) &= \{(p_2, \lambda)\}, & \delta_2(q_1, b, A) &= \{(q_2, \lambda)\}, \\
\delta_1(p_2, b, A) &= \{(p_2, A)\}, & \delta_2(q_2, b, A) &= \{(q_2, \lambda)\}, \\
\delta_1(p_2, c, A) &= \{(p_3, \lambda)\}, & \delta_2(q_2, c, A) &= \{(q_2, A), (q_3, \lambda)\}, \text{ and} \\
\delta_1(p_3, c, A) &= \{(p_3, \lambda)\}.
\end{aligned}
$$

Clearly the languages accepted by these pda's are $L(\mathcal{A}_1) = \{ a^m b^n c^m \mid m, n \geq 1 \}$ and $L(\mathcal{A}_2) = \{ a^k b^{k+1} \mid k \geq 1 \} \cup \{ a^k b^k c^m \mid k, m \geq 1 \}$. Next consider the 2-team pda $\mathcal{T}_1 = (Q_1 \times Q_2, \{a, b, c\}, \{A\}^* \times \{A\}^*, (p^0, q^0), (A, A))$ over $\{\mathcal{A}_1, \mathcal{A}_2\}$. One easily verifies that the language accepted by $\mathcal{T}_1$ is $L_*(\mathcal{T}_1) = L(\mathcal{A}_1) \parallel L(\mathcal{A}_2)$. □

No matter how many component pda's a team pda consists of, no team feature is actually used: each (global) move of a team pda is brought about by a (local) move of an arbitrary one of its component pda's. Any n-team pda thus recognizes the shuffle of n context-free languages. The converse is also true, viz.

Theorem 1. $\mathcal{L}(n\text{-PDA}[-\lambda], *\text{-comp}) = n\text{-}Shuf(CF[-\lambda])$. □

Note that any λ-free n-team pda can be simulated by an n-team pda with λ-moves. Moreover, any n-team pda can be simulated by an $(n + 1)$-team pda: if the n-team pda is composed over $\mathcal{S}$, then it suffices to compose the $(n+1)$-team pda over $\mathcal{S}$ augmented by a pda with an empty transition mapping. However,

Theorem 2. $\mathcal{L}(n\text{-PDA}[-\lambda], *\text{-comp}) \subset \mathcal{L}((n+1)\text{-PDA}[-\lambda], *\text{-comp})$. □

4   Competence in Teams of Pushdown Automata

Until now an n-team pda can move if at least one component pda is competent. A global move is then brought about by the local move of an arbitrary competent pda, i.e. the component pda's of an n-team pda do not cooperate in any way.

In this section we define ways of cooperation between the pda's constituting an n-team pda $\mathcal{T}$ by requiring a precise number of them to be competent before $\mathcal{T}$ can move. These competent pda's are moreover required to be equally competent among each other, i.e. they must have the same symbol on top of their stacks and all together read either the same symbol or λ from the input tape. We distinguish the modes of competence $\leq k$, $=k$, and $\geq k$, for some $k \geq 1$, requiring at most k, exactly k, or at least k component pda's, resp., to be equally competent among each other and allowing no other component pda's to be equally competent with any of them. This resembles maximal competence defined in [2]. From now on we ignore the ≤ 1-mode of competence as it equals the $=1$-mode of competence.

Let us say that in the previous section n-team pda's accepted languages in the *-mode of competence. Note that this is not the same as the $=1$-mode of competence, since in the *-mode of competence an arbitrary one of the possibly many equally competent component pda's is chosen to bring about the global move of $\mathcal{T}$, thus completely disregarding whether or not any other component pda is equally competent with it. Below we will show this with an example.

For the sequel we let $\mathcal{T} = (Q, \Sigma, \Gamma, q^0, Z^0)$ be the n-team pda composed over the set $\mathcal{S} = \{\mathcal{A}_i \mid i \in [n]\}$ of component pda's $\mathcal{A}_i = (Q_i, \Sigma_i, \Gamma_i, \delta_i, q_i^0, Z_i^0)$, we let $f \in \{\leq k \mid k \geq 2\} \cup \{=k, \geq k \mid k \geq 1\}$ be the *modes of competence*, and we say that a natural number ℓ *satisfies* f iff ℓf (e.g. 4 satisfies ≤ 7 because $4 \leq 7$).

$\mathcal{T}$ can *move* from a configuration

$$\tau = ((p_1, \ldots, p_n), aw, (Z_1\beta_1, \ldots, Z_n\beta_n))$$

to a configuration

$$((q_1, \ldots, q_n), w, (\alpha_1\beta_1, \ldots, \alpha_n\beta_n))$$

in *f-comp-mode*, denoted by

$$((p_1, \ldots, p_n), aw, (Z_1\beta_1, \ldots, Z_n\beta_n)) \vdash^f ((q_1, \ldots, q_n), w, (\alpha_1\beta_1, \ldots, \alpha_n\beta_n))$$

if there exists a $J \subseteq [n]$, where $\#J$ satisfies f, such that for all $j \in J$,

$Z_j = X$, for some $X \in \bigcap_{t \in J} \Gamma_t$,
$(q_j, \alpha_j) \in \delta_j(p_j, a, X)$, i.e. all $\mathcal{A}_j$ are equally competent in τ,

and for all $i \in [n] \setminus J$, either

$Z_i \neq X$ or
$\delta_i(p_i, a, X)$ is undefined, i.e. $\mathcal{A}_i$ is not equally competent in τ with above $\mathcal{A}_j$'s.

If $a = \lambda$, then we have a λ-*move*, and an n-team pda without λ-moves is λ-*free*.

$\mathcal{T}$ can thus move from a configuration τ to a configuration τ' in the f-comp-mode if f component pda's are equally competent among each other in τ. A global move of $\mathcal{T}$ is now brought about by all these component pda's changing their local state, reading the first letter of the remaining part of the input word to be read, and replacing the unique symbol on top of their stacks. Consequently, the *language* accepted by $\mathcal{T}$ in f-comp-mode, denoted by $L_f(\mathcal{T})$, is defined as

$$L_f(\mathcal{T}) = \{\, w \in \Sigma^* \mid (q^0, w, Z^0) \vdash^{*f} (q, \lambda, \Lambda) \text{ for some } q \in Q \,\},$$

with $\vdash^{*f}$ as reflexive transitive closure of $\vdash^f$. The family of languages recognized by [λ-free] n-team pda's in f-comp-mode is denoted by $\mathcal{L}(n\text{-PDA}[-\lambda], f\text{-comp})$.

Example 2. (Ex. 1 cont.) As no initial configuration of $\mathcal{T}_1$ has only one competent component pda, the language accepted by $\mathcal{T}_1$ in the $=1$-comp-mode is $L_{=1}(\mathcal{T}_1) = \varnothing$, which does not equal $L_*(\mathcal{T}_1)$. Clearly the language accepted by $\mathcal{T}_1$ in the $=2$-comp-mode or the ≥ 2-comp-mode is the non-context-free language $L_{=2}(\mathcal{T}_1) = L_{\geq 2}(\mathcal{T}_1) = \{\, a^n b^n c^n \mid n \geq 1 \,\}$, while that accepted by $\mathcal{T}_1$ in the ≥ 1-comp-mode or the ≤ 2-comp-mode is the non-context-free language $L_{\geq 1}(\mathcal{T}_1) = L_{\leq 2}(\mathcal{T}_1) = \{\, a^m b^n c^m \mid 1 \leq m \leq n \,\} \cup \{\, a^k b^k c^m \mid 1 \leq k \leq m \,\}$. $\qquad\square$

Note that any λ-free n-team pda in f-comp-mode can be simulated by an n-team pda with λ-moves in f-comp-mode. Moreover, any n-team pda in f-comp-mode can be simulated by an $(n+1)$-team pda in f-comp-mode. Finally,

Theorem 3. *(1)* $L_{\geq 1}(\mathcal{T}) = L_{\leq k}(\mathcal{T})$, *for all* $k \geq n$,
(2) if $\forall J \subseteq [n]$ *with* $\#J = k+1$, $\bigcap_{j \in J} \Sigma_j = \varnothing$ *or* $\bigcap_{j \in J} \Gamma_j = \varnothing$, *then* $L_{=k}(\mathcal{T}) = L_{\geq k}(\mathcal{T})$,
(3) $L_{=k}(\mathcal{T}) = L_{\geq k}(\mathcal{T}) = \varnothing$, *and*
(4) $L_{=n}(\mathcal{T}) = L_{\geq n}(\mathcal{T})$, *for all* $k > n$. $\qquad\square$

We now study the accepting capacity of n-team pda's in the f-comp-mode.

Theorem 4. *Let* $g_1 \in \{=k, \geq k \mid k \geq 2\}$ *and* $g_2 \in \{=1, \geq 1\} \cup \{\leq k \mid k \geq 2\}$. *Then*
(1) $\mathcal{L}((k \cdot n)\text{-PDA}[-\lambda], g_1\text{-comp}) \supset \mathcal{L}(n\text{-PDA}[-\lambda], *\text{-comp})$ *and*
(2) $\mathcal{L}(n\text{-PDA}[-\lambda], g_2\text{-comp}) \supset \mathcal{L}(n\text{-PDA}[-\lambda], *\text{-comp})$. $\qquad\square$

By using the fact that the family of languages recognized by *two-stack pda's* equals $\mathcal{L}(\text{RE})$, we are able to prove that increasing the number of pda's in a team pda need not always lead to an infinite hierarchy.

Theorem 5. $\mathcal{L}(3\text{-PDA}, =2\text{-comp}) = \mathcal{L}(3\text{-PDA}, \geq 2\text{-comp}) = \mathcal{L}(\text{RE})$. $\qquad\square$

As the proof of this theorem uses λ-moves, it remains an open problem to establish the accepting capacity of λ-free n-team pda's, with $n \geq 3$. We conjecture prohibiting λ-moves in general decreases the accepting capacity of n-team pda's.

5   Future Work

We could add final states to pda's and study the accepting capacity of team pda's with acceptance by final states. We could also study the accepting capacity of team pda's with deterministic component pda's. Since the family of languages accepted by deterministic pda's is strictly included in $\mathcal{L}(\text{CF})$, this could result in a different picture. As an initial result, we note that — in analogy with Theorem 1

— the language accepted by an n-team pda with deterministic component pda's in the *-comp-mode and under acceptance by empty stack, equals the shuffle of the languages accepted by its n deterministic component pda's.

In [6], a variety of access control protocols was formally modelled by team automata. The type of protocols modelled was limited, however, because team automata can only deal with pure communication: their constituting component automata can synchronize their actions, but the lack of a private memory blocks them from exchanging information. Since team pda's augment team automata with a (distributed) pushdown memory and thereby allow the flow of information among their consituting component automata, a larger variety of access control protocols can potentially be modelled.

Team pda's seem capable of modelling more groupware protocols in CSCW.

References

1. R.M. Baecker (ed.), *Readings in Groupware and CSCW*, Morgan Kaufmann, 1992.
2. H. Bordihn and E. Csuhaj-Varjú, On competence and completeness in CD grammar systems. *Acta Cybernetica* 12, 4 (1996), 347–361.
3. M.H. ter Beek, E. Csuhaj-Varjú, M. Holzer, and Gy. Vaszil, On Competence in Cooperating Distributed Grammar Systems, parts I-III. TR 2002/1–3, Computer and Automation Research Institute, Hungarian Academy of Sciences, 2002.
4. M.H. ter Beek, E. Csuhaj-Varjú, and V. Mitrana, Teams of Pushdown Automata. TR 2002/4, Computer and Automation Research Institute, Hungarian Academy of Sciences, 2002.
5. M.H. ter Beek, C.A. Ellis, J. Kleijn, and G. Rozenberg, Team Automata for CSCW. In *Proc. 2nd Int. Coll. on Petri Net Technologies for Modelling Communication Based Systems*, Fraunhofer Institute for Software and Systems Engineering, 2001, 1–20.
6. M.H. ter Beek, C.A. Ellis, J. Kleijn, and G. Rozenberg, Team Automata for Spatial Access Control. In *Proc. 7th Eur. Conf. on CSCW*, Kluwer Academic, 2001, 59–77.
7. M.H. ter Beek, C.A. Ellis, J. Kleijn, and G. Rozenberg, Synchronizations in team automata for groupware systems. *CSCW* 12, 1 (2003), 21–69.
8. E. Csuhaj-Varjú and J. Dassow, On cooperating distributed grammar systems. *Journal of Information Processing and Cybernetics EIK* 26 (1990), 49–63.
9. E. Csuhaj-Varjú, J. Dassow, and M. Holzer, On a competence-based cooperation strategy in CD grammar systems. Submitted, 2002.
10. E. Csuhaj-Varjú, J. Dassow, J. Kelemen, and Gh. Păun, *Grammar Systems. A Grammatical Approach to Distribution and Cooperation*, Gordon and Breach, 1994.
11. E. Csuhaj-Varjú and J. Kelemen, Cooperating Grammar Systems: a Syntactical Framework for the Blackboard Model of Problem Solving. In *Proc. AI and Information-control Systems of Robots*, North-Holland, 1989, 121–127.
12. E. Csuhaj-Varjú, C. Martín-Vide, V. Mitrana, and Gy. Vaszil, Parallel Communicating Pushdown Automata Systems. *IJFCS* 11, 4 (2000), 633–650.
13. E. Csuhaj-Varjú, V. Mitrana, and Gy. Vaszil, Distributed Pushdown Automata Systems: Computational Power. To appear in *Proc. 7th. Int. Conf. on Developments in Language Theory*, LNCS, Springer, 2003.
14. J. Dassow and V. Mitrana, Stack Cooperation in Multistack Pushdown Automata. *Journal of Computer and System Sciences* 58, 3 (1999), 611–621.

15. C.A. Ellis, Team Automata for Groupware Systems. In *Proc. Int. Conf. on Supporting Group Work: The Integration Challenge*, ACM Press, 1997, 415–424.
16. J. Grudin, CSCW: History and Focus. *IEEE Computer* 27, 5 (1994), 19–26.
17. L. Kari, A. Mateescu, Gh. Păun and A. Salomaa, Teams in cooperating grammar systems, *Journal of Experimental and Theoretical AI* 7 (1995), 347–359.
18. K. Krithivasan, M. Sakthi Balan, and P. Harsha, Distributed Processing in Automata. *IJFCS* 10, 4 (1999), 443–463.
19. N.A. Lynch, *Distributed Algorithms*, Morgan Kaufmann, 1996.
20. P.H. Nii, Blackboard Systems: The Blackboard Model of Problem Solving and the Evolution of Blackboard Architectures. Part I. *AI Magazine* 7, 2 (1986), 38–53.
21. P.H. Nii, Blackboard Systems. In *Handbook of AI* vol. 4, Addison-Wesley, 1989, 1–82.
22. Gh. Păun and G. Rozenberg, Prescribed teams of grammars. *Acta Informatica* 31 (1994), 525–537.
23. G. Rozenberg and A. Salomaa (eds.), *Handbook of Formal Languages*, Springer, 1997.
24. J. Smith, *Collective Intelligence in Computer Based Collaboration — A Volume in the Computers, Cognition, and Work Series*, Lawrence Erlbaum, 1994.

Algebraic State Machines:
Concepts and Applications to Security

Jan Jürjens

Softw are & Systems Engineering, Informatics, TU Munich, Germany
http://www.jurjens.de/jan − juerjens@in.tum.de

Abstract. The concept of *algebraic state machine* has been introduced
in [3] as a state transition system the states of which are each defined as
an algebra, and that communicate through channels.
To make efficient use of this concept, one needs a formal semantics, as
well as notions of composition and refinement, which are provided in the
present work. T o demonstrate their usefulness for an application area of
major interest, we sho w how to extend algebraic state machines with data
types modelling cryptographic operations and with an adversary model
to reason about security-critical systems. As an example we consider a
cryptographic protocol proposed in the literature.

1 Introduction

A lgebnic state machines (AlgSMs) [3] (based on Abstract State Machines [4])
are state transition systems, the states of which are represented by algebras and
which can communicate through channels. It is motivated by the need to abstract
aw ay from low-level states when describing large systems by state machines. In
this work, we extend this work in several aspects:

- We give a formal semantics for AlgSMs as stream-processing functions.
- We define the composition at the level of algebraic state machines. We prove
  that this composition satisfies useful structural properties (associativity) and
  that it is preserved by the interpretation as stream-processing functions (in
  the sense that the composition of the interpretations of tw oAlgSMs gives
  the interpretation of their composition).
- A w ell-known paradigm of system development is that of *stepwise refinement*: One starts with an abstract specification and refines it in several
  steps to a concrete specification, which is finally implemented. We define
  refinement of AlgSMs wrt. the interfaces defined b y their communication
  mechanisms.
- T o demonstrate their usefulness for an application area of major interest,
  w eshow how to extend AlgSMs with data types modelling cryptographic
  operations and with an adv ersarymodel to reason about securit y-critical
  systems. We define a notion of *secrecy* T odemonstrate usefulness of our
  approach, we formally analyse a security protocol proposed in the literature
  (a varian t of the Internet protocol TLS, which is a successor of SSL), exhibit
  a flaw, propose a correction, and prov e it secure.

M. Broy and A.V. Zamulin(Eds.): PSI 2003, LNCS 2890, 2003., pp. 338–343, 2003.

For space reasons, proofs of the results as well as a discussion of related work has to be omitted from this extended abstract but can be found in the long version.[1]

2   Algebraic State Machines

The idea of connecting abstract state machines using the communication concept of [2] has also been pursued under the name of "interactive ASM" in [6,5,7].

We fix a set $\mathcal{D}$ of data values that can be exchanged between AlgSMs. For a set C of channel names we write $C^{[*]}$ for the set of functions $v : C \to \mathcal{D}^*$ where $\mathcal{D}^*$ is the set of finite sequences in $\mathcal{D}$. Thus v assigns a finite communication history to each of the channels in C.

An *algebraic state machine (AlgSM)* is a state machine where the states are algebras and which is connected through channels with its environment through which it exchanges inputs and outputs: An AlgSM $\mathcal{A}$ is given by

- a set Alg of Σ-algebras (for a signature Σ), which is the set of states of $\mathcal{A}$, also written as State.
- sets I resp. O of input resp. output channel names,
- a state transition function $\Delta : \text{Alg} \times I^{[*]} \to \mathcal{P}(\text{Alg} \times O^{[*]})$,
- and a set of initial states $\text{Alg}^0 \subseteq \text{Alg}$.

An AlgSM is executed as follows:

- one of the initial states is chosen non-deterministically,
- the following step is iterated: the state transition function is applied to the current state and the current channel valuation; from the resulting set, a pair $(S, v) \in \text{Alg} \times O^{[*]}$ is chosen non-deterministically.

As a new contribution, we give an interpretation of AlgSMs as stream-processing functions.

For a set C of channel names we write $C^{\to}$ for the set of functions $v : C \to \mathcal{D}^*)^{\omega}$ (the valuations of the channels in C by infinite communication histories; X^{ω} is the set of infinite sequences $c : \mathbb{N} \to X$). Given $c_0 \in C^{[*]}$ and $c \in C^{\to}$, we write $c_0.c \in C^{\to}$ for the channel valuation such that for each $x \in C$, $c_0.c(x)$ is the sequence the head of which is $c_0(x)$ and the tail of which is $c(x)$. Also, given a set C of channel names, a subset $D \subseteq C$, and a (finite or infinite) communication history $v \in C^{[*]} \cup C^{\to}$, the communication history $v\!\downarrow_D \in D^{[*]} \cup D^{\to}$ is defined by $v\!\downarrow_D(d) = v(d)$ for each channel $d \in D$ (the restriction of v to the channels in D).

An AlgSM $\mathcal{A}$ with sets I resp. O of input resp. output channels and state transition function $\Delta : \text{Alg} \times I^{[*]} \to \mathcal{P}(\text{Alg} \times O^{[*]})$ is interpreted as a function $[\![\mathcal{A}]\!] : I^{\to} \to \mathcal{P}(O^{\to})$, a *stream-processing function* from the input channels in I to the output channels in O, as follows.

---

[1] Available at http://www4.in.tum.de/~juerjens .

We define $f_1 \leq f_2$ for $f_1, f_2 : \mathsf{Alg} \rightarrow (I^\rightarrow \rightarrow \mathcal{P}(O^\rightarrow))$ if and only if $f_1(s)(i) \subseteq f_2(s)(i)$ for all $s \in \mathsf{Alg}$ and $i \in I^\rightarrow$. Then w e define $[\![\_]\!] : \mathsf{Alg} \rightarrow (I^\rightarrow \rightarrow \mathcal{P}(O^\rightarrow))$, $s \mapsto [\![s]\!]$ to be the largest function that satisfies

$$[\![s]\!](i_0.i) \stackrel{\text{def}}{=} \left\{ o_0.\boldsymbol{o} : \exists s' \in \mathsf{Alg}. \Big((s', o_0) \in \Delta(s, i_0) \wedge \boldsymbol{o} \in [\![s']\!](i) \Big) \right\}$$

for all $s \in \mathsf{Alg}$ and $i_0.i \in I^\rightarrow$, with respect to the following relation: Here $i_0.i$ denotes the sequence with head i_0 and tail i. Then for $i \in I^\rightarrow$, w edefine $[\![\mathcal{A}]\!](i) \stackrel{\text{def}}{=} \bigcup_{s \in \mathsf{Alg}^0} [\![s]\!](i)$.

3   Composition

We define (dela yed) composition for tw o AlgSMs $\mathcal{A}_1$ and $\mathcal{A}_2$. It assumes that the communication between components incurs a time delay. The definition is new; it has as counterpart the canonical definition of composition of stream-processing functions, in a way that ensures that the mapping from AlgSMs to stream-processing functions preserves the respective compositions (in the sense that the composition of the in terpretations of tw o AlgSMs gives the interpretation of their composition; see below). Suppose w e are given tw o AlgSMs $\mathcal{A}_i = (\Sigma_i, \mathsf{Alg}_i, I_i, O_i, \Delta_i, \mathsf{Alg}^0{}_i)$ (for $i = 1, 2$) where $\Sigma_i = (S_i, F_i, \mathbf{fct}_i)$, and with $O_1 \cap O_2 = I_1 \cap I_2 = \emptyset$, and $l^{\mathcal{A}_1} = l^{\mathcal{A}_2}$ for the carrier sets of eac h channel $l \in L \stackrel{\text{def}}{=} (O_1 \cup O_2) \cap (I_1 \cup I_2)$. We define their *delayed composition* $\mathcal{A}_1 \odot \mathcal{A}_2 \stackrel{\text{def}}{=} (\Sigma, \mathsf{Alg}, I, O, \Delta, \mathsf{Alg}^0)$ as follo ws:

- $\Sigma \stackrel{\text{def}}{=} (S_1 \uplus S_2 \uplus S_3, F_1 \uplus F_2 \uplus F_3, \mathbf{fct}_1 \uplus \mathbf{fct}_2 \uplus \mathbf{fct}_3)$ where
  - $S_3 \stackrel{\text{def}}{=} \{\mathbf{loc}_l^{\mathcal{A}_1 \odot \mathcal{A}_2} : l \in L\}$ where the sort $\mathbf{loc}_l^{\mathcal{A}_1 \odot \mathcal{A}_2}$ has the same carrier set as $l^{\mathcal{A}_1} = l^{\mathcal{A}_2}$,
  - $F_3 \stackrel{\text{def}}{=} \{\mathbf{feed}_l : l \in L\}$ and
  - $\mathbf{fct}_3(\mathbf{feed}_l) \stackrel{\text{def}}{=} (\mathbf{loc}_l^{\mathcal{A}_1 \odot \mathcal{A}_2})^*$ for $l \in L$.
- $\mathsf{Alg} \stackrel{\text{def}}{=} \{A_1 \uplus A_2 \uplus A_3 : A_1 \in \mathsf{Alg}_1 \wedge A_2 \in \mathsf{Alg}_2 \wedge A_3 \in \mathsf{Alg}(\Sigma_3)\}$ where $\Sigma_3 = (S_3, F_3, \mathbf{fct}_3)$.
- $I \stackrel{\text{def}}{=} (I_1 \cup I_2) \setminus (O_1 \cup O_2)$ and $O \stackrel{\text{def}}{=} (O_1 \cup O_2) \setminus (I_1 \cup I_2)$ with $c^{\mathcal{A}_1 \odot \mathcal{A}_2} = c^{\mathcal{A}_i}$ for $c \in I_i \cup O_i$ (for $i \in \{1, 2\}$).
- For $i \in I^{[*]}$, the state transition function is defined as
  $$\Delta(A_1 \uplus A_2 \uplus A_3, i) \stackrel{\text{def}}{=} \Big\{ (B_1 \uplus B_2 \uplus B_3, \tilde{o}|O) : \tilde{o} \in (O_1 \cup O_2)^{[*]}$$
  $$\wedge \exists \tilde{i} \in (I_1 \cup I_2)^{[*]}. \Big(i = \tilde{i}|_I \wedge (B_1, \boldsymbol{o}|_{O_1}) \in \Delta_1(A_1, \tilde{i}|_{I_1})$$
  $$\wedge (B_2, \boldsymbol{o}|_{O_2}) \in \Delta_2(A_2, \tilde{i}|_{I_2}) \wedge \forall l \in L. (\tilde{i}(l) = \mathbf{feed}_l^{A_3} \wedge \mathbf{feed}_l^{B_3} = o(l)) \Big) \Big\}.$$
- $\mathsf{Alg}^0 \stackrel{\text{def}}{=} \{A_1 \uplus A_2 \uplus A_3 : A_1 \in \mathsf{Alg}^0{}_1 \wedge A_2 \in \mathsf{Alg}^0{}_2 \wedge \forall l \in L. \mathbf{feed}_l^{A_3} = \varepsilon\}$ where ε is the empty sequence.

Here the set of states of $\mathcal{A}_1 \odot \mathcal{A}_2$ is the cartesian product $\mathsf{State}_1 \times \mathsf{State}_2 \times \mathsf{Alg}(\Sigma_3)$ of the sets of states State_1 of $\mathcal{A}_1$ and State_2 of $\mathcal{A}_2$, and the set of

Σ_3-algebras where Σ_3 consists of constants $\mathbf{feed}_l$ storing the contents of each of the local channels $l \in L$. The transitions are constructed as in the case of instantaneous composition, except that the inputs from the local channels are taken from the $\mathbf{feed}_l$ before the transition is fired and the outputs to the local channels are written to $\mathbf{feed}_l$ after the transition is fired. This introduces a delay of one time step into the composition.

Composition is associative if there is no confusion between the sorts and channels:

Theorem 1. *Suppose we are given AlgSMs* $\mathcal{A}_i = (\Sigma_i, \mathsf{Alg}_i, I_i, O_i, \Delta_i, \mathsf{Alg}^0{}_i)$ *(for* $i = 1, 2, 3$*) where* $\Sigma_i = (S_i, F_i, \mathbf{fct}_i)$*. Suppose that for* $i, j \in \{1, 2, 3\}$ *we have* $O_i \cap O_j = I_i \cap I_j = \emptyset$ *and* $l^{\mathcal{A}_i} = l^{\mathcal{A}_j}$ *for the carrier sets of each channel* $l \in (O_i \cup O_j) \cap (I_i \cup I_j)$*. Then* $(\mathcal{A}_1 \odot \mathcal{A}_2) \odot \mathcal{A}_3 = \mathcal{A}_1 \odot (\mathcal{A}_2 \odot \mathcal{A}_3)$*.*

For our result that the mapping from AlgSMs to stream-processing functions preserves composition, we first define *delayed composition* of stream-processing functions. Given stream-processing functions $f_i : I_i^{\rightarrow} \to \mathcal{P}(O_i^{\rightarrow})$ (for $i = 1, 2$) with $O_1 \cap O_2 = I_1 \cap I_2 = \emptyset$, we define the delayed composition $f_1 \odot f_2 : I^{\rightarrow} \to O^{\rightarrow}$ where $I \stackrel{\text{def}}{=} (I_1 \cup I_2) \setminus (O_1 \cup O_2)$ and $O \stackrel{\text{def}}{=} (O_1 \cup O_2) \setminus (I_1 \cup I_2)$ as follows. For $\tilde{i} \in I^{\rightarrow}$, we define

$$f_1 \odot f_2(\tilde{i}) \stackrel{\text{def}}{=} \Big\{ \tilde{o} : \exists i \in (I_1 \cup I_2)^{\rightarrow}, o_1 \in f_1(i|_{I_1}), o_2 \in f_2(i|_{I_2}).$$
$$\Big(\tilde{i} = i|_I \wedge \tilde{o} = (o_1 \cup o_2)|_O \wedge \forall l \in L.i(l) = \varepsilon.(o_1 \cup o_2)(l) \Big) \Big\}$$

where ε is the valuation that maps each channel to the empty sequence. Again, the implicit assumption is that producing an output from an input induces a time delay.

Theorem 2. *For all AlgSMs* $\mathcal{A}_1, \mathcal{A}_2$*, we have* $[\![\mathcal{A}_1 \odot \mathcal{A}_2]\!] = [\![\mathcal{A}_1]\!] \odot [\![\mathcal{A}_2]\!]$*.*

4   Refinement

A useful paradigm of system development is that of *stepwise refinement*: One starts with an abstract specification and refines it in several steps to a concrete specification which is implemented.

We define a notion of *refinement* that allows to proceed from abstract to more concrete specifications in a well-defined way. We also define a notion of *timeless refinement*, which is a relaxation of refinement allowing delays to be inserted. It allows a more flexible treatment, while still offering convenient structural properties.

Definition 1 (Refinement). *Suppose we are given AlgSMs* $\mathcal{A}$ *and* $\mathcal{A}'$*. We say that* $\mathcal{A}'$ *refines* $\mathcal{A}$ *if for each input valuation* $i \in I^{\rightarrow}$*, we have* $[\![A']\!](i) \subseteq [\![A]\!](i)$*.*

Theorem 3. *Composition of AlgSMs and interpretation of AlgSMs as stream-processing functions is preserved by refinement.*

For timeless refinement we define the time abstraction $|c| \in C^\omega$ of a stream $c \in C^\to$ by $|c_0.c| \stackrel{\text{def}}{=} c_0 \hat{} |c|$ (where $\hat{}$ denotes concatenation of sequences). Then for any stream-processing function $f : I^\to \to \mathcal{P}(O^\to)$ we define the *time abstraction* $|f| : I^\omega \to \mathcal{P}(O^\omega)$ by $|f|(i) \stackrel{\text{def}}{=} \{|f(\tilde{i})| : \tilde{i} \in I^\to \wedge |\tilde{i}| = i\}$.

Definition 2 (Timeless refinement). *Suppose we are given AlgSMs $\mathcal{A}$ and $\mathcal{A}'$. We say that $\mathcal{A}'$ refines $\mathcal{A}$ timelessly if for each $i \in I^\omega$, we have $|[\![A']\!]|(i) \subseteq |[\![A]\!]|(i)$.*

Theorem 4. *Interpretation of AlgSMs as stream-processing functions is preserved by timeless refinement.*

5   Security

In the long version of this paper, we demonstrate how one can apply AlgSMs to security analysis.

We consider a variant of the TLS protocol proposed in [1]. We demonstrate that this protocol contains a flaw and propose a corrected version which can be informally specified as follows.

$$C \to S : \mathsf{N_i}, \mathsf{K_C}, \mathsf{Sign}_{\mathsf{K_C^{-1}}}(\mathsf{C} :: \mathsf{K_C})$$
$$S \to C : \{\mathsf{Sign}_{\mathsf{K_S^{-1}}}(\mathsf{k_j} :: \mathsf{N_i} :: \mathsf{K_C})\}_{\mathsf{K_C}}, \mathsf{Sign}_{\mathsf{K_{CA}^{-1}}}(\mathsf{S} :: \mathsf{K_S})$$
$$C \to S : \{\mathsf{s_i}\}_{\mathsf{k_j}}$$

We use AlgSMs to prove the following theorem about the corrected version.

Theorem 5. *Suppose we are given a particular execution of the corrected protocol, a client C, and a number I with $S = S_I$ (where S_i is the server communicating with C in the ith execution round), and suppose that the server S is in its Jth execution round in the current execution when C in its Ith execution round initiates the protocol. Then this execution preserves the secrecy of $C.s_I$ against adversaries whose previous knowledge $\mathcal{K}_A^p$ fulfills the following conditions (where we use prefixing of values by C and S as in object-oriented notation to specify the instance of the client or server a value belongs to).*

– *we have*

$$\Big(\{C.s_I, K_C^{-1}, K_S^{-1}\} \cup \{S.k_j : j \geq J\}$$
$$\cup \{\{Sign_{K_S^{-1}}(X :: C.N_I :: K_C)\}_{K_C} : X \in \mathbf{Keys}\}\Big) \cap \mathcal{K}_A^p = \emptyset,$$

– *for any $X \in \mathbf{Exp}$, $Sign_{K_C^{-1}}(C :: X) \in \mathcal{K}_A^p$ implies $X = K_C$, and*
– *for any $X \in \mathbf{Exp}$, $Sign_{K_{CA}^{-1}}(S :: X) \in \mathcal{K}_A^p$ implies $X = K_S$.*

More details can be found in the long version of this paper.

6   Conclusion

The general context of this work is the need to abstract aw ay from low-level detail and to modularize system models when describing large systems. Towards this aim, [3] introduced the concept of *algebr aic state machines* To make efficient use of this concept, one needs a formal semantics, and composition and refinement, which are provided in the present work. As a major application area, we show ed how to extend AlgSMs with data types modelling cryptographic operations and with an adversary to reason about security-critical systems. As an example we considered a cryptographic protocol proposed in the literature.

T o conclude, the example from the application domain of security-critical systems indicates that AlgSMs are quite a flexible and expressible formal method, which allows to structure a specification in a conv enient way using the concept of channels. The added concepts advance the development of the notion of AlgSMs in that they allow composition and refinement at the level of AlgSMs.

Due to the possible high degree of abstraction provided b y algebraic state machines, this formalism seems to be suitable to consider larger parts of systems beyond security protocols (such as protocol contexts), as planned for future work.

Acknowledgements. Helpful comments from Manfred Broy and Thomas Kuhn are gratefully acknowledged.

References

1. V. Apostolopoulos, V. Peris, and D. Saha. Transport layer security: How much does it really cost? In *Conferenc e on Computer Communiations (IEEE Infocom)*, New Y ork, March 1999.
2. M. Broy and K. Stølen. *Specification and Development of Inter active Systems.* Springer, 2001.
3. M. Broy and M. Wirsing. Algebraic state machines. In T. Rus, editor, *8th International Conference on A lgebraicMethodology and Software T echnolgy (AMAST 2000)*, volume 1816 of *LNCS*. Springer, 2000.
4. Y. Gurevich. Evolving algebras 1993: Lipari guide. In E. Börger, editor, *Specification and Validation Methods*, pages 9–36. OUP, 1995.
5. J. J ürjens. A UML statecharts semantics with message-passing. In *Symposium of Applied Computing 2002*, pages 1009–1013, Madrid, March 11–14 2002. ACM.
6. J. Jürjens. F ormal Semantics for Interacting UML subsystems. In *5th International Conference on F ormal Methods for Open Obje ct-Base dDistributed Systems (FMOODS 2002)*, pages 29–44. IFIP, Kluw er, 2002.
7. J. Jürjens. *Secure Systems Development with UML.* Springer, 2003. In preparation.

Combining Aspects of Reactive Systems

Leonid Kof and Bernhard Schätz

Technische Universität München, Fakultät für Informatik,
Boltzmannstr. 3, D-85748 Garching bei München, Germany
{kof|schaetz}@in.tum.de

Abstract. For reactive systems, a large collection of formal models has
been developed. While the formal relationship between those models is
often carefully analyzed, the methodical implications for selecting or constructing appropriate models for specific application domains are rarely
addressed. We classify and compare different specification methods for
distributed systems concerning communication, behavior, and causality.
We discuss the implications of these dimensions, especially concerning
the combination of their properties.

1 Introduction

In the last thirty years, a variety of different formalisms for specifying distributed
and reactive systems were introduced, like Owicki/Gries [1], CSP [2], CCS [3],
UNITY [4], Esterel [5], Focus [6], to name a few. In general, each of them draws
from a different foundation and is therefore exhibiting its own strengths and
weaknesses. As a consequence, often pragmatic description formalisms like Statecharts end up with a large set of formal models [7] differing in essential aspects.
However, for the engineer it is not always obvious which model to select for a
specific application domain.

In this paper we identify three essential aspects of those formalisms by stripping away the more technical details:

- models of **communication** and **compositionality** as a related issue
- model of **behavior** and **hiding internal structure** as a related issue
- models of **causality** and **action refinement** as a related issue,

each aspect offering different variations to choose from. By classifying formalisms
accordingly, we show that these variations can be chosen independently. More
importantly, there also is a methodological dimension to identify combinations
that are useful concerning the modeling of reactive systems. In Section 2 we
introduce our classification dimensions and different characteristics of each dimension. In Section 2 we start off with the classification of some prominent
formalisms and sketch how less prominent combination could look like. Furthermore, we discuss methodical implications. Finally, in Section 3 we sum up the
results of the previous sections.

M. Broy and A.V. Zamulin (Eds.): PSI 2003, LNCS 2890, pp. 344–349, 2003.

Table 1. Aspects of Reactive Systems

Development Step	Modeling Aspect	Abstraction
Composition ('Observations about components still hold after combing them')	**Communication** ('How does the behavior of one component influence the behavior of others?')	Interference by environment
Modularization ('Observations about components still hold after hiding internal structure')	**Behavior** ('How are observations combined to describe a behavior?')	Scheduling of actions
Action Refinement ('Relation between actions still hold after refining actions')	**Timing** ('How are actions combined to describe an observation?')	Delays between actions

2 Classification

In the following subsections we consider three different aspects of reactive systems: *communication, behavior*, and *causality*. Since in the following we compare those models, we give a short informal list of those common concepts that are used for comparison:

A *component* is a unit of a system capsuling a state and supplying an interface. The *interface* of a component describes the part of the component which can be accessed by other components or the environment, e.g., by means of communication. *Behavior* relates components to (sets of) observations. Using *composition*, components are combined into a new component. An *observation* is a set of events of a component related by a causality relation, describing some form of sequence of actions. An *event* is an observable interaction occurring at the interface of a component, e.g. the communication of a message. *Causality* defines a relation between events of a component, inducing observations in form of executions. By adding *time*, it is possible to describe behavior which is influenced by the fact that no communication takes place by modeling time has passed without communication. *Refinement* relates different behaviors; e.g., behavioral refinement (relating a behavior of a component to a more restricted form of behavior) and structural refinement (relating a component to a network of subcomponents).

As shown in Table 1, the above aspects are related to principles of system description: **Communication** is related to the *compositionality* of a model. **Behavior** is related to the *abstraction* from implementation aspects (e.g., continuity) simplifying the description of a system behavior (e.g., modeling fairness). **Causality** is related to *refining* the interaction of a system, e.g. when abstracting from internal structure or when breaking up an atomic interaction.

For each of these aspects, we describe different variation classes of models. Each variation describes a different level of abstraction from concrete implementations as found in models of reactive systems. The corresponding classes are ordered concerning their capability to support these aspects. For sake of brevity, we only distinguish three classes in each aspect — of course, when considering fine-grained mathematical classifications more complex orders are needed, as, e.g., [8] shows for behavioral models. Since however we focus here on the methodical principles behind these formalisms we restrict these aspects to basic classes and concentrate on the aspect of combining them.

2.1   Modes of Communication

The aspect of communication deals with modes of synchronization between reactive systems, including the ways of exchanging information. As mentioned above, the corresponding methodical aspect is the issue of compositionality, i.e., the capability to deduce the observations of a composed system from the observations of its components. In this dimension, we consider the following range:

Implicit communication: This mode of communication corresponds to implicit communication, e.g. by using (undirected) shared variables. Since no explicit communication mechanism is used, the environment can change the (shared) variables unnoticed by the component. Therefore, compositionality is dependent on the behavior of the environment. This approach is used, e.g., in co-routine approaches like [1] or UNITY [4].

Explicit event based synchronous communication: While this model offers an explicit communication mechanism, synchronization is undirected (there is no designated sender and receiver); synchronization between components takes place by the components agreeing on an event they are all ready to accept. Therefore, when composing components, in this model the possibility of blocking has to be considered. This model of communication is found in TCSP [2] or CCS [3].

Explicit message based asynchronous communication: In this model there is an explicit distinction between sender and receiver; furthermore, the receiver of a message is *input enabled*, i.e. always ready to accept a message. Examples for this model are semantics for asynchronous circuits like [9], reactive modules [10], or stream processing functions like [6].

Note that increasing modularity is related to increasing abstraction from restrictions concerning compositionality: from compositionality with respect to freedom of interference (implicit), via compositionality with respect to deadlock (synchronous), to unrestricted compositionality (asynchronous). The corresponding refinement steps successively add these restrictions (cf., [11]).

2.2   Types of Behavior Modeling

The behavioral aspect focuses on how observations are combined to form a description of the behavior of a system. In denotational models (e.g., traces [9], failures [2], or stream processing functions [6]), observations are defined by the elements of the domain; in algebraic ([12]) or operational models (e.g., CCS

[3], I/O-Automata [13]) observations are defined in terms of states and possible transitions from these states. Since these formalisms describe (potentially) nonterminating systems, infinite observations are included in the behavior of a system. Accordingly, this aspect is related to the abstraction from an operational view of the system including issues like explicit parallelism/true concurrency of events as well as fairness of observations. Consequently, depending on the level of abstraction supplied by the model, phenomena like divergence in TCSP [2] can occur. Combining the issues of fairness and explicit parallelism, we obtain the following range:

Finite: These models essentially support only the description of finite behavior; they do not include a distinction between arbitrary sequentialization and parallel execution. No notion of fairness is supported; divergence can occur in these models. Examples are TCSP [2] or receptive processes [14].

Weak Fairness: While this model also only supports admissible behavior for sequential executions, it also supports explicit parallelism or weak fairness avoiding the treatment of divergence. Examples for this model are continuous stream processing functions [6] or CCS [3].

General Fairness: These systems support general non-admissible behavior or fairness. Examples are TLA [15], or general trace-based descriptions [12].

The methodical aspect of this dimension is the increasing abstraction from scheduling details: from scheduling parallel systems analogously to sequential ones (finite), via a fair scheduling of parallel systems (weak), to a fair scheduling independent of the kind of systems (general). The corresponding refinement steps ensure these implicit fairness assumptions.

2.3 Causality and Time Modeling

Models of causality describe possible relations between the (inter)actions of a component or system. Since those relations describe the unfolding of the communication and behavioral actions over the time, those models always contain some (explicit or implicit) aspect of time. The causality relation should allow for *structural refinement*, i.e., we should be able to replace an abstract component by a network of sub-components often requires augmentation of the causality relation by internal actions of the network. Concerning causality we obtain the following range of this dimension:

Metric Models: These models introduce an explicit labeling of events with (real-valued) time stamps. Non-operational properties like Zeno behavior[1] can arise. Examples for this model are Timed CSP, Timed or Densely-Timed Focus.

Strict Sequentialization: Here, a linear order of events is imposed, making absence of events implicit or explicit. Accordingly, the model excludes causal

---

[1] By Zeno-behavior we characterize those models that do not exclude the occurrence of infinitely many (inter)action in a finite amount of time; see, e.g., [16].

loops and either imposes an interleaving semantics or introduces implicit timing constraints. Examples for this model are trace-based (e.g., asynchronous circuits [9]) or state-based history semantics (TLA [15]).

Unrestricted Causality: Here, no restrictions are imposed on the interaction relation of a system, since an input received by the system can immediately stimulate the production of some output without any delay (*perfect synchrony hypothesis*). This model is used in Esterel [5] or some Statecharts variants [7].

Note that this dimension is ordered with respect to abstraction from timing aspects: from metric models explicitly dealing with real time, via sequentialization abstracting from the passing of time between events, to unrestricted causality abstracting from the introduction of delays. The corresponding refinement steps introduce explicit delays or durations (cf., [17]).

3 Conclusion

The introduced classification scheme supports the analysis of reactive models from a methodical as well as a technical point of view. Such classification is useful when selecting a formalism best suited to capture the aspects of systems for a given application domain. Technically, the classification helps by structuring the choice; methodically, the classification helps by addressing the strengths and weaknesses arising from certain combinations. The independence of these aspects help when 'switching on and off' of certain properties to produce possible formalisms. The ordering within the domains helps to support the relation between different models arranged in a development process.

References

1. Owicki, S., Gries, D.: An Axiomatic Proof Technique for Parallel Programs. Acta Informatica **14** (1976)
2. Hoare, C.A.R.: Communicating Sequential Processes. Prentice-Hall International (1985)
3. Milner, R.: Communication and Concurrency. Series in Computer Science. Prentice Hall (1989)
4. Chandy, K.M., Misra, J.: Parallel Program Design - A Foundation. 2 edn. Addison-Wesley (1989)
5. Berry, G.: The Esterel v5 Language Primer. Technical report, INRIA (2000) `http://www-sop.inria.fr/meije/esterel/esterel-eng.html`; accessed August 19, 2002.
6. Broy, M., Stølen, K.: Specification and Development of Interactive Systems: FOCUS on Streams, Interfaces, and Refinement. Springer (2001) Texts and Monographs in Computer Science.
7. von der Beeck, M.: Comparison of Statecharts Variants. In: Proceedings of FTRTFT94. (1995) LNCS 863.

8. van Glabbeek, R.J.H.: Comparative concurrency semantics and refinement of actions. Technical Report 109, Centrum voor Wiskunden en Informatica (1996) CWI Tracts.
9. Dill, D.L.: Trace Theory for Automatic Hierarchical Verification of Speed Independent Circuits. ACM Distinguished Dissertations. The MIT Press (1989)
10. Alur, R., Henzinger, T.A.: Reactive modules. Formal Methods in System Design: An International Journal **15** (1999) 7–48
11. Schätz, B.: Ein methodischer Übergang von asynchronen zu synchronen Systemen. PhD thesis, Technische Universität München (1998)
12. Bergstra, J.A., Ponse, A., Smolka, S.A.: Handbook of Process Algebra. Elsevier (2001)
13. Lynch, N., Tuttle, M.: An Introduction to Input/Output Automata. CWI Quarterly **2** (1989) 219–246
14. Josephs, M.B.: Receptive process theory. Acta Informatica **29** (1992) 17–31
15. Lamport, L.: Verification and Specification of Concurrent Programs. In Bakker, J., Roever, W.P., G.Rozenberg, eds.: A Decade of Concurrency - Reflexions and Perspectives, Springer Verlag (1993) 347–374 LNCS 803.
16. Shields, M.W.: Semantics of Parallelism. Springer (1997)
17. Scholz, P.: Design of reactive Systgems and their Distributed Implementaion with Statecharts. PhD thesis, Technische Universität München (1998)
18. Parrow, J.: Fairness properties in process algebra with applications in communication protocol verification. PhD thesis, Uppsala University (1985)
19. Davis, J., Schneider, S.: An Introduction to Timed CSP. PRG- 75, PRG Programming Research Group Oxford (1989)
20. Abadi, M., Lamport, L.: An old-fashioned recipe for real time. ACM Transactions on Programming Languages and Systems **16** (1994) 1543–1571

OCL Extended with Temporal Logic

Paul Ziemann and Martin Gogolla

University of Bremen, Department of Computer Science
P.O. Box 330440, D-28334 Bremen, Germany
{ziemann│gogolla}@informatik.uni-bremen.de

Abstract. UML class diagrams have become a standard for modeling the static structure of object-oriented software systems. OCL can be used for formulating additional constraints that can not be expressed with the diagrams. In this paper, we extend OCL with temporal operators to formulate temporal constraints.

1 Introduction

UML class diagrams are popular for modeling the static structure of object-oriented software systems. Syntax and semantics of UML diagrams are semi-formally defined in [8]; OCL, a textual language similar to predicate logic which is used to formulate additional constraints, is also defined there in the same semi-formal way. A formal semantics for UML class diagrams and OCL was given in the current OCL 2.0 OMG submission [2]. OCL expressions used in invariants are evaluated in a single system state. OCL pre- and postconditions characterize operations by considering state transitions, i.e. state pairs.

Temporal logic, as an extension of predicate logic, has been used successfully in the field of software development (see [7] among other approaches). The basic idea of linear temporal logic is to consider not only single states or state pairs, but to care about arbitrary state sequences. By doing so, it is possible to characterize system development by specifying the allowed system state sequences.

In this paper, we present an extension of OCL with important elements of a linear temporal logic. Past and future temporal operators are introduced. Our extended version of OCL, which we call *TOCL* (*Temporal OCL*), allows software engineers to specify constraints on the temporal evolution of a system structure. Since the temporal elements are smoothly integrated in the common OCL syntax, TOCL is easy to use for an engineer familiar with OCL. Another motivation is that several high-level UML/OCL constructs could be reduced to constructs of lower level with additional TOCL constraints. We define the extension by building upon the formal definition of OCL presented in [2]. This paper is a polished version of [10] and a short version of [11].

There is already work to extend OCL with temporal logic in various directions. [9,4] extend OCL with operators of a linear temporal logic. However, the paper does not give a formal foundation of the extension. In [5], the object-based temporal logic BOTL is defined, which is based on the branching temporal logic CTL and a subset of OCL. Inheritance and subtyping are not considered

M. Broy and A.V. Zamulin (Eds.): PSI 2003, LNCS 2890, pp. 351–357, 2003.
© Springer-Verlag Berlin Heidelberg 2003

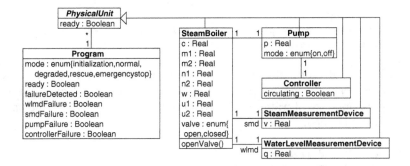

Fig. 1. Object model for the steam-boiler problem

in this approach. [6] presents an OCL extension, equally based on CTL, for specification of state-oriented constraints. This extension concerns system behavior modeled by statechart diagrams; but the development of attributes is not considered there. In [3], OCL is extended with temporal constructs based on the observational mu-calculus. The authors suggest using "templates" with user-friendly syntax which then have to be translated to $\mathcal{O}\mu(\text{OCL})$. However, we think our direct semantics in terms of set theory is useful as well due to its comprehensibility.

2   Basic Idea

To give an idea of the usefulness of a temporal OCL, we demonstrate how parts of the "Steam-boiler control specification problem" [1] can be specified using TOCL. The underlying object model is shown in Fig. 1.

The first invariant states that when a program is in initialization mode, it remains in this mode until all physical units are ready or a failure of the water level measurement device has occurred. We use the temporal operator 'always-until' in this example.

```
context Program inv:
   self.mode = #initialization implies
      always self.mode = #initialization
      until (PhysicalUnit.allInstances->forAll(pu | pu.ready)
            or self.wlmdFailure)
```

In the next invariant we use the 'previous' operator to state that at the beginning of a system run the program has to be in mode 'initialization'.

```
context Program inv:
   previous false implies self.mode = #initialization
```

The following invariant applies the operator 'next' to specify that the mode changes from 'initialization' to 'emergencystop' if a failure of the water level measurement device is detected.

```
context Program inv:
  (self.mode = #initialization and self.wlmdFailure)
  implies next self.mode = #emergencystop
```

When the valve of a steam boiler is open, the water level measured by the water level measurement device (attribute q) will be lower or equal to the normal upper boundary of water level (attribute n2) sometime. Here, the operator 'sometime' is applied.

```
context SteamBoiler inv:
  self.valve=#open implies sometime self.wlmd.q <= n2
```

Of course, TOCL can be used in pre- and postconditions as well. The operation 'openValve()' causes the valve of the steam-boiler to be open until the water level sinks under the normal upper boundary n2. The operator 'always-until' is used in the postcondition.

```
context SteamBoiler::openValve()
  post: always valve = #open until wlmd.q <= n2
```

3   Object Models

In our context, an object model uses all those UML concepts that are essential for modeling structural aspects of a problem domain. An object model can be visualized by a UML class diagram. Instances of an object model (i.e. states of the modeled system) can be visualized by a UML object diagram. Object models are referred to by TOCL constraints and are therefore a prerequisite for the TOCL definition. We adopt the object model definition presented in [2] but extend it with *state sequences*. An *object model*

$$\mathcal{M} = (\text{CLASS}, \text{ATT}_c, \text{OP}_c, \text{ASSOC}, \text{associates}, \text{roles}, \text{multiplicities}, \prec)$$

consists of a set of classes (CLASS) with each class c having attributes (ATT_c) and operations (OP_c) assigned to it. Associations (ASSOC) connect classes with each other. The functions 'associates', 'roles' and 'multiplicities' assign associated classes, role names and multiplicities to associations, respectively. $\prec$ is an irreflexive partial order on the set of classes, representing a generalization hierarchy. An object model specifies the possible states of a system. A *system state*

$$\sigma(\mathcal{M}) = (\sigma_{\text{CLASS}}, \sigma_{\text{ATT}}, \sigma_{\text{ASSOC}}),$$

also called a snapshot of a running system, consists of the existing objects (σ_{CLASS}) with its current attribute values (σ_{ATT}) and links (σ_{ASSOC}) connecting them. We write σ instead of $\sigma(\mathcal{M})$ if the model is clear from the context.

An OCL constraint is evaluated in a single system state. Since TOCL is intended for formulating constraints on the temporal development of a system, a single system state is not sufficient here. We therefore introduce infinite *state sequences* for a model $\mathcal{M}$, denoted as

$$\hat{\sigma}(\mathcal{M}) = \langle \sigma_0, \sigma_1, \ldots \rangle.$$

The order of the states reflects a temporal relationship; that is, the system is in state σ_0 at the beginning, later in state σ_1, and so on. Again, we write $\hat{\sigma}$ instead of $\hat{\sigma}(\mathcal{M})$ if the model is clear from the context. For example, $\sigma_{0\,\text{CLASS}}(c)$ is the set of objects of class c existing in the first state of the sequence. Finite state sequences, which we do not explicitly consider, can be seen as infinite ones with one state that is followed only by empty states, i.e. states without objects.

4   TOCL Types

TOCL is a strongly typed language. We adopt the type system of OCL defined in [2]. Each type t is mapped to its domain by a function I. Each operation on a type t is mapped to a function $I(\hat{\sigma}, i)$, where i is the so called reference index denoting the current state. Therefore, the semantics of an operation can depend on a state sequence and a reference index. However, most operations only depend on the current state or none state at all.

The types of (T)OCL can by divided into several groups. *Integer*, *Real*, *Boolean* and *String* with the expected domains and operations are the basic types. Enumeration types are user-defined; that is, the user specifies the name and a list of possible values for the type. Object types are derived from the object model. There is an object type for each class, having the same name as the corresponding class. The domain of an object type is an infinite set of objects of the class.

Collections of values can be described by the complex types $Set(t)$, $Sequence(t)$, $Bag(t)$, and $Collection(t)$. The parameter t denotes the type of the elements of the set, sequence, or bag (multi-set), respectively. Each type has a special undefined value $\perp$ contained in its domain.

There is a subtype relationship between certain types that is defined by a reflexive partial order $\leq$ on the set of types.

allInstances$_t$: $\rightarrow Set(t)$ and oclIsNew$_t$: $t \rightarrow Boolean$ are two of the operations defined for all object types. In OCL, 'oclIsNew' is only applicable in postconditions. In TOCL, it can be applied in invariants and preconditions as well. The result of 'allInstances$_t$' is the set of objects of type t existing in the current state. This includes instances of child classes of the corresponding class. The operation 'oclIsNew' can be used to check whether an object is new, that is, whether it exists in the current state and not in the preceding. In the first state of a sequence, all existing objects are new. Other operations exist to access attribute values or navigate along links connecting objects. For user-defined operations the user has to provide a OCL expression that specifies the semantics.

5 TOCL Expressions and Constraints

Due to space limitations, we define syntax and semantics of temporal expressions and constraints in this section only informally. The formal definition can be found in [11].

5.1 Temporal Expressions

Syntax and semantics of OCL expressions is defined in [2] by giving six rules each. We do not repeat them here but add further rules for temporal expressions.

Expressions are evaluated in an environment consisting of a state sequence $\hat{\sigma}$, a reference index i denoting the current state, and variable assignment β. The variable assignment influences the evaluation of free variables, the choice of the current state effects the evaluation of object operations like navigation or attribute access. The current state together with the whole state sequence is necessary for the evaluation of temporal expressions.

In the following, we enumerate the temporal expressions and explain their semantics. Let e, e_1 and e_2 be boolean expressions, $a_1, \ldots, a_n$ expressions of types $t_1, \ldots, t_n$, and $\omega : t_1, \ldots, t_n \rightarrow t$ an operation.

'next e' is true if e is true "in the next state"; that is, if e is true with a reference index incremented by one. In all other cases the evaluation results in false. 'always e' is true if e is true in the current state and in all future states of the sequence, otherwise false. An expression 'sometime e' is true if e is true in the current state or in one of the future states. Otherwise it is false. 'always e_1 until e_2' is true if e_1 is true "from now on" until e_2 is true for the first time in future. The expression is also true if e_2 is never true and e_1 is true in all future states. Otherwise it is false. For an expression 'sometime e_1 before e_2' to be true, e_1 just has to be true in at least one future state. One of these has to be before the next future state e_2 is true in (if there is one). When evaluating 'ω@next($a_1, \ldots, a_n$)', the argument expressions are evaluated in the current state but the operation ω is evaluated in the next state. This expressions is also written as '$a_1.\omega$@next($a_2, \ldots, a_n$)'. If a_1 denotes a collection value, an arrow symbol is used instead of the period. Operations such as addition are denoted in infix notation.

The past expressions 'previous e', 'alwaysPast e', 'sometimePast e', 'always e_1 since e_2', 'sometime e_1 since e_2, and the modifier @pre are defined analogously. They behave like the future expressions flipped (with respect to the temporal ordering) across the current state, with the difference that the sequence of past states is bounded by the first state.

5.2 Constraints

A TOCL constraint can either be an invariant or an operation specification. We informally define the slightly modified semantics of invariants. In addition, we give an idea of how the semantics of pre- and postconditions could be defined.

Invariants. An invariant is a condition that must be satisfied in all system states. Let e be a boolean expression with free variables $v_1, \ldots, v_n$. An invariant **context** $v_1 : t_1, \ldots, v_n : t_n$ **inv:** e is *valid in a state sequence* $\hat{\sigma}$ if the following expression is true in the first state:

```
always(
    t₁.allInstances->forAll(v₁:t₁ |
      ...
      tₙ.allInstances->forAll(vₙ:tₙ |
        e
      )...))
```

The expression e is extended to an expression that prepends the 'always' operator and quantifies the declared variables over the set of objects of the respective type existing in the respective state. The fact that an invariant is a condition that must *always* be satisfied is therefore made explicit here. Every OCL invariant is also a TOCL invariant with semantics as expected. If there is no variable declared explicitly but only a type is given as context, the variable 'self' of this type is implicitly declared.

Pre- and Postconditions. Pre- and postconditions are part of operation specifications. They are used to specify conditions to be satisfied before and after the execution of a user-defined operation, respectively.

For an operation specification to be valid in a state sequence, the postcondition must be satisfied in the poststate of all executions of the given operation if the precondition is satisfied in the corresponding prestate. In TOCL, the conditions can either be standard OCL expressions, or boolean past expressions (in preconditions), or boolean future expressions (in postconditions).

To define these semantics formally, a system state would have to hold information about invoked and terminated operations. Then, operation specifications could be reduced to invariants as it is done in [5]. We present this approach in [11].

6 Summary and Conclusions

In this paper we presented TOCL, an extension of OCL with elements of a linear temporal logic. We have started with a description of object models, modeling the static structure of a system. System states have been introduced as snapshots of a running system. Multiple states, which are ordered in time, form state sequences that constitute part of the environment for evaluating TOCL expressions.

We have proceeded with an outline of the TOCL type system. In the central part of the paper, temporal operators have been introduced to combine boolean expressions to new ones. Expressions have been used to form constraints, i.e. invariants and operation specifications (with pre- and postconditions).

There are some issues that are topics of further research. It could be examined to which extent TOCL is capable of describing properties of the various UML diagram types. While TOCL needs a class diagram providing the context, other diagram types (like certain statechart diagrams) could be explained by appropriate TOCL constraints, maybe in part or even completely.

References

1. Jean-Raymond Abrial, Egon Börger, and Hans Langmaack, editors. *Formal Methods for Industrial Applications, Specifying and Programming the Steam Boiler Control (the book grow out of a Dagstuhl Seminar, June 1995)*, volume 1165 of *LNCS*. Springer, 1996.
2. Boldsoft, Rational Software Corporation, and IONA. Response to the UML 2.0 OCL RfP (ad/2000-09-03), June 2002.
   Internet: http://www.klasse.nl/ocl/subm-draft-text.html.
3. Julian C. Bradfield, Juliana Küster Filipe, and Perdita Stevens. Enriching OCL Using Observational Mu-Calculus. In Ralf-Detlef Kutsche and Herbert Weber, editors, *Fundamental Approaches to Software Engineering, 5th International Conference, FASE 2002, held as Part of the Joint European Conferences on Theory and Practice of Software, ETAPS 2002, Grenoble, France, April 8-12, 2002, Proceedings*, volume 2306 of *LNCS*, pages 203–217. Springer, 2002.
4. Stefan Conrad and Klaus Turowski. Temporal OCL: Meeting Specification Demands for Business Components. In Keng Siau and Terry Halpin, editors, *Unified Modeling Language: Systems Analysis, Design and Development Issues*, chapter 10, pages 151–166. Idea Publishing Group, 2001.
5. Dino Distefano, Joost-Pieter Katoen, and Arend Rensink. On a Temporal Logic for Object-Based Systems. In S. F. Smith and C. L. Talcott, editors, *Formal Methods for Open Object-based Distributed Systems*, pages 305–326. Kluwer Academ Publishers, 2000. Report version: TR–CTIT–00–06, Faculty of Informatics, University of Twente.
6. Stephan Flake and Wolfgang Mueller. A UML Profile for Real-Time Constraints with the OCL. In Jean-Marc Jézéquel, Heinrich Hussmann, and Stephan Cook, editors, *UML 2002 - The Unified Modeling Language. Modeling Languages, Concepts, and Tools. 5th International Conference, Dresden, Germany, September/October 2002, Proceedings*, volume 2460 of *LNCS*, pages 179–195. Springer, 2002.
7. Zohar Manna and Amir Pnueli. *The temporal logic of reactive and concurrent systems*. Springer-Verlag New York, Inc., 1992.
8. OMG. *OMG Unified Modeling Language Specification, Version 1.5, March 2003*. Object Management Group, Inc., Framingham, Mass., Internet: http://www.omg.org, 2003.
9. Sita Ramakrishnan and John McGregor. Extending OCL to Support Temporal Operators. In *Proceedings of the 21st International Conference on Software Engineering (ICSE99) Workshop on Testing Distributed Component-Based Systems, LA, May 16-22, 1999*, 1999.
10. Paul Ziemann and Martin Gogolla. An Extension of OCL with Temporal Logic. In Jan Jürjens, Maria Victoria Cengarle, Eduardo B. Fernanez, Bernhard Rumpe, and Robert Sandner, editors, *Critical Systems Development with UML – Proceedings of the UML'02 workshop*, pages 53–62. TUM, Institut für Informatik, September 2002. TUM-I0208.
11. Paul Ziemann and Martin Gogolla. An OCL Extension for Formulating Temporal Constraints. Technical Report 1/03, Universität Bremen, 2003.

The Definition of Transitive Closure with OCL
– Limitations and Applications –

Thomas Baar[*]

Universität Karlsruhe, Fakultät für Informatik
Institut für Logik, Komplexität und Deduktionssysteme
Am Fasanengarten 5, D-76128 Karlsruhe
Fax: +49 721 608 4211,
baar@ira.uka.de

Abstract. The Object Constraint Language (OCL) is based on first-order logic and set theory. As the most well-known application, OCL is used to formulate well-formedness rules in the UML metamodel. Here, the transitive closure of a relationship is defined in terms of an OCL invariant, which seems to contradict classical results on the expressive power of first-order logic.

In this paper, we give sufficient justification for the correctness of the definition of transitive closure. Our investigation reinforces some decisions made in the semantics of UML and OCL. Currently, there is a lively debate on the same issues in the semantics of the upcoming UML 2.0.

1 Introduction

The Object Constraint Language (OCL) is a textual language to annotate UML diagrams (see [5] for a detailed introduction to syntax and application of OCL). For the purpose of this paper we restrict ourselves to invariant expressions in OCL.

The semantics of a UML class diagram is defined formally by the set of admissible object diagrams, where classes, attributes, associations are realized by sets of objects, slots, links [3,4]. Sometimes, an object diagram is called a *state* or *state configuration*.

The semantics of OCL constraints is given in [4] by a formally defined evaluation function which maps, in a given state, any OCL constraint to one of the logical constants true, false, undefined. [1] In admissible states all invariants of the corresponding class diagram must be evaluated to true. Certain restrictions on OCL's syntax ensure that the evaluation of each OCL expression must terminate.

Since every object diagram is admissible unless an invariant is evaluated to false or undefined, OCL has a *loose semantics*. A loose semantics is natural in

---

[*] This work was support by Deutsche Forschungsgemeinschaft (DFG), project Integrierter Deduktiver Softwareentwurf, project number Schm 987/6-3.

[1] The semantics [4] by Richters was adopted by the official language specification, cmp. [3, Chap. 6].

M. Broy and A.V. Zamulin (Eds.): PSI 2003, LNCS 2890, pp. 358–365, 2003.
© Springer-Verlag Berlin Heidelberg 2003

the sense that the classical first-order logic (FOL) is semantically defined in the same way. There are several possibilities for translations of OCL constraints into first-order formulas (see Section 2). Classes in UML class diagrams are typically mapped to types, OCL variables, such as `self`, are mapped to variables with restricted quantification, attributes are mapped to function symbols, etc.

At a first glance, the translation into FOL allows to lift up classical results from FOL to OCL. For example, the logical entailment relation on OCL constraints seems to be semi-decidable, since we can translate invariants into FOL formulas (GÖDEL's Completeness Theorem, 1930). This argumentation ignores a side-condition of UML semantics stipulating object diagrams to contain only finitely many objects. Thus, the translation of invariants into FOL formulas is only correct if the semantics of FOL formulas is restricted to finite models.[2] This makes deduction on OCL invariants more difficult since GÖDEL's Completeness Theorem is not valid on finite models. Moreover, a sound and complete calculus does not exist (TRACHTENBROT, 1950).

Other results from classical logic can certainly be lifted to OCL, e.g. the transitive closure of a binary relation cannot be formalized using FOL regardless of a restriction to finite models.[3]

The metamodel of UML as part of the official language description [3] describes the abstract syntax of UML diagrams in terms of a class diagram and OCL well-formedness rules. Class diagrams are basically defined as graphs, where classes are represented as nodes and associations/generalizations are represented as edges. In order to describe the type system of UML, a class 'has to know' all its superclasses, i.e. the transitive closure of its direct superclasses. In the metamodel, the set of all superclasses is defined using an OCL invariant, which at a first glance contradicts the classical result on the undefinability of transitive closure by FOL formulas. Even so, it is often discussed in the OCL community to substitute, within the metamodel, that definition of transitive closure by informal text, because for 'theoretical reasons' or so we are told.

In this paper, we prove the invariant defining the set of all supertypes to be fully correct. We try to clarify common misunderstandings of classical results by presenting countermodels for apparent FOL definitions of transitive closure. We also discuss the reason why the countermodels do not apply to the definition of all supertypes in the metamodel.

The paper is organized as follows: Section 2 presents the relevant part of the UML metamodel. It also gives a translation into FOL formulas, which provides a more abstract view on the problem. Section 3 enlists countermodels for 'FOL definitions of transitive closure' together with theorems to avoid countermodels. Finally, we draw a conclusion in Section 4.

---

[2] Throughout the paper, we use the term *model* with the meaning it has in classical logic. A *UML model* is in our terminology just a concrete class diagram.

[3] An alternative formulation, of the same result, is the inability of FOL formulas to axiomatize connected, ordered graphs. For finite models, this can be proven using EHRENFEUCHT-FRAÏSSÉ games (see [2] for a detailed account). If infinite models are allowed, this is a consequence of the Compactness Theorem.

2   Transitive Closure in the UML Metamodel

The UML metamodel has proved to be a very intuitive, concise and precise way to describe the syntax of UML diagrams. Thus, the metamodel has the same purpose as an EBNF grammar for formal languages. Also the vocabulary we use in EBNF grammars and in the metamodel are similar syntactical terms, e.g., a grammar for JAVA contains nonterminals like *Assignment*, *Statement*, *Block*, where in the metamodel similar syntactical terms, such as *Class*, *Classifier*, *Association* are realized as metaclasses.

Fig. 1 presents a very small part of the metamodel (cmp. [3, p. 2-14]) and can be read as follows. A *class* in a UML diagram is a special kind of a *classifier* what in turn is a special kind of a *generalizable element*. Each generalizable element can be linked to unspecified many generalizations which in turn are linked to exactly two generalizable elements called child and parent.[4]

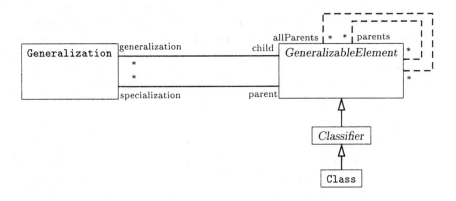

Fig. 1. Part of the UML metamodel, package Core

The dashed associations in Fig. 1 are defined in the metamodel by auxiliary definitions (cmp. [3, p. 2-61]):

```
context GeneralizableElement
    def: parents: Set(GeneralizableElement) =
        self.generalization->collect(gen| gen.parent)

    def: allParents: Set(GeneralizableElement) = self.parents->
        union(self.parents->collect(ge| ge.allParents))
```

Informally speaking, self.parents denotes the set of all direct supertypes and self.allParents denotes the transitive closure of direct supertypes.

It is easy to read the last invariant accordingly to the formal semantics of OCL given in [4] as a mathematical expression (a full translation of OCL and

---

[4] In class diagrams, generalizations are symbolized by generalization arrows from the subclass (child) to the superclass (parent).

UML into FOL can be found in [1]). Let x, y, z be variables for generalizable elements, $Par(x)$ the translation of x.parents, and $APar(x)$ the translation of x.allParents. Then, the OCL definition of allParents can be written as (we substitute the OCL variable self by x, which is a more common variable name in mathematics):

$$APar(x) = Par(x) \cup \{y \mid \exists z \; z \in Par(x) \wedge y \in APar(z)\}$$

This can be further transformed into pure FOL where Par, $APar$ are substituted by two new relation symbols r and r^* with $r(x, y) \leftrightarrow y \in Par(x)$ and $r^*(x, y) \leftrightarrow y \in APar(x)$:

$$r^*(x, y) \leftrightarrow r(x, y) \vee (\exists z \; r(x, z) \wedge r^*(z, y)) \tag{DEF}$$

3   Definition of Transitive Closure and Countermodels

Formula (DEF) is a FOL version of the attempt to define the transitive closure with OCL. Now, we can analyse (DEF) and can construct countermodels where the interpretation of r^* is not the transitive closure of the interpretation of r. Although our argumentation is based on the FOL formula (DEF) it clearly applies to the original OCL formalization as well. Every countermodel of (DEF) can easily be transformed into a non-intended object diagram. Countermodels are presented using the following notation.

NOTATION 1
The formula (DEF) is always interpreted by the structure (U, R, R^*) where U is the universe and the relations R, R^* are interpretations of the relation symbols r, r^*, respectively. We are only interested in models of (DEF). Thus, we always have $R \subseteq R^*$. Elements of U are denoted by a, b, c, possibly decorated with subscripts. A pair (a, b) being an element of a relation S is often denoted as aSb instead of the mathematical notation $(a, b) \in S$.
     There is also a graphical notation for structure (U, R, R^*). The elements of U are displayed as labelled nodes, the elements of R by solid arcs. The elements of R^* not belonging to R are displayed by dashed arcs.
     The transitive closure of a relation S is denoted as $TC(S)$ and defined as usual. Please note, that $TC(S)$ is transitive for any S.
     $TC(S) = \{(a, b) \mid \exists a_1 \dots a_n \; a = a_1 \wedge b = a_n \wedge a_i S a_{i+1} \; for \; i = 1, \dots, n - 1\}$

     The next example presents a model of (DEF) but $R^* \neq TC(R)$. Thus, the formula (DEF) is not a FOL formalization of transitive closure.
EXAMPLE 1 (REFLEXIVE COUNTERMODEL FOR (DEF))

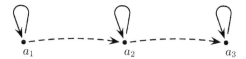

$$a_1 \qquad\qquad a_2 \qquad\qquad a_3$$

Obviously, the relation R^* cannot be the same as $TC(R)$ since R^* is not transitive (the pair (a_1, a_3) is missing).

In the countermodel of Example 3, the relation R^* does not coincide with $TC(R)$ but R^* comprises $TC(R)$. It might arise the question whether this is true in every case. The next Theorem 1 gives an answer and characterizes all models of (DEF) in this respect.

THEOREM 1 (R^* COMPRISES TRANSITIVE CLOSURE)
Let (U, R, R^*) be a model of (DEF). Then,
$$TC(R) \subseteq R^*$$

So far, we have investigated the model of (DEF) without making any assumptions on the interpretation of r. Surely, the formula (DEF) can be fixed in a way that would prevent the countermodel given in Example 3. One attempt could be:
$$r^*(x, y) \leftrightarrow r(x, y) \vee (\exists z\ x \neq z \wedge r(x, z) \wedge r^*(z, y)) \qquad \text{(DEF')}$$

However, from the classical results cited in the introduction, we can conclude the existence of countermodels for any such 'improved formulas'. In the case of (DEF'), cycles of length two are possible in r, which allows as a countermodel for (DEF'):

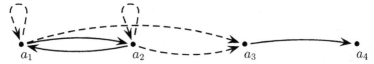

Apparently, this is a hopeless situation, but we should not give up too early. The situation becomes much more comfortable, if we can restrict the interpretation of r appropriately. Suppose, the following axiom is given as an additional information on r:

$$\exists x_1 x_2\ \forall x\ (x = x_1 \vee x = x_2) \wedge \forall yz\ (r(y, z) \leftrightarrow y = x_1 \wedge z = x_2) \qquad \text{(FIXR)}$$

If (FIXR) is valid, the formula (DEF) is a correct definition of transitive closure because in all models of (FIXR, DEF) we have obviously $R = TC(R) = R^*$. Doubtless, the axiom (FIXR) is a very strong restriction on R, but it illustrates the main principle of winning expressiveness by sacrificing universality.

The next Theorem 2 exploits the very same idea and makes two sufficient assumptions explicit. If the models are restricted to be finite and the transitive closure of R does not have any cycles, then (DEF) is a correct definition of the transitive closure. Note, that this assumption on R is a real restriction. For instance, any relation R containing a reflexive pair (a, a) would be not allowed as an interpretation of r.

THEOREM 2 (SOUNDNESS FOR FINITE MODELS, NON-CYCLIC RELATIONS)
Let (U, R, R^*) be a finite model of both (DEF) and axiom (NONCYC):

$$\neg r^*(x, x) \qquad \text{(NONCYC)}$$

Then,
$$TC(R) = R^*$$

Please note, that the finiteness of the model is an essential assumption. If infinite models are allowed, there is a countermodel for (DEF) and (NONCYC) as the next example shows.

EXAMPLE 1 (COUNTER MODEL ON INFINITE UNIVERSE)

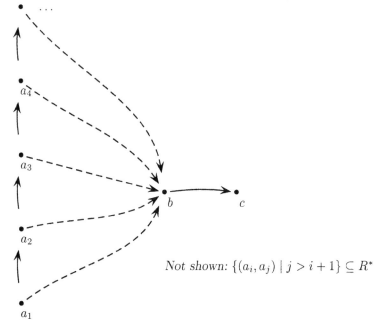

Not shown: $\{(a_i, a_j) \mid j > i + 1\} \subseteq R^*$

In the counter model, an infinite sequence of elements $a_1, a_2, a_3, \ldots$ is assumed where $a_i R a_{i+1}$ for all $i = 1, 2, \ldots$ The relation R^* is not transitive (all pairs (a_i, c) are missing) but have all properties expressed in axioms (DEF) and (NONCYC). The Theorem 2 justifies to call (DEF) a correct axiomatization for transitive closure presuming the two preconditions to be valid. Fortunately, the two preconditions are satisfied for the definition of `allParents` *in the UML metamodel.*

COROLLAR 1 (CORRECT DEFINITION OF `allParents`)
For any object of class `GeneralizableElement` the evaluation of the OCL expression `self.allParents` is always the transitive closure of `self.parents` in any admissible object diagrams for the UML metamodel.

Proof:

We only have to prove that the preconditions of Theorem 2 are satisfied. Clearly, the object diagrams are always finite since the semantics of UML restricts the interpretation of classes to finite sets of objects.

The justification of (NONCYC) has not been mentioned so far, but (NONCYC) is intended for the supertype relationship. Thus, there is a corresponding OCL invariant in the UML metamodel (cmp. [3, p. 2-61]):

context GeneralizableElement
    not self.allParents->includes(self)

4 Conclusion

In this paper we have elaborated a problem which has already caused a lot of confusion and discussions within the OCL community.

Starting with the definition of allParents *in the UML metamodel we investigated a given formalization of the transitive closure. By translation of invariants into first-order logic, the problem was reduced to the axiomatization of transitive closure in first-order logic.*

The classical results were cited. Since software engineers often tend to misunderstand the classical results, we have presented in detail countermodels of the apparent formalization (DEF). We have proven essential properties of all models of (DEF) and pointed out additional preconditions which are sufficient to call (DEF) a correct formalization of the transitive closure. Fortunately, due to the semantics of UML and the OCL invariants given as well-formedness rules in the metamodel, these preconditions are satisfied for our motivating example, the definition of allParents *in the metamodel.*

Our investigation allows also a judgement on the semantics of UML and OCL. As said in the introduction, the restriction to interpret the classes of class diagrams only by finite sets of objects makes things more complicated from the viewpoint of deduction. On the other hand, this decision is an essential precondition to prove the allParents *definition being correct.*

Finally, our investigation has presented a meaningful recursive definition in OCL (note, the definition of allParents *is recursive). This is worth to mention because OCL has currently a simple loose semantics but there is a discussion to substitute the loose semantics by a more complicated fixpoint semantics. At least for the definition of* allParents*, this is absolutely unnecessary.*

Acknowledgement. *I would like to thank Peter H. Schmitt for critical comments on the topic of this paper.*

References

1. B. Beckert, U. Keller, and P. H. Schmitt. *Translating the Object Constraint Language into first-order predicate logic. In* Proceedings, VERIFY, Workshop at Federated Logic Conferences (FLoC), Copenhagen, Denmark, *2002.*
2. H.-D. Ebbinghaus and J. Flum. Finite Model Theory. *Springer, 1995.*
3. OMG. *OMG Unified Modeling Language Specification. Technical Report OMG-UML Version 1.4, Object Mangagement Group, September 2001.*
4. M. Richters. A precise approach to validating UML models and OCL constraints. *PhD thesis, Bremer Institut für Sichere Systeme, Universität Bremen, Logos-Verlag, Berlin, 2001.*
5. J. Warmer and A. Kleppe. The Object Constraint Language: Precise Modeling with UML. *Addison-Wesley, 1998.*

A   Proofs of Theorems

THEOREM 3 (R^* COMPRISES TRANSITIVE CLOSURE)
Let (U, R, R^*) be a model of (DEF). Then,

$$TC(R) \subseteq R^*$$

Proof:

> Indirectly: Let (a, b) be a pair with $(a, b) \in TC(R)$ and $\neg aR^*b$.
> By definition of TC there is n, and there are $a = a_0, a_1, \ldots, a_n = b$
> such that $a_i R a_{i+1}$. By applying (DEF) repeatly we get aR^*a_i for all
> $i = 0, \ldots, n$ contradicting the assumption.

THEOREM 4 (SOUNDNESS FOR FINITE MODELS, NON-CYCLIC RELATIONS)
Let (U, R, R^*) be a finite model of both (DEF) and axiom (NONCYC):

$$\neg r^*(x, x) \qquad \text{(NONCYC)}$$

Then, $$TC(R) = R^*$$

Proof:

> By Theorem 1 we know $TC(R) \subseteq R^*$. It remains to show $R^* \subseteq TC(R)$.
> Indirectly. Assume, there is a pair (a_1, b) with

$$a_1 R^* b \qquad (1)$$

> and

$$(a_1, b) \notin TC(R) \qquad (2)$$

By (2) we know $(a_1, b) \notin R$ and can conclude from (1), (DEF) that there
is a_2 with

$$a_1 R a_2 \wedge a_2 R^* b \qquad (3)$$

and furthermore by (2)

$$(a_2, b) \notin TC(R) \qquad (4)$$

These arguments can be iterated and there are $a_3, a_4, a_5, \ldots$ with

$$a_i R a_{i+1} \wedge a_{i+1} R^* b \wedge (a_{i+1}, b) \notin TC(R) \text{ for } i = 2, 3, 4, \ldots \qquad (5)$$

Since we have assumed U to be finite, there are a_j, a_k with $j < k \leq \|U\| + 1$ and $a_j = a_k$. However, by (5) and (DEF) we can conclude $a_j R^* a_j$ contradicting axiom (NONCYC).

Improving the Consistency Checking Process by Reusing Formal Verification Knowledge*

Rebeca P. Díaz Redondo, José J. Pazos Arias, Ana Fernández Vilas,
Jorge García Duque, and Alberto Gil Solla

Departamento de Enxeñería Telemática. Universidade de Vigo.
36200, Vigo. Spain. Fax number: 34 986 812116
{rebeca, jose, avilas, jgd, agil}@det.uvigo.es

Abstract. At an iterative and incremental requirements capture stage, each iteration implies identifying new requirements, checking their with the current functional specification of the system, and, in many cases, modifying this global specification to satisfy them. In a totally formalized environment, these verifications are usually done applying a model checking algorithm which entails the well-known efficiency problems to check medium-large and large systems. In order to reduce the amount of verifications and, consequently these efficiency problems, we propose reusing previously obtained formal verification results. The ARIFS methodology (*Approximate Retrieval of Incomplete and Formal Specifications*) supports the classification and the efficient retrieval (without formal proofs) of the verification information stored in the repository and, in this paper, we show how to carry out this proposal by using an application example.

1 Introduction

Building large and complex systems, like distributed ones, increases the difficulty of specifying requirements at the beginning of the software process since: (a) these requirements continuously evolve throughout the life-cycle and (b) at early phases, the designer usually has not a deep knowledge about the system. The use of incremental development techniques makes life-cycle models flexible enough to follow these inevitable and often continuous changes. Finally, combining this tendency and the use of formal methods, whose advantages are well-known, it is possible to obtain a totally formalized software process approach which is both iterative and incremental.

Including software reuse in this kind of life-cycles can increase the efficiency of the development process of large and complex systems, specially if software reuse is tackled at early stages of the development process — like at the requirements specification stage. This last practice is widely accepted as a desirable aim, because of the possibility of increasing the reuse benefits [7]. However, there is little evidence in the literature to suggest that software reuse at requirements specification stage is widely practiced.

---

* Partially supported by PGIDT01PX132203PR project (Xunta de Galicia)

M. Broy and A.V. Zamulin (Eds.): PSI 2003, LNCS 2890, pp. 366–380, 2003.

The ARIFS methodology deals with these concerns supporting: (a) the reuse of incomplete specifications — obtained from transient phases of a totally formalized, iterative and incremental requirements specification process — with the aim of saving specification, synthesis and formal verification efforts [3] —; and (b) the reuse of formal verification results to reduce the great computing resources needed to check the consistency of medium-large and large requirements specifications [4]. In this paper, we focus on the last goal and we show how to reuse formal verification information to improve the consistency checking process by using an application example. This proposal entails a big reduction of the formal verification necessities, because we are able to reduce the number of executions of the verification algorithm and/or to reduce the amount of states of the model where the consistency checking is needed. In fact, the application example included in this paper shows these two possibilities.

This paper is organized as follows: the next section summarizes the most remarkable existing works about retrieving reusable components and about improvements in model checking techniques; Section 3 outlines the software development process where the ARIFS methodology is included; Section 4 describes the functional relationship among reusable components which allows managing the repository; in Section 5 we explain how the reuse process is tackled out; in Section 6 the application example is outlined; and, finally, a brief evaluation of the approach and future work are exposed in Section 7.

2   Related Work

Organizing large collections of reusable components is one of the main lacks in software reuse, because providing efficient and effective mechanisms to classify and retrieve software elements from a repository is not an easy problem. Retrieving mechanisms usually rely on the same idea: establishing a *profile* or a set of component's characterizing attributes which is used to classify and retrieve them from a repository. Whenever this profile is based on formal specifications, problems derived from natural language are avoided. The typical *specification matching* process, which offers an exact retrieval, starts expressing the relation between two components by using a logical formula. Then, a theorem prover checks its validity, and only if the prover succeeds, the component is considered to be suitable. The vast number of proofs makes a practical implementation very hard, so in many approaches this number is usually reduced by applying other techniques like: (a) in the proposal of Zaremski and Wing [13], formal proofs are restricted to a small subset of the repository, which is previously selected by using preconditions and postconditions; (b) in REBOUND (RE*use* B*ased* O*n* UND*erstanding*) tool [10] formal proofs are reduced by applying different heuristics, based on the semantic of specifications; (c) NORA/NAMMR tool [11] is basically a *filter pipeline* trying to ensure a *plug-in compatibility*, where there are used *signature matching filters*, *rejection filters* (based on model checking techniques), and, finally, *confirmation filters* (based on Setheo theorem prover, which does not support recursive specifications management).

To sum up, current research lines focus on reusing components at latest stages of the development process, like code, and on using formal descriptions to allow an exact retrieval by applying formal proofs. On the contrary, the ARIFS methodology supports reusing formal components at the requirements specification stage, an early one, and avoiding formal proofs in the retrieval process, that is, providing an approximate retrieval based precisely in the incompleteness of the intermediate models.

On the other hand, model checking is inherently vulnerable to the rather practical problem that the number of states may exceed the amount of computer memory available, which is known as the *state-space explosion problem*. Several effective methods have been developed to solve this problem, although the majority of them try to reduce the state-space: (a) by a symbolic representation of state spaces using BBDs (*Binary Decision Diagrams*) [2]; (b) by partial-order reductions [6] which exploits the fact that for checking many properties it is not necessary to consider all possible ways in which a state space can be traversed; (c) by using equivalence and pre-order relations [8], which transforms models into equivalent, but smaller models that satisfy the same properties; and (d) by a compositional verification, that is, decomposing properties in sub-properties such that each sub-property can be checked for a part of the state space, and the combination of the sub-properties implies the required global property.

Our proposal supplements the previous ones and it also try to reduce the computational necessities of model checking. The underlying idea is reusing formal verification results of the same property in other *functionally similar* incomplete models to the given one. Although in [5] less formalized results (simulation tests) are reused over code components (algorithms), we have not found other proposals sharing our idea of reusing formal verification information at early stages, which increases the reuse benefits.

3   Context

In this section, we briefly describe the first phase of the software development process, SCTL-MUS methodology [9], where the reusing environment is going to be included. The main aim of this phase (*Initial goals*) is achieving a complete and consistent functional specification of the system from user's specification (Fig.1(a)).

In this methodology, functional requirements are specified by using the many-valued logic SCTL [9] (*Simple Causal Temporal Logic*). An SCTL requirement follows the syntax: **Premise** $\Rightarrow \otimes$ **Consequence**, which establishes a causing condition (premise); a temporal operator determining the applicability of the cause ($\Rightarrow \otimes \in \{\Rightarrow, \Rightarrow\odot, \Rightarrow\bigcirc\}$ — referred to as *simultaneously, previously* and *next*—); and a condition which is the effect (consequence). Apart from causation, SCTL adds the concept of *unspecification* which is specially useful to deal with both incomplete and inconsistent information obtained by requirements capture. Although events will be *true* or *false* at the final stage, at intermediate phases of the specification process it is possible that users do not have enough information about them yet, so these events are *unspecified* in these phases. Therefore, it is possible specifying three different values: possible or *true* (1), impossible or *false* (0) and *unspecified* ($\frac{1}{2}$), which is the default value. SCTL requirements are

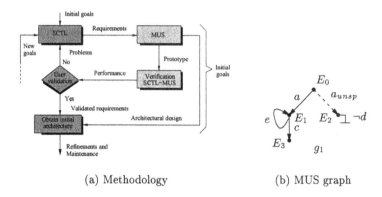

(a) Methodology   (b) MUS graph

Fig. 1. SCTL-MUS Methodology

automatically synthesized to obtain a model or prototype of the system by using MUS [9] (*Model of Unspecified States*), which allows feedback with users. MUS graphs are based on typical labeled-transitions systems, but including another facility: unspecification of its elements. This unspecification is reflected in both events and states of the graph and it is a consequence of the third value of the SCTL logic. Therefore, an event in a state of a MUS graph can be specified to be possible, to be impossible or, in its absence, to be unspecified. Consequently, a state where every single event is unspecified, is called an *unspecified state*. A state where it is not specified any evolution of the model is called a *final state*, consequently, both unspecified states and states where only false events have been specified are final states of a MUS graph. An example of these MUS graphs is shown in Fig. 1(b), where the model g_1 can evolve from one state into another when an event or an action of $\Lambda = \{a, b, c, d, e\}$ occurs or through the special event a_{unsp}. This special event is used whenever the user need to specify a transition, but he does not have enough information about which event is going to enable it. In the initial state of the graph 1(b), E_0, event a is specified as a possible one, that is, system g_1 evolves from this state into state E_1 whenever event a occurs. System g_1 evolves from E_0 into state E_2 through an event which has not been specified yet (a_{unsp}). Since a_{unsp} is not a real event, in subsequent iterations of the requirements capture process, it will evolve to one event of Λ, with the exception of event a, because MUS graphs are deterministic ones. In state E_2 (a final state), event d is an impossible one, which is denoted by $\neg d$, and, finally, state E_3 is a totally unspecified (and a final) state because every event in Λ has not been specified in this state nor as a possible event neither an impossible one[1].

---

[1] Because of simplicity reasons, unspecified events of a state are not represented, only a_{unsp} of E_0 because it implies an evolution of the model.

After the user identifies and specifies a set of new functional requirements which lead to a growth in the system functionality, it is necessary to check the consistency of the current model, that is: if the model already satisfies the new requirements; if it is not able to provide these functional requirements nor in the current iteration neither in future ones (inconsistency); or, if the system does not satisfy the requirements, but it is able to do it (incompleteness). This formal verification is made by using a model checking algorithm which provides different levels of satisfaction of an SCTL requirement in a MUS model. These levels of satisfaction are based on causal propositions: *"an SCTL requirement is satisfied iff its premise is satisfied and its consequence is satisfied according to its temporal operator"*.

As SCTL-MUS methodology adds unspecification concept, the level of satisfaction may not be *false* (nor *true*), just as the boolean logic, in fact, it must have a level of satisfaction related to its unspecification (totally or partially unspecified on the MUS model). Consequently, this methodology defines six levels of satisfaction ($\Phi = \{0, \frac{1}{4}, \frac{1}{2}, \widehat{\frac{1}{2}}, \frac{3}{4}, 1\}$), which are explained in detail in AppendixA (taken from [3]).

4   Classification of Reusable Components in ARIFS

The ARIFS methodology enables classification, retrieval and adaptation of reusable components at the requirements specification phase of the SCTL-MUS methodology. These reusable components gather: (a) its functional specification, which is expressed by a set of SCTL requirements and modeled by the temporal evolution MUS graph; (b) verification information (Section 5) and (c) an interface or *profile* information, which is automatically obtained from its functional characteristics. These profiles allow classifying the reusable components according to their functional characteristics, that is, the underlying idea behind our classification mechanism is that the closer two reusable components are classified in the repository, the more functional similarities they have. Therefore, retrieval criteria must also be based on the functional similarities between reusable components and the query. In order to assess these similarities, we have defined four criteria [3] to distinguish between semantic similarities and structural ones.

The most suitable criterion to reuse verification information is given by the **complete and non finite traces** function, denoted by TC^∞. This function associates with every MUS graph $g \in \mathbb{G}$ a set $TC^\infty(g)$, which is part of the interface or *profile* information of the component whose MUS graph is g. This function is based on the traditional complete trace semantics [12] (obtaining sequences of events linked to every single evolution path of the model), being the main differences that (a) we also take into account both *false* events in order to differentiate them from *unspecified* ones, and (b) non finite evolution paths (unbounded traces and non-terminating traces) of the graph are also reflected in $TC^\infty(g)$.

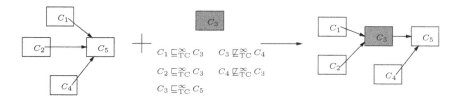

$$TC^\infty(g) = (b\neg d, ac, a(e)+, aec, a(e) + c)$$

For example, figure above shows the result of applying this function to a MUS graph g. In this example, g has five different evolution paths: it can evolve from initial state to a final one where event d is impossible through event b; from initial state to a final one through events a and c; from initial state to a final one through event a, an undetermined number of events e (a non finite evolution path) and, finally, event c; from initial state to a final one through events a, e and c (although trace aec is included in $a(e) + c$, both of them are explicitly included in $TC^\infty(g)$ because of efficient reasons in collating tasks); and from initial state through event a and an infinite number of events e (a non finite evolution path). [2]

For TC^∞, the equivalence relation $=_{TC}^\infty \in \mathbb{G} \times \mathbb{G}$ is given by $g =_{TC}^\infty g' \Leftrightarrow TC^\infty(g) = TC^\infty(g')$, and the preorder $\sqsubseteq_{TC}^\infty \in \mathbb{G} \times \mathbb{G}$ by $g \sqsubseteq_{TC}^\infty g' \Leftrightarrow TC^\infty(g) \sqsubseteq TC^\infty(g')$, that is, $\sqsubseteq_{TC}^\infty$ provides a partial order between equivalence classes or graph sets indistinguishable using TC^∞-observations, so $(\mathbb{G}, \sqsubseteq_{TC}^\infty)$ is a *partially ordered set*, or *poset*. Two graphs g and g' are TC^∞-related iff $g \sqsubseteq_{TC}^\infty g'$ or $g' \sqsubseteq_{TC}^\infty g$. A subset $G_1 \in \mathbb{G}$ is called a *chain* if every two graphs in G_1 are TC^∞-related.

$$C_1 \sqsubseteq_{TC}^\infty C_3 \qquad C_3 \not\sqsubseteq_{TC}^\infty C_4$$
$$C_2 \sqsubseteq_{TC}^\infty C_3 \qquad C_4 \not\sqsubseteq_{TC}^\infty C_3$$
$$C_3 \sqsubseteq_{TC}^\infty C_5$$

Fig. 2. Example of classification in ARIFS

$TC^\infty(g)$ is used to classify reusable components (C) in the lattice after finding its *correct place*, like Fig. 2 shows. That is, it is necessary looking for those components TC^∞-related to C such as C is TC^∞-included on them, and those components TC^∞-related to C such as they are TC^∞-included on C. [3]

5   What and How Is Verification Information Reused?

After running the model checking algorithm, we achieve a set of levels of satisfaction of a SCTL property R in every single state of a MUS graph g. This

---

[2] ( )+ denotes the set of events inside the parenthesis can be repeated an undetermined number of times.

[3] C and C' are TC^∞-related ($C \sqsubseteq_{TC}^\infty C'$ or $C' \sqsubseteq_{TC}^\infty C$) iff their MUS graphs g and g' are also TC^∞-related.

information may be useful to future verifications of the same property — or a subset of it — over the same graph — or over a graph functionally close to it. However and depending on the size of the graph, the management of this amount of information may be difficult, so we also need to store it under a more manageable form. Therefore, we have defined four verification results which summarize this information:

- $\exists \, \Diamond R$ expresses that "*some trace of the system satisfies eventually R*" and its level of satisfaction is denoted by $\models (\exists \, \Diamond R, g)$.
- $\exists \, \Box R$ expresses that "*some trace of the system satisfies invariantly R*" and its level of satisfaction is denoted by $\models (\exists \, \Box R, g)$.
- $\forall \, \Diamond R$ expresses that "*every trace of the system satisfies eventually R*" and its level of satisfaction is denoted by $\models (\forall \, \Diamond R, g)$.
- $\forall \, \Box R$ expresses that "*every trace of the system satisfies invariantly R*" and its level of satisfaction is denoted by $\models (\forall \, \Box R, g)$.

To sum up, the level of satisfaction of R in g, denoted by $\models (R, g)$, is made up of these four results: $\models (R, g) = (\models (\exists \, \Diamond R, g), \models (\forall \, \Diamond R, g), \models (\exists \, \Box R, g), \models (\forall \, \Box R, g))$

The defined classification scheme (Section 4) implies that a component is stored *between* reusable components whose functionalities contain or are contained by it. For instance in Fig. 2, C_1 and C_2 are *functional parts* of C_3, being this one a *functional part* of C_5. In this situation, if we know the level of satisfaction of a property R in C_1 and/or in C_2 and/or in C_5, what is the level of satisfaction of R in C_3? The answer of this question is stored in the **deduction tables** (see Appendix B, taken from [4]) and these results have been obtained after studying how to reuse verification results between two MUS graphs holding a TC^∞-relationship.

Whenever we need to check if an incomplete model g satisfies a property R, we proceed as follows: (1) retrieving the closest components to g whose verification results give information about R; and (2) using the deduction tables to be able to obtain $\models (R, g)$. If the available information is not enough, it is necessary to run the model checking algorithm, but this execution can be reduced depending on the recovered verification information. In fact, it is very probable that we only need to check some states of the graph and so we avoid the exhaustive analysis.

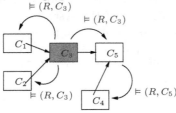

On the other hand, whenever we have new verification information of an incomplete model, we spread out this data across the lattice to improve the learning process of the repository. This expansion is done off-line, so it does not affect the efficiency of the reusing environment, for instance, figure above shows as the verification information linked to C_1, C_2, C_4 and C_5 is updated after C_3 is stored in the repository.

Table 1. MUS graphs of several reusable components of the repository

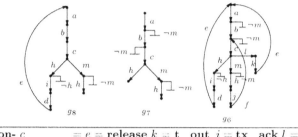

a	=	con-nect	c		=	e	=	release	k	=	t_out	i	=	tx_ack	l	=	loss
					tx_msg												
b	=	con-firm	d		=	f		=	h		=	j				m	=	error
					rx_ack			rx_nack			rx_msg			tx_nack			

6   Applying the Methodology: An Application Example

In this section we apply the described methodology to reduce formal verification tasks at the requirements specification stage of the system modeling a **stop-and-wait** communication protocol, where data traffic is simplex and only data frames may be damaged, but it cannot be completely lost. To sum up, the connection is stablished whenever the sender receives a **confirm** frame after having sent a **connect** frame. After that, the sender fetchs a data frame (event **tx_msg**) and it must wait until an acknowledgment (**ack**) frame arrives before looping back and fetching the next packet. If the sender receives an nacknowledgment (**nack**) frame, it sends the frame again, and this process would be repeated until the frame finally arrived intact. After the sender has transmitted all the data frames, the sender ends the connection transmitting the **release** frame.

We assume that the functionality of our communication protocol is being specified, and the MUS model of the system — which is in an intermediate iteration of the requirements specification phase — is shown in Fig. 3a. At this intermediate stage of the requirements capture process, we need to know if the incomplete model, g, verifies the properties $R_1 \equiv$ (connect $\Rightarrow\bigcirc$ confirm) and $R_2 \equiv$ (rx_msg $\Rightarrow$ error).

Verification of R_1. Property $R_1 \equiv$ (connect $\Rightarrow\bigcirc$ confirm) expresses the following condition: *"just after a connection request occurs, an acceptation of this connection may occurs"*. Hence, we need this property is satisfied by every single possible evolution path of the system, that is, it is a *safety property* [1].

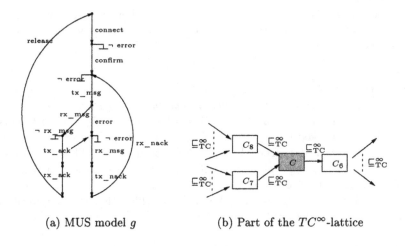

(a) MUS model g (b) Part of the TC^∞-lattice

Fig. 3. MUS model and its correct position in the TC^∞-lattice

We retrieve from our repository (obviously, it is impossible to detail each reusable component here) the closest reusable components to g storing verification information about R_1. We have obtained $\{C_6, C_7, C_8\}$ (Fig.3(b)), whose MUS graphs are shown in Table 1 — where real names of every single event had been replaced by a letter to make it more legible—. Their verification results are as follows: $\vDash (R_1, g_8) = \{1, 1, \frac{1}{2}, \frac{1}{2}\}$, $\vDash (R_1, g_7) = \{1, 1, \frac{1}{2}, \frac{1}{2}\}$ and $\vDash (R_1, g_6) = \{1, 1, \frac{1}{2}, \frac{1}{2}\}$.

Besides that, we know that $\vDash (R_1, E_0|_{g_8}) = 1$ and $\vDash (R_1, E_0|_{g_7}) = 1$. Therefore, after applying the results given by the deduction tables (Appendix B), we obtain the following results:

1. As $\vDash (\exists \Diamond R_1, g_8) = 1$ and $\vDash (\exists \Diamond R_1, g_7) = 1$, then $\vDash (\exists \Diamond R_1, g) = 1$ (see Table 3.(a)).
2. As $\vDash (R_1, E_0|_{g_8}) = \vDash (R_1, E_0|_{g_7}) = 1$, then $\vDash (\forall \Diamond R_1, g) = 1$ (see Property 1).

From the information given by g_6 ($\vDash (\forall \Box R_1, g_6) = \frac{1}{2}$), we deduce that $\phi_2 = \vDash (\forall \Box R_1, g)) \leq_k 1$ (see Table 4.(a)). As $\vDash (\exists \Box R_1, g) \leq_k \vDash (\forall \Box R_1, g)$, then $\phi_1 = \vDash (\exists \Box R_1, g)) \leq_k 1$.[4] Finally and as consequence of the results obtained by applying the deduction tables, we know the following result:

$$\vDash (R_1, g) = \{1, 1, \phi_1 \in \{\tfrac{1}{2}, \tfrac{3}{4}, 1\}, \phi_2 \in \{\tfrac{1}{2}, \tfrac{3}{4}, 1\}\}$$

To sum up, we know, without running the model checking algorithm, that R_1 is a *liveness property* [1] in g — this property is satisfied by every single evolution path of the model ($\vDash (\forall \Diamond R_1, g) = 1$) — and, although it cannot be considered

---

[4] $\leq_k$ partiall ordering is defined in [3] and it is not included here because of space reasons.

as a *safety property* ($\vDash (\forall \,\Box R_1, g) \in \{\frac{1}{2}, \frac{3}{4}, 1\}$), there is not any information prohibiting that if the functional specification increases, it would became true (Appendix A).

Verification of R_2. Property $R_2 \equiv$ (rx_msg $\Rightarrow$ error) expresses that *"in every state of the model where a data reception is enabled, an error must also be allowed"*. This property must be satisfied by every single state of the system unless the one marked by an arrow in Fig. 3a in this case an error must not be allowed, because the data frame has not been retransmitted. Therefore, we would like R_2 to be a *liveness property*, but not a *safety one*. As in the previous section, the following information is recovered: $\vDash (R_2, g_8) = \{1, 1, \frac{1}{4}, 0\}$, $\vDash (R_2, g_7) = \{1, 1, \frac{1}{4}, 0\}$ and $\vDash (R_2, g_6) = \{1, 1, \frac{1}{4}, 0\}$. From which the following verification information can be deduced:

1. As $\vDash (\exists \,\Diamond R_2, g_8) = \vDash (\exists \,\Diamond R_2, g_7) = 1$, then $\vDash (\exists \,\Diamond R_2, g) = 1$ (see Table 3.(a)).
2. $\vDash (\exists \,\Box R_2, g_7) = \vDash (\exists \,\Box R_2, g_8) = \frac{1}{4} \Rightarrow \vDash (\forall \,\Box R_2, g) \in \{0, \frac{1}{4}, \widehat{\frac{1}{2}}\}$ (see Table 3.(c)).
3. As $\vDash (\forall \,\Box R_2, g_8) = \vDash (\forall \,\Box R_2, g_7) = 0$, then, $\vDash (\forall \,\Box R_2, g) = 0$ (see Table 3.(d)).

On the other hand, the verification information linked to g_6 does not add more information (see Table 4). Therefore, the values of $\vDash (R_2, g)$ are the following ones:

$$\vDash (R_2, g) = \{1, \phi_1 \in \Phi, \phi_2 \in \Phi, 0\}, \text{ where } \Phi = \{0, \tfrac{1}{4}, \widehat{\tfrac{1}{2}}, \tfrac{1}{2}, \tfrac{3}{4}, 1\}$$

According to these results, we know that R_2 it is not a *safety property* — just as we wanted, $\vDash (\forall \,\Box R_2, g) = 0$ — and it is satisfied at least for one of the evolution paths of g ($\vDash (\exists \,\Diamond R_2, g) = 1$) — but we need this property to be a *liveness one*, that is, it must be satisfied by every single evolution path of the model. However, applying the deduction tables, we do not know any information about $\vDash (\forall \,\Diamond R_2, g) = \phi_1 \in \Phi$, so to know this result, we would need to apply the model checking algorithm.

However, we will try to reduce the state-space of g before running the model checker. Firstly, we need to know which of the recovered components is the closest one to g according to TC^∞ criterion, that is, which of them need less adaptation effort — addition and/or elimination of sequence of events — to make its functionality the same to g. With this aim, we apply the *functional adaptation* function[5] (see Appendix C), being g_6 the most similar to g according to TC^∞ criterion — Fig. (a) of Table 2 shows the evolution path which has to be added to g to make its functionality the same to g_6 —. Therefore, there are three states of g_6 which are different from g — circled in Fig. (b) of Table 2 —, being responsible for any difference between $\vDash (R_2, g)$ and $\vDash (R_2, g_6) = \{1, 1, \frac{1}{4}, 0\}$.

---

[5] $\{TC^\infty(g) - \rho\} \cup \{TC^\infty(g') - \rho\}$, where $\rho = (TC^\infty(g) \cap TC^\infty(g'))$ — see [3].

Table 2. Refining the state-space

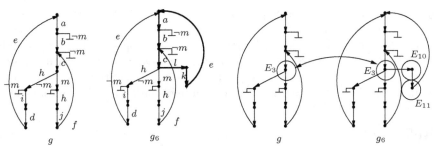

(a) Functional excess of g_6 regarding g (b) States which are different in g and g_6

As R is totally unspecified in E_{10} and in E_{11} ($\models (R_2, E_{10}|_{g_6}) = \models (R_2, E_{11}|_{g_6}) = \frac{1}{2}$), these two states cannot modify the values of $\models (R_2, g)$ from $\models (R_2, g_6)$. However, $\models (R_2, E_3|_{g_6}) = 1$, hence, we need to obtain the level of satisfaction of R_2 in the equivalent state of $E_3|_{g_6}$ in g (Fig. (b) of Table 2), that is, we need to run the model checking algorithm on the state E_3 of g. After that, we obtain that $\models (R_2, E_3|_g) = 1$, hence state E_3 of g_6 does not have any influence in the verification result of R_2 in g, which entails that $\models (R_2, g) = \models (R_2, g_6)$:

$$\models (R_2, g) = \{1, 1, \tfrac{1}{4}, 0\}$$

where it is clear that $\models (\forall \Diamond R_2, g) = 1$, so the property is a *liveness one* in the current model of the system.

To conclude, we have obtained the formal verification results of the property R_2 in the model g without running the model checking algorithm all over the state-space of g, in fact, we only need to run the algorithm in one state of this space, that is, only the 10% of the states were formally checked.

7   Evaluation of the Approach and Future Work

The work introduced in this paper focuses on reusing verification information of incomplete models at the requirements specification stage. We believe reusing this kind of information at early stages increases the reuse benefits and improves the software process. To support this assertion, we need to quantify these bene-fits, that is, obtaining the computational cost of reusing and comparing it with the cost of applying directly the model checking algorithm. However, quantifying the cost of reusing is not easy because it does not only depend on the complex-ity of the reusing algorithms and on the amount of reusable components in the repository, but also on their functional characteristics, which are more difficult to take into account. Besides that, its neccesary to assess some parameters like *recall, precision* and *response time* of the ARIFS methodology which help us to evaluate the approach. In fact, nowadays we are working in a prototype tool, ARIFS tool, to obtain these values.

In order to continue this proposal, we are working on: (a) a *compositional verification*, that is, decomposing properties in sub-properties such that it is possible to reuse verification information about each sub-property, and the combination of the sub-properties implies the required global property; (b) the possibility of reusing verification results of *functionally similar* properties with the given one; and (c) obtaining heuristics which enable predicting the values we need to quantify the benefits of reusing verification information in this environment.

References

1. Bowen Alpern and Ferd B. Schneider. Recognizing Safety and Liveness. *Distributed Computing Journal*, 2:117–126, 1987.
2. R. Bryant. Graph-based Algorithms for Boolean Function Manipulation. *IEEE Transactions on Computers*, 35(8):677–691, 1986.
3. Rebeca P. Díaz Redondo, José J. Pazos Arias, Ana Fernández Vilas, and Belén Barragáns Martínez. ARIFS: an Environment for Incomplete and Formal Specifications Reuse. In *Proc. of Workshop on Formal Methods and Component Interaction.*, volume 66 of *Electronic Notes in Theorethical Computer Science*. Elsevier Science, July 2002.
4. Rebeca P. Díaz Redondo, José J. Pazos Arias, and Ana Fernández Vilas. *Component-Based Software Quality: Methods and Techniques*, volume 2693 of *Lecture Notes in Computer Science (LNCS)*, chapter Reuse of Formal Verification Efforts of Incomplete Models at the Requirements Specification Stage, pages 326–352. Springer Verlag, 2003.
5. I. Keidar, R. Khazan, N. Lynch, and A. Shvartsman. An Inheritance-Based Technique for Building Simulation Proofs Incrementally. In *22nd International Conference on Software Engineering (ICSE)*, pages 478–487, Limerik, Ireland, June 2000.
6. R. Kurshan, V. Levin, M. Minea, D. Peled, and H. Yenigün. Static Partial Order Reduction. *Tools for the Construction and Analysis of Systems, LNCS 1394*, pages 345–357, 1998.
7. W. Lam, J. A. McDermid, and A. J. Vickers. Ten Steps Towards Systematic Requirements Reuse. *Requirements Engineering*, 2:102–113, 1997. Springer Verlag.
8. K. L. McMillan. A Technique of State Space Search based on Unfolding. *Formal Methods in System Design*, 6:45–65, 1995.
9. José J. Pazos Arias and Jorge García Duque. SCTL-MUS: A Formal Methodology for Software Development of Distributed Systems. A Case Study. *Formal Aspects of Computing*, 13:50–91, 2001.
10. J. Penix and P. Alexander. Efficient Specification-Based Component Retrieval. *Automated Software Engineering: An International Journal*, 6(2):139–170, April 1999.
11. J. Schumann and Fischer. NORA/HAMMR: Making Deduction-Based Software Component Retrieval Practical. In *Proc. of the 12th ASE*, pages 246–254, 1997.
12. R. J. van Glabeek. *Handbook of Process Algebra*, chapter The Linear Time - Branching Time Spectrum I: The Semantics of Concrete, Sequential Processes. Elsevier Science, 2001.

13. A. M. Zaremski and J. M. Wing. Specification Matching of Software Components. *ACM Transactions on Software Engineering and Methodology*, 6(4):333–369, October 1997.

A   Levels of Satisfaction of SCTL-MUS Methodology

This appendix outlines a brief description of the six levels of satisfaction of the SCTL-MUS methodology and it was taken from [3].

As SCTL-MUS methodology adds unspecification concept, the level of satisfaction may not be *false* (nor *true*), just as the boolean logic, in fact, it must have a level of satisfaction related to its unspecification (totally or partially unspecified on the MUS model). Consequently, this methodology defines six different levels of satisfaction, which can be partially ordered according to a *knowledge level* ($\leq_k$) (Fig. 4) as follows:

- $\{1, \widehat{\frac{1}{2}}, 0\}$ are the highest knowledge levels. We know at the current stage of the model the final level of satisfaction of the property: 1 or *true* means the requirement is satisfied; 0 or *false* implies the requirement is not satisfied; and $\widehat{\frac{1}{2}}$ or *contradictory or not applicable* means the requirement cannot become *true* or *false*.
- $\{\frac{1}{4}, \frac{3}{4}\}$ are the middle knowledge levels. Although at the current stage of the model, the property is partially unspecified, we know its satisfaction tendency. That is, for the current value $\frac{1}{4}$, in a subsequent stage of specification, the level of satisfaction cannot became 1 (*true*), it will be $\frac{1}{4} \leq_k \phi'$; and for the current value $\frac{3}{4}$, in a subsequent stage of specification, the level of satisfaction cannot became 0 (*false*), it will be $\frac{3}{4} \leq_k \phi'$.
- $\{\frac{1}{2}\}$ is the lowest knowledge level. The property is totally unspecified at the current model's stage and we do not know any information about its future behaviour, that is, it can became $\frac{1}{2} \leq_k \phi'$ in a subsequent stage of specification.

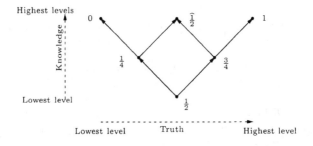

Fig. 4. Knowledge and Truth partial orderings among levels of satisfaction

In short, the level of satisfaction of an SCTL requirement varies according to its closeness to the *true* (or *false*) level of satisfaction. According to this *truth ordering* (Fig. 4), $\Phi = \{0, \frac{1}{4}, \frac{1}{2}, \widehat{\frac{1}{2}}, \frac{3}{4}, 1\}$ is a quasi-boolean lattice with the least upper bound operator $\vee$, the greatest lower bound operator $\wedge$, and the unary operation $\neg$ (defined by horizontal symmetry). The 4-tuple $(\Phi, \vee, \wedge, \neg)$ has the structure of the De Morgan algebra and it is called algebra of MPU [9] (*Middle Point Uncertainty*).

B   Deduction Tables

This appendix contains the **deduction tables** (Tables 3 and 4) which store how to reuse verification information between two MUS graphs holding a TC^{∞}-relationship, and property 1, directly related to this subject. This appendix was taken from [4].

Table 3. Reusing $\models (R, g)$ information to know $\models (R, g')$, where $g \sqsubseteq_{TC}^{\infty} g'$

(a) Results obtained from $\models (\exists \, \Diamond R, g)$

$\models (\exists \, \Diamond R, g) = 0$	$\models (\forall \, \Box R, g') = 0$
$\models (\exists \, \Diamond R, g) = 1$	$\models (\exists \, \Diamond R, g') = 1$
$\models (\exists \, \Diamond R, g) = \widehat{\frac{1}{2}}$	$\models (\forall \, \Box R, g') \geq_k \frac{1}{4}$
$\models (\exists \, \Diamond R, g) = \frac{1}{4}$	

(b) Results obtained from $\models (\forall \, \Diamond R, g)$

$\models (\forall \, \Diamond R, g) = 0$	$\models (\forall \, \Box R, g') = 0$
$\models (\forall \, \Diamond R, g) = 1$	$\models (\exists \, \Diamond R, g') = 1$
$\models (\forall \, \Diamond R, g) = \widehat{\frac{1}{2}}$	$\models (\exists \, \Diamond R, g') \geq_k \frac{3}{4}$
$\models (\forall \, \Diamond R, g) = \frac{3}{4}$	

(c) Results obtained from $\models (\exists \, \Box R, g)$

$\models (\exists \, \Box R, g) = 0$	$\models (\forall \, \Box R, g') = 0$
$\models (\exists \, \Box R, g) = 1$	$\models (\exists \, \Diamond R, g') = 1$
$\models (\exists \, \Box R, g) = \widehat{\frac{1}{2}}$	$\models (\forall \, \Box R, g') \geq_k \frac{1}{4}$
$\models (\exists \, \Box R, g) = \frac{1}{4}$	

(d) Results obtained from $\models (\forall \, \Box R, g)$

$\models (\forall \, \Box R, g) = 0$	$\models (\forall \, \Box R, g') = 0$
$\models (\forall \, \Box R, g) = 1$	$\models (\exists \, \Diamond R, g') = 1$
$\models (\forall \, \Box R, g) = \widehat{\frac{1}{2}}$	$\models (\exists \, \Diamond R, g') \geq_k \frac{3}{4}$
$\models (\forall \, \Box R, g) = \frac{3}{4}$	

Property 1. Let R be an SCTL property which is satisfied in the initial state of a MUS graph g, that is, $\models (R, E_0|_g) = 1$, then we know that $\models (\forall \, \Diamond R, g') = 1$, $\forall g' \mid g \sqsubseteq_{TC}^{\infty} g'$.

Proof. Since $\models (R, E_0|_g) = 1$ and since the initial state of a MUS graph is contained in every single trace of the graph, then $\models (\forall \, \Diamond R, g) = 1$. According to the information stored in Table 3, therefore $\models (\forall \, \Diamond R, g') = 1$, $\forall g' \mid g \sqsubseteq_{TC}^{\infty} g'$.

$\square$

Table 4. Reusing $\models (R, g')$ information to know $\models (R, g)$, where $g \sqsubseteq_{TC}^{\infty} g'$

(a) Results obtained from $\models (\forall \, \Box R, g')$ **(b)** Results obtained from $\models (\exists \, \Diamond R, g')$

$\models (\forall \, \Box R, g') \leq_k 1$	$\models (\exists \, \Diamond R, g) \leq_k 1$	$\models (\exists \, \Diamond R, g') \leq_k 0$	$\models (\exists \, \Diamond R, g) \leq_k 0$
	$\models (\forall \, \Diamond R, g) \leq_k 1$		$\models (\forall \, \Diamond R, g) \leq_k 0$
	$\models (\exists \, \Box R, g) \leq_k 1$		$\models (\exists \, \Box R, g) \leq_k 0$
	$\models (\forall \, \Box R, g) \leq_k 1$		$\models (\forall \, \Box R, g) \leq_k 0$
$\models (\forall \, \Box R, g') = \frac{1}{2}$ or $\models (\forall \, \Box R, g') = \frac{1}{4}$	$\models (\exists \, \Diamond R, g) \in \Phi - \{0\}$	$\models (\exists \, \Diamond R, g') = \frac{1}{2}$ or $\models (\exists \, \Diamond R, g') = \frac{3}{4}$	$\models (\exists \, \Diamond R, g) \in \Phi - \{1\}$
	$\models (\forall \, \Diamond R, g) \in \Phi - \{0\}$		$\models (\forall \, \Diamond R, g) \in \Phi - \{1\}$
	$\models (\exists \, \Box R, g) \in \Phi - \{0\}$		$\models (\exists \, \Box R, g) \in \Phi - \{1\}$
	$\models (\forall \, \Box R, g) \in \Phi - \{0\}$		$\models (\forall \, \Box R, g) \in \Phi - \{1\}$

C   Functional Adaptation Function

This appendix contains the definition of the *functional adaptation function* (Definition 4) which allows us to obtain the adaptation effort between two MUS graphs, that is, the amount of sequence of events that must be added and removed to make their functionality the same. It was taken from [3].

Definition 1. *Let C and C' be two reusable components, the* **functional consensus** *between them, denoted by $\rho(C, C')$, is defined as $\rho(C, C') = TC^{\infty}(g) \sqcap TC^{\infty}(g')$, where g is the MUS graph linked to C and g' the MUS graph linked to C'.*

Definition 2. *Let C and C' be two reusable components, the* **functional deficit** *funcion of C' regarding C, denoted by $\delta(C, C')$, is defined as $\delta(C, C') = TC^{\infty}(g) - \rho(C, C') = TC^{\infty}(g) - (TC^{\infty}(g) \sqcap TC^{\infty}(g'))$, where g is the MUS graph linked to C and g' the MUS graph linked to C'.*

Definition 3. *Let C and C' be two reusable components, the* **functional excess** *function of C' regarding C, denoted by $\varepsilon(C, C')$, is defined as $\varepsilon(C, C') = TC^{\infty}(g') - \rho(C, C') = TC^{\infty}(g') - (TC^{\infty}(g) \sqcap TC^{\infty}(g'))$, where g is the MUS graph linked to C and g' the MUS graph linked to C'.*

Definition 4. *Let C and C' be two reusable components, the* **functional adaptation** *function between them, denoted by $\Delta(C, C')$, is defined as $\Delta(C, C') = \delta(C, C') \cup \varepsilon(C, C')$, where g is the MUS graph linked to C and g' the MUS graph linked to C'. $\Delta(C, C')$ expresses the functional characteristics that being specified by the C are not specified by C' and viceversa.*

Complexity of Model Checking by Iterative Improvement: The Pseudo-Boolean Framework*

Henrik Björklund, Sven Sandberg, and Sergei Vorobyov

Information Technology Department, Box 337, Uppsala University,
751 05 Uppsala, Sweden
{henrikbj,svens}@it.uu.se, vorobyov@csd.uu.se

Abstract. We present several new algorithms as well as new lower and upper bounds for optimizing functions underlying infinite games pertinent to computer-aided verification.

1 Introduction

Infinite two-person adversary full information games are a well established framework for modeling interaction between a system and its environment. A correct system can be naturally interpreted as a player possessing a winning strategy against any strategy of the malicious environment. Respectively, a verification process can be considered as a proof that a system does possess such a strategy. If the system loses, then a winning strategy for the environment encompasses possible system improvements. During the last decades a substantial progress has been achieved both on fitting diverse approaches to computer-aided verification into the game-theoretic paradigm and, simultaneously, on developing efficient algorithms for solving games, i.e., determining the winner and its strategy [6,10,13,18,22,31]. A naturally appealing approach to solving games [12,21,31] consists in taking an initial strategy of the system and gradually 'improving' it, since a non-optimal strategy is outperformed by some counterstrategy of the environment. This allows for improving either the strategy, or the system, or both. In this paper we address the complexity of such an approach in an abstract model based on pseudo-Boolean functions possessing essential properties of games.

Game theory suggests, for numerous types of games, a nice characterization of the optimal solutions for behaviors of rational players, the so-called *Nash equilibria*. The 'only' remaining problem left widely open is: '*What is the exact computational complexity of finding Nash equilibria (optimal strategies) in two-person games with finitely many strategies? Could such games be solved in polynomial time?*' This is a fundamental problem, the solution to which determines whether or not, and to what extent game theory will be applicable

---

* Supported by Swedish Research Council Grants "Infinite Games: Algorithms and Complexity" and "Interior-Point Methods for Infinite Games".

M. Broy and A.V. Zamulin (Eds.): PSI 2003, LNCS 2890, pp. 381–394, 2003.

to solving and optimizing real large-scale games emerging from practical verification of complex reactive systems. The problem is known to belong to the complexity class NP∩coNP (therefore, most probably not NP-complete, luckily!) but is *not known to be polynomial time solvable*. The best currently known algorithms are *exponential* (sometimes *subexponential*). Clearly, superpolynomial algorithms will not allow for practical solutions of the real-life verification games, no matter how fast the progress in hardware continues. Consequently, this problem is one of the most practical and (together with the NP versus P) most fundamental problems in the foundations of computing, complexity theory, and automata theory [27].

In this paper we address the efficiency of iterative improvement algorithms for solving games in the following abstract setting. Consider a game where one of the players has n binary choices, e.g., selects whether to move left or right[1] in n places, and every combination of choices is given a cost, reflecting how good this strategy (combination of choices) is against a perfect adversary. This results in an n-dimensional valued Boolean hypercube, or a *pseudo-Boolean function*. Consequently, everything boils down to optimizing a pseudo-Boolean function. How fast can we optimize such a function? Despite its simplicity, the question appears extremely difficult for the classes of functions with special properties pertinent to games. Not surprisingly, there are not so many strong and general results of this kind in the literature. The best bound in Tovey's survey [30] is $O(2^{n/2})$; Mansour and Singh [25] suggest an $O(2^{0.773n})$ algorithm (for Markov decision processes), and we independently obtain an improved bound $O(2^{0.453n})$ for a similar algorithm in a more general setting [5,8]. Ludwig [24] suggested a subexponential $O(2^{\sqrt{n}})$ algorithm for binary simple stochastic games, which becomes exponential for games of unbounded (non-binary) outdegree. We suggested several [3,6,7,8] subexponential algorithms for games of arbitrary outdegrees.

The development of our theory is primarily motivated by the so-called *parity games*, which are infinite games played on finite directed bipartite leafless graphs, with vertices colored by integers. Two players alternate moving a pebble along edges. The goal of Player 0 is to ensure that the biggest color visited by the pebble infinitely often is even, whereas Player 1 tries to make it odd. The complexity of determining the winner in parity games, equivalent to the Rabin chain tree automata non-emptiness, as well as to the μ-calculus[2] model checking [13,14], is a fundamental open problem in complexity theory [27]. The problem belongs to NP∩coNP, but its PTIME-membership status remains widely open. *Discounted mean payoff* [34] and *simple stochastic games* [11,12], relevant for verification of probabilistic systems, are two other classes to which our theory applies [8].

We exploit the fundamental fact, apparently unnoticed before, that functions arising from such games possess extremely favorable structural properties, close

---

[1] The restriction to two successors is no loss of generality, since a game with non-binary choices may be reduced to binary. However, complexity gets worse, and this issue is dealt with in Section 9.

[2] One of the most expressive temporal logics of programs [13].

to the so-called *completely unimodal functions* [19,33,32,30]. These functions are well known in the field of pseudo-Boolean optimization [9,20], an established area of combinatorial optimization, in which local search [1,30] is one of the dominating methods. The complexity of local search for different classes of functions were carefully investigated [30,19,33]. However, all previously known algorithms for completely unimodal functions were *exponential* [30,9]. A fruitful idea came from linear programming. In the early 90's Kalai [23] and Matoušek, Sharir, Welzl [29,26] came up with strongly subexponential randomized algorithms for linear programming. Later Ludwig [24] adapted it to binary simple stochastic games, and we to binary parity games [28]. We also figured out that Kalai's and Sharir–Welzl's randomized schemes fit perfectly well for completely unimodal optimization [2,5,4] and parity games [28]. Later we succeeded to generalize and adapt those subexponential schemes to create a discrete subexponential algorithm for general (non-binary) parity games [6], and extend it to combinatorial structures (which we call *completely local-global*) more directly reflecting games [7,8,3].

In this paper we present new upper bounds on the number of iterations of various iterative improvement algorithms for optimization of *completely unimodal pseudo-boolean functions* (CUPBFs). Such functions possess several remarkable properties: 1) unique minimum and maximum on every subcube, 2) every vertex has a unique neighborhood improvement signature. The problem of optimizing CUPBFs has been studied before [19,33], but only few and weak bounds are known. Only a very restrictive subclass of decomposable CUPBFs is known to allow for polynomial time randomized optimization. The best known upper bounds are exponential, but it is conjectured that any CUPBF can be optimized in polynomial time [33].

We investigated and compared, both theoretically and practically[3], five algorithms for CUPBF optimization: the Greedy Single Switch Algorithm (GSSA), the Random Single Switch Algorithm (RSSA), the All Profitable Switches Algorithm (APSA), the Random Multiple Switches Algorithm (RMSA), and Kalai-Ludwig's Randomized Algorithm (KLRA). The GSSA and the RSSA have been studied by others in the context of CUPBF optimization. We first proposed the use of the APSA and RMSA in this context in [2]. It turns out that complete unimodality allows, knowing all improving neighbors of a vertex, to improve by simultaneously jumping towards all or some of them. (Actually any 0-1 linear combination of improving directions gives an improvement; this allows for non-local search algorithms that behave surprisingly well in practice.) The only nontrivial lower bound that has been shown is an exponential one for the GSSA [32]. Local search iterative improvement algorithms are appealing, easy to implement, and efficient in practice. But no nontrivial upper bounds are known for those algorithms, except for subclasses of all CUPBFs. We settle several such nontrivial bounds in this paper. The fifth algorithm, KLRA, was first proposed in [24] for solving simple stochastic games, with a subexponential upper bound

---

[3] Our results on practical evaluation and comparison of the algorithms can be found in [2,5,4].

on the expected running time. We show that it can be modified to solve the
CUPBF optimization problem, still in expected subexponential time.

Outline of the paper. In Section 2 we recall the definitions and main results
concerning completely unimodal functions. Section 3 describes five iterative improvement algorithms for completely unimodal functions. Section 4 is devoted to
the random multiple switches algorithm, whereas Section 5 covers single greedy
single random, and all profitable switches algorithms. Section 6 adds random
sampling to the random multiple switches algorithm, while Section 7 does the
same to all other algorithms. Section 8 describes the Kalai-Ludwig-style algorithm. Section 9 generalizes the previous results to completely local-global functions and presents the Sharir-Welzl-style algorithm for these functions.

2   Completely Unimodal Pseudo-Boolean Functions

Parity and simple stochastic games can be solved by maximizing appropriately
defined functions on neighborhood graphs representing sets of strategies. The
prototypical case of such neighborhood graphs is the Boolean hypercube, and the
essential structure of games pertinent to optimization by iterative improvement
is captured, in the first approximation, by completely unimodal functions on
Boolean cubes [19,32,33,30]. Much of the theory we present can be understood
and developed in terms of completely unimodal functions, and until Section 9
we concentrate on this case.

In general, parity and simple stochastic games require less restrictive neighborhood structures and functions. In [7] we succeeded to characterize them as
a class we called *completely local-global* (CLG) functions, defined on Cartesian
products of arbitrary finite sets, rather than on Boolean hypercubes. These functions, considered in Section 9, were crucial in our development [6,7] of subexponential algorithms for parity games with arbitrary outdegree. This is because
reducing such games to binary ones quadratically increases the number of vertices. As a consequence, a straightforward reduction renders subexponential algorithms exponential [6].

Let $H(n)$ denote the *n-dimensional Boolean hypercube* $\{0,1\}^n$, for $n \in \mathbb{N}^+$. A
pseudo-Boolean function is an injective[4] mapping $H(n) \to \mathbb{R}$ associating a real
number to every *n*-dimensional Boolean vector. For $0 \le k \le n$, a *k-dimensional
face* of $H(n)$, or a *k-face*, is a collection of Boolean vectors obtained by fixing $n-k$
arbitrary coordinates and letting the k remaining coordinates take all possible
Boolean values. Faces of dimension 0 are called *vertices*, faces of dimension 1 are
called *edges*. Faces of dimension $n - 1$ are called *facets*. Two vertices that share
an edge are called *neighbors*. Each vertex v in $H(n)$ has exactly n neighbors,
forming the *standard neighborhood* of v on $H(n)$.

---

[4] The standard injectiveness restriction is lifted in Section 9.

Complete Unimodality. A pseudo-Boolean function f is called *completely unimodal* (CUPBF for short) if one of the following four equivalent conditions holds [19,33]:

1. f has a unique local minimum on each face,
2. f has a unique local maximum on each face,
3. f has a unique local minimum on each 2-face,
4. f has a unique local maximum on each 2-face.

Improving directions. Let $f : H(n) \to \mathbb{R}$ be a CUPBF and let v be a vertex on $H(n)$. Number the dimensions of $H(n)$ from 0 to $n-1$. For each $i \in \{0, 1, ..., n-1\}$, let v_i be the neighbor of v that is reached by moving in coordinate i from v. Let p_i be 1 if $f(v) < f(v_i)$, otherwise 0. Then we call $\bar{p} = [p_0, p_1, ..., p_{n-1}]$ the *vector of improving directions* (VID) of v under f.

In the sequel we will usually abuse terminology by identifying a function and a (valued) hypercube it is defined upon. By 'optimizing' we mean '*maximizing*'.

3   Five Iterative Improvement Algorithms

A *standard local-search improvement algorithm* starts in an arbitrary point v_0 of the hypercube $H(n)$ and iteratively improves by selecting a next iterate with a better value from a *polynomial* neighborhood $N(v_i)$ of the current iterate.

Specific instances of the standard algorithm are obtained when one fixes:

1. the neighborhood structure on $H(n)$,
2. the disciplines of selecting the initial point and the next iterate.

Two major local-search improvement algorithms, the *Greedy Single Switch Algorithm (GSSA)* and the *Random Single Switch Algorithm (RSSA)* have previously been investigated and used for optimizing CUPBFs [30]. We also investigate the *All Profitable Switches Algorithm (APSA)* and the *Random Multiple Switches Algorithm (RMSA)*. Strictly speaking, neither APSA, nor RMSA is a local-search algorithm. The first one operates with neighborhood structures which vary depending on the CUPBF being optimized. The second chooses the next iterate from a non-polynomially bounded (in general) neighborhood of the current iterate. Finally, we show how the *subexponential Kalai-Ludwig's Randomized Algorithm (KLRA)* for solving binary simple stochastic games can be modified to optimize CUPBFs, and show that it is subexponential for this problem as well, with expected worst case behavior $2^{O(\sqrt{n})}$. This algorithm has so far been unknown in the field of CUPBF optimization.

Greedy Single Switch Algorithm (GSSA). This is a local-search algorithm that at every iteration chooses the *highest-valued neighbor* of the current vertex as the next iterate. Recall that every vertex of $H(n)$ has exactly n neighbors (in the standard neighborhood). Unfortunately, this algorithm may take *exponentially many* steps to find the maximum of a CUPBF [32].

Random Single Switch Algorithm (RSSA). This is a local-search algorithm that at every iteration chooses uniformly at random one of the *higher-valued neighbors* of the current vertex as the next iterate. This algorithm may also take *exponentially many* iterations to find the global maximum. Although its expected running time for general CUPBFs is unknown, Williamson Hoke [33] has shown, using a proof technique due to Kelly, that the RSSA has expected quadratic running time on any *decomposable* hypercube. Call a facet F an *absorbing facet* if no vertex on F has a higher-valued neighbor that is not on F. A hypercube is called *decomposable* iff it has dimension 1 or has an absorbing facet that is decomposable. This result, together with the fact that in a CUPBF there is a short improving path from any vertex to the maximum (i.e., Hirsch conjecture holds), form grounds for the polynomial time optimization conjecture for CUPBFs [33] (currently open).

All Profitable Switches Algorithm (APSA). The All Profitable Switches Algorithm (APSA) at every iteration computes the VID s of a current iterate v and inverts the bits of v in positions where s has ones to get the new iterate v' (i.e., $v' := v$ XOR s.)

This algorithm may also be seen as a local-search algorithm, but the structure of the neighborhood is not fixed a priori (as for GSSA and RSSA), but rather changes for each CUPBF.

APSA is a stepwise improvement algorithm for CUPBFs because the current iterate v is the unique global minimum on the face defined by fixing all coordinates corresponding to zeros in the VID s. Therefore, the next iterate v' (which belongs to the same face) has a better function value.

Random Multiple Switches Algorithm (RMSA). Like APSA, the Random Multiple Switches Algorithm (RMSA) at every iteration computes the VID s of a current iterate v. However, to get the next iterate v' RMSA inverts bits in v corresponding to a nonempty subset s' of the nonzero bits in s, chosen uniformly at random (i.e., $v' := v$ XOR s'.)

RMSA is a stepwise improvement algorithm for CUPBFs because the current point v is the unique global minimum on the face defined by fixing the coordinates in v corresponding to zeros in s'. Thus the next iterate v', belonging to this face, must have a better function value. Note that RMSA selects at random from a neighborhood that may be *exponentially big* in the dimension. So, strictly speaking, this is not a polynomial local-search improvement algorithm.

Kalai-Ludwig's Randomized Algorithm (KLRA). In a major breakthrough Kalai [23] suggested the first *subexponential* randomized simplex algorithm for linear programming. Based on Kalai's ideas, Ludwig [24] suggested the first *subexponential* randomized algorithm for simple stochastic games with binary choices. We show that Ludwig's algorithm without any substantial modifications performs correctly and with the same expected worst-case complexity

$2^{O(\sqrt{n})}$ for optimizing CUPBFs. Kalai-Ludwig's algorithm may informally be described as follows.

1. Start at any vertex v of $H(n)$.
2. Choose at random a coordinate $i \in \{1, \ldots, n\}$ (not chosen previously).
3. Apply the algorithm recursively to find the best point v' with the same i-th coordinate as v_i.
4. If v' is not optimal (has a better neighbor), invert the i-th component in v', set $v := v'$ and repeat.

4   The Random Multiple Switches Algorithm

The only two algorithms that were previously studied for the CUPBF optimization problem are: 1) the GSSA, 2) the RSSA. The GSSA makes an exponential number of steps on CUPBFs constructed in [32]. If extremely unlucky, the RSSA can make an exponential number of steps on CUPBFs generated by Klee-Minty cubes, but nevertheless its expected runtime on such cubes is $O(n^2)$, quadratic in the number of dimensions. The same expected quadratic upper bound holds for the RSSA running on the class of the so-called *decomposable* CUPBFs (of which Klee-Minty's form a proper subclass) [33, p. 77-78]. Besides these results, there are no other known: 1) nontrivial lower bounds for the problem, 2) better upper bounds for any specific algorithms. Nevertheless, [33, p. 78] conjectures that the RSSA is (expected) polynomial on *all CUPBFs*.

It is worth mentioning, however, that for any CUPBF with optimum v^* and any initial vertex v_0 there is always an improving path from v_0 to v^* of length $hd(v_0, v^*)$, the Hamming distance between v_0 and v^*. Therefore, the 'Hirsch conjecture' about short paths to the optimum holds for CUPBFs (thus the potential existence of 'clever' polynomial time algorithms is not excluded).

Simultaneously, nothing except this 'trivial linear' $\Omega(n)$ lower bound is currently known for the CUPBF optimization problem. For the broader classes of all pseudo-Boolean and all unimin functions[5] there are the $\Omega(2^v/\sqrt{n})$ and the $\Omega(2^v/n^{1.5})$ lower bounds, respectively, for any deterministic algorithms, and the $\Omega(2^{n/2} \cdot n)$ lower bound for any randomized algorithms [30, Thm. 14, p. 66, Coroll. 21, p. 71, Coroll. 19, p. 69].

In view of the above results our new, presented in this section, $O(2^{0.773n}) = O(1.71^n)$ upper bound for our new RMSA (Randomized Multiple Switch Algorithm)[6] should be considered an improvement. The key step consists in exploiting complete unimodality and the next simple lemma, giving a lower bound on the per-step improvement of the target function value by the RMSA, exponential in the number of improving directions in the current vertex.

---

[5] Possessing a unique minimum.
[6] Which is not local-search type. Maybe this is the reason it was not considered in general pseudo-Boolean optimization; it is only correct for CUPBFs.

Lemma 1. *The expected function value improvement of the RMSA step from a vertex v with $i > 0$ improving directions is at least 2^{i-1}.*

This makes the RMSA attractive: we can guarantee that the expected 'value jump' in each step is relatively high, provided, there are many improving directions. If the average number of improving directions per vertex visited during a run of the RMSA were at least k, the algorithm would terminate in at most $O(2^{n-k})$ steps. In particular, $n/2$ average improving directions would give an $O(2^{n/2})$ upper bound. Can we guarantee any nontrivial lower bound on the number of improving directions in any run of the RMSA? Fortunately, the fundamental property that in every completely unimodal cube every possible bit vector of improving directions is present exactly once [33, p. 75-76] allows us to do this. The proof of the following theorem assumes the worst (and seemingly unrealizable) case that the algorithm is always unlucky, selecting a vertex with the *fewest* possible number of improving directions, and the cube generated by these direction is numbered by the *smallest* possible successors of the current value. This forces the worst case and settles an upper bound on the number of RMSA iterations in the worst case.

Theorem 1. *The expected number of iterations made by the RMSA on an n-dimensional CUPBF is less than $2^{0.773n} = 1.71^n$, for sufficiently large n.*

After we obtained the bound from Theorem 1, we were pointed out that a similar bound for the same algorithm, but applied to Markov decision processes, was proved earlier in [25]. Later it became clear that our result is stronger, after we succeeded to reduce simple stochastic games to CLG-functions and CLG-functions to CU-functions [7]. Moreover, we substantially improve the bound from Theorem 1 below $2^{n/2}$ in Section 6 (for a variant of the algorithm).

5   Single Greedy, Single Random, and All Profitable Switches Algorithms

We start with a simple lower bound on the per-step improvement for all three algorithms. This bound is weaker than for the RMSA. Consequently, the upper bounds we can settle for these algorithms are weaker. Nevertheless, the practical behavior of these algorithms shown in experiments [2,5,4] make them very attractive.

Proposition 1. *When the APSA, the GSSA, or the RSSA makes a switch in a vertex with i improving directions the value of the target function increases at least by i (by expected value at least $i/2$ for the RSSA).*

Theorem 2. *For any $0 < \varepsilon < 1$ the APSA, the GSSA,, and the RSSA make fewer than $2^{n-(1-\varepsilon)\log(n)}$ iterations on any n-dimensional CUPBF, for sufficiently large n.*

Remark 1. 1) Note that it is stronger than claiming 'fewer than 2^{n-c} (for a constant $c > 0$)', but 2) weaker than 'fewer than 2^{cn} (for a constant $0 < c < 1$)'. 3) This upper bound is better than the $5/24 \cdot 2^n - 45$ lower bound for any local improvement algorithm on a uniminimax function [30, Thm 23, p. 72].

6   Adding Random Sampling to the RMSA

The RMSA can be considerably improved by adding random sampling. If we start the RMSA from a 'good' vertex, with a value close to the optimum, the RMSA guarantees a reasonably short run before finding it, as is shown in Section 4. The trick is to select a good initial vertex by making an optimal number of random probes picking the one with the best value, and to minimize the overall running time. We call the modified algorithm the RMSA-RS and parameterize it by the number of randomly sampled vertices. For this modified algorithm, a better upper bound can be shown, when we choose the parameter optimally:

Theorem 3. *The RMSA-RS can be parameterized in such a way that its expected running time on an n-dimensional CUPBF is $O(2^{0.453n}) = O(1.37^n)$.*

As described, the RMSA-RS always makes $2^{0.453n}$ random samplings, before starting any optimizations, so its expected best case is $\Omega(2^{0.453n})$. Although other single or multiple switch algorithms we consider have worse known upper bounds, they show much better practical behavior.

7   Adding Random Sampling to the APSA, the GSSA, and the RSSA

As we saw in the previous section, a better bound can be proved for the RMSA when random sampling is added. In this section we show that random sampling also allows for better bounds for the APSA, the GSSA, and the RSSA. The bounds are not as strong, however, as the one for the RMSA with random sampling.

Theorem 4. *For any $0 < \varepsilon < 1/2$ the All Profitable Switches, the Greedy Single Switch, and the Randomized Single Switch Algorithms with initial random sampling of $2^{\frac{n}{2} - (\frac{1}{2} - \varepsilon) \log(n)}$ vertices make less than $2^{\frac{n}{2} - (\frac{1}{2} - \varepsilon) \log(n)}$ iterations on any n-dimensional CUPBF, for sufficiently large n.*

Corollary 1. *With the initial random sampling of $2^{\frac{n}{2} - (\frac{1}{2} - \varepsilon) \log n}$ vertices, for any $\varepsilon \in (0, 1/2)$, the APSA, the GSSA, and the RSSA have running times (expected in the case of RSSA) that are $O(2^{\frac{n}{2} - (\frac{1}{2} - \varepsilon) \log n})$.*

8   Kalai-Ludwig's Algorithm for CUPBFs

We were the first to observe [2] that the Kalai-Ludwig's Randomized Algorithm (KLRA) initially designed for linear programming [23] and later adapted for simple stochastic games [24], works perfectly for CUPBF optimization, also providing *subexponential* expected running time [7]. Modified for CUPBF optimization the KLRA is shown below.

Algorithm 1: Kalai-Ludwig's Algorithm for CUPBFs
KLRA(CUPBF H, initial vertex v_0)
(1)   **if** $dim(H) = 0$
(2)   **return** v_0
(3)   **else**
(4)   choose a random facet F of H containing v_0
(5) $v^* \leftarrow$ KLRA(F, v_0)
(6)   **if** neighbor u of v^* on $H \backslash F$ is better than v^*
(7)   **return** KLRA($H \setminus F, u$)
(8)   **else**
(9)   **return** v^*

It turns out that the algorithm is correct and terminating:

Theorem 5. *For every CUPBF, KLRA terminates and returns the global maximum.*

The following adjusts the theorem and proof in [24] to the case of CUPBFs.

Theorem 6. *The expected running time of KLRA on a CUPBF is $2^{O(\sqrt{n})}$.*

Our experiments on randomly generated CUPBFs [2,5,4] indicate that KLRA performs better than its theoretical subexponential upper bound. Surprisingly,

---

[7] **Added in proof:** Bernd Gärtner pointed out to us that he came up to similar results in [16] (journal version [17]), also building on the ideas of Kalai, Matoušek, Sharir, and Welzl. Rather than using the standard terminology of *completely unimodal functions* [19,32,33,30], B. Gärtner employs a less common and quite inexpressive term *abstract optimization functions* instead, and this unfortunate choice partially explains why his results have not become widely known in pseudo-Boolean optimization. It should be noted, however, that our algorithms and analysis are more general (see the next section), since they apply not only for Boolean cubes, but to hyperstructures (products of simplices) as well. We also allow the functions to take values in *partially* rather than *totally* ordered sets. Additionally, we relax and do not stipulate the "unique sink on every subcube" property. All this is more adequate for games and provides for better complexity bounds. We thank B. Gärtner for his pointers and observations.

the other four algorithms considerably outperform KLRA, although no subexponential bounds are currently known for them. It is reasonable to believe that for some of the algorithms there may be subexponential or better upper bounds. In this work we proved the first nontrivial upper bounds for these algorithms. The bounds we showed are still exponential, but not expected to be tight. Rather, they are to be viewed as a first step towards settling the precise complexity of these algorithms on CUPBFs.

9   Completely Local-Global (CLG) Functions

So far we restricted our attention to binary games. Although every non-binary game can be reduced to a binary one, the resulting number of vertices is proportional to the size of the initial graph. This may give a quadratic blow-up in the number of vertices (e.g., for graphs of linear outdegree), and the $2^{O(\sqrt{n})}$ bound becomes exponential, since n is quadratic in the initial number of vertices. In this section we show how to apply more sophisticated algorithms directly on non-binary structures, maintaining the subexponential bounds. We start with a non-binary generalization of hypercubes.

Definition 1 (Hyperstructure). *For each $j \in \{1, \ldots, d\}$ let $P_j = \{e_{j,1}, \ldots, e_{j,\delta_j}\}$ be a finite set. Call $P = \prod_{j=1}^{d} P_j$ a d-dimensional hyperstructure, or structure for short.*   □

A *substructure* $P' \subseteq P$ is a product $P' = \prod_{j=1}^{d} P'_j$, where $\emptyset \neq P'_j \subseteq P_j$ for all j. If each P'_j has only two elements, then identify P' with H. Call P' a *facet* of P if there is a j such that $P'_k = P_k$ for all $k \neq j$, and P'_j has only one element. Say that $x, y \in P$, are *neighbors* iff they differ in only one coordinate. Thus each $x \in P$ has exactly $\sum_{j=1}^{d}(\delta_j - 1)$ neighbors. The neighbor relation defines a graph with elements of the hyperstructure as nodes, allowing us to talk about paths and distances in the hyperstructure. A structure $P = \prod_{j=1}^{d} P_j$ has d dimensions and $n = \sum_{j=1}^{d} \delta_j$ facets.

Throughout this section, let $\mathcal{D}$ be some partially ordered set. We now consider functions defined on P with values in $\mathcal{D}$. Functions with partially ordered codomains are better suited for games [7].

A *local maximum* of a function $f : P \to \mathcal{D}$ is a vertex in P with value bigger than or equal to all its neighbors. A *global maximum* is a vertex with a function value bigger than or equal to the values of all other vertices. In particular, any global maximum is comparable with all other vertices. Local and global minima are defined symmetrically.

Definition 2 (CLG-function on a hyperstructure). *Let $f : P \to \mathcal{D}$ be a function such that all neighbors have comparable values. Say that f is a CLG-function if the following properties hold on every substructure of P:*

  1. any local maximum of f is also global;
  2. any local minimum of f is also global;
  3. any two local maxima are connected by a path of local maxima;

4. any two local minima are connected by a path of local minima.

By a CLG-structure we mean a *CLG-function* together with the underlying *hyperstructure.*

We note in passing that CLG-functions can be defined on hypercubes as well (with the same four properties), and CUPBFs can be defined: 1) with a partial set $\mathcal{D}$ as co-domain, and 2) on hyperstructures. The relaxation of the co-domain from $\mathbb{R}$ to $\mathcal{D}$ is an advantage (the essential properties rely only on the order of neighbors), important for the applications to games. Many properties are also carried on from hypercubes to hyperstructures, usually with a modified formulation. Multiple switches algorithms, like APSA and RMSA, generalize to hyperstructures as well.

As shown in [7], Algorithm 2 optimizes CLG-functions on hyperstructures in expected time $2^{O(\sqrt{d\log(n/\sqrt{d})}+\log n)}$, where $n = \sum_{j=0}^{d}\delta_j$. For games, where the maximal outdegree is d and $n = O(d^2)$, the bound collapses to $2^{O(\sqrt{d\log d})}$. The algorithm is adapted from the linear programming algorithm by Matoušek, Sharir and Welzl [29,26]. If $\mathcal{P}$ happens to be binary, the algorithm coincides with Kalai-Ludwig's algorithm; see Section 8.

Algorithm 2: MSW-Style Optimization Algorithm

OPTIMIZE(CLG-structure $\mathcal{P}$, initial vertex v_0)

(1)   **if** $\mathcal{P} = v_0$
(2)   **return** v_0
(3)   **else**
(4)   choose a random facet F of $\mathcal{P}$, not containing v_0
(5) $v^* \leftarrow$ OPTIMIZE$(\mathcal{P} \setminus F, v_0)$
(6)   **if** neighbor u of v^* on F is better than v^*
(7)   **return** OPTIMIZE(F, u)
(8)   **else**
(9)   **return** v^*

The importance of CLG-functions stems from the fact that the strategy measures from [24,31,6] are indeed CLG-functions, as shown in [7]. Moreover, CLG-functions on hypercubes can be transformed to CUPBFs by introducing an artificial order on unordered neighbors [7]. Also, CLG-functions on hyperstructures can be transformed analogously to CUPBF-like functions on hyperstructures. Finally, we showed in [7] that any CLG-function reduces to an *LP-type problem,* an abstract framework for linear programming [29] and problems in computational geometry [26,15]. These reductions provide a strong argument for CLG-functions as a link between well-studied areas that look very different on the surface.

CLG-functions simultaneously allow for subexponential and multiple switch algorithms. Although the latter currently have worse known upper bounds, good practical behavior of such algorithms, confirmed by experiments, make them very attractive and competitive [2,5,4]. We hope that a thorough investigation of random walks on the favorable CU- or CLG-structures will allow for improved bounds for multiple switching algorithms, both on the average and in the worst case.

References

1. E. Aarts and J. K. Lenstra, editors. *Local Search in Combinatorial Optimization.* John Wiley & Sons, 1997.
2. H. Björklund, V. Petersson, and S. Vorobyov. Experiments with iterative improvement algorithms on completely unimodal hypercubes. Technical Report 2001-017, Information Technology/Uppsala University, September 2001. http://www.it.uu.se/research/reports/.
3. H. Björklund and S. Sandberg. Algorithms for combinatorial optimization and games adapted from linear programming. In B. ten Cate, editor, *Proceedings of the Eighth ESSLLI Student Session,* 2003. to appear.
4. H. Björklund, S. Sandberg, and S. Vorobyov. An experimental study of algorithms for completely unimodal optimization. Technical Report 2002-030, Department of Information Technology, Uppsala University, October 2002. http://www.it.uu.se/research/reports/.
5. H. Björklund, S. Sandberg, and S. Vorobyov. Optimization on completely unimodal hypercubes. Technical Report 018, Uppsala University / Information Technology, May 2002. http://www.it.uu.se/research/reports/.
6. H. Björklund, S. Sandberg, and S. Vorobyov. A discrete subexponential algorithm for parity games. In H. Alt and M. Habib, editors, *20th International Symposium on Theoretical Aspects of Computer Science, STACS'2003,* volume 2607 of *Lecture Notes in Computer Science,* pages 663–674, Berlin, 2003. Springer-Verlag. Full preliminary version: TR-2002-026, Department of Information Technology, Uppsala University, September 2002.
7. H. Björklund, S. Sandberg, and S. Vorobyov. On combinatorial structure and algorithms for parity games. Technical Report 2003-002, Department of Information Technology, Uppsala University, January 2003. http://www.it.uu.se/research/reports/.
8. H. Björklund, S. Sandberg, and S. Vorobyov. Randomized subexponential algorithms for parity games. Technical Report 2003-019, Department of Information Technology, Uppsala University, April 2003. http://www.it.uu.se/research/reports/.
9. E. Boros and P. L. Hammer. Pseudo-boolean optimization. Technical Report RRR 48-2001, RUTCOR Rutger Center for Operations Research, 2001.
10. E. M. Clarke, O. Grumberg, and D. Peled. *Model Checking.* MIT Press, 2000.
11. A. Condon. The complexity of stochastic games. *Information and Computation,* 96:203–224, 1992.
12. A. Condon. On algorithms for simple stochastic games. *DIMACS Series in Discrete Mathematics and Theoretical Computer Science,* 13:51–71, 1993.
13. E. A. Emerson. Model checking and the Mu-calculus. In N. Immerman and Ph. G. Kolaitis, editors, *DIMACS Series in Discrete Mathematics,* volume 31, pages 185–214, 1997.
14. E. A. Emerson and C. S. Jutla. Tree automata, μ-calculus and determinacy. In *Annual IEEE Symp. on Foundations of Computer Science,* pages 368–377, 1991.

15. B. Gärtner. A subexponential algorithm for abstract optimization problems. *SIAM Journal on Computing*, 24:1018–1035, 1995.
16. B Gärtner. Combinatorial linear programming: Geometry can help. In *RANDOM'98*, volume 1518 of *Lect. Notes Comput. Sci.*, pages 82–96, 1998.
17. B Gärtner. The random-facet simplex algorithm on combinatorial cubes. *Random Structures and Algorithms*, 20(3):353–381, 2002.
18. E. Grädel, W. Thomas, and T. Wilke, editors. *Automata Logics and Infinite Games. A Guide to Current Research*, volume 2500 of *Lecture Notes in Computer Science*. Springer-Verlag, 2003.
19. P. L. Hammer, B. Simeone, Th. M. Liebling, and D. De Werra. From linear separability to unimodality: a hierarchy of pseudo-boolean functions. *SIAM J. Disc. Math.*, 1(2):174–184, 1988.
20. P. Hansen, B. Jaumard, and V. Mathon. Constrained nonlinear 0-1 programming (state-of-the-art survey). *ORSA Journal on Computing*, 5(2):97–119, 1993.
21. A. J. Hoffman and R. M. Karp. On nonterminating stochastic games. *Management Science*, 12(5):359–370, 1966.
22. M. Jurdziński. Small progress measures for solving parity games. In H. Reichel and S. Tison, editors, *17th STACS*, volume 1770 of *Lect. Notes Comput. Sci.*, pages 290–301. Springer-Verlag, 2000.
23. G. Kalai. A subexponential randomized simplex algorithm. In *24th ACM STOC*, pages 475–482, 1992.
24. W. Ludwig. A subexponential randomized algorithm for the simple stochastic game problem. *Information and Computation*, 117:151–155, 1995.
25. Y. Mansour and S. Singh. On the complexity of policy iteration. In *Uncertainty in Artificial Intelligence'99*, 1999.
26. J. Matoušek, M. Sharir, and M. Welzl. A subexponential bound for linear programming. In *8th ACM Symp. on Computational Geometry*, pages 1–8, 1992.
27. C. Papadimitriou. Algorithms, games, and the internet. In *ACM Annual Symposium on Theory of Computing*, pages 749–753. ACM, July 2001.
28. V. Petersson and S. Vorobyov. A randomized subexponential algorithm for parity games. *Nordic Journal of Computing*, 8:324–345, 2001.
29. M. Sharir and E. Welzl. A combinatorial bound for linear programming and related problems. In *9th Symposium on Theoretical Aspects of Computer Science (STACS)*, volume 577 of *Lecture Notes in Computer Science*, pages 569–579, Berlin, 1992. Springer-Verlag.
30. C. A. Tovey. Local improvement on discrete structures. In E. Aarts and Lenstra J. K., editors, *Local Search in Combinatorial Optimization*, pages 57–89. John Wiley & Sons, 1997.
31. J. Vöge and M. Jurdziński. A discrete strategy improvement algorithm for solving parity games. In E. A. Emerson and A. P. Sistla, editors, *CAV'00: Computer-Aided Verification*, volume 1855 of *Lect. Notes Comput. Sci.*, pages 202–215. Springer-Verlag, 2000.
32. D. Wiedemann. Unimodal set-functions. *Congressus Numerantium*, 50:165–169, 1985.
33. K. Williamson Hoke. Completely unimodal numberings of a simple polytope. *Discrete Applied Mathematics*, 20:69–81, 1988.
34. U. Zwick and M. Paterson. The complexity of mean payoff games on graphs. *Theor. Comput. Sci.*, 158:343–359, 1996.

Polynomial Approximations for Model Checking

Nikolai V. Shilov[1,2] and Natalya O. Garanina[2]

[1] Visiting Erskine Fellow, University of Canterbury, Christchurch, New Zealand
nikolai.shilov@cosc.canterbury.ac.nz
[2] Institute of Informatics Systems, Novosibirsk, Russia
shilov@iis.nsk.su

Abstract. The μ-Calculus of D. Kozen (1983) is a very powerful propositional program logic with fixpoints. It is widely used for specification and verification. Model checking is a very popular automatic approach for verification of specifications of finite state systems. The most efficient algorithms that have been developed so far for model checking of the μ-Calculus in finite state systems have exponential upper bounds. A. Emerson, C. Jutla, and P. Sistla studied (1993) the first fragment of the μ-Calculus that permits arbitrary nesting and alternations of fixpoints, and polynomial model checking in finite state systems. In contrast we study lower and upper approximations for model checking that are computable in polynomial time, and that can give correct semantics in finite models for formulae with arbitrary nesting and alternations. A.Emerson, C.Jutla, and P.Sistla proved also that the model checking problem for the μ-Calculus in finite state systems is in $\mathcal{NP} \cap co\text{-}\mathcal{NP}$. We develop another proof (that we believe is a new one) as a by-product of our study.

Keywords: μ-Calculus, model checking, complexity.

1 Preliminaries

The μ-Calculus of D.Kozen (μC) [8] is a very powerful propositional program logic with fixpoints. It is widely used for specification and verification of properties of finite state systems [2]. Due to this reason we restrict ourselves in this paper by finite state systems also. Please refer to [9] for the elementary introduction to μC. The comprehensive definition of μC can be found in a recent textbook [1].

The syntax of μC is constructed from two disjoint alphabets of propositional variables (Prp) and action symbols (Act). It consists of formulae: $\phi ::= (\neg\phi) \mid (\phi \wedge \psi) \mid \langle a \rangle \phi \mid ([a]\phi) \mid (\mu p.\phi) \mid (\nu p.\phi)$, ($p \in Prp$, $a \in Act$, no negative instances of bounded variables). The semantics of μC is defined in models. A model is a triple (D, R, V), where the domain D is a non-empty set, the interpretation R is a total mapping $R : Act \to 2^{D \times D}$, the valuation V is another total mapping $V : Prp \to 2^D$. In every model $M = (D, R, V)$, for every formula ϕ, the semantics $M(\phi)$ is a subset of the domain D that is defined by induction by the formula structure.

M. Broy and A.V. Zamulin (Eds.): PSI 2003, LNCS 2890, pp. 395–400, 2003.

A propositional variable is said to be a propositional constant in a formula iff it is free in the formula. A formula is said to be in a normal form iff negation is applied to propositional constants in the formula only. Due to standard De Morgan laws and duality of $[\,]$ and $\langle\rangle$, μ and ν, every formula of μC is equivalent to some formula in the normal form that can be constructed in polynomial time.

Let us extend μC by some new features: total S5 modalities $\square$ and $\diamond$, and second order (SO) quantifiers $\forall$ and $\exists$. The syntax: $\phi ::= \mu C \mid (\square\phi) \mid (\diamond\phi) \mid (\forall p. \phi) \mid (\exists p. \phi)$. The semantics:

$$- M(\square\psi) = \begin{cases} D, \text{ if } M(\psi) = D \\ \emptyset \text{ otherwise} \end{cases}, \qquad M(\diamond\psi) = \begin{cases} D, \text{ if } M(\psi) \neq \emptyset \\ \emptyset \text{ otherwise} \end{cases},$$

$$- M(\forall p.\psi) = \text{ the greatest lower bound of } \{M_{S/p}(\psi) : S \subseteq D\},$$
$$M(\exists p.\psi) = \text{ the least upper bound of } \{M_{S/p}(\psi) : S \subseteq D\},$$

where ψ, p range over formulae and propositional variables, and $M_{S/p}$ denotes the model that agrees with M everywhere but p: $V_{S/p}(p) = S$.

We also use a variation of the following classical theorem of R. Fagin [5]. (Please refer to [6] for the elementary introduction to descriptive complexity in general and Fagin theorem in particular. For further details refer to [7].)

A set SET of finite structures is in $\mathcal{NP}$ iff there exists a first-order formula FRM that $SET = \{STR : STR \models (\exists P_1...\exists P_m\ FRM)\}$, where $P_1, ... P_m$ are predicate symbols in FRM.

The theorem implies that for every first-order formula FRM the following set of finite structures $\{STR : STR \models (\forall P_1...\forall P_m\ FRM)\}$ is in co-$\mathcal{NP}$. We generalize this claim a little bit.

Assume FRM to be a first-order formula with predicate symbols $P_1, ... P_m$ and $Q_1, ... Q_n$. Assume also that we are interested in finite structures STR where interpretations of $Q_1, ... Q_n$ are some explicit second-order functions $G_1, ... G_n$ of interpretations of $P_1, ... P_m$. In this case we say that FRM is a first-order formula with predicate symbols $P_1, ... P_m$ and second-order functions $G_1, ... G_n$.

Proposition 1. *For all predicate symbols $P_1, ... P_m$, for every first-order formula FRM with predicate symbols $P_1, ... P_m$ and some second-order functions, the following set of finite structures $\{STR : STR \models (\forall P_1...\forall P_m\ FRM)\}$ is in co-$\mathcal{NP}$ provided that all used second-order functions are computable in time polynomial on the structure size.*

2   Upper Bound

The model checking problem for the propositional μ-Calculus in finite state systems is to decide the following set $\{(\phi, M, s) : \phi$ is a μC formula, M is a finite model, and $s \in M(\phi)\}$. The best known complexity class for the model checking problem for μC in finite models is $\mathcal{NP} \cap$ co-$\mathcal{NP}$ [4]. (It is not known whether the problem is (in)complete in any of $\mathcal{NP}$ and co-$\mathcal{NP}$.) A new proof for this upper bound is sketched below.

Proposition 2.

- For every propositional variable p, every $\mu C + S5$ formula θ in the normal form, and every its subformula $(\mu p.\phi)$ that is not nested within the scope of other μ or ν, the following is a tautology: $\theta \leftrightarrow \left(\forall p.\left(\Box(\phi \to p) \to \theta^p_{(\mu p.\phi)} \right) \right)$.
- For every propositional variable q, every $\mu C + S5$ formula θ in the normal form, and every its subformula $(\nu q.\psi)$ that is not nested within the scope of other μ or ν, the following is a tautology: $\theta \leftrightarrow \left(\exists q.\left(\Box(q \to \psi) \wedge \theta^q_{(\nu q.\psi)} \right) \right)$.

(Here and throughout the paper $\to$ and $\leftrightarrow$ stay for standard abbreviations for implication and equivalence, X^Y_Z is the formula obtained by substituting Y for all occurrences of Z in X.)

A formula is said to be in the special prefix form iff it looks as follows:

$(\star)$ $\underbrace{\forall p_n. \exists q_n. \ldots \forall p_1. \exists q_1.}_{n \text{ times}}$

$$\underbrace{\left(\Box(\phi_1 \to p_1) \to \left(\Box(q_1 \to \psi_1) \wedge (\ldots(\Box(\phi_n \to p_n) \to (\Box(q_n \to \psi_n) \wedge \theta))\ldots)\right)\right)}_{n \text{ times}}$$

where n is some integer, all formulae θ, ϕ_1, ψ_1, ..., ϕ_n, ψ_n are quantifier- and fixpoint-free, and without any instance of any of the propositional variables p_1, q_1, ... p_n, q_n under negations.

Corollary 1. *Every formula of the μ-Calculus is equivalent to some formula in the special prefix form that can be constructed in polynomial time.*

In the following proposition we use symbols of second order functions that are interpreted in models by second order functions on sets of states. We introduce these symbols and functions for Skolemization of existential quantifiers in formulae that are in the special prefix forms.

Proposition 3. *Let ξ be an arbitrary formula in the special prefix form $(\star)$. Let g_n, ... g_1 be disjoint symbols of second order functions of 1, ... n arguments respectively. For every model M there exist total second order functions on sets of states $G_n : (2^D)^1 \to 2^D$, ... $G_1 : (2^D)^n \to 2^D$, with values computable in polynomial time, such that the following equality holds:*

$$M(\xi) = M_{(G_1/g_1)\ldots(G_n/g_n)}\left(\forall p_1. \ldots \forall p_n. \right.$$
$$\left. \left(\Box(\bigwedge_{i=1}^{i=n}(\phi_i \to p_i)) \to \theta \right)^{g_n(p_n)\ldots g_1(p_1,\ldots p_n)}_{q_n \ldots q_1} \right).$$

In combination with proposition 1, it implies the following theorem.

Theorem 1. *The model checking problem for the propositional μ-Calculus in finite models is in $\mathcal{NP} \cap \text{co-}\mathcal{NP}$.*

3   Approximating Model Checking

The most efficient algorithms that have been developed so far for model checking of the μC in finite models have exponential upper bounds (ex., [3]). A. Emerson, C. Jutla, and P. Sistla studied the first fragment of the μ-Calculus that permits arbitrary nesting and alternations of fixpoints, and polynomial model checking in finite state systems [4]. The fragment comprises the formulae in the normal form where only closed subformulae can occur in the range of box [ ] and at most one conjunct in every conjunction $\wedge$ is not a closed formula.

We suggest another "fragment" that enjoys polynomial model checking in finite models in spite of nesting and amount of alternations. In contrast to the syntactical definition of the above fragment, the new one has a computational characterization. It exploits a polynomial approximation algorithm presented below. The algorithm calculates lower and upper approximations for semantics of formulae in finite models. If for some formula in some model both approximations are equal, then the algorithm succeeds in calculation of semantics of the formula in the model.

Input a formula ϕ of μC and a finite model M.

Preprocessing. Convert ϕ into the equivalent normal form and then into the equivalent special prefix form (see $\star$). Let two vectors of formulae $\Phi = (\phi_1, ...\phi_n)$ and $\Psi = (\psi_1, ...\psi_n)$ collect all ϕ's and ψ's in ξ.
Let $\underline{P}^j = (\underline{P}_1^j, ...\underline{P}_n^j)$ and $\underline{Q}^j = (\underline{Q}_1^j, ...\underline{Q}_n^j)$ (where $j \geq 0$) be vectors of disjoint variables for sets of states.
Let $\overline{P}^k = (\overline{P}_1^k, ...\overline{P}_n^k)$ and $\overline{Q}^k = (\overline{Q}_1^k, ...\overline{Q}_n^k)$ (where $k \geq 0$) be some other vectors of disjoint variables also for sets of states.
Let $j := 0$ and $k := 0$, $\underline{Q}^0 := (\emptyset, ...\emptyset)$ and $\overline{P}_0 := (D, ...D)$.

Processing.

Repeat
$\underline{P}^j :=$ the least fixpoint of $\lambda S_n...S_1 \cdot \big(M_{(\underline{Q}_n^j/q_n)...(\underline{Q}_1^j/q_1)(S_n/p_n)...(S_1/p_1)}(\Phi) \big)$,
$\underline{Q}^{j+1} :=$ the greatest fixpoint of $\lambda S_n...S_1 \cdot \big(M_{(S_n/q_n)...(S_1/q_1)(\underline{P}_n^j/p_n)...(\underline{P}_1^j/p_1)}(\Psi) \big)$,
$j := j + 1$ **until** $\underline{Q}^j = \underline{Q}^{j-1}$.

Repeat
$\overline{P}^k :=$ the least fixpoint of $\lambda S_n...S_1 \cdot \big(M_{(\overline{Q}_n^k/q_n)...(\overline{Q}_1^k/q_1)(S_n/p_n)...(S_1/p_1)}(\Phi) \big)$,
$\overline{Q}^{k+1} :=$ the greatest fixpoint of $\lambda S_n...S_1 \cdot \big(M_{(S_n/q_n)...(S_1/q_1)(\overline{P}_n^k/p_n)...(\overline{P}_1^k/p_1)}(\Psi) \big)$,
$k := k + 1$ **until** $\overline{Q}^k = \overline{Q}_{k-1}$.

Let $j := j - 1$ and $k := k - 1$.

Output two sets of states: $\underline{M}(\phi) \equiv M_{(\underline{Q}_n^j/q_n)...(\underline{Q}_1^j/q_1)(\underline{P}_n^j/p_n)...(\underline{P}_1^j/p_1)}(\theta)$ and
$\overline{M}(\phi) \equiv M_{(\overline{Q}_n^k/q_n)...(\overline{Q}_1^k/q_1)(\overline{P}_n^k/p_n)...(\overline{P}_1^k/p_1)}(\theta)$.

Proposition 4. *For every formula ϕ of the propositional μ-Calculus, and for every finite Kripke model M, the approximation algorithm returns lower and upper bounds for semantics of the formula in the model: $\underline{M}(\phi) \subseteq M(\phi) \subseteq \overline{M}(\phi)$.*

It implies the following theorem.

Theorem 2. *For every formula ϕ of the propositional μ-Calculus, and for every finite Kripke model M, if $\underline{M}(\phi) = \overline{M}(\phi)$ then $M(\phi) = \underline{M}(\phi) = \overline{M}(\phi)$.*

Let us give an example of the formula that is in the proposed fragment: $FAIR \equiv \nu q.\Big([a]q \ \wedge \ \big(\mu p.(r \vee [a]p)\big)\Big)$. The formula holds in finite models on those states where the propositional constant r holds infinitely often along every infinite a-path that starts from these states. The formula $FAIR$ does not belong to the fragment of A. Emerson, C. Jutla, and P. Sistla, and we do not know whether $FAIR$ is equivalent to some formula in this fragment.

Let us remark also that our "fragment" has no restrictions on nesting and alternations. For every $n \geq 1$ the formula $(\mu x_1.\nu y_1. ...(\mu x_n.\nu y_n.(\bigwedge_{i=1}^{i=n}(x_i \wedge y_i)))...)$ belongs to the "fragment", it has $(2 \times n - 1)$ alternations of fixpoints and the nesting level $2 \times n$.

The Model Checker that utilizes the approximation algorithm is in the process of implementation. It outputs the upper and lower approximations of semantics of the input formulae in the input finite models (that sometimes are their exact semantics). An experimental and theoretical study of its utility is a topic for further research. In our theoretical studies we hope to develop some syntactical conditions for input formulae and easy-to-check semantic conditions for input models that guarantee that the approximation algorithm calculates the exact semantics. At present we can prove a very simple claim of this kind: the algorithm calculates the exact semantics in finite models for all μC formulae without alternations; in particular, it is a correct model checking algorithm for the Computation Tree Logic (CTL [2]). In our experimental study we hope to demonstrate utility of both lower and upper approximations in practical program and system verification.

Acknowledgement. We would like to thank anonymous reviewers for comments and suggestions. Unfortunately we are unable to provide all proof within this extended abstract due to space limitations. But all proofs and the full-body version of the paper are available upon request.

References

1. Arnold A. and Niwinski D. *Rudiments of μ-calculus.* North Holland, 2001.
2. Clarke E.M., Grumberg O., Peled D. *Model Checking.* MIT Press, 1999.
3. Cleaveland R., Klain M., Steffen B. *Faster Model-Checking for Mu-Calculus.* Lecture Notes in Computer Science, v.663, 1993, p.410–422.
4. Emerson E.A., Jutla C.S., Sistla A.P. *On model-checking for fragments of Mu-Calculus.* Lecture Notes in Computer Science, v.697, 1993, p.385–396.

5. Fagin R. *Generalized First-Order Spectra and Polynomial-Time Recognizable Sets.* Complexity of Computations, SIAM-AMS Proc., v.7, 1974, p.27–41.
6. Immerman N. *Descriptive Complexity: A Logician's Approach to Computation.* Notices of the American Mathematical Society, v.42, n.10, 1995, p.1127–1133.
7. Immerman N. *Descriptive Complexity.* 1999, Springer-Verlag
8. Kozen D. *Results on the Propositional Mu-Calculus.* Theoretical Computer Science, v.27, n.3, 1983, p.333–354.
9. Shilov N.V., Yi K. *How to find a coin: propositional program logics made easy.* The Bulletin of the European Association for Theoretical Computer Science, v.75, 2001, p.127–151.

Separating Search and Strategy in Solver Cooperations[*]

Brice Pajot and Eric Monfroy

Institut de Recherche en Informatique de Nantes (IRIN)
University of Nantes – France
{pajot,monfroy}@irin.univ-nantes.fr

Abstract. In the constraint programming community, solver cooperation is now an established paradigm that aims at using several solvers
to improve some kind of limitations or inefficiency imposed by the use
of a unique solver; solver cooperation applications range over several
fields such as heterogeneous domain solving, heterogeneous constraint
forms over the same domain, or distributed problem solving. Meanwhile,
search-languages have emphasised the need to clearly separate the different steps during a constraint problem resolution. In a similar direction,
this paper presents a paradigm that enables the user to properly separate
computation strategies from the search phases in solver cooperations.

1 Introduction and Motivations

Solver cooperation mainly aims at solving the problems inherent to the use of
a single solver. *Cooperation* is defined by a concurrent effort or by an interaction to one end, that is the solving of the initial constraint problem. The use
of constraint cooperation can find numerous applications: distributed problems
(e.g., DCSP solving, embedding of security paradigm), solving of heterogeneous
domain problems (with no existing solvers or only generic solvers), more efficient solving (by gaining from the performances of each solver), and re-use of
previously developed software parts. Describing a strategy is not an easy task;
it needs effective and suited tools. Mainly, cooperations must be supervised by
the user; *cooperation strategies* define the way the solvers interact. They can be
defined with help of a *cooperation strategy language*. The latter, with a suited
framework, enables the user to benefit from the potency of solver cooperation.
Currently, several similar research projects exist. Most of them performs a mix
between the search phase and the computation strategy. *Search* is a common
step of constraint resolution which performs a given walk[1] into the search space
of the problem, whereas the *computation strategy* defines the way of solving the
current sub-problem (w.r.t. the part of the domain being explored). Formerly,
for the solving of a problem with a single solver, the search steps were mixed
with the computational parts; some researchers have thus emphasised the need

---

[*] Financially supported by European project COCONUT IST-2000-26063.
[1] The walk can be described by a *search strategy*.

M. Broy and A.V. Zamulin (Eds.): PSI 2003, LNCS 2890, pp. 401–414, 2003.
© Springer-Verlag Berlin Heidelberg 2003

for separating these tasks by identifying some patterns of reusability. In the same direction, we propose to *clearly separate* these two parts. Moreover, we provide the user with some tools through a *modular solver cooperation framework* and a *cooperation language*. These tools ensure the separation of the four main components which are parts of our system: *Modelling, Search, Strategy, and Solvers*. The novelty of this approach can be tested in a prototypic implementation taking place in the heart of the European project COCONUT which uses solver cooperation.

Numerous previous works on the field of cooperation can be found in the past years. Some tools and frameworks for cooperation of distributed agents already exist (e.g. Manifold [1]). In the more specialised domain of constraints, some works can be found: HELIOS [2] is an heterogeneous distributed cooperative problem solving system that defines an environment where heterogeneous solvers can cooperate. It mainly aims at suppressing the interoperability barriers between the different computing agents but does not offer any facilities for cooperation description. More recently, Monfroy [3] defined a coordination-based chaotic iteration algorithm, for which an implementation has been realized in DICE [4]. Currently, this system does not really allow to define strategies since it is only suitable (devoted) for distributed constraint solving by means of propagation. Thus, the cooperation is reduced to a single kind of strategy (fix point). GMACS [5] is a heterogeneous constraint-solver collaboration framework: it mainly defines a way to combine method and solvers; furthermore, it is based on a graphical approach for describing a collaboration. BALI [6] is a previous experiment in solver collaboration languages; it enables one to define solver strategies, and is based on an environment which is also able to absorb heterogeneity of solver data-types and protocols. One of the problems of BALI and GMACS is the mix between the search part and the resolution part, which does not make easy the task of defining a strategy. More recently, Hofstedt ([7] and its enhanced version [8]) proposed a cooperation framework for constraint problem solving; nevertheless the scope of resolution is more restricted (no optimisation problem resolution, local control, further work needed on mixed integer/real problem solving). Moreover, separating the search step from the global resolution process was successful with, e.g., Localizer [9] or COMET [10] for local search or for SALSA [11] for mixing local and global search. Mosel [12] is a modelling language that aims at combining solvers and solution algorithms; nevertheless, we do not have enough feedback on the success of integrating external user-components into this (easily-extendable said) framework.

This paper is organised as follows. First part relates a conceptual point of view for cooperation/collaboration of solvers. Second part presents a more theoretical framework for the needed notions. Third part introduces the language for describing a cooperation by mainly separating search and resolution parts. And fourth part relates some facts on implementing this kind of cooperation concepts into a framework used for the European project COCONUT.

2   Conceptual Point of View

For the sake of finding a global schema to constraint cooperation, we define the paradigm of constraint programming as :

$$CP = Modelling + Strategy + Solvers + Search$$

It means that each of these parts must be independently provided to the user, and none of them must interlace with another at a given layer. The *Modelling* step enables the user to state his problem whereas *search + strategy* describes the way to solve the problem by means of some given *solvers*. Combining these different parts improves the strength and expressiveness of tools for strategy description, keeping the necessary modularity. Hereafter, the different modules are further detailed.

Constraint Modelling. In essence, constraint problem description is declarative. But the task of representing a problem into a constraint form can become rather tedious, particularly for a non skilled-user. The means of representing a constraint (or by extension an optimisation) problem can be complex. For example, it must offer the ability to describe global constraints (e.g., using $\sum$) or optimisation criteria, by keeping a simple expressive way. Simplifying these tasks is the goal of modelling tools like OPL [13]. On the other hand, using a single solver for constraint problem resolution often leads to arbitrary and meaningless transformations, which can reduce the productivity and efficiency of the global task[2].

Describing a Strategy. A solver-cooperation *strategy* describes the way of combining solver applications in order to find the desired result. In our solver cooperation paradigm, solvers can interact asynchronously. Using cooperations enables one to solve heterogeneous problems that a unique solver cannot; more, it can improve computation time by using intermediate results from other parts. Computation time can also be improved by benefiting from heavily distributed architectures. The latter indeed fully fit in the solver cooperation paradigm. The way to make solvers cooperate is described by *a cooperation strategy*. Mainly, three ways exist:

- The use of a good strategy, i.e., a strategy which is well-established for a given type of problems. It can be fully described by means of a tool (language like BALI or GUI such as GMACS or [14]) or by hard-coding.
- The use of automated strategy discovery. Some form of learning can be used. What can be learned must be defined to use this kind of strategies. Some tracks already exist in automated strategies as in [15] or in automated algorithms with learning [16].

---

[2] Transformation of a non-linear system into a linear one is one of these examples. Here, the meaning of the initial constraint system is lost.

– The use of an intermediate method by describing only some strategy parts (some well-known strategies that are proved to solve a particular problem). Then define rules of the form

$$\bigwedge_i Prop_i(P) \longrightarrow Strat_A$$

Here, $Prop_i$ defines the different problem properties; they can be of numerous types (e.g., syntactic, semantic). Rules are triggered when the current properties of the problem match the required rule properties, and the associated strategy is applied. Nevertheless, some choices have to be done: select a candidate (between fired ones), the way to combine them if we decide to trigger several of them; these choices define some kind of *cooperation strategies*. Note that learning can additionally be used (generating new rules).

Search. *Search* is commonly described as the way the search space is explored. Consider the general paradigm of constraint solving. It consists of giving values to variables such that all the constraints of the problem are satisfied. It can be achieved by giving all possible values to the variable, thus enumerating the candidates of the search-space (could be huge). This kind of labelling can be represented by a *search-tree* (or more generally by a search-graph), where each node is equivalent to valuing a variable. The search-tree leaves define a fully valued problem. Then, the leaf is accepted as a solution if it satisfies all the constraints, else it is suppressed. Doing this complete job is too long and costly. That is why search phase interlaces with pruning phase: constraints are used to prune some inconsistent values (values which can not be candidate due to some constraints) from the domains of variables by using specific techniques (propagation,...). Walking through a search-tree can be achieved in various ways. Some well-know search-strategies are depth-first (we try to reach the leaves) or breadth-first (the search-tree is walked level by level). But, we can have some more-advanced strategies using, for example, heuristic criteria. This process can be made separately from the pure computational part; some tools (e.g.Localizer, COMET, or SALSA) already contribute to this task. The same job can be achieved at a *higher granularity* by using solvers. Using the search phase at the solver granularity (propagation) is enough systematic and uses depth-first algorithms. At the strategy granularity, simple strategies can be used, but most of the time, there are some feedback on the previously-realized computations, which guide the next search step. Similarly to domain-search, some kinds of choice points for the solver-cooperation strategies exist. Thus, they also define a search space that must be partially or totally explored.

3   Theoretical Framework for Cooperation Strategies

Following the analogy with solver resolution, we define the global schema of solver-cooperation resolution as defined by the Fig. 1. It separates the search module from the strategy module. Search guides the global work, but: on the

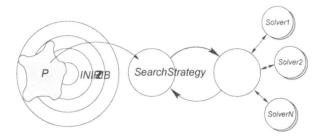

Fig. 1. General cooperation schema

one hand, search is meaningless for some kind of resolutions (e.g., symbolic computations only), and so, not used; on the other hand, the strategy module can give some feedback to help managing the search. For the sake of clarity, we work on an abstract problem P. Instantiation can be further made on a specific constraint framework.

Tools for Strategy Description. For the need of a strategy-description, we must present some useful bricks. Above all, we must define *property checkers*. The latter enable one to verify if a problem respects a given property ϕ. This is useful for using loops or conditionals in strategies.

$$Checker_\phi : P \longrightarrow D$$

where D is an ordered domain defining the acceptance of P by the checker. For example, if $D = B$, then the value is interpreted on the Boolean domain ($\{t, f\}$, and we consider the order $t > f$). Another example could be the set of the three values $\{Rejected, DontKnow, Accepted\}$; it defines some kind of fuzzy acceptance.

A *problem filter* takes a subset of a problem verifying a property ϕ above a certain threshold:

$$Filter_\phi : P, \alpha \longrightarrow P' \text{ s.t. } P' \subseteq P : Checker_\phi(P') \geq \alpha$$

Then let's define more generally a *solver* as a computation unit (an Inference Component):

$$IC_\alpha : P, AdditionalData_\alpha \longrightarrow P$$

Thus, a solver is just a computational part able to apply an arbitrary transformation on a problem (symbolic, domain reduction, relaxation, etc...). Here, $AdditionalData_\alpha$ represents the auxiliary solver-related computation parameters; it can be something like an accuracy parameter, an optimisation parameter, etc... An auxiliary solver-related function enables one to retrieve some information from a given problem.

$$AF_\alpha : P \longrightarrow AdditionalData_\alpha$$

Strategy Choice Points. Applying a strategy leads to make some choices, like the solver to be applied at a given time, the part of the problem the solver applies to or the necessity of launching several concurrent computing instances. These choice-points are called *strategy choice-points* and the way to make these choices define a part of the *cooperation strategy.* A strategy choice-point can be defined generally by the schema on Fig. 2, where: P is the initial problem and P' is the resulting problem of the applied strategy. *Duplicator* defines an atomic operation that duplicates the problem into two branches with the same problem. The duplicator supervises the computational flow: it enables the user to launch sequentially or concurrentially the computations on the different branches. The main purpose is to improve the computation time (using some multiprocess technology). Nonetheless, it adds a time parameter which makes possible to define new time-dependant operators (*First, Bounded − Time*). Next, *Op1* and *Op2* define the operations needed to differentiate the problem on both branches. *Combinator* is a function that tells how to combine both resulting problems. This latter can be of various types (syntactic, semantic, solution-based,...)

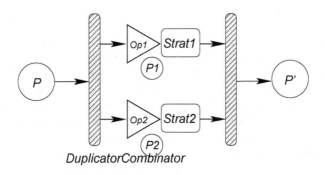

Fig. 2. Strategy choice-point schema

Using this global schema, we can define different strategy choice-points:

1. $P = P_1 \cup P_2$, $P_1 \cap P_2 \neq \emptyset$. This is especially useful when we compute with several solvers which know how to solve only a partial part of the problem (these parts being not distinct). Here, *Op1* and *Op2* can be two filters *Filter1* and *Filter2* on problems. *Filters* extract a sub-part of a problem (relations, variables, ...). Processing this kind of configurations often needs to apply two different strategies.
2. $P = P_1 \cup P_2$, $P_1 \cap P_2 = \emptyset$. This is a particular case of the previous point. It can occurs when a problem is composed of two separated problems (that were linked at a previous step of the global computation), or simply when we can separate data in several parts. There are no requirements on the subsequently applied strategies.

3. $P = P_1 = P_2$ and $Strat1 \neq Strat2$. The problem is duplicated and two different strategies are applied. So, $Op1$ and $Op2$ are both the identity operation. Two different strategies can be "tested". We keep only one of the computed problems, the one that satisfies a given criterion. This work is made by the combinator.

$$P = \left\{ \begin{matrix} Best\_\varPhi \\ DontCare \\ ... \end{matrix} \right\} (P_1, P_2)$$

For example, $Best\_\varPhi$ keeps the problem that best satisfies the property $\varPhi$ and $DontCare$ waits for the two problems keeping randomly only one of them. $Best\_\varPhi$ can be defined with the help of checker as:

$$Best\_\varPhi(P_1, P_2) = \left\{ \begin{matrix} P_1 \textbf{ if } Checker_\varPhi(P_1) > Checker_\varPhi(P_2) \\ P_2 \textbf{ if } Checker_\varPhi(P_1) < Checker_\varPhi(P_2) \\ DontCare(P_1, P_2) \textbf{ else} \end{matrix} \right.$$

Of course, numerous other strategy choice-points can be found, but the above-mentioned ones are of current use.

Computational Flow. A computational flow describes the way the data are processed. A single strategy process can work on data *sequentially*. Using some multiprocess technology enables one to duplicate the computational flow in order to process multiple data simultaneously (independent or not from each others). The main purpose is to process the computation more quickly (parallel or concurrent search), but it also enables the user to take computation time into account.

When no time optimisation is needed, *sequential computation is always possible*. A parallel computation works on a small amount of data divided equally from the initial set in multiple similar processes. Concurrent (or competitive) computations work on the same data with multiple different processes. By nature, parallel or concurrent computations are asynchronous (different processes can have different duration of job completion). As usual, synchronisation of asynchronous flows must be performed in order to combine the resulting problems. Two modules are involved in the computational flow : the *Duplicator* and the *Combinator*. An underlying layer processes the computational flow. The duplicator manages the fact that the processes are executed in a sequential or concurrent way. The combinator enforces the synchronisation of the asynchronous flows (no importance if the flows are executed sequentially or concurrently).

4   Interaction Languages

Now, we must provide the user with a way to describe strategies. Based on an asynchronous framework, the best choice would have been some kind of rules or reactive programming language. Nevertheless, one of the first goals of the project upon which the first implementation relies was to offer some interactive mechanisms. It enables one to have incremental non-planned scenarios like:

1) Model the problem (by any previously discussed way) 2) Launch the computation with one solver 3) Look at the store of constraints and variables (a snapshot of the current computation step) 4) Use another solver to obtain a partial result 5) Launch the computation on another more appropriated solver, and so on... The ability for the user to watch the evolution of his results can lead to more efficiency than a bad autonomous strategy finder. Of course, the user can totally define his strategy with some unknown parameters (e.g., the real solver used) and launch the resolution all at once. Hereafter are detailed the different bricks which compose our language.

The basic Strategy Language. L_{Strat} must not be concerned by any search graph management operations. The operations work on the current problem we are dealing with. What does it mean? Let's take Example 1.

Example 1 (A pure strategy search). **First** : a primitive which launches competitive computing, waits for the first result and drops the other.

```
macro S1 : SolverA, SolverB
macro S2 : SolverB, SolverA
First(S1,S2)
SolverC
```

The S1 macro defines the sequential application of SolverA followed by SolverB; the macro S2 defines the inverted application. In this case, the strategy worker launches two computations according to the given strategies (they can be more complicated including other choice-points). The current flow only continues when one of the branches finishes; the other branch (and all the associated processes) is then stopped. The next operation is processed with the application of SolverC as a sequential operation. This example can be generalised to the Best operation or whatever operation that only returns a single problem.

Remark 1. This example describes the computational flow of a simple strategy; the problem we are working on is implicit. With respect to object orienting programming, we could have a special variable like *this*, which could refer to the implicit treated problem. Nevertheless, the user can use intermediate variables or structures (array, lists, ...) for storing intermediate problems if really needed.

Suppose that we now want to combine the results of two strategies acting on two interlaced problems. This scenario is presented on Example 2.

Example 2 (A concurrent computation).

```
macro S1 : SolverA, SolverC
macro S2 : SolverB, SolverA
Duplicate(Parallel):
    FilterA, S1
  | FilterB, S2
Combine(DomainIntersection)
```

Two macros of sequential solver application ($S1$ and $S2$) are created. Each of them are applied in a competitive manner on one part of the problem and on the other part (resp. filtered by the filter $FilterA$ and $FilterB$). The resulting problems are combined in terms of domain intersection. We can thus deduce that the computation is based on value-assignments of variables. For a value to be solution of the non-splitted problem, it must be a common value of the two computations. Hence, we use the `DomainIntersection` as a combiner for the resulting problems. Of course, numerous other operators (loops, conditionals with use of *checkers*[3], `FixPoint`, . . .), and combinators (problem-based, domain-union, . . .) can be used. Nevertheless, further works with pragmatic examples are needed to establish the correct and minimal set of needed operators.

An additional search language layer. L_{Search} enables the user to manipulate the search graph management operations. This is mainly for advanced manipulation concepts (for the developer of solvers for example) or when the global behaviour does not provide the desired control granularity. This language must be able to duplicate a flow (basically in two parts) by specifying the way to manage the domain-search (depth, heuristic, concurrent/sequential), and the possible branch-cut properties. In fact, search is managed by a generic algorithm for which the particular operations define the behaviour.

```
SEARCH(P_init : Problem)
1   leafs ← {P_init}
2   while (leafs ≠ ∅)
3   do node ← SELECTIONSTRATEGY(leafs)
4       nres ← STRATOP(node)
5       PROPAGSTRATEGY(nres, leafs)
6       if ¬(FAILCONDITION(nres))
7          then if (SOLUTIONCONDITION(nres))
8                  then PROCESSSOLUTION(NRES)
9                  else SEARCHOP(leafs, nres)
```

Here, *leafs* is a set-based datatype, from which we can extract (here, SELECTIONSTRATEGY) or add elements. STRATOP defines the strategy step to be applied on the newly extracted node. PROPAGSTRATEGY specifies a way to inform other parts of the search of some newly discovered information. FAILCONDITION and SOLUTIONCONDITION are respectively two boolean functions which can determine if a node can't be or is a solution of the problem. PROCESSSOLUTION handle the solutions (relatively to the goal : finding one/all solutions, anytime solving). Finally, SEARCHOP deals with the proper search-strategy. Example 3 defines a classical branch and cut search on the continuous domain with this set of operators; the splitted variable is the one with the least domain.

---

[3] checkers are functions able to test if a property is verified on a problem.

Example 3 (Classical branch and cut algorithm).

leafs	Stack, $\cup \equiv$ push, SelectionStrategy $\equiv$ pop
FAILCONDITION	OneOfDomains $= \emptyset$
SOLUTIONCONDITION	DomainSize $< 10^{-6}$
STRATOP	Solver1 (Interval propagation)
PROPAGSTRATEGY	None
PROCESSSOLUTION	Collect all and return the result
SEARCHOP	SplitDomain defined by next both properties
ComputationalFlow	Sequential (or concurential)
VariableChoice	LeastDomainVariable

One ore More Third Additional Language Parts. $L_{SolverX}$ provides some *solver-specific operations* for *SolverX*. It can be for example additional types that are only known by a solver (or a future solver), but necessary for any purpose of the computation. The solver provider is responsible for giving sufficient accessors to its new data.

Example 4 (Retrieving a point from a problem). Given a constraint optimisation problem, we want to give a "good" initial point for a constraint optimisation solver. We hope to find a good starting point with an optimisation solver, i.e., a solver which computes the best point discarding constraints. We must have an accessor function that can give us a "point" from a problem.

```
OptimizationSolverA

sp = PackageSolverB.getPointFromProblem()

ConstraintOptimizationSolverB({starting_point = sp})
```

Our final cooperation language offers the maximal expressiveness with the combination of these languages :

$$L_{Coop} = L_{Strat} + L_{Search} + \sum_i L_{SolverX_i}{}^4$$

5   A Word about the Prototype Implementation

These framework and ideas have been partially implemented into the European project COCONUT (COntinuous CONstraints, Updating the Technology). This latter aims at improving the already-existing benchmarks on difficult optimisation problems on the continuous domain (problems involving real numbers and

---

[4] The combination of languages denoted by + is more a (abusive) convenient way to represent a combination of languages, than a formal semantical way: if L_{Strat} defines the basic syntax of the language and can be used as a standalone language, $L_{SolverX_i}$ can be a "library" or an extension.

interval technology). With this end, we have implemented a component-oriented cooperation framework. Upon this framework, we used a host language to develop the cooperation and search languages. The latter is based roughly on the ideas presented above. Some of the solvers used in this project are: ILOG Cplex, Irin's Stop propagator, and global optimizer, Donlp2, etc...

A Component-Oriented Cooperation Framework. Nowadays, component technology is more and more used, providing a way to develop robust and modular projects. Some well-known component software (Corba, COM, ...) have already been used for a long time, proving the validity of the paradigm mainly for industrial needs, despite their weaknesses for high-performance applications. One may define components as written in the preface of Component Software Szyperski's Book [17],

> Software components are binary units of independent production, acquisition, and deployment that interact to form functioning system.

The main point of the component technology is the framework upon which the components rely. It defines roughly the way of manipulating a component (black/white/glass boxes, component interface) and the way of communicating (protocol, active/passive agents). Fig. 3 presents the component architecture and the involved interactions; the different used components follows the previous discussed separation:

- **Some computing components**. The solvers they encapsulate define the internal behaviour and abilities of the component. The shell the component constitutes enables the solver to communicate with a conform protocol. We may consider no assumption on the fact that a solver works with some underlying technology (parallel or distributed computing, etc...)
- **A strategy component**. It constitutes the strategy part of the previously defined schema. Thus, it manages strategies by the way of some interface or language. Mainly, it sends computation and control messages to the computing instances (solvers) and manage returned results.
- **A search component**. The search space is managed by the way of this component, including storing past states, "computing" next candidate, etc... For the multiprocess computations, the search component can manage several "pointers" on the nodes that are currently processed by the system. It manages the search space by the way of a independent and customisable search strategy.

An auxiliary component database component is used at different steps of the cooperation by the different other components. Its main stored information are: the component *location* (in a local or distributed environment), the *solver properties*, and some *performance feedback*[5].

---

[5] The performance feedback give some material for potential future automated strategies.

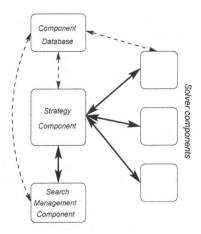

Fig. 3. Global component-interaction schema

Other Features of the Cooperation Framework Prototype.

- C++ as a development language;
- ACE (Adaptive Communication Environment) [18] for communication and asynchronous message processing (including abstraction of low-level network concepts and algorithms using design pattern paradigm);
- Python [19] as a host language. Python is an interpreted object-oriented, and extensible language, upon which we developed the necessary modules.

An example of a simple cooperation described in the prototype is presented hereafter.

Example

```
#!/usr/bin/python2.3    # Python v. 2.3 as an interpreter
from se import *        # Import all basic material
import point            # An helper module provided by Donlp2

# Initialisation
n = SE.init(''problem.txt'')

# First call
p1 = SE.connect(''GlobalOptimiserA'')
n2 = p1.send(n,[(''service'',''propagate'')])

# Second call
v = point.getPointFromNode(n2,point.INF)
p2 = SE.connect(''LocalConstraintOptimiserB'')
nr = p2.send(n2,[(''service'',''solve''),(''x_start'',v), \
(''global'',True)])
```

It is an ad-hoc strategy which calls sequentially two solvers. The first call to a global optimisation solver (`GlobalOptimiserA`) computes a box encapsulating the best point with respect to the optimisation criterion (discarding constraints). The second call to a local constraint optimisation solver uses the lower bounds of the intervals composing the feasible box as a starting point. The syntax explicitly shows the underlying component technology (`connect`, `send`). First part includes the necessary cooperation-strategy modules into Python (the host language). The initialisation step prepares a new search structure with the problem stored in the file `problem.txt`. Then, the user is able to connect to the different known solvers on demand (all the known solvers are imported and thus known, but are not really loaded into memory). To be modular and extendable, most of the options and parameters are passed as a list of couples composed of (`string, value`). Next, we can send a message via a port (here only computation message requests). `getPointFromNode` is an helper function provided by *LocalConstraintOptimiserB* that permits to obtain the starting point from a problem (see ex. 4).

6   Conclusion and Future Works

This paper introduces a new paradigm for constraint programming using cooperation of solvers. It aims at providing a clear separation between the different parts of constraint resolution. It thus defines a global language by assembling several underlying languages. So the main contribution of this paper relies in the search strategy and strategy description. Previous works were mixing the different concepts of search and computational flows what led to difficult descriptions of a reusable strategy. The current prototype relies on a European project where several good solvers can be used for real tests, the main goal of the project being to improve the current existing optimisation benchmarks. Future directions aim at testing more widely the strategies on real problems, which can lead to define a minimal and sufficient set of useful strategy operators. Some kind of automated strategy generation can be introduced by means of rules like those presented quickly in this paper, but further works are nevertheless needed. Besides, the search genericity (local and global search) could be further analysed for solver cooperation (the use of technologies like SALSA or COMET could be possible).

References

1. Arbab, F.: Manifold 2.0 reference manual. Technical report, Centrum voor Wiskunde en Informatica (1997)
2. Aiba, A., Yokota, K., Tsuda, H.: Heterogeneous distributed cooperative problem solving system helios. In: Procs of FGCS'94. (1994)
3. Monfroy, E.: A coordination-based chaotic iteration algorithm for constraint propagation. In: Proceedings of The 15th ACM Symposium on Applied Computing, SAC'00. (2000)

4. Zoeteweij, P.: Coordination-based distributed constraint solving in dice. In: Proceedings of the 18th ACM Symposium on Applied Computing (SAC'2003), ACM Press (2003)
5. Semenov, A., Petunin, D., Kleymenov, A.: Gmacs: the general-purpose module architecture for building cooperative solvers. In: Procs. of the ERCIM/CompulogNet Workshop on Constraint programming. (2000)
6. Monfroy, E.: Solver Collaboration for Constraint Logic Programming. PhD thesis, Centre de Recherche en Informatique de Nancy INRIA-Lorraine (1996)
7. Hofstedt, P., Seifert, D., Godehardt, E.: A framework for cooperating solvers – a prototypic implementation. In: Proceeding of the Worshop of Cosolv 2001. (2001)
8. Franck, S., Hofstedt, P., Mai, P.: A strategy-oriented meta-solver framework. In: Proceeding of FLAIRS 2003. (2003)
9. Michel, L., Van Hentenryck, P.: Localizer: A modeling language for local search. Tech report, Brown University, Computer Science Department (1997)
10. Michel, L., Van Hentenryck, P.: A constraint-based architecture for local search. In: Proceedings of the 17th ACM Conference on Object-Oriented Programming, Systems, Languages, and Applications. (2002)
11. Laburthe, F., Caseau, Y.: SALSA: A language for search algorithms. Lecture Notes in Computer Science **1520** (1998)
12. Colombani, Y., Heipcke, S.: Combining solvers and solution algorithms with Mosel. In: Proceedings of the Fourth International Workshop on Integration of AI and OR techniques in Constraint Programming for Combinatorial Optimisation Problems CP-AI-OR'02. (2002) 277–290
13. Van Hentenryck, P., Perron, L., Puget, J.: Search and strategies in OPL. ACM Transactions on Computational Logic (TOCL) (2000)
14. Monfroy, E., Castro, C.: Basic components for constraint solver cooperations. In: Proceedings of the 18th ACM Symposium on Applied Computing (SAC'2003), ACM Press (2003)
15. Petrov, E., Monfroy, E.: Automatic analysis of composite solvers. In: Proceedings of the 14th Int. Conf. on Tools with Artificial Intelligence (ICTAI), IEEE Computer Society (2002)
16. Caseau, Y., Silverstein, G., Laburthe, F.: Learning hybrid algorithms for vehicle routing problems. TPLP **1** (2001) 779–806
17. Szyperski, C.: Component Software. ISBN: 0-201-17888-5. Addison-Wesley (1998)
18. Schmidt, D., Huston Stephen, C.: C++ Network Programming: Systematic Reuse with ACE and Frameworks. Addison-Wesley Longman (2003)
19. Van Rossum, G., Drake, F.: Python documentation. (2002) http://www.python.org/doc/.

Industrial Application of External Black-Box Functions in Constraint Programming Solver

Vladimir Sidorov[1] and Vitaly Telerman[2]

[1] LEDAS Ltd., 6, Acad. Lavrentjev pr., Novosibirsk, 630090, Russia,
sidorov@iis.nsk.su,
[2] Dassault Systemes, 9, Quai Marcel Dassault, 92150 Suresnes, France,
vitali_telerman@ds-fr.com

Abstract. We examine the problem of interaction between the interval constraint programming solver and external computation algorithms that are considered by the solver as Black Boxes. Some techniques are used in order to resolve a contradiction between the intervals values of the constraint solver and exact values of Black Boxes. The proposed approach was developed and implemented in CATIA CAD/CAM system.

1 Introduction

Over the last ten years, the constraint programming (CP) paradigm has become a very fruitful and viable approach to programming. In this approach, the process of programming consists of generating constraints (domain restrictions) on parameters and solving these constraints by means of general and/or domain-specific methods. At the beginning, constraint programming mostly relied on general-purpose methods (see, e.g., [1,2]). Despite some inefficiency, universal algorithms made it possible for the first time to solve the so-called "mixed" problems, i.e. problems that are a mixture of various kinds of "classical" problems: linear and non-linear equations, inequalities, optimization problems, etc. Obviously, generic methods are usually far too inefficient for solving subproblems that can be handled by specialized, more efficient solvers.

That is why a more realistic point of view has recently become more popular: for solving "mixed" problems, it is more preferable to use specialized algorithms for solving the specific parts of the problem, leaving the rest of the problem to the general-purpose constraint programming methods. For instance, an efficient algorithm such as the Gauss can solve a linear system of equations extracted from a nonlinear constraint problem. In this case, cooperation between all algorithms that are used to solve the original problem must be organized. The goal of this cooperation is to share and exchange data between different solvers in order to tackle new types of problems and/or to speed up computation. A great deal of research has been done in this domain over the last years, particularly in the field of symbolic-numeric algorithms and languages for cooperation of heterogeneous solvers [3,4]. In each case, the following field-independent questions should be answered: how to organize the communication, what is the strategy of cooperation, the problems of correctness, completeness and termination.

M. Broy and A.V. Zamulin (Eds.): PSI 2003, LNCS 2890, pp. 415–422, 2003.
© Springer-Verlag Berlin Heidelberg 2003

All these studies have been performed for solvers implementing mathematical methods and algorithms known in advance. Experiments on these cooperative solvers showed that this approach to solving complex mathematical problems is quite viable, and new research in this field is worthwhile.

However, one should bear in mind that real-world problems are often much more complex than mathematical methods, which are called to solve them. Therefore, we have to "simplify" the reality, and to solve an approximation to a problem. The resulting solution cannot always be regarded as satisfactory, and then we must find an acceptable solution by cut-and-try method.

On the other hand, there exist numerous industrial software packages that have been successfully used to solve narrow, special problems, and either do not allow precise mathematical definition (and classification) or represent proprietary know-how and cannot be described openly.

In this paper, we examine the issue of cooperation between a constraint programming solver and external solvers under the following conditions:

1. The constraint programming solver is an interval solver based on the technology of subdefinite models [2,5].
2. The constraint programming solver does not "know" the algorithms used by the external solvers, and so it has to work by trial and error. Thus, in what follows we will refer to such modules as black boxes.
3. The solver calls the external modules via their public, known interfaces. The objective is to use such black box modules efficiently when solving a constraint programming problem, preferably without losing the remarkable inherent advantages of interval CP solvers.

The need to solve this problem arose in a project that used interval CP solvers NemoNext in the CATIA CAD/CAM system.

NemoNext is an adaptation of the object-oriented constraint programming environment NeMo+, developed in the mid-90's [6], for use in CATIA. Its advantages over NeMo+ include better performance and easier integration into industrial applications. In CATIA, it is included as a solver for systems of equations/inequalities over geometric and/or knowledgeware parameters like weight, density, volume, mass, etc. The task was to ensure that along with the traditional constraints like algebraic equations and inequalities over integer and real intervals, the solver would calculate external functions, modules, or constraints such as, for instance, area and volume measure, calculations of gravity center for complex figures, etc. It is difficult to solve this problem because, as a rule, all such external functions are implemented in the traditional paradigm of programming, i.e., they do not take into account the specifics of interval CP-solvers.

The structure of the paper is as follows. Section 1 discusses the problems arising when setting up the cooperation of the interval CP solver and the external "black boxes," as well as presents the overall architecture of the package. Section 2 examines the data exchange problems between the interval CP solver and the external black boxes. Section 3 presents one example demonstrating viability of this approach. In conclusion, we list the main results and discuss possible future development of this approach.

2 NemoNext — Black Box Cooperation Framework

2.1 NemoNext: Main Characteristics

NemoNext is an object-oriented constraint programming solver, implemented on the base of subdefinite models (SD-models) approach. This approach is based on ideas proposed by A.S. Narin'yani in the early 80s [2]. The main features of the method of SD-models are:

1. A common constraint propagation algorithm that is used to process data of different types. This allows one to solve simultaneously multiple constraints including, e.g., set, Boolean, integer and real variables.
2. Instead of one exact value, a subset of the set of admissible values is associated with each parameter. The most frequently used types of values are intervals (real and integer) and enumerations.
3. Each constraint, for example, $y = cos(x)$, is associated with both interpretation functions, direct and inverse: $y = cos(x)$ and $x = arccos(y)$. As a result, it is possible to solve both direct and inverse problems from the same specification.

The algorithm of computations implemented in NemoNext is a highly parallel data-driven process. Modification of the values of some variables in the common memory automatically results in calling and executing those constraints for which these variables are arguments. The process halts when the execution of constraints does not change the variables of the model. The result of the algorithm is either SUCCESS, in which case the current values of the variables will point to possible values of objects of the model, or FAILURE, which signals that during the execution of the algorithm the value of one of the variables became invalid. It was theoretically proved for this algorithm that it terminates in finitely many steps, the end result does not depend on the specific strategy used to choose constraints for interpretation, and all solutions (if their exist) lies inside the resulting output intervals/enumerations.

2.2 External Black Boxes

A black box is a mapping, which matter is unknown for solver point of view. The only thing the solver knows is its interface. An external black-box is implemented outside the constraint solver by one executable module and has a public interface. We will consider the following types of black boxes:

1. Interval constraint. It implements the direct and all inverse interpretation functions. The parameters values are represented by intervals. Thus, there is no distinction between the input and output arguments of this black box.
2. Interval function. It implements only the direct function, and the parameters values are represented by intervals.
3. N-argument function. It implements the direct function on N-arguments and one result, and parameters values are exact.

4. 1-argument function. It implements the direct function on one argument and one result, and the values of both are exact.

When a black box is connected to NemoNext solver, the following problems must be solved:

1. Merge the subdefinite values (intervals) of NemoNext parameters with the exact values (input and output) of the black box functions (for N- and 1-argument functions).
2. Compute the inverse functions of black box (for all black boxes except Interval constraints) while preserving properties of the constraint solver.

2.3   Strategy of Cooperation

The NemoNext solver considers all external black boxes as external constraints that should be satisfied during the computation. The NemoNext solver knows the black-box interface, and, may be, some additional information. In fact, one specific constraint — the BB-constraint, was implemented in NemoNext in order to provide the interaction of the black box module and the solver. The architecture of this BB-constraint is as follows:

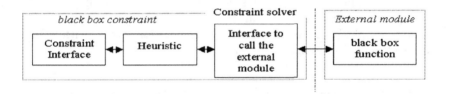

Fig. 1. Connection of a black box to constraint solver

The constraint interface is needed to call the chosen heuristics, as well as to store the best results of the previous computations of the external module. The most important component of this architecture is Heuristics. Heuristics play a vital role in providing the correct values from the constraint solver to the external black box module and getting back the correct results.

It should be noted that one more requirement should be satisfied during the computation: the number of black box calls must be minimized. This requirement is due to the fact that each black box call is much more expensive (in terms of processing time) than all the other NemoNext constraints.

3   Heuristics

3.1   NemoNext: Main Characteristics

Heuristics are used to solve two main problems:

1. Find the minimal and maximal values of the direct function, in order to generate the interval values for NemoNext.
2. Compute the inverse functions of the black box and find their minimal and maximal values, in order to generate the interval values for NemoNext.

The solutions to these problems depend on the type of the black box. In the table below you can see the computation algorithms used by each heuristics.

Heuristics	Type of black box	Extremums of the direct function	Extremums of inverse functions
Simple	Interval constraint	(not necessary)	(not necessary)
InputOutput	Interval function	(not necessary)	Interval Bisection
Gradient	N-argument function	Quickest descent	Coordinate descent
1D Gradient	1-argument function	Quickest descent	Newton's method
1D Quadratic	1-argument function	Quadratic interpolation	Newton's method

Obviously, the interval constraint black boxes can be called from the constraint solver without any heuristics. When the solver computes interval function black boxes, the heuristics are used for finding the minimum and maximum of inverse functions.

All of computation algorithms used in heuristics are well known. Detailed descriptions can be found, e.g., in [7].

The complexity of the heuristics implementation growth with a number of specificities of the problem to be solved:

1. Locality. The minimal and maximal values are found with the help of local search algorithms. These algorithms are sensitive to local extremum points. They were modified to allow the user to increase the probability to find the global maximum or minimum increasing the number of black box calls.
2. Conditional search. Arguments of a black box constraint are always intervals. Thus, all the arguments of a black box function, as well as its result, are bounded by inequalities of the kind $x_{i,low} \leq x_i \leq x_{i,up}$. Denote this region by $D_C = [x_{1,low}, x_{1,up}] \times \ldots \times [x_{N,low}, x_{N,up}]$.
3. Inconsistent points. The domain of a black box function D_f is not known in advance, and usually $D_f \cap D_C \neq D_C$. The domain D_f is determined by the internal constraints of the black box and is generally independent of the type of function or the set of constraints of the NemoNext model. Consequently, each of the algorithms can yield an inconsistent point (leave the domain D_f) in every step, and so they have to be modified to handle these situations.
4. Find only the first solution. Note that calling a black box is usually much slower than processing the remainder of the global problem solved by NemoNext. Therefore, the exact values of arguments returned by the black box can be tested relatively quickly for compatibility with the other constraints of NemoNext. If this set of values satisfies all the constraints of the model, then it is a solution and the algorithms (as well as the entire black box constraint) can be terminated.

5. Find the best solution. The global problem often has multiple solutions, and we need to choose the "best" one. A common approach is to minimize the distance from the solution to an initial point set by the user. In our case it is not necessary to perform slow global search over all solutions of the model. It is sufficient to satisfy the following conditions:

   - If the initial point is a solution, then the algorithm should stop without computations
   - Otherwise, the solution should be close enough (closer than most other solutions) to the initial point.

4   Applications

We will consider one practical example of solving constraint satisfaction problems with two N-arguments black boxes. This example is a part of the engine turbine design: the design of a turbine's blade. The blade is connected to the turbine's disk runner by a bulb, presented in Fig.2. The goal is to find the values of the bulb's parameters, which satisfy not only the geometric constraints like distances and area, but also the engineering ones:

```
/*Centrifugal Force*/    FCbulb = bulbMass*omega^2*bulbRCG;
/*Mass*/                 bulbMass = rho*bulbLength*bulbArea;
/*Spindle speed*/        30.0*omega = Pi*XN2;
/*Real force on the bulb*/ 2.0*P = (FCblade+FCbulb)*cos(alpha);
```

There are two 6-argument black box functions in the model:

```
bulbArea = area(alpha, L1, L2, L3, R1,R2);
bulbRCG = centerofgravity(alpha, L1, L2, L3, R1, R2)+AxeRadius;
```

In the following table we show how the number of calls and computation time of two black boxes depend on the number of their unknown parameters. All the parameters apart from those indicated in the second column are assumed to be constants.

Dimension	Free variables	Heuristics *Gradient*		Heuristics *Gradient* + find first solution	
		centerofgravity	area	centerofgravity	area
1	L1	91	55	9	3
2	L1,L2	561	512	447	36
3	L1,L2,L3	5444	2827	34	4
4	L1,L2,L3,R1	4671	2171	26	3
5	L1,L2,L3,R1,R2	4852	2081	37	4
6	L1,L2,L3,R1,R2,alpha	9308	1391	29	3

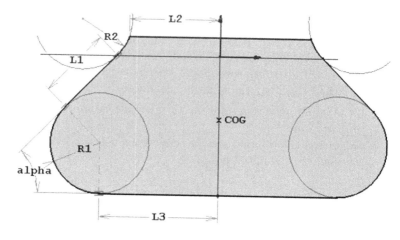

Fig. 2. Drawing for example

5   Conclusion

In this paper we examined the issue of interaction between the NemoNext interval constraint solver and external computation algorithms or modules. In our approach, the external algorithms are closed to NemoNext, and it has to regard them as black boxes. The difficulty of the problem is increased because NemoNext operates in the interval constraint programming paradigm, while the black boxes, as a rule, operate with exact values of parameters, and with the separation of input and output parameters Therefore it was necessary to develop a set of heuristics which were to resolve the contradiction.

This approach was implemented in the project of using interval CP solver NemoNext in the CATIA CAD/CAM system. The results of a number of industrial application scenarios showed the effectiveness of the approach.

The goal of further development is to improve performance, possibly by making the heuristics more specialized.

References

1. Mackworth A. Consistency in Networks of Relations, Artificial Intelligence, vol.8, 1977, p. 99–118.
2. Narin'yani A. S. Sub-definiteness and Basic Means of knowledge representation. Computers and Artificial Intelligence. — Bratislava, 1983. — N5.
3. Marti P., Rueher M. A Distributed Cooperating Constraints Solving System. International Journal on Artificial Intelligence Tools 4, 1 and 2 (1995), 93–113.
4. Granvillers L., Monfroy E., Benhamou F. Symbolic-interval cooperation in constraint programming. In Procs. of ISSAC'2001 (2001), ACM Press. Constraint Programming and Artificial Intelligence:

5. Telerman V., Ushakov D. Subdefinite Models as a Variety of Constraint Programming Proc. of the 8th Internat. Conf. on Tools with Artificial Intelligence, ICTAI'96. — IEEE Computer Society, 1996. — P. 157–163.
6. Shvetsov I., Telerman V., Ushakov D. NeMo+: Object-Oriented Constraint Programming Environment Based on Subdefinite Models // Principles and Practice of Constraint Programming — CP97: Proc. / Ed. by G.Smolka. — Berlin a.o.: Springer-Verlag, 1997. — P. 534–548. — (Lect. Notes Comput. Sci.; 1330).
7. Gurin L. S., Dymarsky Ya. S., Merkulov A. D. Problems and methods of optimal allocation of resources. — Moscow: Sov. radio, 1968. — 463 p. (in Russian)

LGS: Geometric Constraint Solver

Alexey Ershov[1], Ilia Ivanov[1], Serge Preis[2],
Eugene Rukoleev[2], and Dmitry Ushakov[2]

[1] A.P.Ershov Institute of Informatics System,
6, Acad. Lavrentjev pr., 630090 Novosibirsk, Russia
eag@iis.nsk.su, zayats@ledasgroup.com
[2] LEDAS Ltd., 6, Acad. Lavrentjev pr., 630090 Novosibirsk, Russia
{spr, rev, ushakov}@ledasgroup.com
http://lgs.ledasgroup.com

Abstract. In the paper we present LGS — a geometric constraint solver developed at LEDAS Ltd. We review different approaches in geometric constraint solving, present our one, describe in details LGS architecture and the ideas behind it. The main idea of LGS is to decompose the initial problem into a set of simpler ones, to map each instance to a class of problems, and to apply a specialized algorithm to each class. We emphasize key differences of our approach: extendible hierarchy of problem classes, new decomposition techniques, a broad range of numerical algorithms.

1 Introduction

Many software products utilize some form of geometric functionality, CAD systems being one good example. Geometric applications all have a fundamental requirement to maximize the productivity of the end-user by enabling the efficient construction and modification of geometric models. There are many techniques, often called *variational* or *parametric* design, that have been developed to assist the production of geometric models. In brief, these techniques enable end-users to specify and control their geometric models by using *constraints*. Such constraints may include dimensions (distance, angle, radius, etc.), logical relations between objects (incidence, tangency, symmetry, etc.), spatial position and orientation (fixation of coordinates, verticality). All objects and constraints form a variational model and, hence, all modifications made to the model are propagated through the constraints providing consistency with original design intentions.

The main goal of the LGS project is to build a geometric constraint solver effective for both 2D and 3D models[1]. It should work efficiently with models of different complexity, achieving competitive performance compared to industry-standard solvers. The key ability of LGS is solving large systems of simultaneous geometric and engineering constraints[2], naturally arising in variational design.

---

[1] The current version of LGS supports only 2D models.

[2] In the paper we discuss only geometric constraints.

M. Broy and A.V. Zamulin (Eds.): PSI 2003, LNCS 2890, pp. 423–430, 2003.

The rest of this paper is organized as follows. In Sect. 2 we overview different approaches proposed for geometric constraint solving. In Sect. 3 we present the architecture of LGS and main ideas behind it. We conclude with overviewing obtained results and outlining directions of future research.

2   Approaches to Geometric Constraint Solving

We will now briefly review the existing approaches to the solution of geometric constraint problems (a more complete survey can be found, e.g., in [1], and [2] gives a firsthand presentation of the current state of research in this field). These approaches are commonly divided into purely numerical, rule-based, and decomposition methods.

In solvers based on the purely numerical approach, geometric constraints are converted to algebraic ones (which are usually polynomial equations), and the resulting system is solved with a certain set of numerical, usually iterative methods. The Newton method is frequently used, due to its relative simplicity and quick convergence. However, it requires a good initial approximation, does not guarantee convergence to a solution, and is not very fast in the multidimensional case. The homotopy method [3] is gaining in popularity; compared to the Newton method, it is more regular, converges with higher probability to the solution that is nearest to the initial approximation, but its implementation is more complicated. Other common techniques are relaxation methods, the projection method, and other general and specialized methods. Constraint programming methods [4] are unique in their ability to handle non-differentiable and discontinuous constraints, but their performance is not as good. On the whole, the advantage of numerical methods is their ability to solve overconstrained consistent or underconstrained problems[3], while their drawback is in their computational complexity. In addition, changing the model's parameters implies a complete recalculation of the model.

To implement the rule-based approach, constraints are regarded as known facts from which we can infer other facts, corollaries by predefined rules built into the solver [5]. Thus, the fact database is gradually expanded, and as a result we obtain the facts that specify the values of the objects' coordinates, thereby solving the problem. There exist other known methods and their variants based on this approach [6], but current solvers do not as a rule use the rule-based approach.

The third, most interesting approach is to decompose the problem into a tree of subproblems that can be solved one by one. Solvers based on this approach allow localization of changes to the model and do not require complete recalculation. Moreover, by shifting some of the computation complexity from numerical methods to symbolic ones, which are usually polynomially hard, we reduce computation complexity significantly. These solvers simplify the search for all solutions to the problem. The best-known research teams working in this

---

[3] Some authors also use the terms *over-rigid* and *under-rigid*.

field are the Hoffmann group [1], the Clement group [7], and the Owen group [8]. Both the Clement team, which solves geometric models through group analysis on groups of possible motions of geometric objects, and the Owen team, which applies a top-down model decomposition process via identifying 3-connected components in the constraint graph, work in commercial projects and have a relatively small number of publications. The approach of Hoffmann is better known. It allows identification of internally determined parts of the model during bottom-up processing. In what follows, we will be relying on this theory.

3   LGS Architecture

The architecture of LGS (presented on Fig. 1) is modular. It is based on an internal representation that contains all the information about the model. Simultaneously, there exists an external representation defined in terms of API objects and constraints.

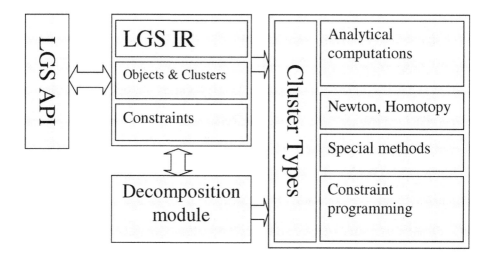

Fig. 1. Architecture of LGS

The internal representation controls all the processes within LGS; it manages the two main problem-solving mechanisms: decomposition (or *clustering*) and then computations. In the decomposition process, the problem is decomposed into subproblems (also called *clusters*) which are analyzed to select the most appropriate computational method and to gather various additional information. The computational methods and additional information are associated with *cluster types*. A cluster type is defined during the analysis phase of clustering and associated with the subproblem in the internal representation. This association is subsequently used in calculations. Based on the results of calculations, the internal representation translates the solution back into API objects, and in the process identifies the objects that have changed.

3.1   LGS API

Application programs interact with LGS through its *API* (*Application Programming Interface*). The construction of a geometric model begins with creating an LGS *context*. A context is a container for geometric objects and constraints. Each of them has a type, and optional lists of parameters and arguments (a list of identifiers of other objects).

Geometric objects are `point` and `polyline`. For poly-lines, functions for accessing the vertices and edges are available. `edge` is an abstract type with the following varieties: `segment` and `elliptic-arc` (the last can also be a closed circle, a closed ellipse, or an arc of a circle).

LGS supports the following *constraints*: `fixation`, `incidence` (the following combinations are possible: two points coincide, two segments coincide, a point lies on a segment or elliptic arc), `distance` (a parameterized constraint fixing the distance between two objects with the following possible combinations: distance between two points, distance between two segments, which implies that they are parallel, or the distance from a point to an edge), `angle` (a parametric constraint with two arguments: a pair of segments; it fixes the angle between the lines passing through the two segments), `angle-OX` (fixes a segment's slope relative to a global coordinate system), `tangency` (a constraint stating that an edge is tangent to an elliptic arc).

There are a variety of *API commands* to control the computations. It is possible to `set-precision` (used in computational algorithms and in identification of the objects that were modified during recalculation of the model), `halt-calculation`, `get-current-state` (OK, no solution, overconstrained system, calculation halted). A special command invokes `recalculate-model`: since LGS is incremental, objects and constraints can be added to the model or removed from it. For these changes to affect the current values of other objects, the model recalculation function must be called explicitly. A group of geometric objects can be moved using parallel translation or rotated by a specified angle relative to an arbitrary point. For parameterized constraints such as distance or angle, the value of the parameter can be changed. In this case recalculation will be faster due to omitting repetition of analysis of the entire model.

3.2   LGS Internal Representation

Geometric objects and constraints discussed above implement the entities declared through the API. The internal representation of LGS is a low-level one and consists of simpler objects and constraints. Decomposition module operates directly on the internal objects and constraints, requires their characteristics such as the number of degrees of freedom (or the number of removed degrees of freedom in the case of constraints). Decomposition presents the structure of a problem in the form of a tree, where every node (also called *a cluster*) is associated with a certain type selected from a predefined hierarchy.

The core is incremental; for each call of an API function that modifies the top-level representation of the problem, the internal and external representations are synchronized, that is, the external objects and constraints are translated into internal ones. If the changes are not limited to the numerical parameters, the decomposition methods are immediately called to update the cluster tree. The result is a message on the new status of the problem: wellconstrained, overconstrained, or underconstrained; in the last case, the system reports whether the structure of the problem was modified as a result of the last changes.

For each problem, the objects specifying the global coordinate system are created in the internal representation. These are two coordinate axes, the origin point and the corresponding constraints. The global coordinate system is used for translating the constraints fixing external objects; these are transformed into the constraints on the distances between the corresponding internal objects and the global coordinate system.

Another special case of translating external constraints is incidence of two points. It has no direct counterpart among the internal constraints and is processed by "merging" two points into one with the appropriate correction of all constraints having these points among their arguments.

Solution of a problem is initiated when a special API command is received. It is performed by traversing the cluster tree depth first and starts at the leaves. A cluster recalculation procedure is a property of its type. Clusters of special types are calculated with the help of analytical methods. Other cluster types are calculated with numerical methods (Newton, homotopy continuation, interval constraints). The mathematical model for these methods is generated according to the following rule. First, the variables representing the coordinates of each geometric object in the model are generated, as well as the internal constraints (such as the main trigonometric equation). Next, the constraints linking these objects are used to generate the equations of the mathematical model.

3.3   Problem Decomposition

To ensure efficiency of calculations, LGS replaces the initial geometric model by a tree-like hierarchical system of submodels, consecutive recalculation of which produces a solution to the initial problem. The submodels are generated by the clustering stage that uses degrees-of-freedom analysis in the constraint graph and allows finding submodels without internal degrees of freedom, or clusters. Some details of clustering are described in this section (a more detailed technical description can be found in [9]).

From the physical standpoint, a cluster is a solid body (since the constraints restrict mutual position of objects in the cluster) and has three external degrees of freedom in two-dimensional space or six in three-dimensional space. From the standpoint of the geometric models containing the cluster, it is equivalent to the local coordinate system and in their context may be regarded as a predefined geometric primitive.

The base algorithm of clustering is searching for maximal flow in a bipartite network whose vertices are geometric objects (including clusters) and binary constraints over them. This algorithm uses a specialized internal representation that is more efficient in the case of incremental computation. Apart from the general flow algorithm, it uses methods that search the model for predefined cluster types, which do not have internal representations but allow analytical solutions or fast numerical algorithms that find solutions. The hierarchy of clusters is constructed incrementally when constraints are added or removed.

The subdivision of the initial problem into subproblems is ambiguous, and so the development of better methods to find clusters in the model is of interest in its own right. Being a symbolic method, clustering is invoked only if the model's dependencies change, rather than just the values of the numerical parameters of its constraints, which saves computational resources in many base manipulations with the model. In addition to the problem of identifying subsystems having zero internal degrees of freedom, clustering solves the problem of identifying structurally overconstrained geometric models, suggesting to the user which constraints in the model are superfluous.

3.4   Cluster Types

Each cluster generated by the clustering phase is associated with the most appropriate node in the tree of cluster types. A cluster type represents a set of geometric models of a similar nature, allowing solution with the same computational method (a *computation function* of a cluster type). Each cluster type has a *discriminator function* that determines whether or not a specific cluster is a representative of this type. Cluster types regarded as sets of geometric models with the natural inclusion relation form a tree-like structure, in which children of the same cluster type are disjoint. When the most similar type is determined for a cluster, the tree is traversed depth-first without backtracking, which yields the most specialized cluster type represented by the cluster. It is expected that during further evolution of the computation engine of LGS the tree of cluster types will be extended by new nodes corresponding to the new efficient computational methods developed to solve special classes of geometric problems.

The root of the cluster type tree is an abstract cluster type with a universal discriminator function. It contains all clusters, and its computation function uses universal methods for solution of systems of equations; depending on the configuration of the solver, these can be Newton-like methods or Interval Constraint Propagation.

In some non-root cluster types, the computation function is modified to ensure more efficient search via finer tuning of computational methods. To solve models with two geometric objects, special analytical methods are used. If at least one of the objects is not a cluster, then the solution is given by an explicit formula; if both of the objects are not clusters, then the solution is unique, and if one of them is a cluster, then there are several solutions.

In the case of multiple solutions, the one that is closer to the initial sketch is selected for further computations. If both objects are clusters, then the solution is obtained by a combination of specialized methods that do not guarantee a solution and a universal method that does. The use of fast, specialized methods for a cluster type, even though they do not guarantee a solution, allows solving some models in a time that is much less than the time needed to solve the problems with the universal method assuring a solution.

If the solution is not found within a certain limit with the methods that do not assure a solution, then the universal method is invoked. This combination of search methods allows reducing the average model solution time.

4 Conclusion

We described a new geometric constraint solver called LGS that encapsulates a lot of state-of-the-art techniques. We proposed a new architecture to a constraint solver — an extendible tree-like hierarchy of cluster types, and presented the ideas behind it.

At the moment of writing this paper, LGS exists in form of 2D prototype solver, but ideas behind LGS now are applied in industrial 3D solver developed by LEDAS Ltd. for a world-leader CAD company. Concerning 2D prototype, we also designed a sample application with sketching capabilities in OpenCASCADE framework [10], this work was performed by Viktor Markin. The last work in the prototype aimed at implementation of elliptic arcs, including introducing new cluster types for new classes of problems, was performed by Alexey Kazakov. Currently LGS solver is being extended with rigid C^1 curves and engineering constraints. Directions of our future research include building representative test base for LGS, improving efficiency by implementing new symbolic techniques, and implementing a 3D solver based on the same approach.

The authors are indebted to anonymous referees for their valuable comments to the previous version of the paper.

References

1. Bouma, W., Fudos, I. and Hoffmann, C.: A Geometric Constraint Solver, in *Computer Aided Design*, Vol.27, No.6, pp. 487–501 (1995)
2. Bruderlin, B. and Roller, D. (eds): Geometric Constraint Solving and Applications, Springer (1998)
3. Lamure, H., Michelucci, D.: Solving Geometric Constraints By Homotopy, in *IEEE Transaction on Visualization and Computer Graphics*, Vol 2, pp. 22–34 (1996)
4. Roukoleev, E. and Ushakov, D.: Constraint Satisfaction and Reasoning in Declarative Geometry with Intervals, in *Proc. ADG 2000*, ETH Zurich, pp. 70–74 (2000)
5. Shpitalni, M. and Lipson H.: Automatic Reasoning for Design Under Geometric Constraints, in *Annals of the CIRP*, Vol. 46/1, pp. 85–89 (1999)
6. Heydon, A. and Nelson, G.: The Juno-2 Constraint-Based Drawing Editor, SRC Research Report 131a (1994)
7. Clement, A., Riviere, A., and Serre, P.: Global Consistency of Dimensioning and Tolerancing, in *Proc. CIRP Int. Seminar on Computer Aided Tolerancing* (1999)

8. Owen, J.: Algebraic Solution for Geometry from Dimensional Constraints, in *ACM Symp. Found. Of Solid Modeling*, pp. 397–407, Austin, Texas (1991)
9. Ershov, A.G.: Enchancing Techniques for Geometric Constraint Solving, LEDAS Preprint 3, Novosibirsk (2002)
10. http://www.opencascade.org

On Strategies of the Narrowing Operator Selection in the Constraint Propagation Method

Yuri G. Dolgov

Novosibirsk State University,
A.P. Ershov Institute of Informatics Systems
Siberian Division of the Russian Academy of Sciences
yorik@sib3.ru

Abstract. This paper presents an approach that allows us to increase efficiency of the constraint propagation method. This approach consists in using a strategy of calls of narrowing operators in the process of computation on the basis of a dynamic system of priorities. Several strategies are described and the results of numerical experiments are discussed.

1 Introduction

The main object in this approach is a constraint that specifies admissible values of variables involved in it. A constraint can be specified by an explicit list of values of variables or by a formula. The problem description is given by a set of constraints and needs no algorithm specification to solve it. The process of solving a problem consists of two steps — deletion of the subdomains which do not contain a solution and search for a solution in the remaining domain. The subdomain deletion is done by the narrowing methods. There exist two classes of narrowing methods — for finite [8] and continuous domains [2,6,7].

One of the main problems of the narrowing methods is a low rate of convergence in some classes of problems, and this difficulty restricts applicability of this approach to large real-life problems. In this paper, we discuss how to increase efficiency of the constraint propagation algorithm for problems with continuous domains and study one of the approaches to this problem.

The paper is organized as follows. Section 2 gives the basic notions of the CP method. Section 3 is devoted to the ways and strategies of its optimization. The results of numerical experiments with these strategies are given in Section 4.

2 Constraint Propagation Method

2.1 The Basic Notions and Definitions

Let us give formal definitions of a constraint and other notions needed in what follows.

M. Broy and A.V. Zamulin (Eds.): PSI 2003, LNCS 2890, pp. 431–437, 2003.

Definition 1. *A constraint on a set of variables* $\{x_1, ..., x_n\}$ *is a subset S of the Cartesian product* $D_{x_1} \times ... \times D_{x_n}$, *where D_{x_i} is the domain of the variable x_i . The constraint is denoted as* $c(x_1, ..., x_n)$.

Definition 2. *CSP, or a constraint satisfaction problem, is a triple* $P = (X, D, C)$, *where $X = \{x_1, ..., x_n\}$ is a set of variables, $D = \{D_{x_1}, ..., D_{x_n}\}$ is a set of their domains, $C = \{c_1, ..., c_n\}$ is a set of constraints.*

Definition 3. *Let $P = (X, D, C)$ be a CSP. We say that value $a_i \in D_{x_i}$ is inconsistent if $\forall a_1 \in D_{x_1}, ..., \forall a_{i-1} \in D_{x_{i-1}}, \forall a_{i+1} \in D_{x_{i+1}}, ..., \forall a_n \in D_{x_n}$ and $\exists c \in C$ such that $c(a_1, ..., a_{i-1}, a_i, a_{i+1}, ..., a_n)$ is false.*

Definition 4. *A reduction operator* $red_c^{x_j}$ *is a function attached to a constraint c and a variable x. Given the domains of all the variables used in c, it returns the domain D_x without the values of x which are inconsistent with the domains of the variables.*

2.2   Constraint Propagation Method

Our main goal is to reduce the domain by removing inconsistent values. In the problems with the finite domains, the most familiar algorithms are AC-3, AC-5, AC-7, these alorithms achieve arc-consistency [8]. For problems with continuous domains, there are special kinds of consistency similar to arc-consistency, such as 2B- (hull-) consistency [1]. Hereinafter we will denote 2B-consistency algorithm as NA (narrowing algorithm). The NA can be described as the following procedure:

```
Procedure NA (X, D, C){
    Queue.Install; (puts all operators in queue)
    While (not Queue.Is_Empty) do (while queue is not empty){
        f = Queue.Pop; (take operator from queue)
        D' = f(D);
        If D' ≠ D then Queue.Put({operators with at
                                      least one intended argument});
        D = D';}
    Return(X, D, C);}
```

In our case the narrowing operators are represented by splitting of the initial system of equations into primitive (unary and binary) relationships. In this case, every primitive relationship makes it possible to express easily every variable through the others.

Let us show how the NA works with narrowing operators given by primitive relationships. Consider the following constraint satisfaction problem:

Variables: $x; D_x = [0, 1]$

Constraints: $x = sin(x)$

Narrowing operators: (a)$red_{x=sin(x)}^{x} = sin(x)$, (b)$red_{x=arcsin(x)}^{x} = arcsin(x)$

In this example, the method works as follows:

Narrowing operator	Narrowing area	Result	Success	Queue
(a)	D_x	[0,0.8414]	+	(b),(a)
(b)	D_x	[0,0.8414]	—	(a)
(a)	D_x	[0,0.7456]	+	(b),(a)
(b)	D_x	[0,0.7456]	—	(a)
(a)	D_x	[0,0.6784]	+	(b),(a)
...				

This example shows us that not all operators equally participate in the process of the domain narrowing. In particular, narrowing is a result of application of the operator (a), whereas operator (b) do not perform any useful actions.

3 Optimization of the Narrowing Algorithm

The problem of the efficient organization of the computational process has been studied in several papers. In particular, paper [10] considers the problem of the determination of a sequence of the calls of the narrowing operators in the algorithms of arc-consistency for finite domains.

Papers [4, 5] present a method for reduction of the number of calls of inefficient narrowing operators for continuous domains. This method allows us to avoid calling operators obviously not reducing the domain, but it does not allow us to reduce the number of calls of operators weakly reducing the domain.

Our work is aimed at the development of strategies of making an efficient selection from the queue of narrowing operators for the continuous domains by reducing a number of calls of the operators not only not reducing the domains, but weakly reducing them as well.

We performed our investigations in the frameworks of the CP-algorithm implemented in the cooperative solver SibCalc [3] that uses a method of splitting of a system into the primitive narrowing operators. It has been stated in [9] that for this kind of systems the order of calls of the operators do not influence the final result but can essentially change the number of the narrowing operators called to obtain the same result. Therefore, our main goal was to create the choice strategies that guarantee the minimal number of calls of the narrowing operators. The main idea of the strategies implemented here is to associate each operator with some numerical parameter that characterizes advisability of its call. This parameter will be called **a priority**.

More than 10 different strategies have been studied and experimentally tested. Most of them did not produce an expected effect, but some strategies appeared to be useful. Further we consider the most successful of the implemented strategies.

Strategy 1. This is the simplest strategy, and it was expected that it should be the most efficient for simple problems. Heuristics used in it are oriented so that to call more frequently the operators with the greatest number of arguments changed at the previous steps. If there are several operators of this kind, any of them may be called. This strategy is:

- At the beginning, all operators get zero priority.
- If a narrowing operator finished working successfully, then priority of every operator such that one of its arguments is a variable with a changed domain is increased by 1.
- The next narrowing operator is chosen randomly from the set of operators with maximal priority. After launching, it gets zero priority.

Strategy 2. This strategy is computationally more sophisticated. To apply it, two additional parameters are connected with each narrowing operator, namely

call_amount — the number of calls

narrowing_amount — the number of successful calls (which result in reduction of the domain).

Heuristics of this strategy turn out so as every narrowing operator should be called at least once at the first step of computations and, later, those operators should be called first that more often reduced the domains of their variables. The strategy consists of the following steps:

- At the beginning, all narrowing operators get zero priority.
- After the regular call of a narrowing operator, *call_amount* related to it increases by 1 and, if the domain was reduced, the parameter *narrowing_amount* also increases by 1. The current priority is calculated by the formula: $priority = max\_priority \cdot \frac{narrowing\_amount}{call\_amount}$
- The next narrowing operator is chosen in random way from the set of operators with the maximal priority. After launching, it gets zero priority.

Strategy 3. This strategy is based on the fact that operators of different kinds reduce a domain in different ways, therefore each narrowing operator is connected with an additional parameter *class_priority* depending on its kind. Heuristics used in this case allow to call the potentially efficient operators and those ones, which significantly reduced the domains at the previous steps, more frequently. To choose the value of a class priority, we have used heuristic reasons for interpretation functions (for example, the narrowing operator $y = exp(x)$ should reduce a domain more efficiently than the operator $y < x$), as well as experimental data obtained in solving a great number of problems with the help of this method. The strategy includes the following steps:

- At the beginning, all narrowing operators get priority equal to the value of *class_priority*.
- After each call of a narrowing operator, its current priority is set equal to *class_priority* if the domain was reduced and to $priority = max(0, priority - 1)$, otherwise.
- The next narrowing operator is chosen in random way from the set of operators with maximal priority.

4 Numerical Experiments

Many experiments have been performed in order to estimate efficiency of the strategies described above. In experiments presented here we consider four strategies — three of them are described above and the fourth is the simplest one, namely, the selection of the next operator without using priorities, in random way, from the set of all operators. This strategy will be called Strategy 0.

The problems with continuous and discrete domains have been considered in our experiments. The results presented below deal only with the continuous domain problems. The tests presented here are the systems of algebraic equations.

Table 1 contains information on the tests. Diagrams 1 and 2 illustrate the qualitative distinctions between strategies under consideration. On these diagrams, data for Strategy 0 is taken as 100%.

Table 1. Descriptions of the problems

Test name	Variables number	Constraints number	Operators number
c2	31	31	401
ellips	5	5	143
kear3	4	4	32
kear12	3	3	74
ode50	51	51	987
trig	2	5	67

- **c2** — a problem of placement on a plane 6 points with given distances between each other and 3 other points. All equations are quadratic equations.
- **ellips** — a problem of finding in three-space all intersection points of an ellipsoid and a curve that are given in parametric form. The system contains polynomial equations of 5th degree with trigonometrical functions.
- **kear3** — a Powell's singular function, test problem N3 from [2] .
- **kear12** — a high-degree polynomial system, test problem N12 from [2].
- **ode50** — a 3-diagonal system of linear equations that describe solving a boundary differential problem on a grid with fifty points.
- **trig** — a system of trigonometrical equations with exponential and logarithmic functions.

The following conclusions on efficiency of the strategies considered here can be derived from the obtained results.

As expected, Strategy 1 requires little computational resources, and experiments prove that the run-time change is proportional to the change in the number of the operator calls. At the same time, it has been found that Strategy 1 is the most efficient for those problems where the operator related to the reduction of a variable domain will most probably reduce this domain in its next call.

Strategy 2 has shown good results on the tests in which a group of the operators that make the main reduction of domains is selected. If all operators

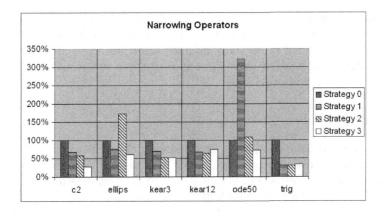

Fig. 1. Relative numbers of narrowing operators

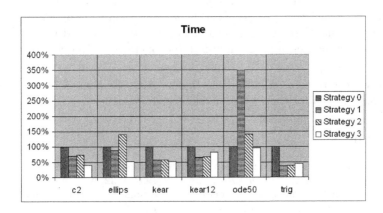

Fig. 2. Relative computing times

reduce the domain equally often, then the strategy becomes inefficient, since in this case operators are chosen in random way. A combination of Strategies 1 and 2 has not resulted in a noticeable decrease in the number of the operator calls, whereas the time required to apply this strategy has significantly increased.

Strategy 3 proved to be the most efficient of all variants. It has been implemented taking into account the data obtained by tracing the constraint propagation method, which made it possible to determine what narrowing operators are the most efficient in practice. On this basis, initial priorities (class priorities) of the operators have been set, and this allowed us to call more often the operators that work more efficiently. Owing to this, the number of "successful" calls (i.e. the calls that result in a real reduction of the variable domains) with the use of this strategy increased from 20-25% to 45-50% and the total number of calls decreased by 40-50%. But the computation time decreased only by 35-45% due to additional costs of the computation of priorities.

Thus, the data obtained so show an evident advantage of Strategy 3 for solution of the majority of problems with the continuous domains. Strategies 1 and 2 can be also used successfully in many cases, but there are some problems such as the application of these strategies to them can result in a significant increase of the computation time.

5   Conclusion

In this paper, we have considered the possibility of an efficiency increase for the constraint propagation method by forming a strategy of the selection of the narrowing operators. We have proposed an approach that uses dynamic priorities of the operators and have considered different variants of priority determination. On the basis of this approach, a large number of the strategies have been implemented and many numerical experiments have been performed. Some experimental results are shown in the paper. In particular, one of the most successful strategies allowed us to decrease the computation time by 35-45%. On this basis, an optimal strategy has been elaborated which is used in the constraint programming method implemented in the cooperative solver SibCalc.

Acknowledgements. The author thanks A.G. Ershov, A.L. Semenov and T.P. Kashevarova for their support and encouragement.

References

1. Benhamou, F., Older, W. Applying interval arithmetic to real, integer and boolean constraints. *Journal of Logic Programming* (1997, v.32, N. 1, pp.1–24.)
2. Kearfott, R.B. Some Test of Generalized Bisection. *ACM Transactions on Mathematical Software* (v.13, 1987, N3,p p.197–220.)
3. Kleymenov, A., Petunin, D., Semenov, A., Vazhev, I. A Model of Cooperative Solvers for Computational Problems. *Proceed. of the 4th International Conference PPAM 2001* (Poland, September. LNCS, v 2328, pp.797–802.)
4. Lhomme, O., Gotlieb, A., Rueher, M., Taillibert, P. Boosting the Interval Narrowing Algorithm. *Proc. JICSLP'96* (MIT Press, pp. 378–392)
5. Lhomme, O., Gotlieb, A., Rueher, M. Dynamic optimization of Interval Narrowing Algorithms. *Journal of Logic Programming* (Elsevier Science Inc. 37(1-3): 165–183, 1998)
6. Older, W., Vellino, A. Constraint Arithmetic on real Intervals. *In Constraint Logic Programming: Selected Research*, edited by F. Benhamou and A. Colmerauer (MIT Press (1993) 175–195)
7. Semenov, A. Solving Integer/Real Nonlinear Equations by Constraint Propagation. *Technical Report N12, Institute of Mathematical Modelling, The Technical University of Denmark* (Lyngby, Denmark, 1994. p. 22)
8. Tsang, E. Foundations of Constraint Satisfaction. Academic Press, Essex (1993)
9. Ushakov, D. Some Formal Aspects of Subdefinite Models. *Prepr. / Siberian Division of Russian Acad. Sci. IIS, Novosibirsk* (No. 49, 1998. p. 23)
10. Wallace, R., Freuder, E. Ordering heuristics for arc consistency algorithms. In *AI/GI/VI'92*, pp. 163–169, Vancouver, British Columbia, Canada, 1992.

PROG$\mathcal{DOC}$ — A New Program Documentation System

Volker Simonis and Roland Weiss

Wilhelm-Schickard-Institut für Informatik, Universität Tübingen
Sand 13, 72076 Tübingen, Germany
{simonis,weissr}@informatik.uni-tuebingen.de

Abstract. Though programming languages and programming styles evolve with remarkable speed today, there is no such evolution in the field of program documentation. And although there exist some popular approaches like Knuth's literate programming system WEB [26], and nowadays JavaDoc [15] or Doxygen [16], tools for managing software development **and** documentation are not as widespread as desirable.

This paper analyses a wide range of literate programming tools available during the past two decades and introduces PROG$\mathcal{DOC}$, a new software documentation system. It is simple, language independent, and it keeps documentation and the documented software consistent. It uses LaTeX for typesetting purposes, supports syntax highlighting for various languages, and produces output in Postscript, PDF or HTML format.

1 Introduction

The philosophy of PROG$\mathcal{DOC}$ is to be as simple as possible and to pose as less requirements as possible to the programmer. Essentially, it works with any programming language and any development environment as long as the source code is accessible from files and the programming language offers a possibility for comments. It is non-intrusive in the sense that it leaves the source code untouched, with the only exception of introducing some comment lines at specific places.

The PROG$\mathcal{DOC}$ system consists of two parts. A so called *weaver* weaves the desired parts of the source code into the documentation, and a *highlighter* performs the syntax highlighting for that code. Source code and documentation are mutually independent (in particular they may be processed independently). They are linked together through special handles which are contained in the comment lines of the source code and may be referenced in the documentation.

PROG$\mathcal{DOC}$ is a good choice for writing articles, textbooks or technical white papers which contain source code examples and it proved especially useful for mixed language projects and for documenting already existing programs and libraries. Some examples of output produced by PROG$\mathcal{DOC}$ are available at [45].

The remainder of this paper is organized as follows: The first three sections will discuss some general aspects of literate programming, give a historical overview of the existing literate programming tools and present some new approaches for software documentation. In section 5, the PROG$\mathcal{DOC}$ system will be introduced and discussed in detail. Finally, section 6 will end the paper with conclusions and an outlook.

M. Broy and A.V. Zamulin (Eds.): PSI 2003, LNCS 2890, pp. 438–449, 2003.
© Springer-Verlag Berlin Heidelberg 2003

2   Some Words on Literate Programming

With an article published 1984 in the Computer Journal [23] Donald Knuth coined the notion of "Literate Programming". Since those days for many people literate programming is irrevocable inter**weave**d with Knuth's WEB [26] and TeX [24] systems.

Knuth justifies the term "literate programming" in [23] with his belief that "... the time is ripe for significantly better documentation of programs, and that we can best achieve this by considering programs to be works of literature." To support this programming style, he introduced the WEB system which is in fact both a language and a suite of utilities. In WEB, the program source code and the documentation are written together into one source file, delimited by special control sequences. The program source can be split into parts which can be presented in arbitrary order. The `tangle` program extracts these code parts from the WEB file and assembles them in the right order into a valid source file. Another program called `weave` combines the documentation parts of the WEB files with pretty printed versions of the code parts into a file which thereupon can be processed by TeX.

This system has many advantages. First of all, it fulfills the "one source" property. Because source code and documentation reside in one file, they are always consistent with each other. Second, the programmer is free to present the code he writes in arbitrary order, thus simplifying it for a human reader to understand the program. This can be done by rearranging code parts, but also by using macros inside the code parts, which can be defined later on in the WEB file. This way a top-down development approach is supported, in which the structure of a program as a whole is presented in the beginning and then subsequently refined, as well as a bottom up design, in which a program is assembled out of low level code fragments defined before. `tangle` will always expand these macros at the right place when constructing the source file out of the WEB file.

Another feature of the WEB system is the automatic construction of exhaustive indexes and cross references by `weave`. Every code part is accompanied by references which link it to all other parts which reference or use it. Also, an index of keywords with respect to code parts is created and the source code is pretty printed for the documentation part. The best way to convince yourself of WEB's capabilities is to have a look at Knuth's TeX implementation [25]. It was entirely written in WEB and is undoubtfully a masterpiece of publishing and literate programming.

2.1   WEB and Its Descendants

Besides its many advantages, the WEB system also has a couple of drawbacks. Many of them apply only to the original WEB implementation of Knuth and have been corrected or worked around in numerous WEB clones implemented thereafter. In this section we will present some of them[1] and discuss their enhancements.

One of the biggest disadvantages of WEB was the fact that it was closely tied to TeX as typesetting system and to Pascal as implementation language. So one of the first flavors

---

[1]   Only systems known to the authors will be mentioned here. A more complete overview may be found at the Comprehensive TeXArchive Network (CTAN) under http://www.ctan.org/tex-archive/web or at http://www.literateprogramming.org.

of WEB was CWEB [27] which extended WEB to C/C++ as implementation languages. It was implemented by Knuth himself together with Silvio Levy. CWEBx [30] is an alternative CWEB implementation with some extensions by Marc van Leeuwen. They both suffer from the same problems like WEB, as they are closely coupled to TEX and the C programming language.

To overcome these language dependencies, noweb [39] (which evolved from spiderWEB) and nuweb [7] have been developed by Norman Ramsey and Preston Briggs, respectively. They are both language independent concerning the programming language, whereas they still use LATEX for typesetting. Nuweb is a rather minimalistic but fast WEB approach with only four control sequences. Both noweb and nuweb offer no pretty printing by default, but noweb is based on a system of tools called filters which are connected through pipes. The current version comes with pretty printing filters for C and Java (see the actual documentation).

Another descendant of an early version of CWEB is FWEB [29]. FWEB initially was an abbreviation for "Fortran WEB", but meanwhile FWEB supports not only Fortran, but C, C++, Ratfor and TEX as well. These languages can be intermixed in one project, while FWEB still supports pretty printing for the different languages. On the other hand, FWEB is a rather complex piece of software with a 140 page user's manual.

Ross Williams' funnelWEB [53] is not only independent of the programming language, but of the typesetting language as well. It defines own format macros, which can be bound to arbitrary typesetting commands (currently for HTML and LATEX).

2.2   General Drawbacks of WEB Based Literate Programming Tools

Though many of the initial problems of the WEB system have been solved in some of the clones, their sheer number indicates that none of them is perfect.

One of the most controversial topics in the field of literate programming is pretty printing where *pretty printing* stands for syntax highlighting[2] **and** code layout and indentation. There are two questions here to consider: Is pretty printing desirable at all, and if yes, how should the pretty printed code look like? The answer is often a matter of personal taste, however there also exist some research results in this area like for example [5].

From a practical point of view it must be stated that doing pretty printing is possible for Pascal, although a look at the WEB sources will tell you that it is not an easy task. Doing it for C is even harder[3]. Taking into account the fact that weave usually processes only a small piece of code, which itself even does not have to be syntactically correct, it should be clear that pretty printing such code in a complex language like for example C++ will be impossible.

To overcome these problems, special tags have been introduced by the various systems to support the pretty printing routines. But this clutters the program code in the WEB file and even increases the problem of the documentation looking completely different

---

[2] *Syntax highlighting* denotes the process of graphically highlighting the tokens of a programming language.

[3] The biggest part of CWEB consists of the pretty printing module. Recognition of keywords, identifiers, comments, etc. is done by a hard coded shift/reduce bottom up parser.

than the source. This can be annoying in a develop/run/debug cycle. As a consequence, the use of pretty printing is discouraged. The only feasible solution could be simple syntax highlighting instead of pretty printing, as it is done by many editors nowadays.

Even without pretty printing and additional tags inserted into the program source, the fact that the source code usually appears rearranged in the WEB file with respect to the generated source file makes it very hard to extend or debug such a program. A few lines of code laying closely together in the source file may be split up to completely different places in the WEB file.

Once this could be called a feature, because it gave the programmer new means of structuring his program code for languages like Pascal which offered no module system or object hierarchy. As analysed in [9] it could be used to achieve a certain amount of code and documentation reuse. However the WEB macro system could also be misused by defining and using macros instead of defining and using functions in the underlying programming language.

Another problem common to WEB systems is their "one source" policy. While this may help to hold source code and documentation consistent, it breaks many other development tools like debuggers, revision control systems and make utilities. Moreover, it is nearly impossible for a programmer not familiar with a special WEB system to debug, maintain or extend code devolved with that WEB.

Even the possibility of giving away only the tangled output of a WEB is not attractive. First of all, it is usually unreadable for humans[4], and second this would break the "one source" philosophy. It seems that most of the literate programming projects realized until now have been one man projects. There is only one paper from Ramsey and Marceau [38] which documents the use of literate programming tools in a team project. Additionally, some references can be found about the use of literate programming for educational purpose (see [8] and [44]).

The general impression confirms Van Wyk's observation in [60] "... that one must write one's own system before one can write a literate program, and that makes [him] wonder how widespread literate programming is or will ever become." The question he leaves to the reader is whether programmers are in general too individual to use some-body else's tools or if only individual programmers develop and use (their own) literate programming systems. The answer seems to lie somewhere in between. Programmers are usually very individual and conservative concerning their programming environment. There must be superior tools available to make them switch to a new environment.

On the other hand, integrated development environments (IDEs) evolved strongly during the last years and they now offer sophisticated navigation, syntax highlighting and online help capabilities for free, thus making many of the features of a WEB system, like indexing, cross referencing and pretty printing become obsolete (see section 3). Finally the will to write documentation in a formatting language like TeX using a simple text editor is constantly decreasing in the presence of WYSIWYG word processors.

---

[4] NuWEB is an exception here, since it forwards source code into the tangled output without changing its format.

2.3 Other Program Documentation Systems

With the widespread use of Java a new program documentation system called JavaDoc was introduced. JavaDoc [15] comes with the Java development kit and is thus available for free to every Java programmer. The idea behind JavaDoc is quite different from that of WEB, though it is based on the "one source" paradigm as well. JavaDoc is a tool which extracts documentation from Java source files and produces formatted HTML output. Consequently, JavaDoc is tied to Java as programming and HTML as typesetting language[5]. By default JavaDoc parses Java source files and generates a document which contains the signatures of all public and protected classes, interfaces, methods, and fields. This documentation can be further extended by specially formatted comments which may even contain HTML tags.

Because JavaDoc is available only for Java, Roland Wunderling and Malte Zöckler created DOC++ [59], a tool similar to JavaDoc but for C++ as programming language. Additionally to HTML, DOC++ can create LaTeX formatted documentation as well. Doxygen [16] by Dimitri van Heesch, which was initially inspired by DOC++, is currently the most ambitious tool of this type which can also produce output in RTF, PDF and Unix man-page format. Both DOC++ and Doxygen can create a variety of dependency-, call-, inclusion- and inheritance graphs, which may be included into the documentation.

These new documentation tools are mainly useful for creating hierarchical, browsable HTML documentations of class libraries and APIs. They are intended for interface descriptions rather than the description of algorithms or implementation details. Although some of them support LaTeX, RTF or PDF output, they are not well suited for generating printed documentation.

Another approach which must be mentioned in this chapter is Martin Knasmüller's "Reverse Literate Programming" system [22]. In fact it is an editor which supports folding and so called *active text elements* [34]. Active text elements may contain arbitrary documentation, but also figures, links or popup buttons. All the *active text* is ignored by the compiler, so no tangle step is needed before compilation. Reverse Literate programming has been implemented for the Oberon system [54].

The GRASP [18] system relies on source code diagramming and source code folding techniques in order to present a more comprehensible picture of the source code, however without special support for program documentation or literate programming. In GRASP, code folding may be done according to the programming language control structure boundaries as well as for arbitrary, user-selected code parts.

3 Software Documentation in the Age of IDEs

Nowadays, most software development is done with the help of sophisticated IDEs (Integrated Development Environments) like Microsoft Visual Studio [32], IBM Visual Age [19], Borland JBuilder [6], NetBeans [35] or Source Navigator [40] to name just a few of them. These development environments organize the programming tasks in so

---

[5] Starting with Java 1.2, JavaDoc may be extended with so called "Doclets", which allow JavaDoc to produce output in different formats. Currently there are Doclets available for the MIF, RTF and LaTeX format (see [49]).

called projects, which contain all the source files, resources and libraries necessary to build such a project.

One of the main features of these IDEs is their ability to parse all the files which belong to a project and build a database out of that information. Because the files of the project can be usually modified only through the builtin editor, the IDEs can always keep track of changes in the source files and update the project database on the fly.

With the help of the project database, the IDEs can offer a lot of services to the user like fast, qualified searching or dependency-, call-, and inheritance graphs. They allow fast browsing of methods and classes and direct access from variables, method calls or class instantiations to their definitions, respectively. Notice that all these features are available online during the work on a project, in contrast to the tools like JavaDoc or Doxygen mentioned in the previous section which provide this information only off-line.

The new IDEs now deliver under such fancy names like "Code Completion" or "Code Insight" features like syntax directed programming [20] or template based programming which have been proposed already in the late seventies by [50,33]. In the past, these systems couldn't succeed because of two main reasons: they where to restrictive in the burden they put on the programmer and the display technology and computing power have not been good enough[6]. However, the enhancements in the area of user interfaces and the computational power available today allow even more: context sensitive prompting of the user with the names of available methods or with the formal arguments of a method, syntax highlighting and fast recompilation of affected source code parts.

All this reduces the benefits of a printed, highly linked and indexed documentation of a whole project. What is needed instead, additionally to the interface description provided by the IDE, is a description of the algorithms and of certain complex code parts. One step into this direction was Sametinger's DOgMA [41,42] tool which is an IDE that also allows writing documentation. DOgMA, like modern IDEs today, maintains an internal database of the whole parsed project. It allows the programmer to reference arbitrary parts of the source code in the documentation while DOgMA automatically creates and keeps the relevant links between the source code parts and the documentation up to date. These links allow a hypertext like navigation between source code and documentation.

While it seems that modern IDEs adopted a lot of DOgMA's browsing capabilities, they didn't adopted its literate programming features. However, systems like NetBeans [35], SourceNavigator [40] or VisualAge [48]) offer an API for accessing the internal program database. This at least would allow one to create extensions of these systems in order to support program documentation in a more comfortable way.

The most ambitious project in this context in the last few years was certainly the "Intentional Programming" project lead by Charles Simonyi [46,47] at Microsoft. It revitalized the idea of structured programming and propagated the idea of programs being just instantiations of intentions. The intentions could be written with a fully fledged WYSIWYG editor which allowed arbitrary content to be associated with the source code. Of course, this makes it easy to combine and maintain software together with the appropriate documentation. Some screen-shots of this impressive system can be found in chapter 11 of [11], which is dedicated solely to Intentional Programming.

---

[6] A good survey about the editor technology available at the beginning of the eighties can be found in [31].

4   Software Documentation and XML

With the widespread use of XML [57] in the last few years it is not surprising that various XML formats have been proposed to break out of the "ASCII Straitjacket" [1] in which programming languages are caught until now. While earlier approaches to widen the character set out of which programs are composed like [1] failed mainly because of the lack of standards in this area, the standardization of UNICODE [51] and XML may change the situation now.

There exist two concurring approaches. While for example JavaML [4] tries to define an abstract syntax tree representation of the Java language in XML (which, by the way, is not dissimilar from the internal representation proposed by the early syntax directed editors) the CSF [43] approach tries to define an abstract XML format usable by most of the current programming languages. Both have advantages as well as disadvantages. While the first one suffers from it's dependency on a certain programming language, the second one will always fail to represent every exotic feature of every given programming language.

A third, minimalistic approach could ignore the syntax of the programming language and just store program lines and comments into as few as two different XML elements. Such an encoding has been proposed by E. Armstrong [3].

However, independent of the encoding's actual representation, once that such an encoding would be available, literate programming and program documentation systems could greatly benefit from it. They could reference distinct parts of a source file in a standard way or they could insert special attributes or even elements into the XML document which could be otherwise ignored by other tools like compilers or build systems. Standard tools could be used to process, edit and display the source files, and internal as well as external links could be added to the source code.

Peter Pierrou presented in [37] an XML literate programming system. In fact it consists of an XML editor which allows one to store source code, documentation and links between them into an XML file. A tangle script is used to extract the source code out of the XML file. The system is very similar to the reverse literate programming tool proposed by Knasmüller, with the only difference that it is independent of the source language and stores its data in XML format. An earlier, but very similar effort described in [14] used SGML as markup language for storing documentation and source code.

Anthony Coates introduced xmLP [10], a literate programming system which uses some simple XML elements as markup. The idea is to use these elements together with other markup elements, for example those defined in XHTML [56], MathML [55] or DocBook [52]. XSLT [58] stylesheets are then used in order to produce the woven documentation and the tangled output files.

Oleg Kiselyov suggested the representation of XML as an s-expression in Scheme called SXML [21]. SXML can be used to write literate XML programs. Different Scheme programs (also called stylesheets in this case) are available to convert from SXML to LaTeX, HTML or pure XML files.

Some of the approaches presented in this section are quite new, but the wide acceptance of XML also in the area of the source code representation of programming languages could give new impulses to the literate programming community. A good starting point for more information on literate programming and XML is the Web site of the OASIS consortium, which hosts a page specifically dedicated to this topic [36].

5 Overview of the PROG$\mathcal{DOC}$ System

With this historical background in mind, PROG$\mathcal{DOC}$ tries to combine the best of the traditional WEB and the new program documentation systems. It releases the "one source" policy, which was so crucial for all WEB systems, thus giving the programmer maximum freedom to arrange his source files in any desirable way. On the other hand, the consistency between source code and documentation is preserved by special handles, which are present in the source files as ordinary comments[7] and which can be referenced in the documentation. PROG$\mathcal{DOC}$'s weave utility pdweave incorporates the desired code parts into the documentation.

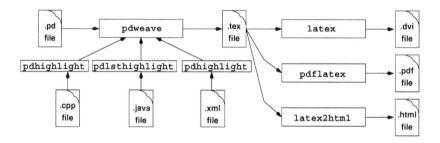

Fig. 1. Overview of the PROG$\mathcal{DOC}$ system

But let us start with an example. Suppose we have a C++ header file called ClassDefs.h with some class declarations. Following this section you can see a verbatim copy of the file:

```
class Example1 {                        double y;
private :                               public :
  int x;                                  explicit Example2(double d) : y(d) {}
public :                                  explicit Example2(int i) : y(i) {}
  explicit Example1(int i) : x(i) {}      explicit Example2(long i) : y(l) {}
};                                        explicit Example2(char c) : y((int)c) {}
                                          void doSomething(); // do something
class Example2 {                        };
private :
```

---

[7] As far as known to the authors, any computer language offers comments, so this seems to be no real limitation.

With ProgDOC, the class may be written as follows:

```
// BEGIN Example1                        double y;
class Example1 {                      // ...
private :                             public :
  int x;                                // BEGIN Constructors
public :                                explicit Example1(double d) : y(d) {}
  explicit Example1(int i) : x(i) {}     explicit Example2(int i) : y(i) {}
};                                        explicit Example2(long i) : y(l) {}
// END Example1                           explicit Example2(char c) : y((int)c) {}
                                          // END Constructors
// BEGIN Example2                         void doSomething(); // do something
class Example2 {                      };
// ...                                // END Example2
private :
```

The only changes introduced so far are the comments at the beginning and at the end of each class declaration. These comments, which of course are non-effective for the source code, enable us to use the new \sourceinput[*options*] {*filename*} {*tagname*} command in the LATEX documentation. This will result in the inclusion and syntax highlighting of the source code lines which are enclosed by the "// BEGIN *tagname*" and "// END *tagname*" lines, respectively.

Consequently the LATEX code presented in the following box

```
''... next we present the declaration
of the class {\tt Example1}:

\sourceinput[fontname=pcr, fontsize=7,
  listing, linenr, label=Example1]
  {ClassDefs.h}{Example1}

as you can see, there is no magic at
all using the {\tt \symbol{92}
sourceinput} command ...''
```

will result in content of the box shown on the right side:

"... next we present the declaration of the class Example1:

Listing 1: ClassDefs.h [Line 2 to 7]

```
class Example1 {
private :
  int x;
public :
  explicit Example1(int i) : x(i) {}
};
```

as you can see, there is no magic at all using the \sourceinput command ..."

The source code appears nicely highlighted, while its indentation is preserved. It is preceded by a caption line similar to the one known from figures and tables which in addition to a running number also contains the file name and the line numbers of the included code. Furthermore, the code sequence can be referenced everywhere in the text with a usual \ref command (e.g. see Listing 1). Notice that the boxes shown here are used for demonstrational purpose and are not produced by the ProgDOC system.

As shown in Fig. 1, ProgDOC isn't implemented in pure LATEX. Instead, the weaver component pdweave is an AWK [2] script while the syntax highlighter pdhighlight is a program generated with flex [13]. It was originally based on a version of Norbert Kiesel's c++2latex filter. It not only marks up the source code parts for LATEX, but also inserts special HTML markup into the LATEX code it produces. In that way an HTML-version of the documentation may be created with the help of Nikos Drakos' and Ross Moore's latex2html [12] utility. However, pdweave is not restricted on pdhighlight as highlighter. It may use arbitrary highlighters which conform to the interface expected by the weaver. And indeed, PROG𝒟𝒪𝒞 provides a second highlighter, called `pdlsthighlight`, which is in fact just a wrapper for the LATEX listings package [17].

Listings 1.1 and 1.2 demonstrate some other features of PROG𝒟𝒪𝒞 like displaying nested code sequences, hiding of code parts which can be thought of as a kind of code folding [22,18] and linking these parts together by either references or active links in HTML/PDF output. Furthermore PROG𝒟𝒪𝒞 is highly customizable. See the PROG𝒟𝒪𝒞 manual [45] for a complete reference.

```
class Example2 {
...
public :
  void doSomething(); // something
};
```

```
explicit Example2(double d) : y(d) {}
explicit Example2(int i) : y(i) {}
explicit Example2(long l) : y(l) {}
explicit Example2(char c) : y((int)c) {}
```

6   Conclusions

This paper listed and discussed most of the literate programming and program documentation systems which have been proposed during the past 20 years and it introduced PROG𝒟𝒪𝒞, the authors' own program documentation system. Even though PROG𝒟𝒪𝒞 is a fully functioning system it also suffers from one drawback criticized in some of the other systems: its tight coupling with LATEX as typesetting system. But PROG𝒟𝒪𝒞 should be thought of as just one incarnation of a very simple, yet powerful idea of keeping source code and documentation synchronised by connecting them through links. The authors' opinion is that nowadays programs are best written with sophisticated IDEs and documentation is best written with powerful word processors, where both of these tools are best suited for their own specific task.

However, importing parts of the source code into the documentation should be just as easy as the import of tables or figures. With today's technology this is only possible with special tools, like PROG𝒟𝒪𝒞. But it is not hard to imagine that one day IDEs will export source code just the way spreadsheet programs export tables. The emerging use of the XML technology may be helpful for this purpose.

Acknowledgements. We want to thank all the users who used PROG𝒟𝒪𝒞 and supplied feedback information to us. Among others these are Martin Gasbichler, Blair Hall and Patrick Crosby. We are truly indebted to Holger Gast, who always answered patiently all our questions and solved many of our problems concerning TEX.

References

1. P. W. Abrahams. *Typographical Extensions for Programming Languages: Breaking out of the ASCII Straitjacket.* ACM SIGPLAN Notices, Vol. 28, No. 2, Feb. 1993

2. A.W. Aho, B.W. Kernighan and P.J.Weinberger. *The AWK Programming Language*. Addison-Wesley, 1988
3. E. Armstrong. *Encoding Source in XML - A strategig Analysis.*
http://www.treelight.com/software/encodingSource.html
4. G. J. Badros. *JavaML: A Markup Language for Java Source Code.* 9th Int. WWW-Conference, Amsterdam, May 2000
5. Ronald M. Baecker, Aaron Marcus. *Human Factors and Typography for More Readable Programs.* Addison-Wesley, 1990
6. Borland Software Corporation. *Borland JBuilder.* http://www.borland.com/jbuilder
7. Preston Briggs. *nuWeb*, http://ctan.tug.org/tex-archive/web/nuweb
8. Bart Childs *Literate Programming, A Practitioner's View* TUGboat, Volume 13, No. 2, 1992, http://www.literateprogramming.com/farticles.html
9. B. Childs and J. Sametinger. *Analysis of Literate Programs from the Viewpoint of Reuse.* Software - Concepts and Tools, Vol. 18, No. 2, 1997, http://www.literateprogramming.com/farticles.html
10. A. B. Coates and Z. Rendon *xmLP - a Literate Programming Tool for XML & Text.* Extreme Markup Languages, Montreal, Quebec, Canada, August 2002, http://xmlp.sourceforge.net/2002/extreme/
11. K. Czarnecki and U. W. Eisenecker. *Generative Programming.* Addison-Wesley, 2000
12. by Nikos Drakos and Ross Moore. *Latex2HTML.*
http://saftsack.fs.uni-bayreuth.de/latex2ht/ or:
http://ctan.tug.org/ctan/tex-archive/support/latex2html
13. Free Software Foundation *The Fast Lexical Analyzer.* http://www.gnu.org/software/flex/
14. D.M. German, D.D. Cowan and A. Ryman. *SGML-Lite – An SGML-based Programming Environment for Literate Programming.* ISACC, Oct. 1996, http://www.oasis-open.org/cover/germanisacc96-ps.gz
15. J. Gosling, B. Joy and G. Steele *"Java Language Specification"* Addison-Wesley, 1996
16. Dimitri van Heesch. *Doxygen.* http://www.doxygen.org
17. Carsten Heinz *"The Listings package"*,
ftp://ftp.dante.de/tex-archive/help/Catalogue/entries/listings.html
18. T. D. Hendrix, J. H. Cross II, L. A. Barowski and K. S. Mathias. *Visual Support for Incremental Abstraction and Refinement in Ada95.* SIGAda Ada Letters, Vol. 18, No. 6, 1998
19. IBM Corporation. *Visual Age C++.* http://www-3.ibm.com/software/ad/vacpp
20. A. A. Khwaja and J. E. Urban. *Syntax-Directed Editing Environments: Issues and Features.* ACM SIGAPP Symposium on Applied Computing, Indianapolis, Indiana, 1993
21. O. Kiselyov. *SXML Specification.* ACM SIGPLAN Notices, Volume 37, Issue 6, June 2002
http://pobox.com/~oleg/ftp/Scheme/xml.html
22. M. Knasmüller. *Reverse Literate Programming.* Proc. of the 5th Software Quality Conference, Dundee, July 1996
23. Donald E. Knuth *Literate Programming* The Computer Journal, Vol. 27, No. 2, 1984
24. Donald E. Knuth *The TeXbook* Addison-Wesley, Reading, Mass., 11. ed., 1991
25. Donald E. Knuth *TeX: The Program* Addison-Wesley, Reading, Mass., 4. ed., 1991
26. Donald E. Knuth *Literate Programming* CSLI Lecture Notes, no. 27, 1992 or Cambridge University Press
27. Donald. E. Knuth and Silvio Levy *The CWEB System of Structured Documentation* Addison-Wesley, Reading, Mass., 1993
28. Uwe Kreppel. *WebWeb.* http://www.progdoc.de/webweb/webweb.html
29. John Krommes. *fWeb.* http://w3.pppl.gov/~krommes/fweb.html
30. Marc van Leeuwen. *CWebx.* http://wallis.univ-poitiers.fr/~maavl/CWEBx/
31. N. Meyrowitz and A. van Dam. *Interactive Editing Systems: Part I and II.* Computing Surveys, Vol. 14, No. 3, Sept. 1982

32. Microsoft Corporation. *Visual Studio.* http://msdn.microsoft.com/vstudio
33. J. Morris and M. Schwartz. *The Design of a Language- Directed Editor for Block-Structured Languages.* SIGLAN/SIGOA Symp. on text manipulation, Portland, 1981
34. H. Mössenböck and K. Koskimies. *Active Text for Structuring and Understanding Source Code.* Software - Practice and Experience, Vol. 27, No. 7, July 1996
35. NetBeans Project. *The NetBeans Platform and IDE.* http://www.netbeans.org
36. The Oasis Consortium. *SGML/XML and Literate Programming.* http://www.oasis-open.org/cover/xmlLitProg.html
37. P. Pierrou. *Literate Programming in XML.* Markup Technologies, Philadelphia, Pensylvania, US, Dec. 1999, http://www.literateprogramming.com/farticles.html
38. N. Ramsey and C. Marceau *Literate Programming on a Team Project* Software - Practice & Experience, 21(7), Jul. 1991, http://www.literateprogramming.com/farticles.html
39. Norman Ramsey *Literate Programming Simplified* IEEE Software, Sep. 1994, p. 97 http://www.eecs.harvard.edu/~nr/noweb/intro.html
40. Red Hat, Inc. *Source Navigator.* http://sourcenav.sourceforge.net
41. J. Samtinger *DOgMA: A Tool for the Documentation & Maintenance of Software Systems.* Tech. Report, 1991, Inst. für Wirtschaftsinformatik, J. Kepler Univ., Linz, Austria
42. J. Samtinger and G. Pomberger *A Hypertext System for Literate C++ Programming.* JOOP, Vol. 4, No. 8, SIGS Publications, New York, 1992
43. S. E. Sandø, The Software Development Foundation *CSF Specification.* http://sds.sourceforge.net
44. Stephan Shum and Curtis Cook *Using Literate Programming to Teach Good Programming Practices* 25th. SIGCSE Symp. on Computer Science Education, 1994, p. 66-70
45. Volker Simonis *The* PROG*DOC* *Program Documentation System* http://www.progdoc.org
46. C. Simonyi. *Intentional Programming - Innovation in the Legacy Age.* IFIP WG 2.1 meeting, june 4th, 1996
47. C. Simonyi. *The future is intentional.* IEEE Computer Magazine, Vol. 32, No. 5, May 1999
48. D. Soroker, M. Karasick, J. Barton and D. Streeter. *Extension Mechanisms in Montana.* Proc. of the 8th Israeli Conf. on Computer Based Systems and Software Engineering, 1997
49. Sun Microsystems, Inc. *The Doclets API.* http://java.sun.com/j2se/javadoc/
50. T. Teitelbaum and T. Reps. *The Cornell Program Synthesizer: A Syntax-Directed Programming Environment.* Communications of the ACM, Vol. 24, No. 9, Sept. 1981
51. The Unicode Consortium. *The Unicode Standard 3.0.* Addison-Wesley, Reading, Mass., 2000, http://www.unicode.org/
52. N. Walsh and L. Muellner. *DocBook: The Definitive Guide.* O Reilly & Associates, 1999, http://www.oasis-open.org/committe/docbook
53. Ross N. Williams. *funnelWeb.* http://www.ross.net/funnelweb/
54. N. Wirth and J. Gutknecht. *The Oberon System.* Software - Practice & Experience, 19(9), 1989, pp. 857–893
55. World Wide Web Consortium. *Mathematical Markup Language.* http://www.w3.org/Math
56. WorldWideWeb Consortium. *Extensible Hypertext Markup Language.* http://www.w3.org/MarkUp
57. The World Wide Web Consortium. *Extensible Markup Language.* http://www.w3.org/XML
58. World Wide Web Consortium. *Extensible Stylesheet Language Transformations.* http://www.w3.org/Style/XSL
59. R. Wunderling and M. Zöckler. *DOC++.* http://www.zib.de/Visual/software/doc++/
60. Christopher J. Van Wyk*Literate Programming Column.* Communications of the ACM, Volume 33, Nr. 3, March 1990. pp. 361–362

Integration of Functional and Timed Testing of Real-Time and Concurrent Systems

Victor V. Kuliamin, Alexander K. Petrenko, Nick V. Pakoulin,
Alexander S. Kossatchev, and Igor B. Bourdonov

Institute for System Programming of Russian Academy of Sciences (ISPRAS),
B. Communisticheskaya, 25, Moscow, Russia
{kuliamin,petrenko,npak,kos,igor}@ispras.ru
http://www.ispras.ru/groups/rv/rv.html

Abstract. The article presents an approach to model based testing of complex systems based on a generalization of finite state machines (FSM) and input output state machines (IOSM). The approach presented is used in the context of UniTesK specification based test development method. The results of its practical applications are also discussed. Practical experience demonstrates the applicability of the approach for model based testing of protocol implementations, distributed and concurrent systems, and real-time systems. This work stems from ISPRAS results of academic research and industrial application of formal techniques in verification and testing [1].

1   Introduction

During last decades more and more processes in industry, individual and social life fall under the influence of software. Software becomes more powerful, and the more powerful it becomes the more assured should be its safety and correctness. In this situation due to well-known human predisposition to errors various formal methods of software verification and validation acquire great importance.

Model based testing use formal models of software requirements to facilitate test development automation and is considered nowadays as one of the main instruments for software quality assurance. First approaches to model based testing appeared at the very rise of computer science. The approach based on finite state machines (FSMs) [2,3] is one of the most widely used of them. FSMs serve as a good modelling mechanism for a long time. But modern software systems are often constructed from distributed, concurrently operating components with intention to satisfy real-time constraints. They are more complex and require more sophisticated modelling methods to capture their complexity and features adequately. Various generalizations of FSM form the foundation of many modern model based testing approaches, which are more suitable for modern software.

Often model based testing of real-time systems is based on so called timed automata [4,5,6], an FSM generalization augmented with temporal attributes. They are used successfully both in testing and model verification areas in research projects. But they are rarely used to model real life systems in industrial

M. Broy and A.V. Zamulin (Eds.): PSI 2003, LNCS 2890, pp. 450–461, 2003.
© Springer-Verlag Berlin Heidelberg 2003

practice. One of the possible causes of this situation is the wide gap between timed automata formalism and formalisms of programming languages used by typical developers. The same gap is inherent to the approaches based on various kinds of temporal logics [7,8], although some commercial tools based on temporal logics are available (see [9]).

The other issue to be noticed is the usual separation of testing of event based communication from testing of unit functionality. But in practice calculations carried out in real-time systems should often be performed with timing restrictions taken into account.

We think that no model based testing approach exists that satisfies all the requirements of real-time or concurrent system testing. So, we have to try some combination of different approaches, which can be determined by three main points.

- The formalism used for description of system behaviour correctness criteria.
- Models used for test goal description and for test sequence generation.
- Means for integrated description of timed and functional (concerning calculations) characteristics of system behaviour.

From the engineering point of view one more issue is important: how to integrate the formalisms used and traditional programming techniques? The good solution of this problem implies that the resulting approach would be suitable for typical software engineers and could be smoothly introduced into industrial practice.

The approach proposed in this article is an extension of UniTesK test development method [10] successfully used for functional testing of complex industrial systems [11] on the base of formal specifications. UniTesK method is based on the following combination of techniques for solution of the problems stated above. Description of system behaviour, or behaviour model, is represented in the form of preconditions and postconditions of target system interface operations and interface data type invariants. The model used for test sequence generation is a FSM in an implicit form (see [10] for details). Usually it can be obtained by abstraction of behaviour model, but sometimes may include some more implementation specifics. The notation used for model is an extension of the programming language used in target system, and the problem of model and implementation integration does not exist.

Thus, three of four questions stated are answered by UniTesK. The open question – how to use this method for specification of timed constraints – is the subject of this article. The general idea is to extend the widely used and effective formalism of FSMs with a minimal set of features to specify concurrency and timed constraints. *Asynchronous finite state machines (AFSMs)* formally defined in the next section are considered to be appropriate for this. Before the definition we also give some background for introduction of new concepts. The third section presents testing approach based on AFSM models and corresponding modifications of UniTesK basic test architecture. Then, the conclusion summarizes the main statements of the work and outlines the future research topics. The appendix reports on some practical applications of the approach.

2   Asynchronous Finite State Machines

The classical approach for FSM based testing of software components can be illustrated by the Fig. 1. The target component is considered as a system that produces one reaction in response for one stimulus provided by the test. The task of testing is to provide a representative collection of test stimuli and to check the correctness of resulting reactions.

Fig. 1. Classical Model of Testing

This approach works well for passive software components. It can also be adapted for active components that produce reactions only in response for stimuli, give one reaction for one stimulus, and the next reaction of which depends only on the sequence of stimuli obtained before.

But what if the target component can produce reactions without any stimuli or can give a sequence of reactions in response for one stimulus? In this case classical FSM model cannot adequately describe the target system behaviour and we have to use more sophisticated approach.

Modern software systems are usually composed from distributed and concurrently working components. Real-time software also is often designed as a collaboration of units working in parallel to satisfy real-time constraints. The testing process for such a unit can be illustrated by the picture on Fig. 2.

Fig. 2. Modern Model of Testing

The difference between these two models cannot be overcome by simple interface transformation. The second model permits production of a sequence of reactions in response for one stimulus, or in absence of any stimulus. Even more complex is dependency of reaction sequence on all the history of interaction between the system and its environment. This kind of behaviour cannot be modelled by FSM in a straightforward way.

Asynchronous finite state machine (AFSM) A is a tuple (V, v_0, I, e, O, T), where

- V is a finite set called *the set of states* of A.
- $v_0 \in V$ is called *the initial state* of A.
- I is a set called *the input alphabet* of A. Its elements are called *input stimuli* of A, or, simply, stimuli.
- $e \notin I$ is called *the empty stimulus*. The set $X = I \cup \{e\}$ is called *extended input alphabet* of A.
- O is a set called *the output alphabet* of A. Its elements are called *reactions* of A.
- $T = R \cup S \cup E$ is a finite set called *the set of transitions* of A. Its parts have the following meaning.
    - $R \subseteq V \times X \times V$ is the set of *receiving transitions*. Note, that receiving transition can be marked with stimulus from I and with the empty stimulus e.
    - $S \subseteq V \times O \times V$ is the set of *sending transitions*.
    - $E \subseteq V \times V$ is the set of *empty transitions*.

We call a state $v \in V$

- *terminal*, if it has no outgoing transitions: $v \notin \pi_1(R) \cup \pi_1(S) \cup \pi_1(E)$. We use here symbol π_i for standard projection $\pi_i : A_1 \times \cdots \times A_n \to A_i$.
- *sending*, if it has only sending or empty outgoing transitions: $v \in \pi_1(S) \cup \pi_1(E) \setminus \pi_1(R)$.
- *receiving*, if it has only receiving outgoing transitions: $v \in \pi_1(R) \setminus \pi_1(S) \cup \pi_1(E)$.
- *mixed*, if it has both receiving and sending or empty outgoing transitions: $v \in \pi_1(R) \cap (\pi_1(S) \cup \pi_1(E))$.

We consider only AFSMs without mixed states. See the definition of AFSM behaviour function at the end of this section and further discussion of possibility of mixed states.

Fig. 3 demonstrates an example of AFSM. We use here widely used notation representing stimulus a as ?a and reaction x as !x. The state 0 is its initial state of the AFSM presented. This AFSM has six states, the input alphabet $\{a, b\}$, and the output alphabet $\{x, y\}$. It also has 4 receiving transitions (one of them is marked with the empty stimulus), 4 sending transitions, and one empty transition. The state 5 is terminal.

We will show later that the behaviour of AFSM presented on Fig. 3 cannot be adequately modelled with any FSM.

To describe how an AFSM A works we need to consider *the input queue* and *the output queue* connected to it. Input queue contains a sequence of stimuli, each of which belongs to extended input alphabet X of A. Output queue collects the sequence of A reactions. Informally, A looks at the head stimulus x of its input

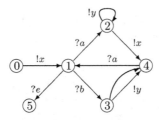

Fig. 3. Example of AFSM

queue and tries to find a transition marked with this stimulus outgoing from its current state. If it can do this, it performs one of such transitions and removes the head stimulus from the input queue. If it cannot, possible reasons can be of four kinds: (1) the current state is terminal and A stops its work; (2) the current state is sending, so A chooses some transition marked with reaction or empty transition and performs it; (3) the current state is receiving and $x = e$, then A does not do anything, but x is removed from the input queue; (4) the current state is receiving and $x \in I$, then the error occurs and A cannot operate any longer. The empty stimulus e is introduced to model the behaviour of a system in the absence of any external stimulus, at least for some time.

A *step* of AFSM A in the state $v \in V$ for the first symbol x in its input queue is defined as nondeterministic choice of one of *the possible transitions,* and corresponding change of the input queue, the output queue, and the current state of A. The set of possible transitions P is determined as follows.

- If v is terminal, $P = \emptyset$. The current state of A and states of its queues remain unchanged.
- If v is sending, $P = \{t \in S \cup E | \pi_1(t) = v\}$. If the transition t chosen belongs to E, the next state of A is $\pi_2(t)$ and its queues are left unchanged. If $t \in S$, the next state is $\pi_3(t)$, the input queue is left unchanged, and the reaction $\pi_2(t)$ is added to the output queue.
- If v is receiving and $x \in X$, $P = \{t \in R | \pi_1(t) = v \wedge \pi_2(t) = x\}$. If this set is not empty, some $t \in P$ is chosen, the next state of A is $\pi_3(t)$, the output queue is left unchanged, and x is removed from the input queue. If $P = \emptyset$ and $x = e$, the state of A and its output queue are left unchanged, and x is removed form the input queue. If $P = \emptyset$ and $x \neq e$, *forbidden input error* occurs.

We consider execution of A for a sequence of stimuli put in its input queue. Such sequence can be finite or infinite. We consider only infinite sequences, because a finite sequence can be represented by the infinite one, obtained by completing the first with infinite sequence of empty stimuli. An *execution* of AFSM A for an infinite input sequence w is a sequence of steps of A, starting from its initial state v_0, while w in its input queue, and the output queue of A is empty. An execution produces some sequence of reactions u, called *the execution result,* in the output queue of A. An execution is *legal*, if it is infinite or ends in a terminal state of A. Illegal execution ends with forbidden input error.

Input sequence w is called *acceptable* for an AFSM A, if all the executions of A for w are legal. *The behaviour function h_A of A is the function defined on the set of its acceptable input sequence. It maps such a sequence w into the set of all possible execution results of A for w.*

Having behaviour functions of AFSMs we can compare them. For example, the behaviour of the AFSM on Fig. 3 cannot be modelled by any FSM, because an FSM cannot produce in response for the input sequence aa the sequence $xy^k x$ for any given natural number k.

We can also choose a subclass $\mathcal{A}$ of all AFSMs and consider behaviour functions of AFSMs from $\mathcal{A}$. In particular, we may allow mixed states in AFSM and define its behaviour in such a state somehow. It is possible to demonstrate (see [12]) that most of the natural ways to define such generalized AFSMs result in state machine classes having the same set of behaviour functions. That is, for each 'generalized AFSM' we can construct the one satisfying the above definition and having the same behaviour function. The only exception is *input output state machines* [13,14], which are usually defined very similar to AFSM, but has no empty stimulus. Their behaviour functions can be realized as behaviour functions of AFSMs, but there exists an AFSM that have behaviour function different from behaviour function of any finite IOSM (see [12] for an example). So, AFSMs present more general class of state machines.

It is easy to construct the AFSM having the same behaviour as a given FSM has. To do so, it is sufficient to add one intermediate state for each FSM transition and to separate each FSM transition into two ones. The first is receiving, marked with the initial transition input stimulus and leads from the starting state of the initial transition to the corresponding intermediate state, and the second is sending and leads from the intermediate state to the end state of the initial transition.

3   Conformance Testing Based on AFSMs

Comparison of behaviour functions of AFSMs can be regarded as the essence of testing based on AFSM models. We say that an AFSM B *conforms* to another AFSM A if for each input sequence w acceptable for A $h_B(w) \subseteq h_A(w)$. This conformance relation is an analogue for reduction relation of FSMs [15].

Having an AFSM model of some software system we can pose a question whether the system works in accordance with the model. It can be regarded as a question on conformance of unknown AFSM, called *the implementation under test*, which we can observe only through its behaviour on sequences of stimuli, to the given one.

To answer this question with the help of testing we should impose some restrictions on the implementation under test. In absence of any restrictions for each given model and sequence of stimuli or even set of such sequences we can construct an implementation that provides the same reactions as model in response for all these sequences, but does not conform to the model. In general case we face with the following problems.

- **Nondeterminism of model.** If behaviour function maps some input sequence into several reaction sequences, then in general we cannot obtain all of them after any finite number of executions. Instead we should lay down some hypothesis on the behaviour of target system. For example, we can suppose that if it works correctly for one trial of given input sequence, it does so for each trial of this sequence. Some approaches to testing based on nondeterministic models use *all results condition* – after some bounded number of trials, we can obtain each possible output (see [16]). In an AFSM one input sequence can map to infinite set of output ones, so all results condition restricts the set of AFSM models we can use for testing.

- **Infinity of behaviour function domain.** Model behaviour function can be defined for infinite set of input sequences. We cannot test all of them, so we should define some *coverage model* – an equivalence on the behaviour function domain – and suppose that if implementation works correctly for one sequence from some equivalence class, then it does so for any one of the same class.

- **Infinity of input sequences.** We define behaviour function on infinite sequences of stimuli. How can we check implementation work for some actually infinite input (that does not end with a sequence of empty stimuli)? We do not know general solution of this problem. Some particular solution can be obtained by choice of actually finite (having only empty stimuli after some step) representatives of coverage classes. Another way is to use for check not only model behaviour function, but some additional predicates on possible serializations of stimuli and reactions, which can assign a verdict on the correctness of output on some finite step.

- **Reaction wait time.** How long should we wait for reactions? This question cannot be solved without restrictions on implementation size (number of states and/or transitions) and introduction of some bound on implementation step execution time. Under those conditions we can calculate upper bounds on reaction wait time.

- **Empty stimulus simulation.** Our empty stimulus is only an abstract representative of active nature of implementation under test. How can we simulate its presence in input sequence? We do not have general answer. One approach is to tap somehow input receipts in the implementation and to trace them. We can do so for systems, which use special function to obtain the status of input queue and for which this function can be substituted. For other systems we can use a special class of models having *time uniform behaviour*. This means that their behaviour does not differ for input sequences, which can be transformed to each other by insertion or removal of empty stimuli. Actually, this class of models is equivalent to finite IOSMs (see [12]). We can also use *the stationary testing*, which is possible when all coverage classes can be represented by sequences without empty stimuli.

We consider testing based on AFSM models in the context of UniTesK technology [10]. This technology provides a full-scale process for test development and testing based on formal specifications of target system behaviour. UniTesK proposes to use two models in test development.

– The first one is the model of system behaviour represented in the form of pre- and postconditions of interface operations and data type invariants. Specifications are automatically transformed into *oracles* – programs that check behaviour of the system under test against specifications. First, the oracle of some target operation checks the precondition and returns precondition violation exception, if it fails. If it holds for the given arguments, the oracle calls the target operation with these arguments. Then, on the base of the result obtained, pre- and post-values of arguments and state variables, it checks the postcondition. So, such an oracle can process any values of arguments and can work with nondeterministic implementation.
– The second model is an FSM used for generation of test sequences. It is called *testing model*. Testing model is usually (but not always) an abstraction of specifications (see [17] for theoretical background of testing model construction). It is represented in the form of *test scenario,* which is an implicit description of the FSM. It has no information on ends of transitions and defines only the data structure of states and a rule of transition firing depending on state data. Test scenario can be developed manually or semi-automatically on the base of behaviour specifications and functionality coverage criterion chosen as a goal of the test.

   During the test the generic FSM traversal mechanism uses scenario to generate an adaptive sequence of input stimuli. Each stimulus is converted into its representation on behaviour model level, then with the help of adapters it is converted into implementation representation, the system produces the response on it, which should be converted back on the level of behaviour model and checked by the appropriate oracle (see [10] for details).

The peculiarity of UniTesK is the implicit representation of state machine model in test scenario. Test designer does not describe states and transitions but specify only the structure of state data (what is to be regarded as state) and input data iterators for each operation under test. The traversal mechanism that uses such a representation should be able to produce a traversal of state machine transitions without knowledge on their ends until their execution.

To use UniTesK for testing real-time and concurrent systems we use AFSM models instead of FSM for test sequence generation and extend the specification constructs. In addition to specifications of interface operations they may contain *asynchronous reaction specifications*. Such a specification also has precondition, saying in what model states this reaction is possible, and postcondition, saying what the resulting state of corresponding transition is. Postconditions can contain timing constraints.

Test suite architecture presented in [10] was also extended. To decide whether the implementation reacts correctly on the input sequence applied we do the following.

1. Collect all the reactions, maybe from several sources (implementation ports). Thus, we know some partial order on reactions, but have no full order on them. This partial order is defined for reactions coming to one port and maybe with the help of timestamps on reactions. Note, that timestamps should be used accurately. They often contain the time of reaction arrival, not the time of its creation. So, in general reactions that arrive on different ports within some short interval cannot be surely ordered.
2. Then, we find all possible serializations of stimuli sent and reactions obtained and all possible sequences of intermediate states in the behaviour model. If we cannot find any, then implementation does not conform to specifications. If we find some, we can consider any of the resulting states as the hypothetic next state of the system and continue the process.

To do this we add to the test suite architecture the component, which generates possible serializations of partially ordered reactions and stimuli. In addition we need AFSM traversal algorithms, which can work with sets of hypothetic current states, or we may use only models that can bring us only to single state after any representative input sequence. In practice we managed to use the second approach (see below the section on applications of AFSMs). The first one is in active research.

4 Practical Applications of AFSMs

The approach to concurrent system testing based on AFSM in UniTesK framework was successfully applied to testing an implementation of IPv6 protocol. The CTesK tool based on C language extension was used in the project.

The system under test was represented by Microsoft Research implementation of Internet Protocol version 6 (IPv6), more precisely, version 1.4 of MSR IPv6 for Microsoft Windows NT/2000. The same test suite was also ported to Windows XP and Windows CE 4.1. The main features tested are the following.

- Packet send and receive, including fragmentation and reassembly of large packets.
- Control messages. As RFC 2463 [18] specifies, IPv6 used Internet Control Messages Protocol version 6 (ICMPv6) to report errors encountered in processing packets and to perform other functions, such as diagnostics. ICMPv6 must be fully implemented by every IPv6 node.
- Neighbour discovery (RFC 2461 [19]), including neighbour solicitation, neighbour advertisement, router solicitation, router advertisements, and redirect.

These features do not exhaust the functionality of IPv6. But their absence or an error in implementation of any of them in the protocol on a node often causes impossibility of normal node work in the IPv6 network.

The specifications were developed in the UniTesK-compliant specification extension of C language on the base of IPv6 specifications presented in RFC documents. The interface specified consists of a set of procedure and non-procedure stimuli and two types of reactions: outgoing IPv6 packets and UDP messages received in sockets. One additional reaction was introduced to specify timing restrictions, namely, timeouts in neighbour discovery protocol.

The following defects were discovered.

- Some series of packets can cause reboot of the system. The error in packet reassembly implementation causes in some cases fatal error in the operating system core.
- A discrepancy between specifications of packet reassembly from fragments and its implementation. This defect was classified as negligible, because it occurs only under specific conditions and does not cause fatal consequences.
- A discrepancy between specification of ICMPv6 Echo function and its implementation. RFC requires that all the responses on ICMPv6 Echo request should be passed to the process initiated the request. MSR IPv6 implementation interface supports passing only of the first response.

The project demonstrated the capabilities of UniTesK approach extended with AFSM models for specification and testing concurrency and real time constraints. The testing performed revealed several defects, while several projects on MSR IPv6 testing carried out simultaneously do not report on their discovery (see [20] for example). The project effort was about 10 man-months, which is much less than the effort of implementation.

The project also revealed some disadvantages C language for representation of abstract software properties specifications. The first is very low level of C language, which hides the logic of abstract model, the second one is manual memory management, which requires much work not related with the matter of specification and test design.

For details see full project reports on [21].

The second project performed according to the method presented in this article is testing of OPC RACE, a peer-to-peer messaging management systems for Nortel Networks. During this project also several errors were found in the implementation.

5   Conclusion

The UniTesK approach for model based testing tries to use notation and concepts familiar for typical developer. This principle was accepted as a compromise that facilitate introduction of formal methods into industrial processes. Sometimes it requires simplification or hiding of theoretical background and advanced techniques used, sometimes forces to exclude promising sophisticated test development techniques from consideration. It provides software engineers with a model based testing technology of moderate complexity that do not require special modelling languages. The article demonstrates the next step in the same direction. The techniques for modelling of concurrency and timing characteristics are represented in an environment familiar for industrial developers.

Introduction of AFSMs in the background of UniTesK technology does not seem to make it much more complex, while gives a set of features especially useful for testing of real-time and concurrent systems. On the base of experience of practical applications [21,22,23], we can say that the approach is quite effective for specification and further conformance testing of protocol implementations, distributed and parallel systems, for testing both functionality and time constraints of real-time systems.

The UniTesK technology is supported by a set of tools developed for different target languages. We already include the support for AFSM based testing in CTesK tool, working with an extension of C, and plan to do so for J@T and .N@T tools, working with Java and C# extensions correspondingly [24,25].

References

1. http://www.ispras.ru/~RedVerst/
2. George H. Mealy. A method for synthesizing sequential circuits. Bell System Technical Journal, 34(5):1045–1079, 1955.
3. E. F. Moore. Gedanken-experiments on sequential machines. Automata Studies, Annals of Maths. Studies, Princeton University Press, no. 34, pp. 129–153, 1956.
4. A. En-Nouaary, H. Fouchal, A. Elqortobi, R. Dssouli, and E. Petitjean. Timed Testing Using Clock Zone Vertices. Technical Report, Departement d'IRO, Universite de Montreal, 1998.
5. D. Clarke and I. Lee. Automatic Test Generation for the Analysis of a Real-time System: Case Study. In 3-rd IEEE Real-time Technology and Applications Symposium, 1997.
6. B. Nielsen and A. Skou. Automated Test Generation from Timed Automata. International Journal on Software Tools for Technology Transfer (STTT), 2002.
7. F. Dietrich, X. Logean, and J. P. Hubaux. Testing Temporal Logic Properties in Distributed Systems. Proc. IFIP Int'l. Wksp. Testing of Commun. Sys., Tomsk, Russia, Aug. 1998.
8. H. Hong, I. Lee, O. Sokolsky, and H. Ural. A Temporal Logic Based Theory of Test Coverage and Generation. International Conference on Tools and Algorithms for Construction and Analysis of Systems (TACAS 2002), April 8–11, 2002.
9. http://www.time-rover.com/main.html
10. I. Bourdonov, A. Kossatchev, V. Kuliamin, and A. Petrenko. UniTesK Test Suite Architecture. Proc. of FME 2002. LNCS 2391, pp. 77–88, Springer-Verlag, 2002.
11. I. Bourdonov, A. Kossatchev, A. Petrenko, and D. Galter. KVEST: Automated Generation of Test Suites from Formal Specifications. FM'99: Formal Methods. LNCS 1708, Springer-Verlag, 1999, pp. 608–621.
12. I. B. Bourdonov, A. S. Kossatchev, V. V. Kuliamin. Classification of Asynchronous Finite State Machines. In Russian. To be printed in works of ISP RAS.
13. P. Zafiropulo, C. H. West, H. Rudin, D. D. Cowan, and D. Brand. Towards Analysing and Synthesizing Protocols. IEEE Transactions on Communications, COM-28(4):651 -660, April 1980.
14. O. Henniger. On test case generation from asynchronously communicating state machines. In M. Kim, S. Kang, K. Hong, eds., Proceedings of the 10-th IFIP International Workshop on Testing of Communicating Systems, Cheju Island, South Korea, 1997. Chapman & Hall.

15. G. von Bochmann, A. Petrenko. Protocol Testing: Review of Methods and Relevance for Software Testing. Proceeding of ISSTA 1994, pp. 109–124.
16. S. Fujiwara and G. von Bochmann. Testing Nondeterministic Finite State Machine with Fault Coverage. IFIP Transactions, Proceedings of IFIP TC6 Fourth International Workshop on Protocol Test Systems, 1991, Ed. by Jan Kroon, Rudolf J. Heijink, and Ed Brinksma, 1992, North-Holland, pp. 267–280.
17. I. Burdonov, A. Kossatchev, and V. Kulyamin. Application of finite automatons for program testing. Programming and Computer Software, 26(2):61–73, 2000.
18. A. Conta and S. Deering, *Internet Control Message Protocol (ICMPv6) for the Internet Protocol Version 6 (IPv6) Specification,* RFC 2463, December 1998.
19. T. Narten, E. Nordmark, and W. Simpson, *Neighbor Discovery for IP Version 6 (IPv6),* RFC 2461, December 1998.
20. http://www.tahi.org
21. http://www.ispras.ru/~RedVerst/RedVerst/White Papers/MSRIPv6 Verification Project/Main.html
22. A. Petrenko, I. Bourdonov, A. Kossatchev, V. Kuliamin. Experiences in using testing tools and technology in real-life applications. Proceedings of SETT'01, India, Pune, 2001.
23. A. K. Petrenko. Specification Based Testing: Towards Practice. Proc. of PSI 2001. LNCS 2244, Springer-Verlag 2001.
24. http://www.atssoft.com
25. http://unitesk.ispras.ru

Test Case Generation for UML Statecharts

Dirk Seifert, Steffen Helke, and Thomas Santen

Technical University of Berlin,
Institute for Software Engineering and Theoretical Computer Science,
Software Engineering Research Group,
Sekr. FR 5-6, Franklinstr. 28/29, 10587 Berlin, Germany,
{seifert,helke,santen}@cs.tu-berlin.de

Abstract. We describe an approach to automatically generate test cases from object-oriented statecharts as they are used in the UML and supported by development tools such as I-Logics Rhapsody.

This work contributes in three respects to using statecharts for specifying and verifying systems. First, it concretizes previously proposed semantics of statecharts by instantiating the abstract data type for the event management and analyzes the resulting specific properties. Second, building on a previously defined conformance relation it discusses two interpretations of *stuttering*. Third, it introduces a compact data structure for representing the statechart semantics that allows for efficient generation of test cases and easily supports both interpretations of stuttering.

1 Introduction

Statecharts [3] are a well accepted notation for specifying reactive systems. They are useful in particular to specify embedded software, such as the software for controllers in automobiles, because the reactive behavior usually is the most important aspect of software in those systems.

Nowadays, there is an active field of research [1,2,4] on defining a semantics of statecharts that is compatible with the object-oriented paradigm [6]. In this paper, we address the problem of generating test cases from object-oriented statecharts. We base our work on Tretmans' foundational research on conformance testing for labeled transition systems [8] and recent adaptions by Latella et al. for UML statecharts [5]. Building on these approaches we address the following three aspects.

First, we give a brief overview of the semantics of object-oriented statecharts that includes a model of observational behavior, distinguishing between input, output, and internal events. The semantics addresses the specific features of object-oriented statecharts: although events may occur simultaneously, they are processed asynchronously and sequentially. Furthermore, like classical statecharts [3], object-oriented ones just ignore events for which no explicit transition is specified. This makes statecharts input enabled, as they will never refuse to process an event.

Second, we define a notion of conforming behavior of one statechart (the implementation) to another (the specification). Actually, we state two interpretations of stuttering [5] that differ in the way they interpret the *default behavior* of ignoring events for which no explicit treatment is specified: one interpretation treats the default behavior strictly,

M. Broy and A.V. Zamulin (Eds.): PSI 2003, LNCS 2890, pp. 462–468, 2003.

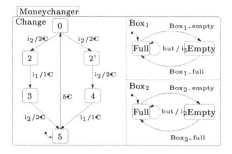

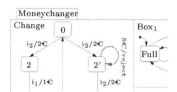

Fig. 1. Statechart for a moneychanger   **Fig. 2.** Handling nonspecified input

allowing the implementation to reduce non-determinism only; the other interpretation treats the default behavior as "don't care" and allows the implementation to extend behavior that the specification does not explicitly prescribe.

Third, we address the problem of exponentially growing semantical representations for statecharts. We introduce a *compact semantic interpretation* of a statechart as a data structure that is considerably smaller than a straightforward representation of the semantics of a statechart. The compact semantic interpretation reflects the observable behavior of a statechart and can serve as input to Tretmans' algorithm [8].

2   Example Specification

The statechart in Fig. 1 describes the behavior of a (simplified) money changing machine. The machine has two reservoirs for coins of 1€ and 2€. Additionally, it has a slot to insert 5€ bills, and a button to request change. When somebody inserts a 5€ bill into the slot and repeatedly presses the button, then the machine will output a number of 1€ and 2€ coins up to a total of 5€.

The statechart has a root state called *Moneychanger* that consists of three orthogonal substates (*and*-states): *Change*, Box_1, and Box_2. The two boxes model reservoirs of 1€ and 2€ coins. A box is in the substate *Full* if its reservoir contains a sufficient number of coins, otherwise it is in the substate *Empty*. If Box_k is in state *Full*, pressing the button of the machine (event *but*) causes a transition from *Full* to itself, which generates an (internal) event i_k. The third orthogonal substate *Change* specifies an algorithm of changing 5€ bills.

3   Foundations

We will see that the semantics of a statechart can be defined as a labeled transition system. Therefore, it is clear that an approach for conformance testing based on labeled transition systems is, in principle, applicable to statecharts. There are, however, two major issues in adapting such an approach to statecharts: first, an adequate conformance relation on statecharts must be defined, and, second, a compact representation of the semantics of a statechart must be found. We address the latter issue in Section 4.

3.1   Statecharts with Asynchronous Signal Events

The considered subset of UML statecharts includes the basic features related to state refinement and orthogonal states, transition priorities, simultaneous occurence of events and the asynchonous and sequential processing of events. The label of a transition has the form *trigger/action*, where *trigger* represents a single event, and *action* is a set of events generated when the transition fires. We omit a formal syntactic description of a statechart here and refer the interested reader to [7].

For the semantic interpretation we associate a labeled transition system to a statechart that resembles the definitions in [4]. Similar definitions can be found in [1,2]. A semantic interpretation SC^s is defined as a 4-tuple $(\Sigma^s, \Sigma_{is}^s, \Lambda^s, \Delta^s)$. A member of the set Σ^s of semantic states is called a *status* and consists of two components $\langle C, Q \rangle$. The first component C is a set of active states, called *active state configuration*. The second component Q is a container of events, called an *event queue*. The event queue contains the events that the statechart has received but has not processed yet. All initial statuses (in Σ_{is}^s) consist of an initial configuration and an empty event queue.

Latella et al. [5] use a parametric abstract data type for the modeling of the environment policy, which abstracts from the exact nature of the event queue. In accordance with the choice made in Rhapsody, we interpret Q as a FIFO queue in the present paper.

For conformance testing we are interested in the observable aspects of a statechart specification. Therefore, we rely on a semantics that hides the internal behavior of SC^s. This becomes obvious in the definition of the transition relation $\Delta^s \subseteq \Sigma^s \times \Lambda^s \times \Sigma^s$ that relates statuses of Σ^s by labeled transitions. We assume that for each statechart a set E is given, which is divided into mutually disjoint sets of internal (unobservable) events E_{int} and observable events E_{obs}. The observable events are again distinctly classified as incoming events in E_{in} and outgoing events in E_{out}. A label in Λ^s is a set of *observable* events, i.e. a subset of $E_{in} \cup E_{out}$. The label {} represents a transition step with unobservable, internal communication only.

The first event in the event queue (the *current event*) determines the set of enabled transitions. The *transition selection algorithm* [6] identifies the maximal sets of non-conflicting transitions as subsets of the set of enabled ones. In general, there is more than one of those sets. This is one source of non-deterministic behavior of a statechart.

Executing the transitions of one non-empty maximal set of non-conflicting transitions yields a new configuration (the *next configuration*) and produces a number of internal and outgoing events. During such a step, a set of incoming events can be received from the global environment simultaneously. The *next status* of SC^s contains the next configuration and the *next queue* that results from deleting the current event from the event queue and appending the internal and incoming events to the queue in any order.

Therefore, the statuses consisting of the next configuration and one of the possible next queues can all be reached from the current status, which is another source of non-determinism in a statechart: the set of the outgoing events and of the incoming events make up the labels of the transitions from the current status to each of the next statuses.

If the set of non-conflicting transitions is empty, then there is no transition starting in a state of the current configuration whose trigger is the current event. In this case the current event will be removed from the queue.

3.2   Conformance Testing

We build on the conformance relation introduced in [5] and on work on test case generation from labelled transition systems [8]. The basic idea of conformance is that an implementation must behave in a manner compatible to the specification. It must not produce a reaction to an input which the specification cannot produce in the same situation. Furthermore, the implementation may produce no output at all if the specification allows that behavior.

A critical issue in determining an adequate conformance relation for statecharts is to decide on the role of transitions in the specification that stem from different interpretations of default behavior. Consider, for example, the statechart of Fig. 1. If the chart is in state 2', and the current event is 5€, then the chart will stay in that configuration while the current event 5€ will be deleted from the event queue.

Fig. 2 shows a statechart that, in the same configuration, reacts differently to a current event of 5€: that chart will produce an event *reject* to make the moneychanger reject the additionally inserted bill and return it to the customer.

Depending on the intuitive interpretation of the default behavior (stuttering), the statechart of Fig. 2 may or may not be acceptable as an implementation of the one of Fig. 1: if the specifiers consider the default behavior as "don't care", because they do not describe it explicitly, then Fig. 2 is an acceptable implementation; if, however, the specifiers do not want an implementation to change the observable behavior of the specification in any case, then Fig. 2 is not acceptable.

4   Test Case Generation

The semantics of a statechart as outlined in Section 3.1 produces very large labelled transition system with much redundancy. One reason is that the set of events generated in one step can be enqueued in the event queue in any possible order — producing statuses (and transitions leading to them) that differ only in the order of events in the event queues. Another reason is that all possible incoming events must be dealt with in all statuses although most of them will just be enqueued and eventually dequeued without causing any observable effect. In the present section, we describe a compact semantic automaton (CSA) as a data structure with much less redundancy. Based on this data structure we derive traces of observable events, which are the input to the testcase generation algorithm.

4.1   Compact Semantic Automaton (CSA)

For the example of the money changing machine, Fig. 3 illustrates the relation between a compact semantic automaton and the corresponding semantic interpretation. The left hand side of the figure shows a part of the semantics of the moneychanger, the center of the figure shows the corresponding CSA, and the right hand side shows an interpretation of the CSA considering all possible incoming events.

In the initial status $\langle C_5, [] \rangle$, the statechart is in the default states and the event queue is empty. The relevant incoming events are 5€, *but* and Box_k_empty. The part shown in

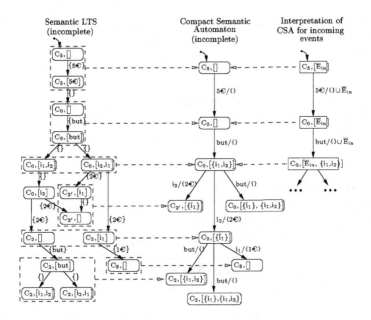

Fig. 3. Compact Representation of a Section of the Semantic Automaton

Fig. 3 considers only what happens if the incoming events 5€ and *but* occur in this order with ample time between them for the moneychanger to completely process 5€ first. Processing *but* in C_0, the charts Box_1 and Box_2 generate the events i_1 and i_2 at the same time. Therefore, there are two transitions leading to statuses with event queues reflecting the possible orders of processing i_1 and i_2. Processing those events non-deterministically leads to one of the configurations C_2 or $C_{2'}$, and so forth.

Combining certain statuses with the same configuration, a compact semantic automaton reduces redundancy. A CSA SC^c is defined as a 4-tuple $(\Sigma^c, \Sigma_{is}^c, \Lambda^c, \Delta^c)$.

In difference to SC^s the *compact status* contains a queue of *sets* of *marked events*. The set of all marked events contains each event $e \in E_{int}$ in two copies, a marked copy $\bar{e}$ and an unmarked copy e.

A member of the queue represents all permutations of the internal events that are generated simultaneously in an atomic synchronous time step. Thus a compact status may represent a number of semantic statuses. The compact status $\langle C_0, [\{i_1, i_2\}] \rangle$ in Fig. 3 represents the semantic states $\langle C_0, [i_1, i_2] \rangle$ and $\langle C_0, [i_2, i_1] \rangle$.

A marked event, such as $\bar{i}_1$ in $\langle C_{2'}, [\{\bar{i}_1\}] \rangle$, represents one that may or may not be present in a member of the event queue: the queue $[\{i_1, i_2\}]$ represents the event queues $[i_1, i_2]$ and $[i_2, i_1]$, and after processing i_2 the resulting queue either is empty (because i_1 has been dequeued) or it only contains i_1. The queue $[\{\bar{i}_1\}]$ represents these alternatives.

The compact statuses of a CSA SC^c are related by labeled transitions. A label in Λ^c has the form *trigger*/*action*^{obs}, where *trigger* represents the *processing* of an event and *action*^{obs} is the set of outgoing events that processing *trigger* produces in one time step.

Additionally, we add a special label δ to Λ^c that indicates possible quiescence [8], i.e. a situation in which the system cannot proceed autonomously.

A CSA does not explicitly represent the observation of incoming events. The triggers of transitions only show when incoming events are processed. Because statecharts are input-enabled, any incoming event can be received at any time. The right-hand side of Fig. 3 shows that explicitly representing those events would result in the set of *marked* incoming events $\overline{E}_{in}$ being the heads of the queues in all compact statuses — which makes it redundant. See [7] for a detailed description of an algorithm for generating a CSA.

4.2 Deriving Event Traces

A test case is a labeled transition system that checks whether a certain part of the observable behavior of an implementation under test conforms to the specification (described by a statechart). To this end, a test case generates stimuli (in E_{in}) for the implementation, and compares its reaction (in E_{out}) to the one the specification prescribes.

To generate test cases based on the CSA for a statechart similar to Tretmans' algorithm [8], it remains to determine the *observable* traces of a specification from the CSA and to produce test cases from these traces. These traces are the basis for the test case generation.

The *incoming* events that stimulate a certain behavior are the triggers of the transitions on a particular path in a CSA. Those transitions mark the points in an execution where the incoming events are processed (c.f. Fig. 3). However, the CSA does not determine when such an event is generated.

In the following, we assume that the processing order of incoming events in the compact semantic automaton is equal to the order of the event generation within the global environment. Thus a statechart can process an event b after an event a only if it receives a before b from the environment. Because the global environment and the implementation under test do not synchronize on the generation of events, we cannot assume a specific order of incoming events and generated outgoing events. Hence, the test case generation procedure must consider any possible order of those events, while preserving the order of outgoing events.

To clarify this point, consider the following path of the CSA in Fig. 3, which is a response to feeding a 5€ bill to the moneychanger and pressing the button two times:

$$5E/\{\} \cdot \text{but}/\{\} \cdot i_2/\{2E\} \cdot i_1/\{1E\} \cdot \text{but}/\{\} \cdot \cdots \Longrightarrow \begin{cases} 5E \cdot \text{but} \cdot \qquad \cdot 2E \cdot 1E \cdot \ldots \\ 5E \cdot \text{but} \cdot 2E \cdot \qquad \cdot 1E \cdot \ldots \\ 5E \cdot \text{but} \cdot 2E \cdot 1E \cdot \qquad \cdot \ldots \end{cases}$$

The last three labels in the path contain the observations *2€, 1€* and *but*. Because the system produces *2€* and *1€* but the environment supplies the event *but*, the latter can occur at any time before, between or after the two other events.

In general, we need to generate all possible interleavings between incoming and outgoing events while preserving causality and the order of events in the respective classes. With this procedure to generate traces from a CSA, we can produce input for Tretmans' testcase generation algorithm.

5 Conclusions

Using a common semantics for object-oriented statecharts, we have implemented the parametric abstract datatype for the modeling of the environment policy by a FIFO-queue and have analyzed the resulting subtleties with respect to testing. The main contribution of our work lies in defining a compact representation for the semantic interpretation. To this end, we introduce a model of observational behavior and introduce two possible interpretations of the implementation relations for UML statecharts.

Two features make the complete semantic description of a non-trivial statechart impracticably large: truly parallel event generation and input-enabledness. To cope with truly parallel event generation, we must consider all permutations of the events that are generated simultaneously in an atomic synchronous time step. For input-enabledness, we must consider the extension of the queue in each atomic synchronous time step by any number of defined incoming events. Each feature results in a tremendously large set of next states for which the CSA provides a compact representation.

Based on the compact semantic representation we use Tretmans' algorithm to generate testcases. In this paper, we describe the principle setting of our approach. We are working on extensions of the theory to inter-object communication and other kinds of events, in particular events carrying data and synchronous events.

References

1. R. Eshuis and R. Wieringa. Requirements level semantics for UML statecharts. In *Proc. Formal Methods for Open Object-Based Distributed Systems, IV*. Kluwer Academic Publishers, 2000.
2. D. Harel and E. Gery. Executable object modeling with statecharts. In *Proc. 18th International Conference on Software Engineering*, pages 246–257, 1996.
3. D. Harel and A. Naamad. The STATEMATE semantics of statecharts. *ACM Transactions on Software Engineering and Methodology*, pages 293–333, 1996.
4. D. Latella, I. Majzik, and M. Massink. Towards a formal operational semantics of UML statechart diagrams. In *Proc. Formal Methods for Open Object-Based Distributed Systems, III*. Kluwer Academic Publishers, 1999.
5. D. Latella and M. Massink. On Testing and Conformance Relations for UML Statechart Diagrams Behaviours. In *Proc. International Symposium on Software Testing and Analysis*, ACM, 2002.
6. OMG – Object Management Group. Unified Modeling Language Specification, Version 1.3, March 2000. www.omg.org.
7. D. Seifert, S. Helke, and T. Santen. Conformance testing for statecharts. Technical Report 2003/1, Technical University of Berlin, 2003.
8. J. Tretmans. Test generation with inputs, outputs, and repetitive quiescence. In *Proc. Workshop on Tools and Algorithms for the Construction and Analysis of Systems*, pages 127–146. Springer-Verlag, 1996.

Conceptual Content Modeling and Management

Joachim W. Schmidt and Hans-Werner Sehring

Technical University Hamburg-Harburg, Software Systems Department,
Harburger Schloßstraße 20, D-21073 Hamburg, Germany
{j.w.schmidt,hw.sehring}@tu-harburg.de

Abstract. Focused views on *entities of interest* — concrete or abstract ones — are often represented by texts, images, speech or other media. Such media views are communicated through visual or audio channels and stored persistently in appropriate containers.

In this paper we extend a computational content-container model into a closely coupled content-concept model intended to capture more of the meaning — and improve the value — of content. Integrated content-concept views on entities are modeled by the notion of *assets*, and our asset language aims at two goals derived from extensive experiences with entity modeling:

1. *Expressiveness*: according to Peirce [29] and others, entity modeling — and, therefore, also asset modeling — has to cover three different perspectives:
   - an entity's inherent *characteristics* (firstness categories);
   - its *relationships* to other entities (secondness categories);
   - the *systematics* behind the first two perspectives (thirdness categories).
2. *Responsiveness*: according to Cassirer [8,47] and others, entity modeling *processes*, in order to be successful have to be
   - *open*, i.e., users of an asset language must be able to adapt their asset models according to the requirements of the entity at hand;
   - *dynamic* in the sense that all aspects of an asset model must be subject to inspection and adaptation at any time.

Our current experiments with asset languages are motivated by the need for a better understanding and integration of content *and* concepts about application entities. We conclude by outlining a component-based implementation technology for open and dynamic asset systems.

1 Introduction: Motivation and Rationale

The management of structured data is well understood in computer science and so is their use in software system engineering [21,46,45]. Data are essentially maintained as content of typed variables or schema-constrained databases, and data access and manipulation is abstracted by functions or transactions and encapsulated by software components.

The object-oriented approach, for example, aims at a seamless support of software development from application analysis through system design to software implementation and provides a methodological basis as well as tool support for the realization of large-scale object systems.

M. Broy and A.V. Zamulin (Eds.): PSI 2003, LNCS 2890, pp. 469–493, 2003.
© Springer-Verlag Berlin Heidelberg 2003

A rapidly increasing class of computer applications use persistent object systems as containers for any kind of (multi-media) content. Such applications face the problem that the computational models by which the container objects are defined say nothing about the application concepts associated with their content. As a consequence, such systems can give only little and incoherent support for content retrieval, presentation, change, explanation, etc.

In this paper we argue that application contents *and* application concepts need to be closely coupled and represented by a single notion which we call an *asset*. Assets represent intimately allied content-concept pairs which represent and signify application entities. The content aspect of an asset holds a media view on an entity while the concept aspect represents its allied concept view.

In section 2 of this paper we first introduce objects as providers of container functionality and then define assets on top of container objects where the concept aspect of an asset is intended to model application aspects of entities and is not restricted to computational purposes. Section 3 discusses the *expressiveness* of an asset language and section 4 outlines such a language. In section 5 the modalities by which an asset language is made available to its users are discussed under the heading of language *responsiveness*. Both asset language expressiveness and responsiveness put particular demands on asset system implementations. Section 6 summarizes aspects of an asset technology. The paper concludes by reporting on ongoing interdisciplinary research and development projects and refers to commercial activities.

In summary, our experiments with asset languages and systems serve essentially two goals:

- advancing large-scale content management by a concept-based view on application content and, vice versa,
- improving the representation of application concepts by means of a generalized notion of content.

2   Adding Meaning to Content

Object-oriented models and technology are highly appropriate in modeling digital containers for various kinds of application content and their presentation media. However, the *meaning* of content, although captured in early phases of object-oriented application analysis and software design, cannot be represented adequately by object-oriented computer languages. Therefore, we propose an asset language capable of representing both computational concepts for containers as well as application concepts for their content.

2.1   Computational Objects as Containers for Application Content

Since the early days of high-level programming the states of computations are modeled by typed variables which hold values from predefined value sets and which can be accessed by predefined operations:

```
var contents: Integer := 0;
```

Here a computational object of variable content is associated with the mathematical concept of integer numbers and is initialized by the specific content *zero*. The specification of high-level programming languages regulates the necessary details of how to use computational objects: their lifetime and visibility or their access from right- and lefthand-side expressions. Since algorithmic programming takes a mathematical view on its application domains the application entities *are* numbers or Booleans and, therefore, there is a perfect match between content — e.g., the mathematical entity *zero* — and the associated mathematical concept of Integer.

In software engineering scenarios where re-usability of designs, code and content is a central issue, computational objects are modeled more explicitly. By an object-based language, for example, we can hide the above integer variable and define integer cells with their own methods and possibly additional properties [1]:

```
object myIntegerCell {
  var contents: Integer := 0;
  method get(): Integer {return self.contents};
  method set(n: Integer) {self.contents := n}; }
```

The cell type, IntegerCellType, is defined by the signature of the above cell object, myIntegerCell. Cells of this kind are perfectly suited for algorithmic computing, i.e., for any application where cell content is modeled by mathematical or logical concepts which are used for computation only.

Fig. 1. Preview thumbnail computed from myImageContainer.contents

Nowadays, however, the majority of applications come from other areas — business enterprises, e-commerce, public administration, logistics, art history etc. — and application entities have to be mapped from their own conceptual context into the computational concepts of a computer language. Object-oriented analysis and design (OOAD) processes support such mapping processes which may result in an `imageContainer` object definition such as

```
object myImageContainer {
    var contents: array of byte := emptyImage;
    method get(): array of byte {return self.contents};
    method set(i: array of byte) {self.contents := i}; }
```

or, for class-based languages [1], in a corresponding class definition, `ImageContainer`. Classes support a more dynamic object generation by

```
myImageContainer := new ImageContainer; ...;
```

Classes also can be re-used for the definition, for example, of specialized containers such as

```
class JPEGContainer refines ImageContainer {
    var ...; ...;
    method getThumbnail(...): SmallJPEGImageCopy
        {... self.contents ...};
    //computes thumbnails from JPEG content and its parameters;
    //may be used for preview etc., see Fig. 1
    method getColorDepth(): Integer {...};
    method getCompressionRate(): Integer {...}; }
```

```
myJPEGContainer := new JPEGContainer; ...;
```

The above example sketches a class which interprets the byte contents in a specific way. Furthermore, it introduces a method `getThumbnail()` which returns a thumbnail version of the object's contents. It is important to note that the contents of computational objects such as `myJPEGContainer` very often serve two purposes:

- *computational* use, e.g., to compute thumbnails from a container's digital content;
- *conceptual* use, e.g., to be interpreted by humans as a thumbnail of some *equestrian statue* (Fig. 1).

Some conceptual model [6] of the notion of *equestrian statue* may have existed as an OOAD document [21] in earlier phases of a software engineering project on iconographic digital libraries but is no more available at runtime.

Consequently, we argue for a language with modeling expressiveness and runtime responsiveness by which we can serve both computational purposes as required for an efficient container technology as well as conceptual purposes as requested for the deeper understanding of the application content maintained by such containers and of the concepts associated with it.

2.2   Content-Concept Pairs as Assets for Entities

As learned from database design and from application software engineering in general, data — or content in the above sense — does not come *out of the blue* but is a result of a careful conceptualization process of the *entities of interest* in some application domain.

In our approach we complement the *media view* on an application entity (as represented by content, see Fig. 1) by a *model view* represented by named and related concepts associated with entities. Content-concept pairs — which we call *assets* (see Fig. 2) — can be defined, queried and manipulated as elements of our *asset language* (see section 4).

In our example domain of *Political Iconography* some person on horseback may be considered as a figure of political relevance and iconographic effect. Such entity may be represented by an asset instance with an asset identifier, say, AID1. The content aspect of asset AID1 may contain an image of the entity at hand as represented by Fig. 1. The concept aspect describes the entity by its *characteristics* (firstness) and by *relationships* to other entities (secondness), for example, AID2 and AID3. Our example asset is defined as an instance of an asset class (thirdness), *EquestrianStatue*, which regulates to some extent the *systematics* behind the bindings to (1) and (2).

A first sketch of asset instance AID1 may look as follows:

```
AID1 → [content {see Fig. 1} | concept sex     male (1) ...
                                artist AID2 (2) ...
                                ruler   AID3

     (2) ...]
                                        EquestrianStatue (3)
```

Our Asset Definition Language is discussed in some detail in section 4. It is based on experiences from entity modeling in database design and software systems engineering.

3   On Expressive Entity Modeling

According to Peirce [29] and others (see, for example, Sowa [39]), *expressive* entity modeling has to cover an entity from three different perspectives:

1. inherent *characteristics* of an entity (Peirce firstness categories);
2. *relationships* between an entity and other entities (Peirce secondness categories);
3. *systematics* of entity *genesis* as provided by the "business procedures" behind legal bindings (Peirce thirdness categories) for perspectives 1 and 2.

As an example for the three perspectives take a human who is modeled as *Person* by the firstness characteristics, age, sex, nationality etc. and as *Employee* by additional secondness relationships to other entities such as his head of division, task assignments, past employments etc. Description on thirdness level

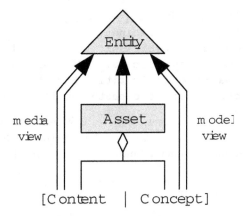

Fig. 2. Entities and Assets, Overview

would further specialize the employee as an *EmployeeOfCompanyABC*, for example, by ABC's specific business procedures for hiring, firing or promoting its personnel or for task assignment (see also section 3.3).

Approaches such as entity-relationship modeling for database design [10] cover essentially the firstness and secondness perspectives. Numerous ER extensions (HERM [45], ..., UML [46]) contribute to the thirdness dimension by various kinds of constraints (invariants, type constraints, pre- and postconditions etc.).

As equally important as the expressiveness of an entity model are the modalities by which such expressive models can be utilized, i.e., their *responsiveness*. Cassirer in his work on *Symbolic Forms* [8,47] studies at length the closely coupled roles of content *and* concept for human domain understanding and emphasizes the *open-dynamic* character of content-concept use. Whitehead, as another example, also states quite clearly, "We must be systematic, but we should keep our systems open" [39]. Responsiveness issues are further discussed in section 5.

To summarize, the rationale behind our content-concept-based asset approach is the assumption that entities are captured by providing both a media view based on content and a model view based on concepts. Our asset language combines computational content management as enabled by advanced object-oriented container technology with insights from the Peirce and Cassirer programs for expressive and responsive conceptual modeling.

3.1   Entity Characteristics

On the level of firstness categories, assets are defined by a choice of *characteristic* properties inherent to an entity. They are modeled by the asset language's base types — String, Integer, Boolean etc. as well as structures over it — or by computational objects as, for example, for Date or SmallJPEGImageCopy.

```
asset someEquestrianStatue {
  content image: JPEGContainer;
  concept characteristic sex: {female, male};
         characteristic paintedAt: Date;
         characteristic title: String;
         characteristic photo: SmallJPEGImageCopy;...}
```

Standard methods such as get, set, etc. need not be defined explicitly but are generated by the asset language compiler together with standard forms for method invocation and parameter binding (see section 6.1).

3.2   Entity Relationships

Asset *relationships* model an entity on the level of secondness, i.e., by its association to or interaction with other entities [38]. Since entities are represented by assets, an asset relationship is essentially a named binding of the asset at hand — the *source* asset — to other assets — the *target* assets. Target asset bindings are initialized by defaults and controlled by target asset classes and their constraints.

```
asset someEquestrianStatue {
  content ...
  concept characteristic ...
         relationship paintedBy: Artist;
         relationship requestBy: Ruler;
         relationship depicted:  Person; ... }
```

3.3   On the Systematics of Entity Genesis

In all mediating organizations, managed companies, organized domains, etc. there are rules by which concrete characteristics and relationships of entities are systematically regulated to some degree. During the analysis and design phase of computerized support systems such systematics of entity genesis — the entity definition on the Peirce thirdness level — are captured by various (semi-)formal approaches. System implementation maps the resulting sets of predicates into conditionals on the software execution level:

- object-oriented software engineering extracts such regulations from textual documents on business procedures and maps them into object designs via semi-formal use-case diagrams [21];
- formal program specification captures program semantics, for example, by invariants as well as pre- and postconditions and applies predicate transformers for code development [19];
- workflow systems have their own pragmatic workflow specification and enactment languages [49], and
- database systems enrich their schema definitions by constraints and triggers which restrict transactions and thus protect database content.

In all cases, thirdness level entity modeling is concerned with the semantics of the set of procedures which handle entities and, therefore, create and change entity descriptions. We concentrate on the use of types and constraints for thirdness level entity modeling and experiment with assets on various levels:

— asset language level: asset type and class definitions as well as constraints on asset characteristics and relationships (*intensional* semantics, see section 4.3);
— asset instance level: *extensional* asset class semantics by representative collections of asset instances; exploited, for example, as training sets for automatic asset classification or for learning scenarios (see section 4.3);
— asset system level: API signatures for process and workflow bindings.

In our approach thirdness issues usually remain underspecified in the sense that details such as binding orders etc. are left open. In an asset's content part there is, however, ample room for all kinds of semi-formal working documents on constraint and procedure specification.

In practice, the firstness and secondness aspects of assets are connected by their use as initialization and manipulation parameters of thirdness "business processes". Looking at assets from such a work perspective we can take a dual position [31]:

— assets for *works to be* which we can bind to, inspect, evaluate, etc.
— assets for *work to do* which we can initialize, put forward, interrupt, resume, refine, undo, redo, etc.

4   Preview of an Asset Definition Language

As with database management, the functionality of an Asset Languages can be subdivided into three subareas: Asset Definition (ADL), Manipulation (AML) and Querying Languages (AQL). In this paper asset definitions are expressed in a linguistic form — by the expressions of our Asset Definition Language — while asset manipulation and querying is performed via interactive, form-oriented interfaces generated from ADL expressions.

4.1   Content Modeling: Asset Container Objects

One of the two indivisible sides of an "asset coin" is its (reference to) content. The content aggregated in an asset is defined in its content part and the entire power of object-oriented container technology is employed here (see section 3):

```
class EquestrianStatue {
  content image: JPEGContainer;
  concept ... }
```

Details of content storage and retrieval regulate, for example,

- **content storage location:** an object store may contain the entire content as indicated in the examples from section 2.1 (`byte array`), or just a reference to externally stored content. In the latter case the container provides (transparent) access to the actual content. In addition issues like caching (for repeating access), archiving (for content vanishing from an external system), mediation (to transparently access more than one external system), etc. may be handled.
- **content delivery mode:** content may be delivered en bloc (as in the case of the byte array) or streamed, QoS parameters [40] might apply, etc.
- **content access modes:** content may be read-only or free for modification. Additional regulations can exist which constrain the access to content (authentication, rights, payment, . . .).

In a content part multiple content objects may be given, e.g., for providing an image in three resolutions:

```
class EquestrianStatue {
  content highResImage: JPEGImageReference; //for print
          onlineImage:  JPEGImageReference; //for web site
          thumbnail:    JPEGImageContainer; //for preview
  concept ... }
```

The possibility of having more than one content container may also be used to have the content presented by different media, or to provide various images of the same content, e.g., photographs from different angles, with changing illumination, etc.

4.2 Conceptual Content Modeling: Asset Characteristics and Relationships

As already outlined in section 3 the concept part of an asset carries various contributions to cover the Peirce program for entity definition. On the level of firstness categories we provide the notion of characteristics. Characteristic attributes can be initialized by default values or objects (of basic or user-defined types). It is important to note, though, that characteristics are not intended for modeling object states but for describing the characteristics of entities.

```
class EquestrianStatue {
  content ...
  concept characteristic sex: {female, male};
          characteristic paintedAt: Date;
                         := new Date{1800 May 20th};
          characteristic title: String
                         := "Bonaparte crossing the Alps";
          characteristic photo: SmallJPEGImageCopy
                         := image.getThumbnail(...);
          ... }
```

Additionally, asset definitions allow the specification of constraints. They add to thirdness properties of assets. By giving a type, a domain restriction is already posed on the characteristics. It can be further narrowed by value or object constraints as in the following example:

```
        ...
characteristic paintedAt: Date
                < new Date{1800 September} and
                > new Date{1800 January};
characteristic title: String
                > "Bonaparte" or > "Napoleon";
characteristic photo: SmallJPEGImageCopy
                res < 100;
    ...
```

Here the characteristic attribute paintedAt is limited to the date interval January to September 1800, and title, once set, has to contain either the string literal "Bonaparte" or "Napoleon" (or both, "Napoleon Bonaparte"). Possible comparators test for equality ("="), lesser ("<"), greater (">"), different ("#"), or similar ("~") values. How the comparator is evaluated depends on the object type. In the case of an object-valued characteristic it can be constrained in each of its attributes. In the above example photo may only have a resolution below 100.

Relationship attributes describe secondness properties of an entity. In the same way as for characteristics, default bindings and constraints can be given for relationships, but based on assets instead of values or objects:

```
class EquestrianStatue {
  content ...
  concept characteristic ...
            ...
        relationship paintedBy: Artist := AID2;
        //AID2 is asset for painter Jacques-Louis David
        relationship requestBy: Ruler := AID3;
        //AID3 is asset for emperor Napoleon Bonaparte
        relationship depicted:Person:=self.requestBy;
        //by default, the bindings to attributes depicted and
        //requestBy are made identical
        ... }
```

Technically relationships are references to other assets. Object-oriented programming languages hide the difference between attributes with value assignment and those with object bindings — i.e., firstness and secondness use of categories (languages like C^{++} make a clear distinction but this is regarded as low-level programming since the choice for using a value or a pointer it is not motivated by the model).

In some conceptual modeling approaches a uniform treatment of attributes of kind "value assignment" and of kind "object binding" is considered an advantage.

However, most object-oriented DDLs [9] as well as UML (via attributes and associations) and many other conceptual modeling languages make the kind of attribute explicit.

Our position in making an explicit distinction between attributes for characteristic values and objects and for relationships to assets is additionally motivated by the support a user gains from asset technology. While the characteristic attributes form the basis for value-based asset querying in the sense of database query languages, the relationship attributes support asset browsing and navigation.

4.3   Remarks on Asset Class Semantics

In our experiments with asset languages we distinguish two ways of defining asset semantics. As outlined so far our asset language has an *intensional* semantics, i.e., is given by (type) predicates which assets of a certain class have to fulfill. A second kind of asset class semantics could be called *extensional* because asset class semantics is based on prescribed asset instances.

Intensional Asset Class Semantics. Intensional asset class definitions are comparable to classes in object-oriented languages and are given by class declarations containing characteristic and relationship attributes with their constraints and default bindings.

As in object-oriented languages our Asset Definition Language allows class refinement. Refined subclasses inherit characteristics and relationships as well as content part from the underlying base class:

```
class EmployeeOfCompanyABC refines Employee {
    concept relationship employer: Company := ABC; }
```

Class definitions as discussed so far are considered static; they can be statically type-checked and compiled. If, however, a class is defined, for example, by the constraint, `Company = ABC`, instead of the initializing assignment, `Company := ABC`, dynamic type checking is required.

Extensional Asset Class Semantics. Extensional definitions of asset semantics is essentially given by collections of `prescribed` asset instances. Currently we are experimenting with collections which are either unordered (sets) or ordered (lists). A second criterion regulates the degree to which such prescribed collections definitively restrict asset instances or not. If a prescribed collection is marked as `final`, users can only select prescribed collection elements and the asset class definition is reduced to an enumeration type:

```
class EquestrianStatue {...}
    prescribed final {AID₁, ..., AIDₙ}
```

Prescribed collections may also be indicated as initial which means that users can start with any element of the collection and modify it within the boundaries drawn by the intensional part of the class definition.

In our flagship project on *Political Iconography* the asset class Equestrian-Statue, for example, is defined by

```
class EquestrianStatue {...}
   prescribed initial AID₁, ..., AIDₙ
```

where the list indicates that order is considered relevant (following Aby Warburg's principle of *good neighborhood*). By starting with a specific element from the list, say, AID_i, a user indicates that — subjectively — this element is considered "closest" to the new asset instance he wants to create.

Examples of host systems exploiting asset class definitions based on prescribed collections are automatic content classifiers for which such instance collections serve as training sets [3,13,52], or e-learning environments presenting the example sets to students (see section 7).

4.4   On Signification Services

A particular service expected from an asset instance are contributions to the identification of the entity which it represents. In our example the value of a distinctive characteristic asset attribute, say, the attribute photo which is computed from the asset's content, may serve as an *iconic* entity signifier. Other characteristics may play the role of *indexical* signifiers. The network of related assets — classes and instances — supports the notion of *symbolic* signifiers [16].

Iconic Signification. Iconic signification is achieved through firstness categories [29]. An iconic signifier resembles for a user some similarity with some entity. An iconic signifier *re-presents* the associated entity and brings it into the user's mind. Those sets of characteristics which make the asset an icon of some entity are distinguished by the keyword icon. In the example below the characteristic attribute photo of an instance of asset class EquestrianStatue signifies some entity iconically. The characteristic sex, however, does not provide any signification service.

Indexical Signification. Indexical signification is, one way or the other, based on the notion of *co-occurrence* and is closely related to Peirce secondness categories [29,16]. There needs to be some matchmaking circumstance by which an indexical signifier and its signified entity are brought together. Asset instances provide, by definition, such co-occurrence between contents and concepts, and asset relationship attributes establish co-occurrence when bound to other asset instances. Furthermore, assets are supposed to support indexical signification of application entities by asset characteristics as, for example, registrationNo:

```
class EquestrianStatue {
  content ...
  concept characteristic sex: {female, male}; ...
          characteristic photo: SmallJPEGImageCopy;
          characteristic registrationNo: Integer;
          ...
          icon  photo;
          index registrationNo; }
```

Symbolic Signification. Symbolic signification makes full use of the categorical structures introduces by asset classes and type systems and is, therefore, closely related to Peirce's thirdness level.

Classes, types and constraints contribute to symbolic signification. If, for example, the definition of `EquestrianStatue` includes a relationship to artists which are constrained to the epoch "Renaissance", then renaissance statues may be signified symbolically via artists.

Well-structured interfaces to large-scale content management systems make extensive use of symbolic signification [17,48].

5   On Asset System Responsiveness

As equally important as the expressiveness of an asset language for entity modeling are the *modalities* by which such expressive models can be utilized, i.e., their *responsiveness*. According to Cassirer [8,47] and others (see, for example, [35]), responsive entity modeling must be

- *open*, i.e., the categories used for entity modeling must not be pre-defined by fixed ontologies but need to be open for adaptation by specialization or generalization as demanded by the application entities at hand;
- *dynamic*, i.e., any aspect of an entity model — all related asset instances as well as their class and type definitions etc. — must be accessible, evaluable and adaptable at any time.

Openness and dynamics together allow asset systems to be constantly adapted, refined and personalized in a process which converges towards the requirements as demanded by its users' tasks.

5.1   Asset System Openness

In the 1920ies Ernst Cassirer already strongly requested that content-concept pairs — which he calls *symbols* [8,47] — be formed in an open context with no restriction to predefined, fixed ontologies for concepts and categories. Humans — Cassirer's *animal symbolicus* — are able to grasp and communicate entities and their media and model views adequately only if concepts can be openly specialized and generalized depending on the modeling needs of the entity at hand. In fact Cassirer considers such differentiation efforts as *the* essential contribution to entity modeling.

In programming, conceptual openness was neglected until the late 60ies when the programming language Simula [14] first introduced object-oriented principles into software simulation systems.

Our notion of assets corresponds closely to the notion of object. While "the *object-oriented* approach to programming is based on an intuitive correspondence between a software simulation of a physical system and the physical system itself" [1], our *asset-oriented* approach to entity modeling aims at an intuitive correspondence between a software representation of a perceptible domain and the perceptible domain itself.

For the domain of *Political Iconography*, for example, our asset application system WEL ([34], see section 7) represents thousands of political concepts related to hundreds of thousands of asset instances which serve essentially as iconic representations of such political concepts.

[1] claims that for applications such as physical systems simulation "objects form natural data abstractions boundaries and help focus on system structure instead of algorithms". For asset-orientation we make a similar claim by referring to the substantially improved

- analogy between asset models and application domains;
- resilience of the asset models;
- reusability of the components of the asset model.

The major single property which supports such demands is the reusability of asset components, i.e., the easy use of an asset in more than one context. As for objects we demand, for example, that asset classes be reused by importing them into other classes and a generic asset class be reused by instantiating it with different parameters.

The subsequent asset class definition specializes equestrian statues depicting only female equestrians:

```
class FemaleEquestrianStatue refines EquestrianStatue{
    concept characteristic sex: {f,m} = f; ... }
```

The technology (see section 6) required for asset system openness resembles to some extent modern object-oriented language compiler technology. However, it also has to address the issue of co-existing populated asset schemata and their cooperation.

5.2   Asset System Dynamics

Besides openness there is a second demand, also already strongly requested by Cassirer. He argues for a maximum of dynamic support for the process of asset system use and improvement. This request is in contrast to systems which force users to leave their actual working process and go through lengthy phases of redefinition, redesign, conversion, etc. Only an open *and* dynamic asset system can be adapted, refined, recompiled, personalized etc., towards the requirements needed by its users' tasks.

A prerequisite of a dynamic asset system is online asset evaluation. While the well-structured concept aspect of assets — asset instance as well as class definitions — can benefit from database query technology, the semi-structured content aspect of assets requires search and indexing technology from information retrieval. Asset systems offer interfaces for combined queries running against both sides, asset content and concepts.

6 Asset Compilation and Configuration Technology

Following our extensive tradition in persistent languages R&D [32,33,24] we are intensely involved in the development of software systems for asset language environments [30]. Our demand for asset system responsiveness in the above sense requires dynamic openness as well as support for asset re-usability and sharing. Such demands disallow asset systems implementation by conventional compiler component and phasing technology:

- dynamic openness implies the need for runtime redefinition and inspection of assets and of their implementing components each time a user supplies a new asset definition or personalizes an existing one;
- re-usability and sharing requires that two asset system components have to cooperate if somebody provides assets for a domain which somebody else wants to use. Such cooperation structures change dynamically with asset definitions;
- working with personalized asset definitions involves that their redefined components have to be able to deal with existing asset instances created according to a schema used previously.

For asset systems implementation we take a two-step approach: the first step is driven by an asset model compiler, the second is based on a module configurator. The compiler translates ADL definitions into a set of modules of different kinds which form the basis for implementing that model. The configurator creates the modular structure of the executable target system for asset modeling and management. This way, we achieve our goal of an open dynamic asset system without paying the performance penalty for runtime interpretation [15] which — as experience from other projects show — could be prohibitively high.

6.1 An Asset Language Compiler

Our model compiler translates ADL asset definitions into the object model of some programming language. The current prototype uses Java as its target language. The compiler generates a set of interfaces and classes which reflect the asset definitions through method declarations which the compiler invents based on the characteristics and the relationships of the assets.

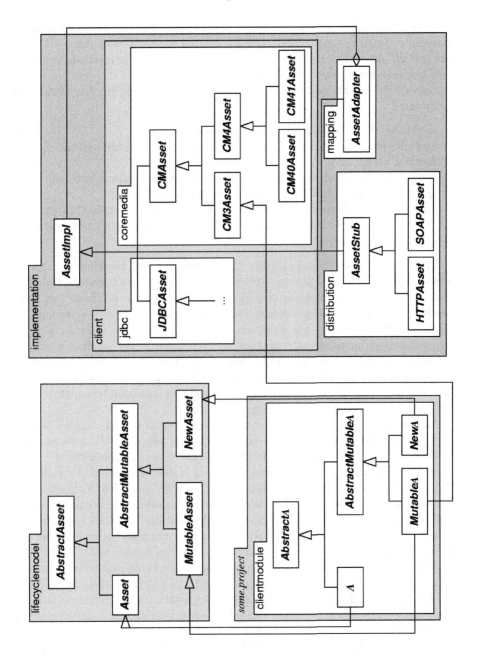

Fig. 3. Compiler generated objects

By and large, the method signatures conform to the JavaBeans standard [41], defining methods according to the name pattern getC() and setC() for a characteristic attribute c and `addR()`, `removeR()`, and `hasR()` for a relationship attribute r. In fact several interfaces are created for each asset class which reflect certain life cycle states of the assets, each with life cycle methods to change state (for a thorough overview see Fig. 3).

Besides the interfaces for the assets themselves a set of auxiliary interfaces is generated:

- iterators [18] to handle collections of assets,
- factories for creating asset instances according to the design pattern "factory method" [18],
- query interfaces for creating query objects, equipping them with the query expression and evaluating them to iterators, and finally
- visitors [18] to distinguish between the possible classes (instead of having a "type switch" operator [1]) of an asset and to determine an asset's state in a type-safe manner.

The interfaces are implemented by classes which reflect the kind of a module (see section 6.2), thus separating relevant concerns of asset system construction. Asset constraints are compiled into the modification methods (set, add, remove), thus having them checked each time a modification is requested (in terms of JavaBeans: they are constrained properties; see also [23]). In addition the modification methods send notifications whenever a modification is applied (bound properties). The value and binding initializations are compiled into the factory methods. In principle all methods of all interfaces are implemented in a way that they can be configured for auditing each invocation to support monitoring of work in progress and archival of works.

As a result of the open dynamics of asset systems the model compiler accepts asset declarations in two modes. One is to simply compile ADL statements as described throughout this paper. In this case the compiler generates the interfaces and classes necessary for the modules of a desired system. To make use of the openness the compiler can also be told that an asset definition refines an existing model. In this case the compiler first computes the integrated model derived from the existing and the new asset declarations and then builds the interfaces and classes. In addition, further classes for mapping between the models are generated for the mapping component outlined in section 6.2.

The compiler has a single front-end for parsing and checking asset definitions in the ADL. For the various kinds of modules to be produced there is one back-end for each one. To be able to generate asset systems with different back-end configurations the compiler is appropriately parameterized. In ongoing research we are working on growing sets of such back-end configurations aiming at a pattern library for asset system generation. For additional technical details please refer to [36].

6.2   On Asset System Modules

For asset system implementation we distinguish several *kinds* of modules. The model compiler creates sets of classes for each instance of a module kind. They form the basis for a domain-specific software architecture with a generated implementation [50]. Since the software artifacts are generated to work in concert we call them *modules*, however, in fact they enjoy essential properties of software *components* [43,2], the most important one being their statelessness.

Statelessness is an essential prerequisite for module exchange at runtime. Statelessness is relevant because the demand for dynamic openness leads to runtime module modification whenever a user changes its asset model. In such cases the model compiler is employed, and the modules built are used to reconfigure the asset management system.

As mentioned above the model compiler adds individual methods to the object classes generated for asset classes. To allow random module combinations all modules have a uniform interface. It is generic so that applications developed against the module interface do not break due to changes requested by dynamic openness. The specific requirements of a concrete model are reflected by the asset parameters of the modules' operations.

So far we have identified five kinds of modules for asset system implementation (sketched in Fig. 4): client modules and server modules as well as modules for mediation, distribution and mapping. These alternatives have satisfied all demands of our current conceptual content management projects, i.e., demands from dynamic openness as well as from non-monotonic and monotonic personalization, replication, access control, etc.

Modules for Asset Clients and for Asset Servers. Modules of the first kind — client modules — are based on persistence and retrieval services as provided by standard components. The individual contribution of a client module is the mapping of objects which represent assets down to the employed standard component and, conversely, the mapping of data retrieved from that component up into the asset model.

ADL expressions serve as abstract descriptions of both application and the data layer (comparable, for example, to the interface modules of [22]). There may be different compiler back-ends for different off-the-shelf technologies, e.g., different database systems. Currently we use JDBC [42] and file access (the top of the generator hierarchy for JDBC can be seen in Fig. 3, package `jdbc`). The back-ends contain the knowledge on how to create a mapping for a particular software product.

The classes generated from an ADL expression to form a client module have to be able to cope with the fact that schemas evolve and that there is data created for outdated schema versions [4]. Since the third-party systems we are using are not capable of allowing populated and versioned schemas to coexist and having the same functions applied to both of them, evolution has to be handled by the asset management system [27]. Old client modules (and the standard component they use) are conserved while fresh client modules for the new model are generated. To access multiple base systems in a uniform way, a mediation module (see next section) is employed. Client and mediation modules together form mediators in the sense of [51].

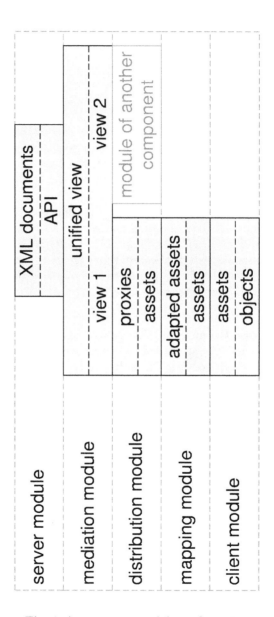

Fig. 4. Asset system module configuration

Server modules are the counterpart of client modules and offer the asset management system functionality as a service to clients. For clients to be able to use such services a standard protocol has to be applied. So far we use XML documents with a schema generated to reflect the asset definitions and transport them by means of HTTP. We have begun work on server module development for WebServices [5] with generated descriptions given in the WDL [11].

Modules for Mediation, Distribution and Mapping. The are three further kinds of modules which are mentioned only briefly in this paper: mediation, distribution and mapping modules.

Mediation modules are capable of delegating calls to other modules and of combining their responses in different ways. They are the crucial part of many module configurations, especially those involving openness.

Distribution modules offer remote communication between two components. They consist of two parts, one for each of the communication partners. Their service is similar to RPC and the two parts correspond to stubs and skeletons. However, instead of using a standardized marshalling format they exchange XML documents with a generated schema (comparable to the suggestion of [37]).

A final module kind which is highly relevant to asset system openness are mapping modules. They support model mapping [4] thus allowing modules generated from different ADL schema revisions to communicate. A mapping module is made up of adapters [18] which convert assets according to the ADL models involved. Adapters wrap an object of a class generated for a base model and fulfill the interface required by the derived model (see package `mapping` in Fig. 3).

Mapping issues are covered by a module kind of its own rather than integrating it into the other kinds of modules so that it can be plugged dynamically [26].

7   Perspective: Interdisciplinary Projects in Conceptual Content Management

The field of algorithmic programming has had from the very beginning a rather clear understanding of its underlying computational models. Nevertheless, experience from countless software engineering projects have been necessary to provide the basis for the development of modern high-level programming languages, their efficient implementation technology and their effective environments for large-scale software development. Following similar arguments we see an urgent need for extensive interdisciplinary project-based experience in conceptual content modeling and management.

Many of the insights leading to the asset approach presented here have been gained in the project *Warburg Electronic Library* [34,7]. The WEL system [48] was developed in an interdisciplinary joint project between the Art History department at Hamburg University and our Software Systems Institute. By now the WEL system has matured to a productive system that is used by hundreds of researchers internationally and is being extended in cooperation with several institutions.

The interdisciplinary WEL project was founded right from the start on extensive domain material on *Political Iconography* and on immense user experience from the area of art history. In the meantime, further content collections and methodological experiences have been provided by other project partners, e.g., from the area of commercial advertisements or from media industry.

Political Iconography (PI) proved to be a perfect application domain for an interdisciplinary project on conceptual content modeling and management. Basically, PI seeks to capture the semantics of key concepts in the political realm under the assumption that political goals, roles, values, means, etc. require mass communication which is implemented by the iconographic use of image-oriented content.

Martin Warnke, our project partner in art history, started his (paper-based) work on PI in the early 80ies. To date he and his colleagues have identified about 1,500 named political concepts and collected more than 300,000 records on iconographic works relevant to PI. In 1990 Warnke was recognized for his work by the Leibniz-Preis, one of the most prestigious research grants in Germany.

A major use of the WEL is its application for educational purposes in e-learning scenarios [25] exploiting its advanced functionality for

- customization of assets to establish thematic views on a domain, and
- personalization of the thematic views by students to construct individualized views.

Fig. 5 outlines the use of customization and personalization in an art history seminar on *Mantua and the Gonzaga*. The all-encompassing PI asset collection (owned by art historian Warnke) is first customized into an asset collection for the seminar project *Mantua and the Gonzaga* (owned by the supervising research assistants). The main objective of individual student projects in that seminar is to further customize and extend the seminar assets, structurally as well as content-wise. Publicizing the final content in some form of media document — a traditional report or an interactive web page — constitutes another educational objective of the seminar.

We conclude by pointing out that many web application projects are essentially online content management projects. Therefore, most of our R&D projects [17,28,44] as well as some of our commercial activities [12,20] profit substantially from our insight in conceptual content modeling and management.

Acknowledgement. We would like to express our thanks to the members of the Software Systems Institute, in particular, Rainer Müller, Michael Skusa, Ulrike Steffens and Axel Wienberg, and Florian Matthes, now Technical University of Munich, Germany. Last but not least our warm thanks to Professor Martin Warnke, Art History Department at the University of Hamburg.

References

1. Martín Abadi and Luca Cardelli. *A Theory of Objects*. Monographs in Computer Science. Springer-Verlag New York, Inc., 1996.

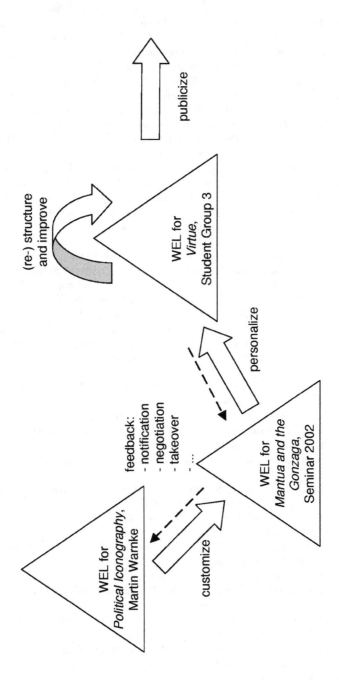

Fig. 5. Asset system for Art History education: A seminar on *Mantua and the Gonzaga*

2. U. Aßmann. *Invasive Software Composition*. Springer-Verlag, 2003.
3. Stefan Berchthold, Bernhard Ertl, Daniel A. Keim, Hans-Peter Kriegel, and Thomas Seidl. Fast Nearest Neighbor Search in High-Dimensional Spaces. In *Proc. 14th IEEE Conf. Data Engineering*. IEEE Computer Society, 1998.
4. Philip A. Bernstein and Erhard Rahm. Data Warehouse Scenarios for Model Management. In Alberto H. F. Laender, Stephen W. Liddle, and Veda C. Storey, editors, *Proc. 19th International Conference on Conceptual Modeling*, volume 1920 of *Lecture Notes in Computer Science*, pages 1–15. Springer-Verlag, 2000.
5. David Booth, Hugo Haas, Francis McCabe, Eric Newcomer, Michael Champion, Chris Ferris, and David Orchard. Web Services Architecture, W3C Working Draft. http://www.w3.org/TR/2003/WD-ws-arch-20030808/.
6. Michael L. Brodie, John Mylopoulos, and Joachim W. Schmidt, editors. *On Conceptual Modelling: Perspectives from Artificial Intelligence, Databases, and Programming Languages*. Topics in Information Systems. Springer-Verlag, 1984.
7. Matthias Bruhn. The Warburg Electronic Library in Hamburg: A Digital Index of Political Iconography. *Visual Resources*, XV:405–423, 2000.
8. Ernst Cassirer. *Die Sprache, Das mythische Denken, Phänomenologie der Erkenntnis*, volume 11-13 Philosophie der symbolischen Formen of *Gesammelte Werke*. Felix Meiner Verlag GmbH, Hamburger Ausgabe edition, 2001-2002.
9. R.G.G. Cattel, Douglas Barry, Mark Berler, Jeff Eastman, David Jordan, Craig Russell, Olaf Schadow, Torsten Stanienda, and Fernando Velez, editors. *The Object Database Standard: ODMG 3.0*. Morgan Kaufmann, 2000.
10. Peter P. Chen. The Enity-Relationship Model: Toward a Unified View of Data. In Douglas S. Kerr, editor, *Proceedings of the International Conference on Very Large Data Bases, September 22-24, 1975, Framingham, Massachusetts, USA*, page 173. ACM, 1975.
11. Roberto Chinnici, Martin Gudgin, Jean-Jacques Moreau, and Sanjiva Weerawarana. Web Services Description Language (WSDL) Version 1.2 Part 1: Core Language. www.w3.org/TR/wsdl12/, June 2003.
12. Homepage of the CoreMedia©© AG. www.coremedia.com, 2003.
13. Nello Cristianini and John Shawe-Taylor. *An Introduction to Support Vector Machines (and other kernel-based learning methods)*. Cambridge University Press, 2000.
14. O. Dahl and K. Nygaard. Simula, an Algol-based simulation language. *Communications of the ACM*, 9(9):671–678, 1966.
15. C.J. Date. *What Not How – The Business Rules Approach to Application Development*. Addison-Wesley, 2000.
16. Terrence W. Deacon. *The Symbolic Species: The Co-evolution of Language and the Brain*. W. W. Norton & Company, Inc., 1997.
17. EURIFT Information Portal. www.eurift.net, 2003.
18. E. Gamma, R. Helm, R. Johnson, and J. Vlissides. *Design Patterns: Elements of Reusable Object-Oriented Software*. Addison-Wesley, 1994.
19. Eric C.R. Hehner. *A Practical Theory of Programming*. Monographs in Computer Science. Springer-Verlag, 1993.
20. Homepage of the infoAsset©AG. www.infoasset.de, 2003.
21. I. Jacobson, G. Booch, and J. Rumbaugh. *The Unified Software Development Process*. Addison-Wesley, 1999.
22. Manfred A. Jeusfeld. Generating Queries from Complex Type Definitions. In Franz Baader, Martin Buchheit, Manfred A. Jeusfeld, and Werner Nutt, editors, *Reasoning about Structured Objects: Knowledge Representation Meets Databases,*

Proceedings of 1st Workshop KRDB'94,, volume 1 of *CEUR Workshop Proceedings*, 1994.

23. H. Knublauch, M. Sedlmayr, and T. Rose. Design Patterns for the Implementation of Constraints on JavaBeans. In *NetObjectDays2000, Erfurt, Germany*. 2000.

24. F. Matthes, G. Schröder, and J.W. Schmidt. Tycoon: A Scalable and Interoperable Persistent System Environment. In Malcom P. Atkinson and Ray Welland, editors, *Fully Integrated Data Environments*, ESPRIT Basic Research Series, pages 365–381. Springer-Verlag, 2000.

25. Hermann Maurer and Jennifer Lennon. Digital Libraries as Learning and Teaching Support. *Journal of Universal Computer Science*, 1(11):719–727, 1995.

26. Mira Mezini, Linda Seiter, and Karl Lieberherr. Component integration with pluggable composite adapters. In *Software Architectures and Component Technology*. Kluwer, 2000.

27. Giorgio De Michelis, Eric Dubois, Matthias Jarke, Florian Matthes, John Mylopoulos, Joachim W. Schmidt, Carson Woo, and Eric Yu. A Three-Faceted View of Information Systems. *Communications of the ACM*, 41(12):64–70, 1998.

28. Rainer Müller, Claudia Niederée, and Joachim W. Schmidt. Design Principles for Internet Community Information Gateways: MARINFO – A Case Study for a Maritime Information Infrastructure. In V. Bertram, editor, *Proceedings of the 1st International Conference on Computer Applications and Information Technology in the Maritime Industries (COMPIT 2000)*, pages 302–322, April 2000.

29. C.S. Peirce. *Collected Papers of Charles Sanders Peirce*. Harvard University Press, Cambridge, 1931.

30. Joachim W. Schmidt, Gerald Schröder, Claudia Niederée, and Florian Matthes. Linguistic and Architectural Requirements for Personalized Digital Libraries. *International Journal on Digital Libraries*, 1(1):89–104, 1997.

31. Joachim W. Schmidt and Hans-Werner Sehring. Dockets: A Model for Adding Value to Content. In Jacky Akoka, Mokrane Bouzeghoub, Isabelle Comyn-Wattiau, and Elisabeth Métais, editors, *Proceedings of the 18th International Conference on Conceptual Modeling*, volume 1728 of *Lecture Notes in Computer Science*, pages 248–262. Springer-Verlag, November 1999.

32. Joachim W. Schmidt. Some High Level Language Constructs for Data of Type Relation. *ACM Transactions on Database Systems*, 2(3):247–261, 1977.

33. J.W. Schmidt and F. Matthes. The DBPL Project: Advances in Modular Database Programming. *Information Systems*, 19(2):121–140, 1994.

34. J.W. Schmidt, H.-W. Sehring, M. Skusa, and A. Wienberg. Subject-Oriented Work: Lessons Learned from an Interdisciplinary Content Management Project. In Albertas Caplinskas and Johann Eder, editors, *Advances in Databases and Information Systems, 5th East European Conference, ADBIS 2001*, volume 2151 of *Lecture Notes in Computer Science*, pages 3–26. Springer, September 2001.

35. Christiane Schmitz-Rigal. *Die Kunst offenen Wissens, Ernst Cassirers Epistemologie und Deutung der modernen Physik*, volume 7 of *Cassirer-Forschungen*. Ernst Meiner Verlag, Hamburg, 2002.

36. Hans-Werner Sehring. *Konzeptorientiertes Content Management: Modell, Systemarchitektur und Prototypen*. PhD thesis, Arbeitsbereich Softwaresysteme, Technische Universität Hamburg-Harburg, Deutschland, 2003.

37. German Shegalov, Michael Gillmann, and Gerhard Weikum. XML-enabled workflow management for e-services across heterogeneous platforms. *The VLDB Journal*, 10(1):91–103, 2001.

38. John Miles Smith and Diane C. P. Smith. Database abstractions: Aggregation. *Communications of the ACM*, 20(6):405–413, 1977.

39. John F. Sowa. *Knowledge Representation, Logical, Philosophical, and Computational Foundations*. Brooks/Cole, Thomson Learning, 2000.
40. W. Stallings. *Networking Standards: A Guide to OSI, ISDN, LAN, and MAN Standards*. Addison-Wesley, 1993.
41. Sun Microsystems. JavaBeans Specification. java.sun.com/products/javabeans/, 2003.
42. Sun Microsystems. JDBC Technology. java.sun.com/products/jdbc/, 2003.
43. C. Szyperski. *Component Software: Beyond Object-Oriented Programming*. Addison-Wesley, 1998.
44. Hompage of the TeFIS project. www.sts.tu-harburg.de/projects/TuTechFoBe/, 1999.
45. Bernhard Thalheim. *Entity-Relationship Modeling: Foundations of Database Technology*. Springer-Verlag, 2000.
46. Unified Modeling Language Resource Center. www.rational.com/uml/, 2003.
47. Donald Verene, editor. *Ernst Cassirer: Symbol, Myth, and Culture. Essays and Lectures of Ernst Cassirer 1935-1945*. Yale University Press, 1979.
48. Homepage of the Warburg Electronic Library. www.welib.de, 2003.
49. Homepage of the Workflow Management Coalition. www.wfmc.com, 2003.
50. S. White and C. Lemus. Architecture Reuse Through a Domain Specific Language Generator. In *Proceedings of the Eighth Workshop on Institutionalizing Software Reuse*, 1997.
51. G. Wiederhold. Mediators in the Architecture of Future Information Systems. *IEEE Computer*, 25:38–49, 1992.
52. Yiming Yang and Jan O. Pedersen. A comparative study on feature selection in text categorization. In *Proc. 14th International Conference on Machine Learning*, pages 412–420. Morgan Kaufmann, 1997.

A Relational Algebra for Functional Logic Deductive Databases*

Jesús Manuel Almendros-Jiménez and Antonio Becerra-Terón

Dpto. de Lenguajes y Computación. Universidad de Almería.
{jalmen,abecerra}@ual.es

Abstract. In this paper, we study the integration of functional logic programming and databases by presenting a data model, and a query and data definition language. The data model is adopted from functional logic programming by allowing complex values. The query and data definition language is based on the use of algebra expressions built from a set of algebra operators over an extended relational algebra. In addition, algebra expressions can be used for defining functions, typical in a functional logic program.

1   Introduction

Database technology is involved in most software applications. For this reason, *functional logic languages* [9] should include database features in order to cover with 'real world' applications and increase its application field.

Relational algebra [7] is a formalism for defining and querying *relational databases* [6]. Relational algebra is based on the use of operators, such as *selection, projection, cross product, join, set union* and *set difference*. Database *views* and *queries* can be defined, in an intuitive way, by using these operators.

In order to integrate functional logic programming and databases, our idea is: (1) to adapt *functional logic programming to databases*, by considering a suitable *data model*; (2) to adapt *the algebra operators* in order to handle the proposed *data model*; (3) to propose a *data definition language* which consists on *expressing conditional rewriting rules by means of algebra operators* and consider a *query language* based on algebra operators; and finally, (4) to provide *semantic foundations* to this integration.

With respect to (1), the underlying data model of functional logic programming is *complex* from a database point of view [1]. Firstly, types can be defined by using *recursively defined datatypes*, such as *lists* and *trees*. Therefore, the attribute values can be *multi-valued*; that is, more than one value (for instance, a set of values enclosed in a list) corresponds to each set of key attributes. In addition, we have adopted a *non-deterministic semantics* from functional-logic programming, recently investigated in the framework CRWL [8]. Under a non-deterministic semantics, values can be *grouped into sets*, representing the set of

---

* This work has been partially supported by the Spanish project of the Ministry of Science and Technology "INDALOG" TIC2002-03968.

M. Broy and A.V. Zamulin (Eds.): PSI 2003, LNCS 2890, pp. 494–508, 2003.

values of the output of a non-deterministic function. Therefore, our data model is complex in a double sense, allowing the handling of: (a) complex values built from recursively defined datatypes, and (b) complex values grouped into sets. Moreover, functional logic programming handles *partial and non-strict* functions, and *possibly infinite data*. Therefore, in our setting, an attribute can be partially defined or, even, include possibly infinite information.

With respect to (2), and in order to deal with recursively defined datatypes, we *generalize the algebra operators* in such a way that, for instance, we can project the elements of a list. In addition, goals and rule conditions in functional logic programming consist on *equality constraints*, which should be solved in order to solve a goal or apply a rule. Therefore, we will generalize *selection* and *projection* operators in a double sense: (a) to restructure complex values, by applying data *constructors* and *destructors* over the attributes of a given relation, and (b) to select tuples whose *totally defined values* satisfy *equality constraints*.

With respect to (3), we propose a *data definition language* which, basically, consists on *database schema, database instance* and *(lazy) function definitions*. For a given database schema, we can define an instance (including *key* and *non-key* attribute values) by means of rules in the form of *algebra expressions*, called *algebraic rules*. In addition, a set of functions can be defined by means of algebraic rules, to be used by queries for handling recursively defined datatypes. The *query language* will also be based on algebra expressions. Lastly, in order to ensure the integration of our framework with functional logic programming, the proposed algebraic rules can be translated into conditional rewriting rules.

Finally, and w.r.t. (4), we will study the *semantics* of the algebra operators and conditions, ensuring that both have the same *expressivity power* as equality constraints. Moreover, we propose a *fixed point operator* definition, which allows computing the *least instance induced* from a set of algebraic rules.

To put an end, let's remark that extended relational algebras have been studied as alternative query languages for *deductive databases* [1] and *constraint databases*[10,5]. Our extended relational algebra is in the line of [1], in which deductive databases handle complex values in the form of *set* and *tuple* constructors. In our case, we generalize the mentioned algebra in order to handle *complex values built from arbitrary recursively defined datatypes*. In addition, our algebra is similar to the proposed algebras for constraint databases, in the sense of dealing with *(equality) constraints*, but here for comparing sets of complex values.

Finally, remark that this work goes towards the design of a functional logic deductive language, whose operational semantics [4,3], as well as an extended relational calculus [2] have also been studied.

The organization of this paper is as follows. In section 2, we will present a short introduction to the syntax of algebraic rules; section 3 will show the data model; section 4 will define the extended relational algebra; section 5 will show the query and data definition language; section 6 will define a fixed point operator which computes the least database instance induced; finally, section 7 will show the main conclusions and future work.

2   Preliminaries

Logic programs and *goals* can be translated into algebra expressions following three basic ideas: *logic variables* are translated into projections, *bounded arguments* into selections and *shared variables* into joins. For instance:

(1)	p(a, a).	**(2)**	p(b, c).
(3)	q(b, a).	**(4)**	r(X, Y) : −p(X, c), q(X, Y).

can be translated into

(1)′	p = (a, a).	**(2)′**	p = (b, c).
(3)′	q = (b, a).	**(4)′**	r = $\pi_{p.1,q.2}(\sigma_{p.2=c}(p) \bowtie_{p.1=q.1} q)$.

Facts are translated into tuple definitions (see **(1)′**, **(2)′** and **(3)′**). With respect to the *rules* and assuming that attribute names are $p.1, \ldots$ for each predicate symbol p, then in rule **(4)**, p(X, c) means "to select the tuples of p with the second attribute equal to c"; that is, $\sigma_{p.2=c}(p)$. Here "=" is intended as the values unifying with c. In addition, the condition p(X, c), q(X, Y) can be intended as a join operation between p and q w.r.t the first attribute of p and q (represented by the shared variable X); that is, $\sigma_{p.2=c}(p) \bowtie_{p.1=q.1} q$. Finally, r projects the first attribute of p (or q) and the second one of q, that is, $\pi_{p.1,q.2}(\sigma_{p.2=c}(p) \bowtie_{p.1=q.1} q)$. Now, a goal : −r(b, X) can be translated into $\pi_{r.2}(\sigma_{r.1=b}(r))$, obtaining as answer the tuple (a). Now, we can consider the following (recursive) program, which succeeds for each natural number built from 0 and s:

(1)	p(0).	*can be translated into*	**(1)′**	p = (0).
(2)	p(s(X)) : −p(X).		**(2)′**	p = $\pi_{s(p.1)}(p)$.

In order to write the original program as an algebra expression, we need to consider projection operators over *complex values*, such as the above translation shows. The meaning of $\pi_{s(p.1)}(p)$ is to project the "successor" of the first attribute of p. This projection operation is even recursive and defines the same relation as the corresponding logic program. Finally, the projection operation also needs to consider the destruction of terms. For instance:

(1)	q(s(0)).	*can be translated into*	**(1)**	q = (s(0)).
(2)	p(X) : −q(s(X)).		**(2)**	p = $\pi_{s.1(q.1)}.(q)$

where $\pi_{s.1(q.1)}(q)$ projects the destruction of the first attribute of q (i.e. s.1(q.1)), by obtaining n whenever the first attribute of q is s(n).

In order to generalize this formalism to functional logic programming, we should assume the following convention. A function f defines an $n + 1$-tuple, whenever the arity of f is n. For instance:

(1)	append([ ], L) := L.
(2)	append([X|L], L1) := [X|append(L, L1)].
(3)	member(X, L) := true ⇐ append(L1, [X|L2]) == L.

can be translated into

(1)′	append := ([ ], L, L).
(2)′	append := $\pi_{[X\|append.1],append.2,[X\|append.3]}(append)$.
(3)′	member := $\pi_{[\|].1(append.2),append.3,true}(\pi_{append.1,[\|].1(append.2),[\|].2(append.2),append.3} == (append))$.

As can be seen, we consider the functions append and member as relations, including *non-ground tuples*; that is, tuples with variables where: (a) these ones are universally quantified (and thus representing an *infinite relation*), and (b) they can be instantiated. For instance, the tuples $([\ ], [0], [0])$ and $([1], [0], [1, 0])$ are (instantiated) tuples of the relation append. Here, the variable L in rule **(3)** is projected, but the strict equality forces the values to be totally defined. This fact is represented by means of the projection $\pi_{\underset{\text{append.3}}{==}}$.

Finally, functions can be either *non-strict* or represent *possibly infinite values*, where $\perp$ is used for representing *non-strictness* and *partial approximations* of infinite values. For instance:

---

(1)	$f(X) := 0.$	*can be translated into*	**(1)$'$**	$f := (X, 0).$
(2)	$g(X) := s(g(X))$		**(2)$'$**	$g := \pi_{g.1, s(g.2)}(g).$

---

where g represents the tuples $(X, \{\perp, s(\perp), s(s(\perp)), \ldots\})$. Now, the equality constraint $f(g(X)) == 0$, which can be written as $\pi_{g.1}(\sigma_{f.2==0}(f \bowtie_{f.1=g.2} g))$, defines as answer the tuple (X), where X is universally quantified.

3   The Data Model

Let's consider job_bonus as an attribute, represented by a complex value of the form j&b(job_name, bonus). Now, the attribute can include the following kinds of information:

$\perp$	undefined information (ni)	*expressing that both person's job name and salary bonus are unknown*
j&b(lecturer, 100)	totally defined information (tdi)	*expressing that a person's job name is lecturer and his(her) salary bonus is 100 €*
j&b(associate, $\perp$)	partially undefined information (pni)	*expressing that we know the job name, but not the salary bonus*

Over these kinds of information, the following *equality relations* can be defined: (1) = (*syntactic equality*); for instance, j&b(associate, $\perp$) = j&b(associate, $\perp$) holds; and (2) == (*strict equality*), expressing that *two values are syntactically equal and totally defined*; for instance, j&b(associate, 250) == j&b (associate, 250) holds, and j&b(associate, $\perp$) == j&b(associate, 250) does not satisfy.

Assuming a set of *data constructors* $c, d, \ldots DC = \cup_{n \geq 0} DC^n$ each one with a given arity, the special symbol $\perp$ with arity 0 (not included in DC), and a set $\mathcal{V}$ of variables $X, Y, \ldots$, we can build the set of *partial c-terms* $CTerm_{DC, \perp}(\mathcal{V})$. In particular, $CTerm_{DC}(\mathcal{V})$ represents the set of *totally defined c-terms*. In addition, we can consider substitutions $Subst_{\perp} = \{\theta : \mathcal{V} \to CTerm_{DC, \perp}(\mathcal{V})\}$ in the usual way.

Now, a *partial ordering* $\leq$ over $CTerm_{DC, \perp}(\mathcal{V})$ can be defined as the least one satisfying: $\perp \leq t$, $X \leq X$, and $c(t_1, ..., t_n) \leq c(t'_1, ..., t'_n)$ if $t_i \leq t'_i$ for all $i \in \{1, ..., n\}$ and $c \in DC^n$. The intended meaning of $t \leq t'$ is that t is *less defined or has less information* than t'. In particular $\perp$ is the *bottom element*. Now, we can build the set of (possibly infinite) cones of c-terms, $\mathcal{C}(CTerm_{DC, \perp}$

$(\mathcal{V})$), and as a particular case, the set of (possibly infinite) ideals of c-terms, $\mathcal{I}(CTerm_{DC,\perp}(\mathcal{V}))$. Cones and ideals can also be partially ordered under the *set-inclusion* ordering (i.e $\subseteq$).

Over cones and ideals, we can define an *equality relation*, $\mathcal{C} == \mathcal{C}'$, which holds whenever *any value* in $\mathcal{C}$ and $\mathcal{C}'$ is *strictly equal*. Finally, we need to consider the *greatest subcone* containing the totally defined values of a cone $\mathcal{C}$, denoted by $Total(\mathcal{C})$, and defined as $Total(\mathcal{C}) = \{\perp\} \cup_{t \in \mathcal{C} \cap CTerm_{DC}(\mathcal{V})} <t>$, where $<t>$ represents the ideal generated by t.

Next, we propose a set of definitions involving the notions related to database schema and instance.

Definition 1 (Database Schemas). *Assuming a Milner's style polymorphic type system, a* database schema S *is a finite set of* relation schemas $R_1, \ldots, R_p$ *of the form:* $R_j(A_1 : T_1, \ldots, A_k : T_k, A_{k+1} : T_{k+1}, \ldots, A_n : T_n)$, $1 \le j \le p$, *wherein the relation names R_j's are a pairwise disjoint set, and the schemas $R_1, \ldots, R_p$ include a pairwise disjoint set of typed attributes[1]* $(A_1 : T_1, \ldots, A_n : T_n)$.

In the relation schema R, $A_1 \ldots A_k$ are *key attributes* and $A_{k+1} \ldots A_n$ represent *non-key attributes*, denoted by the sets $Key(R)$ and $NonKey(R)$, respectively. We denote by $Att(R)$ the attributes of R, $nAtt(R) = n$ and $nKey(R) = k$.

Definition 2 (Databases). *A* database D *is a triple* (S, DC, IF), *where S is a database schema, DC is a set of data constructors, and IF represents a set of (interpreted) function symbols $f, g, \ldots$, each one with an associated arity.*

We denote by $DS(D)$ the set of *defined symbols* of D, which contains relation names, non-key attributes and interpreted function symbols. Interpreted functions can be considered as relations, assuming the following convention. For each $f : T_1 \times \ldots \times T_n \to T_0 \in IF$, we can include in S a relation schema $f(f.1 : T_1, \ldots, f.n : T_n, f.n+1 : T_0)$. As an example of database, we can consider the following one:

Example 1: Person and Job Information

$$S \begin{cases} \texttt{person\_job(\underline{name} : people, age : nat, address : dir, job\_id : job, boss : people)} \\ \texttt{job\_information(\underline{job\_name} : job, salary : nat, bonus : nat)} \\ \texttt{person\_boss\_job(\underline{name} : people, boss\_age : cbossage, job\_bonus : cjobbonus)} \\ \texttt{peter\_workers(\underline{name} : people, work : job)} \end{cases}$$

$$DC \begin{cases} \texttt{john : people, mary : people, peter : people} \\ \texttt{lecturer : job, associate : job, professor : job} \\ \texttt{add : string} \times \texttt{nat} \to \texttt{dir} \\ \texttt{b\&a : people} \times \texttt{nat} \to \texttt{cbossage} \\ \texttt{j\&b : job} \times \texttt{nat} \to \texttt{cjobbonus} \end{cases} \quad IF \begin{cases} \texttt{retention : nat} \to \texttt{nat} \end{cases}$$

---

where S includes the relation schemas `person_job` (storing information about people and their jobs) and `job_information` (storing generic information about jobs), and the *"views"* `person_boss_job`, and `peter_workers`. These ones are considered as views since they will take key values from the relation `person_job`.

---

[1] We can suppose attributes qualified with the relation name when the names coincide.

The first view includes, for each person, pairs in the form of records constituted by: (a) his/her boss and boss' age, by using the complex c-term b&a(people, nat), and (b) his/her job and job bonus, by using the complex c-term j&b(job, nat). The second view includes workers whose boss is peter. In addition, DC includes data constructors for the types people, job, dir, cbossage and cjobbonus, and IF the interpreted function symbol retention which computes the salary without tax. The function retention can be considered as a relation of the form retention(retention.1 : nat, retention.2 : nat). In addition, we can consider database schemas involving *(possibly) infinite databases*. Let's consider the following example:

Example 2: Bidimensional Points and Lines

$$S \left\{ \begin{array}{l} \texttt{2Dpoint}(\underline{\texttt{coord}} : \texttt{cpoint}, \texttt{color} : \texttt{nat}) \\ \texttt{2Dline}(\underline{\texttt{origin}} : \texttt{cpoint}, \underline{\texttt{dir}} : \texttt{orientation}, \texttt{next} : \texttt{cpoint}, \texttt{points} : \texttt{cpoint}, \\ \texttt{list\_of\_points} : \texttt{list(cpoint)}) \end{array} \right.$$

$$DC \left\{ \begin{array}{l} \texttt{north} : \texttt{orientation}, \texttt{south} : \texttt{orientation}, \texttt{east} : \texttt{orientation}, \\ \texttt{west} : \texttt{orientation}, \texttt{northeast} : \texttt{orientation} \ldots \\ [\,] : \texttt{list A}, \quad [\,|\,] : \texttt{A} \times \texttt{list A} \to \texttt{list A} \\ \texttt{p} : \texttt{nat} \times \texttt{nat} \to \texttt{cpoint} \end{array} \right. \qquad IF \left\{ \texttt{select} : (\texttt{list A}) \to \texttt{A} \right.$$

---

wherein the relation schemas 2Dpoint and 2Dline are defined for representing bidimensional points and lines, respectively. The attribute points stores the *(infinite) set* of points of the line, and list_of_points the *(infinite) list* of points of the line. Here, we can see the double use of complex values, that is as a set (implicitly assumed), and a list.

Definition 3 (Schema Instances). *A* schema instance $\mathcal{S}$ *of a database schema* S *is a set of* relation instances $\mathcal{R}_1, \ldots \mathcal{R}_p$, *where each relation instance* $\mathcal{R}_j$ $1 \le j \le p$, *is a (possibly infinite) set of tuples of the form* $(V_1, \ldots, V_n)$ *for the relation* R_j, *with* $n = nAtt(R_j)$ *and* $V_i \in \mathcal{C}(CTerm_{DC,\perp}(\mathcal{V}))$. *In particular, each* V_l *(* $l \le nKey(R_j)$*) satisfies* $V_l \in CTerm_{DC}(\mathcal{V})^2$.

The last condition forces the key values to be one-valued and totally defined. Values can be non-ground where variables are implicitly universally quantified.

Definition 4 (Database Instances). *A* database instance $\mathcal{D}$ *of a database* $D = (S, DC, IF)$ *is a triple* $(\mathcal{S}, \mathcal{DC}, \mathcal{IF})$, *where* $\mathcal{S}$ *is a schema instance,* $\mathcal{DC} = CTerm_{DC,\perp}(\mathcal{V})$, *and* $\mathcal{IF}$ *is a set of function interpretations* $f^{\mathcal{D}}, g^{\mathcal{D}}, \ldots$ *satisfying* $f^{\mathcal{D}} : CTerm_{DC,\perp}(\mathcal{V})^n \to \mathcal{C}(CTerm_{DC,\perp,F}(\mathcal{V}))$ *is monotone for each* $f \in IF^n$, *that is,* $f^{\mathcal{D}} \, t_1 \ldots t_n \subseteq f^{\mathcal{D}} \, t'_1 \ldots t'_n$ *if* $t_i \le t'_i$, *with* $1 \le i \le n$.

The fact of considering the interpreted functions as relations supposes that $\mathcal{IF}$ defines a set of tuples for each $f^{\mathcal{D}} \in \mathcal{IF}$ as follows: $(t_1, \ldots, t_n, V) \in f$ if $V = \{t \mid f^{\mathcal{D}} \, t_1 \ldots t_n = t, \text{ and } t_i \in CTerm_{DC}(\mathcal{V})\}^3$.

Now, database instances can also be *partially ordered* as follows: given a database schema $D = (S, DC, IF)$ and two database instances $\mathcal{D} = (\mathcal{S}, \mathcal{DC}, \mathcal{IF})$

---

[2] Each key value V_j can be considered as an ideal by means of the mapping $V_j \to< V_j >$.

[3] Functions can define partially defined values, but we can lift to totally defined values, by using variables instead of $\perp$ without losing generality.

and $\mathcal{D}' = (\mathcal{S}', \mathcal{DC}', \mathcal{IF}')$, then $\mathcal{D} \sqsubseteq \mathcal{D}'$ iff: (1) $V_i \subseteq V_i'$ for each $k+1 \leq i \leq n$, $(V_1, \ldots, V_k, V_{k+1}, \ldots, V_n) \in \mathcal{R}$ and $(V_1, \ldots, V_k, V_{k+1}', \ldots, V_n') \in \mathcal{R}'$, where $\mathcal{R} \in \mathcal{S}$ and $\mathcal{R}' \in \mathcal{S}'$, are relation instances of $R \in S$ and $k = nKey(R)$; and (2) $f^{\mathcal{D}} t_1 \ldots t_n \subseteq f^{\mathcal{D}'} t_1 \ldots t_n$ for each $t_1, \ldots, t_n \in \mathcal{DC}$, $f^{\mathcal{D}} \in \mathcal{IF}$ and $f^{\mathcal{D}'} \in \mathcal{IF}'$.

As a special case of database instance, we can consider the *bottom database instance*, denoted by $\perp$, where $\mathcal{S}$ is empty, and $f^{\mathcal{D}} t_1 \ldots t_n = < \perp >$ for each $f^{\mathcal{D}} \in \mathcal{IF}$. The bottom database satisfies $\perp \sqsubseteq \mathcal{D}$, for each database instance $\mathcal{D}$. Next, we show an example of database instance for example 1:

Example 1: Database Instance for Person and Job Information

person_job	$\begin{cases} (\texttt{john}, \{\perp\}, \{\texttt{add}('\texttt{6th Avenue}', 5)\}, \{\texttt{lecturer}\}, \{\texttt{mary}, \texttt{peter}\}) \\ (\texttt{mary}, \{\perp\}, \{\texttt{add}('\texttt{7th Avenue}', 2)\}, \{\texttt{associate}\}, \{\texttt{peter}\}) \\ (\texttt{peter}, \{\perp\}, \{\texttt{add}('\texttt{5th Avenue}', 5)\}, \{\texttt{professor}\}, \{\perp\}) \end{cases}$
job_information	$\begin{cases} (\texttt{lecturer}, \{1200\}, \{\perp\}) \\ (\texttt{associate}, \{2000\}, \{\perp\}) \\ (\texttt{professor}, \{3200\}, \{1500\}) \end{cases}$
person_boss_job	$\begin{cases} (\texttt{john}, \{\texttt{b\&a}(\texttt{mary}, \perp), \texttt{b\&a}(\texttt{peter}, \perp)\}, \{\texttt{j\&b}(\texttt{lecturer}, \perp)\}) \\ (\texttt{mary}, \{\texttt{b\&a}(\texttt{peter}, \perp)\}, \{\texttt{j\&b}(\texttt{associate}, \perp)\}) \\ (\texttt{peter}, \{\texttt{b\&a}(\perp, \perp)\}, \{\texttt{j\&b}(\texttt{professor}, 1500)\}) \end{cases}$
peter_workers	$\begin{cases} (\texttt{john}, \{\texttt{lecturer}\}) \\ (\texttt{mary}, \{\texttt{associate}\}) \end{cases}$
retention	$\{ (0, \{0\}) \ldots \ldots (10, \{8\}), \ldots$

As can be seen, each tuple instance includes key and non-key attribute values grouped by sets[4]. Firstly, in the instance of the relation **person_job**, all tuples include the value $\perp$ for the attribute **age**, indicating undefined information (ni). Secondly, the instance of the view **person_boss_job** includes partially undefined (pni), b&a(mary, $\perp$), expressing that **john**'s boss is known (i.e. **mary**), but **mary**'s age is undefined. With respect to the modeling of a (possibly) infinite database, we can consider the following approximation to the instance for the relation schema **2Dline** with (*possibly infinite*) values in their defined attributes:

Example 2: Database Instance for Bidimensional Points and Lines

2Dline	$\begin{cases} (\texttt{p}(0,0), \texttt{north}, \{\texttt{p}(0,1)\}, \{\texttt{p}(0,1), \texttt{p}(0,2), \perp\}, \{[\texttt{p}(0,0), \texttt{p}(0,1), \texttt{p}(0,2)|\perp]\}), \ldots \\ (\texttt{p}(1,1), \texttt{east}, \{\texttt{p}(2,1)\}, \{\texttt{p}(2,1), \texttt{p}(3,1), \perp\}, \{[\texttt{p}(1,1), \texttt{p}(2,1), \texttt{p}(3,1)|\perp]\}), \ldots \end{cases}$

4 Extended Relational Algebra

The projection operator is based on the so-called *projection c-terms*, wherein a projection c-term is a *(labeled) algebra c-term*. Now, we will define both concepts, although, firstly, we need to define the notion of *data destructors*.

Definition 5 (Data Destructors). *Given a set of data constructors DC, we define the set of* data destructors *DD induced from DC as the set $c.idx : T_0 \to T_{idx}$, whenever $c : T_1 \times \ldots \times T_n \to T_0 \in DC$ and $1 \leq idx \leq n$. The semantics of each c.idx is defined as follows: $c.idx(c(t_1, \ldots, t_n)) =_{def} t_{idx}$, and $\perp$ otherwise.*

---

[4] These sets can be ideals or cones but, here, in the examples we will summarize their contents with the maximal elements.

Definition 6 (Algebra C-Terms). *Given a database $D = (S, DC, IF)$, the set of* algebra c-terms *is defined as the set of c-terms built from DC, DD, attributes of D, and variables of $\mathcal{V}$.*

The *projection operator* projects two kinds of elements: (a) algebra c-terms, and (b) totally defined algebra c-terms.

Definition 7 (Projection C-Terms). *A* projection c-term $p, q, \ldots$ *has the form t_A and $\overline{\overline{t_A}}$, where t_A is an algebra c-term.*

$\overline{\overline{t_A}}$ *is a labeled algebra c-term, representing the* set of totally defined c-terms *represented by t_A. A projection c-term denotes a cone or ideal w.r.t. a tuple, depending on whether it combines one-valued or multi-valued attributes.*

Definition 8 (Denotation of Projection C-Terms). *The* denotation *of a projection c-term p in a tuple $V = (V_1, \ldots, V_n) \in \mathcal{R}$ ($R \in S$), w.r.t. a database $D = (S, DC, IF)$ and instance $\mathcal{D} = (\mathcal{S}, \mathcal{DC}, \mathcal{IF})$, denoted by $\llbracket p \rrbracket_V^{\mathcal{D}}$, is defined as follows:*
$\llbracket X \rrbracket_V^{\mathcal{D}} =_{def} < X >$, *if $X \in \mathcal{V}$; $\llbracket A_i \rrbracket_V^{\mathcal{D}} =_{def} \cup_{\psi \in Subst_\perp} V_i \psi$, for all $A_i \in Key(R) \cup NonKey(R)$, and $< \perp >$, otherwise; $\llbracket c(t_1^A, \ldots, t_n^A) \rrbracket_V^{\mathcal{D}} =_{def} < c(\llbracket t_1^A \rrbracket_V^{\mathcal{D}}, \ldots, \llbracket t_n^A \rrbracket_V^{\mathcal{D}}) >^5$, for all $c \in DC^n$; $\llbracket c.idx(t_A) \rrbracket_V^{\mathcal{D}} =_{def} c.idx(\llbracket t_A \rrbracket_V^{\mathcal{D}})$, for all $c.idx \in DD$; and $\llbracket \overline{\overline{t_A}} \rrbracket_V^{\mathcal{D}} =_{def} Total(\llbracket t_A \rrbracket_V^{\mathcal{D}})$.*

We denote by $Att(p)$ (resp. $var(p)$) the attribute names (resp. variables) occurring in a projection c-term p. For instance $\pi_{\text{name},b\&a(\text{boss},\text{age})}^{==}(\texttt{person\_job})$ contains the tuples $(\texttt{john}, \{\perp\})$, $(\texttt{mary}, \{\perp\})$ and $(\texttt{peter}, \{\perp\})$, given that $b\&a(\texttt{boss}, \texttt{age})$ represents a partially defined value in the original relation $\texttt{person\_job}$.

With respect to *selection operator*, we need to define the following: *when a tuple satisfies two kinds of equality relations*: (1) *syntactic equality* (i.e. $=$) and (2) *strict equality* (i.e. $==$).

Definition 9 (Selection Formulas). *A selection formula F has the form: (a) $A = t_A$, where $A \in Key(R)$, $R \in S$, and t_A is an algebra c-term, and (b) $t_A == t_A'$, where t_A and t_A' are algebra c-terms*

Definition 10 (Satisfiability). *A tuple $V \in \mathcal{R}$ ($\mathcal{R} \in \mathcal{S}$) satisfies a selection formula F w.r.t. a database $D = (S, DC, IF)$ and instance $\mathcal{D} = (\mathcal{S}, \mathcal{DC}, \mathcal{IF})$, if $V \models_A F$, where $\models_A$ is defined as follows: $V \models_A A = t_A$, if $\llbracket A \rrbracket_V^{\mathcal{D}} \cap \llbracket t_A \rrbracket_V^{\mathcal{D}} \neq \emptyset$; and $V \models_A t_A == t_A'$, if $\llbracket t_A \rrbracket_V^{\mathcal{D}} == \llbracket t_A' \rrbracket_V^{\mathcal{D}}$*

For instance, let's consider the tuple $(\texttt{john}, \{\perp\}, \{\texttt{add}('\texttt{6th Avenue}', 5)\}, \{\texttt{lecturer}\}, \{\texttt{mary}, \texttt{peter}\})$ from the instance of the relation schema $\texttt{person\_job}$. Now, the selection formulas $\texttt{name} = \texttt{john}$, $\texttt{add.2}(\texttt{address}) == 5$, and $\texttt{boss} == \texttt{mary}$ are satisfied, but $\texttt{age} == 35$, and $\texttt{job\_id} == \texttt{associate}$ are not.

---

[5] To simplify denotation, we write $\{c(t_1^A, \ldots, t_n^A) \mid t_i^A \in C_i\}$ as $c(C_1, \ldots, C_n)$ where $C_i's$ are certain cones.

Definition 11 (Algebra Operators). *Let* $D = (S, DC, IF)$ *and* $\mathcal{D} = (\mathcal{S}, \mathcal{DC}, \mathcal{IF})$ *be a database and a database instance, and let* R, Q *be relation names of* S *(or* IF*), then the* algebra operators *are defined as follows:*

Selection (σ):
$\mathcal{R}' = \sigma_{F_1,\dots,F_n}(R) =_{def} \{V \in \mathcal{R} \mid V \models_A F_1, \dots, F_n\}$ *where* $Key(R') = Key(R)$ *and* $NonKey(R') = NonKey(R)$.

Projection (π):
$$\mathcal{R}' = \pi_{t_1^A,\dots,t_k^A,\overline{\overline{t_{k+1}^A}},\dots,t_n^A}(R) =_{def} \{(\llparenthesis t_1^A \rrparenthesis_V^{\mathcal{D}}, \dots, \llparenthesis t_k^A \rrparenthesis_V^{\mathcal{D}}, \llparenthesis \overline{\overline{t_{k+1}^A}} \rrparenthesis_V^{\mathcal{D}}, \dots, \llparenthesis t_n^A \rrparenthesis_V^{\mathcal{D}}) | V \in \mathcal{R}\}$$
where $t_1^A, \dots, t_k^A$ *are all (possibly destructed) key attributes of* R *and* $t_{k+1}^A, \dots, t_n^A$ *are algebra c-terms, and* $Key(R') = \{t_1^A, \dots, t_k^A\}$ *and* $NonKey(R') = \{\overline{\overline{t_{k+1}^A}}, \dots, t_n^A\}$.

Cross Product $(\times)$:
$\mathcal{P} = R \times Q =_{def} \{(V_1, \dots, V_k, W_1, \dots, W_{k'}, V_{k+1}, \dots, V_n, W_{k'+1}, \dots, W_m) \mid (V_1, \dots, V_k, V_{k+1}, \dots, V_n) \in \mathcal{R}, (W_1, \dots, W_{k'}, W_{k'+1}, \dots, W_m) \in \mathcal{Q}\}$
where $k = nKey(R)$, $k' = nKey(Q)$, $n = nAtt(R)$ *and* $m = nAtt(Q)$, $Key(P) = Key(R) \cup Key(Q)$, *and* $NonKey(P) = NonKey(R) \cup NonKey(Q)$.

Join $(\bowtie)$:
$R \bowtie_{F_1,\dots,F_n} Q =_{def} \sigma_{F_1,\dots,F_n}(R \times Q)$ *with the same conditions as the selection operator.*

Renaming (δ_ρ):
$\mathcal{R}' = \delta_\rho(R)$ *where* $\rho : A_1 A_2 \dots A_n \to B_1 B_2 \dots B_n$, $n = nAtt(R)$, *and* $B_i \neq B_j$ *if* $i \neq j$. $\mathcal{R}'$ *contains the same tuples as* $\mathcal{R}$ *and its schema is* $R'(\rho(A_1), \dots, \rho(A_k), \rho(A_{k+1}), \dots, \rho(A_n))$, *whenever the schema of* R *is* $R(\underline{A_1}, \dots, \underline{A_k}, A_{k+1}, \dots, A_n)$.

Definition 12 (Algebra Expressions). *Given a database* $D = (S, DC, IF)$ *and instance* $\mathcal{D} = (\mathcal{S}, \mathcal{DC}, \mathcal{IF})$, *then the* algebra expressions $\Psi(D)^{\mathcal{D}}$ *are defined as expressions built from a composition of algebra operators over a subset of relation names* $\{R_1, \dots, R_p\}$ *of* S *(and a subset* $\{f_1, \dots, f_r\}$ *of* IF*). In addition, the following conditions must be satisfied:*

(a) Ψ *must be closed w.r.t. key values; that is,* $Key(\Psi) = \cup_{R \in Rel(\Psi)} Key(R)$
(b) Ψ *must be closed w.r.t. data destructors; that is,*
  (b.1) *data destructors* $c.idx(t_A)$ *occur in the form:* $\pi_{c.idx(t_A)}$, $\pi_{c.idx(t_A)=s_A}$, $\pi_{\overline{\overline{c.idx(t_A)}}}$, *and* $\pi_{c.idx(t_A)==s_A}$;
  (b.2) *whenever* $\pi_{c.idx(t_A)}$ *(or* $\sigma_{s_{idx}^A=c.idx(t_A)}$*) occurs in* Ψ, *then* $\pi_{c.i(t_A)}$ *or* $\sigma_{s_i^A=c.i(t_A)}$ *must occur in* Ψ *for each* $1 \leq i \leq n$, *where* $c \in DC^n$; *and*
  (b.3) *whenever* $\pi_{\overline{\overline{c.idx(t_A)}}}$ *(or* $\sigma_{s_{idx}^A==c.idx(t_A)}$*) occurs in* Ψ, *then* $\pi_{\overline{\overline{c.i(t_A)}}}$ *or* $\sigma_{s_i^A==c.i(t_A)}$ *must occur in* Ψ *for each* $1 \leq i \leq n$, *where* $c \in DC^n$

where $Key(\Psi)$ (resp. $Rel(\Psi)$) are the key attribute (resp. relation) names occurring in Ψ.

Algebra expressions are used for expressing *queries* and *algebraic rules*. For instance, next we show several algebra expressions representing queries against the instances of `person_job`, `person_boss_job` and `2Dline`.

Query	Algebra Expression
To obtain lecturer *people and their bosses' addresses whenever these ones are defined*	$\pi_{\text{name},\text{address}'}(\sigma_{\text{name}'=\text{boss, job\_id}==\text{lecturer}}(\delta_{(\rho_1)}(\texttt{person\_job}\times\texttt{person\_job})))$
To obtain associate *people's name, and salary bonus whenever it is defined*	$\pi_{\text{name},\text{j\&b.2(job\_bonus)}}(\sigma_{\text{j\&b.1(job\_bonus)}==\text{associate}}(\texttt{person\_boss\_job}))$
To obtain the direction of p(0,2) *w.r.t* p(0,0)	$\pi_{\text{orientation}}(\sigma_{\text{origin}=\text{p}(0,0),\ \text{points}==\text{p}(0,2)}(\texttt{2Dline}))$

$\rho_1 : \text{name age} \ldots \text{name age} \ldots \rightarrow \text{name age} \ldots \text{name}' \text{age}' \ldots$

5   The Query and Data Definition Language

In this section, we present the query and data definition language based on the extended relational algebra.

Definition 13 (Queries and Query Answers). *A* query *is an algebra expression $\Psi(D)^{\mathcal{D}}$, and $(V_1,\ldots,V_n)$ is an* answer *of $\Psi(D)^{\mathcal{D}}$ if $(V_1,\ldots,V_n)\in\Psi(D)^{\mathcal{D}}$ and $V_i\neq<\perp>$ for all V_i.*

Instances (key and non-key attribute values, and interpreted functions) are defined by means of *algebraic rules*.

Definition 14 (Algebraic Rules). *An* algebraic rule *AR w.r.t. a database D, for a symbol $H\in DS(D)$ of arity n, has the form*

$$H := \pi_{p_1,\ldots,p_n,p}(\Psi(D))$$

indicating that H represents the tuple $(p_1,\ldots,p_n,p)$ obtained from $\Psi(D)$. In this rule,

- *$\Psi(D)$ is an algebra expression, and $(p_1,\ldots,p_n,p)$ can be any kind of projection c-terms;*
- *$(p_1,\ldots,p_n)$ is a* linear tuple *of projection c-terms (each variable and attribute symbol only occurs once), and*
- *extra variables and attributes are not allowed, i.e. $var(p)\subseteq\cup_{1\leq i\leq n}var(p_i)$ and $(Att(p)\cap Att(\Psi(D)))\backslash\cup_{1\leq i\leq n}Att(p_i)=\emptyset$*

Projection operator has been defined for the case $\pi_{t_1^A,\ldots t_k^A,t_{k+1}^A,\ldots t_n^A}$, where each t_i^A is (destructed) key attributes. However in algebraic rules, $p_1,\ldots,p_n,p$ can be any kind of projection c-terms, given they can build new tuples. Whenever the tuple is explicitly declared, we can write rules of the form $H := (p_1, \ldots, p_n, p)$ where p_i are c-terms.

In particular, assuming R of arity k, the rules

$$R := \pi_{p_1,\ldots,p_k}(\Psi(D)) \quad (resp.\ R := (p_1, \ldots, p_k))$$

allow the setting of $p_1, \ldots, p_k$ as key values of the relation R.

Analogously, assuming A of arity $k+1$, the rules

$$A := \pi_{p_1,\ldots,p_k,p}(\Psi(D)) \quad (resp.\ A := (p_1, \ldots, p_k, p))$$

where $A \in NonKey(R)$, set p as value of A for the tuple of R with key values $p_1, \ldots, p_k$.

Finally, interpreted function symbols are represented by rules

$$f := \pi_{p_1,\ldots,p_n,p}(\Psi(D))$$

whenever $f \in IF$ is of arity n, where $p_1, \ldots, p_n$ are the arguments of the function, and p is the function output.

For instance, the instances for the relations person_job, job_ information, and views person_boss_job and peter_workers, can be defined by the following algebraic rules:

Example1 : AlgebraicRulesforPersonandJobInformation

person_job	person_job := (john). person_job := (peter). address := (john, add('6th Avenue', 5)). address := (peter, add('5thAvenue', 5)). job_id := (john, lecturer). job_id := (peter, professor). boss := (john, mary). boss := (mary, peter).
job_information	job_information := (lecturer). job_information := (professor). salary := $\pi_{\text{lecturer,retention.2}}(\sigma_{\text{retention.1}=1500}(\texttt{retention}))$. salary := $\pi_{\text{associate,retention.2}}(\sigma_{\text{retention.1}=2500}(\texttt{retention}))$. salary := $\pi_{\text{professor,retention.2}}(\sigma_{\text{retention.1}=4000}(\texttt{retention}))$. bonus := (professor, 1500).
person_boss_job	person_boss_job := $\pi_{\text{name}}(\texttt{person\_job})$. boss_age := $\pi_{\text{name,b\&a(boss,age')}}(\sigma_{\text{boss=name'}}(\delta_{\text{name...name...}\rightarrow\text{name...name'}}\ldots(\texttt{person\_job}$ $\times \texttt{person\_job})))$. job_bonus := $\pi_{\text{name,j\&b(job\_name,bonus)}}(\sigma_{\text{job\_id=job\_name}}(\texttt{person\_job}$ $\times \texttt{job\_information}))$.
peter_workers	peter_workers := $\pi_{\text{name}}(\sigma_{\text{boss==peter}}(\texttt{person\_job}))$. work := $\pi_{\text{name,job\_id}}(\texttt{person\_job})$.

The right column also contains: person_job := (mary). / address := (mary, add('7thAvenue', 2)). / job_id := (mary, associate). / boss := (john, peter). / job_information := (associate).

Analogously, 2Dpoint and 2Dline can be defined by means of the following algebraic rules:

Example 2 : AlgebraicRulesforBidimensionalPoints and Lines

2Dpoint	$\text{2Dpoint} := (p(0,0))$. $\text{2Dpoint} := \pi_{p(s(p.1(\text{coord})),p.2(\text{coord}))}(\text{2Dpoint})$. $\text{2Dpoint} := \pi_{p.1(\text{coord}),s(p.2(\text{coord})))}(\text{2Dpoint})$. $\text{color} := (p(0,0),1)$. $\text{color} := (p(0,1),1)$.
2Dline	$\text{2Dline} := \pi_{\text{coord},\text{north}}(\text{2Dpoint})$. $\text{2Dline} := \pi_{\text{coord},\text{south}}(\text{2Dpoint})$. $\text{2Dline} := \pi_{\text{coord},\text{east}}(\text{2Dpoint})$. $\text{2Dline} := \pi_{\text{coord},\text{west}}(\text{2Dpoint})$. ... $\text{next} := \pi_{\text{origin},\text{north},p(p.1(\text{origin}),s(p.2(\text{origin})))}(\text{2Dline})$. $\text{next} := \pi_{\text{origin},\text{south},p(p.1(\text{origin}),s.1(p.2(\text{origin})))}(\text{2Dline})$. $\text{next} := \pi_{\text{origin},\text{east},p(s(p.1(\text{origin})),p.2(\text{origin}))}(\text{2Dline})$. $\text{next} := \pi_{\text{origin},\text{west},p(s.1(p.1(\text{origin})),p.2(\text{origin}))}(\text{2Dline})$ ... $\text{points} := \pi_{\text{origin},\text{dir},\text{next}}(\text{2Dline})$. $\text{points} := \pi_{\text{origin},\text{dir},\text{points}'}(\sigma_{\text{next}=\text{origin}'}(\delta_{\rho}(\text{2Dline} \times \text{2Dline})))$. $\text{list\_of\_points} := \pi_{\text{origin},\text{dir},[\text{origin}|\text{list\_of\_points}']}(\sigma_{\text{origin}'=\text{next}}(\delta_{\rho}(\text{2Dline} \times \text{2Dline})))$

$\rho : \text{coord} \ldots \text{coord} \ldots \rightarrow \text{coord} \ldots \text{coord}' \ldots$

Here, **points** is a non-deterministic algebraic rule, which defines an infinite (cone) set of values (i.e. the infinite set of points of the line). Alternatively, **list_of_points** is a deterministic function, which computes the (infinite) list of points of the line.

Finally, we present how to express the same queries and instance definitions by using goals and conditional rewriting rules, typical in functional logic programming.

Definition 15 (Conditional Rewriting Rule). *A conditional (constructor based) rewriting rules [8] has the form:* $H\ t_1 \ldots t_n := r \Leftarrow C$, *where*

- $t_1, \ldots, t_n$ *is a linear tuple of c-terms*
- r *is a* database term, *which consists on terms built from symbols of* $DS(D)$, DC *and* $\mathcal{V}$.
- C *is a set of equality constraints in the form of* $e == e'$, *where* e *and* e' *are database terms*
- *Extra variables are not allowed, that is,* $var(r) \subseteq var(\bar{t})$

In our context, we have three kinds of rules: $R\ t_1 \ldots t_k := true \Leftarrow C$, $A\ t_1 \ldots t_k := r \Leftarrow C$, and $f\ t_1 \ldots t_n := r \Leftarrow C$, for representing relation and non-key attribute names, and interpreted functions, respectively. Key definitions are supposed to be boolean functions, setting $t_1, \ldots, t_k$ as key attribute values. Non-key definitions set r as attribute value for the key values $t_1, \ldots, t_k$; finally, interpreted functions define r as the value of $f\ t_1 \ldots t_n$. In all cases, C plays the role of a condition. As a particular case, queries can be considered as rule conditions. Now, the above queries and algebraic rules can be expressed as follows:

Functional Logic Query	Algebra Expression
boss john == mary.	$\sigma_{\text{name}=\text{john},\ \text{boss}==\text{mary}}(\text{person\_job})$
address (boss X) == Y, job_id X == lecturer.	$\pi_{\text{name},\text{address}'} == (\sigma_{\text{name}'=\text{boss},\ \text{job\_id}==\text{lecturer}}(\delta_{(\rho_1)}(\text{person\_job} \times$ $\text{person\_job})))$
job_bonus X == j&b(associate,Y).	$\pi_{\text{name},\text{j\&b.1}(\text{job\_bonus})} == (\sigma_{\text{j\&b.1}(\text{job\_bonus})==\text{associate}}(\text{person\_boss\_job}))$
points p(0,0) Z == p(0,2).	$\pi_{\text{orientation}}(\sigma_{\text{origin}=p(0,0),\ \text{points}==p(0,2)}(\text{2Dline}))$

$\rho_1 : \text{name}\ \text{age} \ldots \text{name}\ \text{age} \ldots \rightarrow \text{name}\ \text{age} \ldots \text{name}'\ \text{age}' \ldots$

Example 1 : Rewriting Rules for Person and Job Information

person_job	
person_job john := true.	person_job mary := true.
person_job peter := true.	
address john := add('6th Avenue', 5).	address mary := add('7th Avenue', 2).
address peter := add('5th Avenue', 5).	
job_id john := lecturer.	job_id mary := associate.
job_id peter := professor.	
boss john := mary.	boss john := peter.
boss mary := peter.	

job_information	
job_information lecturer := true.	job_information associate := true.
job_information professor := true.	
salary lecturer := retention_for_tax 1500.	
salary associate := retention_for_tax 2500.	
salary professor := retention_for_tax 4000.	
bonus professor := 1500.	

person_boss_job	
person_boss_job Name := person_job Name.	
boss_age Name := b&a(boss Name, address (boss Name)).	
job_bonus Name := j&b(job_id (Name), bonus (job_id (Name))).	

peter_workers	
peter_workers Name := person_job Name ⇐ boss Name == peter.	
work Name := job_id Name.	

Example 2 : Rewriting Rules for Bidimensional Points and Lines

2Dpoint	
2Dpoint p(0, 0) := true.	
2Dpoint p(s(X), Y) := 2Dpoint p(X, Y).	2Dpoint p(X, s(Y)) := 2Dpoint p(X, Y).
color p(0, 0) := 1.	color p(0, 1) := 2.

2Dline	
2Dline X north := 2Dpoint X.	2Dline X south := 2Dpoint X.
2Dline X east := 2Dpoint X.	2Dline X west := 2Dpoint X. ...
next p(X, Y) north := p(X, s(Y)).	next p(X, s(Y)) south := p(X, Y).
next p(X, Y) east := p(s(X), Y).	next p(s(X), Y) west := p(X, Y). ...
points X Z := next X Z.	points X Z := points (next X Z) Z.
list_of_points X Z := [X	list_of_points (next X Z) Z].	

6   Least Induced Database

In this section, we show how to formally obtain the database instance from a set of algebraic rules. With this aim, firstly, we define the *database instance induced from a set of rules*. Secondly, we present a *fixed point operator*, and, finally, we state that the database instance computed by means of the proposed fixed point operator is the *least induced one*.

Definition 16 (Induced Database). *A database instance $\mathcal{D}$ of a database schema D is induced from an algebraic rule of the form*

$$H := \pi_{p_1,\dots,p_n,p}(\Psi(D))$$

where $H \in DS(D)$, iff

- *if $H \equiv R$ and $R(A_1, \dots, A_k, \dots, A_n) \in S$ then: for every $(V_1, \dots, V_k) \in \pi_{p_1,\dots,p_k}(W)$ such that W is an answer of $\Psi(D)^{\mathcal{D}}$, then there exists $(V_1, \dots, V_k, \dots, V_n) \in \mathcal{R}$*
- *if $H \equiv A_i$, $A_i \in NonKey(D)$, and $R(A_1, \dots, A_k, \dots, A_i, \dots, A_n) \in S$ then: for every $(V_1, \dots, V_k, V_i) \in \pi_{p_1,\dots,p_k,p}(W)$ such that W is an answer of $\Psi(D)^{\mathcal{D}}$, then there exists $(V_1, \dots, V_k, \dots, V_i, \dots, V_n) \in \mathcal{R}$*
- *if $H \equiv f$, $f \in IF$ then: for every $(V_1, \dots, V_n, V) \in \pi_{p_1,\dots,p_n,p}(W)$ such that W is an answer of $\Psi(D)^{\mathcal{D}}$, then $f^{\mathcal{D}} V_1, \dots, V_n = V$*

A database instance $\mathcal{D}$ is induced from a set of algebraic rules $AR_1, \ldots, AR_n$, iff $\mathcal{D}$ is induced from every AR_i.

Definition 17 (Fixed Point Operator). *Given a database instance $\mathcal{A} = (\mathcal{S}^A, \mathcal{DC}^A, \mathcal{IF}^A)$ of a database schema $D = (S, DC, IF)$, we define a fixed point operator $T_{\mathcal{P}}(\mathcal{A}) = \mathcal{B} = (\mathcal{S}^B, \mathcal{DC}^B, \mathcal{IF}^B)$ where:*

- *for each database schema $R(A_1, \ldots, A_n) \in S$: $(V_1, \ldots, V_n) \in \mathcal{R}^B, \mathcal{R}^B \in \mathcal{S}^B$ iff $(V_1, \ldots, V_k) \in \pi_{p_1,\ldots,p_k}(W)$, W is an answer of $\Psi(D)^{\mathcal{A}}$, there exists a rule $R := \pi_{p_1,\ldots,p_k}(\Psi(D))$ and $(V_1, \ldots, V_k, V_i) \in \pi_{q_1,\ldots,q_k,q}(Z)$, Z is an answer of $\Omega(D)^{\mathcal{A}}$, and there exists a rule $A_i := \pi_{q_1,\ldots,q_k,q}(\Omega(D))$*
- *for each interpreted function symbol $f \in IF$: $f^B(V_1, \ldots, V_n) = V$, $f^B \in \mathcal{IF}^B$ iff $(V_1, \ldots, V_n, V) \in \pi_{p_1,\ldots,p_n,p}(W)$, W is an answer of $\Psi(D)^{\mathcal{A}}$, and there exists a rule $f := \pi_{p_1,\ldots,p_n,p}(\Psi(D))$*

Starting from the *bottom database instance*, $\perp$, then the fixed point operator computes a chain of database instances $\perp \sqsubseteq A \sqsubseteq A' \sqsubseteq A'', \ldots$ represented by a set of algebraic rules. The following result establishes that the database instance computed by means of the proposed fixed point operator is the least database induced from the set of algebraic rules.

Theorem 1.

- *The fixed point operator $T_{\mathcal{P}}$ has a least fixed point $\mathcal{L} = \mathcal{D}^\omega$ where $\mathcal{D}^0 = \perp$ and $\mathcal{D}^{k+1} = T_{\mathcal{P}}(\mathcal{D}^k)$*
- *For each $\Psi(D)$, V is an answer of $\Psi(D)^{\mathcal{L}}$ iff V is an answer of $\Psi(D)^{\mathcal{D}}$ for each $\mathcal{D}$ induced from the algebraic rules.*

Proof Sketch: By proving that $T_{\mathcal{P}}$ is monotone, that is, $T_{\mathcal{P}}(\mathcal{D}) \sqsubseteq T_{\mathcal{P}}(\mathcal{D}')$ if $\mathcal{D} \sqsubseteq \mathcal{D}'$, and $\mathcal{D}$ is induced from the rules iff $T_{\mathcal{P}}(\mathcal{D}) \sqsubseteq \mathcal{D}$.

7   Conclusions and Future Work

In this paper, we have proposed an integration of functional logic programming and databases by means of a unified syntax and semantics. However, this framework opens new research topics, such as the study of a suitable operational mechanism (as well as the evaluation strategies) in order to efficiently solve queries against a database. On the other hand, we would like to study the extension of our framework for the handling of negative information following the line proposed by [11].

References

1. S. Abiteboul and C. Beeri. The Power of Languages for the Manipulation of Complex Values. *VLDB*, 4(4):727–794, 1995.

2. J.M. Almendros-Jiménez and A. Becerra-Terón. A Safe Relational Calculus for Functional Logic Deductive Databases. *Selected Papers of the WFLP'03. To appear in Electronic Notes on Theoretical Computer Science*, 86(3).

3. J. M. Almendros-Jiménez, A. Becerra-Terón, and J. Sánchez-Hernández. A Computational Model for Funtional Logic Deductive Databases. In *Proc. of ICLP*, LNCS 2237, pages 331–347. Springer, 2001.

4. J. M. Almendros-Jiménez and A. Becerra-Terón. A Framework for Goal-Directed Bottom-Up Evaluation of Functional Logic Programs. In *Proc. of FLOPS*, LNCS 2024, pages 153–169. Springer, 2001.

5. A. Belussi, E. Bertino, and B. Catania. An Extended Algebra for Constraint Databases. *TKDE*, 10(5):686–705, 1998.

6. E. F. Codd. A Relational Model of Data for Large Shared Data Banks. *Communications of the ACM, CACM*, 13(6):377–387, 1970.

7. E. F. Codd. Relational Completeness of Data Base Sublanguages. In *R. Rustin (ed.), Database Systems*, pages 65–98. Prentice Hall, 1972.

8. J. C. González-Moreno, M. T. Hortalá-González, F. J. López-Fraguas, and M. Rodríguez-Artalejo. An Approach to Declarative Programming Based on a Rewriting Logic. *JLP*, 1(40):47–87, 1999.

9. M. Hanus. The Integration of Functions into Logic Programming: From Theory to Practice. *JLP*, 19,20:583–628, 1994.

10. P. Kanellakis and D. Goldin. Constraint Query Algebras. *Constraints*, 1(1–2):45–83, 1996.

11. F. J. López-Fraguas and J. Sánchez-Hernández. Proving Failure in Functional Logic Programs. In *Proc. of the CL*, LNCS 1861, pages 179–193. Springer, 2000.

Implication of Functional Dependencies for Recursive Queries

José R. Paramá, Nieves R. Brisaboa, Miguel R. Penabad, and Ángeles S. Places

Database Lab. Computer Science Dept. Univ. of A Coruña. Campus de Elviña s/n,
15071 A Coruña. Spain. Tf. +34981-167000. Fax. +34981-167160
{parama,brisaboa,penabad}@udc.es,
asplaces@mail2.udc.es

Abstract. After two decades of research in Deductive Databases, SQL99 [12] brings them again to the foreground given that SQL99 includes queries with linear recursion. Therefore some of the problems solved for the relational model demand our attention again.

In this paper, we tackle the *implication of functional dependencies* (also known as the *FD-FD implication problem*) in the deductive model framework. The problem is as follows. *Given P, F, and f, where P is a Datalog program, F is a set of functional dependencies defined on the predicates of P, and f is a fd defined over the predicates of P, is it true that for all databases d defined exclusively on the extensional predicates of P, d satisfies F implies that $P(d)$ –the output database– satisfies f.* Unlike the implication problem of functional dependencies in the relational data model, this problem is undecidable for general Datalog programs.

In this paper, we provide two methods to check if a given set of fds will be satisfied by the output database (without computing such database) for a class of Datalog programs.

1 Introduction

Integrity constraints are general laws that databases must satisfy [15]. They arise naturally in practical applications and restrict the domain of the input databases to a subset of all the possible input databases. Functional dependencies [15] are a type of integrity constraints that all valid databases are required to fulfill through time.

Research in satisfaction of functional dependencies (fds) is very important. Note that for example, violations of other types of constraints as *tuple generating dependency* [15] are due to the lack of complete information about the world (i.e., the lack of certain facts asserted by the tuple-generating dependency), and therefore they can be removed by adding more information to make it complete, such as by treating all given tuple-generating dependencies as additional rules of the program. On the other hand, violations of constraints as the functional dependencies are due to the presence of certain "incorrect" information in the database, such as the same social security number assigned to two persons. There is no way to remove such violations without undoing updates or discarding some

M. Broy and A.V. Zamulin (Eds.): PSI 2003, LNCS 2890, pp. 509–519, 2003.

original information. In the latter case, it is no always clear what portion should be discarded. Therefore, more attention should be paid to the enforcement of constraints of this kind.

Functional dependencies are well studied in the relational data model. However it is more difficult to tackle the problems associated with them in the deductive model framework. One of the most well known problems related with functional dependencies satisfaction in Datalog is the *implication of functional dependencies* (also known as the *FD-FD implication problem*). The problem is as follows: given a Datalog program P and a set of fds F, if the result of applying P to any (extensional) database that fulfills F always produce a database satisfying a new set of functional dependencies (say G), then G is *implied* by F (in P). It has been proven by Abiteboul and Hull [2] that this problem is undecidable for general Datalog programs. Since then, several researchers started to delimit set of Datalog programs where this problem can be decidable.

This problem is important since the computational cost of checking the satisfaction of fds in the input database is less than the computational cost of checking the output database (typically much bigger). New technologies as Data Mining are also interested in this problem [7,6] given that, the implication of functional dependencies entails the discover of new knowledge about the data.

In this work, we provide two methods to check if a given set of fds will be satisfied by the output database without computing such database. With such objective, we introduce a syntactic condition that serves us to decide if a program, which is in a subclass of linear Datalog programs, implies a fd (from a given set of fds). Besides, provided that the scheme of the database is in Boyce Codd Normal Form (BCNF) with respect to the functional dependencies, we offer a syntactic condition that serves us to identify programs that do not imply a specific fd.

The following two examples illustrate the FD-FD implication problem and show us its difficulty.

Example 1. Let $F = \{e : \{1\} \to \{2\}\}$. We shall consider only databases that satisfy F and let $f = p : \{1\} \to \{3\}$. Let $P = \{r_0, r_1\}$, where:

$r_0 : p(X, X, Y) : -e(X, Y).$
$r_1 : p(X, Y, Y) : -e(Y, Y), p(X, X, Y).$

Table 1. d and $P(d)$

d	$P(d)$
$e(1,2)$	$e(1,2)\ \ p(1,1,2)$
$e(2,4)$	$e(2,4)\ \ p(2,2,4)$
$e(4,4)$	$e(4,4)\ \ p(4,4,4)$
	$p(2,4,4)$

Observe in Table 1 that d (the input database) trivially satisfies F. However we can see that the atoms defined over p in the output database $(P(d))$ satisfy the fd f. In fact, we can see that if d satisfies F, $P(d)$ will always satisfy f. This is true given that positions 1 and 3 of the two p-atoms of r_1 have the same variables (and in the same order) and positions 1 and 3 of the p-atom of r_0 have the same variables (and in the same order) as positions 1 and 2 of the e-atom in the body of the rule. □

Example 2. Let $G = \{e : \{1\} \rightarrow \{2\}\}$ and $g = p : \{1\} \rightarrow \{2\}$. Let $P' = \{r_0, r_1\}$ the typical chain program, where:
$r_0 : p(X, Y) : -e(X, Y).$
$r_1 : p(X, Y) : -e(X, Z), p(Z, Y).$

Table 2. d and $P'(d)$

d	$P'(d)$
$e(1, 2)$	$e(1, 2)\ \ p(1, 2)$
$e(2, 3)$	$e(2, 3)\ \ p(2, 3)$
	$p(1, 3)$

We can see in Table 2 that d satisfies G, however the atoms defined over p in the output database do not satisfy the fd g, because $p(1, 2)$ and $p(1, 3)$ violates $p : \{1\} \rightarrow \{2\}$. □

2   Related Work

Although the problem appears for first time in the relational model [10,5], in Datalog the implication problem has also been treated by several researchers [2, 16,9,8] even though, as we have already commented, the problem is not decidable for Datalog programs in general [2].

In order to solve this problem we use a technique called chase. The term "chase" appears for the first time in the lossless-join test of Aho, Beeri, and Ullman [3,15]. Right after that, the chase began to be used to solve problems different from its original motivation (i.e. determining if a certain decomposition is a lossless-join decomposition). Maier, Mendelzon and Sagiv [10] used the chase in order to solve the implication problem of data dependencies and Beeri and Vardi [5] extended the algorithm of Maier, Mendelzon and Sagiv to generalized dependencies.

Gonzalez-Tuchmann [9] used the chase to provide a syntactic condition to solve the FD-FD implication problem for a class of Datalog programs. Wang and Yuan [16] use the chase again as a basic component of an algorithm for testing if a set of integrity constraints (including functional dependencies) IC_1 uniformly implies a set of integrity constraints IC_2 in a Datalog program, provided that IC_1 is preserved by the program.

The problem tackled by Wang and Yuan is slightly different from the problem treated in this paper. They test *uniform* implication, whereas we deal with implication (without uniformity).

New trends also deal with this problem. Lucian Popa considered the problem in the object relational model [14,13]. Siegfried Bell has studied the discovery of functional dependencies from the perspective of Data Mining [7,6].

3 Basic Concepts

We assume the notation and definitions of [15] and then we only define the non-standard concepts. We use $EDB(P)$ to refer the set of EDB predicate names in a Datalog program P and $Pred(P)$ to refer the set of all predicate names in P. Let p be a predicate name in $Pred(P)$ for some program P, we say that P *defines* p if it appears in the head of some rule of P.

We denote variables in Datalog programs by capital letters, while we use lower case letters to denote predicate names. For simplicity, we do not allow constants in programs. Let a_i be an atom, $a_i[n]$ is the term in the nth position of a_i. If N is a set of positions, $a_i[N]$ is the set of terms (of a_i) is such positions. We shall consider the right-hand sides of all fds as singleton sets. By Armstrong's axioms [4], such assumption does not restrict our results.

Let P be a program, let r be a rule and let d be a database. $P(d)$ represents the output of P when its input is d and $r(d)$ represents the output of r when its input is d. Let F be a set of fds, $SAT(F)$ represents the set of all databases over a given Datalog schema $\mathcal{U}$ that satisfy F. Let r and r' be two rules and let F be a set of fds, we say that r and r' are equivalent under F ($r \equiv_{SAT(F)} r'$) if for all database $d \in SAT(F)$, $r(d) = r'(d)$. Let P and P' be two Datalog programs and let F be a set of fds, we say that P and P' are equivalent under F ($P \equiv_{SAT(F)} P'$) if for all database $d \in SAT(F)$, $P(d) = P'(d)$.

We use the symbol, π, like the projection operator of the relational algebra. The output of $\pi_{i_1,\ldots,i_k}[p, P(d)]$ is the projection over the columns $i_1, \ldots, i_k$ of the p-facts of $P(d)$.

Let P be a program and let F and G be sets of fds over $pred(P)$. Consider a fd g defined over p, a predicate name in $pred(P)$. Then we say that g is *implied by F (in P)* [2], denoted by $F \models_P g$, if $P(d)$ satisfies g, for all d in $SAT(F)$ such that d is defined over $EDB(P)$. We say that F *implies G (in P)*, denoted by $F \models_P G$, if $F \models_P g$ for every fd g in G.

Consider two rules, say r and s. Let p_r be the IDB atom[1] in the body of r, h_s the atom in the head of s and b_s the atoms in the body of s. The *expansion (composition)* of r with s, denoted by $r \circ s$, exists if p_r is defined over h_s. It consists in the substitution of p_r by b_s (with a substitution ø, from the variables in h_s to the terms in p_r).

---

[1] We consider only one IDB atom in the body of the rule. The definition can be extended to several IDB atoms straightforward.

Example 3. Let us consider these two rules, $r : p(X, Y) : -e(X, Z), p(Z, Y)$ and $s : p(X, Y) : -e(X, Z_1), e(Z_1, Z_2), p(Z_2, Y)$.

Here, $p_r = p(Z, Y)$ and $h_s = p(X, Y)$. Taking $\emptyset = \{X/Z\}$ we have that $p_r = \emptyset(h_s)$. Then, $r \circ s$ is $p(X, Y) : -e(X, Z), e(Z, Z_1), e(Z_1, Z_2), p(Z_2, Y)$ □

4   The Chase of a Datalog Rule

Let F be a set of fds defined over $EDB(P)$, for some program P. Let r be a rule of P. Let $f = p : \{n\} \to \{m\}$ be a fd in F and let q_1 and q_2 be two atoms in the body of r such that the predicate name of q_1 and q_2 is p, $q_1[n] = q_2[n]$ and $q_1[m] \neq q_2[m]$. Note that $q_1[m]$ and $q_2[m]$ are variables since we are assuming that programs do not contain constants. An *application of the fd f to r* is the uniform replacement in r of $q_1[m]$ by $q_2[m]$ or vice versa.

Definition 1. *Let r be a rule and let F be a set of fds over the predicates in the body of r. The* chase of r *with respect to F, denoted by $Chase_F(r)$, is the rule obtained by applying every fd in F to the atoms in the body of r until no more changes can be made.*

Example 4. Let r be the rule $p(X, Y) : -e(X, Z), e(X, Y), e(Z, Y)$. Let F be the set of fds $F = \{f = e : \{1\} \to \{2\}\}$.

The $Chase_F(r)$ is a new rule $r' = p(X, Y) : -e(X, Y), e(Y, Y)$ obtained after the equalization of Z and Y in the atoms of the original rule r. This equalization is due to the existence of the atoms $e(X, Z)$ and $e(X, Y)$, which have the same variable in the position defined by the left-hand side of the fd $e : \{1\} \to \{2\}$. Thus, Z and Y are equated since they are the variables (of the two atoms $e(X, Z)$ and $e(X, Y)$) in the position defined by the right-hand side of f. Note that r and r' produce the same output when they are evaluated over databases in $SAT(F)$.   □

Because the chase of rules does not introduce new variables, it turns out that the chase procedure always terminates. Applying a fd to a rule r can be performed within time polynomial in the size of r [11,1].

Lemma 1. *Let r be a Datalog rule, F a set of fds over $EDB(r)$ and r' the $Chase_F(r)$. Then, $r' \equiv_{SAT(F)} r$.*

This lemma can be proven readily, we do not include it due to lack of space.

4.1   Equivalence of a Program and the Chase of Its Rules

The definition of the chase of rules can be extended to programs as follows.

Let P be a program. Then *the chase of the rules of a program P with respect to F*, denoted by $ChaseRules_F(P)$, is given by:

$$ChaseRules_F(P) = \{r' \mid r' = Chase_F(r), r \in P\}$$

Corollary 1. *Let P be a program and let F be a set of fds defined over $EDB(P)$. Then $P \equiv_{SAT(F)} ChaseRules_F(P)$.*

Proof. It follows from Lemma 1.   □

5   The Class $\mathcal{P}$ of Linear Datalog Programs

The results of this paper apply to the class $\mathcal{P}$ of linear programs[2] of the following form. The class is composed of linear Datalog programs P definig only one IDB predicate. Furthermore, exactly one of the rules is non-recursive (say r_0), such rule is required to have exactly one atom in its body. Eventually, r_0 must have the following form: $p(\boldsymbol{X}) : -e(\boldsymbol{X})$, where $\boldsymbol{X}$ is a list of distinct variables.

Example 5. The program of Example 2 belongs to the class $\mathcal{P}$.   □

6   Pivoting

Definition 2. *Let r be a rule of a program P in class $\mathcal{P}$ or its chase. Let us denote the atom in the head of r as p_h, and let the predicate name of p_h be p. If the rule is recursive, let p_b be the atom in the body of r whose predicate name is p. Let e_j be an atom in the body of r whose predicate name is e (the EDB predicate name of the atom in the body of the non-recursive rule of P). Then, the argument position i is pivoting in r if $p_h[i] = e_j[i]$ or $p_h[i] = p_b[i]$. A set N of argument positions is pivoting in r if $p_h[N] = e_j[N]$ or $p_h[N] = p_b[N]$.*

Basically, the idea is that if a set of argument positions are pivoting in a rule r, then when r is applied to a database, the constants in the positions of the atoms obtained by r will be in the same order (and positions) as they were in ground atoms or previously derived IDB atoms. That is, if the ground atoms satisfy a fd and the applied rules are pivoting in the positions defined by such fd, then the derived atoms will satisfy such fd as well.

Example 6. Let $P = \{r_0, r_1, r_2\}$ where:
$r_0 : p(X, Y, W, Z) : -e(X, Y, W, Z)$
$r_1 : p(X, Y, W, W) : -a(V, W), e(Y, W, W, V), e(V, Y, W, X), p(X, Y, V, W)$
$r_2 : p(X, Y, W, Q) : -e(X, W, Q, X), p(Y, X, V, V)$

We can see that positions $\{1, 4\}$ are pivoting in r_1 since $p_h[1, 4] = p_b[1, 4]$. However in r_2, positions $\{1, 4\}$ are not pivoting given that $p_h[1, 4] \neq e[1, 4]$ and $p_h[1, 4] \neq p_b[1, 4]$.   □

---

[2] A Datalog program is linear if its rules have at most one IDB atom in their body.

7 A Test to Identify Programs That Imply a fd

The test is based in two conditions. We can assure that a program implies a fd (under a set of fds) if such conditions are satisfied.

Lemma 2. *Let P be a program in class $\mathcal{P}$. Let F be a set of fds defined over $EDB(P)$ and let $f = p\colon \{i_1, \ldots, i_k\} \to \{i_{k+1}\}$, where p is the IDB predicate defined by P. Let e the EDB predicate name in the non-recursive rule of P. If the two conditions showed below are true then $F \models_P f$.*

- *Condition 1 The fd $e\colon \{i_1, \ldots, i_k\} \to \{i_{k+1}\}$ is in F^+,*
- *Condition 2 The set of argument positions $\{i_1, \ldots, i_k, i_{k+1}\}$ are pivoting in $Chase_F(r_i)$ for all recursive rule r_i in P.*

Proof. Let $P' = \{r_0, Chase_F(r_i)\}$, for all recursive rule r_i in P. Let d be a EDB defined over *EDB(P)*. Let us suppose that d satisfies F. Assume that the Conditions 1 and 2 are satisfied. By Condition 1, $P'(d)$ satisfies $e\colon \{i_1, \ldots, i_k\} \to \{i_{k+1}\}$. By Condition 2, $\pi_{i_1, \ldots, i_k, i_{k+1}}[p, P'(d)] = \pi_{i_1, \ldots, i_k, i_{k+1}}[e, P'(d)]$. Then, $P'(d)$ satisfies $p\colon \{i_1, \ldots, i_k\} \to \{i_{k+1}\}$. Finally, $P(d)$ satisfies $p\colon \{i_1, \ldots, i_k\} \to \{i_{k+1}\}$ since by Corollary 1, $P(d) \equiv_{SAT(F)} P'(d)$. □

Example 7. Let $P = \{r_0, r_1\}$, where
$r_0 : p(X, Y, W, Z) : -e(X, Y, W, Z).$
$r_1 : p(X, Y, W, Z) : - a(V, W), a(V, Z), e(Y, W, Z, V), e(V, Y, W, X), p(X, Y, V, W).$

Let $F = \{e\colon \{1\} \to \{4\}, e\colon \{1\} \to \{3\}, e\colon \{2, 3\} \to \{4\}, e\colon \{2, 3\} \to \{1\}, a\colon \{1\} \to \{2\}\}$ and let us consider only databases that satisfy F. Let $f = p\colon \{1\} \to \{4\}$. Note that P is in $\mathcal{P}$. We can see that positions 1 and 4 are not pivoting in r_1. However, if we chase r_1 we obtain the rule:
$Chase_F(r_1) = p(X, Y, W, W) : -a(V, W), e(Y, W, W, V), e(V, Y, W, X), p(X, Y, V, W)$

Observe that positions 1 and 4 are pivoting in $Chase_F(r_1)$, therefore conditions of Lemma 2 are maintained and hence $F \models_P f$. □

8 A Test to Identify Programs That Do Not Imply a fd

Lemma 3. *Let P be a program in class $\mathcal{P}$. Let F be a set of fds over EDB(P) in BCNF. Let $f = p\colon \{i_1, \ldots, i_k\} \to \{i_{k+1}\}$, where p is the IDB predicate defined by P. Let e be the EDB predicate name in the non-recursive rule of P. Assume $e\colon \{i_1, \ldots, i_k\} \to \{i_{k+1}\}$ is left-hand minimal with respect to F. If $F \models_P f$ then the following two conditions must hold:*

- *Condition 1 The minimal fd $e\colon \{i_1, \ldots, i_k\} \to \{i_{k+1}\}$ is in F^+,*
- *Condition 2 For any composition of rules of P $r_c = r_1 \circ \ldots \circ r_n \circ r_0$, where $r_1 \ldots r_n$ are recursive rules of P[3] and r_0 is the non-recursive rule of P, the set of argument positions $\{i_1, \ldots, i_k, i_{k+1}\}$ are pivoting in $Chase_F(r_c)$.*

□

---

[3] Observe that it may be possible to have that $r_i = r_j$, $i, j \in 1 \ldots n$.

Proof. Note that Condition 1 is trivially necessary. Thus, in what follows we assume that is true. Then, assuming that Condition 1 is true and Condition 2 is false, we give a procedure for constructing, for all programs P in $\mathcal{P}$ and for all F defined on predicates in $EDB(P)$, a counterexample database, denoted by d_{count}. d_{count} satisfies the following two conditions:

1. d_{count} is in $SAT(F)$.
2. $P(d_{count})$ is not in $SAT(\{f\})$.

Let P be a program in class $\mathcal{P}$ and let F be a set of fds over $EDB(P)$ in BCNF. Let $f = p : \{i_1, \ldots, i_k\} \to \{i_{k+1}\}$, where p is the IDB predicate defined by P. Let r_{count} be the rule that does not satisfy Condition 2. r_{count} is the $Chase_F(r_c)$, where $r_c = r_1 \circ \ldots \circ r_n \circ r_0$, being $r_1 \ldots r_n$ recursive rules of P (where some of them may be the same rule of P) and r_0 the non-recursive one. Let r_{count} be of the form: $p(X_1, \ldots, X_n) : -L, E$, where L denotes the conjunction of EDB atoms in the body of r_{count} that are not defined over the predicate name e (the predicate name of the atom in the body of the non-recursive rule) and E represents the set of atoms in the body of r_{count} defined over the predicate name e.

From now on, in order to build the counterexample database d_{count}, we consider all the variables in r_{count} (and therefore in L and E) as constants. Let d be the database formed by $L \cup E \cup e_h$, where e_h is an atom constructed as follows:

- $e_h = e(A_1, \ldots, A_n)$
- **for all** $j, 1 \le j \le n$, if $j \in \{i_1, \ldots, i_k\}$, then $A_j = X_j$;
- **else** A_j is a new, distinct constant.

e_h has the same constants as the head of r_{count} in the argument positions defined by the left-hand side of f, and distinct constants anywhere else. Let $d_{count} = Chase_F(d)$. We claim that d_{count} is a counter example of $F \models_P f$. In order to prove that, first we have to prove that the chase of d can be performed without producing any change in L and E and, $e_h[\{i_1, \ldots, i_k\}] = e'_h[\{i_1, \ldots, i_k\}]$, where e'_h is e_h after the chase. The set $E \cup L$ satisfies F because they come from the body of r_{count} that is the chase (w.r.t. F) of r_c. Then, since all EDB atoms in d different from e_h (defined over the predicate name e) are in $SAT(F)$, the first application of a fd over d during the chase must be a fd of the form $e : X \to \{a\}$, let us call such fd g. Observe that g must equate variables of e_h and e_i, an atom in E. We have to prove that $X = \{i_1, \ldots, i_k\}$. Suppose that $X \subset \{i_1, \ldots, i_k\}$, since the scheme of the database is in BCNF, then X is a key. Therefore, $e : \{i_1, \ldots, i_k\} \to \{i_{k+1}\}$ is not minimal, contradiction since we supposed $X \subset \{i_1, \ldots, i_k\}$. Now assume $\{i_1, \ldots, i_k\} \subset X$, in such a case it is not possible to apply g since e_h in positions different from $\{i_1, \ldots, i_k\}$ has new constants that are not present anywhere else.

Observe that all terms in e_h that are not in $\{i_1, \ldots, i_k\}$ are new constants that are not anywhere else, then the equalizations produced by the application of X and any other subsequent fd application will involve always a new constant and a old one. The chase allows to replace the new one by the old one. Since the equalization of the new constant does not affect to the rest of constants (the new one is only in e_h), then L and E are not affected. Since X is key, the chase makes $e_i = e_h$, then e_i or e_h is removed from d_{count} and eventually, there is no possibility to apply any other fd. Hence, the chase ends without applying any change in E and L.

Now we are ready to define the facts in $P(d_{count})$ (say p_1 and p_2) that violate f. p_1 is the head of r_{count} and p_2 is constructed as follows. Let p_2 be the p-fact that we can prove by applying r_0 to $\{e_h'\}$. This implies that $p_2 = p(A_1', \ldots, A_n')$, where $A_1', \ldots, A_n'$ are the constants in e_h'.
Note that:

- d_{count} is in $SAT(F)$ and d_{count} contains only facts about predicates in $EDB(P)$.
- p_2 is in $P(d_{count})$ (by the definition of p_2).
- p_1 is in $P(d_{count})$. This is true since, as we have already seen $d_{count} = E \cup L \cup \{e_h'\}$. Thus, p_1 can be obtained by applying r_{count} to $\{E, L\}^4$.
- p_1 and p_2 violate f. This fact is proven below.

First we prove that $p_1[\{i_1, \ldots, i_k\}]$ is the same as $p_2[\{i_1, \ldots, i_k\}]$ and then we have to prove that $p_1[i_{k+1}]$ is different from $p_2[i_{k+1}]$.

By construction, $p_2[\{i_1, \ldots, i_k\}] = e_h'[\{i_1, \ldots, i_k\}]$. We saw that $e_h[\{i_1, \ldots, i_k\}] = e_h'[\{i_1, \ldots, i_k\}]$. Therefore, $p_2[\{i_1, \ldots, i_k\}] = e_h[\{i_1, \ldots, i_k\}]$. However, by construction of e_h and p_1, $p_1[\{i_1, \ldots, i_k\}] = e_h[\{i_1, \ldots, i_k\}]$. Therefore, $p_1[\{i_1, \ldots, i_k\}] = p_2[\{i_1, \ldots, i_k\}]$.

By construction, $e_h'[i_{k+1}]$ is the same as $p_2[i_{k+1}]$, then since by construction, $p_1[i_{k+1}] \neq e_h[i_{k+1}]$, if $e_h[i_{k+1}]$ does not change during the $Chase_F(d)$ the proof ends, else the proof continues.

If $e_h[i_{k+1}]$ changes during chase, then $e_h' = e_i$, where $e_i \in E$. Thus, we have by construction:

$$e_i[\{i_1, \ldots, i_k\}] = e_h'[\{i_1, \ldots, i_k\}] = p_1[\{i_1, \ldots, i_k\}]$$

However, since in r_{count} the argument positions $\{i_1, \ldots, i_k, i_{k+1}\}$ are not pivoting, we have that $e_i[i_{k+1}] \neq p_1[i_{k+1}]$, hence, $e_h'[i_{k+1}] \neq p_1[i_{k+1}]$. $\square$

Example 8. Let $P = \{r_0, r_1, r_2\}$ where:
$r_0 : p(X, Y, W, Z) : -e(X, Y, W, Z)$
$r_1 : p(X, Y, W, W) : -a(V, W), e(Y, W, W, V), e(V, Y, W, X), p(X, Y, V, W)$
$r_2 : p(X, Y, W, Q) : -e(X, W, Q, X), p(Y, X, V, V)$

Let F be $\{e : \{1\} \to \{4\}\}$. Let f be $p : \{1\} \to \{4\}$. We want to know if $F \models_P f$. Let us check, for example, $r_1 \circ r_2 \circ r_0$:
$p(X, Y, W, W) : -a(V, W), e(Y, W, W, V), e(V, Y, W, X), e(X, V, W, X), e(Y, X, V', V')$
$Chase_F(r_1 \circ r_2 \circ r_0)$ is:
$p(X, Y, W, W) : -a(V, W), e(Y, W, W, V), e(V, Y, W, X), e(X, V, W, X), e(Y, X, V, V)$

---

[4] Remember that E and L do not change during the chase.

Since positions 1 and 4 are not pivoting in $Chase_F(r_1 \circ r_2 \circ r_0)$, hence $F \not\models_P f$.

$\square$

9   Conclusions and Future Work

We have presented a method to check if a fd will be satisfied by the result of applying a recursive query to a database. Clearly it is cheaper to use our method than computing the recursive query and after that checking whether the result satisfies a given fd. Observe that our method determines if a functional dependency is implied (or not implied) without computing the result. Hence, the computational costs associated with our method are the computation of the chase (that can be done in time polynomial in the size of the rule) and the cost of checking if a set of fds are satisfied by the input database, which is typically smaller than the output database.

Finally, as a future work, we will try to find an *if and only if* condition to solve the FD-FD implication problem for the class $\mathcal{P}$ of Datalog programs.

References

1. S. Abiteboul, R. Hull, and V. Vianu. *Foundations of Databases*. Addison Wesley, 1995.
2. S. Abiteboul and R. Hull. Data functions, datalog and negation. In *Proc. Seventh ACM SIGACT-SIGMOD-SIGART Symposium on Principle of Database Systems*, pages 143–153, 1988.
3. A. V. Aho, C. Beeri, and J. D. Ullman. The theory of joins in relational databases. *ACM TODS*, 4(3):297–314, 1979.
4. W. W. Armstong. Dependency structures of data base relationships. In *Proc. 1974 IFIP Congress*, pages 580–583, 1974.
5. C. Beeri and M. Y. Vardi. A proof procedure for data dependencies. *J. ACM*, 31:718–741, 1984.
6. S. Bell and P. Brockhausen. Discovery of constraints and data dependencies in databases (extended abstract). In *European Conference on Machine Learning*, pages 267–270, 1995.
7. S. Bell. Discovery and maintenance of functional dependencies by independencies. In *Knowledge Discovery and Data Mining*, pages 27–32, 1995.
8. N. R. Brisaboa, A. Gonzalez-Tuchmann, H. J. Hernández, and J. R. Paramá. Chasing programs in datalog. In *Proceedings of the 6th International Workshop on Deductive Databases and Logic Programming DDLP98*, pages 13–23. GMD-Forschungzentrum Informationstechnik GmbH 1998 (GMD Report 22), 1998.
9. A. Gonzalez-Tuchmann. *The chase of datalog programs*. PhD thesis, New Mexico State University, Department of Computer Science, Las Cruces, NM 88003-0001, 1995.
10. D. Maier, A. O. Mendelzon, and Y. Sagiv. Testing implications of data dependencies. *ACM TODS*, 4(4):455–469, 1979.
11. D. Maier. *The Theory of Relational Databases*. Computer Science Press, 1983.
12. J. Melton and A. R. Simon. *SQL:1999 Understanding Relational Language Components*. Morgan Kaufmann, 2002.

13. L. Popa, A. Deutsch, A. Sahuguet, and V. Tannen. A chase too far. In *SIGMOD*, pages 273–284, 2000.
14. L. Popa. *Object/Relational Query Optimization with Chase and Backchase*. PhD thesis, University of Pennsylvania, 2000.
15. J. D. Ullman. *Principles of Database And Knowledge-Base Systems*, volume 1. Computer Science Press, 1988.
16. K. Wang and L. Y. Yuan. Preservation of integrity constraints in definite datalog programs. *Information Processing Letters*, 44(4), 1992.

TeXOR: Temporal XML Database on an Object-Relational Database System

Kjetil Nørvåg*, Marit Limstrand, and Lene Myklebust

Department of Computer and Information Science
Norwegian University of Science and Technology
7491 Trondheim, Norway Kjetil.Norvag@idi.ntnu.no

Abstract. Storage costs are rapidly decreasing, making it feasible to store larger amounts of data in databases. This also makes it possible to store previous versions of data in the databases, instead of only keeping the last version. Recently, the amount of data available in XML has been rapidly increasing. In this paper, we describe *TeXOR*, a temporal XML database system built on top of an object-relational database system. We describe the TXSQL query language used in TeXOR for querying temporal XML documents stored in the system, discuss storage alternatives for XML documents in such a system, and some details about the implementation of the current TeXOR prototype.

1 Introduction

Storage costs are rapidly decreasing, making it feasible to store larger amounts of data in databases. This also makes it possible to store previous versions of data in the databases, instead of only keeping the last version. Recently, the amount of data available in XML has been rapidly increasing. One of the advantages of XML is that a document itself contains information that is normally associated with a schema. This makes it possible to do more precise queries, compared to what has been possible with unstructured data. It also has advantages for long-term storage of data: even though the schema has changed, the data itself can contain sufficient information about the contents, so that meaningful queries can be applied to the data.

When previous versions of data are stored in the database, it is possible to search in the historical (old) versions, retrieve documents that were valid at a certain time, query changes to documents, etc. Our main context is storage of XML documents, and querying versions of these. Thus, we will in this paper restrict the discussion to *transaction-time*, i.e., versions are timestamped with the commit time of the transaction that created the versions (in contrast to *valid time*, where a time interval is associated with every tuple/object, denoting when the object is valid in the modeled world).

---

* Corresponding author

M. Broy and A.V. Zamulin (Eds.): PSI 2003, LNCS 2890, pp. 520–530, 2003.

A temporal database can be realized either through an *integrated* approach, in which the internal modules of a DBMS (database management system) are modified or extended to support time-varying data, or through a *stratum* approach, where a middleware layer converts temporal query language statements into conventional statements, executed by an underlying database system [11]. Although we consider the integrated approach as the long-term solution, it is not appropriate for storing and querying temporal XML data *today*, for the simple reason that no such system with product quality exists. Thus, for the time to come, a stratum approach is the most adequate solution. The stratum approach also makes it possible to utilize the existing support for XML data management in the system (including XPath based queries), in addition to benefit from the quality of the system from a database point of view. Another important reason for choosing a stratum approach is the fact that organizations already have made the investment in systems and databases, making it desirable to use existing database systems for ease of integration as well as economical reasons. This is also the reason why we base our system on a widely available commercial object-relational database system instead of a native XML database system.

In order to demonstrate the usefulness of a temporal XML databases in general, and gain experience from actual use of such systems, we have implemented *TeXOR*, a temporal XML database system on top of the commercial object-relational database system Oracle. In this paper, we describe the functionality of TeXOR, and how we implemented it on top of Oracle. It should be emphasized that although Oracle is used in our prototype, the use of JDBC between TeXOR and Oracle means that it should not be too difficult integrating TeXOR with another system that provides support for XML data. It should also be noted that even if we call TeXOR a temporal *XML* database system, it can also be used for storing general temporal data. However, the design decisions have been made and optimized based on the assumption that temporal XML storage will be its most important application.

The organization of the rest of this paper is as follows. In Section 2 we give an overview of related work. In Section 3 we give an overview of storage of XML documents. In Section 4 we describe the functionality provided by TeXOR. In Section 5 we describe the design and implementation of TeXOR. Finally, in Section 6, we conclude the paper and outline issues for further research.

2   Related Work

A model for representing changes in semistructured data (DOEM) and a language for querying changes (Chorel) were presented by Chawathe et al. in [3, 4]. Chorel queries were translated to Lorel (a language for querying semistructured data), and can therefore be viewed as a stratum approach. The work by Chawathe et al. has later been extended by Oliboni et al. [16].

In order to realize an efficient temporal XML database system, several issues have to be solved, including efficient storage of versioned XML documents, efficient indexing of temporal XML documents, and temporal XML query processing. Storage of versioned documents is studied by Marian et al. [12] and Chien et al. [5,7,6]. Chien et al. also consider access to previous versions, but only snapshot retrievals. Temporal query processing is discussed in [13,14].

An approach that is orthogonal, but related to the work presented in this paper, is to introduce valid time features into XML documents. One such approach is presented by Grandi and Mandreoli in [9].

Obviously, our work is heavily inspired by previous work in extending SQL to the temporal domain, for example TSQL2 [17], and previous systems based on the stratum approach. A good overview of the stratum approach, and systems using it, is given in [19].

Other relevant work includes work on temporal document databases [1], temporal object query languages [8], and temporal object database systems [18].

3   Storage of XML Documents

In order to put our work in context, we will in this section give an overview of alternative approaches for storing XML documents.

3.1   Approaches

At first, XML documents were mostly stored as ordinary text files. This is still common. However, in many cases the features provided by DBMSs are desired, for example support for transactions, recovery and querying. As a result several approaches to support these features have been introduced.

Before we describe the approaches in more detail, it can be useful to have in mind that what will be the best approach for a given application, depends very much on whether the XML documents mostly are document-centric (this is often documents meant for human consumption, like books, papers, etc.), or data-centric (this is often documents meant for computer consumption, and that uses XML as a data transport). Many documents also have features of both categories, we call these hybrid documents.

Several approaches to XML storage in DBMSs have been proposed, and can be classified into three categories:

- **XML-enabled database systems:** Traditional database systems (typically object-relational systems), extended with support for XML documents. Examples of XML-enabled database systems are Oracle, IBM DB2, and Microsoft SQL Server. The supported features include storing/retrieving XML documents, as well as query capabilities. Examples of XML-enabled database systems are Oracle, IBM DB2, and Microsoft SQL Server. In general, the XML documents can be stored in two ways:
  - *In CLOBs:*[1] Each document is essentially an attribute in a tuple. In order to make it possible to efficiently query the documents, the contents is indexed (for example in a text index), in order to avoid scans

---

[1] A CLOB is a large object that holds text data, and is similar to a BLOB, which can store any kind of binary data.

of all the documents stored in one relation. One of the most important advantages of this approach is efficient retrieval of single documents (no need for reconstruction/join operations). This is often a good approach for document-centric documents, where retrievals of complete documents/parts of documents are frequent.

- *Mapped to relations:* The documents are mapped to relations, for example using a *table-based mapping* or a *object-relational mapping* (cf. [2] for a more detailed description of the mapping techniques). This is often a good approach for data-centric documents, where we usually are not interested in retrieving the whole documents, only parts of the data stored in it. These documents also often have a regular structure because they are computer-generated, making the mapping easier.

- **Native XML database systems:** These systems define a data model for XML documents (for example the DOM or XPath data model), and all retrieval/storage is based on this model. This makes it possible to support XML-specific features better and more efficiently than the other approaches. Examples of native XML database systems are the Tamino XML Server, eXcelon Extensible Information Server, and X-Hive/DB.

- **Middleware:** Transfer data between XML documents and databases, usually using protocols as ODBC/JDBC. One variant is transferring XML documents into data in tables. Another approach is simply to store the XML documents as CLOBs in the database system. Often, the support for queries when this approach is used, is limited.

4   TeXOR Functionality

In this section we describe the functionality provided by TeXOR. We describe the query language, and how to access the system through the terminal interface and the API.

4.1   The TXSQL Query Language

The TXSQL query language is an extension of the XPath extended SQL query language that Oracle uses, and it also contains support for declaring and querying temporal tables.

Creating Tables. A temporal tables is created by using the t_time modifier in a create table statement. For example, the following statement creates a temporal table where each row contains an oid and an XML document:

```
create table usertable t_time (
    oid number(8),
    xml sys.xmltype)
```

The result of this statement will be `Table created`. Each tuple in such a table contains timestamp(s), but this is transparent to the user. As will be shown later, the data might be stored in more than one Oracle table, in order to make some operations more efficient.

Querying Time in Temporal Tables. Although the timestamps of the tuples normally are hidden, they can be retrieved by explicitly declaring them in the query statement. The (normally hidden) column containing the timestamp is named `t_start`, and is used in `select`-part of queries when querying temporal tables. For example, issuing the following query:

```
select oid, t_start
from usertable
```

gives the following results (the timestamp consists of date and time):

```
oid        t_start
-------------------------
1          20.05.02 12:15:00
2          23.05.02 08:05:00
```

If `t_start` is not included explicitly, the timestamp is not returned. This also applies when using "*". If only "*" is used to retrieve all columns, the timestamp is not returned.

A version in a temporal database is valid in a certain time interval, from `t_start` to `t_end`. Querying the end time `t_end` can be performed similar to querying for the start time as shown above, and the end timestamp is essentially the start timestamp of the next version.

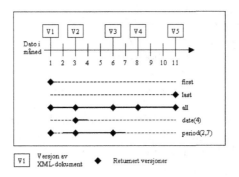

Fig. 1. Some version parameters and the versions they will return

Querying Particular Versions. When querying a temporal table, we often want to restrict the query to particular versions. This could for example be the first version, versions valid at a particular time, or all versions valid during a particular time interval. In TXSQL, the `version` function is used in the `where` part of the `select` statements in order to determine which versions should be involved in the query. In order to specify versions, one of the following parameters is used (also illustrated in Fig. 1, which shows which versions will be returned by using the different parameters):

- `all`: all versions.
- `first`: the first version.
- `last`: the last version (note that in contrast to current versions, a *last* version is not necessarily valid anymore, it could be the last version before deletion).
- `date(timestamp)`: uses a particular timestamp as parameter (we use the DATE type in Oracle for storing timestamps), and returns the versions valid at that time.
- `period(`*timestamp1*`, `*timestamp2*`)`: uses two timestamps as parameters, and returns all versions valid in the period from *timestamp1* to *timestamp2*.

If `version` is not specified, only the current version will be queried, in order to be compatible with non-temporal queries.

Example of use of `version`*:* The following query illustrates how to retrieve all versions of the tuple with a given oid:

```
select x.xml.getClobVal()
from usertable
where oid = 123 and version(all)
```

Note that `xml` is the name of the attribute containing the XMLType data, and that the contents is retrieved by using `getClobVal()`. The result is:

```
x.xml.getClobVal()
-----------------------------------
<name>Per</name><tel>73882934</tel>
<name>Per</name><tel>56894534</tel>
```

4.2   Interface

Users of TeXOR have two interfaces available to the system. One interface is a terminal interface, similar to SQL*Plus in Oracle, and the other is an API for interaction through Java programs.

Terminal Interface. The terminal interface TX has a functionality similar to SQL*Plus in Oracle, but with some extended editing features. From TX the user can connect to the database, enter an TXSQL query, and execute the query. The result from the query is displayed in the terminal window.

API. Even though the terminal interface is nice for testing and experimenting, when using TeXOR from a program, the API is more useful. Using the TeXOR API, the query is submitted as a string to the TeXOR object, and the result can be retrieved by calling another function in the interface.

5   Design of TeXOR

The main part of TeXOR is essentially a middleware layer between the TX/API interfaces and the Oracle DBMS. TeXOR rewrites the TXSQL expressions into SQL, and post-processes the results before they are returned to the user/application. It also manages some extra metadata, for example which tables are temporal tables. The metadata is itself stored in Oracle. In the rest of this section, we will describe in more detail how data is stored. It should again be noted that in the cases where we have several alternative approaches to choose from, the application of XML storage has been the driving decision factor.

5.1   Timestamp Management

There are several alternative approaches to store the timestamp in the database. One is to store the timestamp inside the XML document. However, retrieval of the timestamp is expensive with this alternative. A better alternative in the context we are working, is to store timestamps together with identifier in a separate table. For example, if one table is used to store both historical and current versions, and the user creates a table Usertable with the column XML, the following table will actually be created (and managed):

```
Usertable {oid, xml}
Time_usertable {doc_id, oid, start_time, end_time}
```

The actual storage of timestamps in TeXOR will be described below.

Timestamps will in our system only be used for retrieval/querying purposes, and not for concurrency control or similar purposes. For this reason, it is not critical *when* the timestamp is decided, as long as all document versions stored during one transaction are assigned the same timestamp.[2] If the actual commit timestamp should be used, it would be necessary to postpone until commit time the updates to the table containing the timestamps. This would increase commit time considerably, so that instead, we decide transaction timestamp when the first document is stored in a transaction, and this timestamp also for the other documents stored during this transaction.

---

[2] This is a simplification. For a more thorough discussion on this topic, we refer to [10] and [15].

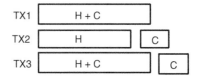

Fig. 2. Storage alternatives

5.2 Storage of Versions

As described previously, XML documents can be stored in Oracle either as 1) CLOBs or 2) by extracting documents into tables. In the TeXOR prototype, only CLOB storage is supported. The main reason for this decision, is that the CLOB alternative 1) permits exact round-trip of documents, and 2) it uses text indexes, which should enhance efficiency for typical XML-queries in our application areas, and in particular for XPath-queries which are supported by this storage alternative.

As illustrated in Fig. 2, there are several alternative approaches for storing a temporal relation:

- TX1: Store both historical (previous) and current versions of the data in one relation. This is the easiest alternative, and in this case the temporal table is essentially the non-temporal equivalent with additional timestamp attributes for start and end time. Although simple to realize, this approach can have problems in some queries for current versions. If a table scan is necessary, it is necessary to scan all the historical versions in addition to the current versions.
- TX2: Store historical and current versions in separate relations. Using this approach, the previous current version is moved to the historical relation when it is updated, and the new current version inserted into the current version relation. Using this approach, only start time is needed in the current version relation, and that might save some space. The most important advantage of this approach is efficient queries for current versions, as all these are stored in a separate table. This table is likely to be much smaller than the size of the historical table.
- TX3: Store current versions in a separate relation, and historical versions plus a copy of current versions in another relation. A possible advantage of this approach is that queries for current versions are efficient, and at the same time queries involving all versions are simple because only one table is involved. However, this is not likely to outweight the disadvantages of using more space, which will in particular be a problem in the case of few versions of each tuple.

Based on the informal arguments given above, we decided to use alternative TX2. This alternative also has the additional advantage of simplifying the vacuuming process, because only historical versions need to be considered. The tables that are created in the ORDBMS for one temporal table in TeXOR, are summarized as an example in Fig. 3.

OID	XML
3	\<name>Ola\</name>
4	\<name>Kari\</name> \<tlf>555 4826\</tlf>
5	\<name>Lise\</name> \<age>26\< /age>

(a) Usertable

DocOID	OID	Start_Time
3	3	20.04.02 12:45:00
1	4	24.04.02 08:05:00
2	5	03.05.02 09:00:00

(b) time_Usertable

OID	XML
1	\<name>Kari\</name> \<tlf>555 2345\</tlf>
2	\<name>Lise\</name> \<age>24\</age>

(c) Usertable_old

DocOID	Oid	Start_Time	End_Time
1	1	02.03.02 12:00:00	24.04.02 08:05:00
2	2	20.03.02 07:15:00	03.05.02 09:00:00

(d) time_Usertable_old

Fig. 3. ORDBMS tables used for one TeXOR temporal table

6   Summary

We have in this paper described stratum temporal XML database management, based on an object-relational database system. In order to provide support for querying temporal data, we designed the TXSQL query language, which is SQL extended with support for querying versions and temporal aspects. The ideas have been realized in the TeXOR prototype, where most aspects described in the paper have been integrated, except vacuuming, granularity control, and some of the version selection support.

As a result of using a stratum approach, some problems and bottlenecks are inevitable. For example, no efficient time-index for our purpose is available, and query optimization can be a problem when part of the "knowledge" is outside the database system. Thus, we suspect that for large amounts of data, where disk accesses are needed, query cost can be high. However, it should be kept in mind that with the improving size of main memory the effect of this is not necessarily disastrous. For example, a desktop computer today often has 512MB or more of main memory.

It should be noted that even if we call TeXOR a temporal XML database system, it can also be used for storing general temporal data. However, the design decisions have been made and optimized based on the assumption that temporal XML storage will be its most important application.

The rationale behind the development of TeXOR was to gain experience in temporal XML data management, and results so far have been useful input to the V2 project, which is another temporal XML database project we are currently working on (see [15]). In the V2 project, we study more in more detail the aspects of efficiency in temporal XML databases. V2 is based on an integrated approach, where also the more low-level parts of the system are implemented.

Acknowledgments. We would like to thank Jon Olav Hauglid for help during the implementation of TeXOR, and for volunteering for the job as database administrator. We would also like to thank Gregory Cobena for providing us with temporal XML testdata.

References

1. M. J. Aramburu-Cabo and R. B. Llavori. A temporal object-oriented model for digital libraries of documents. *Concurrency and Computation: Practice and Experience*, 13(11), 2001.
2. R. Bourret. XML and databases, February 2002 (most recent version available at http://www.rpbourret.com/xml/XMLAndDatabases.htm).
3. S. S. Chawathe, S. Abiteboul, and J. Widom. Representing and querying changes in semistructured data. In *Proceedings of the Fourteenth International Conference on Data Engineering*, 1998.
4. S. S. Chawathe, S. Abiteboul, and J. Widom. Managing historical semistructured data. *TAPOS*, 5(3), 1999.
5. S.-Y. Chien, V. J. Tsotras, and C. Zaniolo. A comparative study of version management schemes for XML documents (short version published at WebDB 2000). Technical Report TR-51, TimeCenter, 2000.
6. S.-Y. Chien, V. J. Tsotras, and C. Zaniolo. Efficient management of multiversion documents by object referencing. In *Proceedings of VLDB 2001*, 2001.
7. S.-Y. Chien, V. J. Tsotras, and C. Zaniolo. Version management of XML documents: Copy-based versus edit-based schemes. In *Proceedings of the 11th International Workshop on Research Issues on Data Engineering: Document management for data intensive business and scientific applications (RIDE-DM'2001)*, 2001.
8. L. Fegaras and R. Elmasri. A temporal object query language. In *Proceedings of the Fifth International Workshop on Temporal Representation and Reasoning*, 1998.
9. F. Grandi and F. Mandreoli. The valid web: An XML/XSL infrastructure for temporal management of web documents. In *Proceedings of Advances in Information Systems, First International Conference, ADVIS 2000*, 2000.
10. C. S. Jensen and D. B. Lomet. Transaction timestamping in (temporal) databases. In *Proceedings of the 27th VLDB Conference*, 2001.

11. C. S. Jensen and R. T. Snodgrass. Temporal data management. *IEEE Transactions on Knowledge and Data Engineering*, 11(1), 1999.
12. A. Marian, S. Abiteboul, G. Cobena, and L. Mignet. Change-centric management of versions in an XML warehouse. In *Proceedings of VLDB 2001*, 2001.
13. K. Nørvåg. Algorithms for temporal query operators in XML databases. In *Proceedings of Workshop on XML-Based Data Management (XMLDM) (in conjunction with EDBT'2002)*, 2002.
14. K. Nørvåg. Temporal query operators in XML databases. In *Proceedings of the 17th ACM Symposium on Applied Computing (SAC'2002)*, 2002.
15. K. Nørvåg. The design, implementation and performance evaluation of the V2 temporal document database system. Technical Report IDI 10/2002, Norwegian University of Science and Technology, 2002. Available from http://www.idi.ntnu.no/grupper/DB-grp/.
16. B. Oliboni, E. Quintarelli, and L. Tanca. Temporal aspects of semistructured data. In *Proceeding of TIME-01*, 2001.
17. R. T. Snodgrass (ed.), I. Ahn, G. Ariav, D. S. Batory, J. Clifford, C. E. Dyreson, R. Elmasri, F. Grandi, C. S. Jensen, W. Käfer, N. Kline, K. G. Kulkarni, T. Y. C. Leung, N. A. Lorentzos, J. F. Roddick, A. Segev, M. D. Soo, and S. M. Sripada. *The TSQL2 temporal query language*. Kluwer Academic, 1995.
18. A. Steiner. *A Generalisation Approach to Temporal Data Models and their Implementations*. PhD thesis, Swiss Federal Institute of Technology, 1998.
19. K. Torp, C. S. Jensen, and R. T. Snodgrass. Stratum approaches to temporal DBMS implementation. In *Proceedings of the 1998 International Database Engineering and Applications Symposium*, 1998.

Functional Dependencies, from Relational to XML

Jixue Liu, Millist Vincent, and Chengfei Liu

School of Computer and Information Science
The University of South Australia
{jixue.liu, millist.vincent, chengfei.liu}@unisa.edu.au

Abstract. The flexibility of XML allows the same data to be represented in many different ways. Some representations may be better than others in that they require less storage or have less redundancy. In this paper we define functional dependencies in XML (XFDs) and investigate their effect on the design of XML documents. We then define two subtypes of XFDs, namely partial and transitive XFDs, which cause the same problems in XML document design as the corresponding types of FDs in relations. We further show that the removal of such types of XFDs can lead to a better document design. On the basis of this, we define the concept of upward XFDs and analyze its use in maximizing the nesting levels in XML documents without introducing redundancy. We further propose guidelines to nesting elements in XML documents.
Keywords: XML, functional dependency, normalization

1   Introduction

XML has become accepted as the universal standard for data interchange and publication on the internet. Because of its flexible syntax, XML allows the same data to be represented in many different ways. Similar to relational databases, some XML documents may be better designed than others in that they may require less storage or have less redundancy. In relational databases, the basis for deciding between different database designs is the theory of functional dependencies and normalization. However, in spite of the variety of integrity constraints that have been defined for XML [6,3,5], functional dependencies in XML (XFDs) have attracted little attention.

A few papers relate to the issue of XFDs [4,7,1]. Only the paper [1] has addressed the issue of how to define FDs in XML. The functional dependencies defined in [1] are on both internal nodes and on leaf nodes of XML trees and a normal form is proposed for XML documents. However, because the internal nodes of a XML tree do not have counterpart in the relational model, the involvement of internal nodes in the XFD definition and normal form in [1] causes difficulties in comparing relational database design techniques to XML document design techniques. This paper adopts a different approach to define XFDs so that the definition of XFDs does not involve internal nodes of XML trees.

M. Broy and A.V. Zamulin (Eds.): PSI 2003, LNCS 2890, pp. 531–538, 2003.
© Springer-Verlag Berlin Heidelberg 2003

The focus of this paper is to define XFDs and then to compare various classes of XFDs with FDs in relations and their effect on XML document design. We do this by firstly define XFDs for XML trees. We note that XFDs are defined on only the leaf nodes of a XML tree to match FDs of relations. The XFDs we define are not on internal nodes of the XML tree because internal nodes have no counterpart in relations. We then define two sub classes of XFDs, partial XFDs and transitive XFDs, and show that they can lead to similar problems in the design of XML documents as the same types of FDs in relational databases. We also show that the design problems can be eliminated if the partial and transitive dependencies are removed. We note that we are not aiming to define a normal form in this paper, we are merely illustrating that some types of XFDs cause the same problems in XML documents as they do in relational database. We believe that the development of appropriate normal forms for XML is a more complex and subtle issue and will address the issue in a forthcoming paper.

Another focus of this paper is to discuss the problem of maximizing the nesting levels of XML documents without introducing redundancy. This is done by defining the concept of upward XFDs. On the basis of this, we propose guidelines to nesting elements of XML documents.

We start our presentation by using an example.

2   An Example

In this section, we give an example of a relation and RFDs on it. We then consider a XML representation of the relation. In the sections following, we define functional dependencies for XML and compare the relational functional dependencies on the relation with the XML functional dependencies on the XML representation.

Table 1. A relation

Did	Eid	Ename	Pid	Pname
d1	e1	john	p1	mining
d1	e2	fred	p2	integration
d2	e1	john	p2	integration

(FD1) Did,Eid → Pid
(FD2) Eid → Ename
(FD3) Pid → Pname

Table 1 depicts a relation that stores the data about departments, employees, projects and their relationships. As the functional dependencies to the right of the table shows, a department is identified by Did. An employee is identified by (Eid) and has a name (Ename). A project has an ID (Pid) and a name (Pname). Each department and employee pair uniquely identifies a project. Furthermore, Eid and Did comprise an key.

We note that FD2 is a partial dependency and FD3 is a transitive dependency. We also note that these functional dependencies are satisfied by the relation instance and because of the partial dependency and the transitive dependency, this relation is not normalized. It is obvious that redundancy exists in the table since, for example, the same employee name "john" is stored twice in the relation.

We now give a XML representation of the relation in Table 1. Because XML syntax allows information to be represented in different structures, there are many correct XML structures for representing Table 1. We have decided to employ the direct translation of each relation tuple to a XML tree branch. The translated XML tree is given in Fig. 1.

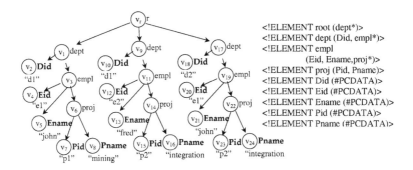

Fig. 1. A XML representation of Table 1

As in its relational counterpart, the XML tree representation has redundancy. In the following sections, we discuss, from a functional dependency point of view, how this redundancy can be avoided during XML document design.

3   XML Functional Dependencies

In this section, we define XML functional dependencies. The notation used in this sections are formally defined in [8].

Let $\mathcal{D}$ be a graph representing an XML DTD which has a unique element called *root*. Let $\mathcal{T}$ be a tree representing an XML instance that conforms to $\mathcal{D}$. A path p is defined to be the path in $\mathcal{D}$ from *root* to an element or an attribute n. A path instance s over p, denoted by $s \prec p$, in $\mathcal{T}$ is a sequence of nodes in $\mathcal{T}$ such that each node is labelled with the corresponding elements (attributes) from p. The intersection of two paths p and q, denoted by $p \cap q$, is the maximum prefix of p and q, which is also a path . The intersection of two path instances of $s \prec p$ and $t \prec q$, denoted by $s \cap t$, is the maximum prefix of s and t, which is also a path instance. If $s \cap t$ is over the path $p \cap q$, s and t are fellows. Let P be a set of path and S be a set of path instances. S is defined to be over P if (1) for every path $p \in P$ there is one and only one instance $s \prec p$ in S; (2) any pair of instances s_i and s_j in S are fellows. The value of S, denoted by $instSetVal(S)$, is defined by the set $\{instval(s)|s \in S\}$ where $instval(s)$ is the constant string on the end node of s. If the end node of s is not a leaf node, $instval(s)$ is not defined. Let P and Q be two path sets. Let S be an instance set over P and T be an instance set over Q. S and T are fellow sets if $\forall s_i \in S$ and $\forall t_j \in T$, s_i and t_j are fellows. When $P = Q$, S and T are fellow sets if $S = T$.

Definition 3.1 (XML functional dependency) A XML functional dependency (XFD) is a statement that P functionally determines Q, denoted by $P \to Q$, where P and Q are two sets of primary paths in a XML DTD $\mathcal{D}$. P is called the left-hand side (LHS) or determinant and Q is called the right-hand side (RHS) or dependent.

A XML tree $\mathcal{T}$ conforming to the DTD **satisfies** the XFD if for any two instance sets T_1 and T_2 over Q, $instSetVal(T_1) \neq instSetVal(T_2)$, then there exist non-empty $\hat{S}_1$, the set of all fellow sets of T_1 over P, and non-empty $\hat{S}_2$, the set of all fellow sets of T_2 over P, such that $\exists S_1 \neq null \in (\hat{S}_1 - \hat{S}_2) \wedge \exists S_2 \neq null \in (\hat{S}_2 - \hat{S}_1)$, $instSetVal(S_1) \neq instSetVal(S_2)$. A XFD is **single RHSed** if there is only one path in Q. Otherwise, it is multiple RHSed. If there is only one path in P or Q, we use the path to replace the path set.

Example 3.1 Let $P=\{\texttt{r.dept.empl.Eid}\}$ and $Q =\{\texttt{r.dept.empl.Ename}\}$. Then the XFD $P \to Q$ is satisfied by the tree in Fig. 1. We arbitrarily choose two instance sets of Q: $T_1 = \{v_r.v_1.v_3.v_5\}$ and $T_2 = \{v_r.v_9.v_{11}.v_{13}\}$. $instSetVal(T_1)=$ $\{\text{"john"}\}\neq$ $instSetVal(T_2)=\{\text{"fred"}\}$. There exist two instance sets $S_1 = \{v_r.v_1.v_3.v_4\}$ and $S_2 = \{v_r.v_9.v_{11}.v_{12}\}$ over P, S_1 being the only fellow set of T_1 and S_2 the only fellow set of T_2, $S_1 \neq S_2$, such that $instSetVal(S_1)=\{\text{"e1"}\}\neq$ $instSetVal(S_2)=\{\text{"e2"}\}$. The tree satisfies the XFD.

Definition 3.2 (XFD implication) Let Σ be a set of XFDs over a DTD $\mathcal{D}$ and $P' \to Q'$ be a XFD over $\mathcal{D}$. Σ implies $P' \to Q'$ if every XML tree $\mathcal{T}$ that conforms to $\mathcal{D}$ and satisfies Σ also satisfies $P' \to Q'$. Then we use Σ^+ to denote all XFDs implied by Σ.

Theorem 3.1 *Let P and Q be path sets over a DTD $\mathcal{D}$. $P \to Q$ implies $P \to q_i$ ($\forall q_i \in Q$); $P \to q_i$ ($\forall q_i \in Q$) implies $P \to Q$.*

Definition 3.3 (Partial XFD) $P \to Q$ is a partial XFD if there exists another XFD $P' \to Q'$ in Σ^+, $Q \cap P = \phi$, such that $P \subset P'$.

Definition 3.4 (Transitive XFD) $P \to Q$ ($P \cap Q = \phi$) is a transitive XFD if there exists another XFD $P' \to P$ ($P' \cap P = \phi$) in Σ^+ and $P' \cap Q = \phi$. $P' \to P$ is called the primary XFD of the transitive XFD.

We use Fig. 1 to show examples. The following XFDs hold over the tree in Fig. 1.

   (XFD1)   `{r.dept.Did, r.dept.empl.Eid} → r.dept.empl.proj.Pid`
   (XFD2)   `r.dept.empl.Eid → r.dept.empl.Ename`
   (XFD3)   `r.dept.empl.proj.Pid → r.dept.empl.proj.Pname`

By the definitions above, we see that XFD2 is partial dependency because we can find XFD1 such that the LHS of XFD2 is contained in the LHS of XFD1. We also see that XFD3 is a transitive dependency because the LHS of XFD3 is the RHS of XFD1. Consequently, these functional dependencies correspond to their flat relation counterparts FD1-FD3 given in Section 2 (see Page 532).

4   Design Issues

In this section, we discuss design issues of XML. We note that in this paper, we aim to improve XML DTD design, but do not propose a normal form. Normal forms in XML have been proposed in [1,4]. The normal form defined in [1] requires XFDs defined on internal nodes. This is not always the case because internal nodes in XML trees do not have counterparts in the relational model. When data in a relational database is exported to XML, the XFDs translated would be primary. The normal form defined in [4] requires functional dependencies defined in a conceptual model which limits its use to those situation where XML document is derived from a high level conceptual models. We believe the problem of normal form is more complex when XFDs do not involve internal nodes or no keys [2] are involved. As a result, we focus on improving XML document design.

In the relational model, if a relation has partial dependencies or transitive dependencies, then the relation potentially has redundancy. The relation can be normalized by decomposing the relation into smaller relations such that the decomposed relations do not have partial or transitive dependencies. This method of normalization can be extended to XML design.

Proposition 4.1 *Let Σ be a set of XFDs over a DTD. Then Σ is redundant if there are partial and transitive XFDs in Σ^+.*

The correctness of the proposition can be shown by the XML tree in Fig. 1 which has redundancy. Note that DTD has redundancy means as long as there exists a tree conforming to the DTD and having redundancy.

A DTD containing partial and transitive XFDs can be transformed to one that does not containing partial and transitive XFDs and redundancy can be removed in this way. The transformation is done by Algorithm E.1 in [8]. The algorithm also transforms XFDs that applicable to the old DTD to those that are applicable to the new DTD. The main idea of the algorithm is to move partial and transitive XFD graphs to the root of the DTD.

When a DTD is transformed from $\mathcal{D}$ to $\mathcal{D}'$, a tree $\mathcal{T}$ conformed to $\mathcal{D}$has to be transformed accordingly to $\mathcal{T}'$ so that $\mathcal{T}'$ conforms to $\mathcal{D}'$. This is done by

Algorithm E.2 in [8]. The algorithm also removes duplicating path instances to make XFD instance tree concise. Fig. 2 shows a XML tree which is transformed from Fig. 1 using the above tree transformation algorithms.

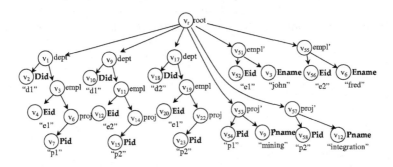

Fig. 2. The normalized tree of Table 1

The existence of partial and transitive functional dependencies is only a necessary conditions for redundancy.

5   Upward XFDs and the Depth of Nesting

Removing redundancy from a XML document is an important rule in XML design as we discussed above. At the same time, a XML document is expected to have maximum depth of nesting. This not only gives a natural representation of application data as done in the nested relations and object-oriented database, but also improves the performance of query execution. For example, in a university application, if Employee is nested under Department and Department is nested under University, then no joins are needed in a query to find employees of a university. However, if Employee, Department, and University are on the same level (no nesting) of a XML design, then answering the query would need to join the document two times, which is very inefficient.

In this section, we investigate the possibility of maximizing the depth of nesting. In other words, we investigate what are guide lines in designing XML DTD such that a DTD has maximum depth and at the same time does not contain redundancy. We do this by firstly defining upward XFDs. In the following definitions, for a path $p = r \cdot l_1 \cdots l_{n-1} \cdot l_n$, the function $parentPath(p)$ is defined to return the path $r \cdot l_1 \cdots l_{n-1}$ and the function $parentEle(p)$ is defined to return the element l_{n-1}. Let $q = r \cdot l'_1 \cdots l'_{m-1} \cdot l'_m$. q is a strict prefix of p if $m < n$ and for $1 \leq i \leq m$, $l'_i = l_i$.

Definition 5.1 Let $\mathcal{F} = \{p_1, ..., p_n\} \to q$ be a XFD. Let $p' = parentPath(p_1) \cap \cdots \cap parentPath(p_n)$. Then $\mathcal{F}$ is upward if $q \cap p'$ is a strict prefix of p'.

For example in Fig. 3, the XFD $r.U.D.Dk \rightarrow r.U.Uk$ is upward because $r.U$ is a strict prefix of $r.U.D$. Similarly, $r.U.D.E.Ek \rightarrow r.U.D.Dk$ is also upward.

Theorem 5.1 *Let $p \rightarrow q$ and $q \rightarrow v$ be two single-LHSed upward XFDs. Then $parentEle(p)$ are child elements of $parentPath(q)$. The redundancy on v, if any, can be removed by running the compact operation defined in [8].*

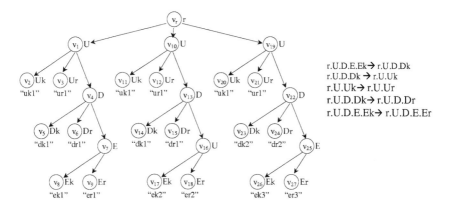

r.U.D.E.Ek➔ r.U.D.Dk
r.U.D.Dk ➔ r.U.Uk
r.U.Uk➔ r.U.Ur
r.U.D.Dk➔ r.U.D.Dr
r.U.D.E.Ek➔ r.U.D.E.Er

Fig. 3. Upward XFDs

The compact operation is defined specifically to remove redundancy at the same time to keep the number of nesting levels when upward transitive dependencies exists. For example in Fig. 3, $r.U.D.Dk \rightarrow r.U.Uk$ and $r.U.D.E.Ek \rightarrow r.U.D.Dk$ are upward XFDs. The XML tree contains redundancy on Ur and Dr. However, here we do not need to restructure the tree. We can simply remove the redundancy by run the compact operation.

For a XFD that is multi-LHSed, it often contains partial XFDs and therefore contains redundancy. The redundancy can be removed by restructuring the design using Algorithms E.1 and E.2 in [8]. However, the algorithms also remove the nesting structure. This concludes that it is not possible to nest elements under a multi-LHSed XFD without introducing redundancy.

In summary, nesting without introducing redundancy is only possible for single-LHSed upward XFDs. The way of constructing nesting can be guided by Theorem 5.1. Furthermore, nesting under multi-LHSed XFDs introduces redundancy.

6   Conclusion

In this paper, we gave our our definition of XML functional dependencies with the aim of comparing the definition with the definition of its relational counterpart. On basis of this, we defined partial and transitive XFDs and studied the inference rules of XFDs. Based on this, we extended the relational normalization method to XML to improve XML document design. We proposed two algorithms for DTD and XML tree normalization. Finally, we investigated the possibility of maximizing the nesting depth of XML design by defining upward XFDs and proposed a guideline for XML design.

References

1. Marcelo Arenas and Leonid Libkin. A normal form for xml documents. *PODS*, 2002.
2. Peter Buneman, Susan Davidson, Wenfei Fan, Carmem Hara, and Wang-Chiew Tan. Keys for xml. *10th www*, May 2001.
3. Peter Buneman, Susan Davidson, Wenfei Fan, Carmem Hara, and WangChiew Tan. Reasoning about keys for xml. *DBPL*, 2001.
4. D.W. Embley and W.Y. Mok. Developing xml documents with guaranteed "good" properties. *ER*, pages 426–441, 2001.
5. Wenfei Fan and Leonid Libkin. On xml integrity constraints in the presence of dtd's. *PODS*, pages 114–125, 2001.
6. Wenfei Fan and Jérôme Siméon. Integrity constraints for xml. *PODS*, pages 23–34, 2000.
7. Mong Li Lee, Tok Wang Ling, and Wai Lup Low. Designing functional dependencies for xml. *VIII Conference on Extending Database Technology (EDBT)*, 2002.
8. Jixue Liu, Millist Vincent, and Chengfei Liu. Functional dependencies, from relational to xml. *http://www.cis.unisa.edu.au/ cisjl/tech_report/subm2-psi03xmlRelFD-DTD.ps*, 2003.

Data-Object Replication, Distribution, and Mobility in Network Environments

Joaquín Pérez O.[1], Rodolfo A. Pazos[1], René Santaolaya[1], Juan Frausto S.[2], Guillermo Rodríguez O.[3], Laura Cruz R.[4], and Maricela Bravo C.[1]

[1] Centro Nacional de Investigación y Desarrollo Tecnológico (CENIDET)
AP 5-164, Cuernavaca, Mor. 62490, México
{jperez, pazos, mari_clau}@sd-cenidet.com.mx
[2] ITESM, Campus Cuernavaca, México
AP C-99, Cuernavaca, Mor. 62589, México
juan.frausto@itesm.mx
[3] Instituto de Investigación Eléctricas, México
AP 475, Cuernavaca, Mor. 62490, México
gro@iie.org.mx
[4] Instituto Tecnológico de Ciudad Madero, México
lcruzr@prodigy.net

Abstract. In this paper we address the problem of replication, allocation and mobility of large data-objects in network environments that may be exposed to significant changes in users' location, usage and access patterns. In these circumstances, if the design is not adapted to the new changes, the system can undergo a severe degradation in data access costs and response time. In order to solve this problem, we propose a formal model to generate a new data-object allocation and replication. The model uses current state information of the system and usage statistical data collected during a given period, and adapts the system to the new users' location and usage patterns so as to minimize communication costs. Implicitly the mathematical model handles mobility and temporality. Model tests have been conducted with satisfactory and promising results. The principles used in the model can be applied to other models for the optimization of resources in network environments like the Web.

1 Introduction

The new requirements of large organizations to carry out their activities in a geographically dispersed way, the development of the communication and Distributed Database Management System (DDBMS) technologies, and the reduction in computer costs, facilitate the implementation of Distributed Database Systems. However, the distribution characteristics offered by commercial DDBMS's should be implemented and managed by expert professionals so that they can provide outstanding benefits.

One of the most difficult problems for the development of databases (DB's) on the Web is the lack of robust methodologies and design assistance tools [1,2,3].

M. Broy and A.V. Zamulin (Eds.): PSI 2003, LNCS 2890, pp. 539–545, 2003.
© Springer-Verlag Berlin Heidelberg 2003

In particular, the logical design is an important factor for the good performance of a distributed system, and determining the data allocation in the system is a complex task. Considering that the nature of distributed systems is dynamic, with changes in network topology, users' location, data access frequencies, costs and resources, the problem becomes even more complex.

Nowadays, the system administrator establishes the initial design of the DB on the Web using his experience and intuition, which remains fixed for some time until he considers that the system has changed significantly. A distributed system with a static design could undergo severe performance degradation because of its inability to adapt to changes in usage, access and data scaling [4,5,6,7]. In this work an approach is proposed to avoid system degradation by designing allocation schemas in an adaptive and scalable way.

A mathematical model is proposed for the design of database-object replication and allocation schemas, starting from the current state of the system and statistical data of usage and access. Experimental tests were carried out with the model to determine its ability to adapt to changes in usage and access patterns and scaling of data.

2   Mathematical Model of Data-Object Replication and Allocation

In order to describe the model and its properties, the following definition is introduced:

Data-object: Entity of a database that requires to be allocated and possibly replicated, which can be an attribute, a relation or a file.

2.1   Description of the Allocation and Replication Problem

The proposed model considers data-objects as independent units that must be allocated in the sites of a network. The model allows generating new allocation schemas that adapt to changes in usage and access patterns of read and write applications; therefore, making the database schema adapt to the dynamic characteristic of a distributed system and avoiding system degradation. The problem consists of allocating data-objects such that the total cost of data transmission for processing all the applications is minimized. The allocation and replication problem is defined as follows:

Assume there are a set of data-objects $O = \{o_1, o_2, \ldots, o_n\}$, a computer communication network that consists of a set of sites $S = \{s_1, s_2, \ldots, s_n\}$, where a set of queries $Q = (q_1, q_2, \ldots, q_n)$ are executed, an initial data-object allocation schema, and the access frequencies of each query from each site. The problem consists of obtaining a new allocation and replication schema that adapts to a new database usage pattern and minimizes transmission costs. Note that a new schema involves mobility of data.

2.2   Objective Function

The integer (binary) programming model proposed consists of an objective function and seven intrinsic constraints. In this model the decision about storing a data-object m, or a replica in site j is represented by a binary variable x_{mj}. Thus, $x_{mj} = 1$ if m is stored in j, and $x_{mj} = 0$ otherwise.

The objective function below (1) models costs using three terms: 1) the transmission cost incurred for processing all the read applications, 2) the transmission cost incurred for processing all the write applications, and 3) the transmission cost for migrating and replicating data-objects between nodes.

$$\min z = \sum_k \sum_j f_{kj} \sum_m \sum_i q_{km} l_{km} c_{ji} w_{jmi} + \sum_k \sum_j cu f'_{kj} \tag{1}$$

$$\sum_m \sum_i q'_{km} l'_{km} c_{ji} x_{mi} + \sum_j \sum_m \sum_i w'_{jmi} c_{ji} d_m$$

where

f_{kj} = emission frequency of read application k from site j, during a given period of time;

f'_{kj} = emission frequency of write application k from site j, during a given period of time;

q_{km} = usage parameter, $q_{km} = 1$ if read application k uses data-object m, otherwise $q_{km} = 0$;

q'_{km} = usage parameter, $q'_{km} = 1$ if write application k uses data-object m, otherwise $q'_{km} = 0$;

l_{km} = number of packets for transporting the items of data-object m required by read application k;

l'_{km} = number of packets for transporting the items of data-object m required by write application k;

c_{ij} = communication cost between sites i and j;

cu = cost for each data-object replication protocol;

w_{jmi} = decision variable, $w_{jmi} = 1$ if from site j data-object m (located at sites i) is used; otherwise $w_{jmi} = 0$;

w'_{jmi} = decision variable, $w'_{jmi} = 1$ if from site j data-object m is replicated to site i; otherwise $w'_{jmi} = 0$;

x_{mi} = decision variable, $x_{mi} = 1$ if data-object m is located at site i; otherwise $x_{mi} = 0$;

d_m = number of packets for moving or replicating data-object m to another site if necessary.

2.3 Problem Intrinsic Constraints

The model solutions are subject to seven constraints, which are formulated in expressions (2) to (8), having the following meaning. Expression (2): each data-object must be stored at least in one site. Expression (3): each data-object must be stored in a site that executes at least one query that uses it. Expressions (4) and (5): variables w_j are forced to adopt values compatible with those of x_{mj}. Expression (6): site storage capacity must not be exceeded by the data-objects stored in each site. Expressions (7) and (8): each replica of a data-object is created at some site from only one copy of the data-object and from a site it was previously located.

$$\sum_j x_{mj} = 1$$
$$\forall m$$

Each object must be stored at last in one site. (2)

$$x_{mi} \le \sum_k q_{km}\varphi_{ki}$$
$$\forall m, i$$

Each data-object m must be stored in a site i that executes at least one query k involving the data-object; where

$$\varphi_{ki} = \begin{cases} 1 & \text{if } f_{ki} > 0 \\ 0 & \text{if } f_{ki} = 0 \end{cases}$$

(3)

$$ns\ x_{mi} - \sum_j w_{jmi} \ge 0$$
$$\forall m, i$$

This constraint forces the value of x_{mi} to 1 when any w_{jmi} equals 1, and induces x_{mi} to 0 otherwise, where

ns = number of sites.

(4)

$$\sum_i w_{jmi} - \theta = 0$$
$$\forall m, j$$

This constraint forces access to one replica of data-object m for each applitacion issued at site j.

$$\theta_{jm} = \begin{cases} 1 & \text{if } \sum_k f_{ki}q_{km} > 0 \\ 0 & \text{if } \sum_k f_{ki}q_{km} = 0 \end{cases}$$

(5)

$$\sum_m p_m x_{mi} CA = CS_i$$
$$\forall i$$

The space occupied by all data-object stored in site j must not exceed te site capacity, where
CS_i = capacity of site i;
p_m = size in bytes of data-object m;
CA = cardinality of the data-object (numbers of rows, if the data-object is a relation or an attribute; number of records, if the data-object is a file)

(6)

$$\sum_j w'_{jmi} - x_{mi} = 0$$
$$\forall m, i$$

One replica of data-object m is created at site i from only one data-object m at site j.

(7)

$$w'_{jmi} - a_{mj} \leq 0$$
$$\forall j, m, i$$

One replica of data-object m is created at site i from the previous location af the data-object m at site j; where
a_{mj} = indicates if data-object m was previously located in site j.

(8)

3   Interpretation of the Allocation and Replication Model

The proposed data-object allocation and replication model implicitly handles changes in users's location, usage and access patterns and scaling of data in order to avoid system degradation. In the following sections an interpretation of the allocation, replication and adaptation capability of the model will be given.

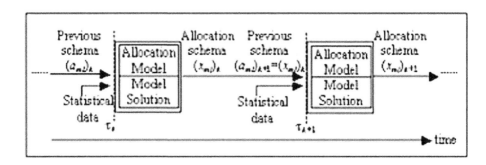

Fig. 1. Temporality of the data allocation model

3.1   Adaptability

When the mathematical model is solved at time τ_k, the inputs are: matrix $(a_{mi})_k = (x_{mj})_{k-1}$ that represents the allocation schema of the system at a time prior to τ_k and the statistics of database usage collected during a given period. The output is the data-object allocation $(x_{mj})_k$ generated at current time τ_k. For the model solution at a subsequent time τ_{k+1}, the allocation schema $(x_{mj})_k$, generated at time τ_k, is assigned to $(a_{mi})_{k+1}$ for representing the previous schema of the system (Fig. 1).

3.2   Scaling of Data

The nature of distributed systems is dynamic; for example, in some time interval the number of sites or access frequencies to data-objects may change positively or negatively. In the proposed model the size of the problem is represented by the matrices and vectors dimensions. In order to take into account problem size changes, it is just necessary to redimension the matrices and vectors used in the model before solving it.

Specifically, redimensioning is made when changes in the following parameters occur: the number of data-objects, the number of queries issued in the system, and the number of computer network sites. Therefore, when the number of sites increases, the number of elements of matrices x_{mj} and a_{mi} is increased too, and the new elements of this last matrix are set to 0.

4   Final Remarks

The experimental results show that the proposed model can be used for generating allocating and replication schemas of large-scale data-objects for the Web. This paper shows that the model incorporates implicitly adaptability, mobility and temporality. In particular, it permits to generate allocation and replication schemas adapted to changes in users' location, usage and access patterns to data-objects, which normally occur during system operation.

The design of allocation and replication schemas is an NP-complete problem, and this characteristic impacts in a decisive way the solution of large scale problems. In the tests carried out an exact method was used to solve the model with very good results regarding solution quality and processing time. A previous version of model was solved using approximate methods, in particular the Threshold Accepting Algorithm, with good results [8,9,10].

Currently, we are formulating a new model to treat data-object replication, in order to apply the model to data hoarding in databases accessed by mobile clients (wireless computation).

References

1. Oszu, M., Valduries, P.: Principles of Distributed Database Systems. Prentice-Hall (1999).

2. Navathe, S., Karlapalem, K., Ra, M.: A Mixed Fragmentation Methodology for Initial Distributed Database Design. In Journal of Computer and Software Engineering, Vol. 3, No. 4 (1995).
3. Florescu, D., Levy, A., Mendelzon, A.: Database Techniques for the World-Wide Web: A Survey. SIGMOD Record, Vol. 27, No.3. (1998) 59-74.
4. Wolfson, O., Jajodia, S., Huang, Y.: An Adaptive Data Replication Algorithm. ACM Transactions on Database Systems, Vol. 22, No. 4 (1997) 255-314.
5. Tamhankar, A.M., Sudha R.: Database Fragmentation and Allocation: An Integrated Methodology and Case Study (1998).
6. Pérez, J.: Integración de la Fragmentación Vertical y Ubicación en el Diseño Adaptivo de Bases de Datos Distribuidas. Ph.D. thesis, ITESM Campus Cuernavaca, Mexico (1999).
7. Lin, X., Oslowska, M., Zhang, Y.: On Data Allocation with the Minimum Overall Communication Costs in Distributed Database Design. In Proceedings of ICCI-93. IEEE Press (1993) 539-544.
8. Kirkpatrick, S., Gellat, C. D., Vecchi, M.P.: Optimization by Simulated Annealing. SCIENCE, Vol. 220, No. 4598 (1983) 671-680.
9. Pérez, J., Romero, D., Frausto, J., Pazos, R.A., Rodríguez, G., Reyes, F.: Dynamic Allocation of Vertical Fragments in Distributed Databases Using the Threshold Accepting Algorithm. In Proceeding of the 10th IASTED International Conference on Parallel and Distributed Computing and Systems, Las Vegas, U.S.A. (1998) 210-213.
10. Pérez, J., Pazos, R.A., Frausto, J., Romero, D., Cruz, L.: Vertical Fragmentation and Allocation in Distributed Databases with Site Capacity Restrictions Using the Threshold Accepting Algorithm. In Lectures Notes in Computer Science, Vol. 1793, Springer-Verlag (2000) 75-81.
11. Wolsey, L.A.: Integer Programming. Wiley-Interscience (1998).

Multi-classification of Patent Applications with Winnow

Cornelis H. A. Koster[1], Marc Seutter[1] and Jean Beney[2]

[1] University of Nijmegen, The Netherlands.
{kees,marcs}@cs.kun.nl
[2] Dept Informatique, INSA de Lyon, France.
jbeney@lisi.insa-lyon.fr

Abstract. The Winnow family of learning algorithms can cope well with large numbers of features and is tolerant to variations in document length, which makes it suitable for classifying large collections of large documents, like patent applications.

Both the large size of the documents and the large number of available training documents for each class make this classification task qualitatively different from the classification of short documents (newspaper articles or medical abstracts) with few training examples, as exemplified by the TREC evaluations.

This note describes recent experiments with Winnow on two large corpora of patent applications, supplied by the European Patent Office (EPO). It is found that the multi-classification of patent applications is much less accurate than the mono-classification of similar documents. We describe a potential pitfall in multi-classification and show ways to improve the accuracy. We argue that the inherently larger noisiness of multi-class labeling is the reason that multi-classification is harder than mono-classification.

1 Introduction

The automatic classification of patent applications is a challenging application area for automatic Text Categorization techniques (for an overview see [13]), due to the large number of features (many thousands of words per document) and the large number of labeled train- and test-documents available. Furthermore, the quality of the labeling is high: each document has been classified carefully by experts highly familiar with the domain at hand.

Traditional classification tasks, as exemplified by the Reuters dataset and most of the collections used in TREC, have been concerned with smaller documents (newspaper stories, medical abstracts) and classes for which few labeled examples are available (between one and a few hundreds). Because of these qualitative and quantitative differences, different problems may arise when classifying patent applications.

M. Broy and A.V. Zamulin (Eds.): PSI 2003, LNCS 2890, pp. 546–555, 2003.

1.1   The EPO Tests

A few years ago, the European Patent Office (EPO) in Rijswijk, the Netherlands, organised an open competition in order to assess the state-of-the-art in supervised learning for document classification (see [8]).

The first EPO test concerned mono-classification of a corpus of 16000 patent applications (EPO1) into 16 disjoint classes (*clusters* of directorates) with a thousand training examples each.

The second test involved a more realistic problem: a multi-classification with many classes, training on a larger number of documents and taking as test documents a large subset of a year's incoming documents.

The University of Nijmegen (KUN) participated in both EPO tests. We demonstrated the suitability of the Balanced Winnow algorithm for the task of classifying patent applications, comparing its performance to that of Rocchio in a number of experiments: a mono-classification of 16000 documents in 16 classes and a multi-classifications of 68418 documents in 44 classes. The largest corpus contained more than 500 000 different terms.

As we have reported in [6], the results of the mono-classification were surprisingly good, but the accuracy in multi-classification on quite similar data was found to be disappointing. In this note, we investigate the reasons for this disparity. Although we find ways to improve the accuracy of multi-classification (see section 3) we must conclude (in section 4) that there are inherent reasons that make it less accurate than mono-classification (section 2).

1.2   The Classification System

The Linguistic Classification System (LCS) developed by the University of Nijmegen (KUN) in the course of the DORO and PEKING Esprit Projects[1] is a generical system for the classification and routing of full-text documents.

The LCS system automatically learns a classification from a corpus of documents labeled with classes. After this training phase it can either be used for testing the classifier obtained on a test collection of documents with a known classification (usually held-out training data), or for producing a classification of new documents without known classification.

The LCS can perform both *mono-classification* (each document belongs to precisely one class) and *multi-classification* (each document belongs to zero or more classes).

The Winnow algorithm, implemented in the LCS, is a heuristical learning algorithm with nice mathematical convergence properties [5]. It iterates repeatedly over the training documents, computing for each class a vector of weights approximating an optimal linear separator between relevant and non-relevant documents [10]. According to [4], the balanced version of the Winnow algorithm can cope with large numbers of features and can tolerate large variations in document length because it uses both positive and negative weights.

---

[1] http://www.cs.kun.nl/peking

2   EPO1: Mono-Classification

The EPO1 corpus of patent material in English consists of 1000 abstracts and
1000 full-text documents for each of 16 classes. Some statistics are given in the
following table:

	documents	lines	words	characters
full-text	16000	7.6M	73.3M	461.1M
abstracts	16000	0.2M	2.0M	12.3M

The material is very homogeneous in document size, and evenly distributed over
the classes. The abstracts, with an average length of 129 words, are in descriptive
prose without tables or formulae. The full text documents are longer (avg 4580
words) and contain some non-linguistic material like tables and formulae.

The only pre-processing applied to the documents was the replacement of
capital letters by the corresponding lowercase letters (decapitalization) and the
replacement of special characters by spaces. In particular, no term stemming
was performed and no stoplist was applied. We relied on the term selection to
eliminate redundant features.

From the labeled full-text documents (the original trainset) a new train and
test set was obtained by randomizing the order and splitting the set (80% training, 20% held out for testing). This training set was trained in epochs of increasing size and the resulting classifier tested on the remaining 20%.

The *learning curves* (micro-averaged precision[2] against number of documents
trained) for abstracts and full-text documents are as follows:

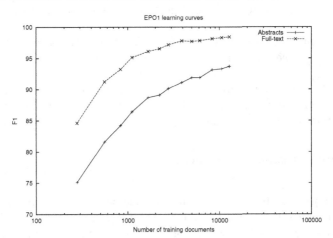

The result is encouraging, with precision on full-text documents exceeding 98
percent at 800 train examples per class, in spite of the large size of the documents. The classes appear to be sufficiently disjoint, and the noise on the labeling

---

[2] The *macro-averaged* precision is the average over all classes of the precision per class,
whereas the *micro-averaged* precision is computed by lumping the classes together.
In mono-classification micro-averaged precision equals recall (any document which
is incorrectly assigned to a class is missing in another class).

appears to be small. At very low numbers of training examples (280 examples, an average of 17.5 examples per class) the precision is already 85 percent. Although learning slows down after about 3000 documents trained, there is still a gradual improvement.

The precision on abstracts is definitely lower. This contradicts (at least for patent applications) the expectation that abstracts should be easier to classify than the corresponding documents because they contain fewer digressions and the words used are more carefully chosen, thus more pertinent. On the contrary, in a patent abstract the lawyers go out of their way to use inclusive, general language. In that light, 93% precision is not bad.

3   EPO2: Multi-classification

The EPO2 corpus contains 68418 labeled documents in English, both in the full-text form and in the form of abstracts. Some statistics:

	documents	lines	words	characters
full-text	68418	44.7M	401.3M	2607.3M
abstracts	68418	1.0M	9.0M	59.5M

For these documents, three different labelings were provided by EPO, of which we consider only one in this paper: a multi-class labeling with 44 directorates. A *directorate* is an organizational unit within EPO, responsible for all patent applications in a certain domain, but many patents belong to more than one domain.

The pre-processing applied to the documents was the same as in the EPO1-test, but this time all terms with a term frequency < 4 were eliminated (TF selection).

The EPO2 test was harder than the previous one, due to the large size of the test material but in particular due to the fact that this test concerned *multi-classification* rather than mono-classification.

3.1   Multi-classification Issues

Conceptually, multi-classification (where each document belongs to zero or more classes) appears to be simpler than mono-classification (where each document belongs to precisely one class), since it can be seen as training an independent binary classifier for each class. In mono-classification, each document is assigned to the class for which it achieves the highest score, which requires the scores of different classes to be comparable.

In multi-classification, each class must have its own *threshold* to determine whether a document with a certain score belongs to that class. In fact the training procedure for multi-classification is the same as that for mono-classification (apart from the fact that each document now may belong to more than one class), but the *selection* of classes for documents is more complicated: rather than assigning each document to the class for which it has the highest score, in multi-classification it is necessary to determine for each class an optimal threshold [1,14] to distinguish between relevant and non-relevant documents for that class.

Another difference concerns the measurement of accuracy: In multi-classification, precision and recall are no longer equal, and we shall use the *micro-averaged F1 value* as a measure of accuracy. The F1-value is a kind of harmonic average of precision and recall.

In the "directorate" classification, an average of 1.43 classes is assigned to each of the 68418 training documents. Therefore each document is a (positive) example for (on the average) 1.43 classes. Calling each <document, class> combination an *example*, the total number of examples is 88000, distributed in such a way that each of the 44 directorates has 2000 examples.

The distribution of the number of classes per document is as follows:

number of classes	1	2	3	4	5	6	7	> 7
number of docs	51981	13745	2323	306	46	13	4	0

3.2   Training on Examples

The 88000 examples were randomly split 80/20 in a train and test set, and classifiers were trained using the Winnow algorithm in eight epochs. The following learning curve (precision, recall and F1-value as a function of the number of documents trained) resulted:

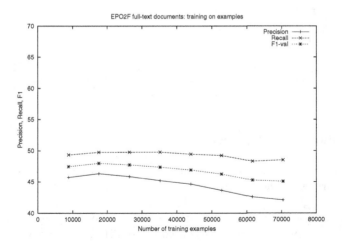

The accuracy reached is low, below 50%. It can be seen that, as more documents are trained, precision, recall and F1-value at first increase, but after some 20000 examples all three deteriorate again. We must be doing something wrong.

3.3   Training on Documents

When training on examples, we do not in any way take into account that some examples pertain to the same document. We are training independent binary classifiers. In training for a certain class, all examples involving that class are seen as *positive* examples, whereas all examples belonging to other classes are seen as *negative* examples for that class. As a consequence, any document belonging to more than one class will be trained both as a positive example and as a negative example for each class to which it belongs!

This will be detrimental for any classification algorithm based on the Vector Space Model (computing the score of a document for some class as an inproduct between class term weights and document term strengths).

In order to prevent a document from being a counterexample to itself, we should be *training on documents* rather than examples, seeing the document as a positive example for each class to which it belongs, and as a negative example for all classes to which it does not belong.

Modifying the train procedure accordingly, and shuffling the documents rather than the examples, we obtain a much better learning curve:

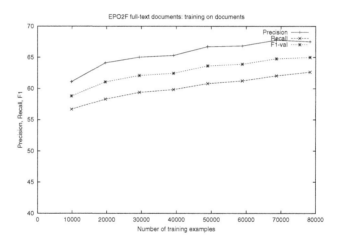

3.4   Training with Optimal Tuning

In the preceding two graphs, as in our original experiment, precision and recall are far apart, with the measure of accuracy (F1) precariously in the middle. In principle it might be caused by a bad choice of thresholds, but the LCS computes on the train set for each class that threshold value which maximizes F1 (not necessarily the point where precision equal recall). The Winnow algorithm has a number of parameters, and the weak point is that we took their values from literature.

After tuning the Winnow parameters on the train set, following the same procedure as in [7], we obtained a much better learning curve:

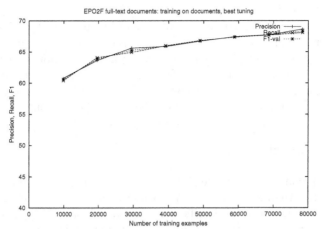

Precision and recall now practically coincide, and when training on 80% of the documents an accuray of .68 is reached.

4   Further Experiments

It is obvious that training on documents results in a better accuracy than training on examples, and tuning can improve the accuracy further, but we may ask ourselves whether this really corresponds to a better ranking of the documents.

4.1   Ranking

In order to study the quality of the ranking, we have made the following Precision/Recall graph (using the treceval utility of TREC) for Winnow trained on examples, on documents and tuned, adding also the curves for the Rocchio algorithm (on examples and documents) for comparison:

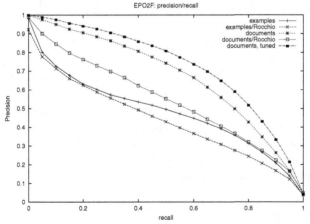

The graphs show clearly that Winnow outperforms Rocchio all the way (as was found in [6]), but also that training on documents rather than examples makes a marked improvement for both algorithms. It is evidently not a good idea to consider multi-class training as the training of independent binary classifiers.

And better tuning of Winnow makes another important improvement at all recall levels. But compared to section 2, the graphs still show that the accuracy achieved in the mono-classification of the EPO1 data is much larger than for the multi-classification of the EPO2 data. Is there an inherent difference between these forms of classification that causes the difference in accuracy?

4.2   Noisy Labeling

We contend that the difference lies mainly in the *noise* in the labeling of the training data. Among the sources of labeling noise mentioned in [11], many are the same for both forms of classification, but multi-classification is particularly prone to *quantization error* (caused by the fact that labels have to be either present or absent, no gradual judgements are allowed).

In the case of the EPO1 corpus, the labeling noise is particularly small because it contains only documents which were unequivocally mono-classified by the experts. A labeling with a "main category" and (zero or more) secondary categories will be much more noisy.

If some percentage of the labels in the trainset have been doled out incorrectly or inconsistently, *no* classification algorithm can be expected to make fewer errors than that percentage in any experiment with held-out data.

In order to obtain an indication of the labeling noise in the EPO1 corpus we therefore performed an experiment on "seen" corpus (training and testing on the same random subset of 50% of the documents), with the following result:

	precision	recall	F1-value
Winnow abstracts	99.61	99.61	99.61
Winnow full-text	100.00	100.00	100.00

Winnow can "explain" the class given to most abstracts and all full-text documents (in the sense that it can find term weights such that they bring the document score to the right side of the threshold). Of course this can also be interpreted as evidence of overtraining on the seen documents. But at least, it is possible to train a classifier which has 100% accuracy on the EPO1 documents.

The boundary condition "each document belongs to precisely one class" provides important information, as can be seen by weakening it to "each document belongs to at most one class". The results for this 0:1 multi-classification of seen EPO1 documents are shown in the next table.

	precision	recall	F1-value
Winnow abstracts	99.87	98.83	99.35
Winnow full-text	100.00	99.80	99.90

The precision is no longer equal to the recall and some .1% of the documents obstinately refuse to be classified in the right category. This is caused by the fact that documents are no longer forced into a class even when their score falls under the threshold of that class. In experiments with a totally different corpus [2], we found that 0:3 multi-classification of unseen mono-classified documents gave a few percent less accuracy than mono-classification.

Training on "seen" EPO2 corpus (0:3 multi-classification, training and testing on the same 80% of the corpus), we obtained the following results:

	precision	recall	F1-value
Winnow abstracts	73.03	72.21	72.62
Winnow full-text	80.12	79.16	79.63

These figures can be taken as an upper limit on the accuracy achievable in multi-classification of EPO2, and are far below those for mono-classification. In this sense, mult-classification is harder than mono-classification.

5   Conclusions and Further Work

The experiments described above confirm that the Winnow algorithm is suitable for the classification of large collections of large documents, such as patent applications, and for this purpose is preferable to Rocchio.

The accuracy in the mono-classification of full-text documents was much better than that of abstracts, contradicting the expectation that abstracts would be easier to classify, because of the more expressive terminology used and the lack of digressions.

We found a potential pitfall in multi-classification (example-based instead of document-based training. Although we managed to diminish the difference in precision and recall between mono-classification and multi-classification by tuning the Winnow parameters, the former remained much more accurate. We argued that this is caused by noise in the labeling of train documents, which is much larger for multi- than for mono-classification, due to the arbitrary labeling of border cases.

The documents were represented quite conventionally, as a bag of words, without any linguistic pre-processing. In particular, no semantical ontology was used and, in contrast to [9], the internal structure of the documents was completely ignored. In spite of this simple document representation, the accuracy of mono-classification is very good.

Our later experiments with other corpora and more informative document representations did not substantiate the expectation that the use of phrases [7], lemmatization and collocations [2] would make an important improvement to the accuracy of automatic classification.

References

1. A. Arampatzis and A. van Hameren (2001), The Score-Distributional Threshold Optimization for Adaptive Binary Classification Tasks. Proceedings ACM SIGIR 2001, pp. 267–275.
2. Nuria Bel, Cornelis H.A. Koster and Marta Villegas (2003), Cross-Lingual Text Categorization. Proceedings ECDL 2003, Springer LNCS 2769, pp 126–139.
3. W.W. Cohen and Y. Singer (1999), Context-sensitive learning methods for text categorization. *ACM Transactions on Information Systems 13*, 1, 100–111.
4. I. Dagan, Y. Karov, D. Roth (1997), Mistake-Driven Learning in Text Categorization. Proceedings 2nd Conference on Empirical Methods in NLP, pp. 55–63.
5. A. Grove, N. Littlestone, and D. Schuurmans (2001), General convergence results for linear discriminant updates. *Machine Learning* 43(3), pp. 173–210.
6. C.H.A. Koster, M. Seutter and J. Beney (2001), Classifying Patent Applications with Winnow, Proceedings Benelearn 2001, Antwerpen, 8pp. http://cnts.uia.ac.be/benelearn2001/
7. C.H.A. Koster and M. Seutter (2002), Taming Wild Phrases. Proceedings 25th European Conference on IR Research (ECIR 2003), Springer LNCS 2633.
8. M. Krier and F. Zaccà (2002), Automatic Categorisation Applications at the European Patent Office. *World Patent Information* 24, pp. 187–196.
9. L. S. Larkey (1999), A patent search and classification system. Proceedings of DL-99, 4th ACM Conference on Digital Libraries, pp 179–187.
10. N. Littlestone (1988), Learning quickly when irrelevant attributes abound: A new linear-threshold algorithm. *Machine Learning*, 2, pp. 285–318.
11. C. Peters and C.H.A. Koster (2003), Uncertainty-based Noise Reduction and Term Selection in Text Categorisation, International Journal of Uncertainty, Fuzziness and Knowledge-Based Systems (IJUFKS) Vol. 11, No. 1, pp 115–137.
12. J.J. Rocchio (1971), Relevance feedback in Information Retrieval, In: Salton, G. (ed.), *The Smart Retrieval system - experiments in automatic document processing*, Prentice - Hall, Englewood Cliffs, NJ, pp 313–323.
13. F. Sebastiani (2001), Machine learning in automated text categorization. ACM Computing Surveys, Vol 34 no 1, 2002, pp. 1–47.
14. Y. Zhiang and J. Callan (2001), Maximum Likelyhood Estimation for Filtering Thresholds, Proceedings of ACM SIGIR 2001, pp. 294–302.

Automatic Evaluation of Quality
of an Explanatory Dictionary
by Comparison of Word Senses[*]

Alexander Gelbukh[1,2], Grigori Sidorov[1],
SangYong Han[2], and Liliana Chanona-Hernandez[3]

[1] Center for Computing Research (CIC), National Polytechnic Institute (IPN),
Av. Juan de Dios Bátiz, Zacatenco, CP 07738, Mexico City, Mexico
{gelbukh,sidorov}@cic.ipn.mx; www.gelbukh.com
[2] Department of Computer Science and Engineering, Chung-Ang University,
221 Huksuk-Dong, DongJak-Ku, Seoul, 156-756, Korea
hansy@cau.ac.kr
[3] Department of Computer Science, Las Americas University,
Mexico City, Mexico
lchanona@mail.com

Abstract. Words in the explanatory dictionary have different meanings (senses) described using natural language definitions. If the definitions of two senses of the same word are too similar, it is difficult to grasp the difference and thus it is difficult to judge which of the two senses is intended in a particular contexts, especially when such a decision is to be made automatically as in the task of automatic word sense disambiguation. We suggest a method of formal evaluation of this aspect of quality of an explanatory dictionary by calculating the similarity of different senses of the same word. We calculate the similarity between two given senses as the relative number of equal or synonymous words in their definitions. In addition to the general assessment of the dictionary, the individual suspicious definitions are reported for possible improvement. In our experiments we used the Anaya explanatory dictionary of Spanish. Our experiments show that there are about 10% of substantially similar definitions in this dictionary, which indicates rather low quality.

1 Introduction

Words in a typical explanatory dictionary have different senses, while only one of which can be meant for a particular occurrence of the word in a particular text. For example, the word "bank" can stand for a financial institution, shore, set, etc., depending on the context. To determine the particular word sense in a given text is important for a number of purposes, such as:

[*] Work done under partial support of Mexican Government (CONACyT, SNI), IPN (CGEPI, COFAA, PIFI), and Korean Government (KIPA Professorship for Visiting Faculty Positions in Korea). The first author is currently on Sabbatical leave at Chung-Ang University.

M. Broy and A.V. Zamulin (Eds.): PSI 2003, LNCS 2890, pp. 556–562, 2003.

- For any kind of understanding of the text. For example, if you are advised to keep your money in a reliable *bank*, would you carry it to a financial institution or a river shore?
- For translating the text. For example, "*my account in the* bank" is to be translated into Spanish as "*mi cuenta en el* banco", whereas "*on the* bank *of the lake*" as "*en la* orilla *del lago*."
- For information retrieval. For example, for a query "*branch banks in Chicago*", a document containing "*There are two Citybank branch banks in the central area of Chicago*" is relevant while "*The hotel is under maple branches at the beautiful bank of Michigan Lake, with an amazing view of Chicago's skyscrapers*" is not.

Such tasks can be performed either manually or automatically. In case of automatic analysis, the task of selection of the intended sense in a given context is called (automatic) word sense disambiguation (WSD) task. This task proved to be quite difficult and is nowadays the topic of active research.

The senses are defined in explicative dictionaries by means of definitions, the latter being the only source of information on a particular sense. A typical WSD algorithm tries to compare the definition of the sense with the surrounding words to guess the meaning intended in a particular context [4]. Thus the quality of disambiguation greatly depends on two factors related to the dictionary that defines the senses:

- Which cases of the use of the given words are considered different senses,
- How these senses are described in the dictionary.

Many dictionaries, including WordNet [11], have been extensively criticized for too fine-grained sense distinction that makes it difficult to choose a particular sense out of a set of very similar or closely related senses. In addition, the difference between very similar senses can disappear in most cases. For example, suppose for the word *window*, a dictionary distinguishes between:

1. the interior of the hole in the wall ("*look through the window*"),
2. the place in the wall where the hole is ("*near the window*"),
3. a frame with the glass in the hole is ("*break the window*"),
4. a computer program interface object ("*the button in the main window*").

Then in many cases can say for sure that in a particular text (for example, "*John came up to the window, broke it and fell out of it*") one of the first three senses was meant (and not the fourth one) but will have difficulties guessing which one of the three because they are too similar. This can happen either because of too fine-grained sense distinction or because of poor wording of the definitions.

Automatic WSD programs are especially sensible to this problem. In frame of WSD it has been even suggested that for practical purposes the senses in the dictionaries should be clustered together to form coarser classifications easier to make clear distinctions [5,7].

In this paper we suggest a method for automatic detection of this problem. It has at least two potential uses:

- To help the lexicographer compiling or maintaining the dictionary to detect potential problems in the system of senses leading to error-prone interpretation,
- To help a human designer or even a software agent [1] to choose a better dictionary to use out of a set of available dictionaries.

Namely, we suggest that in a "good" (for the purposes involving WSD) dictionary the senses of each word are described differently enough to be clearly distinguishable. On the other hand, too similar descriptions of senses of some word indicate a potential problem with the use of the dictionary. To evaluate the similarity between different senses of a word we calculated the share of "equal" words in their definitions in the given explanatory dictionary.

The notion of "equal words" needs clarification. Obviously, equal letter strings represent the same word. In addition, we consider different morphological forms ("take" = "takes" = "took"...) to represent the same word; the process of their identification is called stemming [8]. Finally, we consider two words to be equal if they are synonymous.

We implemented our method for the Anaya explanatory dictionary of Spanish language. We used a synonym dictionary of Spanish for detecting synonyms.

In the rest of the paper, we discuss the algorithm we use for finding similar definitions, the present and the experimental results, and finally draw some conclusions.

2   Algorithm

We calculate a numerical value characterizing the quality of a dictionary as the average similarity between two different word senses of the same word. We also detect specific senses that are too similar, for possible manual merging or improvement of their definitions.

To measure the similarity between two texts (two definitions, in our case) we use an expression based on the well-known Dice coefficient [3,9]. The latter is defined as follows:

$$D(t_1, t_2) = \frac{2 \times W_1 \cap W_2}{|W_1| + |W_2|},\tag{1}$$

where W_1 and W_2 are sets of words in texts t_1 and t_2. This expression characterizes how many words the texts have in common if the words are compared literally. $W_1 \cap W_2$ means that we take the words that exist in both texts.

To take synonymy into account we use a similar but slightly modified expression. Let $W_1 \circ W_2$ be the set of synonymous words in the two definitions calculated as described in 1. Then we determine the similarity as follows:

$$D(t_1, t_2) = \frac{|W_1 \cap W_2| + k\,|W_1 \circ W_2|}{\max\left(|W_1|, |W_2|\right)},\tag{2}$$

We use the maximum value for normalization, because all words from the longer definition can be synonymous to the words from the other one. Consequently we

pre-process all dictionary: POS-tagging, stemming
for each dictionary entry
    for each homonym of the word
        for each unordered pair of its senses $S_1 \neq S_2$
            $D = \frac{similarity(S_1, S_2)}{\max(length(S_1), length(S_2))}$ by (2)
estimate the average D and report too high values of D

Function $similarity(S_1, S_2)$:
    $similarity = 0$; $matched\_words\_list = \emptyset$
    for each word $w_i \in S_1$ except stop-words
        if $w_i \in S_2$ then
            add 1 to $similarity$; add w_i to $matched\_words\_list$
        else for each synonym $s \in synonyms(w_i)$
            if $s \notin matched\_words\_list$ and $s \in S_2$ then
                add k to $similarity$; add s to $matched\_words\_list$ (we use $k = 1$)
                break the cycle
    for each word $w_j \in S_2$ except stop-words
        for each synonym $s \in synonyms(w_j)$
            if $s \notin matched\_words\_list$ and $s \in S_1$ then
                add k to $similarity$; add s to $matched\_words\_list$
                break the cycle

Fig. 1. The algorithm

do not multiply the expression by 2 as in (1). The weighting coefficient k reflects the degree of importance of the synonyms. We use the value $k = 1$ since for the purposes of our experiment it is important to measure the maximum possible similarity. Besides, in our opinion, synonyms should be treated in this calculation with the same importance as literal word intersection, because, by definition, synonyms have similar meanings and normally distinguish only the shades of meaning. Thus, though it is not always possible to substitute one synonym with another in the text, they do express more or less the same concept.

Our algorithm is shown in Fig. 1. For each word in the dictionary, we measured the similarity between its senses. Obviously, words with only one sense were ignored. Since similarity is a symmetrical relation, it was calculated only once for each pair of senses of the word.

Note that we considered homonyms as different words and not as different senses. Normally, this is the way that they are represented in the dictionaries — as different groups of senses. Besides, the homonyms usually have different meanings, so they are of little interest for our investigation.

We measure the similarity in the following way. At the beginning, the similarity score is zero. The words are taken one by one from the first sense in the pair and they are searched in the other sense. If the word is found then the score is incremented. If the word is matched, it is marked (added to the list of matched synonyms) to avoid counting it in the opposite direction while processing the other sense in the pair.

Note that we use normalized words with POS-tags, which allows for matching of any grammatical form. Additionally, this allows for taking into account only significant words and discarding auxiliary words. Unknown words are processed as significant words but only if their length is greater than a given threshold. We used the threshold equal to two letters, i.e., we considered all too short words to be stop-words. We also ignored auxiliary words because normally they do not add any semantic information (like conjunctions or articles), or add some arbitrary information (like prepositions, which frequently depend on the subcategorization properties of verbs).

If the word has no match in the other sense, we search its synonyms in the dictionary of synonyms and check them one by one in the other sense. If the synonym is matched, the score is incremented. At the same time the synonym is marked (added to an auxiliary list of matched synonyms) to avoid repetitive counting. The already marked synonyms are not used for comparisons.

At the next step, the procedure is repeated for the other sense in the pair but only matching of synonyms is performed because the literally matching words have been found already. At the same time, synonyms yet can give additional score because we cannot guarantee that our synonym dictionary is symmetrical (i.e., if A is synonym for B, then B is synonym for A).

Finally, we apply the formula 2 for calculating the modified coefficient of similarity.

3 Experimental Results

We used Anaya dictionary as a source of words and senses. This dictionary has more than 30,000 headwords that have in total more that 60,000 word senses; only 17,000 headwords have more than one sense. We preferred this dictionary to Spanish WordNet (see, for example, [11]) because Spanish WordNet has definitions in English while we were interested in Spanish and used the linguistic tools and synonym dictionary for Spanish.

For morphological processing, we applied Spanish morphological analyzer and generator developed in our laboratory [2].

All definitions in the dictionary were normalized and the POS-tagging procedure was applied [10]. In the experiment, we ignore the possible word senses that were assigned to each word in definition (see [10]) because this procedure gave a certain percent of errors that we try to eliminate here. Word senses in definitions can be taken into account in future experiments.

We also used a synonym dictionary of Spanish that contains about 20,000 headwords. This dictionary is applied at the stage of measuring of the similarity between senses for detecting synonymous words in definitions.

Below we give an example of the data (normalized definitions from Anaya dictionary) that was used. The definition of the word *abad* in one of the senses is as follows:

Abad = Título que recibe el superior de un monasterio o el de algunas colegiatas. (Abbot = Title that receives a superior of a convent or of some churches).

The normalized version of this definition is as follows:

Abad = título#noun que#conj recibir#verb el#art superior#noun de#prep un#art monasterio#noun o#conj el#art de#prep alguno#adj colegiata#noun .#punct
(*Abbot = title#noun that#conj receive#verb a#art superior#noun of#prep a#art convent#noun or#conj of#prep some#adj church#noun*),

where #*conj* is conjunction, #*art* is article, #*prep* is preposition, #*adj* is adjective, #*punct* is punctuation mark, and #*noun* and #*verb* stay for noun and verb. There are some words that were not recognized by our morphological analyzer (about 3%), which are marked as #*unknown*.

The results of applications of the algorithm shown in Fig. 1 are presented in Table 1. Since the similarity is a fraction, some fractions are more probable than others; specifically, due to a high number of short definitions, there were many figures with small denominators, such as $\frac{1}{2}$, $\frac{1}{3}$, $\frac{2}{3}$, etc. To smooth this effect, we represented the experimental results by intervals of values and not by specific values. We present the results for zero similarity separately because there were many senses without any intersection. As one can see, about 1% of

Table 1. Number of sense pairs per intervals

Interval of similarity	Number of sense pairs	Percent of sense pairs
0.00–0.01	46205	67.43
0.01–0.25	14725	21.49
0.25–0.50	6655	9.71
0.50–0.75	600	0.88
0.75–1.00	336	0.49

sense pairs are very similar — they contain more than 50% of equivalent words (with synonyms), and about 10% of sense pairs are significantly similar — they contain more than 25% of equivalent words. 10% is rather large value, so these definitions should be revised in the Anaya dictionary to improve its quality (at least for the purposes of WSD).

4   Conclusions

We proposed a method of automatic evaluation of the quality of the explanatory dictionary by comparison of different senses of each word. We detect and report to the developer the pairs of senses with too similar definitions. We also assess the total quality of the dictionary (with respect to the clarity of distinction of the senses) as an inverse value to the average similarity of the senses of each word. Though it is only one aspect of quality of the dictionaries, it is a rather important feature for all tasks involving WSD, both automatic (for a computer) and manual (for a human user of the dictionary).

The method consists in calculating the relative intersection of senses considered as bags of words; the words are previously POS-tagged and stemmed. During this comparison, both literal intersection and intersection of synonyms of the words are taken into account.

The experiment was conducted for the Anaya dictionary of Spanish. The results show that about 10% of sense pairs are substantially similar (more than 25% of the similar words). This is rather large percentage of similar senses, thus, the dictionary can be improved by rewprding of these definitions, merging these senses, or restructuring the whole entry.

In the future, we plan to perform such experiments with other dictionaries, like, for example, WordNet, and with other languages.

References

1. A. Burton-Jones, V. C. Storey, V. Sugumaran, P. Ahluwalia. Assessing the Effectiveness of the DAML Ontologies for the Semantic Web. In: *Proc. NLDB-2003, Applications of Natural Language to Information Systems.* Lecture Notes in Informatics, Berlin, 2003.
2. Gelbukh, A. and G. Sidorov (2002). Morphological Analysis of Inflective Languages Through Generation. *J. Procesamiento de Lenguaje Natural,* No 29, September 2002, Spain, pp. 105–112.
3. Jiang, J.J. and D.W. Conrad. (1999) From object comparison to semantic similarity. In: *Proc. of Pacling-99 (Pacific association for computational linguistics),* August, 1999, Waterloo, Canada, pp. 256–263.
4. M. Lesk. Automatic sense disambiguation using machine readable dictionaries: How to tell a pine cone from a ice cream cone. In *Proceedings of SIGDOC '86,* 1986.
5. Magnini, B., Strapparava, C. Experiments in Word Domain Disambiguation for Parallel Texts. In: *Proceedings of the ACL Workshop on Word Senses and Multilinguality,* Hong Kong, China, 2000.
6. Manning, C. D. and Shutze, H. (1999) *Foundations of statistical natural language processing.* Cambridge, MA, The MIT press, p. 680
7. A. Suárez and M. Palomar. Word Sense vs. Word Domain Disambiguation: a Maximum Entropy approach In: *Proc. TSD-2002, Text, Speech, Dialogue.* Lecture Notes in Artificial Intelligence, Spriner-Verlag, 2002.
8. Porter, M.F. An algorithm for suffix stripping. *Program,* **14**(3):130–137, 1980.
9. Rasmussen E. (1992) Clustering algorithms. In: Frakes, W. B. and Baeza-Yates, R. *Information Retrieval: Data Structures and Algorithms.* Prentice Hall, Upper Saddle River, NJ, 1992, pp. 419–442.
10. Sidorov G. and A. Gelbukh (2001). Word sense disambiguation in a Spanish explanatory dictionary. In: *Proc. of TALN-2001, Traitement Automatique du Langage Naturel.* Tours, France, July 2-5, 2001, pp. 398–402.
11. *WordNet: an electronic lexical database.* (1998), C. Fellbaum (ed.), MIT, p. 423

An Approach to Automatic Construction of a Hierarchical Subject Domain for Question Answering Systems

Anna V. Zhdanova[1,2] and Pavel V. Mankevich[1,2]

[1] Novosibirsk State University, Novosibirsk 630090, Russia
[2] A.P. Ershov Institute of Informatics Systems, Novosibirsk 630090, Russia
{anna, pavel}@sib3.ru

Abstract. We propose a new statistical algorithm for automatic construction of subject domains that can be used in e-mail or Web question answering systems and ontology generating. The domain hierarchy is extracted from electronic texts written in a natural language, e.g., in English. During the text processing, the quality and quantity of information presented in the texts are being evaluated and then the hierarchical relationships between the pieces of texts are established depending on the derived data. Using this approach, we have created a question answering system which executes hierarchy navigation based on a query analysis including evaluation of the user's conversance with the subject domain. In combination, these steps result in comprehensive and non-redundant answers.

1 Introduction

Development of automatic e-mail or Web question answering systems is of high current interest due to wide commercial applications. The quality of responses provided by such systems is crucially dependent on the data employed in the question processing. Such data are usually extracted from Internet and Intranets. The information presented there is however often redundant, inconsistent and hard to find for users. For these reasons, there is a need in creating software for conversion of texts written in a natural language to databases.

At present, there exist two major approaches to using electronic data for question answering [1]. In the first *database-oriented* approach, the Web fragments are treated as if they were databases; while in the second *information-retrieval* approach, Web data are viewed as an enormous collection of unstructured flat texts. Both directions have their merits and shortcomings. Historically, the first approach, discussed in detail below, is older and more comprehensive (the corresponding studies can be tracked at least back to the middle of the seventies [2]). Most of the previous works following this direction used relational databases [3][4]. This tactics is successful when the original data are presented in the tabular form (e.g., when one deals with price lists or football scores). For data of other types, the process of creating, maintaining and employing a relational database

M. Broy and A.V. Zamulin (Eds.): PSI 2003, LNCS 2890, pp. 563–569, 2003.

is however ineffective, because the use of this data representation is non-trivial and time-consuming. An alternative tactics, allowing one to effectively employ data of various types (e.g., ordinary texts) for message classification and e-mail answering, is based on construction of a hierarchical subject domain [5]. The main shortcoming of the latter method is the yet remaining large amount of manual labor required for database construction (actually, this drawback is inherent for all the versions of the database-oriented approach [1]). To tackle this problem, there is a need in automatic database construction. The related studies are focused on automatic conversion of flat text to hierarchical structures (e.g., to taxonomies of topics) built by employing self-organizing maps [6] and on the hierarchic organization of document collections [7]. The algorithms proposed in the aforementioned studies are however not directly applicable to question answering, i.e., it has not been established that the methods for document clustering will efficiently cope the problem of database construction for question answering systems.

In this work, we present a new method for automatic subject domain construction and use it to build a question answering system. The key novel aspect of our approach is building a hierarchy on the basis of "from simple towards difficult" relationship between its parts. Locating more general and easy for understanding answers (i.e., documents, texts) at the top of the hierarchy and more specific and difficult for understanding answers at the bottom, taking into consideration the user's acquaintance with the subject domain and using the knowledge of the hierarchy elements relationships, we avoid redundancy and insufficiency in question answering.

Our paper is organized as follows. In Section 2, we describe the ideas lying behind our algorithm for automatic construction of the subject domain and also the steps of the algorithm. Section 3 contains evaluation of the performance of our system in terms of recall and precision. Section 4 concludes the presentation.

2   Construction of a Subject Domain

2.1   General Principles

We are interested in the situation when the preliminary information collected for construction of the subject domain is stored in a natural language form, as it often takes place in web-sites and digital libraries. In practice, such information is usually obtained by employing search engines. The main problem in this case is that a user has to browse and read a rather large amount of text in order to get the needed information. This happens mainly because (i) the search engines tend to provide users with links to the web pages containing excessive information instead of the precise answers, and (ii) many useless or irrelevant data are being retrieved as a result.

Subproblem (i) can be skipped by representing the content of the subject domain as a set of meaningful text-units (text documents). Each unit may consist of 20–200 words and its content should be sufficient for providing the user with an answer and for revealing the answer's context. Selecting such text units is a special problem. Although a full-scale discussion of its solution is beyond our present goals, we may note that extended sentences, paragraphs and sections of large texts are likely to be separated in the process of extracting the text units.

Concerning subproblem (ii), it is appropriate to notice that the question answering system should not provide the user with the information he or she already possesses (otherwise, there would be no need in questioning) and the information originating from irrelevant subject domains (e.g., due to polysems) is useless. Our hierarchical model is created to decrease the number of unhelpful and irrelevant texts among those supplied by the question answering system. The hierarchy represents only one subject domain and is based on the use of simple/difficult (also, thus broader/narrower, whole/part) relationships applied to its units' main ideas. The units located at the top represent broader concepts and their content is written in a "simpler" language than the content of the lower units. Thus, the information represented in the units located near the top of the hierarchy is more likely to be familiar to the user. After the user provides an extensive question, the system analyzes the vocabulary of the user's query (i.e., the user's conversance with the subject domain) and decides how far to go within the hierarchy in order to get the relevant unit(s). If the user obtains too broad or too detailed answer, the hierarchical structure makes it possible to navigate from broader to narrower concepts and vice versa.

2.2   Algorithm

The algorithm for automatic construction of the hierarchy incorporates the principles discussed above. Specifically, the units of the hierarchy are ranked from "easy for understanding" (at the top) to "difficult for understanding" (at the bottom). This procedure should be performed so that parent nodes and their descendents are maximally similar semantically.

For construction of the hierarchy, a non zero long list of text units is taken as an input. Initially, the hierarchy is considered to be empty. The steps of the hierarchy construction are as follows:

(i) Rank the units by their weights using the weight function W.

(ii) Choose the unit with the lowest weight and place it as the root (i.e., the top node) of the hierarchy.

(iii) Choose the unit with the lowest weight among the remaining units and calculate the similarity measure S between this unit and each of the already chosen units. Put the newly chosen unit just below the one with the maximum similarity measure.

(iv) Repeat step (iii) until the set of the remaining units is not empty.

The structure of the hierarchy obtained by using the algorithm described above crucially depends on the specific definition of the functions W and S. In our system, the former function is represented as

$$W(u) = 1/ \prod_{w \in u} F(w), \qquad (1)$$

where u is a unit, w is a word, and $F(w)$ is the frequency of the word w in the whole subject domain (i.e., in the processed text units). The function measuring the similarity between two units, u_1 and u_2, is given by

$$S(u_1, u_2) = \frac{\sum_w f(w, u_1) f(w, u_2)}{\left(\sum_w f^2(w, u_1)\right)^{1/2} \left(\sum_w f^2(w, u_2)\right)^{1/2}}, \qquad (2)$$

where $f(w, u)$ is the frequency of the word w in the unit u.

Formula (1) implies that the weight of a text unit directly correlates with its size and the frequency of its words. In other words, the unit's weight is assumed to be proportional to the effort spent by a human on reading it. This assumption is in line with Zipf's theory [8] stating that it takes an effort to recall the meaning of any word during reading or listening, and that frequent (i.e., usual) words are easier to use and understand than rare words. Formula (2) is the same as in the vector-space model [9]. We have tried a few other less founded expressions for the functions W and S (e.g., the number of unique words in a text unit as the weight of the text unit, and the number of common words between two units as their similarity measure) and found that they are inferior compared to Eqs. (1) and (2).

3 Experiments

To illustrate automatic construction of a hierarchical subject domain for question answering systems, we have used a subject domain consisting of 82 text units related to insurance. To test the question answering system based on this domain, we have employed 27 questions concerning these texts. The questions and answers were produced manually on the base of "Frequently Asked Questions" sections of the web sites belonging to insurance companies. The same test has already been used earlier [5] in order to characterize the performance of the question answering system based on the manually constructed subject domain.

By employing our hierarchy construction engine with the formulas (1) and (2), the 82 insurance text units are converted into the hierarchy consisting of six layers in depth. Comparing this hierarchy with the manually built hierarchy indicates that although their structures do not coincide (by superposition) there exist similarities. In both cases, for example, the units from two main subhierarchies of "Insurance" ("Vehicle Insurance" and "Life Insurance") tend to form separate groups. Related to "Vehicle Insurance" and "Life Insurance" fragments of our resulting hierarchy are presented below. Here, numbers (1, 2, etc.) denote hierarchy levels, and strings ("Uninsured motorists", "Liability Insurance", etc.) denote the names of the text units. Location of the records (pairs "number–strings") demonstrates which units are related to which, e.g., here "Personal Injury Protection" is a sub-concept of "Life insurance".

```
2 : Uninsured motorists
    3 : Liability Insurance
    3 : No-Fault Insurance
```

```
                    3 : UM, UIM and collision coverage
                    3 : Underinsured Motorists
                        4 : Liability lingo
                            5 : Liability limits
            2 : Named Non-Owner Policy
                    3 : Extended Non-Owner Liability
                    3 : Drive-Other-Car Endorsement
            2 : Auto replacement coverage
            2 : Fleet Policy
    1 : Life insurance
            2 : Threshold Level
            2 : Personal Injury Protection
            2 : Joint WLI
                    3 : Tax issues
                    3 : The check issue
```

To demonstrate the performance of the question answering system operating with the hierarchical insurance subject domain described above, we show (Fig. 1) the precision-recall curves obtained for the conventional "flat" vector space model, automatically built hierarchy where the weight function W is defined as the number of unique words in a text unit, and the hierarchy as described in Sec. 2.2. Precision is defined as the ratio of the number of units selected correctly to the total number of selected units. Recall is defined as the ratio of the number of correctly selected units to the number of the target units. Both these measures are common for evaluating information retrieval systems [9].

The results for the vector space model are seen to be poor compared to those obtained by using our method employing a hierarchically structured subject domain. For the latter method, it should be noted that the question answering results depend on the choice of the functions employed in subject domain construction and the quality of hierarchy indexing. In particular, the results can be improved by application of different W and S functions and performing lemmatization and synonym recognition for the words of a subject domain. In the future, it would also be useful to test the question answering process on larger data sets.

4   Conclusion

In this paper, we have discussed the principles of automatic construction of a hierarchical subject domain, which are aimed at the question answering tasks. We have described the criteria of the quality of answers and proposed a statistical algorithm for automatic construction of subject domain satisfying these criteria. We have implemented this algorithm and also have created a question-answering module which allows "asking" the system in a natural language and obtaining brief and meaningful answers.

The usefulness of hierarchical subject domains in question answering has already been understood: many of the major search engines build their own Yahoo!-like hierarchies and offer to the users such an option as "Search in the

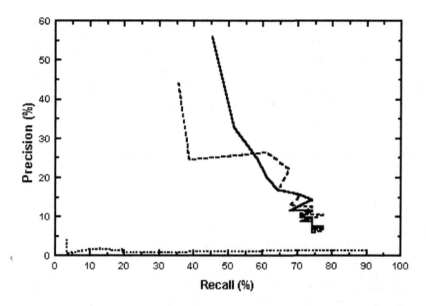

Fig. 1. Precision-recall curves for the flat vector space model (dotted line), the automatically built hierarchy, where W equals to the number of unique words in a text unit (dashed line), and the basic automatically built hierarchy (solid line)

Selected Category". Yet, even the largest question answering systems build their catalogues manually. This process consumes time and labor and is often far from perfect: the manually built hierarchies significantly depend on the creator's points of view, educational standards, etc., which may result in inadequate performance of the system. Furthermore, most of the question answering systems provide links to web-pages instead of brief answers and do little apart from pattern matching when it comes to semantic analysis of the query. Such approaches make it probable to lose needed details in the information flow and spend appreciable extra time on dealing with large web pages. Our results indicate that many of these shortcomings can be removed by employing automatically constructed subject domains.

In a general context, our work is a step towards obtaining two needed but yet unattained things: efficient question answering systems and automatically generated ontologies. In fact, the results obtained in our work can be directly applied to construction of such ontologies, i.e., to automatic extraction of data from natural language texts. The idea of augmenting ordinary Web documents with semantic annotations and other metadata is very promising, because it allows to easily find and compare information presented on the Web in different ways. The attempts to solve the latter problem are usually based on the linguistic methods. In particular, Llorens et al. [10] propose to analyze noun phrases and verbal structures found within electronic documents. Sundblad [11] describes retrieving the needed term relationships from the TREC9 question corpora. In both cases, the researchers employ preliminary processing of large amount of texts but report a small number of extracted hierarchies. This shortcoming is directly related to the use of phrase structures. In contrast, the statistical methods are independent of phrase structures. For this reason, we believe that using a combination of linguistic and statistical methods may be more efficient, and accordingly, statistical methods can significantly contribute to the automatic generation of ontologies.

Acknowledgement. The authors thank F.G. Dinenberg, A.L. Semenov and D.V. Shishkin for useful discussions.

References

1. Lin, J. The Web as a Resource for Question Answering: Perspectives and Challenges. In *Proceedings of the Third International Conference on Language Resources and Evaluation, LREC'02* (2002).
2. Levin, D.Ya., Narin'yani, A.S. An Experimental Miniprocessor: Semantic-Oriented Analysis. In *Natural Language Interaction with Computer* (Computer Center of the Siberian Branch of the USSR Academy of Sciences, Novosibirsk, 1978), pp. 223–233 (in Russian).
3. Dinenberg, F.G., Levin, D.Ya. Natural Language Interfaces for Environmental Data Bases. In *Applications of Natural Language to Information Systems*, edited by R.P. van de Riet *et al.* (IOS Press, Amsterdam, 1996).
4. Cheblakov, G.B., Dinenberg, F.G., Levin, D.Ya., Popov, I.G., Zagorulko, Yu.A. Approach to Development of a System for Speech Interaction with an Intelligent Robot. In *Perspectives of System Informatics - PSI 1999 (LNCS 1755)*, edited by D. Bjørner *et al.* (Springer, Berlin, 1999), pp. 517–529.
5. Zhdanova, A.V., Shishkin, D.V. Classification of E-mail Queries by Topic: Approach Based on Hierarchically Structured Subject Domain. In *Intelligent Data Engineering and Automated Learning - IDEAL 2002 (LNCS 2412)*, edited by H. Yin *et al.* (Springer, Berlin, 2002), pp. 99–104.
6. Freeman, R., Yin, H. Self-Organising Maps for Hierarchical Tree View Document Clustering Using Contextual Information. In *Intelligent Data Engineering and Automated Learning - IDEAL 2002 (LNCS 2412)*, edited by H. Yin *et al.* (Springer, Berlin, 2002), pp. 123–128.
7. Vinokourov, A., Girolami, M. A Probabilistic Framework for the Hierarchic Organisation and Classification of Document Collections. *J. Intellig. Inform. Systems*, **18**, 153–172 (2002).
8. Zipf, G. K. *Human Behavior and the Principle of Least Effort.* (Addison-Wesley, Cambridge, MA, 1949).
9. Manning, C.D., Schutze, H. *Foundations of Statistical Natural Language Processing* (The MIT Press, Cambridge, MA, 2001).
10. Lloréns, J., Astudillo, H. Automatic Generation of Hierarchical Taxonomies from Free Text Using Linguistic Algorithms. In *Advances in Object-Oriented Information Systems (LNCS 2426)*, edited by J.-M. Bruel et al. (Springer, Berlin, 2002), pp. 74–83.
11. Sundblad, H. Automatic Acquisition of Hyponyms and Meronyms from Question Corpora. In *Proceedings of the 15th European Conference on Artificial Intelligence, ECAI'02* (IOS Press, Amsterdam, 2002).

Author Index